STUDY GUIDE

for

EIGHTH EDITION

BUSINESS LAW

Legal Environment, Online Commerce, Business Ethics, and International Issues

HENRY CHEESEMAN

PEARSON

Boston Columbus Indianapolis New York San Francisco Upper Saddle River
Amsterdam Cape Town Dubai London Madrid Milan Munich Paris Montreal Toronto
Delhi Mexico City Sao Paulo Sydney Hong Kong Seoul Singapore Taipei Tokyo

Executive Editor: Stephanie Wall
Editorial Project Manager: Karen Kirincich
Production Project Manager: Nancy Freihofer
Senior Manufacturing Buyer: Megan Cochran

www.pearsonhighered.com

ISBN-10:   0-13-296998-X
ISBN-13: 978-0-13-296998-7

Table of Contents

1 | LEGAL HERITAGE AND THE DIGITAL AGE

Chapter Overview

This chapter discusses the significance of the concept of law and its functions in our society in terms of overseeing the behavior that takes place within it by individuals, businesses, and organizations. Even though the meaning of law is vast, law in general is a set of standards and rules by which we justify our actions and which is the basis of consequences and sanctions. The philosophy of law, various schools of thought on its development, and the importance of flexibility in its application are also examined. The history and development of our laws and courts along with interpretation as it pertains to technology, growth of commerce and the standards of society are what bring about changes and new laws.

Objectives

Upon completion of the exercises in this chapter, you should be able to:
1. Define law.
2. Describe the functions of law.
3. Explain the development of the U.S. legal system.
4. List and describe the sources of law in the United States.
5. Discuss the importance of the U.S. Supreme Court's decision in Brown v. Board of Education.

Practical Application

You should be able to understand the basis, development, and need for law, the importance of flexible interpretation of the law, and the framework by which laws are established.

Helpful Hints

You should read each chapter and complete or read the corresponding study guide exercises. The Refresh Your Memory exercise will determine the materials on which you need to place more emphasis. The Critical Thinking Exercise will help to assess your ability to analyze and apply the legal concepts you have learned to the facts given in the exercise. The Sample Quiz, which is composed of true/false, multiple choice and short answer questions, is provided as a means of assessing your mastery of the chapter.

Essentials for a Well-Written Critical Thinking Exercise

Critical Thinking exercises should be approached in a methodical way. Each exercise should be read twice, the first time to get a feel for the facts and determine what is being asked of you and the second time to spot the issues presented. Once you know what the question is asking you to do, you can mark up the facts with a pen and place possible applicable legal terms from the chapter you have just studied next to the fact to which it pertains. In order to prepare a well-written answer, it is imperative that you prepare an outline that is organized by either the topic or legal issues that will be discussed. Demonstrate how the facts in your exercise meet the requirements of the legal principle(s) you are discussing.

There are two sides to every story just as there are two sides to every argument. When applicable, give reasoning for both sides. If you are applying case law that you have studied, be sure to show how the case(s) apply to the facts you've been given, based upon the similarity of both scenarios. If the case is not supportive of your analysis, you may indicate this point with a brief explanation and continue with the issues for which you have strong support.

Finally, make sure that you have utilized all of the relevant facts and applied the pertinent law in analyzing these facts. It is your reasoning and application of the main objectives of the chapter that will help to determine your competency of the information given to you. If you approach these types of exercises as challenging, fun, and practical, you will begin to appreciate their usefulness in your everyday life. A sample answer is given at the end of the chapter and is to be used as a guide. Answers will vary based on the law and analysis applied by individual students.

Study Tips

Law is a set of standards and rules by which we justify our conduct and actions and the violation of which is subject to consequences and sanctions. The description of a law is usually made with its function in mind. Functions of the law include the following:

- To shape moral standards.
- To maintain the status quo.
- To facilitate planning.
- To maximize individual freedom.
- To keep the peace.
- To promote social justice.
- To facilitate orderly change.
- To provide a basis for compromise.

Various scholars have stated their philosophies on the development of the law. There are several schools of jurisprudential thought. You will notice that each adjective describing each school gives you a hint as to the reasoning behind the title of each school. For example, the Command School would be easy to remember, as a commander has been defined as a person who holds rank, such as a higher official. As such, it is easy to remember that the law changes when the ruler (or commander) changes. The following mnemonic may help you to remember the main schools of thought:

A cranky squirrel commands natural history!

A — The **Analytical School** asserts that the law is formed by logic.
C — The **Critical Legal Studies School** does not believe in rules for settling disputes, but applying rules of fairness to each circumstance.
S — The **Sociological School** believes that law is a way to form social behavior and attain sociological goals.
C — The **Command School** espouses that the law changes when the ruler changes.
N — The **Natural Law School** maintains that the basis of law should be on morality and ethics.
H — The **Historical School** believes that changes in societal norms are eventually demonstrated in the law. These scholars rely on precedent to solve modern problems.

Foundation of American Law

The American common law was derived from England and its laws. It is helpful to understand a brief history of how our laws developed.

English Common Law

These laws developed from judge-issued opinions that became precedent for other judges to decide similar cases. Local judges, appointed by the king, were given the responsibility of administering the law in a uniform manner.

Law Courts

The judges issued their opinions in cases that later set the precedent for deciding the same types of cases. Legal procedure was stressed over merit, and monetary awards were all that was available in a law court.

Equity Courts

A court that is based on fairness when deciding cases.

Merchant Courts

A court that dealt with only the law of merchants and their commercial disputes; eventually this court was combined with the regular court system.

Sources of Law

- Constitution — The supreme law of the land that provided for the structure of the federal government. This structure established the legislative, executive, and judicial branches of government. Those powers not given to the federal government by the Constitution are reserved for the states.

- Treaties — Compacts or agreements between two or more nations that become a part of the Constitution.

- Statutes — A set of state or federal laws that describes conduct that must be followed by those the statute was designed to protect. These laws are organized by topic in code books. An example would be the Uniform Commercial Code.

- Ordinances — Laws that are created and enforced by local governments including counties, school districts, and municipalities. An example would be a traffic law.

- Executive Orders — These are laws that are made by the president or state governors.

- Judicial Decisions — Federal and state issued decisions about individual lawsuits.

The Doctrine of *Stare Decisis*

A rule of law set forth by higher courts, which becomes precedent for lower court decisions. In addition to the benefit of helping to establish uniformity of law, this doctrine makes it easier for individuals and businesses to determine what the law is.

Refresh Your Memory

The following exercise will give you the opportunity to test your memory of the principles given in this chapter. Read the question twice and place your answer in the blank provided. Review the chapter material for any question that you are unable to answer or remember.

1. _____ is the philosophy or science of law.

2. _____ philosophers emphasize a moral theory of law— that is, law should be based on morality and ethics.

3. The _____ School proposes that legal rules are unnecessary and are used as an obstacle by the powerful to maintain the status quo.

4. The Law and Economics School is also called the _____.

5. The _____ can be divided into cases decided by the law courts, equity courts, and merchant courts.

6. The only relief available at _____ was a monetary award for damages.

7. _____ courts were under the authority of the lord chancellor.

8. The _____ of the United States of America is the supreme law of the land.

9. The _____ branch has the power to interpret and determine the validity of the law.

10. _____ is written law enacted by the legislative branch of the federal and state governments that establishes certain courses of conduct that covered parties must adhere to.

11. Basic zoning laws is an example of _____.

12. An order issued by a member of the executive branch of the government is a(n) _____ order.

13. A decision about an individual lawsuit issued by a federal or state court is called a _____.

14. Based on the common law tradition, past court decisions become _____ for deciding future cases.

15. Adherence to precedent is called the doctrine of _____.

Critical Thought Exercise

Following the genocide, torture, rape, and murder of thousands of civilians in Rwanda in 1994, sixty-three individuals were tried for genocide and crimes against humanity. Numerous persons were sentenced to life sentences.

Many of those prosecuted objected to being tried outside Rwanda for acts committed within Rwanda. The accused further objected to being prosecuted for acts that were not deemed criminal by their own leaders or national laws.

You are asked to address a large convention sponsored by a nationalist group that argues against any person ever being subjected to criminal punishment by an international court for acts committed within their home country.

Your argument should address the following issues while trying to explain whether or not you feel prosecutions by an international body are lawful and justified:
1. What law is being violated when someone commits a crime against humanity?
2. Who has the authority to enforce laws against genocide and crimes against humanity?
3. Should a citizen of a sovereign nation be subjected to punishment by an international tribunal for acts committed within their home country?
4. Who is responsible for the prosecution of these crimes?

Please compose your answer to the Critical Thinking Exercise using a separate sheet of paper or your computer word processing program.

Practice Quiz

True/False

16. _____ Businesses that are organized in the United States are subject to its laws, but not to the laws of other countries in which they do business.

17. _____ Laws in the U.S. are not set to evolve with changes in social norms.

18. _____ The Law and Economics School of jurisprudential thought holds that rights are not worth protecting if it is too costly from an economic viewpoint.

19. _____ The Critical Legal Studies School of jurisprudential thought seeks to restrict the subjective decision-making powers of judges.

20. _____ Sociological philosophers are unlikely to adhere to past law as precedent.

21. _____ The Historical School maintains that law is shaped by logic.

22. ____ Within a state, the state constitution precedes the U.S. Constitution.

23. ____ Executive orders are an example of codified law.

24. ____ Administrative agencies are created by the judicial branch of government.

25. ____ Treaties are considered to be a part of the supreme law of the United States of America.

26. ____ Statutes are enacted by Congress and state legislatures.

27. ____ The authority to enact ordinances lies solely with the state legislatures.

28. ____ Ordinances are not codified into code books.

29. ____ State courts of one state are not required to follow the legal precedent established by the courts of another state.

30. ____ The doctrine of *stare decisis* provides that each court decision is independent and should stand on its own.

Multiple Choice

31. Law is described as _____.

A. a study of fundamental problems, such as those connected with existence, knowledge and language
B. a body of rules of action or conduct prescribed by controlling authority, and having binding legal force
C. a system that builds and organizes knowledge in the form of testable explanations and predictions
D. a group of hypotheses employed to explain a phenomenon

32. The Supreme Court case decision on the case of Brown v. Board of Education was important because it exhibited _____.

A. the use of the affirmative action policy
B. the state's supremacy over federal rulings
C. the scope of flexibility of the law
D. the importance of following precedence

33. Proponents of the _____ School of jurisprudence emphasize a moral theory of law, where law is based on morality and ethics, and is discovered by human reasoning and making choices between good and evil.

A. Natural Law
B. Analytical
C. Historical
D. Sociological

34. The Analytical School of jurisprudence maintains that the law should be _____.

A. based on social behavior
B. shaped by logic
C. set by the ruling class
D. based on morality

35. Which school of jurisprudence views law as a sort of evolutionary process, where changing norms of society will be reflected in the law?

A. the Historical School of jurisprudence
B. the Sociological School of jurisprudence
C. the Analytical School of jurisprudence
D. the Natural Law School of jurisprudence

36. Imposing a ban on public smoking can serve as an example of a law that adheres to the _____ School of jurisprudence.

A. Command
B. Law and Economics
C. Sociological
D. Analytical

37. Proponents of the Command School of jurisprudence will assert that the law is _____.

A. a means to achieve and advance sociological goals
B. developed, communicated, and enforced by the ruling party
C. a collection of a society's traditions and customs that has developed over the centuries
D. based on human reasoning, and humans' choosing power between what is good and evil

38. What is considered as the supreme law of the land in the United States?

A. judicial decisions issued by the state courts
B. the Constitution of the United States of America
C. the federal statutes passed by the United States Congress
D. executive orders passed by the President

39. The _____ branch of the federal government has the power to enforce the law.

A. judicial
B. legislative
C. commissary
D. executive

40. The branch of the federal government that has the power to enact laws is the

_____.

A. judiciary
B. legislature
C. consulate
D. executive

41. A(n) _____ is a compact made between two or more nations.

A. amendment
B. charter
C. treaty
D. statute

42. What would be an example of codified law in the United States?

A. judicial rulings
B. treaties
C. federal statutes
D. executive orders

43. Ordinances are codified laws that are issued by _____.

A. local government bodies
B. the state legislature
C. Supreme Court judges
D. the President

44. _____ are established by the legislative and executive branches of the federal government to enforce and interpret statues enacted by the Congress and state legislatures.

A. Commissaries
B. State courts
C. Councils
D. Administrative agencies

45. Stare decisis is the doctrine of _____.

A. providing proof to assert a fact in court
B. separating powers between state and religion
C. adhering to legal precedent
D. ensuring all legal rights are provided to a person when otherwise deprived of them

Short Answer

46. List the functions of the law.

_____

_____

47. Differentiate between the Historical School of jurisprudence and the Sociological School of jurisprudence.

_____

_____

48. Explain the three courts under the English common law.

_____

_____

49. Why was the Merchant Court established under the English common law?

_____

_____

50. What are the three branches of government created by the Constitution of the United States of America?

_____

_____

51. Who is empowered to enact an ordinance? Give an example of an ordinance.

_____

_____

52. What is the difference between judicial decisions and precedents?

_____

_____

53. Explain the doctrine of *stare decisis* and how it has influenced the legal system.

_____

_____

54. Give an account of how the digital age has affected lawmaking in the United States.

_____

_____

55. List the various schools of jurisprudential thought.

_____

_____

Answers to Refresh Your Memory

1. Jurisprudence [p. 8]
2. Natural law [p. 8]
3. Critical Legal Studies [p. 9]
4. Chicago School [p. 9]
5. English common law [p. 10]
6. law courts [p. 11]
7. Chancery/ Equity [p. 11]
8. Constitution [p. 12]
9. judicial [p. 12]
10. Statute [p. 13]
11. ordinance [p. 14]
12. executive [p. 14]
13. judicial decision [p. 15]
14. precedent [p. 15]
15. *stare decisis* [p. 15]

Critical Thought Exercise Model Answer

The Origins of Law

In its most basic form, law is comprised of the rules created by the controlling authority of a society, usually its government. These rules are given legal force and effect and control the actions of the individuals within the society. Most law is created by each society within a country and is referred to as national law. Law that is created by way of treaties, customs, and agreements between nations is international law.

For most countries, national law finds its foundation in the philosophies of legal positivism, which assumes that there is no law higher than the laws created by the government, and legal realism, which stresses a realistic approach that takes into account customary practices and present day circumstances.

In the area of international law, the philosophy of natural law plays an important role. Natural law holds that there is a universal law that is applicable to all human beings that is higher than any law created by an individual society or government. Certain conduct, such as genocide and crimes against humanity, are deemed to be without any possible moral justification, regardless of the existence or nonexistence of any national law concerning these types of acts.

When a nation or segment of a society within a nation engages in conduct that violates natural law, it is no defense to this conduct that the government or society advocates or condones the conduct.

Justification for International Criminal Tribunals and an International Criminal Court

The nations of the world have collectively agreed for over 50 years that international courts capable of resolving disputes and addressing crimes against humanity are needed. This need has been filled by the United Nations.

The members of the United Nations consent to the jurisdiction of the international courts as a way to advance their rights in the international arena. Until 1998, the International Court of Justice (ICJ) was the principal judicial organ of the United Nations. The ICJ, located in The Hague, Netherlands, began operating in 1946. The prior court had been in the same location since 1922. In 1998, the International Criminal Court (ICC) was also created.

The ICJ operates under a statute that is part of the Charter of the United Nations. The ICJ lacks power to address situations such as the Holocaust and genocide in Cambodia because it can only hear cases between states. It has no jurisdiction over individuals.

Prior to the formation of the ICC, the United Nations members formed criminal tribunals to address war crimes and crimes against humanity that have been committed during specific periods of time. These tribunals were given authority to prosecute individuals who were responsible for these severe criminal acts.

The overall purpose of these tribunals was to pursue peace and justice in the affected areas. The International Criminal Tribunal for Rwanda was established for the prosecution of persons responsible for genocide and other serious violations of international humanitarian law committed in the territory of Rwanda between 1 January 1994 and 31 December 1994. The tribunal was also authorized to prosecute Rwandan citizens responsible for genocide and other such violations of international law committed in the territory of neighboring States during the same period.

An international criminal court has been called the missing link in the international legal system. The International Court of Justice at The Hague handles only cases between States, not individuals. Without an international criminal court for dealing with individual responsibility as an enforcement mechanism, acts of genocide and egregious violations of human rights often go unpunished. No one was held accountable for the over two-million people killed by the Khmer Rouge in Cambodia in the 1970s. The same was true for murders of men, women, and children in Mozambique, Liberia, El Salvador, and other countries.

Defining International Crimes

When each instance of genocide or crimes against humanity has taken place, a specific statute had to be created which not only set up the tribunal, but defined the crimes that were to be prosecuted. The jurisdiction of the tribunal only extended to those crimes and that time period covered in the statute.

In the statute establishing the International Criminal Tribunal for Rwanda, specific definitions for genocide, crimes against humanity, and violations of the Geneva Convention were set forth in detail. To address crimes against humanity, the ICTR statute established "...the power to prosecute persons responsible for the following crimes when committed as part of a widespread or systematic attack against any civilian population on national, political, ethnic, racial or religious grounds: (a) Murder; (b) Extermination; (c) Enslavement; (d) Deportation; (e) Imprisonment; (f) Torture; (g) Rape; (h) Persecutions on political, racial and religious grounds; (i) Other inhumane acts." (ICTR Statute, Article 3.)

Need for International Prosecution

Without the international tribunals, those responsible could easily flee to other countries and avoid being held accountable for their acts of genocide. This was particularly true in the case of Rwanda, where the perpetrators simply went across the border into neighboring countries to hide when pursued. They would then reenter Rwanda and continue the killing when they were able. Rwanda was unable to handle the apprehension and prosecution of those responsible because the government of Rwanda had broken down and lacked the power to enforce peace. The need for international prosecution also arises when the controlling government and its leaders are the actual perpetrators, such as in the case of Yugoslavia. The government in power may actually mandate that the criminal acts be carried out as part of an "ethnic cleansing." This was true in both Nazi Germany and in Yugoslavia in the 1990s.

Deterrence and Responsibility for Prosecutions in the Future

Nations agree that criminals should normally be prosecuted by national courts in the countries where the crimes are committed. When the national governments are either unwilling or unable to act to restore peace and seek justice, there needs to be an institution in place to address the horrors of genocide and crimes against humanity. In the past, perpetrators had little chance of being caught, much less prosecuted. The new ICC seeks to create a deterrent effect. Those responsible for murder, terrorism, genocide, and violations of the Geneva Convention will know that they will be pursued throughout the world. Additionally, the loopholes inherent in the tribunal process will be eliminated. The ineffective nature of the ICTR is shown by the fact that the murder of thousands of people from 1995-1999 will go unpunished because the ICTR was only authorized to prosecute those crimes committed in 1994.

Without an international institution to address crimes such as those committed in Rwanda, the perpetrators of the worst crimes in history would go unpunished. The members of the United Nations have decided that they desire the protection afforded by an international criminal court.

Answers to Practice Quiz

True/False

16. False. Businesses that are organized in the United States are subject to its laws. They are also subject to the laws of other countries in which they operate. [p. 3]

17. False. U.S. law evolves and changes along with the norms of society, technology, and the growth and expansion of commerce in the United States and the world. [p. 5]

18. True. The Law and Economics School believes that promoting market efficiency should be the central goal of legal decision making. [p. 9]

19. True. The Critical Legal Studies School proposes that legal rules are unnecessary and are used as an obstacle by the powerful to maintain the status quo. Under this theory, subjective decision making by judges would be permitted. [p. 9]

20. True. The Sociological School of jurisprudence asserts that the law is a means of achieving and advancing certain sociological goals. The followers of this philosophy, known as realists, believe that the purpose of law is to shape social behavior. [p. 8]

21. False. The Historical School of jurisprudence believes that the law is an aggregate of social traditions and customs that have developed over the centuries. [p. 8]

22. False. The Constitution of the United States of America is the supreme law of the land. This means that any law—whether federal, state, or local—that conflicts with the U.S. Constitution is unconstitutional and, therefore, unenforceable. [p. 12]

23. False. Executive order is issued by the president and governors of states. It regulates the conduct of covered parties. It is not a codified law. [p. 14]

24. False. The legislative and executive branches of federal and state governments are empowered to establish administrative agencies to enforce and interpret statutes enacted by Congress and state legislatures. [p. 14]

25. True. The U.S. Constitution provides that the president, with the advice and consent of two-thirds of the Senate, may enter into treaties with foreign governments. Treaties become part of the supreme law of the land. [p. 12]

26. True. The U.S. Congress is empowered by the Commerce Clause and other provisions of the U.S. Constitution to enact federal statutes to regulate foreign and interstate commerce. [p. 13]

27. False. State legislatures often delegate lawmaking authority to local government bodies, including cities and municipalities, counties, school districts, water districts, and such. [p. 14]

28. False. Ordinances are codified laws. [p. 14]

29. True. The courts of one jurisdiction are not bound by the precedent established by the courts of another jurisdiction, although they may look to each other for guidance. [p. 15]

30. False. Adherence to precedent is called the doctrine of *stare decisis*. The doctrine of *stare decisis* promotes uniformity of law within a jurisdiction.

Multiple Choice

31. B. Law is that which must be obeyed and followed by citizens, subject to sanctions or legal consequences; a body of rules of action or conduct prescribed by controlling authority and having binding legal force. [p. 3]

32. C. U.S. law evolves and changes along with the norms of society, technology, and the growth and expansion of commerce in the United States and the world. [p. 5]

33. A. The Natural Law School of jurisprudence postulates that the law is based on what is correct. Natural law is discovered by humans through the use of reason and choosing between good and evil. [p. 8]

34. B. The Analytical School of jurisprudence maintains that the law is shaped by logic. The emphasis is on the logic of the result rather than on how the result is reached. [p. 8]

35. A. The Historical School of jurisprudence believes that the law is an aggregate of social traditions and customs that have developed over the centuries. It believes that changes in the norms of society will gradually be reflected in the law. [p. 8]

36. C. The Sociological School of jurisprudence asserts that the law is a means of achieving and advancing certain sociological goals. The followers of this philosophy believe that the purpose of law is to shape social behavior. [p. 8]

37. B. The philosophers of the Command School of jurisprudence believe that the law is a set of rules developed, communicated, and enforced by the ruling party rather than a reflection of the society's morality, history, logic, or sociology. [p. 8]

38. B. The Constitution of the United States of America is the supreme law of the land. This means that any law—whether federal, state, or local—that conflicts with the U.S. Constitution is unconstitutional and, therefore, unenforceable. [p. 12]

39. D. The U.S. Constitution has created three branches of the federal government and given them different powers. The executive branch (president) has the power to enforce the law. [p. 12]

40. B. The legislative branch (Congress) is that branch of the federal government that has the power to make (enact) the law. [p. 12]

41. C. A compact made between two or more nations. Treaties become part of the supreme law of the land. [p. 12]

42. C. Statutes are written laws that establish certain courses of conduct that covered parties must adhere to. Federal statutes are organized by topic into code books. This is often referred to as codified law. [p. 13]

43. A. Local government bodies such as cities and municipalities, counties, school districts, water districts are empowered to adopt ordinances. Ordinances are codified. [p. 14]

44. D. The legislative and executive branches of federal and state governments are empowered to establish administrative agencies to enforce and interpret statutes enacted by Congress and state legislatures. [p. 14]

45. C. Doctrine of *Stare Decisis* is based on the common law tradition. Past court decisions become precedent for deciding future cases. [p. 15]

Short Answer

46. The primary functions served by the law in the U.S. are:
a. Keeping the peace
b. Shaping moral standards
c. Promoting social justice
d. Maintaining the status quo
e. Facilitating orderly change
f. Facilitating planning
g. Providing a basis for compromise
h. Maximizing individual freedom
[p. 4]

47. The various schools of jurisprudential thought are:
a. Natural Law School
b. Historical School
c. Analytical School
d. Sociological School
e. Command School
f. Critical Legal Studies School
g. Law and Economics School
[p. 8]

48. The Historical School of jurisprudence believes that the law is an aggregate of social traditions and customs that have developed over the centuries. It believes that changes in the norms of society will gradually be reflected in the law. The Sociological School of jurisprudence asserts that the law is a means of achieving and advancing certain sociological goals. The followers of this philosophy believe that the purpose of law is to shape social behavior. [p. 8]

49. The English common law can be divided into cases decided by the law courts, equity courts, and merchant courts.
Law Courts- The judges at these courts were charged with administering the law in a uniform manner. It emphasized the form (legal procedure) over the substance (merit) of a case. The only relief available at law courts was a monetary award for damages.
Chancery Courts- These courts were under the authority of the Lord Chancellor. The chancellor's remedies were called equitable remedies because they were shaped to fit each situation.
Merchant Courts- The merchants who traveled about England and Europe developed certain rules to solve their commercial disputes. These rules—known as the Law Merchant—were based on common trade practices and usage. Eventually, a separate set of courts was established to administer these rules called the Merchant Court. [p. 11]

50. As trade developed during the Middle Ages, the merchants who traveled about England and Europe developed certain rules to solve their commercial disputes. These rules, known as the "law of merchants," or the Law Merchant, were based on common trade practices and usage. Eventually, a separate set of courts was established to administer these rules. This court was called the Merchant Court. In the early 1900s, the Merchant Court was absorbed into the regular law court system of England. [p. 11]

51. The U.S. Constitution established the structure of the federal government. It created three branches of government and gave them the following powers:
a. The legislative branch (Congress) has the power to make (enact) the law.
b. The executive branch (President) has the power to enforce the law.
c. The judicial branch (courts) has the power to interpret and determine the validity of the law. [p. 12]

52. State legislatures often delegate lawmaking authority to local government bodies, including cities and municipalities, counties, school districts, water districts, and such. These governmental units are empowered to adopt ordinances. Zoning laws, building codes, sign restrictions, and such are examples of ordinance. [p. 14]

53. In a judicial decision, a judge or justice usually explains the legal reasoning used to decide the case. These opinions often include interpretations of statutes, ordinances, and administrative regulations and the announcement of legal principles used to decide the case. A precedent is a rule of law established in a court decision. Lower courts must follow the precedent established by higher courts. [p. 15]

54. Adherence to precedent is called the doctrine of *stare decisis*. The doctrine of *stare decisis* promotes uniformity of law within a jurisdiction, makes the court system more efficient, and makes the law more predictable for individuals and businesses. A court may later change or reverse its legal reasoning if a new case is presented to it and change is warranted. [p. 15]

55. The electronic age arrived before new laws were written that were unique and specific for this environment. Courts have applied existing laws to the new digital environment by requiring interpretations and applications. In addition, new laws have been written that apply specifically to this new environment. The U.S. Congress has led the way, enacting many new federal statutes to regulate the digital environment. [p. 17]

2 | COURTS AND JURISDICTION

Chapter Overview

This chapter examines and compares the state court systems and the federal court system. It provides an overview of the types of cases the various courts can hear as well as both state and federal jurisdictional issues. Emphasis is placed on the meanings associated with Supreme Court decisions. Finally, an explanation of the different types of jurisdiction is given.

Objectives

Upon completion of the exercises in this chapter, you should be able to:
1. Describe state court systems.
2. Describe the federal court system.
3. List and describe the types of decisions that are issued by the U.S. Supreme Court.
4. Compare the jurisdiction of state courts with that of federal courts.
5. Define personal jurisdiction, standing to sue, and venue.

Practical Application

You should be able to understand which court and system are proper for hearing particular cases, as well as be able to differentiate between the various types of courts. You should be able to assess when or why a case has been brought in federal court. You should have a broader understanding of the various types of U.S. Supreme Court decisions. You should be able to determine whether an individual has a stake in the outcome of a lawsuit sufficient to have standing to sue, as well as be able to analyze jurisdictional and venue issues surrounding a case.

Helpful Hints

This chapter may be a little confusing, as there appear to be so many different types of courts, all of which hear different types of cases. It is recommended that you diagram the state and federal court systems, branching each of the various courts off of the applicable state or federal court system. Page 25 of your text gives an example of how one diagram can be utilized. You should also place two to four main points next to each type of court. For example, if you are working on the state court systems, in particular the limited-jurisdiction trial court, you may want to note that they are sometimes called inferior trial courts, hear matters that are specialized, and list some of the examples of the types of cases that are heard in this type of court. As you proceed in this manner, you will find that you have created a flow chart of the courts that will be easy to visualize when determining the answers to text and real life situations. Next, review this chapter's study guide, and then complete the Refresh Your Memory exercise followed by the Critical Thought Exercise and Sample Quiz.

Study Tips

The laws and their development that you became familiar with in Chapter One as well as the court systems you are learning about in this chapter are analogous to the base layer of a specialty cake. It is by knowing the appropriate law and court within the proper court system that you will be able to apply the correct legal principles to situations as they occur. The areas of law in the chapters that follow will provide the upper layers and frosting to this unique cake. The essential ingredients of adhering to the proper time and procedural requirements along with satisfying the essential substantive elements for various legal actions are what provide balance to this legally created pastry if you will.

There are two main court systems in the United States, the federal and the state court systems. It is important to know which court system has the proper jurisdiction to hear the case that has been prepared. The following list breaks down each court system, highlighting some important points to remember about each court system as well as the courts within each system.

State Court Systems

A general fact about the state court systems is that every state, as well as the District of Columbia, has one. The majority of states have at least four types of state court systems that are discussed below.

Limited-Jurisdiction Trial Court (Inferior Trial Courts) – These trial courts in most cases can hear specialized cases such as those involving family law, probate, traffic matters, juvenile issues, misdemeanors, and civil cases that do not exceed a set dollar amount. An attorney trying a case in this type of court may introduce evidence and illicit testimony. If the case does not result in a favorable outcome for one of the parties to the lawsuit, that party may appeal his/her case to an appellate court or a general-jurisdiction court. Many states also have a small claims court wherein a party on his/her own behalf brings a civil case worth a small dollar amount. If a party in a small claims case loses, then that party may also appeal to the general-jurisdiction trial court or an appellate court.

General-Jurisdiction Trial Court. – A general-jurisdiction trial court can be found in every state. The trial testimony and evidence that is preserved on record allow these courts to be called the courts of record. This court hears felonies, cases above a certain dollar amount and cases not heard by the inferior trial courts.

Intermediate Appellate Court – This court hears appeals from trial courts and decides if the trial court erred, thereby justifying a reversal or modification of the decision. The entire trial court record or just the important parts of the record may be reviewed. At this level of the court system, a party may not introduce new evidence or testimony. The decision of this appellate court may be appealed to the highest state court.

Highest State Court – The majority of states have a supreme court, which is the highest court in the state court system. The job of a state Supreme Court is to hear appeals from the intermediate appellate court. Once again, no new evidence or testimony is allowed. Once this court has made its decision, it becomes final. However, if there is a question of law, then the state supreme court's decision May be granted review by the U.S. Supreme Court.

Federal Court System

The United States Constitution states that the federal government's judicial power lies with the Supreme Court. In addition to this judicial power, Congress was allowed to establish inferior, or special, courts that include the U.S. district courts and the U.S. courts of appeal.

Special Federal Courts –. The nature of these courts is to hear limited types of cases such as those involving federal tax laws, law suits against the United States, international commercial disputes, and cases involving bankruptcy.

U.S. District Courts – These courts are the federal courts' general-jurisdiction courts.

U.S. Courts of Appeal – These courts are the intermediate appellate courts of the federal court system. The U.S. courts of appeal hear appeals from the cases already heard by the U.S. district courts. As with the state court systems, no new evidence or testimony may be introduced by a party.

Court of Appeals for the Federal Circuit – Even though this is a United States appellate court, its jurisdiction is special as it is able to review the decisions made in the Patent and Trademark Office, the Court of International Trade, and the Claims Court.

The U.S. Supreme Court – This high court of our land is administered by a president-appointed chief justice and is made up of nine nominated justices. This court hears cases from the federal circuit courts of appeal, from some federal district and special federal courts, as well as the highest state courts. A special note of interest is that a petition for certiorari must be made to the Supreme Court if a petitioner wants his/her case reviewed. If the court decides to review the case, then a writ of certiorari is issued provided there is a constitutional or other important issue involved in the case. No new evidence or testimony may be introduced at this level.

Federal and State Courts Jurisdiction

In order for a federal court to hear a case, the case must involve a federal question, or diversity of citizenship. It's important to distinguish these two concepts. A case involving a federal question deals with treaties, federal statutes, and the U.S. Constitution. There need not be a set dollar amount to bring this type of case. Compare this to cases involving diversity of citizenship whereby the cases need to be between citizens of different states or a citizen of a country and a citizen of a state or a citizen of a state and a foreign country with the foreign country acting as the plaintiff in a law suit. These types of cases require that the controversy exceed $75,000.00. If the dollar amount isn't met, then the appropriate state court must hear the case.

Court Jurisdiction to Hear a Case

In order to bring a lawsuit, a person must have a stake in the outcome of the lawsuit. This is known as standing to sue.

The court must also have the proper jurisdiction to hear the case. You must be familiar with subject matter jurisdiction, *in personam*, *in rem*, and *quasi in rem* jurisdiction. You must be familiar with the use of the long-arm statutes and when they are permitted to be used over nonresidents.

Which court is the proper venue to hear my case?

The law mandates that lawsuits be heard by the court with jurisdiction that is closest to where the incident happened or where the parties live.

Refresh Your Memory

1. Limited- jurisdiction trial courts are also referred to as _____ trial courts.

2. A(n) _____ court is also known as court of record.

3. The U.S. Court of _____ hears cases brought against the United States.

4. The geographical area served by each court of appeal is referred to as a _____.

5. The highest court in the land is the _____ of the United States.

6. A petition asking the Supreme Court to hear a case is called _____.

7. _____ is an official notice that the Supreme Court will review a case.

8. If a majority of the justices agree as to the outcome of a case but not as to the reasoning for reaching the outcome, it is a _____ decision.

9. A justice who does not agree with a decision can file a _____ that sets forth the reasons for his or her dissent.

10. _____ cases are cases arising under the U.S. Constitution, treaties, and federal statutes and regulations.

11. Admiralty, antitrust, patent, and so on are examples of _____ jurisdiction.

12. The plaintiff must have some stake in the outcome of the lawsuit. This is called _____.

13. A court may have jurisdiction to hear and decide a case because it has jurisdiction over the property of the lawsuit. This is called _____ jurisdiction.

14. _____ is a concept that requires lawsuits to be heard by the court with jurisdiction that is nearest the location in which the incident occurred or where the parties reside.

15. _____ clause is a contract provision that designates a certain state's law or country's law that will be applied in any dispute concerning nonperformance of the contract.

Critical Thought Exercise

You are a district manager of marketing for Intestine Smart, Inc., a California corporation, makers of Colon Grenade, a colon-cleansing drug. You have negotiated the sale of over 4 million dollars worth of this product from Prescript Co., another California corporation, which operates pharmacies under the names of Col On, Goodstuff Co., and Drugs 2 Go. These pharmacies are located primarily in California, but Prescript Co. has now expanded into 22 states including Utah.

Enticed by a Goodstuff ad in the Utah Free Press for Colon Grenade, Alice Thinstone bought the drug at Goodstuff Co. and used it. Within a week, Thinstone suffered a ruptured colon. Alleging that the injury was caused by Colon Grenade, Thinstone sued Prescript Co. and Intestine Smart in a Utah state court.

You have received a letter from the CEO of Intestine Smart, Ms. Sheila Snob, threatening to fire you and demanding to know why Intestine Smart is being subjected to a lawsuit in Utah, since she has never been informed of any sales of the product to companies outside of California.

Your assigned task is to draft a memo to your boss, Ms. Snob, and explain to her whether Intestine Smart must respond to the suit and defend against it in Utah. Explain the legal theory and the reasons for your opinion.

Please compose your answer to the Critical Thinking Exercise using a separate sheet of paper or your computer word processing program.

Practice Quiz

True/False

16. _____ In small claims courts, it is necessary that the parties are represented by a lawyer at all times.

17. _____ The decisions handed down by the general jurisdiction trial courts are appealable to an intermediate appellate court or the state supreme court.

18. _____ Appellate court decisions are final and cannot be appealed to any higher courts.

19. _____ No new evidence or testimony is heard in the state supreme courts.

20. _____ In the United States, each state has only a single district court.

21. _____ The highest court in the land is the Supreme Court of the United States, which is located in Washington, DC.

22. _____ The Chief Justice of the Supreme Court is elected by the Associate Justices of the U.S. Supreme Court.

23. _____ The decisions of the U.S. Supreme Court can be appealed to higher courts.

24. _____ The U.S. Congress gives the Supreme Court discretion to decide what cases it will hear.

25. _____ A petitioner must file a petition for certiorari, asking the Supreme Court to hear the case.

26. _____ A tie decision by the U.S. Supreme Court sets a precedent for later cases.

27. _____ A justice who agrees with the outcome of a case but not the reason proffered by other justices can issue a dissenting opinion that sets forth his or her reasons for deciding the case.

28. _____ For federal question cases to be brought to a federal court, the dollar amount of the controversy must exceed $75,000.

29. _____ A plaintiff, by filing a lawsuit with a court, gives the court in personam jurisdiction over himself or herself.

30. _____ A change of venue may be requested in order to find a jury that is not prejudiced.

Multiple Choice

31. _____ are courts that hear cases of a general nature that are not within the jurisdiction of limited-jurisdiction trial courts.

A. Inferior trial courts
B. Intermediate appellate courts
C. Courts of record
D. State supreme courts

32. Decisions of the _____ are final unless a question of law is involved that is appealable to the U.S. Supreme Court.

A. highest state courts
B. courts of records
C. courts of appeals
D. general-jurisdiction trial courts

33. The geographical area served by each U.S. court of appeals is referred to as a _____.

A. district
B. circuit
C. range
D. county

34. Which of the following courts was created by Article III of the U.S. Constitution?

A. U.S. Court of Appeals
B. U.S. Tax Court
C. U.S. Supreme Court
D. U.S. Court of Federal Claims

35. The _____ hears cases brought against the United States.

A. U.S. Court of Federal Claims
B. U.S. Tax Court
C. U.S. Supreme Court
D. U.S. District Court

36. Which of the following statements is true of the U.S. Supreme Court?

A. The U.S. Supreme Court does not hear any new evidence or testimony in reviewed cases.
B. The U.S. Supreme Court hears appeals only from the federal circuit courts of appeals.
C. The U.S. Supreme Court's decisions are appealable.
D. The U.S. Supreme Court does not grant any oral hearings to the parties.

37. _____ refers to an official notice that the Supreme Court will review a case.

A. En banc review
B. *Stare decisis*
C. Writ of certiorari
D. *Sua sponte*

38. In the U.S. Supreme Court, if all the justices voting agree as to the outcome and reasoning used to decide a case, it is a _____ decision.

A. tie
B. unanimous
C. majority
D. plurality

39. Mary has already won her case at the U.S. Court of Appeals. When the case is reviewed by the Supreme Court, only eight judges are present. Four of the judges vote for Mary while the other four vote against her. Which if the following will be the result of this case?

A. The case will be sent to the U.S. Court of Appeals for a review.
B. Mary will win and the case will set a precedent for later cases.
C. The case will be reviewed again by the U.S. Supreme Court when all the judges are present.
D. Mary will win the case as she had already won at the U.S. Court of Appeals.

40. Which of the following is true about a plurality decision of the Supreme Court?

A. It settles the case and sets the precedent for later cases.
B. It affirms the decision of the lower court.
C. It settles the case but does not set the precedent for later cases.
D. It causes the case to be reviewed again at later date.

41. In which of the following cases do federal courts have exclusive jurisdiction?

A. suits against the United States
B. federal question cases
C. cases involving sales and lease contracts
D. diversity of citizenship cases

42. In which of the following cases do federal and state courts have concurrent jurisdiction?

A. bankruptcy cases
B. patents cases
C. antitrust cases
D. diversity of citizenship cases

43. _____ refers to jurisdiction to hear a case because of jurisdiction over the property of the lawsuit.

A. Private jurisdiction
B. *Quasi in rem* jurisdiction
C. *In rem* jurisdiction
D. In personam jurisdiction

44. _____ refers to a concept that requires lawsuits to be heard by the court with jurisdiction that is nearest the location in which the incident occurred or where the parties reside.

A. Jurisdiction
B. Doctrine of *stare decisis*
C. Circuit
D. Venue

45. _____ refers to a contract provision that designates a certain state's law or country's law that will be applied in any dispute concerning nonperformance of the contract.

A. Arbitration clause
B. Forum-shopping
C. Choice of law clause
D. Forum selection clause

Short Answer

46. Describe the state court systems.

_____

_____

47. Explain the functions of the special federal courts.

_____

_____

48. Explain the jurisdiction of the U.S. Supreme Court.

_____

_____

49. What are the various types of decisions that can be issued by the Supreme Court?

_____

_____

50. What is diversity of citizenship? Explain its jurisdiction.

_____

_____

51. Explain concurrent jurisdiction.

_____

_____

52. Discuss the need and significance of the long-arm statute.

_____

_____

53. Compare and contrast between *in rem* and *quasi in rem* jurisdiction.

_____

_____

54. Explain the concept of venue. When may a change of venue be requested?

_____

_____

55. Describe the need for forum-selection and choice of law clauses.

_____

_____

Answers to Refresh Your Memory

1. inferior [p. 20]
2. general- jurisdiction [p.20]
3. Federal Claims [p. 24]
4. circuit [p. 24]
5. Supreme Court [p. 26]
6. petition for certiorari [p. 27]
7. writ of certiorari [p. 27]
8. plurality [p. 28]
9. dissenting opinion [p. 28]
10. Federal question [p. 29]
11. exclusive federal [p. 31]
12. standing to sue [p. 32]
13. *in rem* [p. 33]
14. venue [p. 34]
15. choice-of-law [p. 34]

Model Answer to Critical Thought Exercise

To: Ms. Snob
From: Student, District Manager, Intestine Smart Inc.
Re: Response to Lawsuit in Utah State Court

This is a question involving jurisdiction. Jurisdiction is the authority of a court to hear a case. There are three types of jurisdiction: 1) *In personam* whereby the court has jurisdiction over the parties to a lawsuit; 2) *In rem* jurisdiction which is when the court has jurisdiction to hear a case because of jurisdiction over the property involved in the lawsuit; and 3) *quasi in rem* jurisdiction; where jurisdiction is allowed a plaintiff who obtains a judgment in one state to try to collect the judgment by attaching the property of the defendant located in another state.

Even though you were never informed of any sales of Colon Grenade outside of the state of California, we may be required to respond to the suit and defend against it in Utah based on the following reasons:

1) Even though our company wasn't physically located in Utah when Alice Thinstone suffered a ruptured colon, she may apply the principles surrounding the theory set forth in *International Shoe Co. v. Washington,* 326 U.S. 310 wherein the court said that "the Due Process Clause permits jurisdiction over a defendant in any state in which the defendant has 'certain minimum contacts' such that the maintenance of the suit does not offend traditional notions of fair play and substantial justice." Arguably by selling our product to Prescript Co., which operates in 22 states, including Utah, we are receiving the benefit of increased sales, albeit indirectly from Utah resident Alice Thinstone. Further, as was expressed in the court's ruling in *Calder v. Jones,* 465 U.S. 783, 104 S.Ct. 1482, 79 L.Ed.2d 804 (1984), Intestine Smart should "reasonably anticipate being hauled into court" in Utah as it is reasonably foreseeable that Colon Grenade would be sold in different states given the fact that Prescript Co. operates in 22 states, with Utah being one of them. If it is found that Intestine Smart, Inc., had sufficient minimum contacts with the forum State of Utah and that the sale of its product there afforded Intestine Smart the benefits of the laws of the forum state, then we will be required to defend ourselves in a suit in Utah state court.

2) It may be argued that we assumed the risk that our product would be sold to an out-of-state resident as we knowingly and voluntarily negotiated the sale of the Colon Grenade product with Prescript Co., a business operating in several states. Also, we should not be allowed to reap only the benefits of profit from our sales and shirk our corporate ethical responsibility to not harm those to whom our product is sold.

In conclusion, Ms. Snob, it would be in our best interest to respond to the lawsuit filed against us. If we are able to show that there was some other intervening act (such as improper use of Colon Grenade by Ms. Thinstone, some other medical condition that could have had the same result, etc.) responsible for Ms. Thinstone's ruptured colon and that Colon Grenade in no way caused her injury, we may be successful in defending against the suit. We could really secure a feather in our cap if we could demonstrate that despite an alleged forseeability of the injury alleged, the use of Colon Grenade could not have possibly caused the result complained of by Ms. Thinstone. *(Note: A higher degree of understanding is demonstrated by a student who incorporates the reasoning given in this paragraph, as this material is not addressed until later in the text.)*

Answers to Practice Quiz

True/False

16. False. In small claims courts, the parties must appear individually and cannot have lawyers represent them. [p. 20]

17. True. General-jurisdiction trial courts hear cases that are not within the jurisdiction of limited-jurisdiction trial courts, such as felonies, civil cases more than a certain dollar amount, and so on. The decisions handed down by these courts are appealable to an intermediate appellate court or the state supreme court, depending on the circumstances. [p. 20]

18. False. Appellate court decisions are appealable to the state's highest court. [p. 21]

19. True. The function of a state's highest court is to hear appeals from intermediate appellate state courts and certain trial courts. No new evidence or testimony is heard. [p. 21]

20. False. There are 94 U.S. district courts. There is at least one federal district court in each state and the District of Columbia, and heavily populated states have more than one district court. [p. 24]

21. True. The highest court in the land is the Supreme Court of the United States, also called the U.S. Supreme Court, which is located in Washington, DC. The Court is composed of nine justices who are nominated by the president and confirmed by the Senate. [p. 26]

22. False. The Chief Justice of the Supreme Court is appointed by the President of the U.S. [p. 26]

23. False. The Supreme Court, which is an appellate court, hears appeals from federal circuit courts of appeals and, under certain circumstances, from federal district courts, special federal courts, and the highest state courts. The Supreme Court's decision is final. [p. 27]

24. True. The U.S. Constitution gives Congress the authority to establish rules for the appellate review of cases by the Supreme Court, except in the rare case in which mandatory review is required. Congress has given the Supreme Court discretion to decide what cases it will hear. [p. 27]

25. True. Petition for certiorari is a petition asking the Supreme Court to hear a case. [p. 27]

26. False. If there is a tie decision, the lower court decision is affirmed. Such votes are not precedent for later cases. [p. 28]

27. False. A justice who agrees with the outcome of a case but not the reason proffered by other justices can issue a concurring opinion that sets forth his or her reasons for deciding the case. [p. 28]

28. False. There is no dollar-amount limit on federal question cases that can be brought in federal court. [p. 29]

29. True. A court's jurisdiction over a person is called in *personam* jurisdiction. A plaintiff, by filing a lawsuit with a court, gives the court in *personam* jurisdiction over himself or herself. [p. 32]

30. True. Pretrial publicity may prejudice jurors located in the proper venue. In such cases, a change of venue may be requested so that a more impartial jury can be found. [p. 34]

Multiple Choice

31. C. General-jurisdiction trial courts or courts of record hear cases that are not within the jurisdiction of limited-jurisdiction trial courts, such as felonies, civil cases more than a certain dollar amount, and so on. [p. 20]

32. A. The highest court in a state court system hears appeals from intermediate appellate state courts and certain trial courts. Decisions of highest state courts are final unless a question of law is involved that is appealable to the U.S. Supreme Court. [p. 21]

33. B. The geographical area served by each court is referred to as a circuit. There are 13 circuits in the federal court system. [p. 24]

34. C. Article III of the U.S. Constitution provides that the federal government's judicial power is vested in one Supreme Court. This court is the U.S. Supreme Court. [p. 24]

35. A. The special federal courts established by Congress have limited jurisdiction. The U.S. Court of Federal Claims hears cases brought against the United States. [p. 24]

36. A. The Supreme Court hears appeals from federal circuit courts of appeals and, under certain circumstances, from federal district courts, special federal courts, and the highest state courts. No new evidence or testimony is heard. [p. 26]

37. C. Writ of certiorari is an official notice that the Supreme Court will review a case. [p. 27]

38. B. If all the justices voting agree as to the outcome and reasoning used to decide a case, it is a unanimous decision. Unanimous decisions are precedent for later cases. [p. 27]

39. D. If there is a tie decision, the lower court decision is affirmed. [p. 28]

40. C. If a majority of the justices agree as to the outcome of a case but not as to the reasoning for reaching the outcome, it is a plurality decision. A plurality decision settles the case but is not precedent for later cases. [p. 28]

41. A. Federal courts have exclusive jurisdiction to hear cases involving federal crimes, antitrust, bankruptcy, patent and copyright cases, suits against the United States, and admiralty cases. [p. 29]

42. D. State courts have concurrent jurisdiction with federal courts to hear cases involving diversity of citizenship and federal questions over which federal courts do not have exclusive jurisdiction. [p. 31]

43. C. A court may have jurisdiction to hear and decide a case because it has jurisdiction over the property of the lawsuit. This is called *in rem* jurisdiction. [p. 33]

44. D. Venue requires lawsuits to be heard by the court of the court system that has jurisdiction to hear the case that is located nearest to where the incident occurred, where witnesses and evidence are available, and such other relevant factors. [p. 34]

45. C. Parties often agree in contracts as to what state's law or country's law will apply in resolving a dispute. These clauses are called choice-of-law clauses. [p. 35]

Short Answer

46. State court systems include the following:
Limited-Jurisdiction Trial Courts – State limited-jurisdiction trial courts, which are sometimes referred to as inferior trial courts, hear matters of a specialized or limited nature.
General-Jurisdiction Trial Courts – These courts hear cases that are not within the jurisdiction of limited-jurisdiction trial courts, such as felonies, civil cases more than a certain dollar amount, and so on.
Intermediate Appellate Courts – An appellate court reviews either pertinent parts or the whole trial court record from the lower court.
State Supreme court – It is the highest court in a state court system; it hears appeals from intermediate appellate state courts and certain trial courts. [p. 20]

47. The special federal courts established by Congress have limited jurisdiction.
They include the following:
• U.S. Tax Court – The U.S. Tax Court hears cases that involve federal tax laws.
• U.S. Court of Federal Claims – The U.S. Court of Federal Claims hears cases brought against the United States.
• U.S. Court of International Trade – The U.S. Court of International Trade handles cases that involve tariffs and international trade disputes.
• U.S. Bankruptcy Court – The U.S. Bankruptcy Court hears cases that involve federal bankruptcy laws.
• U.S. Court of Appeals for the Armed Forces – The U.S. Court of Appeals for the Armed Forces exercises appellate jurisdiction over members of the armed services.
• U.S. Court of Appeals for Veterans Claims – The U.S. Court of Appeals for Veterans Claims exercises jurisdiction over decisions of the Department of Veterans Affairs.
[p. 24]

48. The highest court in the land is the Supreme Court of the United States, also called the U.S. Supreme Court. The Court is composed of nine justices who are nominated by the president and confirmed by the Senate. The president appoints one justice the Chief Justice of the U.S. Supreme Court, who is responsible for the administration of the Supreme Court. The Supreme Court, which is an appellate court, hears appeals from federal circuit courts of appeals and, under certain circumstances, from federal district courts, special federal courts, and the highest state courts. No new evidence or testimony is heard. The Supreme Court's decision is final. [p. 26]

49. The Supreme Court can issue several types of decisions:
Unanimous Decision – If all the justices voting agree as to the outcome and reasoning used to decide a case, it is a unanimous decision.
Majority Decision – If a majority of the justices agree as to the outcome and reasoning used to decide a case, it is a majority decision.
Plurality Decision – If a majority of the justices agree as to the outcome of a case but not as to the reasoning for reaching the outcome, it is a plurality decision.
Tie Decision – Sometimes the Supreme Court sits without all nine justices being present. There may be a tie decision in such cases. [p. 28]

50. Diversity of citizenship occurs if a lawsuit involves (1) citizens of different states or (2) a citizen of a state and a citizen or subject of a foreign country. If there is diversity of citizenship, the plaintiff may bring the case in either state or federal court. If a plaintiff brings a diversity of citizenship case in federal court, it remains there. If the plaintiff brings a diversity of citizenship case in state court, it will remain there unless the defendant removes the case to federal court. Federal courts must apply the relevant state law to diversity of citizenship cases. [p. 29]

51. State courts have concurrent jurisdiction with federal courts to hear cases involving diversity of citizenship and federal questions over which federal courts do not have exclusive jurisdiction. If a case involving concurrent jurisdiction is brought by a plaintiff in federal court, the case remains in federal court. If the plaintiff brings a case involving concurrent jurisdiction in state court, the defendant can either let the case be decided by the state court or remove the case to federal court. If a case does not qualify to be brought in federal court, it must be brought in the appropriate state court. [p. 31]

52. In most states, a state court can obtain jurisdiction in a civil lawsuit over persons and businesses located in another state or country through the state's long-arm statute. These statutes extend a state's jurisdiction to nonresidents who were not served a summons within the state. The nonresident defendant in the civil lawsuit must have had some minimum contact with the state such that the maintenance of that lawsuit in that state does not offend traditional notions of fair play and substantial justice. The exercise of long-arm jurisdiction is generally permitted over nonresidents who have (1) committed torts within the state, (2) entered into a contract either in the state or that affects the state (and allegedly breached the contract), or (3) transacted other business in the state that allegedly caused injury to another person. [p. 32]

53. A court may have jurisdiction to hear and decide a case because it has jurisdiction over the property of the lawsuit. This is called *in rem* jurisdiction. Sometimes a plaintiff who obtains a judgment against a defendant in one state will try to collect the judgment by attaching property of the defendant that is located in another state. This is permitted under *quasi in rem* jurisdiction, or attachment jurisdiction. [p. 33]

54. Venue requires lawsuits to be heard by the court of the court system that has jurisdiction to hear the case that is located nearest to where the incident occurred, where witnesses and evidence are available, and such other relevant factors. Occasionally,

pretrial publicity may prejudice jurors located in the proper venue. In such cases, a change of venue may be requested so that a more impartial jury can be found. [p. 34]

55. Parties sometimes agree in their contract as to what state's courts, what federal court, or what country's court will have jurisdiction to hear a legal dispute should one arise. Such clauses in contracts are called forum-selection clauses or choice of forum clauses. In addition to agreeing to a forum, the parties also often agree in contracts as to what state's law or country's law will apply in resolving a dispute. These clauses are called choice-of-law clauses. [p. 34]

3 | JUDICIAL, ALTERNATIVE, AND E-DISPUTE RESOLUTION

Chapter Overview

This chapter examines the pretrial litigation process, as well as the concepts involved with dismissals and pretrial judgments and settlement conferences. Emphasis is placed on the importance of a cost-benefit analysis when bringing, maintaining, and defending a lawsuit. The pretrial litigation process, court use of e-filings, and the stages of a trial, as well as appeal are explained. Non-judicial alternatives, such as arbitration and mediation are also discussed.

Objectives

Upon completion of the exercises in this chapter, you should be able to:
1. Describe the pretrial litigation process.
2. Describe how a case proceeds through trial.
3. Describe how a trial court decision is appealed.
4. Explain the use of arbitration and other nonjudicial methods of alternative dispute resolution.
5. Describe e-courts and e-dispute resolution.

Practical Application

You should be able to be familiar with the costs and benefits of bringing and defending a lawsuit. You should have a broader understanding of the pretrial litigation process and the various procedural requirements. You will become familiar with the reasoning behind dismissals, pretrial judgments, and settlement conferences. You should be able to understand the sequence of events associated with a trial as well as the option of appeal after the judgment has been rendered. You will be able to discern whether nonjudicial alternatives may be an option to you depending on the situation that is presented.

Helpful Hints

The pre-litigation process is similar to playing a board game, as an individual must proceed through various steps in order to reach a final goal. If you view discovery as a means of determining your opponent's strategy, it will assist you in reaching the most desirable outcome in a case. Review of this chapter's study sheet and completion of the Refresh Your Memory exercise followed by the Critical Thought Exercise and Sample Quiz are all helpful in committing the various pretrial, trial, and appeal processes.

Study Tips

The laws and their development that you became familiar with in Chapter One as well as the court systems you learned about in Chapter two are analogous to the base layer of a specialty cake. It is by knowing the appropriate law and court within the proper court system that you will be able to apply the correct legal principles to situations as they occur. The areas of law in the chapters that follow will provide the upper layers and frosting to this unique cake. The essential ingredients of adhering to the proper time and procedural requirements along with satisfying the essential substantive elements for various legal actions are what provide balance to this legally created pastry if you will.

Litigation, as you know, is the process of bringing, maintaining, and defending a lawsuit. It is through the pretrial litigation process that we are able to do just that. The process of discovery enables us to adequately prepare a case. Some of the most common forms of discovery include depositions, interrogatories, the production of documents, and physical and mental examinations. Once a case is set for trial, a variety of methodical steps are enacted to determine liability in a case. Of course, the individual who loses has the option of appeal. Note, should a person determine that litigation is not the best way to handle a situation; there are a variety of alternative dispute resolution choices that may be more suitable to the individual or particular case.

What are the advantages and disadvantages of bringing and defending a lawsuit?

It is very important to consider all of the factors involved when deciding to sue or defend a lawsuit. This is known as the cost-benefit analysis. This is a commonsense decision that can be made by weighing how much money will be won or lost in light of your chances of winning or losing against the costs to litigate, expenses associated with employees being released from work, as well as prejudgment interest provided by the law. Other emotional considerations such as the impact on the relationship of the parties and their reputations, as well as the mental aggravation and turmoil that may manifest itself should also be factored in. A caveat of the potential for error in the legal system must not be discarded in balancing whether or not it is wise to bring or defend a lawsuit.

When can a lawsuit be brought?

This refers to federal and state government time limitations regarding the period of time the plaintiff has the right to sue a defendant. Statutes of limitations will vary depending on the type of lawsuit involved.

What is involved in the pretrial litigation process?

The pretrial litigation process is an essential ingredient in the foundational layer of the legal process. You must be familiar with the various important pleadings of complaint, answer, cross-complaint, and reply when initiating and responding to a lawsuit. You will need to know about the different types of discovery and what activities both parties may participate in to discover facts of the case from one another as well as witnesses before trial. The primary types of discovery are depositions, interrogatories, production of documents, and physical and mental examinations. A familiarity with the pretrial motions of judgment on the pleadings, and motion for summary judgment should be developed to create an understanding that some lawsuits in whole or in part should not go to trial. You should be aware of the purpose of a settlement conference and realize that if a settlement is not forthcoming, this tool is important in identifying the main trial issues.

What are the stages of a trial?

A legal trial is much like a performance at a theater. There are those who are performing the case in a methodical fashion from beginning to end. In using this comparison, the program of a trial would read in the following order: jury selection, opening statements, the plaintiff's case, the defendant's case, rebuttal, rejoinder, closing arguments, jury instructions, with the jury deliberation and the entry of judgment acting as the end of the show. The sequel to the trial in a civil case is the appeal, which can be brought by either the plaintiff or the defendant. In a criminal trial, the appeal can only be brought by the defendant. Opening and responding briefs may be filed with the court. The drama of this performance is in the appellate court finding an error of law in the record, in which case the lower court decision will be reversed.

What other choices does a person have?

Sometimes, using the court system to resolve disputes results in a great expenditure of money and time. In order to alleviate these concerns, alternative dispute resolution methods are being utilized to resolve disputes rather than using litigation. Some of the alternatives that are available include mediation, conciliation, mini-trial, fact-finding, and a judicial referee.

Refresh Your Memory

The following exercise will give you the opportunity to test your memory of the principles given in this chapter. Read the question twice and place your answer in the blank provided. Review the chapter material for any question that you are unable to answer or remember.

1. _____ is the process of bringing, maintaining, and defending a lawsuit.

2. The paperwork that is filed with the court to initiate and respond to a lawsuit is referred to as the _____.

3. A court order that directs the defendant to appear in court and answer the complaint is called a _____.

4. If the defendant does not answer the complaint, a _____ is entered against him or her.

5. The act of a court to combine two or more separate lawsuits into one lawsuit is called _____.

6. A _____ occurs when a group of plaintiffs collectively bring a lawsuit against a defendant.

7. A _____ establishes the period during which a plaintiff must bring a lawsuit against a defendant.

8. A _____ is oral testimony given by a party or witness prior to trial.

9. _____ are written questions submitted by one party to a lawsuit to another party.

10. The defendant's attorney can call additional witnesses and introduce other evidence to counter the rebuttal. This is called the _____.

11. The trial court usually issues a _____ that sets forth the reasons for the judgment.

12. An appellant is also called a _____.

13. _____ is a procedure whereby the parties to a legal dispute engage in discussions to try to reach a voluntary settlement of their dispute.

14. A _____ is an impartial third party who hears and decides the dispute.

15. A _____ is a voluntary private proceeding in which lawyers for each side present a shortened version of their case to the representatives of both sides.

Critical Thought Exercise

You are the manager at the Green-R-Us, an organic health food store in a small town in Tennessee. Three weeks ago, one of your employees reported that there had been an incident on their shift where a customer had slipped and fallen when a large cup of tofu "coffee" had been spilled near the cash register. The drink had been spilled by the customer immediately ahead of the customer who had slipped and fallen. Since your employee was the only employee on duty at the time, he had finished the transaction for the customer, logged off of the cash register, and asked the remaining customer to wait while he went to the back of the store to retrieve a mop to clean up the spill and warned the customer to avoid the spill. When the employee returned, that customer was on the floor after slipping in the spilled drink. Your employee offered to call an ambulance, but the customer declined and left the store to return to their bicycle and peddle away.

You have been called to a meeting with the owner, who has just received a letter from an attorney for Mr. Lott A.Cashe, who is the customer who slipped and fell in your store. Mr. Cashe is demanding that your store pay damages for the injuries he sustained when he slipped and fell in your store. He maintains that he has sustained back, neck, hip, knee, and ankle injuries as result of this accident with medical bills in the amount of $2,240. He states that he has missed work, incurring $2,500 in lost income. He asserts that he has been unable to care for his four children on his own and has incurred $1,600 in paying for unanticipated child care. He states that he has been unable to drive and has sustained $480 in hiring taxis to take him to necessary medical appointments. Additionally, he claims that there are other miscellaneous expenses related to his injuries, as well as the pain and suffering and inconvenience that cannot be quantified, that he believes to be compensable at $3,000. The total amount of damages he is demanding is $9,820.

The owner of the Greens-R-Us has asked that you review Mr. Cashe's demands and advise him as to how you think he should proceed, since the incident happened on your watch. He has held a preliminary consultation with his attorney of one hour. His lawyer has estimated that an immediate settlement could be made for the amount requested for no additional fee on her part. A negotiated settlement could require 20 to 30 hours of her time. Taking the case to court could take 100 hours or more of her time in preparation and an additional 10 hours in court. His attorney charges $150 per hour, with a charge of $300 for court time.

Write a memo to the owner outlining how you think the owner should reply to Mr. Cashe's demands and explaining your reasons for your advice.

Please compose your answer to the Critical Thinking Exercise using a separate sheet of paper or your computer word processing program.

Practice Quiz

16. _____ The complaint and summons are served on the plaintiff.

17. _____ An answer is the defendant's written response to a plaintiff's complaint that is filed with the court and served on the plaintiff.

18. _____ A class action is a court order directing the defendant to appear in court and answer the complaint.

19. _____ A reply is a document filed by the original plaintiff in response to the defendant's cross-complaint.

20. _____ The act of people interested in the lawsuit joining as parties to an existing lawsuit is called arbitration.

21. _____ The statute of limitations for all lawsuits in the United States is two years.

22. _____ A plaintiff can appeal for the extension of the statute of limitations and sue the defendant.

23. _____ The motion for summary judgment alleges that if all the facts presented in the pleadings are taken as true, the party making the motion would win the lawsuit when the proper law is applied to these asserted facts.

24. _____ Motions for summary judgment are supported by evidence outside of the pleadings.

25. _____ A pretrial hearing is also known as a settlement conference.

26. _____ In a jury trial, the judge is the trier of fact.

27. _____ *Voir dire* is the process whereby the jurors ask prospective judges questions to determine whether they would be biased in their decisions.

28. _____ After a witness is sworn in, he or she is cross-examined by the plaintiff's attorney.

29. _____ Only the defendant can appeal in a criminal case.

30. ____ Negotiation is a procedure whereby the parties choose an impartial third party to hear and decide the dispute.

Multiple Choice

31. _____ refers to the document a plaintiff files with the court that serves on the defendant to initiate a lawsuit.

A. Rejoinder
B. Order
C. Appeal
D. Complaint

32. Which of the following terms denotes the defendant's written response to a plaintiff's complaint that is filed with the court and served on the plaintiff?

A. answer
B. summons
C. rejoinder
D. rebuttal

33. In which of the following cases is a default judgment entered?

A. A defendant admits all the allegations in the complaint.
B. There is insufficient evidence to resolve the dispute.
C. A defendant does not file a written response to a plaintiff's complaint.
D. The court believes that the lawsuit can be settled before/without trial.

34. Which of the following can be filed by the defendant of a lawsuit?

A. answer
B. complaint
C. reply
D. injunction

35. In which of the following cases does a class action occur?

A. There are no factual disputes to be decided by the jury.
B. A group of plaintiffs collectively bring a lawsuit against a defendant.
C. The defendant has multiple grounds for appeal.
D. The plaintiff does not reply to the defender's cross-complaint.

36. The statute of limitations establishes the period within which _____.

A. a motion for judgment on the pleadings can be made by either party
B. a defendant must file a written answer against a plaintiff's complaint
C. a defendant can file a cross-complaint against the plaintiff
D. a plaintiff must bring a lawsuit against a defendant

37. The term _____ refers to the oral testimony given by a party or witness prior to trial.

A. deposition
B. class action
C. interrogatory
D. intervention

38. _____ are written questions submitted by one party to a lawsuit to another party.

A. Depositions
B. Interrogatories
C. Rejoinders
D. Summons

39. Which of the following motions asserts that there are no factual disputes to be decided by the jury, and that the judge can apply the proper law to the undisputed facts and decide the case without a jury?

A. motion for judgment notwithstanding the verdict
B. motion for judgment on the pleadings
C. motion for a directed verdict
D. motion for summary judgment

40. What is the purpose of a pretrial hearing?

A. requesting the other party to produce all documents relevant to the case
B. assessing the factual accuracy of the deposition of witnesses
C. facilitating the settlement of a case before it goes to trial
D. instructing the judge to decide the case without a jury

41. Which of the following statements is true of the plaintiff's case?

A. The plaintiff's attorney examines the witnesses during cross-examination.
B. The defendant's attorney can ask questions only about the subjects that were brought up during the direct examination.
C. The defendant's attorney examines the witnesses during re-direct examination.
D. Documents and other evidence have to be introduced before the first witness is subject to direct examination.

42. What is jury deliberation?

A. jurors considering the evidence and attempting to reach a decision
B. jurors re-questioning a particular witness from one of the parties
C. jury and the judge disagreeing on the outcome of the case
D. jurors being replaced in case of illness or disqualification

43. The appealing party in an appeal is called a(n) _____.

A. appellate
B. appellee
C. petitioner
D. respondent

44. Which of the following is a method of alternative dispute resolution?

A. pretrial hearing
B. settlement conference
C. appeal
D. fact- finding

45. A(n) _____ is a voluntary private proceeding in which lawyers for each side present a shortened version of their case to the representatives of both sides.

A. pretrial hearing
B. mini-trial
C. arbitration
D. appeal

Short Answer

46. What are the major phases of pretrial litigation process?

_____

_____

47. What are the different types of pleading?

_____

_____

48. What are the major forms of discovery?

_____

_____

49. Explain the two pretrial motions.

_____

_____

50. Differentiate between trials with and without jury.

_____

_____

51. What are the different stages of trial?

_____

_____

52. What can a party to a lawsuit do if he or she is displeased with the trial court's judgment?

_____

_____

53. What are the different forms of alternative dispute resolution?

_____

_____

54. What is the advantage of a mini-trial?

_____

_____

55. Describe e-courts and e-dispute resolution.

_____

_____

Answers to Refresh Your Memory

1. Litigation [p. 41]
2. pleadings [p. 41]
3. summons [p. 42]
4. default judgment [p. 42]
5. consolidation [p. 43]
6. class action [p. 43]
7. statute of limitations [p. 45]
8. deposition [p. 45]
9. Interrogatories [p. 46]
10. rejoinder [p. 49]
11. written memorandum [p. 50]
12. petitioner [p. 50]
13. Negotiation [p. 52]
14. arbitrator [p. 52]
15. mini-trial [p. 54]

Model Answer to Critical Thought Exercise

To: Owner, Greens-R-Us
From: Student, Manager, Greens-R-Us

Re: Response to Mr. Cashe's Claims

Essentially, this is what is called a "nuisance suit", because a business will often settle, as the costs for defending suits of this kind generally outweigh any "savings" of winning in court.

The report given by our employee shows that Mr. Cashe was aware of and warned of the spill. No one saw him fall, as he was on floor when the employee returned with the mop. Mr. Cashe declined medical attention at the time, and walked away with no apparent injury.

Documentation of Mr. Cashe's purported injuries and related expenses is necessary to ensure that his injuries are legitimate and the result of this accident. This information can be used to quash an unfounded claim, to negotiate a fair settlement based on accurate data, or as discovery for a court case.

If Mr. Cashe provides some or all of the requested documentation, we would then need to evaluate whether agreeing to a settlement would be less expensive than defending against his claim in court. Our attorney has estimated that it would cost between $1,500 and $4,500 for her services in the event of a settlement. She estimates that her services would cost at least $10,500 if the case were to go to court. There would also be the costs for additional wages and lost time to be in court for employees acting as witnesses or representing the store, transportation costs, clerical costs, and other miscellaneous expenses.

An initial request for documentation from Mr. Cashe could be made by us, rather than the attorney. If his claim is spurious, such a request may be sufficient for him to drop his claim. A letter from our attorney could add weight to our request for documentation and provide additional discouragement for any bogus claims. The time required for such a letter would be minimal.

If Mr. Cashe proceeds with his claim and provides the necessary documentation, it would appear that a settlement would be in our best interests, as attorney fees alone would make the defense against this claim in court more expensive than is the proposed amount of the settlement.

It is imperative that Mr. Cashe provide documentation of his injuries and related expenses prior to negotiating a settlement. We must not settle a claim unless that claim is legitimate, or we will have many such claims by those looking for an easy windfall.

Answers to Practice Quiz

True/False

16. False. The complaint and summons are served on the defendant. [p. 42]

17. True. The defendant, the party who is being sued, must file an answer to the plaintiff's complaint. In the answer, the defendant admits or denies the allegations contained in the plaintiff's complaint. [p. 42]

18. False. A class action occurs when a group of plaintiffs collectively bring a lawsuit against a defendant. [p. 43]

19. True. The original plaintiff must file a reply (answer) to the cross-complaint. The reply, which can include affirmative defenses, must be filed with the court and served on the original defendant. [p. 43]

20. False. The act of people interested in the lawsuit joining as parties to an existing lawsuit is called intervention. [p. 43]

21. False. Federal and state governments have established statutes of limitations for each type of lawsuit. Most are from one to four years, depending on the type of lawsuit. [p. 45]

22. False. If a lawsuit is not filed within this time period, the plaintiff loses his or her right to sue. [p. 45]

23. False. A motion for summary judgment asserts that there are no factual disputes to be decided by the jury and that the judge should apply the relevant law to the undisputed facts and decide the case. [p. 47]

24. True. Motions for summary judgment, which can be made by either party, are supported by evidence outside the pleadings. Affidavits from the parties and witnesses, documents, depositions, and such are common forms of evidence. [p. 47]

25. True. Federal court rules and most state court rules permit the court to direct the attorneys or parties to appear before the court for a settlement conference, or pretrial hearing. [p. 47]

26. False. The judge sits as the trier of fact in nonjury trials. [p. 48]

27. False. *Voir dire* is the process whereby the judge and attorneys ask prospective jurors questions to determine whether they would be biased in their decisions. [p. 49]

28. False. After a witness has been sworn in, the plaintiff's attorney examines the witness. This is called direct examination. [p. 49]

29. True. In a civil case, either party can appeal the trial court's decision once a final Judgment is entered. Only the defendant can appeal in a criminal case. [p. 50]

30. False. Negotiation is a procedure whereby the parties to a legal dispute engage in discussions to try to reach a voluntary settlement of their dispute. [p. 52]

Multiple Choice

31. D. To initiate a lawsuit, the party who is suing (the plaintiff) must file a complaint in the proper court. [p. 41]

32. A. The defendant's answer is filed with the court and served on the plaintiff. In the answer, the defendant admits or denies the allegations contained in the plaintiff's complaint. [p. 42]

33. C. If the defendant does not answer the complaint, a default judgment is entered against him or her. A default judgment establishes the defendant's liability. The plaintiff then has only to prove damages. [p. 42]

34. The defendant, the party who is being sued, must file an answer to the plaintiff's complaint. [p. 42]

35. B. A class action occurs when a group of plaintiffs collectively bring a lawsuit against a defendant. [p. 43]

36. D. A statute of limitations establishes the period during which a plaintiff must bring a lawsuit against a defendant. If a lawsuit is not filed within this time period, the plaintiff loses his or her right to sue. [p. 45]

37. A. A deposition is oral testimony given by a party or witness prior to trial. The deposition of a witness can be given voluntarily or pursuant to a subpoena (court order). [p. 45]

38. B. Interrogatories are written questions submitted by one party to another party. The questions must be answered in writing within a stipulated time. [p. 46]

39. D. Motion for summary judgment asserts that there are no factual disputes to be decided by the jury and that the judge can apply the proper law to the undisputed facts and decide the case without a jury. These motions are supported by affidavits, documents, and deposition testimony. [p. 47]

40. C. Federal court rules and most state court rules permit the court to direct the attorneys or parties to appear before the court for a settlement conference, or pretrial hearing. One of the major purposes of such hearings is to facilitate the settlement of a case. [p. 47]

41. B. A plaintiff bears the burden of proof to persuade the trier of fact of the merits of his or her case. This is called the plaintiff's case. The defendant's attorney can ask questions only about the subjects that were brought up during the direct examination. [p. 49]

42. A. After the judge reads the jury instructions, the jury retires to the jury room to consider the evidence and attempt to reach a decision. This is called jury deliberation. [p. 49]

43. C. In a civil case, either party can appeal the trial court's decision once a final judgment is entered. The appealing party is called the appellant, or petitioner. [p. 50]

44. C. Alternative dispute resolution (ADR) is a method of resolving disputes outside the court judicial system. Fact-finding is a form of ADR. [p. 52]

45. B. A mini-trial is a voluntary private proceeding in which lawyers for each side present a shortened version of their case to the representatives of both sides. The representatives of each side who attend the mini-trial have the authority to settle the dispute. [p. 54]

Short Answer

46. The pretrial litigation process can be divided into the following major phases: pleadings, discovery, pretrial motions, and settlement conference.
Pleadings – The paperwork that is filed with the court to initiate and respond to a lawsuit is referred to as the pleadings.
Discovery – The legal process provides for a detailed pretrial procedure called discovery.
Pretrial motions – There are several pretrial motions that parties to a lawsuit can make to try to resolve or dispose of all or part of a lawsuit prior to trial. The two pretrial motions are motion for judgment on the pleadings and motion for summary judgment.
Settlement conference – Federal court rules and most state court rules permit the court to direct the attorneys or parties to appear before the court for a settlement conference, or pretrial hearing. [p. 41, 45, 47]

47. The different types of pleading are:
Complaint – A document filed by a plaintiff with a court and served with a summons on the defendant. It sets forth the basis of the lawsuit.
Answer – A document filed by a defendant with a court and served on the plaintiff. It usually denies most allegations of the complaint.
Cross-complaint and reply – A document filed and served by a defendant if he or she countersues the plaintiff. The defendant is the cross-complainant, and the plaintiff is the cross-defendant. The cross-defendant must file and serve a reply (answer). [p. 43]

48. The major forms of discovery are as follows:
Deposition – A deposition is oral testimony given by a party or witness prior to trial.
Interrogatories – Interrogatories are written questions submitted by one party to a lawsuit to another party.
Production of documents – One party to a lawsuit may request that the other party produce all documents that are relevant to the case prior to trial. This is called production of documents.
Physical or Mental Examination – In cases that concern the physical or mental condition of a party, a court can order the party to submit to certain physical or mental examinations to determine the extent of the alleged injuries. [p. 46]

49. Motion for Judgment on the Pleadings – A motion for judgment on the pleadings can be made by either party once the pleadings are complete. This motion alleges that if all the facts presented in the pleadings are true, the party making the motion would win the lawsuit when the proper law is applied to these facts.
Motion for Summary Judgment – The trier of fact (i.e., the jury or, if there is no jury, the judge) determines factual issues. A motion for summary judgment asserts that there are

no factual disputes to be decided by the jury and that the judge should apply the relevant law to the undisputed facts and decide the case. [p. 47]

50. Pursuant to the Seventh Amendment to the U.S. Constitution, a party to a civil action at law is guaranteed the right to a jury trial in a case in federal court. If either party requests a jury, the trial will be by jury. If both parties waive their right to a jury, the trial will occur without a jury. The judge sits as the trier of fact in nonjury trials. Lawyers for each party and the judge can ask prospective jurors questions to determine whether they would be biased in their decisions. Biased jurors can be prevented from sitting on a particular case. [p. 48]

51. The different stages of trial are:
Jury Selection – The pool of potential jurors is usually selected from voter or automobile registration lists. Individuals are selected to hear specific cases through a process called *voir dire*.
Opening Statements – Each party's attorney is allowed to make an opening statement to the jury at the beginning of a trial.
The Plaintiff's Case – A plaintiff bears the burden of proof to persuade the trier of fact of the merits of his or her case. This is called the plaintiff's case.
The Defendant's Case – The defendant's case must (1) rebut the plaintiff's evidence, (2) prove any affirmative defenses asserted by the defendant, and (3) prove any allegations contained in the defendant's cross-complaint.
Rebuttal and Rejoinder – After the defendant's attorney has finished calling witnesses, the plaintiff's attorney can call witnesses and put forth evidence to rebut the defendant's case. This is called a rebuttal. The defendant's attorney can call additional witnesses and introduce other evidence to counter the rebuttal. This is called the rejoinder.
Closing Arguments – At the conclusion of the presentation of the evidence, each party's attorney is allowed to make a closing argument to the jury.
Jury Instructions, Deliberation, and Verdict – Once the closing arguments are completed, the judge reads jury instructions (or charges) to the jury. This is called jury deliberation, which can take from a few minutes to many weeks. After deliberation, the jury reaches a verdict.
Entry of Judgment – After the jury has returned its verdict, in most cases the judge will enter a judgment to the successful party, based on the verdict. [p. 48]

52. In a civil case, either party can appeal the trial court's decision once a final judgment is entered. Only the defendant can appeal in a criminal case. The appeal is made to the appropriate appellate court. A notice of appeal must be filed by a party within a prescribed time after judgment is entered. An appellate court will reverse a lower court decision if it finds an error of law in the record. [p. 50]

53. The different forms of alternative dispute resolution are:
Negotiation – Negotiation is a procedure whereby the parties to a legal dispute engage in discussions to try to reach a voluntary settlement of their dispute.
Arbitration – In arbitration, the parties choose an impartial third party to hear and decide the dispute.

Mediation – Mediation is a form of negotiation in which a neutral third party assists the disputing parties in reaching a settlement of their dispute.

Mini-Trial – A mini-trial is a voluntary private proceeding in which lawyers for each side present a shortened version of their case to the representatives of both sides.

Fact-Finding – In some situations, called fact-finding, the parties to a dispute employ a neutral third party to act as a fact-finder to investigate the dispute.

Judicial Referee – If the parties agree, the court may appoint a judicial referee to conduct a private trial and render a judgment. [p. 52]

54. Mini-trials serve a useful purpose in that they act as a substitute for a real trial, but they are much briefer and not as complex and expensive to prepare for. Because the strengths and weaknesses of both sides' cases are exposed, the parties are usually more realistic regarding their own positions and the merits of settling the case prior to an expensive, and often risky, trial. [p. 54]

55. Electronic courts, or e-courts, also referred to as virtual courthouses, are substantially being used by courts. Technology allows for the electronic filing—e-filing—of pleadings, briefs, and other documents related to a lawsuit. In addition, technology allows for the scanning of evidence and documents into a computer for storage and retrieval and for e-mailing correspondence and documents to the court, the opposing counsel, and clients. Scheduling and other conferences with the judge or opposing counsel are held via telephone conferences and e-mail. Many courts have instituted electronic document filing and tracking. In some courts, e-filing of pleadings and other documents is now mandatory. [p. 56]

4 | CONSTITUTIONAL LAW FOR BUSINESS AND E-COMMERCE

Chapter Overview

This chapter details the functions of the United States Constitution and provides a solid overview of the legal framework under which our government operates. Emphasis is placed on the concepts of federalism and the separation of powers, as well as the federal government's power to regulate foreign, interstate, and local commerce. You will gain familiarity with the First Amendment and its application to the Internet. The concepts of substantive and procedural due process, equal protection, and the constitutional limits on e-commerce are also explored.

Objectives

Upon completion of the exercises in this chapter, you should be able to:
1. Describe the concept of federalism and the doctrine of separation of powers.
2. Define and apply the Supremacy Clause of the U.S. Constitution.
3. Explain the federal government's authority to regulate interstate commerce and foreign commerce.
4. Explain how the freedoms of speech, assembly, religion, and the press are protected by the First Amendment and how commercial speech may be limited.
5. Explain the doctrines of equal protection and due process.

Practical Application

You should be able to understand the importance of the Commerce Clause and the government's reasoning behind regulation of commerce. You should also be able to understand what types of speech are protected and the limitations on speech. You should be able to understand and apply the various standards of review in equal protection cases. It is important to understand the difference between substantive due process and procedural due process.

Helpful Hints

This chapter should be approached much as you would approach the weighing of and need for various elements in a scientific laboratory. The chapter begins with a discussion on the powers given to the federal government and those that are reserved for the states. The chapter discusses the creation, need, and function of balancing the three branches of government. The importance and impact of the commerce clause on the government and its place in business are examined. The limitations on the First Amendment Freedom of Speech based on the type of speech and restrictions on the government concerning Freedom of Religion are discussed. The important balancing of classification as set forth in a government regulation against governmental standards in equal protection cases are scrutinized. As you review the study tips section and complete the various chapter exercises, it is beneficial to weigh the governmental interest against what is being protected.

Study Tips

Constitution of the United States of America

The two major functions that the U.S. Constitution serves are to create the three branches of the federal government (i.e., the executive, legislative, and judicial) and allocate powers to these branches, as well as to protect individual rights by limiting the government's ability to restrict those rights.

Federalism

This refers to our country's form of government. The states and the federal government share powers. Sometimes the federal law and state law conflict. When this happens, the federal law prevails.

Branches of the Federal Government

You should familiarize yourself with the legislative, executive, and judicial branches of government and know what function each branch serves, as well as how each affects one another.

State and Local Government Regulation of Business – "Police Power"

States are able to regulate intrastate and a large amount of interstate business that takes place within its borders. The police power given to the states allows the states to make laws that protect or promote the health, safety, morals, and welfare of its citizens.

Bill of Rights

You should know that the Bill of Rights is the ten amendments to the United States Constitution. Also, the two rights that are heavily emphasized are the Freedom of Speech and the Freedom of Religion as per the First Amendment.

Freedom of Speech

It is important to realize that this freedom extends only to speech and not conduct. You should also familiarize yourself with the types of speech. It is helpful to list them and place the protection each is given next to them. The following demonstrates an easy way to do this.

Political Speech – fully protected
Commercial Speech – An example would be advertising. Speeches used by businesses are subject to time, place, and manner restrictions.

Offensive Speech – Speech that is offensive to a lot of people is also subject to time, place, and manner restrictions.

Unprotected Speech includes dangerous speech, fighting words, defamatory language, child pornography, and obscene speech.

Note that with obscene speech, the states can define the meaning of obscene speech. It has been stated that obscene is where the average person's prurient interest is appealed to, and the work is patently offensive, thereby describing the sexual conduct in accordance with the state law and the work is in need of serious literary, artistic, political, or social value.

Freedom of Religion

The Constitution mandates that local, state and federal governments be neutral regarding religion. There are two religion clauses in the First Amendment between which you should know the difference:

- The Establishment Clause prohibits the government from establishing a state religion or promoting one religion over another.

- The Free Exercise Clause prevents the government from making laws that inhibit or prohibit people from participating in or practicing their chosen religion.

Commerce

This is a very important term to know. As you may recall, the Commerce Clause of the Constitution has the greatest impact on business than any other clause. In order to fully appreciate as well as understand this importance, you need to know the following:

- The difference between interstate and intrastate commerce is that interstate involves instrumentalities of trade moving across state borders. Compare this to intrastate where commerce is moving within the state.

- The traditional role of government in regulating interstate commerce was to regulate only commerce that moved in interstate commerce. Whereas modernly the federal government may regulate local commerce if it has an impact on commerce as a whole.

- If state law burdens interstate commerce, then the law is declared void and unconstitutional.

The Equal Protection Clause

This clause of the Fourteenth Amendment states that a state cannot "deny to any person within its jurisdiction the equal protection of the laws." Though it primarily applies to state and local governments, it also applies to federal government action. You must know the three standards for review of equal protection cases:

- *Strict Scrutiny* is applied when there is a classification that is a suspect class, such as race.

- *Intermediate Scrutiny* is applied when the classification is based on a protected class that is not race, such as age and sex.

- The *Rational Basis Test* is applied when neither a suspect nor protected class is involved. All that is needed is a justifiable reason for the law trying to be enacted.

The Due Process Clause

This clause is provided for in the Fifth and Fourteenth Amendments as both have a due process clause. The Fifth Amendment applies to the federal government whereas the Fourteenth Amendment applies to state and local government. The crux of this clause is that no individual shall be deprived of life, liberty, or property without due process of law. There are two types of due process:

- Substantive due process refers to the content of the law. It must be clear, not too broad, and worded in such a way that a "reasonable person" could understand the law in order to obey it.

- Procedural due process requires that a person be given notice and an opportunity to be heard before his/her life, liberty, or property is taken.
    - The Just Compensation Clause, which states the government must pay to the owner just compensation for taking an individual's property, is included here.

Privileges and Immunities Clause

This clause prohibits states from enforcing laws that unduly favor their own residents, thereby resulting in discrimination against residents of other states.

Refresh Your Memory

The following exercise will give you the opportunity to test your memory of the principles given in this chapter. Read the question twice and place your answer in the blank provided. Review the chapter material for any question that you are unable to answer or remember.

1. _____ are certain powers delegated to the federal government by the states.

2. The legislative branch is _____; that is, it consists of the U.S. Senate and the U.S. House of Representatives.

3. The president is selected by the _____, whose representatives are appointed by state delegations.

4. The concept of federal law taking precedence over state or local law is commonly called the _____ doctrine.

5. The _____ Act establishes the requirements for conducting casino gambling and other gaming activities on tribal land.

6. Power that permits states and local governments to enact laws to protect or promote the public health, safety, morals, and general welfare is called the _____.

7. The _____ guarantees certain fundamental rights to natural persons and protects these rights from intrusive government action.

8. _____ speech cannot be prohibited or regulated by the government.

9. Defamatory language and obscene speech are examples of _____.

10. The _____ prohibits the government from either establishing a government-sponsored religion or promoting one religion over another.

11. _____ Clause of the Fourteenth Amendment provides that a state cannot "deny to any person within its jurisdiction the equal protection of the laws."

12. _____ test is a test that is applied to classifications based on race.

13. The _____ Clause provides that no person shall be deprived of "life, liberty, or property" without due process of the law.

14. The _____ process form of due process requires that the government give a person proper notice and hearing of legal action before that person is deprived of his or her life, liberty, or property.

15. _____ Clause prohibits states from enacting laws that unduly discriminate in favor of their residents.

Critical Thought Exercise

Larry Brown is a very religious person and is very active in the anti-abortion movement. While Brown travels the streets of his hometown of Westerfield, Illinois, he plays taped sermons and spiritual music that support his religious and political views. The City of Westerfield enacted an ordinance that prohibited the playing of car sound systems at a volume that would be "audible" at a distance greater than fifty feet. Brown was arrested and convicted for violating the ordinance. Brown appealed his conviction on the grounds that the ordinance violated his right to free speech and free exercise of his religious beliefs. The City of Westerfield countered that noise coming from Brown's car could pose a hazard if he and other drivers were unable to hear emergency vehicles as they approached, and as such, the ordinance was a proper exercise of the police power possessed by the State of Illinois.

Was the playing of sermons by Brown protected by the Free Speech and Free Exercise clauses of the First Amendment to the United States Constitution?

Please compose your answer to the Critical Thinking Exercise using a separate sheet of paper or your computer word processing program.

Practice Quiz

True/False

16. ____ In federalism, the federal government and the state governments share powers.

17. ____ Reserved powers are delegated to the judiciary by the President of the United States.

18. _____ Checks and balances built into the Constitution ensure that amendments to the Constitution are not contradictory to existing laws.

19. _____ The Supremacy Clause establishes that the fundamental legal and political authority is vested in the citizens of the U.S.A.

20. _____ Indian Gaming Regulatory Act establishes the requirements for conducting casino gambling and other gaming activities on tribal land.

21. _____ State governments do not have the power to regulate commerce with foreign nations.

22. _____ If the federal government has chosen not to regulate an area of commerce despite possessing the Commerce Clause powers to regulate it, the area is subject to Dormant Commerce Clause.

23. _____ E-commerce is not subject to the Commerce Clause of the Constitution, as most businesses that conduct e-commerce over the Internet do not have any physical location.

24. _____ The Bill of Rights establishes the United States as a federal nation and divides power between the center and the states.

25. _____ Lila, a newspaper columnist from Chicago, is unhappy with the soaring price of fuel in the U.S. She publishes an article that criticizes the government's refusal to offer gasoline at a subsidized price. This is an example of fully protected speech.

26. _____ Advertising is categorized as limited protected speech.

27. _____ The Establishment Clause guarantees that there will be no state-sponsored religion.

28. _____ The Equal Protection Clause of the Fourteenth Amendment provides that a state cannot promote one religion over other religions.

29. _____ Intermediate scrutiny test is applied to classifications based on a protected class other than race.

30. _____ Substantive due process requires that that the government give a person proper notice and hearing of legal action before that person is deprived of his or her life, liberty, or property.

Multiple Choice

31. When the states ratified the Constitution, they delegated _____ powers to the federal government.

A. reserved
B. enumerated
C. police
D. statutory

32. Reserved powers are given to the _____ by the Constitution.

A. federal government
B. judiciary
C. U.S. Congress
D. state governments

33. The _____ is responsible for making federal law.

A. President
B. state governments
C. Supreme Court
D. legislative branch

34. Why have checks and balances been built into the U.S. Constitution?

A. to keep a check on the number and frequency of amendments made to the Constitution
B. to prevent any one of the three branches of the government from becoming too powerful
C. to ensure the judiciary is not biased or corrupt
D. to ensure that people of all races and ethnicities are uniformly represented

35. The _____ provides that federal law takes precedence over state or local law.

A. Bill of Rights
B. Preemption doctrine
C. Due Process Clause
D. Free Exercise Clause

36. The Indian Gaming Regulatory Act sets the terms of _____ activities on tribal land.

A. mining
B. hunting and gathering
C. agriculture and animal rearing
D. casino gambling

37. Which of the following statements is true of the United States' Foreign Commerce Clause?

A. Direct regulation of foreign commerce by the federal government violates the Commerce Clause.
B. A state can enact a law that forbids a foreign country from doing business in that state, if that country engages in activities that are not condoned by that state.
C. Regulation of foreign commerce by state governments is unconstitutional.
D. A state government is only permitted to regulate foreign trade indirectly.

38. Which of the following statements is true of states' police power?

A. They are given the authority to enact laws that regulate the conduct of business.
B. The states are allowed to regulate army activities within their borders.
C. Police power restricts states from regulating inter-state commerce, although it happens within their borders.
D. The police force of a state is controlled by the federal police department.

39. The first ten amendments to the U.S. Constitution are collectively known as the
_____.

A. Due Process clause
B. Bill of Rights
C. Privileges clause
D. Articles of Confederation

40. Which of the following statements is true about the freedom of speech guaranteed by the Bill of Rights?

A. The Freedom of Speech clause was added to the Constitution in the third amendment.
B. There is no provision for fully protected speech in the Constitution.
C. The Freedom of Speech clause protects speech only, not conduct.
D. Burning the American flag in protest to a federal government military action is in violation of the Freedom of Speech clause.

41. Jerome wears a t-shirt that bears a picture of the current U.S. president. Under this picture, there are words which imply that the President is doing a bad job of running the country. In accordance to the Freedom of Speech Clause, which of the following is valid?

A. Jerome wearing that t-shirt is an instance of limited protected speech.
B. Jerome could be arrested as his t-shirt violates the Freedom of Speech doctrine.
C. Criticizing the current president is fully protected speech and Jerome cannot be prosecuted.
D. Wearing that t-shirt makes Jerome liable for prosecution on the basis of defamatory language.

42. The _____ clause prevents the government from enacting laws that either prohibit or inhibit individuals from participating in or practicing their chosen religions.

A. Due Process
B. Privileges
C. Establishment
D. Free Exercise

43. A(n) _____ test is applied to classifications of people based on a suspect class.

A. cogent basis
B. intermediate scrutiny
C. rational basis
D. strict scrutiny

44. Which of the following provisions is made by the Due Process clauses?

A. Violation of freedom of speech makes the violator liable for immediate prosecution with due process of the law.
B. No state can regulate foreign trade directly or indirectly without due process of the law.
C. Motions for amendments to the constitution cannot be made without a majority in the parliament.
D. No person shall be deprived of life, liberty, or property without due process of the law.

45. The _____ clauses in the Constitution collectively prohibit states from enacting laws that unduly discriminate in favor of their residents.

A. Due Process
B. Equal Protection
C. Privileges and Immunity
D. Establishment

Short Answer

46. How is power divided between the federal government and the state governments?

_____

_____

47. How is the federal government divided? Why are checks and balances necessary?

_____

_____

48. Explain the regulation of commerce with Native American Tribes.

_____

_____

49. How does the U.S. government regulate e-commerce?

_____

_____

50. Explain the Bill of Rights.

_____

_____

51. What are the three categories of speech according to the U.S. Supreme Court?

_____

_____

52. What are the two religion clauses under the First Amendment?

_____

_____

53. What are the three different standards of review for deciding whether the government's different treatment of people or businesses violates or does not violate the Equal Protection Clause?

_____

_____

54. What are the two categories of due process?

_____

_____

55. Explain Privileges and Immunities Clause.

_____

_____

Answers to Refresh Your Memory

1. Enumerated powers [p. 62]
2. bicameral [p. 62]
3. Electoral College [p. 62]
4. preemption [p. 64]
5. Indian Gaming Regulatory [p. 66]
6. police power [p. 67]
7. Bill of Rights [p. 69]
8. Fully protected [p. 70]
9. unprotected speech [p. 72]
10. Establishment Clause [p. 75]
11. Equal Protection [p. 76]
12. Strict scrutiny [p. 76]
13. Due Process [p. 77]
14. procedural due [p. 77]

15. Privileges and Immunities Clause [p. 78]

Critical Thought Exercise Model Answer

States possess police powers as part of their inherent sovereignty. These powers may be exercised to protect or promote the public order, health, safety, morals, and general welfare. Free Speech that has political content, such as the speech being used by Brown, has traditionally been protected to the fullest extent possible by the courts. Free speech includes the right to effective free speech. Amplification systems can be used as long as the speech does not harass or annoy others in the exercise of their privacy rights at an inappropriate time or in an inappropriate location. Thus, Brown would have greater leeway to play his sermons in a commercial district during the day than he could to blast then in a residential neighborhood at midnight. The Free Exercise Clause provision in the First Amendment to the Constitution prohibits Congress from making a law "prohibiting the free exercise" of religion. The Free Exercise Clause guarantees that a person can hold any religious belief that he or she wants. When religious practices are at odds with public policy and the public welfare, the government can act. Brown has the absolute right to listen to his sermons and preach them to others. However, he cannot engage in this activity if it causes a danger to the safety of others. The question that is not answered by the facts is whether the distance of fifty feet is to prevent annoyance or a danger to drivers upon the streets and highways. Without a showing by Westerfield that music and speech that is audible from fifty feet is actually dangerous to drivers, Brown is free to play his sermons and spiritual music in a manner that is annoying to others.

Answers to Practice Quiz

True/False

16. True. Federalism is the U.S. form of government in which the federal government and the 50 state governments share powers. [p. 62]

17. False. Any powers that are not specifically delegated to the federal government by the Constitution are reserved to the state governments. These are called reserved powers. [p. 62]

18. False. Certain checks and balances are built into the Constitution to ensure that no one branch of the federal government becomes too powerful. [p. 62]

19. False. Supremacy Clause establishes that U.S. Constitution and federal treaties, laws, and regulations are the supreme law of the land. [p. 64]

20. True. In the late 1980s, the federal government authorized Native American tribes to operate gaming facilities. Congress passed the Indian Gaming Regulatory Act,7 a federal statute that establishes the requirements for conducting casino gambling and other gaming activities on tribal land. [p. 66]

21. True. The Commerce Clause of the U.S. Constitution gives the federal government the exclusive power to regulate commerce with foreign nations. [p. 66]

22. True. Dormant Commerce Clause applies to a situation in which the federal government has the Commerce Clause power to regulate an area of commerce but has chosen not to regulate that area of commerce. [p. 68]

23. False. A significant portion of the sales of goods, licensing of intellectual property, and sales of services are accomplished through e-commerce. Because e-commerce is commerce, it is subject to the Commerce Clause of the U.S. Constitution. [p. 68]

24. False. The Bill of Rights guarantees certain fundamental rights to natural persons and protects these rights from intrusive government action. [p. 69]

25. True. Fully protected speech is speech that the government cannot prohibit or regulate. [p. 70]

26. True. Two major forms of limited protected speech are offensive speech and commercial speech. Advertising is commercial speech. [p. 72]

27. True. The Establishment Clause prohibits the government from either establishing a government-sponsored religion or promoting one religion over another. [p. 75]

28. False. The Equal Protection Clause of the Fourteenth Amendment provides that a state cannot "deny to any person within its jurisdiction the equal protection of the laws." [p. 76]

29. True. The lawfulness of government classifications based on a protected class other than race (e.g., gender) is examined using an intermediate scrutiny test. [p. 76]

30. False. The substantive due process category of due process requires that government statutes, ordinances, regulations, and other laws be clear on their face and not overly broad in scope. [p. 77]

Multiple Choice

31. D. Enumerated powers are certain powers delegated to the federal government by the states. [p. 62]

32. D. Any powers that are not specifically delegated to the federal government by the Constitution are reserved to the state governments. These are called reserved powers. [p. 62]

33. D. The legislative branch is responsible for making federal law. This branch is bicameral; that is, it consists of the U.S. Senate and the U.S. House of Representatives. [p. 62]

34. D. Checks and balances is a system built into the U.S. Constitution to prevent any one of the three branches of the government from becoming too powerful. [p. 62]

35. D. The concept of federal law taking precedence over state or local law is commonly called the preemption doctrine. [p. 64]

36. D. Indian Gaming Regulatory Act is a federal statute that establishes the requirements for conducting casino gambling and other gaming activities on tribal land. [p. 66]

37. C. The Commerce Clause of the U.S. Constitution gives the federal government the exclusive power to regulate commerce with foreign nations. This is called the Foreign Commerce Clause. [p. 66]

38. A. Police power permits states and local governments to enact laws to protect or promote the public health, safety, morals, and general welfare. This includes the authority to enact laws that regulate the conduct of business. [p. 68]

39. D. In 1791, the 10 amendments that are commonly referred to as the Bill of Rights were approved by the states and became part of the U.S. Constitution. The Bill of Rights guarantees certain fundamental rights to natural persons and protects these rights from intrusive government action. [p. 69]

40. C. Bill of Right guarantees freedom of speech. The First Amendment's Freedom of Speech Clause protects speech only, not conduct. [p. 70]

41. C. Political speech is an example of fully protected speech. Thus, the government could not enact a law that forbids citizens from criticizing the current president. [p. 70]

42. A. The Free Exercise Clause prohibits the government from interfering with the free exercise of religion in the United States. [p. 75]

43. D. Any government activity or regulation that classifies persons based on a suspect class (e.g., race, national origin, and citizenship) or involves fundamental rights (e.g., voting) is reviewed for lawfulness using a strict scrutiny test. [p. 76]

44. D. Due Process Clause provides that no person shall be deprived of "life, liberty, or property" without due process of the law. [p. 77]

45. C. Article IV of the Constitution contains the Privileges and Immunities Clause, which provides that "The Citizens of each State shall be entitled to all Privileges and Immunities of Citizens in the several states." [p. 78]

Short Answer

46. The federal government and the 50 state governments share powers. When the states ratified the Constitution, they delegated certain powers—called enumerated powers—to the federal government. For example, the federal government is authorized to regulate interstate commerce and foreign affairs. Any powers that are not specifically delegated to the federal government by the Constitution are reserved to the state governments. These are called reserved powers. State governments are empowered to deal with local affairs. For example, states enact laws that provide for the formation and regulation of partnerships and corporations. Cities adopt zoning laws that designate certain portions of the city as residential areas and other portions as business and commercial areas. [p. 62]

47. The federal government is divided into three branches:
a. Legislative branch – Article I of the Constitution establishes the legislative branch of the federal government. The legislative branch is responsible for making federal law. This branch is bicameral; that is, it consists of the U.S. Senate and the U.S. House of Representatives.
b. Executive branch – Article II of the Constitution establishes the executive branch of the federal government by providing for the election of the president and vice president. The president is not elected by popular vote but instead is selected by the Electoral College, whose representatives are appointed by state delegations. The executive branch of government is responsible for enforcing federal law.
c. Judicial branch – Article III of the Constitution establishes the judicial branch of the federal government by establishing the U.S. Supreme Court and providing for the creation of other federal courts by Congress. The judicial branch is responsible for interpreting the U.S. Constitution and federal law.
Certain checks and balances are built into the Constitution to ensure that no one branch of the federal government becomes too powerful. [p. 62]

48. In general, the United States treats Native Americans as belonging to separate nations, similarly to the way it treats Spain or France; however, it still considers Native Americans "domestic dependent" nations with limited sovereignty. Today, many Native Americans live on reservations set aside for various tribes. In the late 1980s, the federal government authorized Native American tribes to operate gaming facilities. Congress passed the Indian Gaming Regulatory Act, a federal statute that establishes the requirements for conducting casino gambling and other gaming activities on tribal land. This act allows Native Americans to negotiate with the states for gaming compacts and ensures that the states do so in good faith. If a state fails to do so, the tribe can bring suit in federal court, forcing the state to comply. Today, casinos operated by Native Americans can be found in many states. Profits from the casinos have become an important source of income for members of certain tribes. [p. 65]

49. The advent of the Internet has caused a revolution in how commerce is conducted. The Internet and other computer networks permit parties to obtain website domain names and conduct business electronically. This is usually referred to as electronic commerce or e-commerce. Some businesses that conduct e-commerce over the Internet do not have

any physical location, whereas many "brick-and-mortar" businesses augment their traditional sales with e-commerce sales as well. Currently, a significant portion of the sales of goods, licensing of intellectual property, and sales of services are accomplished through e-commerce. Because e-commerce is commerce, it is subject to the Commerce Clause of the U.S. Constitution. [p. 68]

50. In 1791, the 10 amendments that are commonly referred to as the Bill of Rights were approved by the states and became part of the U.S. Constitution. The Bill of Rights guarantees certain fundamental rights to natural persons and protects these rights from intrusive government action.
Examples – Fundamental rights guaranteed in the First Amendment include freedom of speech, freedom to assemble, freedom of the press, and freedom of religion.
Most of these rights have also been found applicable to so-called artificial persons (i.e., corporations). Originally, the Bill of Rights limited intrusive action by the federal government only. Intrusive actions by state and local governments were not limited until the Due Process Clause of the Fourteenth Amendment was added to the Constitution in 1868. [p. 69]

51. Fully Protected Speech – Fully protected speech is speech that the government cannot prohibit or regulate.
Limited protected speech – It is the speech that the government may not prohibit but that is subject to time, place, and manner restrictions. Two major forms of limited protected speech are offensive speech and commercial speech.
Unprotected speech – It is the speech that is not protected by the First Amendment and may be forbidden by the government. Dangerous speech, fighting words that are likely to provoke a hostile or violent response from an average person, speech that incites the violent or revolutionary overthrow of the government, defamatory language, child pornography, and obscene speech are types of unprotected speech. [p. 72]

52. Establishment Clause – The U.S. Constitution requires federal, state, and local governments to be neutral toward religion. The Establishment Clause prohibits the government from either establishing a government-sponsored religion or promoting one religion over another. Thus, it guarantees that there will be no state-sponsored religion.
Free Exercise Clause – The Free Exercise Clause prohibits the government from interfering with the free exercise of religion in the United States. Generally, this clause prevents the government from enacting laws that either prohibit or inhibit individuals from participating in or practicing their chosen religions. [p. 75]

53. The three standards of review are:
Strict scrutiny test – Any government activity or regulation that classifies persons based on a suspect class (e.g., race, national origin, and citizenship) or involves fundamental rights (e.g., voting) is reviewed for lawfulness using a strict scrutiny test.
Intermediate scrutiny test – The lawfulness of government classifications based on a protected class other than race (e.g., gender) is examined using an intermediate scrutiny test.

Rational basis test – The lawfulness of all government classifications that do not involve suspect or protected classes is examined using a rational basis test. [p. 76]

54. The categories of due process are:
Substantive Due Process – The substantive due process category of due process requires that government statutes, ordinances, regulations, and other laws be clear on their face and not overly broad in scope. The test of whether substantive due process is met is whether a "reasonable person" could understand the law to be able to comply with it. Laws that do not meet this test are declared void for vagueness.
Procedural Due Process – The procedural due process form of due process requires that the government give a person proper notice and hearing of legal action before that person is deprived of his or her life, liberty, or property. [p. 77]

55. Article IV of the Constitution contains the Privileges and Immunities Clause, which provides that "The Citizens of each State shall be entitled to all Privileges and Immunities of Citizens in the several states." The Fourteenth Amendment contains the Privileges or Immunities Clause, which provides that "No State shall make or enforce any law that shall abridge the privileges or immunities of the citizens of the United States." Collectively, the clauses prohibit states from enacting laws that unduly discriminate in favor of their residents. Note that the clauses apply only to citizens; they do not protect corporations or aliens. [p. 78]

5 | INTENTIONAL TORTS AND NEGLIGENCE

Chapter Overview

This chapter provides a good understanding of the intentional torts against persons and property. The tort of negligence, as well as applicable defenses to this cause of action, is explained in a methodical fashion. The special negligence doctrines such as negligence per se, negligent infliction of emotional distress, and res ipsa loquitur are examined. The torts of disparagement and fraud, which can contribute to unfair competition, are discussed. The doctrine of strict liability is reviewed.

Objectives

Upon completion of the exercises in this chapter, you should be able to:
1. List and describe intentional torts against persons.
2. List and explain the elements necessary to prove negligence.
3. Describe the business-related torts of disparagement and fraud.
4. Describe special negligence doctrines.
5. Define and apply the doctrine of strict liability.

Practical Application

You should be able to recognize the various intentional torts, as well as negligence, and apply the elements associated with each to real life and hypothetical situations. You should have a greater understanding of the concept of strict liability and the purpose of punitive damages.

Helpful Hints

This chapter lends itself towards organization in that you can sort the torts by whether they are intentional or unintentional. The elements of the tort of negligence are easily remembered if you list the elements vertically and diagram causation horizontally. This is displayed for you in the study tips section of this chapter. The tort of misrepresentation is easily remembered by using the mnemonic given under the study tips section. Once you have these organizational skills mastered for the main sections in this chapter, the other information given is very easy to remember. Many of the cases you will review in this chapter will be easy for you to understand as they pertain to many companies with which you may be familiar.

Study Tips

The first organizational step you should take is to learn the intentional torts based upon their application. You should be cognizant of some of the fine nuances associated with some of these torts. It is often easier to list the elements of the tort rather than state its technical definition. One of the most important things you should remember about the intentional torts as a whole is to look at the fact pattern or case being given to you and determine if the tortfeasor had the intent to do the act. If there is nothing in the facts to indicate this, then maybe the tortfeasor's action could be classified as negligent. If this is the case, then you will have to proceed through the various steps based on the flow chart given under the negligence heading in this chapter. Student learning styles will vary, so both methods are given. The pages that follow will assist you in studying the torts that are discussed in this chapter.

Tort

A tort is a civil wrong for which an individual or business may seek compensation for the injuries that have been caused. Compensation for these injuries may include damages for mental distress, loss of wages, pain and suffering, past and future medical expenses. In a tort situation where the victim dies, a wrongful death action may also be an option.

Intentional Torts Against Persons

Assault – The intentional threat of immediate harm or offensive contact or any action that arouses reasonable apprehension of imminent harm.

Assault list of elements with special nuances
- *intentional*
- *placing of another*
- *in immediate* – Note that future threats are not actionable.
- *apprehension* –The victim must be fearful of what appears to be an inevitable contact. The victim must be aware of the tortuous act. The victim's reaction must be one of fear as opposed to laughter which would negate the element of apprehension.
- *of harmful or offensive contact*

Battery – The intentional, unauthorized harmful or offensive touching of another without consent or legal privilege.

Battery list of elements with special nuances
- *intentional*
- *unauthorized*
- *harmful* or *offensive* – A kiss may be considered offensive by some.
- *touching* – The touching of an accessory such as a purse that is attached to the victim may be enough to satisfy this element.
- *of another*
- *without consent* or *legal privilege* – You should be aware of the merchant's protection statutes, which sometimes have a role in the privilege arena of this tort.

Other interesting notations on battery are that the victim does not have to be aware of the battery for the tort to occur. The victim may be sleeping when it happens or have his or her back turned when the battery occurs. Battery and assault can occur together; however, the victim would need to show awareness in order to fully prove the elements of assault.

Transferred Intent Doctrine – When one individual intends to injure one person but injures another individual, the law transfers the perpetrator's intent from the person the harm was originally meant for to the actual victim, who may then bring a lawsuit against the wrongdoer.

False Imprisonment – The intentional mental or physical confinement of another without consent or legal privilege.

False Imprisonment list of elements with special nuances:
- *intentional*
- *mental* or *physical* – An example of mental confinement may be through an assertion of legal authority or by one in a superior position. Physical confinement may include barriers or threats of physical harm.
- *confinement* – Be careful with this element as future threats or moral pressure does not satisfy this element. Also, if there is a reasonable means of escape, this element may be difficult to prove.
- *of another*
- *without consent* or *legal privilege* – This element will be difficult to establish if a merchant is involved. This aspect of tort law is discussed below.

Shoplifting and Merchant Protection Statutes – Since merchants lose thousands of dollars every year from shoplifters, many states have enacted statutes to protect them. These statutes are often referred to as shopkeeper's privilege. There are three important aspects of this type of statute that will absolve a merchant from liability of false imprisonment allegations.

Merchant Protection Statutes nuances
- There must be reasonable grounds for detaining and investigating the shoplifter.
- The suspected shoplifter can be detained for only a reasonable time.
- The investigations must be conducted in a reasonable manner.

Misappropriation of the Right to Publicity – This tort is an attempt by another to appropriate a living person's name or identity for commercial purposes. A classic example of this would be individuals who sell cheaper versions of a famous performer's concert merchandise.

Invasion of the Right to Publicity – It involves a violation of an individual's right to live his/her life without unwarranted or undesired publicity.

Truth is not a defense to this tort, as the fact does not have to be untrue. If the fact is one of public record, this tort cannot be claimed. Examples include wiretapping and reading hand-delivered as well as the e-mail of another.

Defamation of Character – This tort involves an intentional or accidental untrue statement of fact made about an individual to a third party.

Defamation of Character list of elements with special nuances
- *intentional* or *accidental* – May be overheard accidentally
- *untrue statement of fact* – Be careful as truth is always a defense.
- *published to a third party* – The third party can see or hear the untrue statement.

You should be aware of some of the other important aspects of defamation of character. Libel is written defamation and slander is oral defamation. Some types of media such as television and radio broadcasts come under the category of libel, as the courts view them as permanent in nature since the original scripts were composed prior to broadcasting the defamatory content. Opinions are not actionable, as it is not considered to be an untrue statement of fact. Public figures such as movie stars, celebrities, and other famous people must show that the statement was knowingly made or made with reckless disregard of the statement's falsity; malice must be shown.

Disparagement – This tort involves an untrue statement made by a person or business about another business's reputation, services, products, etc. This tort is also known as product disparagement or trade libel. The defendant must have made the statement intentionally to a third party knowing that what he or she was saying was not true.

Intentional Misrepresentation (Fraud) – It is the intentional defrauding of a person out of money, property, or something else of value. This tort lends itself nicely towards a mnemonic that will assist you in remembering its elements. The mnemonic is MIS JD.

M   Misrepresentation of material fact that was false in nature
I   Intentionally made to an innocent party
S   Scienter (knowledge) of the statement's falsity by the wrongdoer
J   Justifiable reliance on the false statement by the innocent party
D   Damages were suffered by the injured party

Intentional Infliction of Emotional Distress
- intentional or reckless
- extreme and outrageous conduct – The conduct must go beyond the bounds of decency.
- by one individual
- against another
- that causes severe emotional distress – Many states require a physical injury, illness, or discomfort. However, states that are more flexible in their interpretation of this element have found that humiliation, fear, and anger will satisfy this element. Some states no longer require that the severity of the emotional distress be shown.

Malicious prosecution – A lawsuit in which the original defendant sues the original plaintiff. In the second lawsuit, the defendant becomes the plaintiff and vice versa.

Unintentional Torts (Negligence)

In order to be successful in a negligence cause of action, one must show that a duty of care was owed to the plaintiff, that the defendant breached this duty, that the defendant was the actual and proximate cause of plaintiff's injuries, and that the plaintiff suffered damages.

Duty of Care

You should know the general duty of care which states that we all owe one another a duty of due care so as to not subject others to an unreasonable risk of harm. This duty is based on the reasonable person standard. An example of when this general duty of care is owed is the situation involving an invitee. An invitee, such as a plumber, is one who is invited onto the land of another for the mutual benefit of both people. The duty of ordinary care is also owed to a licensee, such as an encyclopedia salesperson, who with consent comes onto the land of another for his or her own benefit. An owner does not owe a general duty of care to a trespasser, but does owe a duty not to willfully or wantonly injure a trespasser. Children are measured against other children of similar age and experience.

There are certain situations where a higher standard of care is owed, such as with professionals, innkeepers, common carriers, taverns and bartenders, social hosts, and paying passengers riding in a vehicle of another.

Breach of Duty

If a duty, albeit general and or special, has been established and it is found that the defendant has not acted as a reasonable person would, the court may find a breach of the duty of care.

Causation

It is important to remember that the plaintiff must show that the defendant was the actual (factual) and proximate (legal) cause of the plaintiff's injuries. Further, the defendant must be the direct cause of the plaintiff's injuries. If this cannot be established, plaintiff must show that the injuries that occurred were foreseeable in that it would be the type of injury one would expect from the activity the defendant was engaged in. It is best to diagram this element horizontally in order to remember its nuances. Please see below.

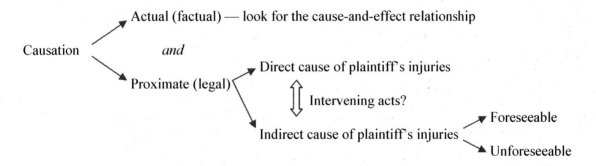

Damages

The plaintiff must have actually suffered an injury or damages.

Special Negligence Doctrines

Professional Malpractice
Professionals are held to the standard of a reasonable professional. Liability is known as malpractice. You should be cognizant of the medical professional who acts as a good Samaritan. Medical professionals are relieved of liability for injury caused by their ordinary negligence when rendering aid to victims in need of emergency care.

Negligent Infliction of Emotional Distress
Though this is not an intentional tort, it is being placed here as it is a tort that is not only against individuals, but is one that some courts are recognizing when defendant's negligent conduct causes the plaintiff to suffer severe emotional distress. This tort requires the plaintiff's relative was injured or killed and that plaintiff suffered the severe distress at the same time he or she observed the accident. Some jurisdictions require the plaintiff suffer some sort of physical injury while other states do not mandate this element.

Negligence per se and *res ipsa loquitur* are special negligence doctrines that are important to be aware of as they are special in their establishment of the element of duty as well as assisting in the plaintiff's burden of proof in a negligence case.

Negligence Per Se – This doctrine involves the violation of a statute that proximately causes the plaintiff's injuries. There must be a statute that was enacted to prevent the type of injury suffered by the plaintiff and the plaintiff must be within the class of persons the statute was designed to protect.

Res Ipsa Loquitur – This doctrine means "the thing speaks for itself." This is an important doctrine as there is a presumption of negligence where the plaintiff proves that the defendant had exclusive control of the instrumentality or circumstances that caused the plaintiff's injuries and the injury that the plaintiff suffered wouldn't have ordinarily occurred, "but for" someone's negligence.

Defenses Against Negligence

Superseding or Intervening Event – Under negligence, a person is liable only for foreseeable events. Therefore, an original negligent party can raise a superseding event or an intervening event as a defense to liability.

Contributory negligence states that if a plaintiff is partially at fault for causing his or her own injuries, then the plaintiff is barred from recovering damages.

Comparative negligence doctrines assess damages by the plaintiff's percentage of fault. This is known as pure comparative negligence. If the plaintiff is in a jurisdiction that adopts the partial comparative negligence doctrine, then plaintiff must be less than fifty percent negligent in causing his or her injuries. If the plaintiff is over fifty percent negligent, then recovery is barred and the defendant is not liable.

Assumption of the Risk is a defense that states that a defendant may assert indicating that the plaintiff knowingly and voluntarily entered into a risky activity that resulted in injury.

Strict Liability

This is a tort that involves liability without fault if the activity that the defendant is engaged in places the public at risk of injury despite reasonable care being taken. Examples of activities that qualify for this categorization include fumigation, storage of explosives, and blasting.

Refresh Your Memory

The following exercise will give you the opportunity to test your memory of the principles given in this chapter. Read the question twice and place your answer in the blank provided. Review the chapter material for any question that you are unable to answer or remember.

1. _____ is (1) the threat of immediate harm or offensive contact or (2) any action that arouses reasonable apprehension of imminent harm.

2. Throwing a rock or shooting an arrow at a person with the intention to hit him/her is an example of _____.

3. The intentional confinement or restraint of another person without authority or justification and without that person's consent constitutes _____.

4. The merchant protection statute is also known as _____.

5. _____ is a false statement that appears in a letter, newspaper, magazine, book, photograph, movie, video, and so on.

6. The intentional defrauding of a person out of money, property, or something else of value is called _____, also known as fraud or deceit.

7. _____ refers to the obligation people owe each other—that is, the duty not to cause any unreasonable harm or risk of harm.

8. A _____ is a test the courts attempt to determine how an objective, careful, and conscientious person would have acted in the same circumstances and then measure the defendant's conduct against that standard.

9. The actual cause of negligence is also known as _____.

10. The liability of a professional who breaches his or her duty of ordinary care is called _____.

11. _____ is a tort in which the violation of a statute or an ordinance constitutes the breach of the duty of care.

12. _____ is a statute that relieves medical professionals from liability for ordinary negligence when they stop and render aid to victims in emergency situations.

13. An intervening event is also known as a _____ event.

14. _____ provides that a plaintiff must be less than 50 percent responsible for causing his or her own injuries to recover under comparative negligence.

15. A liability without fault is also known as _____.

Critical Thought Exercise

Chip North is a 22-year-old racing enthusiast who went to a car race at Trona International Speedway. North was excited because he had obtained a seat close to the track near the finish line. North's ticket came with five others in a sealed envelope that was imprinted in a large font with the following:

"WARNING!
Your seating for this event is in a very
DANGEROUS AREA

Debris and fluids from race cars may be ejected or sprayed from the
race surface into your seating area in the event of a crash or malfunction
of a race vehicle. Please ask to change your seating if you do not desire to
ASSUME THE RISK OF SERIOUS INJURY."

The envelope is opened by North's younger brother, who does not pay any attention to the envelope and discards it after removing the tickets. During the race a car crashes into the wall in front of North's seat and sprays him with burning gasoline, causing severe injuries. North sues Trona Speedway for negligence for subjecting him to a known danger by seating him and others so close to the racetrack. Trona Speedway denies any liability based upon the warning on the envelope and the known risk that spectators take when attending a race. At trial, which side should prevail?

Please compose your answer to the Critical Thinking Exercise using a separate sheet of paper or your computer word processing program.

Practice Quiz

True/False

16. _____ Locking one door to a building when other exits are not locked is also false imprisonment.

17. _____ Placing someone in a "false light" constitutes an invasion of privacy.

18. _____ Most courts hold that defamatory statements in radio and television broadcasts are considered slander.

19. _____ The publication of opinions is usually not actionable.

20. _____ Misappropriation of the right to publicity is an untrue statement made by one person or business about the products, services, property, or reputation of another business.

21. _____ Scienter refers to unintentional conduct.

22. _____ An indignity, an annoyance, rough language, or an occasional inconsiderate or unkind act does not constitute outrageous behavior.

23. _____ Throwing a lit match on the ground in the forest and causing a fire is a breach of a duty of care.

24. _____ If a defendant's negligent act has breached a duty of care owed to the plaintiff, this breach is actionable even if the plaintiff does not suffer any injury or injury to his or her property.

25. _____ An actual cause of negligence is also known as the legal cause.

26. _____ The violation of a statute that proximately causes an injury is res ipsa loquitur.

27. _____ Res ipsa loquitur applies in cases where the defendant had exclusive control of the instrumentality or situation that caused the plaintiff's injury.

28. _____ Good Samaritan laws protect medical professionals from liability for their ordinary negligence as well as gross negligence.

29. _____ An original negligent party can raise a superseding event or an intervening event as a defense to liability.

30. _____ The doctrine of contributory negligence holds that a plaintiff who is partially at fault for his own injury cannot recover against the negligent defendant.

Multiple Choice

31. Which of the following is an example of an intentional tort?

A. battery
B. negligent infliction of emotional distress
C. negligence per se
D. res ipsa loquitur

32. Sometimes a person acts with the intent to injure one person but actually injures another. The _____ applies to such situations.

A. res ipsa loquitur
B. Good Samaritan laws
C. transferred intent doctrine
D. contributory negligence

33. Reading someone else's mail or wiretapping someone's telephone are examples of:
A. defamation of character.
B. invasion of the right to privacy.
C. misappropriation of the right to publicity.
D. disparagement.

34. An oral defamatory statement is _____.

A. libel
B. assault
C. battery
D. slander

35. Trade libel and slander of title are also known as _____.

A. fraud
B. scienter
C. disparagement
D. negligence

36. Which of the following is true of fraud?

A. It is the intentional defrauding of a person out of money, property, or something else of value.
B. The wrongdoer makes a false representation of material or immaterial fact.
C. The innocent party may or may not justifiably rely on the misrepresentation.
D. The innocent party may or may not be injured.

37. Which of the following is true with regard to tort of outrage?

A. Repeated annoyances coupled with threats are considered outrageous.
B. Tort of outrage is unintentional.
C. The tort requires publication to a third party.
D. The tort requires physical contact between the plaintiff and defendant.

38. _____ is a test used to determine whether a defendant owes a duty of care.

A. Reasonable person standard
B. *Negligence per se*
C. *Res ipsa loquitur*
D. Contributory negligence

39. Proximate cause is also known as:

A. causation in fact.
B. actual cause.
C. legal cause.
D. intervening cause.

40. A doctor who amputates a wrong leg is liable for _____.

A. negligent infliction of emotional distress
B. negligence per se
C. res ipsa loquitur
D. professional malpractice

41. If a defendant is in control of a situation in which a plaintiff has been injured and has superior knowledge of the circumstances surrounding the injury, the plaintiff might have difficulty proving the defendant's negligence. In such a situation, the law applies the doctrine of _____.

A. negligence per se
B. professional malpractice
C. res ipsa loquitur
D. negligent infliction of emotional distress

42. Tom negligently hits Mark with a ball. While carrying him to the hospital, their car meets with an accident and Mark dies. Though Tom is liable for the injury caused to Mark, he is not liable for his death as the car accident was a(n) _____.

A. assumption of the risk
B. comparative negligence
C. proximate cause
D. superseding event

43. Which of the following is a defense against negligence that a defendant can use against a plaintiff?

A. Assumption of risk
B. Unintentional tort
C. Disparagement
D. Assault

44. States that have adopted partial comparative negligence, apply _____ in case a plaintiff is more than fifty per cent responsible for his or her injuries.

A. comparative negligence
B. contributory negligence
C. comparative fault
D. absolute fault

45. The doctrine of _____ holds that (1) there are certain activities that can place the public at risk of injury even if reasonable care is taken and (2) the public should have some means of compensation if such injury occurs.

A. professional malpractice
B. unintentional tort
C. strict liability
D. transferred intent

Short Answer

46. What are the three categories of torts?
_____
_____

47. Briefly explain the doctrine of transferred intent
_____

48. What are the requirements to prove the tort of defamation of character by a plaintiff?
_____
_____

49. What is the difference between slander and libel?
_____
_____

50. What is the difference between actual cause and proximate cause?
_____
_____

51. What is the purpose of Good Samaritan laws?
_____
_____

52. Explain the two defenses against negligence.

_____

_____

53. What assumptions are made under the defense of assumption of risk?

_____

_____

54. What is the difference between contributory negligence, comparative negligence, and partial comparative negligence?

_____

_____

55. When is strict liability imposed?

_____

_____

Answers to Refresh Your Memory

1. Assault [p. 85]
2. battery [p. 85]
3. false imprisonment [p. 86]
4. shopkeeper's privilege [p. 86]
5. Libel [p. 88]
6. intentional misrepresentation [p. 89]
7. Duty of care [p. 91]
8. reasonable person standard [p. 91]
9. causation in fact [p. 94]
10. professional malpractice [p. 96]
11. *Negligence per se* [p. 97]
12. Good Samaritan law [p. 98]
13. superseding [p. 98]
14. Partial comparative negligence [p. 100]
15. strict liability [p.100]

Critical Thought Exercise Model Answer

The tort of negligence occurs when someone suffers injury because of another's failure to exercise the standard of care that a reasonable person would exercise in similar circumstances. The operator of a facility where a sporting event takes place has a duty to provide safe seating for the spectators unless the risk of injury is assumed and accepted by the spectators. Spectators at a baseball game assume the risk that a ball may be hit into the stands and strike them. Spectators at a hockey game do not assume this same risk because pucks are not usually hit high enough over the protective glass to strike spectators. A plaintiff, who voluntarily enters into a risky situation, knowing the risk involved, will not be allowed to recover. This is the defense of assumption of risk. The requirements of this defense are (1) knowledge of the risk and (2) voluntary assumption of the risk. If North had actually been given knowledge of the risk, he may have voluntarily assumed that risk by sitting close to the racetrack. However, six tickets were placed in one envelope that was opened by someone other than North. Trona Speedway cannot argue that North voluntarily assumed a risk for which he was not given notification. The knowledge of risk may be implied from the general knowledge of spectators at a particular type of event, such as baseball. There is no indication that North or any other spectator would know of the danger associated with sitting in a seat for which a ticket was sold. Because North did not assume the risk of being injured by burning gasoline while a spectator at the race, Trona is still liable for negligence.

Answers to Practice Quiz

True/False

16. False. Locking one door to a building when other exits are not locked is not false imprisonment. [p. 86]

17. True. Sending an objectionable telegram to a third party and signing another's name would place the purported sender in a false light in the eyes of the receiver. [p. 88]

18. False. Most courts hold that defamatory statements in radio and television broadcasts are considered libel because of the permanency of the media. [p. 88]

19. True. The statement "My lawyer is lousy" is an opinion and is not defamation. Hence, it is not actionable. [p. 88]

20. False. Disparagement is an untrue statement made by one person or business about the products, services, property, or reputation of another business. [p. 89]

21. False. Scienter refers to intentional conduct. [p. 89]

22. True. Repeated annoyances or harassment coupled with threats are considered outrageous. [p. 89]

23. True. A failure to exercise care or to act as a reasonable person would act is a breach of the duty of care. [p. 91]

24. False. Even though a defendant's negligent act may have breached a duty of care owed to the plaintiff, this breach is not actionable unless the plaintiff suffers injury or injury to his or her property. [p. 92]

25. False. An actual cause is also called causation in fact. [p. 94]

26. False The violation of a statute that proximately causes an injury is negligence per se. [p. 97]

27. True. *Res ipsa loquitur* is a tort in which the presumption of negligence arises because (1) the defendant was in exclusive control of the situation and (2) the plaintiff

would not have suffered injury but for someone's negligence. The burden switches to the defendant to prove that he or she was not negligent. [p. 97]

28. False. Good Samaritan laws protect medical professionals only from liability for their ordinary negligence, not for injuries caused by their gross negligence or reckless or intentional conduct. [p. 98]

29. True. Under negligence, a person is liable only for foreseeable events. Therefore, an original negligent party can raise a superseding event or an intervening event as a defense to liability. [p. 98]

30. False. The doctrine of contributory negligence holds that a plaintiff who is partially at fault for his own injury cannot recover against the negligent defendant. [p. 100]

Multiple Choice

31. A. Battery is unauthorized and harmful or offensive physical contact with another person that causes injury. It is an intentional tort. [p. 85]

32. C. Under the transferred intent doctrine, the law transfers the perpetrator's intent from the target to the actual victim of the act. [p. 86]

33. B. The law recognizes each person's right to live his or her life without being subjected to unwarranted and undesired publicity. A violation of this right constitutes the tort of invasion of the right to privacy. [p. 88]

34. D. A slander is an oral defamation of character. For example, The statement "My lawyer has been disbarred from the practice of law," when she has not been disbarred, is an untrue statement of fact and is actionable as defamation. [p. 88]

35. C. A disparaging statement is an untrue statement made by one person or business about the products, services, property, or reputation of another business. It is also known as trade libel, product disparagement, and slander of title. [p. 89]

36. A. Fraud occurs when a wrongdoer deceives another person out of money, property, or something else of value intentionally. [p. 89]

37. A. An indignity, an annoyance, rough language, or an occasional inconsiderate or unkind act does not constitute outrageous behavior. However, repeated annoyances or harassment coupled with threats are considered outrageous. [p. 89]

38. A. Reasonable person standard is a test used to determine whether a defendant owes a duty of care. This test measures the defendant's conduct against how an objective, careful, and conscientious person would have acted in the same circumstances. [p. 91]

39. C. A point along a chain of events caused by a negligent party after which this party is no longer legally responsible for the consequences of his or her actions is called a proximate cause.. [p. 94]

40. D. Professionals, such as doctors, lawyers, architects, accountants, and others, owe a duty of ordinary care in providing their services. A professional who breaches this duty of care is liable for the injury his or her negligence causes. This liability is commonly referred to as professional malpractice. [p. 96]

41. C. *Res ipsa loquitur* is a tort in which the presumption of negligence arises because (1) the defendant was in exclusive control of the situation and (2) the plaintiff would not have suffered injury but for someone's negligence. The burden switches to the defendant to prove that he or she was not negligent. [p. 97]

42. D. A superseding event is an event for which a defendant is not responsible. The defendant is not liable for injuries caused by the superseding or intervening event. [p. 98]

43. A. Assumption of the risk is a defense a defendant can use against a plaintiff who knowingly and voluntarily enters into or participates in a risky activity that results in injury. [p. 98]

44. B. Several states have adopted partial comparative negligence, which provides that a plaintiff must be less than 50 percent responsible for causing his or her own injuries to recover under comparative negligence; otherwise, contributory negligence applies. [p. 100]

45. C. Strict liability is liability without fault. That is, a participant in a covered activity will be held liable for any injuries caused by the activity, even if he or she was not negligent. [p. 100]

Short Answer

46. There are three categories of torts are (1) intentional torts, (2) unintentional torts (negligence), and (3) strict liability. [p. 85]

47. Sometimes a person acts with the intent to injure one person but actually injures another. The transferred intent doctrine transfers the perpetrator's intent from the target to the actual victim of the act. The victim can then sue the defendant. [p. 86]

48. The tort of defamation of character requires a plaintiff to prove that:
1. The defendant made an untrue statement of fact about the plaintiff.
2. The statement was intentionally or accidentally published to a third party. In this context, publication simply means that a third person heard or saw the untrue statement. It does not require appearance in newspapers, magazines, or books. [p. 88]

49. A false statement that appears in a letter, newspaper, magazine, book, photograph, movie, video, and so on is called a libel; whereas, oral defamation of character is called slander. [p. 88]

50. A defendant's negligent act must be the actual cause, also called causation in fact, of the plaintiff's injuries. Proximate cause or legal cause is a point along a chain of events caused by a negligent party after which this party is no longer legally responsible for the consequences of his or her actions. [p. 94]

51. Good Samaritan law relieves medical professionals from liability for ordinary negligence when they stop and render aid to victims in emergency situations. [p. 98]

52. The two defenses against negligence are:
1. Superseding event- An event for which a defendant is not responsible. The defendant is not liable for injuries caused by the superseding or intervening event.
2. Assumption of the risk- A defense a defendant can use against a plaintiff who knowingly and voluntarily enters into or participates in a risky activity that results in injury. [p. 98]

53. The defense of assumption of risk assumes that the plaintiff (1) had knowledge of the specific risk and (2) voluntarily assumed that risk. [p. 98]

54. Contributory negligence is a doctrine that says a plaintiff who is partially at fault for his or her own injury cannot recover against the negligent defendant. Comparative negligence is a doctrine under which damages are apportioned according to fault. Partial comparative negligence provides that a plaintiff must be less than 50 percent responsible for causing his or her own injuries to recover under comparative negligence. [p. 100]

55. Strict liability is imposed for abnormally dangerous activities that cause injury or death, such as crop dusting, blasting and fumigation. [p. 100]

6 | PRODUCT AND STRICT LIABILITY

Chapter Overview

This chapter discusses the multiple tort principles that are available to injured parties as a result of defectively made products. Negligence, misrepresentation, and strict liability are the standard causes of action that are available. Many individuals including purchasers, users, lessees, and even innocent bystanders who are injured by a defective product may seek recovery under the legal theory called product liability. This chapter will help you understand how manufactures, sellers, lessors, and others involved with the defective product may be held liable for the injuries caused to others who were injured by the product. Emphasis is placed upon the duties that are required of manufacturers as well as others in the chain of distribution.

Objectives

Upon completion of the exercises in this chapter, you should be able to:
1. Describe and distinguish among the several legal theories of product liability.
2. Define the doctrine of strict liability.
3. Identify and describe defects in manufacture and design.
4. Identify and describe defects of failure to warn and in packaging.
5. Describe the damages recoverable in a product liability lawsuit.

Practical Application

You should be able to establish a basis for a product liability lawsuit by identifying the different types of legal theories and their elements. You should be able to identify the proper party against who to assess liability, identify and apply potential defenses, and be familiar with the types of damages that are available.

Helpful Hints

This chapter is a good chapter for reviewing the concepts of negligence and misrepresentation that you learned in the last chapter and allows you to build upon your knowledge of torts. It is important to learn the duties that are owed by those who manufacture, sell, or lease products that are defectively made so that you will be able to select the appropriate cause of action to bring against the proper party. In the Study Tips section that follows, the necessary elements for the causes of action in a product liability lawsuit and the proper parties against whom suit should be brought are listed. By studying the causes of action in this manner, it will assist you in committing the entire concept of product liability to memory.

Study Tips

Product liability

The liability of manufacturers, sellers, and others for the injuries caused by defective production.

Negligence and Fault

In order to be successful in a negligence action based on products liability, the plaintiff must first establish that a duty was owed and thereafter breached by the defendant. There are several types of duties that are owed, any of which can be breached alone or in combination with the others. These duties as well as who owes the duty (which is listed in parenthesis) include:

- the duty to assemble the product safely. (the manufacturer)
- the duty to properly design the product. (the manufacturer)
- the duty to inspect or test the product. (the manufacturer)
- the duty to properly package the product. (the manufacturer)
- the duty to warn of any dangerous propensities that the product may have. (the manufacturer and possibly the retailer and/or wholesaler)

Of course a breach of any of these duties gives rise to a negligence cause of action of which the plaintiff must demonstrate that the defendant was the actual as well as proximate cause of his or her injuries. The interesting part of this aspect is that there may be more than one defendant who is being sued for negligence, and as such, each may assert that the other was a supervening act that breaks the chain of proximate causation thereby making him or her the indirect cause of the plaintiff's injuries.

- The plaintiff will have a difficult time in proving a negligence cause of action based upon product liability as it is often a challenge determining who was negligent. Any one of the parties that suit will be brought against could have caused the plaintiff's injuries. The potential parties in a negligence cause of action may include the manufacturer, the retailer, a possible wholesaler, and maybe even a repairperson. Any one of these parties could singly or together have caused the plaintiff's injuries.

Misrepresentation

A plaintiff bringing a lawsuit based on misrepresentation will do so because of the fraud associated with the quality of the product. Only those who relied on the misrepresentation and thereafter suffered injury may bring a cause of action under this tort.

- Though misrepresentation is not the most common cause of action of which to base a product liability action on, it can be utilized if the plaintiff shows the seller or lessor made a misrepresentation concerning the product's quality or did not reveal a defect in the product. Manufacturers, sellers, and lessors are potential defendants for this type of cause of action.

Strict Liability

The basis behind strict liability is to impose liability regardless of whose fault it is. As you learned in the previous chapter, strict liability is often imposed when a defendant is engaged in an ultra-hazardous activity. Strict liability is also imposed upon lessors and sellers who are in the business of leasing and selling products. Casual sellers are exempt from the facet of being in the business of leasing and selling products. A casual seller is someone who is not a merchant.

- Be careful as strict liability involves products and not services. If the situation involves both, the court will look at the prevalent element in order to determine whether or not strict liability applies.

- Who may be liable under a strict liability theory?
  - **All in the Chain of Distribution Are Liable.**
  - All manufacturers, distributors, wholesalers, retailers, lessors, manufacturers of sub-components may be held strictly liable for the injuries caused by the product.
    - Note that if one or more of the parties in the chain of distribution are held liable in a strict liability lawsuit, the parties may seek indemnification by bringing a separate cause of action against the negligent party.
  - Special notation concerning entrepreneur liability for a defective product - Entrepreneurs may avoid the concern of being named in a product liability lawsuit by taking the cautionary measure of purchasing a products liability insurance policy. This will help minimize or eliminate the costs associated with such a lawsuit. Note that any amount of damages above and beyond what the policy covers will be the responsibility of the business.

- Who may recover under strict liability?
  - Purchaser or lessee, family members, guests, employees, customers, and persons who passively enjoy the benefits of the product, as well as bystanders injured by the defective product.

- What damages can be recovered under strict liability?
  - Personal injury with some jurisdictions limiting the dollar amount of the award.
  - Property damage, which is recoverable in most jurisdictions.
  - Lost income which is recoverable in some jurisdictions.
  - Punitive damages are recoverable if the plaintiff can show that the defendant intentionally injured him or her or acted maliciously for his or her safety.

- Elements in a strict liability cause of action: First, a defect must be shown. Several types of defects exist.

  Manufacturing defect – A failure on the manufacturer's part to properly assemble, test, or check the product's quality.

  Design defect – This defect involves the application of a risk-utility analysis. The court will weigh the gravity of the danger from the design, the likelihood that injury will result from the design, and the availability as well as expense of producing a safer different design against the utility of the design. The crashworthiness doctrine falls under this category of defect, as the courts have held that automobile manufacturers have a duty when designing automobiles to take into account the possibility of a second collision from within the automobile. A failure to protect occupants from foreseeable dangers may result in a lawsuit based upon strict liability.

Packaging defect – A manufacturer has a duty to design and provide safe packages for their products so that they are either tamperproof or indicate if they have been tampered with. This type of defect has particular application in the pharmaceutical industry.

Failure to warn is viewed as a defect – Manufacturers as well as sellers have a duty to warn users about the dangerous aspects of a product. The warning must be clear and conspicuous on the product. A failure to warn may subject those in the chain of distribution to a lawsuit based on strict liability.

Miscellaneous defects – There are other defects that can give rise to a strict liability cause of action: the failure to safely assemble a product, failure to provide adequate instructions for the safe use or assembly of a product, failure to adequately test a product or select proper component parts or materials, and failure to properly certify the product.

- Defenses to a product liability lawsuit: There are many *defenses* that may have applicability in a product liability lawsuit.

  Supervening Event – No liability exists if the product is materially altered or modified after it leaves the seller's possession and the modification or alteration causes the injury.

  Generally Known Dangers – If a product is generally known to be dangerous and a seller fails to warn of this, then liability may attach. However, placing a safety feature on a generally known dangerous product may assist in limiting or absolving liability.

  Government Contractor Defense – A government contractor must show that the government provided precise specifications for the product and the contractor did in fact conform to those specifications. Further that the government was warned by the contractor of any known product defects or dangers.

  Assumption of the Risk – Even though a defendant may utilize this defense by showing that the plaintiff knew and appreciated the risk involved and voluntarily assumed the risk, this defense is not widely used.

  Misuse of Product – The main aspect the defendant must prove is that the plaintiff has abnormally misused the product and that such misuse was unforeseeable. If the misuse was foreseeable, the seller of the product will remain liable.

  Statute of Limitations and Repose – A failure to bring a cause of action within the allowed time frame will relieve the defendant of liability. Many jurisdictions state that the statute of limitations begins to run when the plaintiff suffers an injury. Other states feel this is unfair to the seller and have created statutes of repose that limit the liability a seller has by setting a time frame in terms of years from when the product was first sold.

  Contributory and Comparative Negligence – If a person is found to have been negligent in contributing to his or her own injuries, this will not prevent him or her from recovering in a strict liability cause of action as it would under an ordinary negligence cause of action. Further, the courts have applied the defense of comparative negligence, thereby apportioning the damages based upon the negligence of each of the parties.

Refresh Your Memory

The following exercise will give you the opportunity to test your memory of the principles given in this chapter. Read the question twice and place your answer in the blank provided. Review the chapter material for any question that you are unable to answer or remember.

1. _____ is a tort related to defective products in which the defendant has breached a duty of due care and caused harm to the plaintiff.

2. _____ is a tort doctrine that makes manufacturers, distributors, wholesalers, retailers, and others in the chain of distribution of a defective product liable for the damages caused by the defect, irrespective of fault.

3. _____ refers to all manufacturers, distributors, wholesalers, retailers, lessors, and subcomponent manufacturers involved in a transaction.

4. _____ refers to monetary damages that are awarded to punish a defendant who either intentionally or recklessly injured the plaintiff.

5. A defect in manufacture occurs when a manufacturer fails to _____.

6. _____ is a doctrine that says automobile manufacturers are under a duty to design automobiles so they take into account the possibility of harm from a person's body striking something inside the automobile in the case of a car accident.

7. _____ refers to a defect that occurs when a manufacturer does not place information about the dangers of using a product on its packaging, causing injury if the dangers are unknown.

8. When the containers of a product are not tamperproof, it is termed as a _____.

9. _____ is a defect that occurs when a manufacturer does not provide detailed directions for safe assembly and use of a product.

10. _____ refers to an alteration or a modification of a product by a party in the chain of distribution that absolves all prior sellers from strict liability.

11. To assert _____ as a defense, the defendant must prove that the plaintiff knew and appreciated the risk of the product.

12. _____ refers to a statute that requires an injured person to bring an action within a certain number of years from the time that he or she was injured by a defective product.

13. _____ refers to a statute that limits the seller's liability to a certain number of years from the date when the product was first sold.

14. The term _____ refers to a defense that says a person who is injured by a defective product but has been negligent and is partially responsible for his or her own injuries cannot recover from the defendant.

15. The term _____ refers to the doctrine which applies to strict liability actions that says a plaintiff who is contributorily negligent for his or her injuries is responsible for a proportional share of the damages.

Critical Thought Exercise

Bruce Owens bought a Chevrolet Suburban from General Motors Corp. (GMC). Four years later, Owens crashed into the rear of another car while commuting to work. The speed of Owens' vehicle at the time of the crash was estimated to be less than 35 miles per hour. A properly functioning seatbelt will restrain the driver from impacting the steering wheel and the windshield during a crash at 40 miles per hour. During the crash, the seatbelt that Owens was properly wearing broke away from its anchor, causing Owens to be thrust against the steering wheel and into the windshield. Owens received a fractured skull, broken ribs, and a fractured left ankle. Owens sued GMC, Chevrolet, and the dealership that sold the vehicle to him. Owens claimed in his suit that because the seat belt broke, the defendants were strictly liable for his injuries. Investigation determined that the seatbelt anchor was both inadequate to sustain the forces involved in restraining a person during a crash and had been installed in a manner that increased the likelihood of failure during a crash.   Are the defendants strictly liable to Owens?

Please compose your answer to the Critical Thinking Exercise using a separate sheet of paper or your computer word processing program.

Practice Quiz

True/False

16. _____ The liability of manufacturers, sellers, lessors, and others for injuries caused by defective products is commonly referred to as product liability.

17. _____ Under the doctrine of strict liability, a plaintiff cannot recover punitive damages for reckless conduct of the defendant.

18. _____ In a negligence lawsuit, parties who were not actually negligent are also liable to the plaintiff.

19. _____ Intentional misrepresentation occurs when a seller or lessor conceals a defect in a product.

20. _____ The doctrine of strict liability holds the manufacturers of a defective product solely liable for injuries caused by that product.

21. _____ A defendant who has not been negligent but who is made to pay a strict liability judgment can bring a separate action against the negligent party in the chain of distribution to recover its losses.

22. _____ Privity of contract between the plaintiff and the defendant is not required in a strict liability suit.

23. _____ Plaintiffs can allege multiple product defects in one lawsuit.

24. _____ Failure to properly assemble a product constitutes a defect in design by the manufacturer.

25. _____ Courts can apply a consumer expectation test to evaluate the adequacy of a product's design.

26. _____ A defect in manufacture occurs when the manufacturer fails to warn customers about the dangerous propensities of its products.

27. _____ Manufacturers and others in the chain of distribution are not strictly liable for failure to provide adequate instructions on assembly and use of a product.

28. _____ Inadequate testing of a product can support a product liability lawsuit based on strict liability.

29. _____ Under the defense of contributory negligence, if Mary is partially responsible for her injuries, then she can recover partial damages from the defendant.

30. _____ Any alteration or modification of a product after it leaves the seller's possession can make the seller strictly liable for injuries caused by the product.

Multiple Choice

31. Intentional misrepresentation occurs when a seller or lessor _____.

A. fails to warn customers about the dangerous propensities of a product
B. shows negligence in product design
C. fails to assemble a product carefully
D. conceals a defect in a product

32. Which of the following statements is true about strict liability?

A. It applies only to manufacturers of a defective product.
B. It is liability without fault.
C. It requires privity of contract between the plaintiff and the defendant.
D. It covers casual sales and transactions.

33. According to the doctrine of strict liability, which of the following parties is strictly liable for injuries caused by a defective product?

A. only the manufacturers of the products
B. only the parties directly involved in the sale of the product to the customer
C. all parties providing services related to the product
D. all parties in the chain of distribution

34. Betty buys a lawnmower, manufactured by FlatPlanes, Inc., from Harvey's department store. A defect in the design of the blades causes the lawnmower to kick back on operation, injuring Betty. Which of the following remedial actions is Betty entitles to?

A. Betty can sue Harvey's department store for negligence.
B. Betty can sue either Harvey's department store or FlatPlanes, Inc. for strict liability.
C. Betty can only sue FlatPlanes, Inc. for strict liability as they manufactured the defective lawnmower.
D. Betty can only sue Harvey's department store for strict liability as they sold her the defective lawnmower.

35. Which of the following statements is true about the strict liability doctrine?

A. Privity of contract between the injured party and defendant is mandatory.
B. Injured bystanders cannot recover damages under the strict liability doctrine.
C. Parties in the chain of distribution are strictly liable only to the customer who buys the product.
D. Injured bystanders are entitled to the same protection as the consumer or user.

36. Mary was getting a ride home in John's new car. On the way, a malfunctioning brake caused an accident and both Mary and John were injured. Which of the following statements is true of this situation?

A. Mary can recover from a strict liability lawsuit against the manufacturer of John's car.
B. Mary can file a strict liability lawsuit against John.
C. Mary can file a negligence lawsuit against the dealership that sold John his car.
D. John can file a negligence lawsuit against the dealership from which he bought the car.

37. Companies that manufacture products to government specifications are not liable if such products cause injury because _____.

A. the companies have government contractor defense
B. the use of these products entails generally known dangers
C. these products are abnormally misused
D. people assume the risk when using these products

38. A man tries to swallow a pen as part of a circus act. The pen becomes lodged in his throat and he is taken to a hospital for immediate medical attention. The man sues the company that manufactured the pen. Which of the following would be the best defense for the pen manufacturer in this lawsuit?

A. They can claim that the product carried generally known dangers.
B. They can claim that the product was abnormally misused.
C. They can claim that the injury was caused by a supervening event.
D. They can claim that the plaintiff had assumed the risk when buying the product.

39. Bill buys a truck and replaces the regular tires with large tires to turn the vehicle into a monster truck. When he tries to drive the truck, the oversized tires cause the truck to roll over and crash. Bill then files a strict liability lawsuit against the truck manufacturer to recover for his injuries. Which of the following is the best defense for truck manufacturer in this lawsuit?

A. government contractor defense
B. assumption of the risk
C. generally known danger
D. supervening event

40. A pharmaceutical company has disclosed a list of side effects of its new prescription drug. A consumer, taking the drug in the right doses, suffers from one of these side effects and sues the company for product liability. Which of the following would be the pharmaceutical company's defense in this lawsuit?

A. The consumer was injured due to a supervening event.
B. The consumer had assumed the disclosed risks when purchasing the drug.
C. The side effects suffered by the consumer were generally known dangers of the drug.
D. The consumer abnormally misused the drug.

Short Answer

41. Handy Dandy makes a meat slicing machine that contains a sharp blade for thin cuts of meat. What must Handy Dandy and those stores who sell the meat slicing machine do to protect themselves from product liability suits?

_____

_____

42. When does the statute of limitations begin to run in a product liability cause of action?

_____

43. Who, or what, is included in the chain of distribution?

_____

44. What is the defense of generally known dangers?

_____

45. If a bicycle manufacturer discovers that the front tire is not properly mounted or installed due to a bolt that is improperly made, what must the manufacturer do?

_____

46. Slimy Sid's Sedans, a used car dealer, represents to Donna Dimsy that the car she is about to buy has a better engine than any brand new car she could find. After she purchases it, the engine blows up on the freeway she is driving on, causing massive burns to 70 percent of Donna's body. On what tort can Donna base her cause of action against Slimy Sid's?

_____

_____

47. When does the statute of repose begin to run?

_____

48. Paul is a worker on an assembly line for a treadmill manufacturer where he is responsible for putting the safety handrails on each machine. The demand for the treadmills has been high and as such, the production line speed has increased dramatically. Paul becomes sloppy trying to keep up with the speed of production and fails to tighten down the safety rail on a machine that Fanny Fitness purchases. Fanny injures herself after losing her balance on the treadmill when the safety handrail detached itself from the machine. What duty has Paul breached?

_____

49. What type of breach is required to be proved in a negligence suit for product liability, but not under strict liability?

_____

50. Name five common types of product defects.

_____

51. Which analysis may the court apply to evaluate the adequacy of a product's design?

_____
_____

52. When may a seller be relieved of liability for the misuse of a product?

_____

53. What is the effect of a supervening event on the liability of a manufacturer of a product?

_____

54. What is the primary difference between using the theories of negligence or misrepresentation and the theory of strict liability?

_____
_____

55. What does privity of contract require that would make product liability suits difficult for plaintiffs to bring against some manufacturers and sellers?

_____

Answers to Refresh Your Memory

1. Negligence [p. 106]
2. Strict liability [p. 107]
3. Chain of distribution [p. 108]
4. Punitive damages [p. 109]
5. adequately check the quality of a product [p. 110]
6. Crashworthiness [p. 113]
7. Failure to warn [p. 113]
8. Failure to warn [p. 113]
9. Failure to provide adequate instructions [p. 114]
10. Supervening event [p. 115]
11. assumption of the risk [p. 115]

Critical Thought Exercise Model Answer

In order to establish strict liability, Owens must establish the following requirements:
(1) *The defendant must sell the product in a defective condition.* The anchor was unable to perform as intended because it was poorly designed and was also installed incorrectly. Either reason makes the product defective. (2) *The defendant was in the business of selling this product.* GMC, Chevrolet, and the dealership are all in the business of selling Suburbans. (3) *The product must be unreasonably dangerous to the user because of its defect.* A vehicle without a safely functioning seatbelt that can properly restrain a passenger during a crash is very dangerous. There is no valid reason for a manufacturer not to install a working seatbelt. (4) *The plaintiff must incur physical injury.* Owens was severely injured. (5) *The defective condition must be the proximate cause of the injury.* We know that Owens was propelled into the steering wheel and windshield because the seatbelt did not restrain him. The speed of the crash was within limits where the seatbelt should have worked properly. (6) *The goods must not have substantially changed from the time of sale to the time of injury.* There are no facts showing any modification to the seatbelt while owned by Owens.

All of the elements needed to establish strict liability for the defective product are present. When a product is defective, as in this case, all defendants in the chain of distribution, from the manufacturer to the distributor to the dealer, have joint and several liability for the injury to plaintiff. Owens may recover against all the defendants in this case.

Answers to Practice Quiz

True/False

16. True. The liability of manufacturers, sellers, lessors, and others for injuries caused by defective products is commonly referred to as product liability. [p. 106]

17. False. In product liability cases, a court can award punitive damages if it finds that the defendant's conduct was committed with intent or with reckless disregard for human life. [p. 109]

18. False. In a negligence lawsuit only a party who was actually negligent is liable to the plaintiff. [p. 106]

19. True. Intentional misrepresentation occurs when a seller or lessor either (1) affirmatively misrepresents the quality of a product or (2) conceals a defect in it. [p. 106]

20. False. All parties in the chain of distribution of a defective product are strictly liable for the injuries caused by that product. [p. 108]

21. True. A defendant who has not been negligent but who is made to pay a strict liability judgment can bring a separate action against the negligent party in the chain of distribution to recover its losses. [p. 108]

22. True. Privity of contract is not required between the plaintiff and defendant because strict liability is a tort defense. [p. 109]

23. True. Plaintiffs can allege multiple product defects in one lawsuit. [p. 110]

24. False. A defect in manufacture occurs when the manufacturer fails to (1) properly assemble a product, (2) properly test a product, or (3) adequately check the quality of a product.[p. 110]

25. True. In evaluating the adequacy of a product's design, a court may apply a risk–utility analysis. Some courts apply a consumer expectation test, which requires a showing that the product is more dangerous than the ordinary consumer would expect. [p. 111]

26. False. Failure to warn of dangerous propensities is a defect that will support a strict liability action. [p. 113]

27. False. Failure to provide adequate instructions for the safe assembly and use of a product is a defect that subjects the manufacturer and others in the chain of distribution to strict liability. [p. 114]

28. True. Defects that support a finding of product liability based on strict liability include inadequate testing of products, inadequate selection of component parts or materials, and improper certification of the safety of a product.[p. 114]

29. False. Under the defense of contributory negligence, a party who is partially at fault for causing her own injuries is barred from recovering damages from the defendant in a product liability action. [p. 116]

30. False. The manufacturer or seller is not liable if a product is materially altered or modified after it leaves the seller's possession and the alteration or modification causes an injury. [p. 115]

Multiple Choice

31. D. Answer D is correct, as intentional misrepresentation occurs when a seller or lessor either (1) affirmatively misrepresents the quality of a product or (2) conceals a defect in it. [p. 106]

32. B. Answer B is correct as strict liability is liability without fault.[p. 107]

33. D. Answer D is correct, as all parties in the chain of distribution of a defective product are strictly liable for the injuries caused by that product.[p. 108]

34. B. Answer B is correct, as all parties in the chain of distribution of a defective product are strictly liable for the injuries caused by that product.[p. 108]

35. D. Answer D is correct, as strict liability is a tort doctrine, privity of contract between the plaintiff and the defendant is not required. In other words, the doctrine applies even if the injured party had no contractual relations with the defendant.[p. 109]

36. A. Answer A is correct as all parties in the chain of distribution of a defective product are strictly liable for the injuries caused by that product. Thus, all manufacturers, distributors, wholesalers, retailers, lessors, and subcomponent manufacturers may be sued and assessed liability under the doctrine of strict liability in tort.[p. 109]

37. A. Answer A is correct, as defense and other contractors that manufacture products to government specifications are not usually liable if such a product causes injury. This is called the government contractor defense. [p. 114]

38. B. Answer B is correct, as a manufacturer or seller is relieved of product liability if the plaintiff has abnormally misused the product.[p. 115]

39. D. Answer D is correct as. the manufacturer or seller is not liable if a product is materially altered or modified after it leaves the seller's possession and the alteration or modification causes an injury. Such alteration or modification is called a supervening event. [p. 115]

40. B. Answer B is correct as the doctrine of assumption of the risk can be asserted as a defense to a product liability action. For this defense to apply, the defendant must prove that (1) the plaintiff knew and appreciated the risk and (2) the plaintiff voluntarily assumed the risk. [p. 115]

Short Answer

41. Handy Dandy and those stores who sell the meat slicing machine must place a proper and conspicuous warning on the meat slicer to be insulated from strict liability, as they have a duty to warn consumers and users about the dangerous propensities of the product. [p. 106]

42. The statute of limitations in a product liability cause of action begins to run when the plaintiff suffers an injury. [p. 115]

43. All manufacturers, distributors, wholesalers, retailers, lessors, and subcomponent manufacturers involved in a transaction are included in the chain of distribution. [p. 108]

44. This defense acknowledges that certain products are inherently dangerous and are known to the general population to be so. [p. 114]

45. The bicycle manufacturer must notify the purchasers and users of the defect and correct the defect. [p. 106]

46. Donna can base her cause of action against Slimy Sid's Sedans on intentional misrepresentation because Slimy Sid affirmatively misrepresented the quality of the engine and concealed the defects in the engine. [p. 106]

47. The statute of repose begins to run when the product is first sold. [p. 115]

48. Paul has breached the duty to assemble the product carefully. [p. 110]

49. Strict liability does not require the injured person prove that the defendant breached a duty of care. [p. 107]

50. Defect in manufacture, defect in design, failure to warn, defect in packaging, and failure to provide adequate instructions. [p. 110]

51. In evaluating the adequacy of a product's design, a court may apply a risk–utility analysis.[p. 111]

52. The seller is relieved of product liability if the plaintiff has abnormally misused the product, if there has been an unforeseeable misuse of the product. [p. 115]

53. A supervening event absolves all prior parties in the chain of distribution of liability, thus a manufacturer would be absolved of liability if there is a supervening event after the product leaves the manufacturer. [p. 115]

54. The tort theories of negligence and misrepresentation require the plaintiff to prove that the defendant(s) are at fault for the injuries they have sustained. Strict liability is liability without fault. [p. 106-107]

55. Privity of contract requires that there be a contractual relationship between the plaintiff and defendant, which would preclude plaintiffs from bringing suit against manufacturers or sellers if the plaintiff had not purchased the product directly from that manufacturer or seller. [p. 109]

7 | INTELLECTUAL PROPERTY AND CYBER PIRACY

Chapter Overview

Intellectual property consists of trade secrets, patents, trademarks, and copyrights. This chapter explores the remedies for infringement of the rights that are attached to them. You will also become familiar with the protection that is attached to technology based intellectual property.

Objectives

Upon completion of the exercises in this chapter, you should be able to:
1. Describe the business tort of misappropriating a trade secret.
2. Describe how an invention can be patented under federal patent laws and the penalties for patent infringement.
3. List the items that can be copyrighted and describe the penalties of copyright infringement.
4. Define trademark and service mark and describe the penalties for trademark infringement.
5. Define cyber piracy and describe the penalties for engaging in cyber infringement of intellectual property rights.

Practical Application

You should be able to distinguish among a copyright, trademark, and patent, and determine whether or not an infringement has occurred. You will become familiar with various intellectual property acts, their applications, and which laws will afford the greatest protection to the creator.

Helpful Hints

The easiest way to study the material is to categorize all of the information and acts in a methodical fashion that is consistent throughout the chapter. The Study Tips section that follows attempts to organize the information for you so that studying becomes more manageable.

Study Tips

Each intellectual topic area is organized in the same fashion so that it becomes habit for you to learn the information in a logical manner. When studying, it will help you to have someone ask you the questions under each heading to determine what you have learned.

Trade Secrets

<u>What is a trade secret?</u> A product, formula, pattern, design compilation of customer data or any other business secret.

<u>What is considered a violation of a trade secret?</u> The defendant, usually an employee, must have obtained the trade secret through unlawful means, such as theft, bribery, or industrial espionage.

<u>Does an owner of a trade secret have any obligations under the law?</u> Yes, he or she must take all reasonable precautions to protect his or her trade secret. If the owner does not protect his or her trade secret, then there is no protection under the law for it.

<u>What laws afford protection of a trade secret?</u>
State unfair competition laws, which may include the Uniform Trade Secrets Act. The federal Economic Espionage Act of 1996 makes it a federal crime to steal another person's trade secrets.

<u>What may the owner recover if he or she is successful in a trade secret action?</u>
The owner may recover profits, damages, and procure an injunction to stop the offender from using or revealing the trade secret. Under the Economic Espionage Act, organizations may be fined up to $10 million dollars per criminal act and individuals may get up to 15 years of prison time per violation. Fines and prison terms increase if the act benefited a foreign government.

Patents

<u>What is required to get a patent?</u> An invention that is novel, useful, and non-obvious.

<u>What types of things can be patented?</u> Processes, machines, improvements of existing machines, compositions of matter, asexually reproduced plants, designs for an article of manufacture, living material invented by a person

<u>How does an individual get a patent?.</u> Briefly stated, an individual applies for a patent with the Patent and Trademark Office and is assigned a number. While waiting for approval, the individual may affix the terminology "patent pending" on the thing to be protected.

<u>What other laws are available to help inventors?</u> Under the American Inventors Protection Act of 1999, an inventor may file a provisional application with the Patent and Trademark Office pending the final completion and filing of a patent application. The inventor has "provisional rights" for three months pending the filing of a final application.

<u>Federal Law and Patents</u> – The Federal Patent Statute protects patented inventions from infringement. There are no state patent laws.

<u>Law to be aware of</u> – The <u>Public Use Doctrine</u> (also called the one-year "on sale" doctrine) states that a patent may not be granted if the invention was used by the public for more than one year prior to the filing of the patent application. This law encourages timely patent applications.

<u>What may the patent holder recover in a successful patent infringement action?</u> A patent holder may recover money equal to a reasonable royalty rate on the sale of the infringed article, damages such as loss of customers, an injunction preventing future infringing action, and an order requiring destruction of the infringing material. If the court finds that the infringement was intentional, then it may award treble the damages.

Copyrights

<u>What can be copyrighted?</u> Only tangible writings that can be physically seen may be copyrighted. This includes books, sermons, greeting cards, jewelry, and glassware.

<u>What is required in order to get a copyright?</u> The work must be the original, tangible work of the author. Notice is not required; however, it is recommended that notice be placed on the work so as to prevent the claim of innocent infringement. Registration with the U.S. Copyright Office is voluntary and can be done at any time during the copyright period.

<u>What laws afford protection of an individual's work?</u>
Copyright Term Extension Act of 1998 – This act added 20 years to existing copyrighted work and to future copyrighted works. For individual copyright holders, copyright protection is for the life of the author plus 70 years. For a corporate copyright holder, protection is ninety-five years from the year of first publication or 120 years from the year of creation, whichever is shorter.

The Digital Millennium Copyright Act – This act "prohibits the unauthorized access to copyrighted digital works by circumventing the wrapper or encryption technology that protects the intellectual property." Civil and criminal penalties are imposed under this act. Actual damages, treble damages, attorney's fees, and injunction and statutory damages are some of the remedies available. Criminal penalties in the form of fines and prison time may also be ordered. The level of protection of digital copyrighted works has risen as a result of this act.

The No Electronic Theft Act (NET act) provides from criminalizing certain types of copyright infringement. It "prohibits any person from willfully infringing a copyright for either the purpose of commercial advantage or financial gain, or by reproduction or distribution even without commercial advantage or financial gain, including by electronic means where the retail value exceeds $1,000. Penalties include up to one year imprisonment and fines up to $100,000.

<u>Can work be used even if it is copyrighted?</u> Under the Fair Use Doctrine, certain limited, unauthorized use of copyrighted materials is permitted without it being an infringement. Quotations from a review or criticism of a work, brief news report quotations, a small reproduction of a work by a teacher in order to teach a lesson, and reproduction of a work in a judicial or legislative hearing are considered fair use.

<u>What may an individual recover in a successful copyright infringement action?</u> The plaintiff may recover any profit made by the infringer, damages suffered by the plaintiff, an order to impound or destroy the infringing work, an injunction to prohibit future infringement, and statutory damages in lieu of actual damages may be awarded.

Trademarks

<u>What can be trademarked?</u> Marks such as distinctive marks, symbols, names, words, mottos, or slogans can be trademarked.

<u>Note the difference between a trademark and other marks, such as a service mark, certification mark, or a collective mark.</u>
- Service mark – Used to set apart the services of the holder from the competition. *Ex:* Weight Watchers
- Certification mark – A mark used to certify that goods are of a certain quality or come from a certain geographical location. Ex: Santa Maria Tri-Tip Sandwiches
- Collective mark –A mark used by associations or cooperatives, etc. Ex: Big Brothers of America

<u>What is the purpose of a trademark?.</u> To protect the owner's investment and goodwill in a mark.

<u>What is needed to qualify for protection of a mark?</u> The mark must have acquired secondary meaning or be distinctive. A term that becomes descriptive loses its distinction and its protection.

<u>How does an individual register a trademark?</u> Trademarks are registered with the U.S. Patent and Trademark Office in Washington, D.C. The original mark is valid for 10 years and renewable for an unlimited number of 10-year periods. The registered user may use the trademark symbol, however, it is not necessary. Registration is permitted if a mark was in use in commerce or the individual verifies a good faith intention to use the mark within six months of registration.

<u>What laws protect a trademark?</u>
The Federal Lanham Trademark Act, which was intended to protect the owner's investment and goodwill in a mark and prevent consumer confusion.

The Federal Dilution Act of 1995 protects famous marks from dilution. There are three requirements under this act that must be met: (1) the mark must be famous; (2) used for commercial purposes by the other party; and (3) the use must cause dilution of the distinctive aspect of the mark. The purpose of this act is to stop those who try to benefit from others monetary and creative efforts in promoting their famous marks. Many situations that call for the use of this act's protection are domain name cases.

Refresh Your Memory

The following exercise will give you the opportunity to test your memory of the principles given in this chapter. Read the question twice and place your answer in the blank provided. Review the chapter material for any question that you are unable to answer or remember.

1. Intellectual property falls into a category of property known as _____.

2. A(n) _____ is a product formula, pattern, design, compilation of data, customer list, or other covert business information.

3. A closely guarded formula for a recipe protected by a soft drink manufacturer would be considered as an example of a _____.

4. If a competitor reverse engineers a trade secret, then the competitor is _____..

5. A competitor can lawfully use a rival's trade secret if the competitor got the trade secret by means of _____.

6. A _____ is a grant by the federal government upon the inventor of an invention for the exclusive right to use, sell, or license the invention for a limited amount of time.

7. A _____ is a patent that protects the functionality of a patent.

8. _____ is a legal right that gives the author of qualifying subject matter, and who meets other requirements established by law, the exclusive right to publish, produce, sell, license, and distribute the work.

9. In terms of copyright law, the use of copyrighted material in a satire or parody would be an example of _____.

10. Uploading copyrighted material to an unauthorized web site by a non-copyright holder would count as an act of copyright infringement under the _____.

11. _____ is any trade name, symbol, word, logo, design, or device used to identify and distinguish goods of a manufacturer or seller or services of a provider from those of other manufacturers, sellers, or providers.

12. A _____ mark is mark that confirms that a seller of a product or service has met certain geographical location requirements, quality standards, material standards, or mode of manufacturing standards established by the owner of the mark.

13. A mark that indicates that a person has met the standards set by an organization and is a member of that organization is known as a(n) _____ mark.

14. A _____ is a term for a mark that has become a common term for a product line or type of service and therefore has lost its trademark protection.

15. _____ is a type of trademark dilution where a famous mark is linked to products of inferior quality or is portrayed in an unflattering, immoral, or reprehensible context likely to evoke negative beliefs about the mark's owner

Critical Thought Exercise

Lindsey and Tony decide to establish an Internet business called Our Business is E-Business (OBE) in Greenport, while enrolled at Green Valley College. The business sells electronic equipment including computers, CD players, home theater systems, and PDAs. The merchandise is high quality, but sales have been in a slump due to competition. They need more sales to keep the business operating. Lindsey and Tony add you as a partner with a one-third interest for your investment of $20,000. Lindsey comments that if all the students who were listening to the latest hits from artists like Linkin Park, O-Town, and Sheryl Crow would buy a piece of equipment from them, OBE would be an overnight success. Lindsey purchased CDs from twelve popular music artists and establishes a link for listening to this music once an item is purchased from OBE. For every $100 spent on OBE merchandise, the customer can listen to an hour of music for free. Lindsey and Tony have not been making very much profit on each individual sale, especially since many items sold by OBE are relatively inexpensive, such as remote controls, surge protectors, CD cases, and audio/video cables. As a partner, you are worried that there may be something wrong with using the artists' music to help sell OBE merchandise. You ask Tony and Lindsey to remove the link to the free music from the OBE Internet site. Mainly because sales have increased by 30 percent since the music link was added to the OBE site, they vote against you and insist that the music link remain part of the site unless you can prove to them that it is not in the best interest of OBE to continue with the "free music" offer.

Prepare a memorandum to your partners on the intellectual property rights that may be involved in your situation and the consequences of any infringement for OBE.

Please compose your answer to the Critical Thinking Exercise using a separate sheet of paper or your computer word processing program.

Practice Quiz

True/False

16. _____ Intellectual property falls into a category of property known as intangible rights.

17 _____ A patent can only be claimed for a limited amount of time.

18. _____ Abstractions and scientific principles cannot be patented unless they are part of the tangible environment.

19. _____ If an invention is obvious, then it does not qualify for a patent.

20. _____ The patent term begins to run from the date the patent is issued.

21 _____ In the United States, the first person to invent an item or a process is given patent protection over a later inventor who was first to file a patent application.

22. _____ Non-patented inventions that have been in public use for over a year can still be patented.

23. _____ Utility patents for inventions are valid for 20 years.

24. _____ A utility patent is a patent that may be obtained for the ornamental nonfunctional design of an item.

25. _____ Copyright for a work can only be claimed once the U.S. Copyright Office issues it.

26. _____ After the copyright period runs out, the work enters the public domain.

27. _____ A trademark is only issued if the registrant proves he has used the mark in commerce.

28 _____ The trademark symbols "TM" and "SM" can be used with marks that have been not been registered.

29. _____ A party has to be a member of an organization to use a certification mark.

30. _____ Ordinary words or symbols that have taken on a secondary meaning will qualify as marks.

Multiple Choice

31. .Which of the following would be considered to be a part of intellectual property?

A. buildings
B. vehicles
C. business contracts
D. patents

32. Apart from recovering damages, and recovering profits made by the offender, successful plaintiffs in a misappropriation of a trade secret case can also _____.

A. obtain the offender's trademarks or brand name as payoff
B. ask for transfer of any of the offender's patents to the plaintiff
C. ask to acquire the offender's trade secrets as payoff
D. obtain an injunction prohibiting the offender from divulging the trade secret

33. What is a patent number?

A. a number assigned to a patent during application
B. a number assigned to a patent when the patent is pending
C. a number assigned to a patent once the patent is granted
D. a number assigned to a patent when it comes under investigation

34. According to the public use doctrine for patents, _____.

A. a patent will not be granted if the invention was already in public use for one year before filing application
B. an invention cannot be used in the public domain prior to it being granted a patent
C. the inventor has to test his invention in the public domain, to measure its validity, before being granted a patent
D. the invention will come into the public domain once its term period has expired

35. Which of the following provisions does the American Inventors Protection Act make?

A. It lets the inventor apply for a provisional right application.
B. It allows the inventor to ask for an immediate patent on his invention.
C. It protects the invention from going public before the patent is issued.
D. It does not let non-patent holders to challenge the inventor's patent.

36. Which of the following types of patents is valid only for a period of 14 years?

A. utility patent
B. process patent
C. business method patent
D. design patent

37. Which of the following is suitable for copyrighting?

A. buildings
B. musical compositions
C. business methods
D. product logos

38. What is the period of copyright protection provided for individuals under the Sonny Bono Copyright Term Extension Act of 1998?
A. Individuals are granted 120 years copyright protection from the year of creation of the work.
B Individuals are granted 95 years copyright protection from the year of first publication of the work.
C. Individuals are granted copyright protection for their lifetime plus 70 years.
D. Individuals are granted 20 years of copyright protection, after which it has to be renewed for a fee.

39. How is a copyright different from a patent?
A. Copyrights are applied for inventions, while a patent is applied for tangible writings.
B. Patents have a limited term period, while copyrights carry lifelong terms.
C. Patents fall under the federal law, while copyrights fall under state law.
D. Copyrights should be novel, and useful, while patents need not be so.

40. Which of the following intellectual properties is protected by the Lanham Act?
A. trademark
B. trade secret
C. copyright
D. patent

Short Answer

41. What is the owner of a trade secret obliged to do?

_____

42. What does the registration of a trademark serve to do?

_____

43. What was the purpose of Congress enacting the Federal Patent Statute?

_____

44. Give examples of three things that may be patented.

_____

45. Under current patent law, when does the patent term begin to run?

_____

46. When does copyright infringement occur?

_____

47. How has the Digital Millennium Copyright Act changed the traditional fair use doctrine?

_____

_____

48. Give three examples of tangible writings that are afforded copyright protection.

_____

49. What is meant by the terminology "secondary meaning"?

_____

50. Give at least three examples of things that cannot be trademarked.

_____

51. Give three examples of trade names that have become generic and are no longer protected under trademark law.

_____

52. What is meant by the term "dilution" in the context of the federal Dilution Act?

_____

53. What are the three fundamental requirements that must be met by a trademark under the federal Dilution Act in order to qualify for its protection?

_____

54. What provision does the Trademark Dilution Revision Act make?

_____

55. Give one example of each of the following: trademark, service mark, certification mark, and collective mark.

_____

Answers to Refresh Your Memory

1. intangible property [pp.121]
2. trade secret [p. 122]
3. trade secret [p. 122]
4. allowed to use the trade secret but not the original trademark [p. 122]
5. reverse engineering [p. 122]
6. patent [p. 124]
7. utility patent [p. 124]
8. Copyright [p. 128]
9. application of fair use doctrine [p. 130]
10. No Electronic Theft Act [p. 131]
11. Trademark [p. 132]
12. certification [p. 133]
13. collective membership [p. 133]
14. generic name [p. 136]
15. Tarnishment [p. 138]

Critical Thought Exercise Model Answer

To: Tony and Lindsey
From: Your Partner
Re: Possible Copyright Infringement

Copyrights are designed to protect the rights of artists while preserving the public's right to benefit from the works of these artists. Use of copyrighted material is legal only if there is permission from the copyright holder or there is permissible use under the fair use doctrine. The fair use doctrine allows limited use of copyrighted material for a specific purpose, such as education, editorial comment, parody, criticism, news reporting, research, and scholarship. Fair use does not apply to situations where the use is for a commercial purpose. A court will also examine the effect the use will have upon the potential market for the value of the copyrighted material. Because we are using the music to enhance our sales, this is an impermissible commercial use. Though we are not copying the music, we may be liable for contributory infringement if a court finds that we, with knowledge of the infringing activity, induce, cause, or materially contribute to the infringing conduct of another. We are making it possible for customers to have access to a copy of the music. Contributory infringement includes a simple link to a Web site with infringing files on it. Liability extends to both the linking site and the site where the files are located. We are not only linking to copyrighted material but we are knowingly and willingly hosting the files with the intent of distributing the music. The penalties for this activity are up to five years in prison and a fine of $250,000 for the first offense.

A solution to this problem is to obtain a license from the copyright holder that would allow us to use the music with their permission. The license fee will be negotiable and we may be able to obtain it for a very fair price when we explain the limited use and nature of our business. The artist may consider the limited use to be a form of free publicity, much like play time on a radio station. The failure to cease using copyrighted material subjects all three of us to civil and criminal penalties. Failure to cure this infringement violated your fiduciary duty to me as a partner. If you do not immediately get OBE in compliance with 17 U.S.C Section 101 et seq., I will be forced to terminate our partnership.

Answers to Practice Quiz

True/False

16. True. Intellectual property falls into a category of property known as intangible rights, which are not tangible physical objects. [p. 121]

17. True. A patent is a grant by the federal government upon the inventor of an invention for the exclusive right to use, sell, or license the invention for a limited amount of time. [p. 124]

18. True. Abstractions and scientific principles cannot be patented unless they are part of the tangible environment. [p. 125]

19. True. If an invention is nonobvious, it qualifies for a patent; if it is obvious, then it does not qualify for a patent.[p. 125]

20. False. The patent term begins to run from the date the patent application is filed (instead of when the patent is issued, as was previously the case). [p. 127]

21. True. The United States still follows the first-to-invent rule rather than the first-to file rule followed by some other countries. Thus, in the United States, the first person to invent an item or a process is given patent protection over a later inventor who was first to file a patent application.[p. 127]

22. False. Under the one-year "on sale" doctrine, also called the public use doctrine, a patent may not be granted if the invention was used by the public for more than one year prior to the filing of a patent application. [p. 127]

23. True. Utility patents for inventions are valid for twenty years. [p. 126]

24. False A design patent is a patent that may be obtained for the ornamental nonfunctional design of an item. [p. 128]

25.False. The U.S. Court of Appeals for the Federal Circuit in Washington, DC, was created in 1982. This is a special federal appeals court that hears appeals from the Board of Patent Appeals and Interferences of the U.S. Patent and Trademark Office and federal courts concerning patent issues. [p. 124]

26.True. After the patent period runs out, the invention or design enters the public domain, which means that anyone can produce and sell the invention without paying the prior patent holder. [p. 127]

27. True. A registrant must prove either that he has used the intended mark in commerce (e.g., actually used in the sale of goods or services) or states that he intends to use the mark in commerce within six months from the filing of the application.[p. 132]

28. True. TM and SM are used to designate unregistered trademarks and service marks, respectively. [p. 132]

29. False. A certification mark is a mark usually owned by a nonprofit cooperative or association. A party does not have to be a member of the organization to use the mark.. [p. 133]

30. True. Ordinary words or symbols that have taken on a secondary meaning can qualify as marks. [p. 134]

Multiple Choice

31. D. Answer D is the correct answer, intellectual property falls into category of property known as intangible rights, which are not tangible physical objects. Intellectual property includes patents, copyrights, and trademarks. [p. 121]

32. D. Answer D is the correct answer; generally, a successful plaintiff in a misappropriation of a trade secret action can (1) recover the profits made by the offender from the use of the trade secret, (2) recover for damages, and (3) obtain an injunction prohibiting the offender from divulging or using the trade secret. [p. 122]

33. C. Answer C is the correct answer. If a patent is granted, the invention is assigned a patent number. [p. 124]

34. A. Answer A is the correct answer. According to the public use doctrine, a patent may not be granted if the invention was used by the public for more than one year prior to the filing of a patent application. [p. 127]

35. A. Answer A is the correct answer. Congress enacted the American Inventors Protection Act, which permits an inventor to file a provisional application. [p. 127]

36. D. Answer D is correct. A design patent is valid for fourteen years.[p. 128]

37. B. Answer B correctly. Only tangible writings—writings that can be physically seen—are subject to copyright registration and protection. [p. 128]

38. C. Answer C is the correct answer. According to the Sonny Bono Copyright Term Extension Act of 1998 extended copyright protection individuals are granted copyright protection for their lifetime plus seventy years. [p. 129]

39. B. Answer B is the correct answer. Patents on articles of manufacture and processes have 20 years term period and design patents have 14 years term period. Individual holder has life of author plus 70 years term period. [p. 137]

40. A. Answer A is correct. In 1946, Congress enacted the Lanham (Trademark) Act, 5 commonly referred to as the Lanham Act, to provide federal protection to trademarks, service marks, and other marks. [p. 132]

Short Answer

41. The owner of a trade secret is obliged to take all reasonable precautions to prevent that secret from being discovered by others. [p. 122]

42. Registering a trademark serves to give constructive notice that the mark is the registrant's personal property. [p. 132]

43. The Federal Patent Statute provides an incentive for inventors to invent, make their inventions public, and protects against infringement. [p. 124]

44. Answers will vary; any three of the following: machines; processes; compositions of matter; improvements to existing machines, processes, or compositions of matter; designs for an article of manufacture; asexually reproduced plants; living material invented by a person. [p. 124-125]

45. The patent term begins to run from the date the application is filed. [p. 127]

46. Copyright infringement occurs when a party copies a substantial and material part of another's work without permission. [p. 130]

47. The DMCA has made it illegal to even access the copyrighted material by breaking through the digital wrapper or encryption technology that protects the work. [p. 131]

48. Answers will vary, however examples include books, magazines, musical compositions, lectures, and greeting cards to name a few. [p. 129]

49. A secondary meaning is when an ordinary term has become a brand name. [p. 134]

50. Answers will vary. Examples include the flag of the United States, immoral or scandalous remarks, geographical names standing alone, surnames standing alone. [p 134]

51. Answers will vary, including Frisbee, trampoline, Tollhouse cookies, and cornflakes. [p. 137]

52. Dilution is the lessening of the capacity of a famous mark to identify and distinguish the goods and services of the trademark holder, irrespective of whether or not there is competition between the owner of the mark and the other party. [p. 138]

53. The mark must be famous. The use by the other party must be commercial. The use must cause dilution of the distinctiveness of the mark. [p. 139]

54. The act provides that a dilution plaintiff need not show that it has suffered actual harm to prevail in its dilution lawsuit. [p. 138]

55. Answers will vary: Trademark – Coca-Cola, Big Mac; Service mark – FedEx, Big Brown; Certification mark – Real California Cheese; Collective Mark – Washington Apple, Grown in Idaho. [pp. 133-134]

8 | CRIMINAL LAW AND CYBER CRIMES

Chapter Overview

This chapter presents business and online crimes. You will be able to differentiate between a felony and a misdemeanor, and be able to define the various crimes and elements that help to establish liability for each. The chapter provides an overview of criminal procedure from arrest through trial. The Racketeer Influenced and Corrupt Organization Act (RICO), Foreign Corrupt Practices Act, and the safeguards provided in the Fourth, Fifth, Sixth and Eighth Amendments to the U.S. Constitution are examined.. The law as it pertains to Internet crimes is reviewed.

Objectives

Upon completion of the exercises in this chapter, you should be able to:
1. List and describe the essential elements of a crime.
2. Describe criminal procedure, including arrest, indictment, arraignment, and the criminal trial.
3. Identify and define business and white-collar crimes.
4. List and describe cyber crimes.
5. Explain the constitutional safeguards provided by the Fourth, Fifth, Sixth, and Eighth Amendments to the U.S. Constitution.

Practical Application

You should be able to identify the different types of crimes, including those involving the Internet, and identify the elements necessary to establish liability. You should be able to understand and explain the criminal process, beginning with the arrest through to trial. You should be able to apply the safeguards that are afforded under the United States Constitution.

Helpful Hints

It is helpful to distinguish between what a felony is versus a misdemeanor. It is easier to remember the crimes that are involved if you categorize them based on whether the crimes are against individuals, property, or the Internet. In order to remember the aspects of criminal procedure that accompanies the crime itself, it is helpful to draw a horizontal time line listing the various stages of the criminal process. It is important to be aware of the statutory acts such as the Racketeer Influenced and Corrupt Organization Act and the Foreign Corrupt Practices Act.

Study Tips

Background Information

- The U.S. leads the world in terms of humanity and sophistication in the criminal law system.

- In the United States, a person is presumed innocent until proven guilty.
- Guilt must be established beyond a reasonable doubt.
- The United States Constitution gives the accused certain safeguards.

Crime

A crime is a violation of a duty owed to society that has legal consequences and which requires the individual to make amends to the public.

Sources of Criminal Law

- Statutes are the main source.
- Penal codes –detailed, well-defined criminal activities, with sanctions for violations.
- State and federal regulatory statutes

Parties to a Criminal Action

- The government is the plaintiff in a criminal action, represented by an attorney called a prosecutor.
- The accused is the defendant, represented by a defense attorney. The government will provide a free attorney if the defendant is unable to afford representation.

Important Facts to Know about Felonies

- They are the most serious types of crimes.
- Crimes that are inherently evil (*mala in se*) are considered to be felonies.
- Crimes such as murder, rape, bribery, and embezzlement are felonies in most jurisdictions.
- Imprisonment is the usual punishment; however, the death penalty is imposed in some jurisdictions for the crime of first-degree murder.
- Federal law requires mandatory sentencing for certain crimes.
- Some states require mandatory sentencing for certain crimes.
- A number of statutes provide for the degrees of crime and the penalties for each.

Important Facts to Know about Misdemeanors

- They are less serious than felonies.
- Crimes that are prohibited by society (*mala prohibita*) but not inherently evil are categorized as a misdemeanor.
- Crimes such as burglary, regulatory statute violations, and robbery are examples of misdemeanors.
- These types of crimes have punishments that are less severe than felonies.
- Punishment includes imprisonment for less than a year and/or a fine.

Violations Are Neither a Felony nor a Misdemeanor

- Examples of a violation include jaywalking and traffic violations. A fine is the only punishment allowable unless a jury trial is granted.

Elements of a Crime

Two necessary elements to be shown when proving a person is guilty of a crime:

Criminal Act
- The defendant must have performed the wrongful act. The performance of the wrongful act is also known as the *actus reus*.
- The performing or failure to do a certain act can satisfy this element.
- A defendant's thought of doing the crime will not satisfy the criminal act element. The wrongful act must have been carried out.
- Criminal acts can bring about civil law actions that have their basis in tort.

Criminal Intent
- The defendant must have the necessary state of mind (specific or general intent) when he/she performed the act. This intent is also referred to as the *mens rea*.
- It is important to differentiate between specific and general intent.
    o Specific intent is demonstrated when the accused intentionally or with knowledge or purposefully performs the prohibited act.
    o General intent is proven where there is a lesser amount of culpability.
- The jury may deduce the type of intent based upon the defendant's actions.
- There is no crime where there is no *mens rea*. If the act that was performed was an accident, then *mens rea* cannot be established.
- Strict or absolute liability for a prohibited act means that *mens rea* is not required. Violation of an environmental statute is an example where absolute liability would be imposed.

Criminal Procedure

There are several pretrial procedures as well as the trial itself that you need to be familiar with. The pretrial procedure involves the arrest, indictment, arraignment, and plea bargaining.

Arrest
- The police must have a warrant based upon probable cause before a person can be arrested.
    o Probable cause has been defined as the existence of objective, articulated facts that would raise in the mind of a reasonable person that a crime has been committed or is about to be committed.
- A search without a warrant is allowed when the crime is in progress, those involved in the crime are fleeing from the scene or there is a great chance that the evidence will be destroyed. Probable cause is still required even in the absence of a warrant.
- After the accused is arrested, a booking takes place. The booking involves the recording of the arrest as well as the standard fingerprinting.

Bail Bond
- A bail amount is usually set after a person is arrested.
- If the accused posts bond, he or she will be released from prison until trial.
- The accused can post bond himself, or pay a professional bail bonds person to post bail.

Indictment or Information
- The indictment or information involves the formal charges that must be brought against the accused before being brought to trial.

- The government evaluates those charged with serious crimes. If there is enough evidence to hold the accused for trial, an indictment is then issued and the accused is held for trial.
- For crimes with a lesser magnitude, a judge will determine if there is sufficient evidence to hold the accused for trial. An information is issued upon confirmation that the evidence is sufficient and the accused is then held over for trial.

Arraignment

- Once an information or indictment is issued, the accused is informed of the charges against her or him and is requested to enter a plea.
- The accused may enter a guilty, not guilty, or nolo contendere plea. If the latter is chosen, the accused does not admit guilt, but agrees to a penalty. Nolo contendere pleas may not be used later on in a civil proceeding. Acceptance of the nolo contendere pleading is optional.

Plea Bargaining

- This involves an agreement between the government and the accused whereby the accused admits to a lesser offense in exchange for the government's imposition of a lesser penalty.
- The rationale behind plea bargaining is to minimize overcrowding of prisons, avoid trial risks, and to save costs associated with trial.

The Criminal Trial

- All jurors must agree unanimously before the accused is found guilty.
- The defendant may appeal if he or she is found to be guilty.
- Even if one juror disagrees, the accused will not be found guilty.
- If the defendant is innocent, the government cannot appeal.
- If a unanimous decision does not come to fruition, the jury will be hung in terms of what they decided. The government then has the option of retrying the case before a new jury or judge.

Common Crimes

The most common crimes against persons and property are given below. It is important for you to be aware of the necessary elements of a particular crime in order to prove that it has or has not been committed.. When you are given a certain set of facts, it is important to analyze them and determine their applicability to each of the requisite elements of the crime you are trying to prove.

Murder

- The unlawful killing of a human being by another with aforethought of malice.
- Most states have several degrees of murder.

Felony Murder Rule

- Where murder is committed in the commission of another felony, even though the perpetrator did not originally plan to commit a murder, most states hold the perpetrator liable for murder.
- Intent for the crime of murder is inferred from the intent to commit the other crime.

Robbery

- The taking of personal property of another using fear or force.
- Note that a pickpocket does not qualify as a robber as there is no fear or force.

Burglary
- At common law, burglary was the "breaking and entering a dwelling at night" with the intent to commit a felony therein.
- Compare the common definition to the modern expansion, which includes daytime thefts of offices and commercial buildings. The breaking element is no longer a requirement in many jurisdictions. If there has been an unauthorized entry through an unlocked door or window, this will be sufficient.

Larceny
- At common law, larceny was the "wrongful and fraudulent taking of another person's personal property."
- Personal property includes trade secrets, computer programs, tangible property, and other types of business property.
- Examples of larceny include automobile theft, car stereo theft, and pickpocketing.
- The perpetrator need not use force or go into a building in order to commit this crime.
- Some jurisdictions categorize the larceny as either grand or petit based upon the value of the goods that were taken.

Theft
- In those jurisdictions that do not categorize crimes in terms of robbery, larceny, and burglary, the crimes of this nature are under the heading of theft. These jurisdictions then label the theft as petit or grand depending on the value of the goods taken.

Receiving Stolen Property
- If a person knowingly receives stolen property with the intent to deprive its rightful owner of that property, they may be found to have committed the crime of receiving stolen property. The stolen property may be personal property, money, stock certificates, or anything tangible.
- An important notation is that the element of knowledge may be inferred from the circumstances.

Arson
- The crime of arson at common law was defined as "the malicious or willful burning of the dwelling house of another person."
- Modernly, the term dwelling includes all buildings including public, commercial, and private ones.

White Collar Crimes

Many crimes are often committed by businesspersons and are generally characterized by cunning and deceit. The most important of these crimes are discussed below.

Forgery
- This crime involves the fraudulent making or alteration of a written document, which affects the legal liability of another person.
- Examples include falsifying public records and counterfeiting as well as imitating another person's signature on a check or altering the amount of the check.
  - Note that one spouse may sign his or her spouse's check and deposit it into a joint account without it being designated as forgery. There is no intent to defraud in this situation.

Embezzlement
- A statutory crime involving the fraudulent conversion of property by a person to whom another individual's property was entrusted.
- Employer's representatives, agents, or employees usually commit this crime.
- The main element to be aware of is the fact that the property was entrusted to the individual who ultimately absconded with it.

Bribery
- When one individual gives money, property, favors, or anything of value to another in exchange for a favor in return, this is known as bribery. This is often referred to as a kickback or a payoff.
- Intent is an essential element of this crime.
- If the offeree accepts the bribe, he or she is then also guilty of the crime.
- The offeror can be guilty of the crime without the offeree accepting the bribe.
- The Foreign Corrupt Practices Act of 1977 requires firms to keep accurate records as they pertain to foreign transactions. American companies may not bribe a foreign official, political party or candidate in an attempt to influence new business or retention of a continuing business. Knowledge is a key element in making the conduct as described above a crime. Punishment includes fines and imprisonment.

Extortion
- Extortion involves the obtaining of property of another with or without his or her consent by use of actual or threatened force, violence, or fear.
- The truth or falsity of the information does not matter.
- Examples of extortion include when one person threatens another that a piece of information will be exposed unless money or property is given to the extortionist. This is known as blackmail.
- Extortion of public officials is referred to as extortion "under color of official right."

Criminal Fraud
- This crime is known as false pretenses or criminal fraud or deceit as the accused obtains title to the property through trickery.
- Included under this crime is the crime of mail and wire fraud. The government will prosecute a suspect if the mail or wires are used to defraud another individual.
- Mail Fraud, Wire Fraud, and Internet Fraud. Federal law prohibits the use of mails or wires to commit fraud on another person. These statutes are often used when there is insufficient evidence to prosecute the real crime and have a maximum penalty of 20 years in prison.

Money Laundering
- The process of running the proceeds from illegal activity through a legitimate business to clean it by burying the illegal proceeds under layers of bogus transactions posted on the books of the legitimate business.
- The Money Laundering Control Act forbids knowingly engaging in a monetary transaction through a financial institution involving property gained from illegal activity in excess of $10,000.
- The Act also forbids knowingly engaging in a financial transaction involving proceeds of illegal activity.
- Sanctions include fines of up to the greater of $500,000 or twice the amount of the property involved and up to 20 years in prison, as well as forfeiture of property to the government.

Criminal Conspiracy
- When two or more people agree to commit a crime.
- A party must commit an overt act to further the crime.
- Actual commission of the crime is unnecessary.
- The government may bring this charge if the criminals have been thwarted or there is insufficient evidence to prosecute the planned crime.

Corporate Criminal Liability
- At common law, the courts held that corporations lacked the *mens rea* needed to commit a crime.
- Modernly, corporations are being held criminally liable for the acts of their managers, employees, and agents. Since imprisonment is not feasible, they are being fined or having their franchise or license taken away.
- The corporate officers, employees, or directors are held personally liable for crimes that they personally commit regardless if it was done for personal gain or for the corporation. If a corporate manager fails to appropriately supervise his or her subordinate, the manager may be held criminally liable for the subordinate's criminal activities.

The Racketeer Influenced and Corrupt Organizations Act (RICO)
- It is a federal crime to acquire or maintain an interest in or conduct or participate in an "enterprise" through a "pattern" of "racketeering activity."
- Examples of racketeering activity include gambling, robbery, arson, deals involving narcotics, bribery, mail fraud, etc.
- Punishment includes fines, imprisonment, and forfeiture of any property or business interests that were obtained as a result of the RICO violations.
- The government can also seek business reorganization, dissolution, and the dissolution of the defendant's interest in an enterprise as part of civil penalties for RICO violations.

Constitutional Safeguards

Protection Against Unreasonable Search and Seizure
- The Fourth Amendment plays an important role in protecting corporations and persons from *unreasonable searches and seizures* by the government. "It permits people to be secure in their person, houses, papers, and effects."
  - Note that regulated businesses as well as those who are involved in hazardous industries are subject to warrantless searches.
- *Exclusionary Rule.* Searches may not go beyond the area specified in the warrant. If evidence is obtained as a result of an unreasonable search or seizure, it will be considered tainted. This evidence may not be used against the accused, but can be used against other individuals.
  - The "good faith" exception to the exclusionary rule states that illegally obtained evidence may be used against the accused if the police officers that obtained the evidence believed in good faith that they were acting in accordance with a lawful search warrant.

Privilege Against Self-Incrimination
- The Fifth Amendment states "no person shall be compelled in any criminal case to be a witness against himself."
- The privilege against self-incrimination is applicable to individuals, not corporations and partnerships.

- o Be aware though that private papers such as personal diaries of businesspersons are protected from disclosure.
- *Miranda Rights.* The Supreme Court upheld the right of the accused to be warned that they had the protection against self-incrimination. Statements or confessions obtained from a suspect prior to receiving their "Miranda warning" can be excluded from evidence at trial.
- Attorney-Client Privilege and Other Privileges. *The attorney-client privilege* is provided for in the Fifth Amendment. The Fifth Amendment also recognizes the psychiatrist/psychologist-patient privilege, priest/minister/rabbi-penitent privilege, spouse-spouse privilege, and parent-child privilege.
    - o Federal courts do not recognize an accountant-client privilege, though many state courts do.
- Immunity from Prosecution. The government consents to not use any evidence given by an individual against that person. Immunity is usually granted when the government wants information from an individual who has asserted his or her Fifth Amendment privilege against self-incrimination. If immunity is granted, the individual loses his or her Fifth Amendment protection.

Other Constitutional Protections
- Fifth Amendment Protection Against Double Jeopardy. The Fifth Amendment via its double jeopardy clause states a person may not be tried twice for the same crime. Compare this to where the accused has committed several crimes. The accused may be tried for each of the crimes without being in violation of the double jeopardy rule. If the acts are violations in different jurisdictions, each jurisdiction may try the accused.
- Sixth Amendment Right to a Public Jury Trial. The Sixth Amendment gives the accused the right to be tried by an impartial jury, to cross-examine witnesses against the accused, to have a lawyer's assistance and to have a speedy trial.
- Eighth Amendment Protection against Cruel and Unusual Punishment. This amendment protects the accused from abusive or torturous punishments.

Refresh Your Memory

The following exercise will give you the opportunity to test your memory of the principles given in this chapter. Read the question twice and place your answer in the blank provided. Review the chapter material for any question that you are unable to answer or remember.

1. A collection of criminal statutes is referred to as a(n) _____.

2. _____ include environmental laws, securities laws, and antitrust laws and provide for criminal violations and penalties.

3. _____ are the most serious of crimes, and are considered to be inherently evil.

4. A(n) _____ is considered a less serious crime; not inherently evil but prohibited by society; and is punishable by fines or imprisonment for one year or less.

5. A person found speeding is considered to have committed a(n) _____.

6. _____ crimes require that the perpetrator either knew or should have known that his or her actions would lead to harmful results.

7. A(n) _____ is a document for a person's detainment, based on a showing of probable cause that the person committed a crime.

8. _____ is defined as the substantial likelihood that a person either committed or is about to commit a crime.

9. A(n) _____ is a charge of having committed a crime, usually a felony, based on the judgment of a grand jury.

10. A(n) _____ is an agreement in which the accused admits to a lesser crime than charged, and in return, the government agrees to impose a lesser sentence than might have been obtained had the case gone to trial.

11. A jury that cannot come to a unanimous decision about the defendant's guilt is called a _____.

12. The wrongful or fraudulent taking of another's personal intangible properties like trade secrets, computer programs, and other business property is considered as a(n) _____.

13. _____ is a crime that involves the willful or malicious burning of a building.

14. The fraudulent making or alteration of a written document that affects the legal liability of another person is called _____.

15. _____ is the fraudulent conversion of property by a person to whom that property was entrusted.

Critical Thought Exercise.

Build-Rite Construction Company of Santa Maria, Jamaica, receives a copy of an invoice for $160,000 of supplies from Hayward Lumber. Tom Cheat, owner of Build-Rite, notices that the invoice states that the company name is Build-Right Contractors and gives the company office address as Santa Maria, California. The invoice contains three different account numbers that Cheat discovers are all assigned to Build-Right. Cheat pays the invoice but does nothing to correct the account numbers. During the next 14 months, Cheat has his employees order over $800,000 worth of materials from Hayward Lumber via the Internet, using the account numbers assigned to the California company. When the bills come due each month, Build-Right pays for the materials sent to Build-Rite, thinking that they have been shipped to one of their own construction sites. Cheat builds over 200 luxury vacation homes in Jamaica and has the funds from the sale of the homes sent to his accounts in the Bahamas, where his brother runs a one-person bank. The credit of Build-Right is ruined when they discover the misuse of their account numbers and refuse to pay the balance of over $300,000 charged to their accounts. Several banks pull their funding of Build-Right projects and equipment is seized. Build-Right has to temporarily lay off 180 employees.

What crime, if any, has been committed by Tom Cheat or his company? Who may be prosecuted? What law will apply? What steps should Build-Right take to help it recover financially and prevent this from happening again in the future?

Please compose your answer to the Critical Thinking Exercise using a separate sheet of paper or your computer word processing program.

Practice Quiz

True/False

16. _____ A person charged with a crime in the United States is presumed guilty until proven innocent.

17. _____ A crime is the violation of a statute for which the government imposes a punishment.

18. _____ If the accused cannot afford a private defense lawyer, the government will provide one free of charge.

19. _____ In a criminal lawsuit, guilt has to be proven beyond any reasonable doubt.

20. _____ A *nolo contendere* plea can be used as evidence of liability against the accused at a subsequent civil trial.

21 _____ The case against the accused is dismissed if neither an indictment nor information statement is issued.

22. _____ Crimes committed by businesspersons are referred to as blue-collar crimes.

23 _____ Extortion of private persons is commonly referred to as blackmail.

24. _____ The government can forfeit any property involved in a money laundering offense.

25. _____ Persons injured by a RICO violation can bring a private civil RICO action against the violator.

26. _____ The Fifth Amendment protects people from unreasonable search and seizure by the government.

27. _____ Warrantless searches are permitted where it is likely that evidence will be destroyed.

28 _____ A confession obtained from a person who has not been read the *Miranda* rights is not admissible in court.

29. _____ The attorney-client privilege can only be raised by the defendant.

30. _____ The Eighth Amendment prohibits capital punishment.

Multiple Choice

31. Who is the plaintiff in a criminal lawsuit?

A. the respondent
B. the government
C. a private party
D. the victim

32. Which two elements are required to find a defendant guilty of an intent crime?

A. criminal act and criminal intent
B. victim and criminal intent
C. criminal act and proof of gain
D. motive and criminal intent

33. When is a criminal said to be judgment proof?

A. when the criminal has not been read his Fifth Amendment rights prior to his arrest
B. when the criminal has been deemed to be insane
C. when the criminal does not have the money to pay a civil judgment
D. when the criminal is found to be unfit to go to prison

34. At what stage of the criminal procedure is the accused asked to enter a plea?

A. when the accused is being booked
B. when the accused is taken to an arraignment
C. when the accused is being arrested
D. while an indictment or information statement is being issued

35. Which of the following crimes is an example of a white-collar crime?

A. larceny
B. arson
C. forgery
D. battery

36. _____ is a crime in which one person gives another person money, property, favors, or anything else of value for a favor in return.

A. Battery
B. Bribery
C. Larceny
D. Embezzlement

37. The crime of _____ involves the obtaining of property from another, with his or her consent, induced by wrongful use of actual or threatened force, violence, or fear.

A. bribery
B. extortion
C. money laundering
D. embezzlement

38. Which one of the following types of protection does the Fourth Amendment provide to U.S. citizens?

A. protection against self-incrimination
B. protection against being tried for the same case twice
C. protection from unreasonable search and seizure by the government
D. protection from cruel and unusual punishment for a criminal defendant

39. Under which of the following circumstances is a warrantless search permitted?

A. if evidence is not in plain view
B. if evidence is likely to be destroyed
C. if the suspect has been previously convicted
D. if there is no probable cause

40. Which of the following Amendments protects criminal defendants from cruel and unusual punishment, and also protects criminals from torture?

A. Fifth Amendment
B. Fourth Amendment
C. Eighth Amendment
D. Fourteenth Amendment

Short Answer

41. What are the two elements that must be proven for one to be found guilty of most crimes?

_____

42. Who has the burden of proof if a person is charged with a crime?

_____

43. What types of things are not protected from disclosure under the Fifth Amendment?

_____

44. Give three examples of privileges that exist under the Fifth Amendment.

_____

45. What is the definition for the crime of robbery?

_____

46. What is required for the crime of receiving stolen property?

_____

47. Mr. Sly convinces Suzy Sweet to withdraw all of her money and invest in his water well that he claims to bottle as the water of youth. He has Suzy believe that her investment will triple in a month. Mr. Sly takes her money and flees the country to live in Barbados. What crime has Mr. Sly committed?

_____

48. What does the Fourth Amendment protect persons and corporations from?

_____

49. How may an accused be prosecuted twice or more without violating the double jeopardy clause of the Fifth Amendment?

_____

50. What is the definition of a crime?

_____

51. What does a plea of nolo contendere mean?

_____

52. What is a hung jury?

_____

53. What is the good faith exception to the exclusionary rule?

_____

54. What is the attorney-client privilege?

_____

55. What protection does the accountant-client relationship have?

_____

Answers to Refresh Your Memory

1. penal code [p. 144]
2. Regulatory statutes [p. 144]
3. Felonies [p. 145]
4. misdemeanor [p. 145]
5. violation [p. 145]
6. General intent [p. 146]
7. arrest warrant [p. 147]
8. Probable cause [p. 147]
9. indictment [p. 149]
10. plea bargain [p. 149]
11. hung jury [p. 150]
12. larceny [p. 151]
13. Arson [p. 152]
14. forgery [p. 152]
15. Embezzlement [p. 152]

Critical Thought Model Answer

Obtaining title to property through deception or trickery constitutes the crime of theft by false pretenses. This crime is commonly referred to as fraud. When the fraud is accomplished by the use of mails or wires, a federal offense has taken place. Because Cheat assumed the identity of Build-Right, the offense of identity theft may have been committed. The use of new technology, especially computers and the Internet, make this offense hard to prevent and extremely damaging to the victim.

Cheat may be both criminally and civilly liable under the Racketeer Influenced and Corrupt Organization Act (RICO). RICO makes it a federal crime to acquire or maintain an interest in, use income from, or conduct or participate in the affairs of a criminal enterprise through a pattern of racketeering activity. The commission of two or more enumerated crimes within a ten-year period establishes the pattern of activity. The enterprise can be a corporation, partnership, sole proprietorship, business, or organization. The Build-Rite construction company suffices as a criminal enterprise. The use of the Internet previously created a problem if wires were not used for transmission of the fraudulent communication. The statutes concerning wire fraud have been amended to include Internet activity within the definition of wire fraud. If the profits from the building of the condominiums had been invested in or maintained by Build-Rite, the assets would have been subject to forfeiture.

Unfortunately, the funds have been transferred to a bank in the Bahamas. The Bahamas have joined the Cayman Islands as a location where the bank secrecy laws protect the identity and amount of account deposits. The assets of Build-Rite are subject to forfeiture as are the proceeds sent to the Bahamas. Cheat is liable for multiple criminal offenses, if he can be apprehended. The employees of Build-Rite will incur criminal liability only if they knew that the account numbers were being misused. To remedy the situation, Build-Right should create a secure electronic signature for all account transactions. They can insist that all orders over a certain amount be confirmed by a separate e-mail with a password. The FTC should be consulted for advice and help in getting equipment released and credit with the banks restored.

Answers to Practice Quiz

True/False

16. False. A person charged with a crime in the United States is presumed innocent until proven guilty. [p. 144]

17. True. A crime is defined as any act done by an individual in violation of those duties that he or she owes to society and for the breach of which the law provides that the wrongdoer shall make amends to the public. [p. 144]

18. True. If the accused cannot afford a private defense lawyer, the government will provide one free of charge.[p. 145]

19. True. For the government to prove that the accused is guilty of the crime charged the accused must be found guilty beyond a reasonable doubt.[p. 144]

20. False. A *nolo contendere* plea cannot be used as evidence of liability against the accused at a subsequent civil trial. [p. 149]

21. True. The case against the accused is dismissed if neither an indictment nor information statement is issued. [p. 149]

22. False. Many crimes are referred to as white-collar crimes because they are most often committed by business managers and employees. [p. 144]

23. True. Extortion of private persons is commonly referred to as blackmail. [p. 145]

24. True. The violation of the Money Laundering Control Act subjects any property involved in or traceable to the offense to forfeiture to the government. [p. 154]

25. True. Persons injured by a RICO violation can bring a private civil RICO action against the violator to recover for injury to business or property. [p. 155]

26. False. The Fourth Amendment to the U.S. Constitution protects persons and corporations from overzealous investigative activities by the government. It protects the rights of the people from unreasonable search and seizure by the government. [p. 157]

27. True. Warrantless searches are permitted only (1) incident to arrest, (2) where evidence is in "plain view," or (3) where it is likely that evidence will be destroyed. [p. 157]

28. True. Any statements or confessions obtained from a suspect before he or she has been read the *Miranda* rights can be excluded from evidence at trial. [p. 161]

29. False. Either the client or the attorney can raise their attorney-client privilege. [p. 161]

30. False. The Eighth Amendment protects criminal defendants from cruel and unusual punishment. However this clause does not prohibit capital punishment. [p. 162]

Multiple Choice

31. B. Answer B is correct. In a criminal lawsuit, the government (not a private party) is the plaintiff. [p. 145]

32. A. Answer A is correct. Two elements must be proven for a person to be found guilty of an intent crime, (1) criminal act (*actus reus*) and (2) criminal intent (*mens rea*). [p. 146]

33. C. Answer C is correct. In many cases, a person injured by a criminal act will not sue the criminal to recover civil damages because the criminal is often judgment proof—that is, the criminal does not have the money to pay a civil judgment. [p. 147]

34. B.. Answer B is correct. If an indictment or information is issued, the accused is brought before a court for an arraignment proceeding, during which the accused is (1) informed of the charges against him and (2) asked to enter a plea. [p. 149]

35. C. Answer C is correct as extortion white-collar crimes involves forgery. The crime of forgery occurs if a written document is fraudulently made or altered and that change affects the legal liability of another person.[p. 152]

36. B. Answer B is correct as bribe is a crime in which one person gives another person money, property, favors, or anything else of value for a favor in return. [p. 152]

37. B. Answer B is correct. The crime of extortion involves the obtaining of property from another, with his or her consent, induced by wrongful use of actual or threatened force, violence, or fear. [p. 153]

38. C. Answer C is correct. The Fourth Amendment to the U.S. Constitution protects persons and corporations from overzealous investigative activities by the government. It protects the rights of the people from unreasonable search and seizure by the government. [p. 157]

39. B. Answer B is correct. Warrantless searches are permitted only (1) incident to arrest, (2) where evidence is in "plain view," or (3) where it is likely that evidence will be destroyed. [p. 157]

40. C. Answer C is correct. The Eighth Amendment protects criminal defendants from **cruel** and unusual punishment. [p. 162]

Short Answer

41. Most crimes require both a criminal act and criminal intent to find a person guilty of a crime. [p. 146]

42. The government has the burden of proof in prosecuting a person for a crime. [p. 147]

43. Because only natural persons may claim the privilege against self-incrimination, business records of corporations and partnerships are generally not protected from disclosure, even if those records will incriminate individuals who can claim the privilege. [p. 160]

44. Answers will vary. Examples include psychiatrist/psychologist-patient privilege, priest/minister/rabbi-penitent privilege, spouse-spouse privilege, doctor-patient. [p. 161]

45. Robbery is the taking of personal property from another by the use of fear or force. [p. 151]

46. It is a crime for a person to (1) knowingly receive stolen property, and (2) intend to deprive the rightful owner of that property. [p. 151]

47. Mr. Sly has committed the crime of false pretenses, or fraud, in that he obtained Suzy's money through deceit and trickery. [p. 154]

48. Generally, the government does not have the right to search individual or business premises without a search warrant. [p. 157]

49. If the same criminal act violates the laws of two or more jurisdictions, each jurisdiction is free to prosecute the accused without violating the double jeopardy clause. [p. 162]

50. Any act done by an individual in violation of those duties that he or she owes to society and for the breach of which provides that the wrongdoer shall make amends to the public. [p. 144]

51. The accused agrees to the imposition of a penalty but does not admit guilt. [p. 149]

52. A jury that cannot come to a unanimous decision about the defendant's guilt. [p. 150]

53. This exception allows illegally obtained evidence to be introduced against the accused if the police officers who conducted the unreasonable search reasonably believed that they were acting pursuant to a lawful search warrant. [p. 157]

54. The attorney-client privilege is invoked when a client tells his or her attorney about his or her case without fear that the attorney will be called as a witness against his or her client. [p. 161]

55. The accountant-client privilege is not recognized by the federal courts. Many states have enacted statutes that recognize this privilege in state courts. [p. 161]

9 | NATURE OF TRADITIONAL AND E- CONTRACTS

Chapter Overview

There are a variety of circumstances under which an individual will enter into a contractual situation in his or her lifetime. This chapter is intended to provide you with a broad overview of the different types of contracts, the requirements for contract formation, the sources of contract law, and the role of technology in contract law.

Objectives

Upon completion of the exercises in this chapter, you should be able to:
1. Define contract.
2. List the elements necessary to form a valid contract.
3. Distinguish between bilateral and unilateral contracts.
4. Describe and distinguish between express and implied-in-fact contracts.
5. Describe and distinguish among valid, void, voidable, and unenforceable contracts.

Practical Application

You should be able to determine whether or not a contract has been formed, as well as the type of contract that is involved. You should be able to recognize whether or not equity will play a role in the situation you are assessing. You should be more aware of the difficulties that individuals face when entering into electronic contracts and the licensing of computer information, as well as the importance of the Uniform Computer Information Transaction Act in these matters.

Helpful Hints

This chapter lends itself toward organization. As you attempt to learn the area of contract law, it is helpful to know what a contract is as well as and the necessary requisites for its formation. It is beneficial to list the various types of contracts with an example of each to help you remember and differentiate between them. As you study various fact situations, it is important in contract law that you read the hypotheticals and/or cases line by line, being careful to examine the facts, as they may or may not be controlled by the contract principles that you have learned. In contract law, slight variations in wording or sequence of events can change the outcome.

Study Tips

The following study tips have been organized in a manner that will assist you in easily learning the concepts involved in this chapter.

Definition of a Contract

An agreement between two or more parties that is enforceable in equity or a court of law.

- **Parties to a contract**:
  - *The offeror.* The one who is making the offer;
  - *The offeree.* The one who is the individual to whom the offer is made.

- **Elements of a contract**: In order to have a valid contract, there must be:
  - *An offer and acceptance.* Both, together, equate to an agreement.
  - *Consideration.* A legally sufficient bargained-for exchange. Be careful with this element, as gift promises, moral obligations, past consideration, and illusory promises are considered insufficient consideration.
  - *Contractual capacity.* The legal ability to enter into the contract. This is another area in which to watch for issues, as minors, intoxicated individuals, and those who have been adjudged insane may not have the requisite capacity to understand the nature of the transaction into which they are entering.
  - *Lawful object.* Contracts to accomplish illegal goals are contrary to public policy and are void. An example of this would be a contract entered into to kill another individual in order to receive an insurance policy's proceeds.

- **Defenses to the enforcement of a contract**: Two defenses can be used to block the enforcement of a contract.
  - *Genuineness of assent.* Assent to a contract must be genuine and cannot have been obtained through duress, undue influence, or fraud.
  - *Writing and form.* Certain contracts must be in writing or must be in a particular form.

Sources of Contract Law

- *Common law of contracts.* This law was developed from early court decisions that eventually became precedent for subsequent decisions. Many of the principles developed under the common law are still the same today.
- *Uniform Commercial Code (UCC).* The purpose of this law is to establish a uniform system of commercial law in the United States. It is important to note that the UCC takes precedence over common law.
- *Restatement (Second) of Contracts.* Though this compilation of contract law principles is law, it is used more often as a guide due to its statutory nature as opposed to law.

Objective Theory of Contracts

This theory applies to both express and implied-in-fact contracts. It does not matter whether or not the contract is express or implied-in-fact; the court will still apply the reasonable person standard. This means, would a reasonable person conclude that the words and conduct of the parties as well as surrounding circumstances were enough to demonstrate that the parties intended to create a contract? Subjective intent is irrelevant as it is the objective intent based on the reasonable person standard that will be examined.

E-Commerce

Electronic contracts and the licensing of computer information provide the base for much of the cyberspace economy. E-commerce contract provide special problems of contract formation, enforcement, and the provision of consumer protection. Often, traditional contract rules apply. Many states, as well as the federal government, have enacted laws that specifically regulate e-commerce transactions.

- *The Uniform Computer Information Transactions Act (UCITA).* This act targets a majority of the legal issues that are faced when conducting e-commerce over the Internet. Since a majority of the states have adopted some or all of the act, it is anticipated to become the foundation for the creation and enforcement of cyberspace licenses and contracts.

Classifications of Contracts

- **Bilateral and Unilateral** Contracts
  - *Bilateral contract.* This type of contract involves a promise for a promise. For example, "I promise to wash your car if you promise to take me to the movies." Acceptance is in the form of a promise.
  - *Unilateral contract.* This type of contract involves a promise for performance. For example, "If you mow the lawn, I will pay you $10.00." There is no contract until the offeree performs the requested act of mowing the lawn. Acceptance is in the form of performance.
- **Formal and Informal Contracts**
  - *Formal contracts.* A formal contract is one requiring a special method or form to create it. Some examples of formal contracts are contracts under a state's wax seal, a recognizance for example in the form of a bond, negotiable instruments as per the Uniform Commercial Code, and letters of credit which are also governed by the Uniform Commercial Code.
  - *Informal contracts.* All contracts that do not require a special form or method to create are considered informal contracts.
- **Valid, Void, Voidable, and Unenforceable Contracts**
  - *Valid contract.* A valid contract is one that meets all of the required elements to establish a contract.
  - *Void contract* – A void contract is one that does not have any legal affect.
  - *Voidable contract.* A voidable contract is one that enables one party to avoid his or her contractual obligations. Examples of where this situation may exist absent certain exceptions are contracts entered into by minors, insane individuals, intoxicated persons, those acting under undue influence, duress, or fraud, and where there is a mutual mistake.
  - *Unenforceable contract.* If there is a legal defense to the enforcement of the contract, the contract is unenforceable. An example of this would by if a writing such as the case with the purchase of real estate is required to be in writing as per the Statute of Frauds.
- **Executed and Executory Contracts**
  - *Executed contract.* If both parties have performed their required obligations under the contract, the contract is said to be executed.
  - *Executory contract.* If only one side has fully performed his or her obligations of the contract, the contract is said to be executory.

Express and Implied Contracts

- **Express contracts.** Simply stated, these are either oral or written agreements between two parties. An example would be an oral agreement to buy someone's radio and a written agreement to buy someone's home.
- **Implied-in-fact contracts.** This type of contract is implied on the conduct of the parties. There are certain requirements that must be met before a court will find that this type of contract exists. These requirements are:
    o The plaintiff gave services or property to the defendant.
    o The plaintiff expected compensation for the property or services. In other words the property or services were not gifts.
    o Even though the defendant could have refused to accept the property or services given by the plaintiff, he or she did not.
- **Quasi-contracts.** The term quasi-contract is an equitable one and is also known as implied-in-law contract. The Court will create a contract, even though there is not an actual contract between the parties, if the plaintiff provided goods or services to the defendant without compensation. Further reinforcement for the creation of a quasi-contract exists when it is shown that it would be unjust not to require the defendant to pay for the benefit received.

Equity

The equity courts of England developed a set of rules whose foundation was premised on fairness, moral rights, and equality. Equity principles were applied when the remedy at law was not adequate or in the interest of fairness, equitable principle had to be applied.

Refresh Your Memory

The following exercise will give you the opportunity to test your memory of the principles given in this chapter. Read the question twice and place your answer in the blank provided. Review the chapter material for any question that you are unable to answer or remember.

1. The _____ states that the intent to contract is judged by the reasonable person standard and not by the subjective intent of the parties.

2. According to the objective theory of contracts, the intent to enter into an express or implied-in-fact contract is judged by the _____.

3. The _____ establishes uniform legal rules for the formation and enforcement of electronic contracts and licenses.

4. A contract is _____ if the offeror's promise is answered with the offeree's promise of acceptance.

5. A contract is _____ if the offeror's offer can be accepted only by the performance of an act by the offeree.

6. Yvonne finds a carpenter to do some repairs for her house and tells him that if he finishes the job within Saturday, she would pay him $1,000. This offer creates a(n) _____ contract

7. An offeror uses blackmail to make an offeree sign a contract that involves the sale of the offeree's house. The contract is _____.

8. If a contract is required to be in writing under the Statute of Frauds but is not, the contract is _____.

9. A contract that has been fully performed on both sides is called an _____ contract.

10. Contracts that have been fully performed by one side but not by the other are classified as _____ contracts.

11. An oral agreement to purchase a neighbor's bicycle is a(n) _____ contract.

12. A(n) _____ is stated orally or in written words.

13. In a(n) _____ contract, agreement between parties is inferred from their conduct.

14. A(n) _____ is an equitable doctrine whereby a court may award monetary damages to a plaintiff for providing work or services to a defendant even though no actual contract existed.

15. _____ is a doctrine that permits judges to make decisions based on fairness, equality, moral rights, and natural law.

Critical Thought Exercise

Ricky Boggs, a 27-year-old country singer, was severely injured in an automobile accident. Boggs was airlifted by Bishop County Air Ambulance to Bishop Trauma Center for surgery and treatment. Boggs slipped into a coma and after seven weeks was transported to Bishop County Extended Care Hospital. Boggs remained in the hospital for fourteen months before he died without ever having regained consciousness. The total charges assessed by Bishop County for the care of Boggs exceeded $370,000.00. After he died, Bishop County sued Boggs' estate to recover the expenses of the air ambulance, trauma treatment, surgery, hospital stay, and extended care. Was there a contract between Bishop County and Boggs? If so, how much can Bishop County recover from the estate?

Please compose your answer to the Critical Thinking Exercise using a separate sheet of paper or your computer word processing program.

Practice Quiz

True/False

16. _____ Provision of services qualifies as a "consideration" for an enforceable contract.

17. _____ Agreement to a contract requires an offer by the offeror and an acceptance of the offer by the offeree.

18. _____ If the law requires that a contract be in writing, failure of such a contract to be in writing does not impact its enforcement.

19. _____ Common law of contracts refers to contract law developed primarily by state courts.

20. _____ Restatement of the Law of Contracts is the agreed upon federal law in the United States.

21. _____ Under the objective theory of contracts, the subjective intent of a party to enter into a contract is irrelevant.

22. _____ Companies are not permitted to issue licenses by e-commerce.

23. _____ The UCITA does not require state legislature to become law of a state.

24. _____ If ambiguity is detected while determining the type of contract, it is presumed to be a bilateral contract.

25. _____. A unilateral contract can be accepted without the performance of an act by the offeree.

26. _____ A letter of credit is considered an informal contract as it does not have a special method of creation.

27. _____ If one of the parties to a contract can enforce the contract, it is considered valid.

28. _____ A voidable contract is also termed as an unenforceable contract.

29. _____ A contract that has been fully performed by both sides is called an executory contract.

30. _____ A quasi-contract is an equitable doctrine whereby a court may award monetary damages to a plaintiff for providing work or services to a defendant even though no actual contract existed.

Multiple Choice

31. Which of the following is an acceptable consideration for a contract?

A. arrest
B. penalty
C. money
D. sentence

32. Which of the following statements is true about contracts?

A. The offeror is the party to whom an offer to enter into a contract is made.
B. An offeree is the authority that supervises the signing of a contract.
C. A contract is created when the offer is made and before it is accepted.
D. To have an enforceable contract, there must be mutual assent by the parties.

33. Which of the following is true of the UCC?

A. The UCC aims to create a uniform system of accounting among the 50 states.
B. The common law of contracts normally takes precedence over the provisions of the UCC.
C. Article 2 of the UCC prescribes a set of uniform rules for the creation and enforcement of rules of taxation.
D. Article 2A of the UCC prescribes a set of uniform rules for the creation and enforcement of contracts for the lease of goods.

34. Which of the following is true of the Restatement of the Law of Contracts?

A. It serves as a reference for guidance in contract disputes.
B. It does not identify negotiable instruments as formal contracts.
C. Its goal is to create a uniform system of commercial law among the 50 states.
D. It is the absolute federal law for contracts drafted in the U.S.A.

35. Which of the following is true of UCITA?

A. It establishes the rules for operation of franchises in the U.S.A.
B. It does not become law until a state adopts it as a statute.
C. It solely deals with the formation of electronic contracts, not licenses.
D. It addresses most of the legal issues that are encountered while starting an entrepreneurial venture.

36. Which of the following is an informal contract?

A. check
B. bank draft
C. lease
D. recognizance

37. What is recognizance?

A. a party's acknowledgement in court that he or she will pay a specified sum of money if a certain event occurs
B. a sealed document that contains a formal contract whose contents are known to both parties and the referee who supervised its signing
C. a sealed document that contains an informal contract whose contents are known only to the parties
D. a party's acknowledgement in court that he or she is not liable to pay any money if a certain event occurs

38. Which of the following is a necessary condition for a contract to be considered valid?

A. It is enforceable by both the parties.
B. It is enforceable by at least one of the parties.
C. It can be voided by one of the parties.
D. It can be voided by both parties.

39. Which of the following is true of enforcing a contract?

A. A contract is only considered valid if it is enforceable by both parties.
B. In an unenforceable contract, at least one party has the option to void his or her contractual obligations.
C. Void contracts are enforceable in cases involving mutual mistakes.
D. Parties may voluntarily perform a contract that is unenforceable.

40. Which of the following statements is true of the doctrine of quasi-contract?

A. It allows a court to award monetary damages to a defendant because no actual contract existed between the parties.
B. It applies only where there is an enforceable contract between the parties.
C. It is an equitable doctrine intended to prevent unjust enrichment.
D. Agreement between parties to a quasi-contract has been inferred from their conduct.

Short Answer

41. Give two defenses that may be raised to the enforcement of contracts.

_____

42. When is a contract created?

_____

43. What is the difference between an executor contract and an executed contract?

_____

_____

44. When is a unilateral contract accepted?

_____

45. What happens if there is any ambiguity as to whether a contract is unilateral or bilateral in nature?

_____

46. Jan Ruiz, a business owner, says to Mary Munoz, a decorator, "If you promise to wallpaper my waiting room by December 1, I will pay you $600.00." Mary promises to do so. What type of contract has been created?

_____

47. Dr. Kurt Crandall says to Collin Jones, a contractor, "If you have the extra rooms to my office built and ready to see patients by May 5, I will pay you $25,000." What type of contract may have been created?

_____

48. What type of contract is formed where Anthony says to Paul, "I will give you $10,000 if you help my friend Joe rob A & B liquor"?

_____

49. Why is the Uniform Commercial Code important to the law of contracts?

_____

50. Why was the Uniform Computer Information Transactions Act developed?

_____

51. If Alan has painted George's entire house except for the front door, may George revoke his offer to pay Alan for painting his house? Why or why not?

_____

_____

52. What type of agreement exists where the agreement between the parties has been inferred from their conduct?

_____

53. What does the objective theory of contracts hold?

_____

_____

_____

54. When is a quasi-contract imposed?

_____

55. What is the result if both parties to a contract avoid their contractual obligations?

_____

Answers to Refresh Your Memory

1. objective theory of contracts [p. 171]
2. reasonable person standard [p. 171]
3. UCITA [p. 172]
4. bilateral contract [p. 172]
5. unilateral [p. 172]
6. unilateral [p. 172]
7. voidable [p. 174]
8. unenforceable [p. 174]
9. executed [p. 174]
10. executory [p. 174]
11. express [p. 174]
12. express contract [p. 174]
13. implied-in-fact [p. 174]
14. quasi-contract [p. 176]
15. Equity [p. 177]

Critical Thought Exercise Model Answer

For parties to have an express contract, the terms of the agreement must be fully and explicitly stated in words, either oral or written. If there is no express agreement, an implied-in-fact contract may be created in whole or in part from the conduct of the parties, rather than their words. In this case, Boggs was unconscious, so he never manifested an assent to any agreement to pay for services, either by his words or conduct. In this type of situation, a plaintiff may have to rely upon a theory of quasi-contract. A Quasi-contract is a fictional contract imposed on parties by a court in the interests of fairness and justice. Quasi-contracts are usually imposed to avoid unjust enrichment of one party at the expense of another. Society wants medical personnel to come to the aid of injured persons without regard to the existence of a contract before services are rendered. This is especially true in an emergency situation where life may be in jeopardy. Though Boggs never consented to an agreement, it would be unfair for Bishop County to render medical treatment to Boggs to save his life and then receive no compensation. Boggs would then be unjustly enriched at the expense of Bishop County. The amount of recovery, however, is not dependent upon the charges assessed by the county. Because Boggs was never able to bargain for the amount or extent of services, the court will only allow Bishop County to recover the reasonable value of the medical services rendered. The $370,000.00 in bills will be scrutinized by the court and reduced if they exceed a reasonable cost for Boggs' treatment.

Answers to Practice Quiz

True/False

16. True. Money, personal property, real property, provision of services, and such qualify as consideration. [p. 170]

17. True. To have an enforceable contract, there must be an agreement between the parties. This requires an offer by the offeror and an acceptance of the offer by the offeree. [p. 169]

18. False. The law requires that certain contracts be in writing or in a certain form. Failure of such a contract to be in writing or to be in proper form may be raised against the enforcement of the contract. [p. 170]

19. True. Contract law developed primarily by state courts are common law of contracts. [p. 170]

20. False. The Restatement of the Laws of Contract is not law. However, lawyers and judges often refer to it for guidance in contract disputes because of its stature.[p. 171]

21. True. Under the objective theory of contracts, the subjective intent of a party to enter into a contract is irrelevant.. [p. 171]

22. False. Companies such as Microsoft Corporation, Google Inc., Facebook, Inc., and other technology companies license the use of their software over the Internet. [p. 171]

23. True. The UCITA is a model act that does not become law until a state legislature adopts it as a statute for the state.[p. 172]

24. True. If there is any ambiguity as to which it is, it is presumed to be a bilateral contract. [p. 172]

25. False. A contract is unilateral contract if the offeror's offer can be accepted only by the performance of an act by the offeree. [p. 172]

26. False. A letter of credit is an agreement by the issuer of the letter to pay a sum of money upon the receipt of an invoice and other documents. Letters of credit are governed by the UCC. Formal contracts are contracts that require a special form or method of creation. [p. 173]

27. True. A valid contract is enforceable by at least one of the parties. [p. 173]

28. False. A void contract has no legal effect. It is as if no contract had ever been created. With an unenforceable contract, there is some legal defense to the enforcement of the contract. A void contract is not also termed as an unenforceable contract.[p. 174]

29. False. A contract that has not been performed by both sides is called an executory contract.[p. 174]

30. True. The equitable doctrine of quasi-contract, also called implied-in-law contract, allows a court to award monetary damages to a plaintiff for providing work or services to a defendant even though no actual contract existed between the parties. [p. 176]

Multiple Choice

31. C. Answer C correctly states that money, personal property, real property, provision of services, and such qualify as consideration. [p. 170]

32. D. Answer D is correct. To have an enforceable contract, there must be an agreement between the parties. This requires an offer by the offeror and an acceptance of the offer by the offeree. There must be mutual assent by the parties. [p. 169]

33. D. Answer D correctly states that Article 2A (Leases). Article 2A (Leases) prescribes a set of uniform rules for the creation and enforcement of contracts for the lease of goods. These contracts are referred to as lease contracts.[p. 171]

34. A. Answer A is correct, as the Restatement of the Law of Contracts is not law. However, lawyers and judges often refer to it for guidance in contract disputes because of its stature. [p. 171]

35. B. Answer B is correct. The UCITA is a model act that does not become law until a state legislature adopts it as a statute for the state.[p. 172]

36. C. Answer C is correct. Valid informal contracts (e.g., leases, sales contracts, service contracts) are fully enforceable and may be sued upon if breached. [p. 173]

37. A. Answer A is correct. In a recognizance, a party acknowledges in court that he or she will pay a specified sum of money if a certain event occurs. [p. 173]

38. B. Answer B is correct. A valid contract is enforceable by at least one of the parties.[p. 173]

39. D. Answer D is correct. With an unenforceable contract, there is some legal defense to the enforcement of the contract. If a contract is required to be in writing under the Statute of Frauds but is not, the contract is unenforceable. The parties may voluntarily perform a contract that is unenforceable.. [p. 174]

40. C. Answer C is correct. The doctrine of quasi-contract is intended to prevent unjust enrichment and unjust detriment.[p. 176]

Short Answer

41. Two defenses that may be raised against the enforcement of contracts are genuineness of assent, and writing and form. [p. 170]

42. A contract is created when an offer made by the offeror is accepted by the offeree. [p. 169]

43. An executory contract occurs when one or both parties have not yet completed performance under the contract. An executed contract occurs when both parties have completed performance under the contract. [p. 174]

44. A unilateral contract is accepted when the offeree performs the act required under the contract. [p. 172]

45. The contract is presumed to be a bilateral contract. [p. 172]

46. A bilateral contract was created the moment that Mary promised to wallpaper the waiting room. [p. 172]

47. Dr. Crandall's offer created a unilateral contract whereby the offer can be accepted only by the contractor's performance of the requested act. [p. 172]

48. A void contract, as entering into a contract to commit a crime has no legal effect. [p. 174]

49. It helps to establish a uniform system of commercial law among the 50 states. [p. 171]

50. It was developed to establish uniform legal rules for the formation and enforcement of electronic contracts and licenses. [p. 172]

51. No, George may not revoke his offer as Alan has substantially completed the entire house with the exception of the front door. [p. 173]

52. There is an implied-in-fact contract. [p. 174]

53. This theory holds that the intent to enter into an implied-in-fact contract or an express contract is judged by the reasonable person standard, which looks at whether a reasonable person would conclude that the parties intended to make a contract after considering the circumstances and actions of the parties. [p. 171]

54. A quasi-contract is imposed where one party confers a benefit on another who keeps the benefit and it would be unjust not to require that person to pay for the benefit received. [p. 176]

55. Both parties are released from their contractual obligations. [p. 174]

10 | AGREEMENT

Chapter Overview

The previous chapter discussed the requirements for the formation of a contract, as well as the various types of contracts. This chapter expands upon the requirement of agreement. You will learn what constitutes a valid offer and the various ways that an offer can be terminated. Offers such as rewards, advertisements, auctions, and counteroffers are discussed. You will discover the many ways that an acceptance can be affected, with special emphasis on the mailbox rule.

Objectives

Upon completion of the exercises in this chapter, you should be able to:
1. Define agreement, offer, and acceptance.
2. Describe the required terms of an offer and describe the terms that can be implied in an offer.
3. Describe special forms of offers, including Internet auctions.
4. Define counteroffer and describe the effects of a counteroffer.
5. Describe how offers are terminated by acts of the parties and by operation of law.

Practical Application

You should be able to recognize whether or not a valid offer has been made and whether or not the essential terms are included within it. You should be able to determine whether an offer has been properly terminated and whether the mailbox rule applies. You should be able to draft a simple offer by utilizing the information contained in this chapter.

Helpful Hints

Each chapter, especially in the area of contracts, builds on one another. It is vital that you understand the information given in each chapter and know how to apply it to given fact situations. Your initial analysis of a potential contract should begin with the offer. You should use a mental checklist of what is required to establish a valid offer. If one of the elements is missing, then ask yourself whether there is a rule of law that may apply to satisfy that missing element. Next, you should determine whether or not you are examining a special offer such as a reward, an advertisement, auction, or counteroffer. Quickly review your mental checklist of any special rules that may apply to these types of offers. Before you proceed any further, look at the facts and assess whether or not the offer has been terminated. Next, ask whether there has been an acceptance to the offer you have analyzed. If so, you need to address the issue of whether the acceptance was proper. Examine whether the offer specified a means of acceptance, the time for acceptance, method of communication, and the mailbox rule. The Study Tips section that follows gives easy to remember lists of what is required for the aspects of this chapter.

Study Tips

Agreement

Definition: The manifestation by two or more persons of the substance of a contract. It requires an *offer* and an *acceptance*.

Offer

Definition. As per Section 24 of Restatement (Second) of Contracts: "The manifestation of willingness to enter into a bargain, so made as to justify another person in understanding that his assent to that bargain is invited and will conclude it."

Objective Intent: The offeror must objectively intend to be held to the offer. Remember objective intent is gauged against a reasonable person in the same or similar circumstances.
- Were mere preliminary negotiations going on between the parties? If the offeror is asking a question as opposed to making a statement of intent to bargain, it is probably an invitation to make an offer and not indicative of the offeror's present intent to contract.
- Was the offer made in anger, jest, or undue excitement?. If any of these exist, the objective intent is missing and the offer cannot result in a valid contract.
- Offers made as an expression of opinion are not enforceable promises.

Express Terms: The offer's terms must be definite or reasonably certain.
- Were the terms clear so that the offeree was able to accept or reject the terms of the offer?
- Did the offer contain an identification of the parties, identification of the subject matter, the consideration to be paid, and the time for performance? If the answer is yes, then the offer will probably be considered definite and certain.

Implied Terms: Were there any implied terms?
- Common Law: If any of the terms were missing, the offer would fail.
- Modern Law: There is more leniency, as the court will supply a missing term if a reasonable term can be implied, such as for price and time or performance.

Communication: The offer has to be communicated to the offeree. Without communication, there can be no acceptance.

Special Offers

Advertisements: These are treated as invitations to make an offer.
- The exception to it being an invitation is if the offer is definite or specific that it is obvious that the advertiser had the present intend to be bound by the advertisement, then it will be considered to be an offer.

Rewards: An offer to pay a reward is an offer to form a unilateral contract.
- The two requirements to accept a reward are that the offeree had knowledge of the reward before completing the requested act and he or she performed the requested act.

Auctions: Usually a seller uses an auctioneer to offer to sell his or her goods.
- Auctions are with reserve as they are usually considered an invitation to make an offer. The seller can withdraw his or her goods from the sale and refuse the highest bid.
- Note, that if the auction is without reserve, the seller must accept the highest bid and cannot take his or her goods back.

Termination of an Offer by the Parties

An offer may be terminated by the parties by revoking the offer, rejecting the offer, or by a counteroffer made by the offeree. These three means of terminating an offer are discussed below.

Revocation of An Offer by the Offeror: At common law, the offeror could revoke his or her offer any time before the offeree accepted.
- The revocation may be express or implied by the offeror or a third party.
- The majority of states rule that the revocation is not effective until it is received.
- Revocation of an offer made to the public may be revoked by communicating in the same way that the offer was made for the same length of time.
- Option Contract: Prevention of revocation by the offeror is accomplished through an option contract.
  - The offeree usually pays the offeror money to keep the offer open for an agreed-upon period of time.
  - During this period of time the offeror agrees not to sell the subject matter of the offer to anyone else.
  - Death or incompetency does not terminate the option contract, unless it was a personal service contract.

Rejection of an Offer by the Offeree: The rejection may be express or implied by the offeree's conduct.
- The rejection is not effective until it is received.
- An acceptance by the offeree after the offeree has rejected the offer is construed as a counteroffer.

Counteroffer by the Offeree: It terminates the original offer.
- It creates a new offer that the original offeror is now free to accept or reject.

Termination of the Offer by Operation of Law

An offer may be terminated by operation of law in several situations. It can be terminated by destruction of the subject matter or by death or incompetency of the offeror or offeree, by a supervening illegality, or by lapse of time.

Destruction of the Subject Matter: The offer is terminated if the subject matter of the offer is destroyed through no fault of either party before the offer is accepted.
- An example of this would be if a boat that was listed for sale sank and was unable to be recovered, the offer would automatically terminate

Death or Incompetency of the Offeror or Offeree: Death of either the offeror or offeree terminates the offer.

- Incompetency of the offeror or offeree terminates the offer.
- Notice of the death or incompetency is not a requirement.
- Death or incompetency will not terminate an option contract unless it was a personal service contract.

Supervening Illegality: If the object of the offer is made illegal before the offer is accepted, the offer terminates.

- For example, if a bog frog becomes an endangered species after an offer is made for its sale to pet stores, but before the pet stores accept, the offer is terminated.
- Many times statutes are enacted that make the object of the offer illegal.

Lapse of Time: The offer sometimes limits the time in which it can be accepted.

- The time begins to run from the time it is actually received by the offeree and extends until the stated time period ends.
- If no time is stated in the offer, then the offer terminates within a "reasonable time" and on a case-by-case basis.
- If an offer is made over the telephone or face to face, then the offer usually terminates after the conversation.

Acceptance

Defined: Simply stated, an acceptance is an outward manifestation of assent to be bound by the terms of the offer as assessed by the reasonable person standard.

Who Can Accept an Offer?
- Only the offeree can accept the offer to create a contract.
- If an offer is made to more than one person, each person has the power to accept the offer.
- If an acceptance is made by one party, it terminates the offer as to the other individuals to whom the offer was made.
- If a joint offer has been made, the offer must be accepted jointly.

Unequivocal Acceptance: Known as the "mirror image rule", it states that the offeree must accept the offeror's terms.
- Grumbling acceptances do form contracts.
- Acceptances, however, that add conditions to them are not unequivocal and thus fail.

Silence as Acceptance: The general rule is that silence is not held to be an acceptance despite the offeror stating it is. There are several exceptions to the general rule.
- Where the offeree by his words intended his silence to mean acceptance.
- A signed agreement by the offeree allowing continued delivery until notice was given.
    - o For example, if Sid continued to buy crafts from a monthly craft club then his silence would indicate acceptance until he notifies the craft club that he wants to discontinue his membership.
- Prior course of dealings by the parties where silence is construed as an acceptance.
- The offeree accepts the benefit of goods or services given by the offeror even though the offeree had the opportunity to reject the services or goods.

Time of Acceptance: The Mailbox Rule. Also known as the acceptance-upon-dispatch rule.

- Acceptance is effective when it is placed in the mailbox, or dispatched, even if it gets lost along the way.
- The rule does not apply if a rejection is sent first and then an acceptance is mailed.
- The acceptance has to be properly dispatched.
    - o It has to be properly addressed, packaged, and have proper postage applied.
    - o Under common law, if the acceptance wasn't properly dispatched, it wasn't effective unless received by the offeror.

Mode of Acceptance: The usual rule is that the offeree must accept by an authorized mode of communication.

- Express authorization. The offer can state how it is to be accepted.
    - o Note: If the offeree uses a different means to communicate his or her acceptance instead of the means stipulated to be the parties, then the acceptance is ineffective.
- Implied authorization. May apply where it is customary in similar transactions between the parties, or prior dealings or usage of trade. Implied authorization will be allowed "by any medium reasonable in the circumstances." Section 30 of the Restatement Second.

Refresh Your Memory

The following exercise will give you the opportunity to test your memory of the principles given in this chapter. Read the question twice and place your answer in the blank provided. Review the chapter material for any question that you are unable to answer or remember.

1. A(n) _____ is a voluntary exchange of promises between two or more legally competent persons to do, or refrain from doing, an act.

2. Section 24 of the Restatement (Second) of Contracts defines a(n) _____ as the manifestation of willingness to enter into a bargain, so made as to justify another person in understanding that his assent to that bargain is invited and will conclude it.

3. The _____ theory of contracts states that the intent to contract is judged by the reasonable person standard and not by the subjective intent of the parties.

4. A term in a contract that can reasonably be supplied by the courts is referred to as a(n) _____.

5. An invitation to make an offer or an actual offer is referred to as a(n) _____.

6. A(n) _____ is a withdrawal of an offer by the offeror that terminates the offer.

7. A response by an offeree that contains terms and conditions different from or in addition to those of the offer is called a(n) _____.

8. An agreement that an offeror will not sell his property for a specified period subsequent to the offeree paying consideration to the offeror is referred to as a(n) _____.

9. If a fire destroys an office building that has been listed for sale, the offer is automatically terminated due to _____.

10. An offer is terminated on the grounds of "supervening illegality" when _____.

11. An offer is terminated on the grounds of "lapse of time" if _____.

12. _____ is a manifestation of assent by the offeree to the terms of the offer in a manner invited or required by the offer as measured by the objective theory of contracts.

13. The legal power to accept an offer belongs to the _____.

14. The mirror image rule states that _____.

15. The _____ states that an acceptance is effective when it is dispatched, even if it is lost in transmission.

Critical Thought Exercise.

Gus Vincent sent invitations to a number of potential buyers to submit bids for the mineral rights to his 2,000-acre parcel in upstate New York on the outskirts of the City of Hudson. Seven bids were received, including the highest bid from International Mining and Cement Company, LTD. (IMC). Vincent then decided to hold onto the land for a few more years and never responded to any of the bidders. IMC claimed that a contract had been formed by submission of its winning bid and sued Vincent for breach of contract. Did a contract exist?

Please compose your answer to the Critical Thinking Exercise using a separate sheet of paper or your computer word processing program.

Practice Quiz

True/False

1. _____ A contract requires an offer and an acceptance.

2. _____ An offer is not effective until it is actually received by the offeree.

3. _____ An agreement is created when the offeree receives the offer.

4. _____ The offer must be communicated to the offeree for the offer to be effective.

5. _____ Identification of the parties of a contract would be an express term.

6. _____ Advertisements are considered to be invitations to make an offer.

7. _____ In an auction with reserve, the bidder can withdraw his bid after an acceptance has been indicated from the offeror.

8. _____ In auction without reserve, the seller is the offeree.

9. _____ An offeror can revoke his or her offer even after an agreement or acceptance has been reached.

10. _____ During a counteroffer, the previous offeror remains the offeror.

11. _____ An option contract is terminated upon the death of the offeror.

12. _____ An offer is terminated if the subject matter of the offer is destroyed.

13. _____ If no time is stated in an offer, then the offer stays valid indefinitely.

14. _____ Bilateral contracts is accepted only upon the offeree's performance of the required act.

15. _____ Under the mailbox rule, an acceptance is only effective when it is received.

Multiple Choice

16. Which of the following statements is true of an offer that was not communicated?

A. The offer stays valid for 30 days from the date of creation.
B. The offer cannot be accepted by the offeree if not communicated.
C. The offeree can claim an offer that was not communicated.
D. It is considered to be an implied term.

17. Which of the following would be considered an offer to form a unilateral contract?

A. advertisement
B. auction without reserve
C. reward offer
D. auction with reserve

18. Which of the following is true for legally claiming a reward?

A. A promise of completing the requested act is sufficient for a claimant to claim the reward.
B. Knowledge of the reward before completing the requested act is necessary to claim the reward.
C. The claimant can claim the reward even if he or she came to know of the reward subsequent to completing the act.
D. The offeror cannot withdraw the reward once the offer has been placed in the public domain.

19. In which of the following types of offers does the seller offer the goods for sale?

A. revocation
B. reward
C. auction with reserve
D. auction without reserve

20. Which of the following is true for an auction with reserve?

A. The seller retains the right to refuse the highest bidder.
B. Invitations to make an offer are not allowed.
C. Goods cannot be withdrawn from sale after the offer has been made.
D. A bid once made cannot be withdrawn and is legally binding.

21. Which of the following is true for an auction without reserve?

A. The bidder is considered the offeror.
B. The seller need not accept the highest bid.
C. The goods on sale cannot be withdrawn.
D. The auctioneer is not allowed to set a minimum bid.

22. Which of the following is true about an option contract?

A. If the offeree chooses not to buy the property then money paid in consideration must be returned.
B. If money is paid as consideration, then that is not applied to the sale price.
C. Death or incompetency of either party terminates an option contract.
D. The offer cannot be revoke during the option period.

23. Which of the following contradicts the mirror image rule?

A. silence as acceptance
B. option contract
C. counteroffer
D. acceptance-upon-dispatch

24. _____ is a stipulation in an offer that says the acceptance must be by a specified means of communication.

A. Option contract
B. Mirror image rule
C. Implied authorization
D. Express authorization

25. The term _____ refers to a mode of acceptance that is indicated from what is customary in similar transactions, usage of trade, or prior dealings between the parties.

A. express authorization
B. implied authorization
C. option contract
D. unequivocal acceptance

Short Answer

26. How may offers made to the public be revoked?

_____

27. If Homer asked Ernie, "Would you be interested in selling your car to me?" Would this be a valid offer? Why or why not?

_____

28. In what ways may an offer be rejected?

_____

29. What happens if the subject matter of an offer is destroyed by a fire?

_____

30. What happens if the terms of an offer are not definite and certain?

_____

31. If Teddy puts an offer in an envelope to sell his 1950-style juke box to Marla for $10,000, but fails to send it, what is the result?

_____

32. If Marcia places an ad in the Sunset News Press offering a reward for her lost cat Barney and she lets the ad run for five weeks, what must she do to revoke the ad?

_____

33. If Sue says to Julius, "I think $3,500 is too high for your old truck. I will pay you $2,500 instead." What is the effect of Sue's statement?

_____

34. What is the result if a flood from a broken pipe destroys the bolts of silk fabric Martha was intending to buy?

_____

_____

35. Omar decides to sell Jane his motor home for $60,000, provided she decides by May 1. Omar is adjudged insane before Jane makes her decision. What is the effect of Omar's insanity?

_____

36. What does the mirror image rule require?

_____

37. What is an option contract?

_____

38. If Mario offers to sell Jennifer two pallets of freshly picked bananas for $150.00 on Monday, but Jennifer waits for almost a month to accept his offer, what defense does Mario have if he has already sold the two pallets of bananas to someone else?

_____

39. Why is silence usually not considered an acceptance even if the offeror states that it is?

_____

40. Under the common law, what was the effect of an acceptance that was not properly dispatched?

_____

Answers to Refresh Your Memory

1. agreement [p. 182]
2. offer [p. 184]
3. objective [p. 184]

4. implied term [p. 185]
5. advertisement [p. 186]
6. revocation [p. 187]
7. counteroffer [p. 188]
8. option contract [p. 189]
9. destruction of the subject matter [p. 189]
10. a statute or court decision deems an object of the offer unlawful [p. 189]
11. the offer is not accepted within a stated time period [p. 189-190]
12. Acceptance [p. 182]
13. offeree [p. 184]
14. the offeree must accept the terms as stated in the offer [p. 191]
15. mailbox rule [p. 192]

Critical Thought Exercise Model Answer

To have an offer that is capable of acceptance, three elements must be present: (1) There must be a serious, objective intention by the offeror; (2) The terms of the offer must be reasonably certain, or definite, so that the parties and the court can ascertain the terms of the contract; and, (3) The offer must be communicated to the offeree. There appears to be sufficient information in the bid to find definite terms. Sending the request for a bid to IMC fulfilled the communication requirement. The issue centers on whether the request for a bid was accompanied by a serious intent to be bound by the offeror. Intent is not determined by the subjective intentions, beliefs, or assumptions of the offeror. What meaning Vincent attached to his invitation to bid is not relevant. Intent is determined by what a reasonable person in the offeree's position would conclude the offeror's words and actions meant. A request or invitation to negotiate is not an offer. It only expresses a willingness to discuss the matter and possibly enter into a contract after further negotiations. A reasonable person in the position of IMC would not conclude that the invitation evidenced an intention to enter into a binding agreement. As in construction contracts, an invitation to submit a bid is not an offer, and the bidding party does not bind the party who requests bids merely by submitting a bid. The party requesting the bids is free to reject all the bids or not act at all. Vincent was not bound by the bid of IMC merely because it was the highest submitted. Vincent never manifested an intent to be bound by the invitation to bid and he remained free to reject the bid of IMC or simply change his mind and take no action at all..

Answers to Practice Quiz

True/False

16. True. A contract requires an offer and an acceptance. [p. 182]

17. True. An offer is not effective until it is actually received by the offeree.[p. 184]

18. False. The offeree has the power to create an agreement by accepting the offer.[p. 184]

19. True. The offer must be communicated to the offeree for an offer to be effective. [p. 184]

20. True. To be considered definite, an offer (and contract) generally must contain the following terms: (1) identification of the parties, (2) identification of the subject matter and quantity, (3) consideration to be paid, and (4) time of performance. Complex contracts usually state additional terms. [p. 184]

21 True. As a general rule, advertisements for the sale of goods, even at specific prices, generally are treated as invitations to make an offer.[p. 186]

22. False. In an auction with reserve a contract is formed only when the auctioneer strikes the gavel down or indicates acceptance by some other means. The bidder may withdraw his or her bid prior to that time.[p. 187]

23. False. In an auction without reserve, the seller is the offeror, and the bidders are the offerees. [p. 187]

24. False. Under the common law, an offeror may revoke (i.e., withdraw) an offer any time prior to its acceptance by the offeree. [p. 187]

25. False. A counteroffer by the offeree simultaneously terminates the offeror's offer and creates a new offer. Offerees' making of counteroffers is the norm in many transactions. A counteroffer terminates the existing offer and puts a new offer into play. The previous offeree becomes the new offeror, and the previous offeror becomes the new offeree. [p. 188]

26. False. The death or incompetency of either party does not terminate an option contract unless the contract is for the performance of a personal service.[p. 189]

27. True. An offer terminates if the subject matter of the offer is destroyed through no fault of either party prior to the offer's acceptance.[p. 189]

28. False. If no time is stated in an offer, the offer terminates after a "reasonable time" dictated by the circumstances.[p. 190]

29. False. Acceptance of a bilateral contract occurs when the offeree dispatches the acceptance by an authorized means of communication.[p. 192]

30. False. Under the mailbox rule rule, the acceptance is effective when it is dispatched, even if it is lost in transmission. [p. 192]

Multiple Choice

31. B. Answer B is correct, an offer cannot be accepted if it is not communicated to the offeree by the offeror or a representative or an agent of the offeror. [p. 185]

32. C. Answer C is correct, an offer to pay a reward (e.g., for the return of lost property or the capture of a criminal) is an offer to form a unilateral contract. [p. 186]

33. B. Answer B is correct, to be entitled to collect the reward, the offeree must (1) have knowledge of the reward offer prior to completing the requested act and (2) perform the requested act.[p. 187]

34. D. Answer D is correct, in an auction without reserve, the seller is the offeror, and the bidders are the offerees. [p. 187]

35. A. Answer A is correct. In an auction with reserve the seller retains the right to refuse the highest bid and withdraw the goods from sale. [p. 187]

36. C. Answer C is correct. In an auction without reserve, the seller must accept the highest bid and cannot withdraw the goods from sale. [p. 187]

37. D. Answer D is correct. An offeree can prevent the offeror from revoking his or her offer by paying the offeror compensation to keep the offer open for an agreed-upon period of time. This creates what is called an option contract. [p. 189]

38. C. Answer C is correct. To meet the mirror image rule, the offeree must accept the terms of the offer without modification. Any attempt to accept the offer on different terms constitutes a counteroffer, which rejects the offeror's offer.[p. 191]

39. D. Answer D is correct. An offer can stipulate that acceptance must be by a specified means of communication (e.g., registered mail, telegram). Such stipulation is called express authorization.[p. 192]

40. B. Answer B is the correct. Implied authorization is a mode of acceptance that is implied from what is customary in similar transactions, usage of trade, or prior dealings between the parties. [p. 192]

Short Answer

41. Offers made to the public may be revoked by communicating the revocation by the same means used to make the offer [p. 188]

42. No, it is not a valid offer; it is a preliminary negotiation in that Homer is asking if Ernie is interested in selling his car. [p. 183-184]

43. An offer may be rejected by the offeree's express words (oral or written) or conduct [p. 188]

44. The offer automatically terminates. [p. 189]

45. The courts cannot enforce the contract or determine an appropriate remedy for its breach if the terms of the offer are not definite and certain. [p. 184]

46. The offer cannot be accepted if it is not communicated to the offeree. [p. 184]

47. Marcia must communicate the revocation in the Sunset News Press for five weeks, as the general rule is that revocation of offers made to the public must be by the same means and for the same length of time as the original offer. [p. 188]

48. Sue has made a counteroffer that in effect terminated the original offer from Julius and created a new offer. [p. 188]

49. The offer is automatically terminated by operation of law as the subject matter, here the bolts of silk fabric, was destroyed through no fault of either party (flooding from a broken pipe) prior to the offer being accepted. [p. 189]

50. The offer automatically terminates since there is no contract prior to Omar being adjudged insane. [p. 189]

51. The mirror image rule requires the offeree to accept the offeror's terms. Acceptance must be unequivocal. [p. 191]

52. An option contract is one in which an offeror is prevented from revoking his or her offer by receiving compensation from the offeree to keep the offer open for an agreed-upon period of time. [p. 189]

53. An offer terminates when a stated time period ends. If no time is stated, an offer terminates after a reasonable time. A reasonable time for perishable items, such as bananas may be a very short time. [p. 190]

54. This rule is intended to protect offerees from being legally held to offers because they did not respond. [p. 191]

55. Under common law, if an acceptance was not properly dispatched, it was not effective until it was actually received by the offeror. [p. 192]

11 | CONSIDERATION AND PROMISSORY ESTOPPEL

Chapter Overview

This chapter explores the element of consideration, or in lay person's terms, "something of legal value given in exchange for a promise." Upon reviewing this chapter, you will understand what is meant by consideration, as well as its significance in the formation of a contract. The material provided in this chapter will enable you to analyze promises that are not supported by consideration, as well as enforceable promises that are lacking consideration.

Objectives

Upon completion of the exercises contained in this chapter, you should be able to:
1. Define consideration and describe the requirements of consideration.
2. Define gift promise and identify whether gift promises are enforceable.
3. Describe contracts that lack consideration, such as those involving illegal consideration, an illusory promise, a preexisting duty, or past consideration.
4. Define accord and satisfaction of a disputed claim.
5. Define and apply the equitable doctrine of promissory estoppel.

Practical Application

You should be able to recognize whether there is sufficient consideration in a contractual situation to become part of the basis of the bargain between the parties. You should be able to recognize what type of consideration is being given. You should be able to determine whether a contract will or will not be enforceable if consideration is lacking.

Helpful Hints

It will be beneficial to you to break down the definition of consideration into several parts and give an example for each. It would be helpful to analyze the cases given at the end of the chapter in your text and attempt to apply the contract principles you have learned up to this point.

As you begin to analyze the cases at the end of the chapter, it is important to make a notation of the issues you spot in the case itself. You will do a more thorough job if you analyze the cases line by line, which will enable you to address the legal concerns that may be present in each fact situation. Each contract question should be read twice before being answered. You will find that making an outline of your answer before writing it is very useful, as it provides a means to organize and prepare a rough draft before your final response to each question is written.

Study Tips

Consideration

- Defined: "Something of legal value."

Examples: money, property, forbearance of a right, the provision of services, or anything else of legal value

- Presumption: A written contract is presumed to be supported by consideration.

Requirements of Consideration: There are two requirements for consideration.
- Something of legal value must be given, and
  - Legal Value is established if the promisee suffers a legal detriment or the promisor receives a legal benefit.
- There must be a bargained-for exchange.
  - Bargained-for Exchange refers to the exchange that parties engage in that lead to an enforceable contract.

Gift Promise

Gift promises and gratuitous promises by themselves are not enforceable
- If the promisee offers to do something in exchange for either of these two types of promises, then consideration is established.
- A completed gift promise cannot be rescinded for lack of consideration.

Contracts Lacking Consideration

Illegal Consideration: A contract based on illegal consideration is void. A promise to refrain from doing an illegal act will not be enforceable as illegal consideration is part of the bargained-for exchange.
- Example: "If you pay me $5,000, I will not damage your brand new car!"

Illusory Promises: If the parties enter into a contract, but one or both of them choose not to perform, then consideration will be lacking.
- Example: Fred says to Jim, "I will paint your garage if I feel like it."

Preexisting Duty: If a person promises to perform an act or do something he or she is already under an obligation to do, then the promise is unenforceable because no new consideration has been given. In other words, the individual had a preexisting duty.
- Exception: If a party encounters substantial unforeseen difficulties while performing his or her contractual duties and the parties modify their contract to accommodate these difficulties, no new consideration is necessary.

Past Consideration: When a party to a contract promises to compensate another for work that has been performed in the past, then the situation involving past consideration exists. A contract must be supported by new consideration in order to be binding.

Special Business Contracts

Output Contracts: The seller agrees to sell all of its production to one buyer.

Requirements Contracts: The buyer contracts to purchase all of the requirements for an item from a single seller.
- Example, Kurt has an Internet store that he wishes to sell leather purses in. After doing his research, he contacts Abbot, an international wholesaler who gives him the best price of anyone in the market. Kurt and Abbot agree that Kurt will purchase all of his leather purse requirements from Abbot.

Best Efforts Clause: This clause usually states that one or both of the parties will use their best efforts to achieve the objective of the contract. It's important to remember that the courts have held that imposition of the duty to use best efforts is sufficient consideration to make a contract enforceable.

Settlement of Claims

Accord: An accord is an agreement where both parties agree to accept something different in satisfaction of the original contract.

Satisfaction: Simply stated, this is the performance of the accord.

Equity: Promissory Estoppel

The purpose of promissory estoppel is to give a remedy to a person who has justifiably relied upon another's promise, but that person takes back his or her promise. Because there is no agreement or consideration, the recipient of the promise cannot sue based on breach of contract. This doctrine estops the promisor from revoking his or her promise and thereby prevents unjust enrichment by the promisor.
- *Elements of Promissory Estoppel*
  - The promisor made a promise.
  - The promisor should have expected that the promise would induce the promisee to rely on the promise.
  - The promisee relied on the promise and took action based on the promise that caused a detriment to the promisee.
  - Injustice would occur if the promise were not enforced.

Refresh Your Memory

The following exercise will give you the opportunity to test your memory of the principles given in this chapter. Read the question twice and place your answer in the blank provided. Review the chapter material for any question that you are unable to answer or remember.

1. _____ is defined as something of legal value given in exchange for a promise.

2. _____ is an exchange that parties engage in that leads to an enforceable contract.

3. _____ is a promise that is unenforceable because it lacks consideration.

4. Gift promises are also known as _____.

5. If parties enter into a contract but one or both of the parties can choose not to perform their contractual obligations, the contract lacks consideration. Such promises are known as _____.

6. Illusory promise is a promise that lacks _____.

7. A promise lacks consideration if a person promises to perform an act or do something he is already under an obligation to do. This is called a _____.

8. Promise based on the past performance of the promise is called _____.

9. In a(n) _____, the seller agrees to sell all of its production to a single buyer.

10. A _____ is a contract in which a buyer agrees to purchase all of its requirements for an item from one seller.

11. _____ is an agreement whereby the parties agree to accept something different in satisfaction of the original contract.

12. The performance of an accord is called _____.

13. _____ is accord and satisfaction performed together.

14. Promissory estoppel is also known as _____.

15. _____ is an equitable doctrine that prevents the withdrawal of a promise by a promisor if it will adversely affect a promisee who has adjusted his or her position in justifiable reliance on the promise.

Critical Thought Exercise

David Johnson was a well-known businessman in Connecticut and was considering a political career. Johnson desired to enter the race for his local congressional seat. Johnson had a 21-year-old daughter, Stacey, who had studied theater at an Ivy League School and was ready to seek her fame and fortune in movies. When no roles in movies were forthcoming, Stacey was offered a lucrative contract to perform in adult films. David Johnson was afraid that his daughter's pornographic film career would cause great embarrassment to his family and ruin his political career. Stacey would not listen to her father and was anxious to make the adult films. Mr. Johnson offered his daughter $750,000 if Stacey refrained from making any adult films or any other film that involved nudity for a period of ten years. The offer by Mr. Johnson was conveyed to Stacey in a letter. Stacey agreed to her father's offer and stated in a return letter that she would use his promise to motivate her to lead a more moral life. Stacey rejected the offers to make adult films and refrained from making any film wherein she appeared nude for a period of ten years. At the end of ten years, Stacey requested that her father pay the $750,000 as promised. Mr. Johnson refused to pay the money, stating that Stacey had given him nothing in return for his promise except a promise to be a good person. Mr. Johnson asserted that the agreement lacked legally sufficient consideration. Was a contract formed that was supported by consideration?

Please compose your answer to the Critical Thinking Exercise using a separate sheet of paper or your computer word processing program.

Practice Quiz

True/False

16. _____ To be enforceable, a contract must be supported by consideration.

17. _____ Promissory estoppel is an equity doctrine that permits parties to enforce of a contract that includes consideration.

18. _____ A promise is something of legal value given in exchange of a consideration.

19. _____ Forbearance of a legal right can be provided as consideration.

20. _____ Considerations can only be monetary or economic in nature.

21. _____ For a gift promise to be enforceable, the promisee must offer a consideration.

22. _____ Contracts based on illegal consideration are valid.

23. _____ Illusory promises are enforceable if one of the parties has performed their contractual obligation.

24. _____ A promise based on past consideration is not enforceable.

25. _____ A new promise can include a past consideration for it to be enforceable.

26. _____ In an output contract, the buyer agrees to make all of its purchase from one buyer.

27. _____ A requirements contract is unenforceable due to lack of consideration.

28. _____ Imposition of the best-efforts duty provides sufficient consideration to make a contract enforceable.

29. _____ An accord is enforceable even though no new consideration is given.

30. _____ Promissory estoppels can be invoked for cases that include consideration.

Multiple Choice

31. _____ is an equity doctrine that permits a court to order enforcement of a contract that lacks consideration.

A. Promissory estoppel
B. Gift promise
C. Illusory promise
D. Option contract

32. A contract is said to have legal value if _____.

A. the promisee suffers a legal detriment
B. the promisor suffers a legal detriment
C. both the promisor and the promisee receive a legal benefit
D. the promisee receives a legal benefit

33. To meet contractual legality, considerations must be _____.

A. beneficial to both parties involved
B. bargained-for exchange of promise for performance
C. mentioned in writing in the contract
D. detrimental to both parties involved

34. Which of the following can convert a gift promise into an enforceable promise?

A. if the promisee receives a legal benefit
B. if the promisor offers a consideration
C. if the promisee offers a consideration
D. if the promisor suffers a legal detriment

35. Which of the following is true of a gift promise?

A. A gift promise can be enforced in a court of law.
B. The promisee can take legal action if the promisor does not uphold the promise.
C. A gift promise contains considerations.
D. A completed gift promise cannot be cancelled for lack of consideration.

36. _____ is a promise to refrain from doing an unlawful act, and therefore is a promise that will not support a contract.

A. Illegal consideration
B. Illusory promise
C. Preexisting duty
D. Gift promise

37. An illusory contract lacks consideration because:

A. one or both parties can choose not to perform their contractual obligations.
B. the person promises to perform an act or do something he is already under an obligation to do.
C. the consideration promised is unlawful and therefore void.
D. the compensation paid is for work done in the past.

38. Mary buys a lottery ticket and promises to buy her friend Sharon a new pair of shoes if she checks the lottery results while Mary is away. Sharon agrees to do so, provided she has the time for it. What kind of contract do Mary and Sharon have?

A. preexisting duty
B. illusory promise
C. illegal consideration
D. past consideration

39. A promise lacks consideration if a person promises to perform an act or do something he is already under an obligation to do. This is called a(n) _____.

A. illegal consideration
B. illusory promise
C. gift promise
D. preexisting duty

40. Corey desperately needs to get to the airport and decides to take his neighbor Tanner's help. Tanner agrees to help and drives Corey to the airport. Upon arrival at the airport, Corey promises to pay Tanner $25 towards gas money. Which of the following contracts does Corey's promise fall under?

A. illegal consideration
B. past consideration
C. preexisting duty
D. illusory promise

41. Which of the following is true for a buyer with an output contract?

A. The buyer is obliged to buy all the goods sold from the seller.
B. The buyer can choose to buy when and what he wants from the seller.
C. The buyer cannot sue the seller in case the seller plans to share its output with another buyer.
D. The buyer cannot enforce the best-efforts clause in the output contract.

42. Poweroxi Inc. produces rocket propellant fuel that is used in space shuttles. NASA is an agency that requires rocket propellant fuel to send its rockets to space. NASA enters into a contract with Poweroxi Inc. to purchase all of the propellant fuel it will need this year from Poweroxi. What would this contract be an example of?

A. option contract
B. output contract
C. requirements contract
D. yield contract

43. _____ is an agreement whereby the parties agree to accept something different in satisfaction of the original contract.

A. Counteroffer
B. Mirror image acceptance
C. Promissory estoppel
D. Accord

44. Which of the following is true for an accord?

A. It is enforceable even though no new consideration is given.
B. The non-breaching party cannot enforce the original contract if the accord is not satisfied.
C. The accord terminates the original contract.
D. An accord is only reached when both parties of the contract fail to meet their contractual obligations.

45. Which of the following is true for applying promissory estoppels to a contract?

A. Both parties must suffer legal detriment.
B. They can be applied for gift promise contracts.
C. They can be applied for illusory promise contracts.
D. Injustice would be caused if the promise were not enforced.

Short Answer

46. What is contract consideration?

_____
_____

47. What are the requirements of a consideration?

_____
_____

48. Explain gift promises. Why are gift promises unenforceable by law?

_____
_____

49. Explain the promises that lack consideration.

_____

_____

50. Explain the preexisting duty principle in private sector contracts.

_____

_____

51. What is the difference between an output contract and a requirement contract?

_____

_____

52. What is a best-efforts contract?

_____

_____

53. What is accord and satisfaction in contractual terms?

_____

_____

54. Give an account of promissory estoppels.

_____

_____

55. What are the requirements for the doctrine of promissory estoppel to apply?

_____

_____

Answers to Refresh Your Memory

1. Consideration [p. 197]
2. bargained-for exchange [p. 197]
3. Gift promise [p. 198]
4. gratuitous promises [p. 198]
5. illusory promise [p. 200]
6. consideration [p. 200]
7. preexisting duty [p. 200]
8. past consideration [p. 201]
9. output contract [p. 201]
10. requirements contract [p. 202]
11. Accord [p. 202]
12. satisfaction [p. 202]
13. compromise [p. 202]
14. detrimental reliance [p. 202]
15. Promissory estoppel [p. 202]

Critical Thought Exercise Model Answer

The fact that a party has made a promise does not mean that the promise is enforceable. In contract law, a basis for the enforcement of promises is consideration. Consideration is the value given in return for a promise. It is usually broken into two parts: (1) something of legally sufficient value must be given in exchange for the promise, and (2) there must be a bargained-for exchange. Something of legally sufficient value may consist of (1) a promise to do something that one has no prior legal duty to do, (2) the performance of an action that one is otherwise not obligated to perform, or (3) the refraining from an action that one has a legal right to undertake. Stacey has the legal right to enter into a contract to perform in adult movies. She has suffered a detriment by forfeiting income that she was legally entitled to obtain. The second element of consideration is that it must provide the basis for the bargain that was struck between the parties to the agreement. The consideration given by the promisor must induce the promisee to incur a legal detriment and the detriment incurred must induce the promisor to make the promise. This keeps the promise from being a gift. Stacey was induced to refrain from making adult films by the promise of her father to pay her $750,000. She was anxious to make the films and did not sign the contract offered to her because of Mr. Johnson's promise. Keeping his daughter out of adult films is what induced Mr. Johnson to make his promise to pay her money. Therefore, the agreement between Mr. Johnson and Stacey was supported by legally sufficient consideration. Because Stacey fulfilled the requested act and suffered the detriment requested by Mr. Johnson, he is now legally obligated to pay her $750,000.00.

Answers to Practice Quiz

True/False

16. True. To be enforceable, a contract must be supported by consideration, which is broadly defined as something of legal value. It can consist of money, property, the provision of services, the forbearance of a right, or anything else of value. [p. 197]

17. False. Promissory estoppel is an equity doctrine that permits a court to order enforcement of a contract that lacks consideration. [p. 197]

18. False. Consideration is defined as something of legal value given in exchange for a promise. [p. 197]

19. True. Consideration can come in many forms. Forbearance of a legal right can be provided as consideration. Accepting an out-of-court settlement in exchange for dropping a lawsuit is an example of consideration. [p. 197]

20. False. Consideration can come in many forms. The most common types consist of either a tangible payment or the performance of an act. Less usual forms of consideration include the forbearance of a legal right and noneconomic forms of consideration. [p. 197]

21. True. Gift promises are unenforceable because they lack consideration. To change a gift promise into an enforceable promise, the promisee must offer to do something in exchange. [p. 198]

22. False. A contract cannot be supported by a promise to refrain from doing an illegal act because that is illegal consideration. Contracts based on illegal consideration are void. [p. 200]

23. False. If parties enter into a contract but one or both of the parties can choose not to perform their contractual obligations, the contract lacks consideration. Such promises, which are known as illusory promises [p. 200]

24. True. Past consideration is not consideration for a new promise; therefore, a promise based on past consideration is not enforceable. [p. 201]

25. False. Past consideration is not consideration for a new promise. Hence, it is not enforceable. [p. 201]

26. False. In an output contract, the seller agrees to sell all of its production to a single buyer. [p. 201]

27. False. A requirements contract is a contract in which a buyer agrees to purchase all of its requirements for an item from one seller. Such contracts are enforceable under law. [p. 202]

28. True. A best-efforts contract is a contract which contains a clause that requires one or both of the parties to use their best efforts to achieve the objective of the contract. The imposition of the best-efforts duty provides sufficient consideration to make a contract enforceable. [p. 202]

29. True. An accord is enforceable even though no new consideration is given because the parties reasonably disagreed as to the value of the goods or services contracted for. [p. 202]

30. False. Promissory estoppel (or detrimental reliance) is an equity doctrine that permits a court to order enforcement of a contract that lacks consideration. [p. 202]

Multiple Choice

31. A. Parties cannot subsequently assert lack of consideration to undo the performed contract, if the contract lacked consideration. Promissory estoppel is an equity doctrine that permits a court to order enforcement of a contract that lacks consideration. [p. 197]

32. A. A contract is considered to be supported by legal value if (1) the promisee suffers a legal detriment or (2) the promisor receives a legal benefit. [p. 197]

33. B. To be enforceable, a contract must arise from a bargained-for exchange. [p. 197]

34. C. To change a gift promise into an enforceable promise, the promisee must offer to do something in exchange—that is, in consideration—for the promise. [p. 198]

35. D. Gift promises are unenforceable because they lack consideration. A completed gift promise cannot be rescinded for lack of consideration. [p. 199]

36. A. A contract cannot be supported by a promise to refrain from doing an illegal act because that is illegal consideration. Contracts based on illegal consideration are void. [p. 200]

37. A. If parties enter into a contract but one or both of the parties can choose not to perform their contractual obligations, the contract lacks consideration. Such promises, which are known as illusory promises are unenforceable. [p. 200]

38. B. Illusory promise is a contract into which both parties enter but in which one or both of the parties can choose not to perform their contractual obligations. Thus, the contract lacks consideration. [p. 200]

39. D. Preexisting duty is something a person is already under an obligation to do. A promise lacks consideration if a person promises to perform a preexisting duty. [p. 200]

40. B. Past consideration is a prior act or performance. Past consideration is not consideration for a new promise; therefore, a promise based on past consideration is not enforceable. [p. 201]

41. A. In an output contract, the seller agrees to sell all of its production to a single buyer. [p. 201]

42. C. A requirements contract is a contract in which a buyer agrees to purchase all of its requirements for an item from one seller. [p. 202]

43. D. In some situations, one of the parties to a contract believes that he or she did not receive what he or she was due. This party may attempt to reach a compromise with the other party. If the two parties agree to a compromise, a settlement of the claim has been reached. The settlement agreement is called an accord. [p. 202]

44. A. An accord is enforceable even though no new consideration is given because the parties reasonably disagreed as to the value of the goods or services contracted for. [p. 202]

45. D. Promissory estoppel is an equity doctrine that permits a court to order enforcement of a contract that lacks consideration. Promissory estoppel is applied to avoid injustice. [p. 202]

Short Answer

46. Consideration must be given before a contract can exist. Consideration is defined as something of legal value given in exchange for a promise. Consideration can come in many forms. The most common types consist of either a tangible payment, e.g., money, property, or the performance of an act, e.g., providing legal services. Less usual forms of

consideration include the forbearance of a legal right, e.g., accepting an out-of-court settlement in exchange for dropping a lawsuit, and noneconomic forms of consideration, e.g., refraining from "drinking, using tobacco, swearing, or playing cards for a specified time period. Written contracts are presumed to be supported by consideration. [p. 197]

47. Consideration consists of two elements: (1) Something of legal value must be given and (2) there must be a bargained-for exchange.
1. Legal value. Under the modern law of contracts, a contract is considered to be supported by legal value if (1) the promisee suffers a legal detriment or (2) the promisor receives a legal benefit.
2. Bargained-for exchange. To be enforceable, a contract must arise from a bargained-for exchange. In most business contracts, the parties engage in such exchanges. The commercial setting in which business contracts are formed leads to this conclusion. [p. 197]

48. Gift promises, also called gratuitous promises, are unenforceable because they lack consideration. To change a gift promise into an enforceable promise, the promisee must offer to do something in exchange—that is, in consideration—for the promise. For example, on May 1, Mrs. Colby promises to give her son $10,000 on June 1. When June 1 arrives, Mrs. Colby refuses to pay the $10,000. The son cannot recover the $10,000 because it was a gift promise that lacked consideration. If, however, Mrs. Colby promises to pay her son $10,000 if he earns an "A" in his business law course and the son earns the "A," the contract is enforceable and the son can recover the $10,000. A completed gift promise cannot be rescinded for lack of consideration. [p. 198]

49. The following are the promises that lack consideration:

Illegal Consideration – A contract cannot be supported by a promise to refrain from doing an illegal act because that is illegal consideration. Contracts based on illegal consideration are void.

Illusory Promise – If parties enter into a contract but one or both of the parties can choose not to perform their contractual obligations, the contract lacks consideration. Such promises, which are known as illusory promises, are unenforceable.

Preexisting Duty – A promise lacks consideration if a person promises to perform an act or do something he is already under an obligation to do. This is called a preexisting duty. The promise is unenforceable because no new consideration has been given.

Past Consideration – Problems of past consideration often arise when a party promises to pay someone some money or other compensation for work done in the past. Past consideration is not consideration for a new promise; therefore, a promise based on past consideration is not enforceable. [p. 200]

50. In the private sector, the preexisting duty rule often arises when one of the Parties to an existing contract seeks to change the terms of the contract during the course of its performance. Such midstream changes are unenforceable: The parties have a preexisting duty to perform according to the original terms of the contract. Sometimes a party to a contract runs into substantial unforeseen difficulties while performing his or her contractual duties. If the parties modify their contract to accommodate these unforeseen

difficulties, the modification will be enforced even though it is not supported by new consideration. [p. 201]

51. Output Contract – In an output contract, the seller agrees to sell all of its production to a single buyer. Output contracts serve the legitimate business purposes of (1) assuring the seller of a purchaser for all its output and (2) assuring the buyer of a source of supply for the goods it needs.
Requirements Contract – A requirements contract is a contract in which a buyer agrees to purchase all of its requirements for an item from one seller. Such contracts serve the legitimate business purposes of (1) assuring the buyer of a uniform source of supply and (2) providing the seller with reduced selling costs. [p. 201]

52. A best-efforts contract is a contract which contains a clause that requires one or both of the parties to use their best efforts to achieve the objective of the contract. The courts generally have held that the imposition of the best-efforts duty provides sufficient consideration to make a contract enforceable. Real estate listing contracts often require a real estate broker to use his or her best efforts to find a buyer for the listed real estate. Contracts often require underwriters to use their best efforts to sell securities on behalf of their corporate clients. Both of these contracts would be enforceable. Of course, a party can sue another company for failing to use its promised best efforts. [p. 202]

53. In some situations, one of the parties to a contract believes that he or she did not receive what he or she was due. This party may attempt to reach a compromise with the other party, e.g., by paying less consideration than was provided for in the contract. If the two parties agree to a compromise, a settlement of the claim has been reached. The settlement agreement is called an accord. If the accord is performed, it is called a satisfaction. This type of settlement is called an accord and satisfaction, or a compromise. [p. 202]

54. Promissory estoppels are equity doctrines that permit a court to order enforcement of a contract that lacks consideration. Promissory estoppel is applied to avoid injustice. It is usually used to provide a remedy to a party who has relied on another party's promise, but that party has withdrawn its promise and is not subject to a breach of contract action because consideration is lacking. The doctrine of promissory estoppel prevents the promisor from revoking his or her promise based on lack of consideration. Therefore, the person who has detrimentally relied on the promise for performance may sue the promisor for performance or other remedy the court feels is fair to award in the circumstances. [p. 202]

55. For the doctrine of promissory estoppel to apply, the following elements must be shown:
1. The promisor made a promise.
2. The promisor should have reasonably expected to induce the promisee to reply on the promise.
3. The promisee actually relied on the promise and engaged in an action or forbearance of a right of a definite and substantial nature.
4. Injustice would be caused if the promise were not enforced. [p. 203]

12 | CAPACITY AND LEGALITY

Chapter Overview

This chapter's primary emphasis entails the capacity to enter into contracts and the lawfulness of certain contracts. You will learn about the obligations minors, intoxicated and insane individuals have under contracts into which they enter. Contracts that are contrary to statutes, or those that are unconscionable, are examined in this chapter.

Objectives

Upon completion of the exercises contained in this chapter, you should be able to:
1. Define and describe the infancy doctrine.
2. Define legal insanity and intoxication and explain how they affect contractual capacity.
3. Identify illegal contracts that are contrary to statutes and those that violate public policy.
4. Describe covenants not to compete and exculpatory clauses and identify when they are lawful.
5. Define unconscionable contract and determine when such contracts are unlawful.

Practical Application

You should be able to determine the extent to which an incapacitated individual will be responsible when entering into a contract. You should be able to determine whether the rules of law regarding the infancy doctrine, legal insanity, and intoxication will have an impact on any contracts into which you may enter. You should be able to determine whether covenants not to compete, as well as exculpatory clauses, are lawful based on the knowledge you should have obtained. Your knowledge should enable you to determine whether or not a contract may be unconscionable, void, or voidable.

Helpful Hints

This chapter lends itself toward simple organization based on who may be involved in a contractual situation and what type of clause with which the parties are concerned. The rules are very straightforward and simple to learn. It is beneficial to explore the critical legal thinking cases at the end of the chapter in your text and to answer the Critical Thought Exercise contained herein. The more exposure you have to situations involving capacity and legality, the easier and more recognizable these issues will become for you.

Study Tips

Capacity and Legality

- The law generally presumes that parties who enter into a contract have the capacity to do so, but issues involving capacity for which a contract can be affected usually involve minors, intoxicated or insane individuals.

- A contract with an illegal purpose is void and cannot be enforced against either party.
- An unconscionable contract, the terms of which are so oppressive or manifestly unfair that enforcement would be unjust, are unenforceable.

Minors

- *Defined.* At Common Law, females under 18 years of age and males under 21 years of age.
    - Most states have statutes specifying the age of majority.
    - Most prevalent age of majority is 18 years old for males and females.
    - Any age below the statutory age of majority is called the period of minority.

Infancy Doctrine: This doctrine gives minors the right to disaffirm most contracts they have entered into with adults. It serves as a minor's protection against unscrupulous adults who may want to take advantage of a minor. It is an objective standard.
- A minor may choose whether or not to enforce the contract.
    - If both parties are minors, both parties have the right to cancel the contract.
- A minor cannot disaffirm as to part of a contract and affirm as to another part of the contract.

Disaffirmance: The act of a minor to cancel a contract under the infancy doctrine.
- A minor may disaffirm a contract in writing, orally, or by conduct; no formalities are needed.
- It must be done prior to reaching the age of majority or a reasonable time thereafter.
    - Reasonableness is assessed on a case-by-case basis.

Minor's Duty of Restoration: If either party has not performed the contract, the minor only needs to disaffirm the contract.
- *Minor's Duty of Restoration.* Upon disaffirmance of the contract, the minor must return the goods to the adult, even if the goods are lost, destroyed, consumed, or depreciated in value.
- *Minor's Duty of Restitution.* In a majority of states, the minor will be required to put the adult in status quo upon disaffirming the contract if the minor was intentionally or grossly negligent in his or her conduct thereby causing the adult's property to lose value. Some states require the minor to make restitution of the reasonable value of the item when disaffirming any contract.

Ratification: Simply defined: To accept. A minor may ratify a contract before reaching the age of majority or a reasonable time thereafter. If disaffirmance does not occur in this time frame, it is considered accepted.
- Ratification may be expressed, impliedly, or by conduct.
- Ratification relates back to the inception of the contract.

Parents' Liability for Their Children's Contracts: If the parents have not sufficiently provided for their children's necessaries of life, then they are liable for their children's contracts.
- *Exception:* If a minor becomes emancipated by voluntarily leaving home and living apart from his or her parents and can support him or herself, then the parents have no duty to support their child. This is looked at on a case-by-case basis.

Necessaries of Life: Minors must pay for the necessaries of life for which they contract.
- *Examples:* food, clothing, tools of the trade, medical services, education.
- The minor is required to pay the reasonable value of the services or goods.
- Statutes exist that make minors liable for certain contracts.

- o Examples of some of these special types of contracts as per the statutes include child support, education, medical, surgical, and pregnancy cares to name a few.

Mentally Incompetent Persons

In order for a person to be relieved of his or her duties under a contract, the law mandates that the person have been legally insane at the time he or she entered into the contract.

- *Legal Insanity.* Legal insanity is determined by using the *objective cognitive understanding test* which involves determining whether the person was incapable of understanding or comprehending the nature of the transaction.
  - o The following do not qualify as insanity: delusions, light psychological or emotional problems, or weakness of intellect.

Adjudged Insane: If an individual is adjudged insane, the contract is void.

Insane, but not Adjudged Insane: The contract is voidable by the insane person. The other party does not have the option to avoid the contract unless that party doesn't have the contractual capacity either.

- The other party must put the insane party back to the status quo. The sane party must also be placed back to the status quo if he or she was unaware of the other party's insane condition.
- *Liability of insane people:* Under a quasi-contract, insane individuals are liable for the reasonable value for the necessaries of life that they receive.

Intoxicated Persons

Contracts entered into by intoxicated individuals are voidable by that person. Intoxication may be by alcohol or drugs.

- The contract is voidable only if the person was so intoxicated that he or she was incapable of understanding or comprehending the nature of the transaction.
  - o Note that some states will only allow the person to disaffirm the contract if he or she was forced to become intoxicated.
- The intoxicated party must be returned to the status quo.
  - o The intoxicated person must return the consideration under the contract, thereby making restitution to the other party and returning him or her to the status quo.
- Intoxicated persons are liable in quasi-contract to pay the reasonable value for the necessaries that they receive.

Legality

The object of a contract must be lawful or the contract is void and unenforceable.

Contracts Contrary to Statutes: Contracts to perform activities prohibited by statutes are illegal and void.

Usury laws: These laws set an upper limit on the annual rate that can be charged on certain loans. They are enacted to protect borrowers from loan sharks. Consequences for violating these laws include criminal and civil penalties.

Contracts to Commit Crimes: Contracts to commit criminal acts are void. However, if the object of the contract became illegal after the contract was entered into because of a governmental statute, both parties no longer have to perform under the contract.

Gambling Statutes: All states have some sort of regulation or prohibition concerning gambling,
- *Lotteries, wagering, and games of chance.* Consequences for violating these laws also include criminal and civil penalties.

Effect of Illegality: Illegal contracts are void. Neither party can sue for enforcement of the contract. If such a contract is executed, the court will leave the parties where it finds them.
- *Exception.* Innocent persons who were legitimately ignorant of the law or the fact that made the contract illegal.
- *Exception.* Persons who were induced to enter into the contract through fraud, duress, or undue influence.
- *Exception.* Persons who entered into the contract, but who withdrew before the illegal act was performed.
- *Exception.* Some states allow the less-at-fault party to recover restitution from the more-at-fault party.

Contracts Contrary to Public Policy: If the contract has a negative impact on society or impacts public safety or welfare, it is void.
- *Immoral contracts.* These contracts may be against public policy, such as a contract that requests sexual favors. Societal beliefs and practices are used as a guide in determining what immoral conduct is.

Special Business Contracts

Contract in Restraint of Trade: Contracts that unreasonably restrain trade are unlawful.
- Price-fixing agreements are contracts that restrain trade.

Licensing Statutes: All states require that certain occupations and professions be licensed in order to practice.
- The regulatory statutes concern those that protect the public.
  - *Example.* An unlicensed doctor may not collect payment for services that a regulatory statute requires a licensed person to provide.
- The revenue-raising statutes are made to raise money for the government. Their purpose is to gather revenue. Protecting the public is not a consideration with this type of statute.
  - *Example.* A licensed attorney who fails to pay the annual renewal fee can recover payment for services rendered.

Exculpatory Clause: An exculpatory clause relieves one or both parties from tort liability under a contract. This type of clause can relieve a party from ordinary negligence but not be used in cases of gross negligence, intentional torts, fraud, or willful conduct. Courts do not condone exculpatory clauses unless the parties have equal bargaining power.

Covenant Not to Compete: These types of ancillary contracts are lawful if reasonableness can be demonstrated based on the line of business protected, the duration of the restriction and the geographical area that is being protected. The court can refuse to enforce it or alter it to make it reasonable if there is a need.

Unconscionable Contracts

Some contracts are so unfair that they are unjust. The public policy based doctrine of unconscionability allows the courts to refuse to enforce the contract, refuse to enforce the unconscionable clause but enforce the rest of the contract, or limit the application of any unconscionable clause in order to avoid an unconscionable result.

- *Contracts of Adhesion.* Many consumer contracts are form contracts that do not allow for negotiation and which must be signed in order to obtain particular goods or services.
    - These contracts are generally lawful, even where there is disparity in the bargaining power of the parties.

Elements of Unconscionability:
- The parties possessed severely unequal bargaining power.
- The dominant party unreasonably used its unequal bargaining power to obtain unfair terms.
- The subservient party had no reasonable alternative.

Refresh Your Memory

The following exercise will give you the opportunity to test your memory of the principles given in this chapter. Read the question twice and place your answer in the blank provided. Review the chapter material for any question that you are unable to answer or remember.

1. A _____ is a person who has not reached the age of majority.

2. To protect minors, the law recognizes the _____, which gives minors the right to disaffirm (or cancel) most contracts they have entered into with adults.

3. _____ states that a minor is obligated only to return the goods or property he or she has received from the adult in the condition it is in at the time of disaffirmance.

4. _____ is the act of a minor after the minor has reached the age of majority by which he or she accepts a contract entered into when he or she was a minor.

5. The parental duty of support terminates if a minor becomes _____.

6. _____ is a state of contractual incapacity, as determined by law.

7. A person declared legally insane by a proper court or administrative agency is called _____.

8. State _____ set an upper limit on the annual interest rate that can be charged on certain types of loans.

9. _____ is a situation in which both parties are equally at fault in an illegal contract.

10. _____ licensing statute is a licensing statute enacted to protect the public.

11. Licensing statutes enacted to raise money for the government are called _____ statutes.

12. An _____ is a contractual provision that relieves one (or both) of the parties to a contract from tort liability.

13. Covenant not to compete is also known as _____.

14. _____ are preprinted forms whose terms the consumer cannot negotiate and that they must sign in order to obtain a product or service.

15. _____ is a contract that courts refuse to enforce in part or at all because it is so oppressive or manifestly unfair as to be unjust.

Critical Thought Exercise

You manage a small bicycle shop and sell a very good product, with some bikes costing $2,000. A young man comes into your store and wants to buy a mountain bike for $1,200. He has the cash. You are very happy to sell it to him. He tells you that he is an ambitious high school student who is taking classes at the local university and needs a bicycle that is capable of handling the large hills between the high school and college so that he can make it to class.

Two years later, the young man comes into the shop and tells you that yesterday was his eighteenth birthday, and after drinking a great deal of alcohol, he rode his bike down the Cuesta Grade and crashed into a Ford Expedition. He hands you a piece of bent frame and states that this is all that was left of the bicycle when he went back to the accident scene this morning. He asks for his $1,200 back as he now "desires to undo the contract."

Will you agree to the full refund? Why or why not?

Please compose your answer to the Critical Thinking Exercise using a separate sheet of paper or your computer word processing program.

Practice Quiz

True/False

16. ____ The infancy doctrine binds an adult to the minor's decision on a contract.

17. ____ The infancy doctrine gives adults the right to disaffirm contracts entered with minors.

18. ____ A minor can disaffirm a contract any time after reaching the age of majority.

19. ____ The duty of restitution states that a competent party should be placed in status quo by the minor upon disaffirmance of a contract.

20. ____ The parental duty of support is terminated if a minor becomes emancipated.

21. ____ Minors are not obligated to pay for the necessaries of life that they contract for.

22. ____ A person who was legally insane at the time of entering a contract is relieved of his or her duties from the contract.

23. ____ The court-appointed guardian is the only person who has the legal authority to enter into contracts on behalf of a person who has been adjudged insane.

24. ____ In a contract involving a competent person and a person who is insane but not adjudged insane, the competent party can void the contract.

25. ____ A contract with an intoxicated person is not voidable by the other party if that party had contractual capacity.

26. ____ The intoxicated person is not legally obligated to return consideration, received under the contract, to the competent party.

27. ____ If the object of a contract becomes illegal after the contract is entered into, the parties are discharged from the contract.

28. ____ Judges can define morality based on their individual views.

29. ____ An exculpatory clause must be reciprocal to be considered enforceable.

30. ____ An exculpatory clause that results from superior bargaining power is usually found to be void.

Multiple Choice

31. The _____ is a legal principle that allows minors to cancel most contracts they have entered into with adults.

A. duty of restoration
B. duty of restitution
C. infancy doctrine
D. contract of adhesion

32. Which of the following is true about a minor's right to disaffirm a contract?

A. A minor must reach the age of majority to disaffirm a contract.
B. Contracts that come under the necessaries of life can be disaffirmed by minors.
C. A minor can disaffirm a contract any time prior to reaching the age of majority.
D. Minors are exempt from duty of restoration during the period of minority.

33. _____ is a rule that states that a minor is obligated only to return the goods or property he or she has received from the adult in the condition it is in at the time of disaffirmance.

A. Emancipation doctrine
B. Duty of restitution
C. Infancy doctrine
D. Duty of restoration

34. _____ is a rule that states that if a minor has transferred money, property, or other valuables to the competent party before disaffirming the contract, that party must place the minor in status quo.

A. Emancipation doctrine
B. Duty of restitution
C. Infancy doctrine
D. Duty of restoration

35. _____ is the act of a minor after he or she has reached the age of majority, by which he or she accepts a contract entered into when he or she was a minor.

A. Exculpation
B. Ratification
C. Restitution
D. Emancipation

36. If a minor ratifies a contract while still being a minor, _____.

A. the minor has to hold the adult in status quo in case of disaffirmance
B. the minor is bound by the terms of the contract
C. the minor is exempt from the duty of restitution
D. the contract can still be disaffirmed by the minor

37. The act or process of a minor voluntarily leaving home and living apart from his or her parents is referred to as _____.

A. restitution
B. restoration
C. emancipation
D. adhesion

38. Which of the following is true of a contract where one of the parties is insane but not adjudged insane?

A. The contract is only voidable by the insane person.
B. The contract is voidable by the competent party.
C. Only the court appointed legal guardian to the insane person can modify contracts.
D. The non-insane person must be placed in status quo if the insane person voids the contract.

39. _____ set an upper limit on the interest rate that can be charged on certain types of loans.

A. State usury laws
B. Federal banking reforms
C. Congressional committees
D. Chambers of commerce

40. Which of the following is an example of a contract contrary to statutes by its very existence?

A. a contract of adhesion
B. a contract between two minors
C. a contract where one party is insane but not adjudged insane
D. a usurious loan contract

41. What is the doctrine of *in pari delicto* with reference to contracts?

A. It is a situation in which both parties are equally at fault in an illegal contract.
B. It is a situation where one party has unknowingly signed a contract to commit crimes.
C. It is a special exemption right to circumvent usury laws.
D. It gives minors the right to disaffirm a contract.

42. According to the regulatory licensing statute, _____.

A. only licensed persons can recover payment for services
B. unlicensed persons can recover payment for services
C. persons breaching a revenue-raising statute cannot recover payment for services
D. all government-licensed persons have to pay an annual fee to renew their licenses

43. _____ is a licensing statute with the primary purpose of increasing earnings for the government.

A. Usury statute
B. Ratification statute
C. Revenue raising statute
D. Regulatory licensing statute

44. A(n) _____ is a contractual provision that relieves one or both of the parties to a contract from tort liability.

A. contract of adhesion
B. exculpatory clause
C. duty of restitution
D. fundamental breach

45. A(n) _____ is a contract that courts refuse to enforce in part or at all because it is so oppressive or manifestly unfair as to be unjust.

A. quasi-contract
B. contract of adhesion
C. contract in restraint of trade
D. unconscionable contract

Short Answer

46. Explain the infancy doctrine.

_____

_____

47. What is the minor's duty of restoration in a disaffirmed contract?

_____

_____

48. Describe parents' liability for their children's contracts.

_____

_____

49. What are the two standards developed by law concerning contracts of mentally incompetent persons?

_____

_____

50. Explain the law for contracts entered into by intoxicated persons.

_____

_____

51. What is the usury law?

_____

_____

52. What are gambling statutes?

_____

_____

53. Explain regulatory licensing statute and revenue-raising statute.

_____

_____

54. What does the exculpatory clause imply?

_____

_____

55. Explain the noncompete clause.

_____

_____

Answers to Refresh Your Memory

1. minor [p. 207]
2. infancy doctrine [p. 207]
3. Duty of restoration [p. 208]
4. Ratification [p. 209]
5. emancipated [p. 209]
6. Legal insanity [p. 210]
7. adjudged insane [p. 210]
8. usury laws [p. 211]
9. *In pari delicto* [p. 213]
10. Regulatory [p. 215]
11. revenue-raising [p. 215]
12. exculpatory clause [p. 216]
13. noncompete clause [p. 217]
14. Contracts of adhesion [p. 218]
15. Unconscionable contract [p. 218]

Critical Thought Exercise Model Answer

In almost all states, the age of majority for contractual purposes is eighteen years old. With some exceptions, the contracts entered into by a minor are voidable at the option of the minor. For a minor to exercise their option to disaffirm a contract, he or she only needs to manifest an intent not to be bound by the contract. The contract can normally be disaffirmed at any time during minority or for a reasonable time after attaining the age of majority. When a minor disaffirms a contract, all property that he or she has given to the adult as consideration must be returned to the minor. Upon disaffirmance, most states require that the minor need only return the goods or money that were the subject of the contract, provided that the minor still has the goods or money. The minor may disaffirm the contract even if the goods are lost, stolen, damaged, or destroyed. A minor may not disaffirm a contract for necessaries, such as food, clothing, shelter, and medical services. However, the minor remains liable for the reasonable value of the goods used when the goods are deemed a necessary. Transportation is normally not considered a necessary. The young man who purchased the bike told me that he was only in high school. This should have put me, as the agent for the store, on notice that I was dealing with a minor. It is irrelevant that the minor drank alcohol before he crashed the bicycle. I will be obligated to return the total purchase price unless my store is in one of the few states that require the minor to put me in the same position as before the contract. In that state, the minor would only be entitled to a refund of the purchase price minus the cost of the damage to the bicycle. Since the bicycle was destroyed, no refund would be warranted.

Answers to Practice Quiz

True/False

16. True. Under the infancy doctrine, a minor has the option of choosing whether to enforce a contract. The adult party is bound to the minor's decision. [p. 207]

17. False. Infancy doctrine allows minors to disaffirm (cancel) most contracts they have entered into with adults. The adult party is bound to the minor's decision. [p. 207]

18. False. A minor can expressly disaffirm a contract orally, in writing, or through his or her conduct. The contract may be disaffirmed at any time prior to the person's reaching the age of majority plus a "reasonable time." [p. 207]

19. False. Duty of restitution states that if a minor has transferred money, property, or other valuables to the competent party before disaffirming the contract, that party must place the minor in status quo. [p. 208]

20. True . Emancipation occurs when a minor voluntarily leaves home and lives apart from his or her parents. The parental duty of support terminates if a minor becomes emancipated. [p. 209]

21. False. Minors are obligated to pay for the necessaries of life that they contract for. Otherwise, many adults would refuse to sell these items to them. [p. 209]

22. True. To be relieved of his or her duties under a contract, a person must have been legally insane at the time of entering into the contract. This state is called legal insanity. [p. 210]

23. True. Any contract entered into by a person who has been adjudged insane is void. That is, no contract exists. The court-appointed guardian is the only one who has the legal authority to enter into contracts on behalf of the person who has been adjudged insane. [p. 210]

24. False. Any contract entered into by an insane but not adjudged insane person is voidable by the insane person. Unless the other party does not have contractual capacity, he or she does not have the option to void the contract. [p. 210]

25. True. Most states provide that contracts entered into by certain intoxicated persons are voidable by those persons. The contract is not voidable by the other party if that party had contractual capacity. [p. 210]

26. False. The intoxicated person generally must return the consideration received under the contract to the other party and make restitution that returns the other party to status quo. [p. 211]

27. True. Some contracts have illegal objects. A contract with an illegal object is void and therefore unenforceable. These contracts are called illegal contracts. [p. 211]

28. False. Judges are not free to define morality based on their individual views. Instead, they must look to the practices and beliefs of society when defining immoral conduct. [p. 214]

29. False. An exculpatory clause (also called a release of liability clause) is a contractual provision that relieves one (or both) of the parties to a contract from tort liability. Such clauses do not have to be reciprocal. [p. 217]

30. True. One of the elements to prove that a contract or a clause in a contract is unconscionable is that the parties possessed severely unequal bargaining power. [p. 218]

Multiple Choice

31. C. To protect minors, the law recognizes the infancy doctrine, which gives minors the right to disaffirm (or cancel) most contracts they have entered into with adults. [p. 207]

32. C. A minor can expressly disaffirm a contract orally, in writing, or through his or her conduct. The contract may be disaffirmed at any time prior to the person's reaching the age of majority plus a "reasonable time." [p. 207]

33. D. Generally, a minor is obligated only to return the goods or property he or she has received from the adult in the condition it is in at the time of disaffirmance, even if the item has been consumed, lost, or destroyed or has depreciated in value by the time of disaffirmance. This rule is called the duty of restoration. [p. 208]

34. B. If a minor has transferred consideration to a competent party before disaffirming the contract, that party must return the consideration to the minor. If the consideration has been sold or has depreciated in value, the competent party must pay the minor the cash equivalent. This action is called the duty of restitution. [p. 208]

35. B. If a minor does not disaffirm a contract either during the period of minority or within a reasonable time after reaching the age of majority, the contract is considered ratified (accepted). [p. 208]

36. D. Any attempt by a minor to ratify a contract while still a minor can be disaffirmed just as the original contract can be disaffirmed. [p. 208]

37. C. The parental duty of support terminates if a minor becomes emancipated. Emancipation occurs when a minor voluntarily leaves home and lives apart from his or her parents. [p. 209]

38. A. Any contract entered into by an insane but not adjudged insane is voidable by the insane person. Unless the other party does not have contractual capacity, he or she does not have the option to void the contract. [p. 210]

39. A. State usury laws set an upper limit on the annual interest rate that can be charged on certain types of loans. The limits vary from state to state. Lenders who charge a higher rate than the state limit are guilty of usury. [p. 211]

40. D. State usury laws set an upper limit on the annual interest rate that can be charged on certain types of loans. It is a contract contrary to existing statutes. [p. 211]

41. A. *In pari delicto* a situation in which both parties are equally at fault in an illegal contract. [p. 213]

42. A. Generally, unlicensed persons cannot recover payment for services where he or she does not have the required license. [p. 215]

43. C. Licensing statutes enacted to raise money for the government are called revenue-raising statutes. A person who provides services pursuant to a contract without the appropriate license required by such a statute can enforce the contract and recover payment for services rendered. [p. 215]

44. B. An exculpatory clause (also called a release of liability clause) is a contractual provision that relieves one (or both) of the parties to a contract from tort liability. An exculpatory clause can relieve a party of liability for ordinary negligence. [p. 216]

45. D. When a contract is so oppressive or manifestly unfair as to be unjust, the law has developed the equity doctrine of unconscionability to prevent the enforcement of such contracts. A contract found to be unconscionable under this doctrine is called an unconscionable contract. [p. 218]

Short Answer

46. To protect minors, the law recognizes the infancy doctrine, which gives minors the right to disaffirm (or cancel) most contracts they have entered into with adults. This right is based on public policy, which reasons that minors should be protected from the unscrupulous behavior of adults. In most states, the infancy doctrine is an objective standard. If a person's age is below the age of majority, the court will not inquire into his or her knowledge, experience, or sophistication. Generally, contracts for the necessaries of life, are exempt from the scope of this doctrine. Under the infancy doctrine, a minor has the option of choosing whether to enforce a contract (i.e., the contract is voidable by a minor). The adult party is bound to the minor's decision. If both parties to a contract are minors, both parties have the right to disaffirm the contract. [p. 207]

47. Generally, a minor is obligated only to return the goods or property he or she has received from the adult in the condition it is in at the time of disaffirmance, even if the item has been consumed, lost, or destroyed or has depreciated in value by the time of

disaffirmance. This rule, called the duty of restoration, is based on the rationale that if a minor had to place the adult in status quo upon disaffirmance of a contract, there would be no incentive for an adult not to deal with a minor. [p. 208]

48. Generally, parents owe a legal duty to provide food, clothing, shelter, and other necessaries of life for their minor children. Parents are liable for their children's contracts for necessaries of life if they have not adequately provided such items. The parental duty of support terminates if a minor becomes emancipated. Emancipation occurs when a minor voluntarily leaves home and lives apart from his or her parents. The courts consider factors such as getting married, setting up a separate household, or joining the military in determining whether a minor is emancipated. Each situation is examined on its merits. [p. 209]

49. The law has developed two standards concerning contracts of mentally incompetent persons: (1) adjudged insane and (2) insane but not adjudged insane.
Adjudged Insane – In certain cases, a relative, a loved one, or another interested party may institute a legal action to have someone declared legally (i.e., adjudged) insane. If after hearing the evidence at a formal judicial or administrative hearing the person is adjudged insane, the court will make that person a ward of the court and appoint a guardian to act on that person's behalf. Any contract entered into by a person who has been adjudged insane is void.
Insane but Not Adjudged Insane – If no formal ruling has been made about a person's sanity but the person suffers from a mental impairment that makes him or her legally insane—that is, the person is insane but not adjudged insane—any contract entered into by this person is voidable by the insane person. Unless the other party does not have contractual capacity, he or she does not have the option to void the contract. [p. 210]

50. Most states provide that contracts entered into by certain intoxicated persons are voidable by those persons. The intoxication may occur because of alcohol or drugs. The contract is not voidable by the other party if that party had contractual capacity. Under the majority rule, the contract is voidable only if the person was so intoxicated when the contract was entered into that he or she was incapable of understanding or comprehending the nature of the transaction. In most states, this rule holds even if the intoxication was self-induced. Some states allow the person to disaffirm the contract only if the person was forced to become intoxicated or did so unknowingly. [p. 210]

51. State usury laws set an upper limit on the annual interest rate that can be charged on certain types of loans. The limits vary from state to state. Lenders who charge a higher rate than the state limit are guilty of usury. These laws are intended to protect unsophisticated borrowers from loan sharks and others who charge exorbitant rates of interest. Most states provide criminal and civil penalties for making usurious loans. Some states require lenders to remit the difference between the interest rate charged on the loan and the usury rate to the borrower. Other states prohibit lenders from collecting any interest on the loan. Still other states provide that a usurious loan is a void contract, permitting the borrower not to have to pay the interest or the principal of the loan to the lender. [p. 211]

52. All states either prohibit or regulate gambling, wagering, lotteries, and games of chance via gambling statutes. States provide various criminal and civil penalties for illegal gambling. There are many exceptions to wagering laws. Many states have enacted statutes that permit games of chance under a certain dollar amount, bingo games, lotteries conducted by religious and charitable organizations, and the like. Many states also permit and regulate horse racing, harness racing, dog racing, and state-operated lotteries. [p. 213]

53. Regulatory licensing statute – Statutes may require persons or businesses to obtain a license from the government to qualify to practice certain professions or engage in certain types of businesses. These statutes, which are enacted to protect the public, are called regulatory licensing statutes. Generally, unlicensed persons cannot recover payment for services where he or she does not have the required license.
Revenue-raising statute – Licensing statutes enacted to raise money for the government are called revenue-raising statutes. A person who provides services pursuant to a contract without the appropriate license required by such a statute can enforce the contract and recover payment for services rendered. [p. 215]

54. An exculpatory clause (also called a release of liability clause) is a contractual provision that relieves one (or both) of the parties to a contract from tort liability. An exculpatory clause can relieve a party of liability for ordinary negligence. It cannot be used in a situation involving willful conduct, intentional torts, fraud, recklessness, or gross negligence. Exculpatory clauses are often found in leases, sales contracts, sporting event ticket stubs, parking lot tickets, service contracts, and the like. Such clauses do not have to be reciprocal. [p. 216]

55. Entrepreneurs and others often buy and sell businesses. The sale of a business includes its "goodwill," or reputation. To protect this goodwill after the sale, the seller often enters into an agreement with the buyer not to engage in a similar business or occupation within a specified geographic area for a specified period of time following the sale. This agreement is called a covenant not to compete, or a noncompete clause. Covenants not to compete that are ancillary to a legitimate sale of a business or employment contract are lawful if they are reasonable in three aspects: (1) the line of business protected, (2) the geographic area protected, and (3) the duration of the restriction. [p. 217]

13 | GENUINENESS OF ASSENT AND UNDUE INFLUENCE

Chapter Overview

The requirements for creation of a contract as well as agreement, capacity, and consideration have been discussed in the preceding chapters. However, even though an individual may consent to a contract, if his or her assent is not genuine, the contract may be unenforceable. This chapter emphasizes the areas of mistake, misrepresentation, duress, and undue influence.

Objectives

Upon completion of the exercises in this chapter, you should be able to:
1. Explain genuineness of assent.
2. Explain how mutual mistake of fact excuses performance.
3. Explain the elements of intentional misrepresentation (fraud).
4. Describe duress.
5. Define equitable doctrine of undue influence.

Practical Application

You should be able to recognize whether a mistake, as it applies to a contractual situation, is a unilateral or a mutual mistake and state the particulars for each. You should be able to decide whether or not a fraudulent misrepresentation, or another type of fraud, exists and the remedies that are available for the same. You should be able to understand the impact of both physical and economic duress, as well as undue influence, upon a contractual situation. The information in this chapter will help you in developing a sense of what is genuine assent.

Helpful Hints

The five areas with which you should be familiar are divided into easily remembered sections in the Study Tips section. Differentiating between the types of fraud can be confusing, so it is important that you gain exposure to as many cases and examples as possible. The exercises given in this chapter will help to enhance the exercises given at the end of the chapter in the text.

Study Tips

Genuineness of Assent and Undue Influence

The areas of mistake, misrepresentation, duress, and undue influence impact whether or not a party's assent to a contract is genuine, or if other factors influenced his or her consent to enter into the contract in the first place.

- Assent must be present to have an enforceable contract.
- Assent may be accomplished by express words or conduct.

Mistake

Mistakes occur when one or both of the parties have an incorrect belief about the subject matter, value, or some other area of the contract.

Unilateral Mistake. This occurs when one party is mistaken about a material fact concerning the subject matter of the contract. Generally, the mistaken party usually will not be allowed to rescind the contract.

- *Exceptions.*
    - If one party is mistaken and the other party knew or should have known about the mistake, then the mistake is treated like a mutual mistake and rescission is allowed.
    - If a unilateral mistake is made because of a clerical or mathematical error and is not because of gross negligence.
    - The gravity of the mistake makes enforcing the contract unconscionable.

Mutual Mistake of material fact. A mistake made by both parties concerning a material fact that is important to the subject matter of the contract. Either party may rescind the contract if there has been a mutual mistake of a past or existing material fact, as there has been no meeting of the minds between the parties as the subject matter is in dispute.

- *What is considered to be a material fact?*
    - Anything that is significant to the subject matter of the contract.
    - An ambiguity may qualify as a mutual mistake of material fact.

Ambiguity is confusion as to the meaning of a word or term in the contract.

Mutual Mistake of Value. The contract remains enforceable because the subject matter is not in dispute and the parties are only mistaken as to the value.

Fraud

Fraudulent misrepresentation as an inducement to enter into a contract – The innocent party's assent is not genuine and the contract is voidable. The remedies that are available are rescission and restitution or enforce the contract and sue for damages.

Proving Fraud. A plaintiff must prove all of the elements of fraud to seek protection from enforcement of a contract. The mnemonic you utilized in Chapter 4 is applicable here. The mnemonic is MISJD.

M – Misrepresentation of a material fact that was false in nature
I – Intentionally made to the innocent party
S – Scienter (knowledge) of the statement's falsity by the wrongdoer
J – Justifiable reliance on the false statement by the innocent party
D – Damages were suffered by the injured party

- *Material misrepresentation of fact.* The misrepresentation can be verbal or written words, or conduct of a party, regarding a past or existing material fact.
    - Generally, opinions or predictions do not constitute fraud.
- *Intent to deceive.* The person making the misrepresentation must have had either knowledge of the falsity or insufficient knowledge of the veracity of the fact.
    - Intent can be inferred from the circumstances.

- *Reliance on the misrepresentation.* The innocent party must have justifiably relied on the misrepresentation. Such justification is usually found unless there was knowledge of the misrepresentation or the assertion was so extravagant so as to be obviously false.
- *Injury to the innocent party.* The innocent party must prove the misrepresentation caused economic injury.
    - Damages are the difference between the value of the property as represented and the actual value of the property.
    - Alternatively, the buyer can rescind the contract and recover the purchase price.

Fraud in the Inception. Also known as fraud in the factum, the person is deceived on what he or she is signing. The contract is void.

Fraud in the Inducement. The person knows what he or she is signing, but has fraudulently been induced to enter into the contract. The contract is voidable by the innocent party.

Fraud by Concealment. This fraud occurs where one party specifically conceals a material fact from the other party.

Silence as Misrepresentation. One need not divulge all facts to the other party; however, if the nondisclosure would cause death or bodily injury or there is a fiduciary relationship or federal or state statutes require that a fact be disclosed, then fraud may be implied.

Misrepresentation of Law. The general rule is that this is not actionable as fraud. However, if one party to the contract is a professional who should know the law and misrepresents the law intentionally to a less knowledgeable party, this will be enough to allow rescission of the contract.

Innocent Misrepresentation. This occurs when a party makes a statement of fact that he or she honestly believes is true even though it is not. The injured party may rescind the contract but may not seek damages. This type of misrepresentation is sometimes treated as a mutual mistake.

Duress

Duress occurs when one party threatens to do a wrongful act unless the other party enters into a contract. Duress can occur via threats of physical harm or extortion or to bring or not drop a criminal lawsuit.
- Physical duress. This occurs when someone threatens to physically harm another if they do not sign a contract.
- The threat to bring or not drop a civil lawsuit is not duress, unless it's a frivolous suit.

Equity: Undue Influence

Rescission based on undue influence is allowed if it can be shown that a fiduciary or confidential relationship existed between the parties and the dominant party unduly used his or her influence to persuade the servient party to enter into a contract. This contract is voidable.

Refresh Your Memory

The following exercise will give you the opportunity to test your memory of the principles given in this chapter. Read the question twice and place your answer in the blank provided. Review the chapter material for any question that you are unable to answer or remember.

1. A court may permit the rescission of a contract based on the equitable doctrine of _____.

2. A(n) _____ occurs where one or both of the parties to a contract have an erroneous belief about the subject matter, value, or some other aspect of the contract.

3. _____ is an action to undo a contract.

4. A(n) _____ occurs when only one party is mistaken about a material fact regarding the subject matter of the contract.

5. A(n) _____ fact is a fact that is important to the subject matter of a contract.

6. Knowledge that a representation is false or that it was made without sufficient knowledge of the truth is called _____.

7. Scienter is also known as _____.

8. To recover damages, the innocent party must prove that the fraud caused him or her _____ injury.

9. Fraud in the inception is also known as _____.

10. _____ is a fraud that occurs when the party knows what he or she is signing but has been fraudulently induced to enter into the contract.

11. The _____ will be allowed as grounds for rescission of the contract if one party to the contract is a professional who should know what the law is and intentionally misrepresents the law to a less sophisticated contracting party.

12. A(n) _____ occurs when a person makes a statement of fact that he or she honestly and reasonably believes to be true even though it is not.

13. _____ occurs when one party threatens to do some wrongful act unless the other party enters into a contract.

14. If someone threatens to physically harm another person unless that person signs a contract, this is _____.

15. _____ occurs when one person (the dominant party) takes advantage of another person's mental, emotional, or physical weakness and unduly persuades that person (the servient party) to enter into a contract.

Critical Thought Exercise

At Rip-Off Motors, an exotic used car dealership, you are the general manager and Slick is your dishonest salesman. Slick told a potential customer, Dupe, that the Porsche he was interested in purchasing had been driven only 25,000 miles in four years and had never been in an accident. Dupe hired Grease, a mechanic, to appraise the condition of the car. Grease said that the car probably had at least 75,000 miles on it and probably had been in an accident. In spite of this information, Dupe still thought the car would be a good buy for the price, which was still lower than a Porsche with 75,000 miles. Dupe bought the car and it immediately developed numerous mechanical problems which would cost over $10,000 to repair. Dupe has now come back to Rip-Off Motors and is seeking to have you rescind the contract on the basis of Slick's fraudulent misrepresentations of the car's condition. If you rescind the contract, it will cause the dealership to lose over $13,000.

Write a letter to either: A) Dupe, if you are refusing to rescind the contract, or B) Mr. Big, the owner of Rip-Off Motors, if you intend to rescind the contract and suffer the loss. Explain the reasons for your decision, citing authority for your action.

Please compose your answer to the Critical Thinking Exercise using a separate sheet of paper or your computer word processing program.

Practice Quiz

True/False

16. _____ Assent of a party to a contract may be manifested in any manner sufficient to show agreement, including conduct.

17. _____ Mistakes in clerical or mathematical errors which are not the result of gross negligence are considered unilateral mistakes.

18. _____ In most cases of unilateral mistake, the mistaken party is permitted to rescind the contract.

19. _____ If there has been a mutual mistake, the contract cannot be rescinded.

20. _____ A unilateral mistake occurs if both parties know the object of the contract but are mistaken as to its value.

21. _____ When a mutual mistake of value occurs, the contract remains enforceable by either party.

22. ____ A misrepresentation of a material fact is actionable as fraud only if it occurs by words.

23. ____ Contracts involving fraud in the inception are void.

24. ____ A misrepresentation of law is actionable as fraud as the innocent party cannot know every legal detail that applies to the situation.

25. ____ Innocent misrepresentation is treated as a mutual mistake.

26. ____ Duress is a situation in which one party threatens to do a wrongful act unless the other party enters into a contract.

27. ____ Duress is said to have occurred only where a threat involved a physical harm.

28. ____ A threat to bring a civil lawsuit constitutes duress only when such a suit is frivolous or brought in bad faith.

29. ____ Taking advantage of another person's mental, emotional, or physical weakness and unduly persuading that person to enter into a contract constitutes duress.

30. ____ For a situation to be considered "undue influence," the persuasion by the wrongdoer must overcome the free will of the innocent party.

Multiple Choice

31. _____ is an action to undo a contract.

A. Recession
B. Rescission
C. Restitution
D. Inception

32. Heather chooses to buy a scarf at Macy's and reads the price on the tag as $50. She uses her credit card to pay for the scarf, but post-purchase, she notices that the price tag actually says $500. This is an instance of a(n) _____.

A. unilateral mistake
B. mutual mistake of value
C. innocent misrepresentation
D. bilateral mistake

33. In which of the following cases of assent is the rescission of a contract unenforceable?

A. misrepresentation of a material fact
B. mutual mistake of value
C. silence as misrepresentation
D. innocent misrepresentation

34. _____ is a mistake made by both parties concerning an object that is important to the subject matter of a contract.

A. Mutual mistake of value
B. Elementary unilateral mistake
C. Mutual mistake of material fact
D. Fraud by concealment

35. A contract in which both parties are mistaken about the value of the object of the contract is considered _____.

A. unenforceable
B. unconscionable
C. void
D. non-rescindable

36. Intentional misrepresentation is commonly referred to as _____.

A. erroneous misrepresentation
B. duress
C. fraud
D. undue influence

37. To prove fraud, which of the following elements must be shown?

A. The wrongdoer intended to deceive the innocent party.
B. The innocent party was the one who detected fraud.
C. The wrongdoer assumed a false identity.
D. The innocent party knew the wrongdoer.

38. What is scienter?

A. undue influence used on a party to a contract
B. knowledge that a representation is false
C. another term for duress
D. damages given to a victim of fraud

39. The measure of damages, recovered from a misrepresentation, is _____.

A. the actual value of the property
B. the represented value of the property
C. twice the actual value of the property which includes punitive damages
D. the difference between the value of the property as represented and the actual value of the property

40. Contracts involving fraud in inducement are _____.

A. valid
B. void
C. non-rescindable
D. voidable

41. Which of the following occurs when one party intentionally hides a material fact from another party?

A. fraud in the inducement
B. silence as misrepresentation
C. fraud in concealment
D. misrepresentation of law

42. Which of the following is not actionable as fraud?

A. silence as misrepresentation
B. misrepresentation of law
C. marriage to obtain rights of immigration
D. identity theft

43. Which of the following constitutes duress?
A. an event that occurs when one person consciously decides to induce another person to rely and act on a misrepresentation
B. a situation in which one person takes advantage of another person's mental, emotional, or physical weakness and unduly persuades that person to enter into a contract
C. the knowledge that a representation is false or that it was made without sufficient knowledge of the truth
D. a threat to commit extortion unless someone enters into a contract

44. Which of the following is true of duress?

A. It is liable for fraud.
B. A threat should involve physical harm for it to be actionable as duress.
C. Intoxicating a person to sign a contract is considered duress.
D. It is a threat issued to make another person sign a contract.

45. Which of the following is true of undue influence in entering contracts?

A. A fiduciary or confidential relationship must have existed between the parties for undue influence to be proven.
B. Undue influence is not grounds for prosecution, as the innocent party has complete freedom to evaluate the terms of the contract.
C. A contract that is entered into because of undue influence is not voidable.
D. Undue influence need not require the overcoming of the innocent party's free will.

Short Answer

46. How is a mistake different from fraud?

_____

_____

47. Distinguish between unilateral mistake and mutual mistake.

_____

_____

48. What elements should be shown to prove fraud?

_____

_____

49. What is a material fact? Explain misrepresentation of material fact.

_____

_____

50. Explain the element of injury to the innocent party with reference to fraud.

_____

_____

51. List the various types of fraud.

_____

_____

52. Explain silence as misrepresentation.

_____

_____

53. What is misrepresentation of law?

_____

_____

54. What is duress?

_____

_____

55. Explain the equitable doctrine of undue influence.

_____

_____

Answers to Refresh Your Memory

1. undue influence [p. 222]
2. mistake [p. 222]
3. Rescission [p. 222]
4. unilateral mistake [p. 222]
5. material [p. 223]
6. scienter [p. 225]
7. guilty mind [p. 225]
8. economic [p. 225]
9. fraud in the factum [p. 225]
10. Fraud in the inducement [p. 225]
11. misrepresentation of law [p. 226]
12. innocent misrepresentation [p. 226]
13. Duress [p. 228]
14. physical duress [p. 228]
15. Undue influence [p. 228]

Critical thought Exercise Model Answer

Dear Mr. Dupe:

I agree with you that my salesman, Slick, made a misrepresentation to you concerning the mileage and condition of the Porsche you purchased. In order for you to recover damages for the tort of fraud, you must show: (1) a misrepresentation of a material fact; (2) an intent on the part of Slick to deceive you; and, (3) you, the innocent party, must have justifiably relied on the misrepresentation. In our situation, you took the car to an independent mechanic, Grease, who informed you that the car had greater mileage than represented by Slick and had probably been in an accident. You decided that the car was still a good value despite this additional information. You did not rely upon the misrepresentations of my salesman when you purchased the car. As a result, you are not entitled to damages for fraud, nor are you entitled to rescind the agreement.

Yours truly,
General Manager

Answers to Practice Quiz

True/False

16. True. Assent may be manifested in any manner sufficient to show agreement, including express words or conduct of the parties. [p. 222]

17. True. A unilateral mistake occurs when only one party is mistaken about a material fact regarding the subject matter of the contract. A unilateral mistake occurs because of a clerical or mathematical error that is not the result of gross negligence. [p. 222]

18. False. In most cases of unilateral mistake, the mistaken party will not be permitted to rescind the contract. The contract will be enforced on its terms. [p. 222]

19. False. If there has been a mutual mistake, the contract may be rescinded on the grounds that no contract has been formed because there has been no "meeting of the minds" between the parties. [p. 223]

20. False, A mutual mistake of value exists if both parties know the object of the contract but are mistaken as to its value. [p. 224]

21. True. When a mutual mistake of value occurs, the contract remains enforceable by either party because the identity of the subject matter of the contract is not at issue. [p. 224]

22. False. A misrepresentation of a material fact by the wrongdoer may occur by words (oral or written) or by the conduct of a party. [p. 224]

23. True. Fraud in the inception, or fraud in the factum, occurs if a person is deceived as to the nature of his or her act and does not know what he or she is signing. Contracts involving fraud in the inception are void rather than just voidable. [p. 225]

24. False. A misrepresentation of law is not actionable as fraud. The innocent party cannot generally rescind the contract because each party to a contract is assumed to know the law that applies to the transaction, either through his or her own investigation or by hiring a lawyer. [p. 226]

25. True. An innocent misrepresentation occurs when a person makes a statement of fact that he or she honestly and reasonably believes to be true even though it is not. Often, innocent misrepresentation is treated as a mutual mistake. [p. 226]

26. True. Duress occurs when one party threatens to do some wrongful act unless the other party enters into a contract. Such a contract is not enforceable against the innocent party. [p. 228]

27. False. Duress occurs when one party threatens to do some wrongful act unless the other party enters into a contract. Duress can also occur where a threat does not involve physical harm. [p. 228]

28. True. A threat to bring (or not drop) a civil lawsuit, does not constitute duress unless such a suit is frivolous or brought in bad faith. [p. 228]

29. False. Undue influence occurs when one person (the dominant party) takes advantage of another person's mental, emotional, or physical weakness and unduly persuades that person (the servient party) to enter into a contract. [p. 228]

30. True. The persuasion by the wrongdoer must overcome the free will of the innocent party. A contract that is entered into because of undue influence is voidable by the innocent party. [p. 228]

Multiple Choice

31. B. Rescission is an action to undo a contract. The law permits rescission of some contracts made in mistake. [p. 222]

32. A. A unilateral mistake occurs when only one party is mistaken about a material fact regarding the subject matter of the contract. [p. 222]

33. B. A mutual mistake of value exists if both parties know the object of the contract but are mistaken as to its value. Here, the contract remains enforceable by either party because the identity of the subject matter of the contract is not at issue. [p. 224]

34. C. A material fact is a fact that is important to the subject matter of a contract. An ambiguity in a contract may constitute a mutual mistake of a material fact. [p. 223]

35. D. A mutual mistake of value exists if both parties know the object of the contract but are mistaken as to its value. Here, the contract remains enforceable by either party because the identity of the subject matter of the contract is not at issue. [p. 224]

36. C. Fraud is an event that occurs when one person consciously decides to induce another person to rely and act on a misrepresentation. [p. 224]

37. A. Fraud is an event that occurs when one person consciously decides to induce another person to rely and act on a misrepresentation. To prove a fraud, it must be shown that the wrongdoer intended to deceive the innocent party. [p. 224]

38. B. Knowledge that a representation is false or that it was made without sufficient knowledge of the truth is called scienter or guilty mind. [p. 225]

39. D. The measure of damages is the difference between the value of the property as represented and the actual value of the property. This measure of damages gives the innocent party the "benefit of the bargain." [p. 225]

40. D. Fraud in the inducement is fraud that occurs when the party knows what he or she is signing but has been fraudulently induced to enter into the contract. Such contracts are voidable by the innocent party. [p. 225]

41. C. Fraud by concealment occurs when one party takes specific action to conceal a material fact from another party. [p. 226]

42. B. A misrepresentation of law is not actionable as fraud. The innocent party cannot generally rescind the contract because each party to a contract is assumed to know the law that applies to the transaction, either through his or her own investigation or by hiring a lawyer. [p. 226]

43. D. Duress is a situation in which one party threatens to do a wrongful act unless the other party enters into a contract. The threat to commit extortion unless someone enters into a contract constitutes duress. [p. 228]

44. D. Duress is a situation in which one party threatens to do a wrongful act unless the other party enters into a contract. [p. 228]

45. A. Undue influence occurs when one person (the dominant party) takes advantage of another person's mental, emotional, or physical weakness and unduly persuades that person (the servient party) to enter into a contract. To prove undue influence a fiduciary or confidential relationship must have existed between the parties. [p. 228]

Short Answer

46. A mistake occurs where one or both of the parties to a contract have an erroneous belief about the subject matter, value, or some other aspect of the contract.
Mistakes may be either unilateral or mutual. The law permits rescission of some contracts made in mistake. A misrepresentation occurs when an assertion is made that is not in accord with the facts. An intentional misrepresentation occurs when one person consciously decides to induce another person to rely and act on a misrepresentation. Intentional misrepresentation is commonly referred to as fraudulent misrepresentation, or fraud. When fraudulent misrepresentation is used to induce another to enter into a contract, the innocent party's assent to the contract is not genuine, and the contract is voidable by the innocent party. The innocent party can either rescind the contract and obtain restitution or enforce the contract and sue for contract damages. [p. 222, 224]

47. A unilateral mistake occurs when only one party is mistaken about a material fact regarding the subject matter of the contract. In most cases of unilateral mistake, the mistaken party will not be permitted to rescind the contract.
Mutual mistake is a mistake made by both parties. The two kinds of mutual mistakes are:
Mutual Mistake of a Material Fact – A party may rescind a contract if there has been a mutual mistake of a material fact. A material fact is a fact that is important to the subject matter of a contract.
Mutual Mistake of Value – A mutual mistake of value exists if both parties know the object of the contract but are mistaken as to its value. Here, the contract remains enforceable by either party because the identity of the subject matter of the contract is not at issue. [p. 223]

48. To prove fraud, the following elements must be shown:
1. The wrongdoer made a false representation of material fact.
2. The wrongdoer intended to deceive the innocent party.

3. The innocent party justifiably relied on the misrepresentation.
4. The innocent party was injured. [p. 224]

49. A material fact is a fact that is important to the subject matter of a contract. A misrepresentation of a material fact by the wrongdoer may occur by words (oral or written) or by the conduct of a party. To be actionable as fraud, the misrepresentation must be of a past or existing material fact. This means that the misrepresentation must have been a significant factor in inducing the innocent party to enter into the contract. It need not have been the sole factor. Statements of opinion or predictions about the future generally do not form the basis for fraud. [p. 224]

50. To recover damages, the innocent party must prove that the fraud caused him or her economic injury. The measure of damages is the difference between the value of the property as represented and the actual value of the property. This measure of damages gives the innocent party the "benefit of the bargain." In the alternative, the buyer can rescind the contract and recover the purchase price. [p. 225]

51. The various types of fraud are as follows:
a. Fraud in the Inception
b. Fraud in the Inducement
c. Fraud by Concealment
d. Silence as Misrepresentation
e. Misrepresentation of Law
f. Innocent Misrepresentation [p. 225, 226]

52. Generally, neither party to a contract owes a duty to disclose all the facts to the other party. Ordinarily, such silence is not a misrepresentation unless (1) nondisclosure would cause bodily injury or death, (2) there is a fiduciary relationship (i.e., a relationship of trust and confidence) between the contracting parties, or (3) federal and state statutes require disclosure. The Restatement (Second) of Contracts specifies a broader duty of disclosure: Nondisclosure is a misrepresentation if it would constitute a failure to act in "good faith." [p. 226]

53. Usually, a misrepresentation of law is not actionable as fraud. The innocent party cannot generally rescind the contract because each party to a contract is assumed to know the law that applies to the transaction, either through his or her own investigation or by hiring a lawyer. There is one major exception to this rule: The misrepresentation will be allowed as grounds for rescission of the contract if one party to the contract is a professional who should know what the law is and intentionally misrepresents the law to a less sophisticated contracting party. [p. 226]

54. Duress occurs when one party threatens to do some wrongful act unless the other party enters into a contract. If a party to a contract has been forced into making the contract, the assent is not voluntary. Such a contract is not enforceable against the innocent party. Thus, if someone threatens to physically harm another person unless that person signs a contract, this is physical duress. If the victim of the duress signs the

contract, it cannot be enforced against the victim. Duress can also occur where a threat does not involve physical harm. [p. 228]

55. The courts may permit the rescission of a contract based on the equitable doctrine of undue influence. Undue influence occurs when one person (the dominant party) takes advantage of another person's mental, emotional, or physical weakness and unduly persuades that person (the servient party) to enter into a contract. The persuasion by the wrongdoer must overcome the free will of the innocent party. A contract that is entered into because of undue influence is voidable by the innocent party. [p. 228]

14 | STATUE OF FRAUDS AND EQUITABLE EXCEPTIONS

Chapter Overview

Once a contract has been established, it is important to examine the subject matter of the contract to determine whether or not the contract was required to be in writing and if there are any issues regarding the proper form that it might have to be in. This chapter explores the Statute of Frauds and the contracts that are required to be in writing. It discusses if and when prior oral or written agreements between the parties on the same subject matter can be utilized to explain what the parties intended. Explanations of how the court may interpret the parties' contract language as well as whether several documents or references may constitute a contract are discussed.

Objectives

Upon completion of the exercises in this chapter, you should be able to:
1. List the contracts that must be in writing under the Statute of Frauds.
2. Explain the effect of noncompliance with the Statute of Frauds.
3. Describe how the Statute of Frauds is applicable to the UCC sale of goods and leases.
4. Describe the formality of the writing of contracts and the parol evidence rule.
5. Define the equitable doctrines of part performance and promissory estoppel.

Practical Application

You will be able to determine which documents comprise a contract based on the expressions used by the parties and the location of the documents. You should be able to recognize contractual situations that require the application of the Statute of Frauds and whether or not the writing requirement can be satisfied in the absence of a writing. You should be able to assess whether there are any issues concerning parol evidence and if any exceptions exist.

Helpful Hints

Since most of this chapter concentrates on the Statute of Frauds, it is beneficial to thoroughly understand this concept. A mnemonic is provided for you to accomplish this objective. Once this primary goal has been fulfilled, the remaining information will easier for you to apply and learn.

Study Tips

Statute of Frauds

Certain kinds of contracts must be in writing in order to memorialize the significant terms and prevent misunderstanding or fabrications, otherwise known as fraud. The mnemonic given below will help give you an easy way to remember which contracts are required to be in writing.

Mr. Dibbles Places Many Fancy Real Estate Ads.

Mr.	–	Contracts in consideration of **M**arriage
Dibbles	–	**D**ebt of another
Places	–	**P**art Performance
Many	–	**M**ust be performed within one year
Fancy	–	**F**or goods $500 or more
Real Estate	–	Transfers of ownership interests in **Real Estate** such as mortgages, leases
Ads	–	**A**gency contracts

Writing Requirement. Though they vary from state to state, every state has a Statute of Frauds.
- An executory contract that is not in writing, though required to be by the Statute of Frauds, is unenforceable.
- An executed contract that is not in writing, though required to be, cannot be rescinded on the ground of noncompliance with the Statute.

Contracts Involving Interests in Real Property. Contracts that transfer an ownership interest in land must be in writing. This includes mortgages, leases, life estates, and most easements.
- Real property includes the land, its buildings, trees, soil, minerals, timber, plants, crops, and permanently affixed things to the buildings (fixtures).

One Year Rule. If a contract cannot be performed by its own terms within one year, it must be in writing. If it can be performed within one year, the contract can be oral.
- Modifications that extend the time past one year need to be in writing.

Guaranty Contract. A collateral or guaranty contract occurs where one person agrees to answer for the debts or duties of another individual.
- The first (original) contract, between the debtor and creditor, need not be in writing.
- The second (guaranty) contract, between the guarantor and the creditor, must be in writing.
- *The "main purpose" exception.* Also known as the leading object exception, states that if the main purpose of the transaction and the oral contract is to benefit the guarantor, the guaranty contract need not be in writing.

Contract for the Sale of Goods. The Uniform Commercial Code requires contracts for the sale of goods that cost $500 or more to be in writing in order to be enforceable.
- Modifications that cause the contract price to rise to $500 or more must be in writing.

Contract for the Lease of Goods. Contracts for the lease of goods with payments of $1000 or more must be in writing in order to be enforceable under the Uniform Commercial Code.
- Modifications that cause lease payments to rise to $1,000 or more must be in writing.

Agent's Contracts. Agent's contracts to sell real estate must be in writing under the equal dignity rule, which states that if the underlying contract must be in writing, so too must the agent's contract.

Promises Made in Consideration of Marriage. These types of contracts must be in writing for the most obvious reason, to determine ownership of property and assist in determining benefits and property distribution upon death or dissolution of the same.

Equity: Part Performance

This involves the situation where there is an oral contract for the sale of land or other transfer of interest in real property and there is some sort of partial performance.

- In order for the partial performance to act as an exception to the Statute of Frauds, many courts require that the purchaser either take possession of the property and pay part of the purchase price or make valuable improvements on the land.
- If part performance can be shown, the oral contract will be ordered to be specifically performed in order to prevent an injustice.

Formality of the Writing

A contract does not have to be drafted by a lawyer or formally typed to be binding. A contract can be a letter, telegram, invoice, sales receipts, checks, or handwritings on scraps of paper.

Required Signature. The contract must be signed by the party to be charged.
- A signature can be a nickname, initial, a symbol, and even the letter 'X.'

Integration of Several Writings. An entire writing need not be in a single document to be enforceable. Several writings can be combined or *integrated* to form a single written contract.
- *Incorporation by reference.* Integration may be accomplished by expressly referring to it in one document that refers to and incorporates another document in it.

Interpreting Contract Words and Terms. The parties may explain the words and terms used in the contract. Some contracts contain a glossary that defines the terms and used in a contract. If the words and terms are not defined, the courts will interpret using the following standard.
- *Ordinary words* are given the meaning as stated in the dictionary.
- *Technical words* are given their technical meaning.
- *Specific terms* qualify general terms.
- *Typed words* prevail over preprinted words.
- *Handwritten words* prevail over preprinted and typed.
- If an ambiguity exists, it will be resolved against the party who drafted the contract.
- If both parties are in the same sort of trade, then the words used in the trade will be given their meaning as per trade usage.
- Interpretation will be to advance the object of the contract.

Parol Evidence Rule

The parol evidence rule states that if a written contract is a complete and final expression of the parties' agreement, any prior oral or written statements that alter, contradict, or are in addition to the terms of the written contract are inadmissible in any court proceeding concerning the contract.
- Any words outside of the four corners of the contract are called parol evidence.

Merger, or Integration, Clause. This clause, which expressly reiterates the Parol Evidence Rule, can be included in the contract.

Exceptions to the Parol Evidence Rule. There are several exceptions to the Parol Evidence Rule. Parol evidence may be admitted in court if
- The evidence shows that a contract is void or voidable because of fraud, misrepresentation, duress, undue influence, or mistake.

- The evidence explains ambiguous language.
- The evidence concerns a prior course of dealing or course of performance or a usage of trade.
- The evidence fills in the gaps in a contract, such as a missing price term.
- The evidence corrects an obvious clerical or typographical error, which allows the court to reform the contract.

Promissory Estoppel

Promissory estoppels, also known as equitable estoppels, is an exception to the Statute of Frauds. The effect of this doctrine is to estop the promisor from raising the Statute of Frauds as a defense. It involves an oral promise that is enforceable if three conditions are met.
- The promise induces action or forbearance of action by another,
- The reliance on the oral promise was foreseeable, and
- Injustice can be avoided only by enforcing the oral promise.

Refresh Your Memory

The following exercise will give you the opportunity to test your memory of the principles given in this chapter. Read the question twice and place your answer in the blank provided. Review the chapter material for any question that you are unable to answer or remember.

1. _____ is a state statute that requires certain types of contracts to be in writing.

2. _____ includes the land itself, buildings, trees, soil, minerals, timber, plants, crops, fixtures, and things permanently affixed to the land or buildings.

3. _____, also known as deed of trust, is an interest in real property given to a lender as security for the repayment of a loan.

4. Mortgage is also known as _____.

5. A _____ is the transfer of the right to use real property for a specified period of time.

6. _____ is an interest in real property for a person's lifetime; upon that person's death, the interest will be transferred to another party.

7. _____ easements must be in writing to be enforceable, while implied easements need not be written.

8. A _____ occurs when one person agrees to answer for the debts or duties of another person.

9. In a guarantee situation, the original contract, or primary contract, is between the _____ and the _____.

10. _____ is a person who agrees to pay a debt if the primary debtor does not.

11. _____ says that agents' contracts to sell property covered by the Statute of Frauds must be in writing to be enforceable.

12. _____ is an equitable doctrine that allows the court to order an oral contract for the sale of land or transfer of another interest in real property to be specifically performed if it has been partially performed and performance is necessary to avoid injustice.

13. _____ is any oral or written words outside the four corners of a written contract.

14. _____ clause, also known as integration clause, is a clause in a contract that stipulates that it is a complete integration and the exclusive expression of the parties' agreement.

15. _____, also known as equitable estoppel is an equitable doctrine that permits enforcement of oral contracts that should have been in writing. It is applied to avoid injustice.

Critical Thought Exercise

On February 1, Professor Herbert was hired by your company's vice president as the company historian at a rate of $1,400 per month for as long as Herbert lived, with $700 to be paid on the first and fifteenth of each month. Herbert was paid regularly for eight months and then the president decided that he didn't like Herbert digging into company history. No further payments were made to Herbert. Herbert claimed that the company had breached the oral contract and brought suit, seeking damages of $1,400 per month for the rest of his life. The company president asserts that the contract is not enforceable because contracts that cannot be performed within one year must be in writing under the Statute of Frauds.

Draft a memorandum to the president advising him as to the applicable law and whether you believe the company will be able to defend against Herbert's claim based upon the one-year rule.

Please compose your answer to the Critical Thinking Exercise using a separate sheet of paper or your computer word processing program.

Practice Quiz

True/False

16. ____ If an oral contract that should have been in writing under the Statute of Frauds is already executed, neither party can seek to rescind the contract on the grounds of noncompliance with the Statute of Frauds.

17. ____ Trees, crops, minerals, and timber are barred from being included in contracts involving interests in real property.

18. ____ Built-in cabinets in a house would be considered as permanent parts of the real property.

19. ____ A lease is an interest in real property given to a lender as security for the repayment of a loan.

20. ____ A life estate will be transferred to another party in the event of the holder's death.

21. ____ An easement is a form of real property security given by a borrower to a lender.

22. ____ According to the Statute of Frauds, an executory contract that cannot be performed by its own terms within one year of its formation must be in writing.

23. ____ In a guaranty situation, there is only one contract among three parties.

24. ____ The primary contract in a guarantee situation is between the debtor and the creditor.

25. ____ Equal dignity rule says that agents' contracts to sell property covered by the Statute of Frauds must be in writing to be enforceable.

26. ____ If Johnny made an oral contract with Peter to sell Peter his truck for $15,000, Johnny's eventual refusal to sell the truck is considered breach of contract.

27. ____ Any writing—including letters, telegrams, invoices, sales receipts, checks, and handwritten agreements written on scraps of paper—can be an enforceable contract.

28. ____ The signature of the person who is enforcing the contract is necessary.

29. ____ A person's nickname or initials that indicate his or her intent are not considered binding signatures.

30. ____ Placing several documents in the same envelope indicates implied integration.

Multiple Choice

31. The _____ requires certain contracts to be in writing.

A. part performance exception
B. Statute of Frauds
C. equal dignity rule
D. common law of contracts

32. Which of the following is an exception to the Statute of Frauds?

A. merger clause
B. agents' contracts
C. contracts under promissory estoppel
D. prenuptial agreement

33. Which of the following is considered "real property?"

A. a club membership
B. fifty-one percent partnership in a firm
C. a fixture permanently affixed to a building
D. diamond jewelry

34. Which of the following is an interest in real property given to a lender as security for the repayment of a loan?

A. lease
B. easement
C. life estate
D. mortgage

35. Ida moves to New York from Poland and wants to live in an apartment. However, she does not have sufficient money to buy one. Her colleague Henry allows Ida to live in his old apartment for a year, if she pays him $25,000. This contract would be considered a(n) _____.

A. installment
B. mortgage
C. lease
D. easement

36. Which of the following interests in real property transfers to another person after the present holder's death?

A. easement
B. life estate
C. EMI
D. mortgage

37. The _____ states that an executory contract which cannot be performed by its own terms within one year of its formation must be in writing.

A. one-year rule
B. common law of contracts
C. merger clause
D. parol evidence rule

38. A(n) _____ occurs when one person agrees to answer for the debts or duties of another person.

A. guaranty contract
B. mortgage
C. main purpose exception
D. implied integration

39. In a guaranty situation, the original contract is between the _____.

A. creditor and the guarantor
B. creditor and the lessee
C. debtor and the guarantor
D. debtor and the creditor

40. The _____ states that if the main purpose of a transaction and an oral collateral contract is to provide pecuniary benefit to the guarantor, the collateral contract does not have to be in writing to be enforced.

A. merger clause
B. parol evidence rule
C. collateral contract rule
D. leading object exception

41. The _____ says that agents' contracts to sell property covered by the Statute of Frauds must be in writing to be enforceable.

A. merger clause
B. equal dignity rule
C. doctrine of equity
D. common law of contracts

42. Section 2-201(1) of the Uniform Commercial Code is the basic Statute of Frauds provision for _____.

A. all contracts involving interests in real property
B. lease contracts
C. sales contracts
D. mortgage contracts

43. Which of the following statements is true of signature on a written contract?

A. The contract should be signed by the party who seeks enforcement.
B. A person's nickname or initials are not binding legal signatures.
C. The signature must appear at the end of the writing.
D. The signature of the person who is enforcing the contract is not necessary.

44. Which of the following statements is true of interpreting contract words and terms?

A. Specific terms are presumed to qualify general terms.
B. Preprinted words prevail over handwritten words.
C. Where a preprinted form contract is used, preprinted words prevail over typed words.
D. If there is an ambiguity in a contract, the ambiguity will be resolved in favor of the party who drafted the contract.

45. Under which of the following conditions does a promissory estoppel provide for the enforceability of an oral contract?

A. when enforcing the oral promise provides for faster resolution of the case
B. when the reliance on the oral promise was unforeseeable
C. when the promise induces action or forbearance of action by another
D. when the oral promise provides for reduced damages to the defendant

Short Answer

46. What are the various contracts involving interests in real property?

_____

_____

47. Explain the one-tear rule.

_____

_____

48. When does a guarantee contract occur?

_____

_____

49. Explain the main purpose exception.

_____

_____

50. Explain UCC: Contract for the Lease of Goods

_____

_____

51. What is the doctrine of part performance?

_____

_____

52. What does the Statute of Frauds state about signatures?

_____

_____

53. How does the court interpret undefined words and terms?

_____

_____

54. What are the exceptions to parol evidence rule?

_____

_____

55. Explain the doctrine of promissory estoppel.

_____

_____

Answers to Refresh Your Memory

1. Statute of Frauds [p. 233]
2. Real property [p. 234]
3. Mortgage [p. 234]
4. deed of trust [p. 234]
5. lease [p. 234]
6. Life estate [p. 234]
7. Express [p. 234]
8. guarantee contract [p. 236]
9. debtor; creditor [p. 236]
10. Guarantor [p. 236]
11. Equal dignity rule [p. 237]
12. Part performance [p. 239]
13. Parol evidence [p. 241]
14. Merger [p. 241]
15. Promissory estoppel [p. 242]

Critical Thought Exercise Model Answer

Each state has a Statute of Frauds under which certain types of contracts must be in writing to be enforceable. The primary purpose of the statute is to ensure that there is reliable evidence of the existence and terms of certain types of contracts that are deemed important. These types of contracts include those involving interests in land, contracts that cannot by their terms be performed within one year from the date of formation, those that create collateral promised for one person to answer for the debt or duty of another, and contracts for the sale of goods priced at $500 or more. Contracts that cannot, by their own terms, be performed within one year from the day after the contract is formed must be in writing to be enforceable. The test for determining whether an oral contract is enforceable under the one-year rule of the statute is not whether the agreement is likely to be performed within one year from the date the contract was formed but whether performance within a year is possible. When performance within one year is impossible, the contract is unenforceable if it was not in writing. An exception to this "possibility of performance within one year" standard is raised by a lifetime employment contract. Some states rely upon the traditional view that the contract can be performed within one year because a person may die within the first year. The modern view is that a lifetime employment contract anticipates a relationship of long duration, well in excess of one year. These states hold the view that to allow an oral contract for lifetime employment would eviscerate the policy underlying the Statute of Frauds and would invite confusion, uncertainty, and outright fraud. The determination of the enforceability of this oral contract for lifetime employment for Professor Herbert will depend upon whether the jurisdiction adopts the traditional or modern view of the one-year rule.

Answers to Practice Quiz

True/False

16. False. If an oral contract that should have been in writing under the Statute of Frauds is already executed, neither party can seek to rescind the contract on the grounds of noncompliance with the Statute of Frauds. [p. 234]

17. False. Real property includes the land itself, buildings, trees, soil, minerals, timber, plants, crops, fixtures, and things permanently affixed to the land or buildings. [p. 234]

18. True. Certain items of personal property that are permanently affixed to the real property are fixtures that become part of the real property. [p. 234]

19. False. A lease is the transfer of the right to use real property for a specified period of time. [p. 234]

20. True. On some occasions, a person is given a life estate in real property. The person has an interest in the real property for the person's lifetime, and the interest will be transferred to another party on that person's death. [p. 234]

21. False. An easement is a given or required right to use another person's land without owning or leasing it. [p. 234]

22. True. According to the Statute of Frauds, an executory contract that cannot be performed by its own terms within one year of its formation must be in writing. This is called the one-year rule. [p. 235]

23. False. In a guaranty situation, there are at least three parties and two contracts. [p. 236]

24. True. In a guarantee situation, the first contract, which is known as the original contract, or primary contract, is between the debtor and the creditor. It does not have to be in writing. [p. 236]

25. True. Many state Statutes of Frauds require that agents' contracts to sell real property covered by the Statute of Frauds be in writing to be enforceable. The requirement is often referred to as the equal dignity rule. [p. 237]

26. False. According to Section 2-201(1) of the Uniform Commercial Code (UCC), the sales contracts for the sale of goods costing $500 or more must be in writing. [p. 238]

27. True. A written contract does not have to be either drafted by a lawyer or formally typed to be legally binding. Thus, any writing—including letters, telegrams, invoices, sales receipts, checks, and handwritten agreements written on scraps of paper—can be an enforceable contract. [p. 239]

28. False. The Statute of Frauds and the UCC require a written contract, whatever its form, to be signed by the party against whom enforcement is sought. The signature of the person who is enforcing the contract is not necessary. [p. 239]

29. False. A person's last name, first name, nickname, initials, seal, stamp, engraving, or other symbol or mark that indicates the person's intent can be binding. The signature may be affixed by an authorized agent. [p. 240]

30. True. Placing several documents in the same container (e.g., an envelope) may also indicate integration. Such an action is called implied integration. [p. 240]

Multiple Choice

31. B. Every U.S. state has enacted a Statute of Frauds that requires certain types of contracts to be in writing. This statute is intended to ensure that the terms of important contracts are not forgotten, misunderstood, or fabricated. [p. 233]

32. C. There are several equitable exceptions to the Statute of Frauds. The doctrine of promissory estoppel is one of them. [p. 233]

33. C. Real property includes the land itself, buildings, trees, soil, minerals, timber, plants, crops, fixtures, and things permanently affixed to the land or buildings. [p. 234]

34. D. Borrowers often give a lender an interest in real property as security for the repayment of a loan. This action must be done through the use of a written mortgage or deed of trust. [p. 234]

35. C. A lease is the transfer of the right to use real property for a specified period of time. [p. 234]

36. B. On some occasions, a person is given a life estate in real property. The person has an interest in the real property for the person's lifetime, and the interest will be transferred to another party on that person's death. [p. 234]

37. A. According to the Statute of Frauds, an executory contract that cannot be performed by its own terms within one year of its formation must be in writing. This one-year rule is intended to prevent disputes about contract terms that may otherwise occur toward the end of a long-term contract. [p. 235]

38. A. A guaranty contract occurs when one person agrees to answer for the debts or duties of another person. Guaranty contracts are required to be in writing under the Statute of Frauds. [p. 236]

39. D. In a guaranty situation, there are at least three parties and two contracts. The first contract, which is known as the original contract, or primary contract, is between the debtor and the creditor. [p. 236]

40. D. If the main purpose of a transaction and an oral collateral contract is to provide pecuniary benefit to the guarantor, the collateral contract is treated like an original contract and does not have to be in writing to be enforced. This exception is called the main purpose exception, or leading object exception, to the Statute of Frauds. [p. 236]

41. B. Many state Statutes of Frauds require that agents' contracts to sell real property covered by the Statute of Frauds be in writing to be enforceable. The requirement is often referred to as the equal dignity rule. [p. 237]

42. C. Section 2-201(1) of the Uniform Commercial Code (UCC) states that sales contracts for the sale of goods costing $500 or more must be in writing. [p. 238]

43. D. The Statute of Frauds and the UCC require a written contract, whatever its form, to be signed by the party against whom enforcement is sought. The signature of the person who is enforcing the contract is not necessary. [p. 239]

44. A. Specific terms are presumed to qualify general terms. For example, if a provision in a contract refers to the subject matter as "corn," but a later provision refers to the subject matter as "feed corn" for cattle, this specific term qualifies the general term. [p. 240]

45. C. Under the Statute of Frauds, the oral promise is enforceable against the promisor if the promise induces action or forbearance of action by another [p. 242]

Short Answer

46. The various contracts involving interests in real property are:
Mortgages – Borrowers often give a lender an interest in real property as security for the repayment of a loan. This action must be done through the use of a written mortgage or deed of trust.
Leases – A lease is the transfer of the right to use real property for a specified period of time. Most Statutes of Frauds require leases for a term more than one year to be in writing.
Life estates – On some occasions, a person is given a life estate in real property. In other words, the person has an interest in the real property for the person's lifetime, and the interest will be transferred to another party on that person's death. A life estate is an ownership interest that must be in writing under the Statute of Frauds.

Easements – An easement is a given or required right to use another person's land without owning or leasing it. Easements may be either express or implied. Express easements must be in writing to be enforceable, while implied easements need not be written. [p. 234]

47. According to the Statute of Frauds, an executory contract that cannot be performed by its own terms within one year of its formation must be in writing. This one-year rule is intended to prevent disputes about contract terms that may otherwise occur toward the end of a long-term contract. If the performance of the contract is possible within the one-year period, the contract may be oral. The extension of an oral contract might cause the contract to violate the Statute of Frauds if the original term and the extension period exceed one year. [p. 235]

48. A guaranty contract occurs when one person agrees to answer for the debts or duties of another person. Guaranty contracts are required to be in writing under the Statute of Frauds. In a guaranty situation, there are at least three parties and two contracts. The first contract, which is known as the original contract, or primary contract, is between the debtor and the creditor. It does not have to be in writing (unless another provision of the Statute of Frauds requires it to be). The second contract, called the guaranty contract, is between the person who agrees to pay the debt if the primary debtor does not (i.e., the guarantor) and the original creditor. The guarantor's liability is secondary because it does not arise unless the party primarily liable fails to perform. [p. 236]

49. The "Main Purpose" Exception If the main purpose of a transaction and an oral collateral contract is to provide pecuniary (i.e., financial) benefit to the guarantor, the collateral contract is treated like an original contract and does not have to be in writing to be enforced.5 This exception is called the main purpose exception, or leading object exception, to the Statute of Frauds. This exception is intended to ensure that the primary benefactor of the original contract (i.e., the guarantor) is answerable for the debt or duty. [p. 236]

50. Section 2A-201(1) of the Uniform Commercial Code (UCC) is the Statute of Frauds provision that applies to the lease of goods. It states that lease contracts involving payments of $1,000 or more must be in writing. If a lease payment of an original lease contract is less than $1,000, it does not have to be in writing under the UCC Statute of Frauds. However, if a modification of the lease contract increases the lease payment to $1,000 or more, the modification has to be in writing to be enforceable. The most recent revision to UCC 2A-201 requires that lease contracts involving payments of $20,000 or more must be in writing to be enforceable. A state must adopt this amendment for it to become effective. However, most states have not enacted this change. [p. 238]

51. If an oral contract for the sale of land or transfer of other interests in real property has been partially performed, it may not be possible to return the parties to their status quo. To solve this problem, the courts have developed the equitable doctrine of part performance. This doctrine allows the court to order such an oral contract to be specifically performed if performance is necessary to avoid injustice. For this

performance exception to apply, most courts require that the purchaser either pay part of the purchase price and take possession of the property or make valuable improvements on the property. [p. 239]

52. The Statute of Frauds and the UCC require a written contract, whatever its form, to be signed by the party against whom enforcement is sought. The signature of the person who is enforcing the contract is not necessary. Thus, a written contract may be enforceable against one party but not the other party. Generally, the signature may appear anywhere on the writing. In addition, it does not have to be a person's full legal name. The person's last name, first name, nickname, initials, seal, stamp, engraving, or other symbol or mark (e.g., an X) that indicates the person's intent can be binding. The signature may be affixed by an authorized agent. If a signature is suspected of being forged, the victim can hire handwriting experts and use modern technology to prove it is not his or her signature. [p. 239]

53. If the parties have not defined the words and terms of a contract, the courts apply the following standards of interpretation:
a. Ordinary words are given their usual meaning according to the dictionary.
b. Technical words are given their technical meaning, unless a different meaning is clearly intended.
c. Specific terms are presumed to qualify general terms. For example, if a provision in a contract refers to the subject matter as "corn," but a later provision refers to the subject matter as "feed corn" for cattle, this specific term qualifies the general term.
d. If both parties are members of the same trade or profession, words will be given their meaning as used in the trade (i.e., usage of trade). If the parties do not want trade usage to apply, the contract must indicate that.
e. Where a preprinted form contract is used, typed words in a contract prevail over preprinted words. Handwritten words prevail over both preprinted and typed words.
f. If there is an ambiguity in a contract, the ambiguity will be resolved against the party who drafted the contract. [p. 240]

54. There are several major exceptions to the parol evidence rule. Parol evidence may be admitted in court if it:
a. Shows that a contract is void or voidable (e.g., evidence that the contract was induced by fraud, misrepresentation, duress, undue influence, or mistake).
b. Explains ambiguous language.
c. Concerns a prior course of dealing or course of performance between the parties or a usage of trade.
d. Fills in the gaps in a contract (e.g., if a price term or time of performance term is omitted from a written contract, the court can hear parol evidence to imply the reasonable price or time of performance under the contract).
e. Corrects an obvious clerical or typographical error. The court can reform the contract to reflect the correction. [p. 241]

55. The doctrine of promissory estoppel, or equitable estoppel, is another equitable exception to the strict application of the Statute of Frauds. The version of promissory

estoppel in the Restatement (Second) of Contracts provides that if parties enter into an oral contract that should be in writing under the Statute of Frauds, the oral promise is enforceable against the promisor if three conditions are met: (1) The promise induces action or forbearance of action by another, (2) the reliance on the oral promise was foreseeable, and (3) injustice can be avoided only by enforcing the oral promise. Where this doctrine applies, the promisor is estopped (prevented) from raising the Statute of Frauds as a defense to the enforcement of the oral contract. [p. 242]

15 | THIRD-PARTY RIGHTS AND DISCHARGE

Chapter Overview

This chapter examines third-party rights under contracts entered into by other individuals, in particular assignees and intended third-party beneficiaries. It explores conditions to performance and the various ways to discharge the duty of performance. The assignment and delegation of contractual duties are also discussed.

Objectives

Upon completion of the exercises contained in this chapter, you should be able to:
1. Describe assignment of contract rights and what contract rights are assignable.
2. Define intended beneficiary and describe this person's rights under a contract.
3. Define covenant.
4. Distinguish between conditions precedent, conditions subsequent, and concurrent conditions.
5. Explain when the performance of a contract is excused because of objective impossibility or commercial impracticability.

Practical Application

Upon mastering the concepts in this chapter, you should be able to recognize whether or not a contract may be assigned or delegated and any liabilities that may have been incurred as a result of the assignment or delegation. You should be able to determine if a third party to a contract has any rights as a beneficiary to the contract. You should be able to analyze questions and real-life situations concerning the various ways a contract may be discharged by law.

Helpful Hints

It can be difficult to keep the parties straight in contracts involving more than two parties, so it can be helpful to diagram the transaction, as in your text. It is helpful to imagine yourself as the person being given an assignment of a right or a delegation of a duty when analyzing the question or hypothetical, so that the concepts become clear. Do not let the titles of assignee, assignor, delegatee, delegator, or obligor and obligee overwhelm you. It is easier to learn the concept behind the titles first, so that the party's actions and the impact will become second nature to you.

Study Tips

Third-Party Rights and Discharge

The parties to a contract are said to be in privity of contract and have a legal obligation to perform the duties specified in their contract which can be enforced in court.
- The duty of performance may be discharged by agreement, excuse of performance, or by operation of law.

- Third parties do not generally have rights under other people's contracts
  - *Exception.* Assignees, to whom rights are subsequently transferred.
  - *Exception.* Intended beneficiaries, to whom contracting parties intended to give rights under the contract.

Assignment of a Right

The transfer of contractual rights is called an assignment of rights or an assignment.

Form of Assignment. No formalities are necessary. However, words to express the intent of the assignor are carefully examined.
- Words such as *transfer*, *give*, and *convey* have been used to express intent in an assignment.
- *Obligor.* The party who owes a duty of performance under a contract.
- *Obligee.* The party who is owed a duty of performance under a contract.
- *Assignor.* The obligee who transfers the right to receive performance.
- *Assignee.* The party to whom the right to receive performance has been transferred.

Personal Service Contracts. Generally, these contracts are not assignable.
- The parties can expressly agree that the contract can be assigned.

Assignment of Future Rights. The general rule is that a person may not assign a currently nonexisting right that he or she is expecting in the future.

Contract Where Assignment Would Materially Alter the Risk. Contracts where assignment would materially alter the risk of the obligor cannot be assigned.
- A classic example would be assigning your homeowner's insurance to a friend of yours who cannot afford it.

Assignment of Legal Action. An individual may not assign the right to sue for the violation of personal rights. A legal right that arises from a breach of contract can be assigned.

Effect of an Assignment of a Right. The assignee stands in the shoes of the assignor. The assignor is entitled to performance by the obligor.
- The assignment extinguishes all rights of the assignor against the obligor.
- An obligor can assert any defenses he or she had against the assignor or assignee.

Notice of Assignment. The assignee must notify the obligor about the assignment and the performance by the obligor must be given to the assignee. If there is no notice given to the obligor, he or she can continue performing under the contract to the assignor. The assignee's only recourse is to sue the assignor for damages.
- If the obligor knows of the assignment but continues to perform to the assignor, the assignee can sue the obligor for payment. He or she will also have to pay to the assignor and to the assignee. Further he or she may sue the assignor for damages.

Anti-assignment Clause. This clause prohibits the assignment of rights under the contract.

Approval Clause. An approval clause is one in which the obligor must approve any assignment.

Successive Assignments of the Same Right. If the obligee fraudulently or mistakenly assigns the same right to successive parties, several rules can be used to determine the true assignee.

- *The American Rule.* The New York Rule is used by the majority of states and states that the first assignment in time prevails regardless of notice.
- *The English Rule.* This rule states that the first to give notice prevails.
- *The Possession of Tangible Token Rule.* Under either the American or English rule, if the assignor makes a successive assignment of a contract right that is represented by a tangible token, such as a savings passbook, stock certificate, etc., the first assignee who receives delivery of the tangible token prevails over subsequent assignees.

Delegation of a Duty

The delegation of a duty is a transfer of contractual duties by the obligor to another party for performance. Generally, no special words or formality are required.
- *Delegator.* The obligor who transferred his or her duty.
- *Delegatee.* The party to whom the duty has been transferred.
- *Obligee.* The party to whom the duty is owed.

Duties That Can and Cannot Be Delegated.
- If an obligee has a substantial interest in having the obligor perform the duty, the duty cannot be delegated.
    - *Personal service contracts.* These contracts require the discretion, expertise, and the exercise of personal skills.
    - *Material variation of the duty.* A contract whose performance would materially vary if the obligor's duties were delegated cannot be delegated.
- Where contracts have been entered into with a company, rather than an individual, the company can designate any of its qualified employees to perform the contract.

Effect of Delegation of Duties.
The delegator remains legally liable for the performance of the contract, thereby being subjected to a lawsuit if the delegatee does not perform properly.
- *Assumption of duties.* If the word assumption or a similar term is contained in the delegation, then there has been an assumption of duties. The obligee can sue the delegatee for nonperformance or negligent performance on the contract. The delegator remains liable also.

Anti-delegation Clause.
The parties to a contract can specify that the duties under the contract cannot be delegated. These clauses are usually enforced.
- Some courts allow totally impersonal duties to be delegated despite such a clause.

Assignment and Delegation.
Circumstances where there is both an assignment of rights and a delegation of duties.
- The modern view holds that if there is an assignment of rights, there has also been a delegation of duties.

Third-Party Beneficiaries

Third parties who claim rights under contracts are either intended or incidental.

Intended Beneficiaries.
Third-party beneficiaries to whom the contracting parties intended to give rights under the contract.
- *Donee beneficiary.* The third-party beneficiary to whom the contracting parties intended to confer a benefit or gift under a donee beneficiary contract. If the promisor fails to perform, the donee beneficiary can sue the promisor under the contract.

- o *Promisee.* The contracting party who directs that the benefit be conferred on another.
- o *Promisor.* The contracting party who agrees to confer performance for the benefit of the third party.
- o *Donee beneficiary.* The third party on whom the benefit is to be conferred.
- *Creditor beneficiary.* In a creditor beneficiary contract, the original creditor on a contract becomes the creditor beneficiary on a second contract between the original debtor and a new debtor. If the new debtor fails to pay the creditor beneficiary, the creditor beneficiary can either enforce the original contract or the second contract for payment.
  - o A creditor beneficiary contract usually arises as follows:
    - A debtor borrows money from a creditor to buy an item.
    - The debtor enters into an agreement to pay the creditor back with interest.
    - The debtor thereafter sells the item to another individual before the loan is paid off.
    - The new buyer then promises the debtor that he or she will pay the balance of the loan amount to the creditor.

Incidental Beneficiary. An incidental beneficiary is one who is unintentionally benefited by other people's contracts and has no rights to sue under the contract.

- The public and taxpayers are only incidental beneficiaries to any contracts entered into by the government on their behalf.

Covenant

A covenant is an unconditional promise to perform. Nonperformance of a covenant equals a breach of contract giving the other party the right to sue.

Conditions

A conditional promise is not as definite as a covenant. The promisor's duty to perform depends on whether or not a condition has been or not been met. A conditional promise become a covenant once the condition is met.

- Words like *if, on condition that, provided that, when, after, as soon as* indicate a condition.

Condition Precedent. The occurrence or nonoccurrence of an event before a party is obligated to perform under the contract.

- *Condition precedent based on satisfaction.* There are two tests to determine whether this unique form of condition precedent has been met.
  - o The personal satisfaction test. This is a subjective test whereby the person is to act in good faith in matters involving personal taste and comfort.
  - o The reasonable person test. This is an objective test that is used to judge contracts involving mechanical fitness and most commercial transactions. This is used when a third person is involved who is used to judge another's work.
  - o Time of performance as a condition precedent. If a party is not jeopardized by a delay, this will be considered a minor breach.
    - If *"time is of the essence,"* performance by the stated time is an express condition. This will be considered a breach of contract if performance is not rendered by the start date.

Condition Subsequent. This condition exists when a contract provides that the occurrence or nonoccurrence of an event automatically excuses the performance of an existing duty to perform.

- In the Restatement (Second) of Contracts, there is no distinction between a condition precedent and a condition subsequent.

Concurrent Conditions. This condition occurs when both parties render performance at the same time.

Implied Condition. Any of the above conditions may be considered to be express or implied in nature. A condition is implied from the situation surrounding the contract and the parties' conduct.

Discharge of Performance

There are three ways to discharge a party's duty under a contract: by mutual agreement of the parties, by impossibility of performance, or by operation of law.

Discharge by Agreement. The parties mutually agree to discharge their contract.
- *Mutual rescission.* The parties to a contract can mutually agree to discharge or end their contractual duties.
- *Substituted contract.* The parties can enter into a new contract that revokes and discharges a prior contract.
- *Novation.* This agreement substitutes a new party for one of the original contracting parties. All three must be in unison regarding the substitution.
- *Accord and Satisfaction.* The settlement of a contract dispute where the parties accept something different than originally agreed upon and performance of the same. If an accord is not satisfied when it is due, the injured party may enforce the accord or the original contract.

Discharge by Impossibility. This excuse of nonperformance is excused if the contract becomes objectively impossible to perform.
- Example: Death of a promissory in a personal service contract.
- Example. Destruction of the subject matter prior to performance.
- Example: A supervening illegality makes performance of the contract illegal.

Force Majeure Clause. These types of clauses are where the parties agree in their contract as to the events that will excuse nonperformance of the contract. These typical force majeure clause excuses nonperformance caused by natural disasters.
- Modernly, labor strikes and shortages of materials excuse performance under this clause.

Statute of Limitations. The statutory frame in which to bring a lawsuit.
- The UCC gives four years as the limit to bring a cause of action based on breach of contract.

Refresh Your Memory

The following exercise will give you the opportunity to test your memory of the principles given in this chapter. Read the question twice and place your answer in the blank provided. Review the chapter material for any question that you are unable to answer or remember.

1. The state of two specified parties being in a contract is called _____.

2. A party who owes a duty of performance under a contract is called the _____ .

3. An oblige who transfers the right to receive performance is called a(n) _____ .

4. _____ is a clause that prohibits the assignment of rights under the contract.

5. The _____ , also known as New York Rule, provides that the first assignment in time prevails, regardless of notice.

6. The _____ rule provides that the first assignee to give notice to the obligor.

7. An obligor who transfers his or her duty is called a(n) _____ .

8. A situation where there is a valid delegation of duties but the delegatee has not assumed the duties under a contract, the delegation is called a(n) _____ .

9. A third party who is not in privity of contract but who has rights under the contract and can enforce the contract against the promisor is called the _____ .

10. A contract entered into with the intent to confer a benefit or gift on an intended third party is called _____ .

11. A party who is unintentionally benefited by other people's contracts is called an _____ .

12. A(n) _____ is an unconditional promise to perform.

13. _____ is an objective test that applies to commercial contracts and contracts involving mechanical fitness.

14. A(n) _____ agreement substitutes a third party for one of the original contracting parties.

15. _____ is a clause in a contract in which the parties specify certain events that will excuse nonperformance.

Critical Thought Exercise

The Rocky Mountain Plumbing Company (RMP), which you manage, is very successful and has an excellent reputation. Your business is known for its fairness, prompt performance, and superior work. After a severe earthquake of 7.4 on the Richter scale, billions of dollars worth of pipe damage occurred to hundreds of structures in the area serviced by your company. RMP has signed several huge contracts to repair or replace plumbing for government buildings, hospitals, and three hotels owned by Alexis. Each of these contracts will be for $800,000 or more.

You are uncertain if RMP will be able to meet the deadlines set in the contracts as the urgency of the work needing to be done to so many buildings might call for more time. You have the option of assigning some of the work to Bob's Plumbing, a far less reputable company, or making other arrangements with the county, the hospital district, and Alexis. You are afraid that if you inform people that RMP is unable to perform the contracts on time, it may lose the contracts along with the huge profits they will bring.

Your partners share your skepticism about meeting the deadlines and want to hire Bob's Plumbing immediately without mentioning it to any of the parties involved.

RMP's partners request that you draft a memorandum advising them of the options and risks involved with each option.

Please compose your answer to the Critical Thinking Exercise using a separate sheet of paper or your computer word processing program.

Practice Quiz

True/False

16. _____ Privity of contract refers to the transfer of contractual rights by an obligee to another party.

17. _____ A party who is owed a right under a contract is called the obligor.

18. _____ Terms such as sell, convey, and give indicate the intent to transfer a contract right.

19. _____ A person is permitted to assign a currently nonexistent right that he or she expects to have in the future.

20. _____ The obligor can raise any personal defenses he or she may have directly against the assignee.

21. _____ Anti-assignment clause in a contract prohibits the assignment of rights under the contract.

22. _____ Approval clauses require that the assignee approve any assignment of a contract.

23. _____ The party to whom the duty is owed is the delegatee.

24. _____ In a case of assumption of duties, the delegatee is not liable for nonperformance.

25. _____ An assignment and delegation occurs when there is a transfer of both rights and duties under a contract.

26. _____ The promisee is the contracting party who agrees to confer performance for the benefit of the third person.

27. ____ An incidental beneficiary has no rights to enforce or sue under other people's contracts.

28. ____ A covenant is an unconditional promise to perform.

29. ____ A reasonable person test is a subjective test that applies to contracts involving personal taste and comfort.

30. ____ A statute of limitations establishes the time period during which a lawsuit must be brought.

Multiple Choice

31. An obligee who transfers the right to receive performance is called the _____.

A. subsequent assignor
B. assignor
C. obligor
D. assignee

32. A legal right that arises out of a breach of contract is _____.

A. considered a future right
B. not assignable
C. subject to approval clause
D. assignable

33. Who should provide a notice of assignment to the obligor?

A. facilitator
B. assignor
C. obligee
D. assignee

34. Which of the following is true in the event that an assignee does not provide a notice of assignment to the obligor?

A. The assignee cannot sue the obligor to recover payment.
B. The assignee cannot sue the assignor for damages.
C. The obligor's only recourse is to sue the assignee for damages.
D. The assignee's only course of action is to sue the obligee for damages.

35. A(n) _____ is used if the obligor does not want to deal with or render performance to an unknown third party.

A. novation agreement
B. approval clause
C. anti-assignment clause
D. anti-delegation clause

36. Approval clauses require that the _____ approve any assignment of a contract.

A. obligor
B. obligee
C. assignor
D. assignee

37. Which of the following is an illustration of the possession of tangible token rule?

A. The right of collecting $10,000 is recorded in the assignee's savings account passbook.
B. An obligee who is owed $10,000 assigns the right of collection $5,000 each to two assignees.
C. The assignee can re-assign the right only to a sub-assignee selected by the obligee.
D. An obligee cannot assign a right to collection of more than once.

38. A(n) _____ occurs when there is a transfer of both rights and duties under a contract.

A. discharge
B. declaration of duties
C. assumption of duties
D. assignment and delegation

39. A(n) _____ is an original creditor who becomes a beneficiary under the debtor's new contract with another party.

A. creditor beneficiary
B. donee beneficiary
C. incidental creditor
D. subsequent assignee

40. Which of the following is true of incidental beneficiaries?

A. A creditor beneficiary is an unintended beneficiary.
B. An incidental beneficiary cannot sue under other people's contracts.
C. An intended third-party beneficiary cannot enforce the contract against the promisor.
D. Incidental beneficiary is a third party who is benefitted intentionally.
41. Which of the following phrases describes the term covenant?

A. successive assignments of a right
B. a breach of contract
C. mutual rescission of a contract
D. an unconditional promise to perform

42. _____ refers to a condition that requires the occurrence of an event before a party is obligated to perform a duty under a contract.

A. Concurrent condition
B. Condition subsequent
C. Condition precedent
D. Implied condition

43. _____ refers to a condition whose occurrence or nonoccurrence of a specific event automatically excuses the performance of an existing contractual duty to perform.

A. Condition subsequent
B. Condition precedent
C. Concurrent condition
D. Implied condition

44. In which of the following conditions is a party's absolute duty to perform conditioned on the other party's absolute duty to perform?

A. condition precedent
B. concurrent condition
C. condition subsequent
D. implied condition

45. The injured party loses the right to sue if the lawsuit is brought after the ____ expires.

A. privity of contract
B. notice of assignment
C. statute of limitations
D. future right

Short Answer

46. Explain the process of transfer of rights.

_____

_____

47. What is notice of assignment?

_____

_____

48. What are the various rules that apply to successive assignment?

_____

_____

49. What are the duties that cannot be delegated?

_____

_____

50. What are the effects of delegation of duties?

_____

_____

51. What are the two types of third-party beneficiaries?

_____

_____

52. What are the two tests developed by the court to determine whether the condition precedent based on satisfaction has been met?

_____

_____

53. What are the different methods for discharging a contract by mutual agreement?

_____

_____

54. In what circumstances is the nonperformance of contractual duties is excused?

_____

_____

55. Explain the statute of limitations.

_____

_____

Answers to Refresh Your Memory

1. privity of contract [p. 247]
2. obligator [p. 247]
3. assignor [p. 247]
4. Anti-assignment clause [p. 249]
5. American rule [p. 250]
6. English [p. 250]
7. delegator [p. 250]
8. declaration of duties [p. 251]
9. intended third-party beneficiary [p. 252]
10. donee beneficiary contract [p. 252]
11. incidental beneficiary [p. 254]
12. covenant [p. 255]
13. Reasonable person test [p. 256]
14. novation [p. 259]
15. force majeure [p. 259]

Critical Thought Exercise Model Answer

To: RMP Partners
From: Your Partner
RE: Options for performing the contracts

The obligor in a contract must be careful to refrain from informing the obligee that he or she is unable to perform. This may cause the obligee to treat the statement as an anticipatory repudiation and a breach. Therefore, RMP should pursue an option that does not create a breach. It is lawful to transfer the duties under a contract to another party. This delegation of duties does not relieve the party making the delegation of the obligation to perform in the event that the party to whom the duty has been delegated. No special form is required to create a valid delegation of duties. Some duties cannot be delegated, such as when performance depends upon the special skills of the obligor, when the contract expressly prohibits delegation, when special trust has been placed in the obligor, or when performance by a third party will vary materially from that expected by the obligee. These contracts were awarded to us because we are capable of handling the work. This does not mean that Bob's Plumbing is incapable of performing the same duties. RMP would be within its rights to delegate the duties under one or more of the contracts to Bob's Plumbing. RMP would remain liable for any breach of the contract by Bob's Plumbing. Because Bob's Plumbing is a far less reputable company than RMP, we may not want to expose ourselves to greater liability. Another safer option is to enter into a novation with one or more of the obliges and Bob's Plumbing which will allow a new contract to be formed between Bob's Plumbing and an obligee and then extinguish our contract. This will relieve us of any liability under that particular contract, but it will also cause us to lose the profit from the contract and hurt our reputation. Our reputation will be hurt worse if we become embroiled in a contract dispute with the schools and hospital, not to mention a very influential businessperson, Alexis. We should calculate how much of the business we can handle and then approach the parties involved in the smaller contracts and suggest a novation. If the novation is refused, we will then have no choice but to delegate some of the work to Bob's Plumbing.

Answers to Practice Quiz

True/False

16. False. Privity of contract is the state of two specified parties being in a contract. [p. 247]

17. False. A party who owes a duty of performance under a contract is called the obligor. [p. 247]

18. True. Generally, no formalities are required for a valid assignment of rights. Words or terms, such as sell, transfer, convey, and give, are sufficient to indicate intent to transfer a contract right. [p. 247]

19. False. A person cannot assign a currently nonexistent right that he or she expects to have in the future. [p. 248]

20. True. The obligor can also raise any personal defenses (e.g., participation in the assignor's fraudulent scheme) he or she may have directly against the assignee. [p. 249]

21. True. Some contracts contain an anti-assignment clause that prohibits the assignment of rights under the contract. [p. 249]

22. False. Approval clauses require that the obligor approve any assignment of a contract. [p. 249]

23. False. A party to whom a duty has been transferred is called a delegate. [p. 250]

24. False. In case of assumptions of duties, the obligee can sue the delegatee and recover damages from the delegatee for nonperformance or negligent performance by the delegatee. [p. 251]

25. True. An assignment and delegation occurs when there is a transfer of both rights and duties under a contract. If the transfer of a contract to a third party contains only language of assignment, the modern view holds that there is corresponding delegation of the duties of the contract. [p. 252]

26. False. The promisor is the contracting party who agrees to confer performance for the benefit of the third person. [p. 252]

27. True. Incidental beneficiary is a party who is unintentionally benefited by other people's contracts. An incidental beneficiary has no rights to enforce or sue under other people's contracts. [p. 254]

28. True. In contracts, parties make certain promises to each other. A covenant is an unconditional promise to perform. Nonperformance of a covenant is a breach of contract that gives the other party the right to sue. [p. 255]

29. False. Reasonable person test is an objective test that applies to commercial contracts and contracts involving mechanical fitness. [p. 256]

30. True. Every state has a statute of limitations that applies to contract actions. Under these statutes, if an aggrieved party does not bring suit for breach of contract during a designated period after a breach of contract has occurred, he losses the right to sue. [p. 259]

Multiple Choice

31. B. An oblige who transfers the right to receive performance is called an assignor. The party to whom the right has been transferred is called the assignee. [p. 247]

32. D. A legal right that arises out of a breach of contract may be assigned. [p. 248]

33. D. When an assignor makes an assignment of a right under a contract, the assignee is under a duty to notify the obligor that (1) the assignment has been made and (2) performance must be rendered to the assignee. [p. 249]

34. A. If the assignee fails to provide notice of assignment to the obligor, the obligor may continue to render performance to the assignor, who no longer has a right to it. [p. 249]

35. C. Some contracts contain an anti-assignment clause that prohibits the assignment of rights under the contract. Such clauses may be used if the obligor does not want to deal with or render performance to an unknown third party. [p. 249]

36. A. Some contracts contain an approval clause. Such clauses require that the obligor approve any assignment of a contract. Where there is an approval clause, many states prohibit the obligor from unreasonably withholding approval. [p. 249]

37. A. The possession of tangible token rule provides that under either the American or English rule, if the assignor makes successive assignments of a contract right that is represented by a tangible token, such as a stock certificate or a savings account passbook, the first assignee who receives delivery of the tangible token prevails over subsequent assignees. [p. 250]

38. D. An assignment and delegation occurs when there is a transfer of both rights and duties under a contract. If the transfer of a contract to a third party contains only language of assignment, the modern view holds that there is corresponding delegation of the duties of the contract. [p. 252]

39. A. A creditor beneficiary contract usually arises in the following situation:

1. A debtor borrows money from a creditor to purchase some item. 2. The debtor signs an agreement to pay the creditor the amount of the loan plus interest 3. The debtor sells the item to another party before the loan is paid. 4. The new buyer promises the original debtor that he will pay the remainder of the loan amount to the original creditor. [p. 253]

40. B. In many instances, the parties to a contract unintentionally benefit a third party when a contract is performed. In such situations, the third party is referred to as an incidental beneficiary. An incidental beneficiary has no rights to enforce or sue under other people's contracts. [p. 254]

41. D. In contracts, parties make certain promises to each other. A covenant is an unconditional promise to perform. Nonperformance of a covenant is a breach of contract that gives the other party the right to sue. [p. 255]

42. C. If a contract requires the occurrence (or nonoccurrence) of an event before a party is obligated to perform a contractual duty, this is a condition precedent. [p. 256]

43. A. A condition subsequent exists when there is a condition in a contract that provides that the occurrence or nonoccurrence of a specific event automatically excuses the performance of an existing duty to perform. [p. 257]

44. B. Concurrent conditions arise when the parties to a contract agree to render performance simultaneously—that is, when each party's absolute duty to perform is conditioned on the other party's absolute duty to perform. [p. 257]

45. C. Every state has a statute of limitations that applies to contract actions. Under these statutes, if an aggrieved party does not bring suit for breach of contract during a designated period after a breach of contract has occurred, he loses the right to sue. [p. 259]

Short Answer

46. The transfer of contractual rights is called an assignment of rights. A party who owes a duty of performance under a contract is called the obligor. A party who is owed a right under a contract is called the obligee. An obligee who transfers the right to receive performance is called an assignor. The party to whom the right has been transferred is called the assignee. The assignee can assign the right to yet another person called a subsequent assignee, or subassignee. [p. 247]

47. When an assignor makes an assignment of a right under a contract, the assignee is under a duty to notify the obligor that (1) the assignment has been made and (2) performance must be rendered to the assignee. If the assignee fails to provide notice of assignment to the obligor, the obligor may continue to render performance to the assignor, who no longer has a right to it. The assignee cannot sue the obligor to recover payment because the obligor has performed according to the original contract. The assignee's only course of action is to sue the assignor for damages. [p. 249]

48. The following rules apply to successive assignment:
American Rule (New York rule) – The American rule (or New York Rule) provides that the first assignment in time prevails, regardless of notice.
English Rule – The English rule provides that the first assignee to give notice to the obligor (the person who owes the performance, money, duty, or other thing of value) prevails.
Possession of Tangible Token Rule – The possession of tangible token rule provides that under either the American or English rule, if the assignor makes successive assignments of a contract right that is represented by a tangible token, such as a stock certificate or a savings account passbook, the first assignee who receives delivery of the tangible token prevails over subsequent assignees. [p. 250]

49. If an obligee has a substantial interest in having an obligor perform the acts required by a contract, these duties cannot be transferred. This restriction includes obligations under the following types of contracts:
a. Personal service contracts calling for the exercise of personal skills, discretion, or expertise

b. Contracts whose performance would materially vary if the obligor's duties were delegated [p. 251]
50. Where there has been a delegation of duties, the liability of the delegatee is determined by the following rules:
a. Assumption of Duties. Where a valid delegation of duties contains the term assumption or other similar language, there is an assumption of duties by the delegatee. Here, the obligee can sue the delegatee and recover damages from the delegatee for nonperformance or negligent performance by the delegatee.
b. Declaration of Duties. Where there is a valid delegation of duties but the delegatee has not assumed the duties under a contract, the delegation is called a declaration of duties. Here, the delegatee is not liable to the oblige for nonperformance or negligent performance and the obligee cannot recover damages from the delegatee. [p. 251]

51. Intended Beneficiary – When parties enter into a contract, they can agree that the performance of one of the parties should be rendered to or directly benefit a third party. Under such circumstances, the third party is called an intended third-party beneficiary. An intended third-party beneficiary can enforce the contract against the party who promised to render performance.
Incidental Beneficiary – In many instances, the parties to a contract unintentionally benefit a third party when a contract is performed. In such situations, the third party is referred to as an incidental beneficiary. An incidental beneficiary has no rights to enforce or sue under other people's contracts. [p. 252, 254]

52. Personal Satisfaction Test – The personal satisfaction test is a subjective test that applies if the performance involves personal taste and comfort (e.g., contracts for interior decorating, contracts for tailoring clothes). The only requirement is that the person given the right to reject the contract acts in good faith.
Reasonable Person Test – The reasonable person test is an objective test that is used to judge contracts involving mechanical fitness and most commercial contracts. Most contracts that require the work to meet the satisfaction of a third person (e.g., engineer, architect) are judged by this standard. [p. 256]

53. The different methods for discharging a contract by mutual agreement are:
a. Mutual Rescission – If a contract is wholly or partially executory on both sides, the parties can agree to rescind (i.e., cancel) the contract. Mutual rescission requires parties to enter into a second agreement that expressly terminates the first one.
b. Substituted Contract – The parties to a contract may enter into a new contract that revokes and discharges an existing contract. The new contract is called a substituted contract.
c. Novation – A novation agreement (commonly called novation) substitutes a third party for one of the original contracting parties. The new substituted party is obligated to perform a contract.
d. Accord and Satisfaction – The parties to a contract may agree to settle a contract dispute by an accord and satisfaction. The agreement whereby the parties agree to accept something different in satisfaction of the original contract is called an accord. The performance of an accord is called a satisfaction. [p. 258]

54. Under the following circumstances, the nonperformance of contractual duties is excused:
a. The death or incapacity of the promisor prior to the performance of a personal service contract
b. The destruction of the subject matter of a contract prior to performance
c. A supervening illegality that makes performance of the contract illegal [p. 259]

55. Every state has a statute of limitations that applies to contract actions. Under these statutes, if an aggrieved party does not bring suit for breach of contract during a designated period after a breach of contract has occurred, he losses the right to sue. Time periods vary from state to state. The usual period for bringing a lawsuit for breach of contract is one to five years. [p. 259]

16 | REMEDIES FOR BREACH OF TRADITIONAL AND E-CONTRACTS

Chapter Overview

This chapter focuses on the differences between the types of performance in a contract and the effects of each. It clarifies the types of legal damages and equitable remedies that are available. The torts associated with contracts and the significance of punitive damages are explained.

Objectives

Upon completion of the exercises in this chapter, you should be able to:
1. Describe complete, substantial, and inferior performance of contractual duties.
2. Describe compensatory, consequential, and nominal damages awarded for the breach of traditional and e-contracts.
3. Explain rescission and restitution.
4. Define the equitable remedies of specific performance, reformation, and injunction.
5. Describe torts associated with contracts.

Practical Application

You should be able to determine whether a minor or material breach has occurred in a contract and what legal or equitable remedies may be available for the breach. You will have a better grasp of the requirements for seeking the equitable remedies of specific performance, injunction, and reformation. You will be familiar with the torts that can accompany contracts and whether punitive damages may be an option.

Helpful Hints

It is important that you learn the terminology associated with this chapter in order to know which types of remedies apply to certain situations. Some mnemonics for the equitable remedies of injunction as well as specific performance have been provided to assist you in committing to memory what is required for these equitable remedies. The material will be easier to grasp if you list and learn the legal remedies separately from the equitable remedies.

Study Tips

Remedies for Breach of Contract

There are three levels of performance of a contract, complete, substantial, and inferior. Various remedies at law, as well as equitable remedies, may be available to the nonbreaching party.

Performance and Breach

Each contracting party owes an absolute duty to perform under the contract, unless that duty has been discharged or excused.

Complete Performance. This type of performance happens when a party to a contract gives performance exactly as outlined in the party's contract. A contract that is fully performed is said to be executed. A contracting party's unconditional and absolute offer to perform will also discharge a party's obligations under the contract.

Substantial Performance: Minor Breach. This type of performance happens when a party to a contract gives performance that only has a little bit left to do before it will be considered completely performed. The nonbreaching party has several options available to him or her:
- He can convince the breaching party to lift the performance so that it completes the contract.
- He may deduct the costs to repair the defect from the contract price and give the remaining amount under the contract to the breaching party.
- If the breaching party has been paid, the innocent party may sue the breaching party to recover the cost of repair.

Inferior Performance: Material Breach. A material breach happens when a party gives inferior performance of his or her contractual obligations so that it destroys or impairs the purpose of the contract. The courts will examine each case individually to determine materiality of the breach.
- A material breach releases the nonbreaching party from further performance.
- The nonbreaching party may rescind the contract and seek restitution of any monies paid.
- The nonbreaching party can sue for breach of contract and ask for damages.

Anticipatory Breach. Anticipatory repudiation happens when one party lets the other party know in advance that he or she will not perform, or may not perform, the contractual duties when they come due. The repudiator may expressly state this or his or her conduct may show it.
- The nonbreaching party's obligations are discharged immediately.
- The nonbreaching party may sue for breach of contract immediately without waiting for performance to become due.

Monetary Damages

Monetary damages are available for either minor or material breaches of contract. The types of monetary damages include compensatory, consequential, liquidated, and nominal damages.

Compensatory Damages. These damages to compensate a nonbreaching party for the loss of the bargain. These were designed to "make the person whole again." The court determines how much will be awarded based upon the type of contract involved.
- *Sale of a Good.* The measure of compensatory damages for a breach of sales contract is the difference between the contract price and the market price at the time and place of delivery of the goods.
- *Construction Contract.* The amount of compensatory damages available for breach depends upon the status of the construction project itself. In other words, it depends on the stage of completion that the project is in when the breach happens. The contractor may recover the profits that he or she might have made on the contract if the owner breaches before the construction begins.

- *Employment Contract.* Recovery based on an employer breaching equals lost wages or salary as compensatory damages. If the employee breaches, the employer can recover the costs of hiring a new employee plus any salary increase to pay the replacement.

Mitigation of Damages. The law places a duty on the nonbreaching party to avoid and reduce the resulting damages, known as mitigating the damages. A party's duty of mitigation will be based on the type of contract involved.

Consequential Damages. These types of damages are foreseeable damages that happen because of circumstances not related to the contract itself. In order to recover consequential damages, the breaching party must be aware or have reason to know that the breach will cause special damages to the other party.

Liquidated Damages. Sometimes the parties to a contract agree in advance as to the amount of damages that will be payable in the event of a breach, known as liquidated damages.
- It must be shown that
    - the actual damages are difficult or impracticable to determine and
    - the liquidated amount must be reasonable in the circumstances.
- This is an exclusive remedy regardless of what the actual damages later are assessed as being.
- *A liquidated damages clause as a penalty.* If the actual damages are clearly able to be determined in advance and if the liquidated damages are unconscionable or excessive.
    - When a liquidated damages clause is viewed as a penalty, it is unenforceable.

Nominal Damages. These damages are awarded based on principle and are usually a very small amount. No real financial loss is suffered when a party brings a suit based upon principle.

Enforcement of Remedies. Once a judgment has been rendered, an attempt to collect it is made. If the breaching party fails to satisfy the judgment, the court may issue two types of writs:
- Writ of Attachment. The writ orders the sheriff to seize the breaching party's property that he or she has in his or her possession and to sell the property to satisfy the judgment. Not all property can be sold, depending on the applicable state exemptions.
- Writ of Garnishment. Wages, bank accounts, and other property owned by the breaching party that is being handled by a third party must be paid to the non-breaching party. There are federal and state laws limiting the amount of wages or salary that can be garnished.

Rescission and Restitution

Rescission is an action to undo a contract where there has been a material breach of contract due to fraud, duress, undue influence, or mistake. The parties must make restitution of the consideration they received under the contract if they are going to rescind it. Restitution requires that they must return the goods, property, money, or other consideration that was received from the other property. Notice of the rescission is required.

Equitable Remedies

If the remedy at law is not adequate, then the equitable remedies of specific performance, reformation, and injunction may be available so that an injustice may be prevented.

Specific Performance. This is a discretionary remedy the courts may award if the subject matter is unique and a service contract is not involved.

Reformation. This is an equitable remedy that allows the court to rewrite the parties' contract to reflect their true intentions.

Injunction. An injunction is an equitable remedy that prohibits a person from doing a certain act.

Torts Associated with Contracts

If a party demonstrates that a contract-related tort has occurred, tort damages will also be available to a party. These include compensation for pain and suffering, emotional damages, possible punitive damages, and personal injury. The torts in this area include interference with contractual relations and breach of implied covenant of good faith and fair dealing.

- **Punitive Damages.** These are usually not recoverable for breach of contract. However, if certain tortuous conduct such as fraud or intentional conduct is associated with the nonperformance of a contract, punitive damages in addition to actual damages may be awarded to punish the defendant.

Intentional Interference with Contractual Relations. This tort occurs when a third party induces a contracting party to breach the contract with another party.

- A third party will not be held to have induced a breach if the breach already existed between the original parties.

Breach of Implied Covenant of Good Faith and Fair Dealing. This tort, also known as the tort of bad faith, is implied in certain types of contracts whereby the parties are held to act in "good faith" and deal fairly in also aspects in obtaining the contract's objective.

Refresh Your Memory

The following exercise will give you the opportunity to test your memory of the principles given in this chapter. Read the question twice and place your answer in the blank provided. Review the chapter material for any question that you are unable to answer or remember.

1. _____ is a situation in which a party to a contract renders performance exactly as required by the contract.

2. Poole Contractors makes a contract with Delta Resources to pay $50,000 for the supply of 500 truckloads of sand within next week. Delta Resources delivers the sand in two days after the contract was made. Poole Contractors pays the $50,000 promised in the contract. This is an instance of _____.

3. A(n) _____ breach of a contract occurs when a party renders inferior performance of his or her contractual obligations.

4. _____ occurs when one contracting party informs the other that he or she will not perform his or her contractual duties when due.

5. _____ place the nonbreaching party in the same position as if the contract had been fully performed.

6. _____ damages are awarded when the nonbreaching party sues the breaching party even though no financial loss has resulted from the breach.

7. Parties to a contract agree in advance to pay _____ damages if the contract is breached.

8. _____ is an action to undo a contract.

9. _____ is a term that denotes the return of goods or property received from the other party to undo a contract.

10. A _____ is an order of the court that enables a government officer to seize property of the breaching party and sell it at auction to satisfy a judgment.

11. A _____ is an order of the court that orders that wages, bank accounts, or other property of the breaching party held by third persons be paid to the nonbreaching party to satisfy a judgment.

12. An award of _____ orders the breaching party to perform the acts promised in a contract.

13. _____ refers to an equitable doctrine that permits the court to rewrite a contract to express the parties' true intentions.

14. A court order that prohibits a person from doing a certain act is termed as a(n) _____.

15. Kimberly Inc., a jewelry store, and JKCent, a retailer, draft a contract that permits JKCent to retail Kimberly's jewelry in its stores. However, the parties discover a minor clerical error six months into the contract and the court rewrites their contract. This is an instance of _____.

Critical Thought Exercise.

The Cheersville Fire Department (CFD) entered into a written contract on 2-17-07 with American Emergency Truck Co. (AET) for the purchase of a $290,000.00 ladder/pump truck. The contract set forth a delivery date of 9-1-07, as insisted upon by CFD. According to CFD Chief Sam Miller, their 1932 pumper truck was not going to last beyond that date and time was of the essence. On 8-1-07, the CFD truck died and was not able to be repaired. The Cheersville Town Council voted to wait until the new truck arrived on September 1, 2007, instead or renting another old truck from Friendsville Fire District. On 8-15-07, AET notified CFD that the truck would not be ready for delivery until 10-1-07. The Town Council again decided to wait without renting another truck. Cheersville notified AET that its truck was out of service and the new truck was desperately needed by 9-1-07. On 9-15-07, a major fire damaged the Cheersville School. The fire started in the kitchen and could have easily been controlled with normal fire fighting equipment. The damage to the school was estimated to be approximately $2,800,000.

AET denies any liability. The truck was delivered by AET on 10-5-07. You are on the Cheersville Town Council and have been assigned the task of drafting a memorandum for the council detailing the following: (1) Whether Cheersville has grounds to sue American Emergency Truck; (2) What damages would be recoverable from AET; and (3) What defenses AET may assert.

Please compose your answer to the Critical Thinking Exercise using a separate sheet of paper or your computer word processing program.

Practice Quiz

True/False

16. _____ Strict performance by a party discharges that party's duties under the contract.

17. _____ Tender of performance discharges a party's contractual obligations.

18. _____ Minor breach occurs when a party renders substantial performance of his or her contractual duties.

19. _____ Material breach of a contract occurs when a party renders considerable performance of his or her contractual obligations.

20. _____ A nonbreaching party cannot rescind the contract in the event of a material breach.

21. _____ In an anticipatory breach, the nonbreaching party does not have the right to sue the breaching party until performance is due.

22. _____ Monetary damages can be recovered only for material breach.

23. _____ If the employee breaches the contract, the employer can recover the costs to hire a new employee.

24. _____ Consequential damages are unforeseeable damages.

25. _____ Nominal damages are awarded when no financial loss resulted from the breach.

26. _____ Mitigation of damages is a nonbreaching party's legal duty toward avoiding or reducing damages caused by a breach of contract.

27. _____ Parties to a contract agree upon liquidated damages after the contract has been breached.

28. _____ Restitution is an action to undo a contract.

29. _____ Writ of garnishment is an order of the court that enables a government officer to seize property of the breaching party and sell it at auction to satisfy a judgment.

30. _____ Intentional interference with contractual relations arises when a third party induces a contracting party to breach the contract with another party.

Multiple Choice

31. Which of the following statements is a true of a breach of contract?

A. Strict performance by a party discharges that party's duties under the contract.
B. Inferior performance constitutes a minor breach of contract.
C. Substantial performance constitutes a material breach.
D. The most common remedy for a breach of contract is an award of equitable remedies.

32. Which of the following terms refers to an unconditional and absolute offer by a contracting party to perform his or her obligations under a contract?

A. injunction
B. writ of garnishment
C. tender of performance
D. writ of attachment

33. Which of the following statements is true of discharge of contracts?

A. Anticipatory breach discharges the breaching party's obligations to the contract.
B. Substantial performance is sufficient to discharge a contract.
C. Tender of performance discharges a party's contractual obligations.
D. Tender is a conditional offer by contracting party to perform his or her obligations under the contract.

34. When does a minor breach occur?

A. when a party rescinds the contract before actual work on the contract has commenced
B. when a party renders substantial performance of his or her contractual duties
C. when the party who is being offered goods or services rescinds the contract
D. when the party who is offering goods or services rescinds the contract

35. Which of the following constitutes material breach?

A. inferior performance
B. substantial performance
C. anticipatory repudiation
D. rescission without notification

36. When a party commits an anticipatory breach, the nonbreaching party _____.

A. must wait until the performance was due before suing
B. is immediately discharged from his or her own duties
C. cannot seek damages because he or she received advance notice of the breach
D. loses his or her right to sue after the due-date for performance is reached

37. Which of the following terms refers to a nonbreaching party's legal duty to avoid or reduce damages caused by a breach of contract?

A. tender of performance
B. mitigation of damages
C. liquidation of damages
D. disclaimer of consequential damages

38. Which of the following statements is true of mitigation of damages?

A. The breaching party must make efforts to mitigate damages resulting from the breach of contract.
B. If an employer breaches an employment contract, he or she owes a duty to mitigate damages by trying to find substitute employment for the employee.
C. The extent of mitigation of damages required is common to all kinds of contracts.
D. If an employer breaches a contract, the employee is only required to accept comparable employment.

39. Which of the following is used in case of a breach of contract that cannot be adequately compensated through a legal remedy?

A. mitigation of damages
B. liquidation of damages
C. equitable remedies
D. tort remedies

40. Which of the following torts arises when a third party induces a contracting party to breach the contract with another party?

A. intentional interference with contractual relations
B. breach of the covenant of good faith and fair dealing
C. tort of bad faith
D. malicious breach of contractual relations

Short Answer

41. Where there has been a material breach of contract, what may the nonbreaching party do?

_____

42. What is meant when someone says that he has substantially performed under a contract?

_____

43. What two remedies restore the parties to the position they held before the contract?

_____

44. What is the measure of compensatory damages for a breach of contract involving the sale of goods?

_____

45. What can an employee whose employer has breached an employment contract recover in damages?

_____

46. If there has been inferior performance of a contract, what may the nonbreaching party seek in a court of law?

_____

47. If the Soft Sponge Corporation has breached its contract with its employee Barbara, what is Barbara required to do in terms of mitigating her damages and any employment that is offered to her?

_____

48. What type of law applies when determining the damages available for a breach of a sales contract involving goods?

_____

49. If Shawna wishes to rescind her contract with Elmer, what is she required to do?

_____

50. If Bob demonstrates a contract-related tort has occurred, what types of tort damages may he recover?

_____

51. Give a purpose for an equitable remedy.

_____

52. If an owner breaches a construction contract, what type of damages may the contractor recover?

_____

53. What factors do the courts consider when viewing whether or not an employee has mitigated his or her damages when seeking substitute, comparable employment after an employer has breached an employment contract?

_____

54. In order to be liable for consequential damages, what must be shown about the breaching party?

_____

55. What is required under the implied covenant of good faith and fair dealing?

_____

Answers to Refresh Your Memory

1. Strict performance [p. 265]
2. strict performance [p. 265]
3. material [p. 266]
4. Anticipatory repudiation [p. 269]
5. Compensatory damages [p. 269]
6. Nominal [p. 271]
7. liquidated [p. 270]
8. Rescission [p. 274]
9. Restitution [p. 274]
10. writ of attachment [p. 274]
11. writ of garnishment [p. 274]
12. specific performance [p. 274]
13. Reformation [p. 276]
14. injunction [p. 276]
15. reformation [p. 276]

Critical Thought Exercise Model Answer

Before either party to a contract has a duty to perform, one of the parties may make an assertion or do an act that indicates they will not perform their obligations under the contract at a future time. This is called an anticipatory repudiation of the contract and is treated as a material breach. The nonbreaching party may immediately bring an action for damages, wait to see if the breaching party changes their mind, or may seek specific performance by the breaching party. When AET notifies CFD that it will not be able to deliver the truck as promised, CFD must decide what course of action it will take. The damages that may be sought would be any increase in cost that CFD has to pay to obtain the truck from another seller plus any consequential or incidental damages. In this situation, CFD needs the truck more than it needs money damages. The CFD had a duty to protect the citizens of Cheersville and another truck is not readily obtainable. The truck that was being built for CFD by AET was somewhat unique and failure to perform the contract would create great hardship for CFD. However, CFD had to make an election at the time of the breach, which took place on 8-15-07. Because CFD failed to elect to pursue specific performance, they will be left with an action for damages. Specific performance is not available at this late point in time as the truck was actually delivered on 10-5-07. CFD will seek consequential damages for the damage caused to the Cheersville School. AET will be liable for those damages if they were reasonably foreseeable at the time of the breach or fire occurred. CFD had previously notified AET that their truck was old and would not last in service beyond 9-1-07. CFD again told AET of the urgency when the truck was taken out of service on 8-1-07. Knowing the need for the truck and the fact that CFD was without a truck after 8-1-07, AET continued to promise to perform the contract. The damages to the school were probably foreseeable as they are the type of damages that would occur if CFD was without a truck.

AET will have two possible defenses to the contract. The most obvious is that Cheersville failed to fulfill its duty of mitigation of damages. This rule requires the plaintiff to have done whatever was reasonable to minimize the damages caused by the defendant. CFD failed to take any action to mitigate their damages. The city council decided to not rent a replacement truck even after their only truck was taken out of service. Because they failed to mitigate their damages, Cheersville will have their damages reduced by those amounts they could have prevented. In this case, the facts state that the damages to the school could have been minimized if a temporary replacement truck had been obtained. A rental was available from Friendsville and Cheersville failed to mitigate their damages by renting the truck. The second defense that AET may assert is that Cheersville agreed to a modification of the contract when they did not pursue any action when notified of the delay in the delivery date. This defense is weak because Cheersville notified AET that it desperately needed the truck by the original contract date of 9-1-07. Cheersville did nothing that could be deemed as acquiescence in the request by AET to extend the delivery date. Therefore, no modification of the original agreement was ever accomplished. Cheersville will prevail in their breach of contract suit, but the amount of damages will be relatively small due to Cheersville's failure to mitigate damages.

Answers to Practice Quiz

True/False

16. True. Complete (or strict) performance by a party discharges that party's duties under the contract. [p. 265]

17.True. Tender of performance, or tender, also discharges a party's contractual obligations. [p.265]

18. True. A minor breach is a breach that occurs when a party renders substantial performance of his or her contractual duties. [p. 265]

19. False. A material breach of a contract occurs when a party renders inferior performance of his or her contractual obligations that impairs or destroys the essence of the contract. [p. 266]

20. False. Where there has been a material breach of contract, the nonbreaching party may rescind the contract and seek restitution of any compensation paid under the contract to the breaching party. [p. 266]

21. False. In an anticipatory breach (or anticipatory repudiation) the nonbreaching party also has the right to sue the repudiating party when the anticipatory breach occurs; there is no need to wait until performance is due. [p. 269]

22. False. Where there has been a breach of a contract, the nonbreaching party may recover monetary damages from a breaching party. [p. 269]

23. True. If the employee breaches the contract, the employer can recover the costs to hire a new employee plus any increase in salary paid to the replacement. [p. 270]

24. False. Consequential damages are foreseeable damages that arise from circumstances outside a contract. [p. 270]

25. True. Nominal damages are awarded when the non–breaching party sues the breaching party even though no financial loss has resulted from the breach. [p. 271]

26. True. Mitigation of damages is a nonbreaching party's legal duty to avoid or reduce damages caused by a breach of contract. [p. 271]

27. False. Under certain circumstances, the parties to a contract may agree in advance to the amount of damages payable upon a breach of contract. These damages are called liquidated damages. [p. 272]

28. False. Restitution is the return of goods or property received from the other party to rescind a contract. [p. 274]

29. False. A writ of garnishment orders that wages, bank accounts, or other property of the breaching party that is in the hands of third parties be paid over to the nonbreaching party to satisfy the judgment. [p. 274]

30. True. Intentional interference with contractual relations usually arises when a third party induces a contracting party to breach a contract with another party. [p. 277]

Multiple Choice

31. A. Answer A is the correct answer. Complete (or strict) performance by a party discharges that party's duties under the contract. [p. 265]

32. C. Answer C is the correct answer. Tender of performance, is an unconditional and absolute offer by a contracting party to perform his or her obligations under the contract. [p. 265]

33. C. Answer C is correct, as tender of performance, or tender, discharges a party's contractual obligations. [p. 265]

34. B. Answer B is correct, minor breach is a breach that occurs when a party renders substantial performance of his or her contractual duties. [p. 265]

35. A. Answer A is correct a material breach of a contract occurs when a party renders inferior performance of his or her contractual obligations that impairs or destroys the essence of the contract. [p. 266]

36. B. Answer B is correct,. Where there is an anticipatory repudiation, the nonbreaching party's obligations under the contract are discharged immediately. [p. 269]

37. B. Answer B is correct,. Mitigation of damages refers to a nonbreaching party's legal duty to avoid or reduce damages caused by a breach of contract. [p. 271]

38. D. Answer D is correct. If an employer breaches an employment contract, the employee owes a duty to mitigate damages by trying to find substitute employment. The employee is only required to accept comparable employment. [p. 271]

39. C. Answer C is correct. Equitable remedies are available if there has been a breach of contract that cannot be adequately compensated through a legal remedy. [p. 274]

40. A. Answer A is correct, intentional interference with contractual relations is a tort that arises when a third party induces a contracting party to breach the contract with another party. [p. 277]

Short Answer

41. The nonbreaching party may rescind the contract and seek restitution of any compensation paid under the contract to the breaching party. [p. 274]

42. Contract performance that deviates only slightly from complete performance. [p. 265-266]

43. Rescission, which means to undo a contract, and restitution, which is the return of goods, property, money, or other consideration received from the other party to a contract. [p. 274]

44. The difference between the contract price and the market price. [p. 269]

45. Lost wages or salary as compensatory damages. [p. 270]

46. The nonbreaching party may either (1) rescind the contract and recover restitution or (2) affirm the contract and recover damages. [p. 266]

47. She is required to seek comparable employment. [p. 271]

48. The UCC (Uniform Commercial Code) applies when determining damages for a breach of a sales contract involving goods. [p. 269]

49. Shawna must give Elmer notice. [p. 274]

50. Bob may recover compensation for personal injury, pain and suffering, emotional distress and possibly punitive damages. [p. 277]

51. To prevent unjust enrichment. [p. 274]

52. The contractor may recover profits. [p. 270]

53. The courts consider such things as compensation, rank, status, job description, and geographical location when determining the comparability of jobs. [p. 271]

54. The breaching party must know or have reason to know that the breach will cause special damages to the other party in order to be liable for consequential damages. [p. 270]

55. The parties are held to the express terms of the contract and are required to act in "good faith" and to deal fairly in all aspects of the contract. [p. 277]

17 | E-COMMERCE AND DIGITAL LAW

Chapter Overview

This chapter explores e-commerce by giving a thorough explanation of the Internet, the World Wide Web, electronic mail, and domain names. Other topics that are analyzed are the domain name Anticybersquatting Act, e-contracts and their writing and signature requirements, e-licensing, licensing, and breach of license agreements. The remedies available to the licensor and licensee for the breach of a licensing agreement under UCITA are also assessed.

Objectives

Upon completion of the exercises in this chapter, you should be able to:
1. Describe the laws that apply to e-mail contracts, e-commerce, and Web contracts.
2. Describe e-licensing and the provisions of the Uniform Computer Information Transactions Act (UCITA).
3. Describe the provisions of the federal Electronic Signatures in Global and National Commerce Act (E-Sign Act)
4. Describe laws that protect privacy in cyberspace.
5. Define Internet domain names and describe how domain names are registered and protected.

Practical Application

You should be comfortable enough with the terminology to apply the concepts associated with e-contracts and licensing to real life situations involving both online and traditional ways of accomplishing these tasks.

Helpful Hints

The best approach to studying this chapter is to become familiar with the terminology, and the application of the concepts will follow. For some students, the technology- based vocabulary will be relatively easy due to having been exposed to the use of a computer. However, for those who are just beginning their exposure to computers, this chapter will provide you with a good start so that you will be able to apply the various electronic requirements to contracts and licensing.

Study Tips

Each section follows the text, and builds upon one another so that you may get the big picture when applying the terminology and laws to the primary areas of focus of contracts and licensing. When studying, it will help you to have someone ask you the questions under each heading to determine what you have learned.

Internet Law and E-Commerce

Through e-commerce, consumers and businesses can purchase almost any good or service over the internet from websites and registered domain names. Licensing agreements for information and software are routinely made electronically. Federal and state laws have sought to modify old laws or write new laws to fit these new methods of doing business.

The Internet

The Internet or the Net is a collection of millions of computers that provide a network of electronic connections between computers.

The World Wide Web. The World Wide Web consists of millions of computers that support a standard set of rules for the exchange of information called Hypertext Transfer Protocol (HTTP). Web-based documents are formatted using common code language such as Java and Hypertext Markup Language.
*   Web Sites. A Web site is composed of electronic documents known as Web pages. Web sites with their own individual unique online addresses and pages are stored on servers all around the world which are operated by Internet Service Providers (ISPs). Individuals may view these sites and pages by using web browsers. These pages contain a variety of multimedia content including text images, video, sound, and animation

E-mail and Websites

Electronic mail, or e-mail, is an instantaneous means of communication in the form of electronic writing from one individual to another. Each individual has his or her own unique Web address. In some instances, e-mail has replaced some paper and telephone correspondence.

CAN-SPAM Act. The Controlling the Assault of Non-Solicited Pornography and Marketing Act, enacted by Congress in 2003, actually approves businesses to use spam so long as they do not lie. It does not allow victims to bring civil actions against spammers. The act
*   prohibits spammers from using falsified headers in e-mail messages, including the originating domain name and e-mail address,
*   prohibits deceptive subject lines that mislead a recipient of the contents or subject matter of the message,
*   requires that recipients of spam be given the opportunity to opt out and not have the spammer send e-mail to the recipient's address, and
*   requires spammers who send sexually oriented e-mail to properly label it as such.

Internet Service Provider (ISP). Internet service providers provide access to the internet to consumers and businesses. They provide e-mail accounts, Internet access, storage on the Internet, and a variety of access devices and services. Web-hosting services allow users to create their own websites and provide storage space for website users.
*   Under the federal Communications Decency Act of 1996, providers are not considered to be the publisher or speaker of information provided by another content provider, so are generally not responsible for the content transmitted over their networks by users and websites.

Electronic Communications Privacy Act (ECPA). This act makes it a crime to intercept an electronic communication at the point of transmission, while in transit, when stored by a router or server, or after receipt by the intended recipient.
*   Electronic communications include transfers of signals, writings, images, sounds, data or intelligence of any nature.
*   The act allows some accesses that do not violate its provisions:

      o   The provider of the electronic communication service, such as an employer, may access stored e-mail.

      o   Government and law enforcement entities that are investigating suspected illegal activity pursuant to a valid warrant may access electronic communications.

- The act provides criminal penalties and access to civil suits for damages.

Domain Names

A domain name is a unique name that identifies the Web site of an individual or company. Domain names can be obtained by choosing a name that has not been chosen and registering it with a database like "Whois" or Network Solutions Inc. Registration requires completion of a registration form and a minimal payment per year. See pages 266 of your text for the most commonly used top-level extensions for domain names.

Anticybersquatting Consumer Protection Act (ACPA). This act was promulgated in 1999 to target cybersquatters who register Internet domain names of famous companies and people to hold them hostage by demanding payments of ransom from the famous person or company.

- The act requires that two criteria be met:
  - o   That the name must be famous and
    - ▪   Trademarked names of famous actors, actresses, singers, and stars apply.
  - o   That the domain name must have been registered in bad faith.
    - ▪   The courts may look at the extent to which the domain name resembles the holder's name or famous person's name, whether goods or services are sold under the name, the holder's offer to sell or transfer the name, and whether the holder has obtained multiple Internet domain names of famous individuals.
- The act has remedies available to plaintiffs
  - o   The court may issue a cease-and-desist order as well as an injunction.
  - o   A plaintiff may opt for statutory damages between $1,000 and $300,000 in lieu of proving damages.

E-Contracts

E-contracts require all of the same elements necessary to form a regular contract. Individuals can prove the existence of these contracts by printing out the e-mail or Web contract and its prior e-mail or Web negotiations.

Electronic Signature in Global and National Commerce Act (E-SIGN Act). This act, enacted in 2000, seeks to put electronic contracts on par with traditional paper contracts.

- **Writing Requirement of Statute of Frauds Met.** The act recognizes electronic contracts as meeting the writing requirement of the Statute of Frauds. The act requires that
  - o   consumers must consent to receiving electronic records and contracts,
  - o   a consumer must be able to show that they have access to electronic records in order to have met the "receiving electronic records" requirement, and
  - o   businesses must tell consumers that they have the right to receive hard-copy documents of their transaction.
- **E-Signatures Recognized as Valid.** The act gives an electronic signature the same effect as a pen-inscribed signature on paper. Electronic signatures can be verified in three ways:
  - o   By something the signatory knows, such as a secret password, pet's name, etc.

o By something a person has, such as a smart card, which looks like a credit card and stores personal information.
o By biometrics, which uses a device that digitally recognizes fingerprints or the retina or iris of the eye.

E-Licensing

Because of the difficulties associated with forming contracts over the Internet, as well as their enforcement, the Uniform Computer Information Transaction Act was created.

Uniform Computer Information Transaction Act (UCITA). This act provides an exhaustive set of uniform rules that sets the standard for performance and enforcement of computer information transactions. This act creates contract law for the licensing of information technology rights. For purposes of this act, a computer information transaction is an agreement to create, transfer, or license computer information or informational rights. [UCITA Sec.102 (a)(11)]. A state makes UCITA law by way of a state statute. Further, federal law preempts UCITA.

Licensing. Licensing is an agreement with owners of intellectual property and information rights to transfer limited rights in the property or information to parties for specified purposes and limited duration is a license.
- Licensor. The one who owns the intellectual property or information rights and obligates him- or herself to transfer rights in the property or information to the licensee.
- Licensee. The party who is given limited rights in or access to the intellectual property of information rights.
- Exclusive license. A license for a specified duration in which the licensor will not grant to any other person rights in the same information.

Refresh Your Memory

The following exercise will give you the opportunity to test your memory of the principles given in this chapter. Read the question twice and place your answer in the blank provided. Review the chapter material for any question that you are unable to answer or remember.

1. The computers that constitute the World Wide Web use a standard set of rules known as _____ for the exchange of information.

2. The CAN-SPAM Act _____.

3. _____ are companies that provide consumers and businesses with access to the Internet.

4. The _____ recognizes electronic contracts as meeting the writing requirement of the Statute of Frauds for most contracts.

5. Under the E-SIGN Act, an e-signature can be verified by using _____.

6. A(n) _____ is any computer system that has been established by a seller to accept orders.

7. The _____ establishes a uniform and comprehensive set of rules that govern the creation, performance, and enforcement for computer information transactions.

8. A(n) _____ refers to a contract that transfers limited rights in intellectual property and informational rights.

9. A(n) _____ is an owner of intellectual property or informational rights who transfers rights in the property or information to another party.

10. A(n) _____ refers to a party who is granted limited rights in or access to intellectual property or informational rights owned by another party.

11. A(n) _____ is a contract by which the owner of software or a digital application grants limited rights to the owner of a computer or digital device to use the software or digital application for a limited period and under specified conditions.

12. A(n) _____ is a detailed and comprehensive written agreement between a licensor and a licensee that sets forth the express terms of their agreement.

13. The _____ is a federal statute that makes it a crime to intercept an electronic communication at the point of transmission, while in transit, when stored by a router or server or after receipt by intended recipient.

14. A(n) _____ uniquely identifies an individual's or company's website.

15. _____ is the most widely used domain extension in the world, and is preferred by businesses.

Critical Thought Exercise

The James Co. of New York has been in the business of retail chocolate and confection sales since 1923. As the Internet has developed, James has started doing business by e-mail. Mrs. Dubyah communicates with James by numerous e-mails, negotiating the sale of 300 one-pound chocolate Easter eggs. They agree that the price will be $18 per egg and they will be shipped for arrival in Maryland 10 days before Easter. James produces the eggs and ships them in a timely manner. At the last minute, Mrs. Dubyah decides to order her Easter gifts from another company. When the shipment arrives in Maryland, Mrs. Dubyah wants to reject the shipment and order her eggs from a friend in Oklahoma. As the business secretary for Mrs. Dubyah, you are responsible for advising Mrs. Dubyah on business matters and executing her contracts as instructed.

Write a brief memorandum to Mrs. Dubyah, explaining to her your position on whether she can rely upon the Statute of Frauds as a defense to a damages claim by James Co. and whether the shipment should be accepted.

Please compose your answer to the Critical Thinking Exercise using a separate sheet of paper or your computer word processing program.

Practice Quiz

True/False

16. _____ The UCITA provides rules for contracts involving computer information transactions and software and information licenses.

17. _____ The World Wide Web consists of computers that support a standard set of rules for the exchange of information, called Hypertext Transfer Protocol.

18. _____ Each website has a unique online address.

19. _____ E-mail contracts are enforceable even if they don't meet traditional contract requirements.

20. _____ The CAN-SPAM Act does not can spam but instead approves businesses to use spam as long as they do not lie.

21. _____ ISPs provide e-mail accounts to users, Internet access, and storage on the Internet.

22. _____ The E-SIGN Act is a not a federal statute and state legislatures are required to adopt it in order for it to become state law.

23. _____ Counteroffers are not effective against electronic agents.

24. _____ The UCITA does not become law until a state's legislature enacts it as a state statute.

25. _____ The UCITA makes it illegal to access another person's stored e-mail.

26. _____ The ECPA provides that stored electronic communications may not be accessed by the party or entity providing the electronic communication service.

27. _____ A network extension is a unique name that identifies an individual's or company's website.

28. _____ The .biz extension is used for large-business and corporate websites.

29. _____ Registering a domain name of another party's trademarked name or famous person's name in bad faith is called cybersquatting

30. _____ The ACPA is federal statute that permits trademark owners and famous persons to recover domain names that use their names where the domain name has been registered by another person or business in bad faith.

Multiple Choice

31. Which of the following is true of the World Wide Web?

A. Only businesses—not individuals—can have their own websites.
B. Individuals need not register with a service provider to access the web.
C. A website can have several online addresses.
D. Each website must have a unique online address.

32. Which of the following acts regulates spam e-mail on the Internet?

A. Anticybersquatting Consumer Protection Act
B. Controlling the Assault of Non-Solicited Pornography and Marketing Act
C. Communications Decency Act
D. Uniform Computer Information Transactions Act

33. What does the Communications Decency Act of 1996 provide?

A. Businesses can send spam e-mails, as long as they don't lie.
B. ISPs are not liable for the content transmitted over their networks by e-mail users and websites.
C. Businesses are liable for invading the right to privacy if they send unsolicited e-mails.
D. The number of servers an ISP can access in a geographical location is limited.

34. Jessica wants to buy a laptop from the Tenn Computers website. Before confirming the purchase, the website asks her to provide biometric identification using an electronic scanner. This is an example of _____.

A. e-licensing
B. an e-signature
C. an exclusive license
D. cybersquatting

35. Which of the following is true of the UCITA?

A. It establishes a uniform set of rules that prohibit all forms of cybersquatting.
B. It defines which technologies should be used to create a legally binding signature in cyberspace.
C. It aims at eliminating all domain names registered in bad faith.
D. It governs the creation, performance, and enforcement for computer information transactions.

36. An exclusive license is defined as _____.

A. a license that grants access to exclusive information for a limited period
B. a license that restricts the licensee to some information only
C. a license that is granted to only one party for a specific period
D. a license that grants licensees only a few rights in intellectual property

37. The ECPA is a federal statute that _____.

A. establishes that businesses are allowed send spam e-mails, as long as they do not lie
B. rules that ISPs are not liable for the content transmitted over their networks by e-mail users and websites
C. establishes that an e-signature is as effective as a pen-and-paper signature
D. makes it a crime to intercept an electronic communication at the point of transmission.

38. Which of the following entities does the ECPA permit to access stored electronic communication?

A. law enforcement entities performing an investigation
B. the owner of the website where the user has an e-mail account
C. the Internet service provider
D. the bank where an account holder keeps his finances

39. Jonathan Smith, a neurosurgeon in Oregon, wants to start a website that makes it possible for neurosurgeons across the world to work on cases in collaboration. Which of the following domain extensions is most apt for Smith's website?

A. .com
B. .coop
C. .biz
D. .pro

40. The _____ is a federal statute that permits trademark owners and famous persons to recover domain names that use their names where the domain name has been registered by another person or business in bad faith.

A. UCITA
B. ACPA
C. ICANN
D. ECPA

Short Answer

41. For what does the Uniform Computer Information Transaction Act provide?

_____

42. What remedies does the Anticybersquatting Consumer Protection Act provide?

_____

43. Which act enabled electronic signatures to be sufficient to form an enforceable contract?

_____

44. What is the result, if any, if the UCITA provisions are unenforceable?

_____

45. What does .com represent?

_____

46. What extension is an unrestricted global name that may be used by businesses, individuals, and organizations?

_____

47. Who can use the extension .pro?

_____

48. What does the Communications Decency Act provide?

_____

49. What is the biggest challenge when someone uses a digital signature?

_____

50. What is a web contract?

_____

51. What may an aggrieved party do if he or she thinks that prior to the performance date the other party might not deliver performance when due?

_____

52. What is an electronic agent?

_____

53. Give an example of a domain name extension that is most commonly used by ISPs, Web-hosting companies, and other businesses that are directly involved in the infrastructure of the Internet.

_____

54. What are the three ways in which a digital signature can be verified?

_____

55. What are the exceptions of the Electronic Communications Privacy Act (ECPA)?

_____

Answers to Refresh Your Memory

1. HTTP [p. 282]
2. prohibits the messages themselves from containing graphic sexually explicit material [p. 283]
3. ISPs [p. 284]
4. E-SIGN Act [p. 286]
5. a smart card [p. 286]
6. electronic agent [p. 287]
7. UCITA [p. 288]
8. license [p. 288]
9. licensor [p. 288]
10. licensee [p. 288]
11. e-license [p. 289]
12. licensing agreement [p. 289]
13. ECPA [p. 289]
14. domain name [p. 290]
15. .com [p. 291]

Critical Thought Exercise Model Answer

It is understood that e-mail is a convenient way to negotiate and agree on contract terms and to ultimately agree on a final contract. Assuming that all the elements to establish a valid contact are present, the fact that the contract is communicated by e-mail does not prevent the agreement from being valid and enforceable. The subject matter, parties, price, and delivery terms have all been negotiated and agreed upon. While this is a contract for goods exceeding $500 that requires a written contract, there is no reason why the e-mails cannot be printed and used as the required writing. The e-mails will amply demonstrate the parties' intent and desire to enter into the agreement. The ordering of the eggs by Mrs. Dubyah by e-mail will have no less effect than a written letter. Thus, e-mail contracts meet the writing requirement for enforceable contracts.

Mrs. Dubyah is therefore advised to accept the shipment and pay for it as agreed. The Statute of Frauds will not supply a viable defense and it would be unethical for her to cancel the order based merely upon a whim.

Answers to Practice Quiz

True/False

16. True. Uniform Computer Information Transactions Act (UCITA) is a model state law that creates contract law for the licensing of information technology rights. [p. 287]

17. True. The World Wide Web, also called the Web, consists of millions of computers that support a standard set of rules for the exchange of information called Hypertext Transfer Protocol (HTTP). [p. 282]

18. True. Websites and web pages are stored on servers throughout the world, which are operated by Internet service providers (ISPs). They are viewed by using web-browsing software such as Microsoft Internet Explorer. Each website has a unique online address. [p. 282]

19. False. E-mail contracts are enforceable as long as they meet the requirements necessary to form a traditional contract. This includes agreement, consideration, capacity, and lawful object. [p. 283]

20. True. In effect, the CAN-SPAM Act does not can spam but instead approves businesses to use spam as long as they do not lie. [p. 283]

21. True. ISPs provide e-mail accounts to users, Internet access, and storage on the Internet. [p. 284]

22. False. In 2000, the federal government enacted the Electronic Signatures in Global and National Commerce Act (E-SIGN Act). This act is a federal statute enacted by Congress and therefore has national reach. [p. 286]

23. True. Most web pages use electronic ordering systems that do not have the ability to evaluate and accept counteroffers or to make counteroffers. Most state laws recognize this limitation and provide that an e-contract is formed if an individual takes action that causes the electronic agent to cause performance or promise benefits to the individual. Thus, counteroffers are not effective against electronic agents. [p. 287]

24. True. The UCITA does not become law until a state's legislature enacts it as a state statute. [p. 288]

25. False. The ECPA makes it illegal to access stored e-mail as well as e-mail in transmission. [p. 289]

26. False. The ECPA provides that stored electronic communications may be accessed without violating the law by the party or entity providing the electronic communication service. [p. 290]

27. False. Domain name is a unique name that identifies an individual's or company's website. [p. 290]

28. False. biz extension is used for small-business websites. [p. 291]

29. True. Sometimes a party will register a domain name of another party's trademarked name or famous person's name. This is called cybersquatting. [p. 292]

30. True. Anticybersquatting Consumer Protection Act (ACPA) is a federal statute that permits trademark owners and famous persons to recover domain names that use their names where the domain name has been registered by another person or business in bad faith. [p. 292]

Multiple Choice

31. D. Answer D is the correct answer. Websites and web pages are stored on servers throughout the world, which are operated by Internet service providers (ISPs). They are viewed by using web-browsing software such as Microsoft Internet Explorer. Each website has a unique online address. [p. 282]

32. B. Answer B is correct. In 2003, Congress enacted the federal Controlling the Assault of Non-Solicited Pornography and Marketing Act (CAN-SPAM Act).1 The act (1) prohibits spammers from using falsified headers in e-mail messages, including the originating domain name and e-mail address; (2) prohibits deceptive subject lines that mislead a recipient about the contents or subject matter of the message; (3) requires that recipients of spam be given the opportunity to opt out and not have the spammer send e-mail to the recipient's address; and (4) requires spammers who send sexually oriented e-mail to properly label it as such. [p. 283]

33. B. Answer B is correct. A provision in the federal Communications Decency Act of 1996 provides: "No provider or user of an interactive computer service shall be treated as the publisher or speaker of any information provided by another information content provider."2 Thus, ISPs are not liable for the content transmitted over their networks by e-mail users and websites. [p. 285]

34. B. Answer B is correct. Digital signature can basically be verified by biometrics, which uses a device that digitally recognizes fingerprints or the retina or iris of the eye. [p. 287]

35. D. Answer D is correct. The Uniform Computer Information Transactions Act (UCITA) is a model act that establishes a uniform and comprehensive set of rules that govern the creation, performance, and enforcement for computer information transactions. [p. 288]

36. C. Answer C is correct. An exclusive license means that for the specified duration of the license, the licensor will not grant to any other person rights in the same information. [p. 289]

37. D. Answer D is correct. Electronic Communications Privacy Act (ECPA) is a federal statute that makes it a crime to intercept an electronic communication at the point of transmission, while in transit, when stored by a router or server or after receipt by intended recipient. There are some exceptions to this law. [p. 289]

38. A. Answer A is correct. The ECPA provides that stored electronic communications may be accessed without violating the law by the following: 1. the party or entity providing the electronic communication service. The primary example would be an employer who can access stored e-mail communications of employees using the employer's service. 2. Government and law enforcement entities that are investigating suspected illegal activity. Disclosure would be required only pursuant to a validly issued warrant. [p. 290]

39. D. Answer D is correct. .pro extension is available to professionals, such as doctors, lawyers, and consultants. [p. 291]

40. B. Answer B is correct. Anticybersquatting Consumer Protection Act (ACPA) is A federal statute that permits trademark owners and famous persons to recover domain names that use their names where the domain name has been registered by another person or business in bad faith. [p. 292]

Short Answer

41. It provided for uniform and comprehensive rules for contracts involving computer information transactions and software information licenses. [p. 282]

42. It provides for the issuance of a cease-and-desist order and injunctions by the court. Monetary damages can also be awarded with the plaintiff opting for damages as provided by statute or he or she may prove his or her damages. [p. 292]

43. The Electronic Signature in Global and National Commerce Act. [p. 286]

44. Any provisions of the UCITA that are preempted by federal law are unenforceable to the extent of the preemption. [p. 288]

45. This extension represents the word *commercial* and is the most widely used extension in the world. [p. 291]

46. .info [p. 291]

47. This extension is available to professionals, such as doctors, lawyers, consultants, and other professionals. [p. 291]

48. Communications Decency Act is a federal statute that provides that Internet service providers (ISPs) are not liable for the content transmitted over their networks by e-mail users and websites. [p. 285]

49. The biggest challenge when someone uses a digital signature is making sure he or she is the person he or she claims to be. [p. 287]

50. Web contract is a contract that is entered into by purchasing, leasing, or licensing goods, services, software, or other intellectual property from websites operated by sellers, lessors, and licensors. [p. 285]

51. The aggrieved party may make a demand for adequate assurance of due performance from the other party. [p. 271]

52. An electronic agent is any computer system that has been established by a seller to accept orders. [p. 287]

53. .net [p. 291]

54. A digital signature can basically be verified in one of three ways: 1. By something the signatory knows, such as a secret password, pet's name, and so forth 2. By something a person has, such as a smart card, which looks like a credit card and stores personal information 3. By biometrics, this uses a device that digitally recognizes fingerprints or the retina or iris of the eye. [p. 287]

55. The ECPA provides that stored electronic communications may be accessed without violating the law by the following: 1.The party or entity providing the electronic communication service. 2. Government and law enforcement entities that are investigating suspected illegal activity. Disclosure would be required only pursuant to a validly issued warrant. [p. 290]

18 | FORMATION OF SALES AND LEASE CONTRACTS

Chapter Overview

This chapter focuses on the formation and requirements of sales and lease contracts. The requirements and exceptions as they pertain to modification, the Statute of Frauds, and parol evidence are explored. Various key sections of the Uniform Commercial Code are explored in terms of their flexibility and applicability to sales and lease contracts.

Objectives

Upon completion of the exercises in this chapter, you should be able to:
1. Describe sales contracts governed by Article 2 of the Uniform Commercial Code (UCC).
2. Describe lease contracts governed by Article 2A of the UCC.
3. Describe the formation of sales and lease contracts.
4. Define the UCC's firm offer rule, additional terms rule, and written confirmation rule.
5. Describe how Revised Article 2 (Sales) and Article 2A (Leases) permit electronic contracting.

Practical Application

You should be able to determine what is necessary and acceptable to form valid sales or lease contracts. Your studies should provide you with the knowledge you need to modify, explain, or validate either of these types of contracts should the need arise.

Helpful Hints

It is important to remember that basic contract principles also apply to sales and lease contracts, so you are not learning all new material. By reviewing the elements of basic contract formation, and adding to it, you will have a better chance at retaining the information. As you study this chapter, keep the Uniform Commercial Code's leniency in mind when forming sales and lease contracts. When you are analyzing a fact situation or a contract, it is advisable to read and analyze each line separately so that you do not miss any potential issues.

Study Tips

This chapter focuses on Article 2 (Sales) and Article 2A (Leases) of the Uniform Commercial Code. It is easier to study this chapter if you learn the scope of each of these articles. Article 2 involves transactions in goods and Article 2A involves consumer and finance leases.

Uniform Commercial Code (UCC)

The Uniform Commercial Code (UCC) was created as a model act to provide uniform laws to govern commercial transactions. For the UCC to become law in a state, that state must adopt the statute. Every state has adopted all or a majority of the UCC, except for Louisiana, which has adopted only parts of the statute.

Article 2 (Sales)

All states, except for Louisiana, have adopted this article of the UCC.

What is a Sale? A sale is the passing of title from a seller to a buyer for a price.

What are goods? Goods are tangible things that are movable at their identification.
- Money, intangible items, bonds, patents, stocks, and land and not considered to be goods.
- Things that are severable from the land can be goods.

Goods versus Services. Services are not covered under Article 2; however, when there is a mixed sale of both goods and services, if the goods dominate the transaction, then Article 2 does in fact apply. Each case involving a mixed sale is examined individually.

Who is a Merchant? A merchant is a person who deals in goods of the kind involved in the transaction or one who holds himself out to have a particular skill or knowledge peculiar to goods involved in the transaction.
- Article 2 applies to all sales regardless of a person's status of being or not being a merchant in the transaction.
- Note that some sections of Article 2 apply only to merchants and express the special rules of duty placed upon merchants.

Article 2A (Leases)

This article applies to personal property leases, which also involves the formation, performance, and default of leases.

Definition of Lease. A lease is the conveyance of the right to the possession and use of the named goods for a set time period in return for certain consideration.
- Lessor. The person who transfers the right of possession and use of the goods under the lease.
- Lessee. The person who obtains the right to possession and use of goods under a lease.

Finance Lease. This involves three parties, the lessor, the lessee, and the vendor (supplier). Here the lessor is not a manufacturer or supplier of goods, but still acquires title to the goods or the right to use and possess in connection with the lease terms.

Formation of Sales and Lease Contracts: Offer

As with other contracts, both sales and lease contracts require an offer and acceptance in order to be properly formed.

Open Terms. The court will look at the parties' intent to make a contract and then determine if there is a reasonably certain basis for giving an appropriate remedy. When open terms are allowed to be read into the contract, this is referred to as gap-filling rules.
- Open Price Term. If a price in a contract is missing, the court will imply a "reasonable price" at the time of delivery.
- Open Payment Term. In the absence of an agreement on payment terms, payment is due at the time and place where the buyer is to receive the goods.
- Open Delivery Term. If there is no agreed-upon place of delivery, then delivery is to take place at the seller's place of business.

- Open Time Term. The contract must be performed within a reasonable time if there is no provision in the parties' contract for a set specified time of performance.
- Open Assortment Term. This occurs when the buyer is given the option of choosing the goods from an assortment of goods.

UCC Firm Offer Rule. This rule states an exception to the common law rule regarding revocation of offers. It states that a merchant who offers to buy, sell, or lease goods and gives a written and signed assurance on a separate form that the offer will be held open cannot revoke the offer for the time stated or, if no time is stated, for a reasonable time. The maximum amount of time permitted under this rule is three months [UCC 2-205, 2A-205].

Consideration. Consideration is required in the formation of sales and lease contracts. Unlike common law, however, the UCC indicates that modification of sales and lease contracts do not require consideration, but they do require the element of good faith.

Formation of Sales and Lease Contracts: Acceptance

At common law and under the UCC, a contract is created when the buyer or lessee sends his or her acceptance to the offeror, not upon receipt.

Method and Manner of Acceptance. Acceptance may be accomplished in any manner and by any reasonable medium of acceptance.
- If a buyer makes an offer, then the seller's acceptance is signified by either the seller's prompt promise to ship or his or her prompt shipment of conforming or nonconforming goods.
- Acceptance of the goods by the buyer occurs if after the buyer has a reasonable opportunity to accept the goods, either indicates that the goods are conforming, or signifies that he or she will keep the goods regardless of their nonconformity, or if he or she fails to reject the goods within a reasonable period of time after delivery of the goods.

UCC Permits Additional Terms. At common law, an offeree's acceptance had to mirror the image of the offer. If additional terms were included, it was considered a counteroffer. The UCC, however, has given flexibility to this rule.
- If one or both parties are nonmerchants, any additional terms become proposed additions to the contract.
    - o The proposed additions do not terminate the offer nor does it constitute a counteroffer.
    - o If the offeree's proposed additions are accepted by the offeror, they become part of the contract.

"Battle of the Forms". If both parties are merchants, additional terms become part of the contract unless the acceptance is expressly conditional on assent to the terms of the offer or the additional terms materially alter the terms of the original contract or the offeror notifies the offeree that he or she is rejecting the additional terms.

Accommodation Shipment. A shipment of nonconforming goods is not considered an acceptance if the seller reasonably notifies the buyer that the shipment is being offered as an accommodation to the buyer.
- An accommodation shipment is considered a counter-offer from the seller to the buyer.

UCC Statute of Frauds

Goods costing $500 or more and lease payments of $1,000 or more must be in writing. The agreement must be signed by the party to be charged.

Exceptions to the Statute of Frauds. These sales and lease situations do not have to meet the writing requirement of the Statute of Frauds:
- Specially Manufactured Goods
- Admissions in Pleadings or Court
- Part Acceptance

UCC Written Confirmation Rule. If both parties are merchants and one of the parties to the oral contract sends written confirmation within a reasonable time after entering into the contract and the other merchant does not object to the contract within ten days of his or her receipt of the confirmation, then the Statute of Frauds is satisfied.

When Written Modification is Required. If the parties state that the modification must be in writing, then it has to be. However, in general, an oral modification is sufficient if it does not violate the Statute of Frauds.

Parol Evidence. A rule that states that a written contract is the complete and final expression of the party's agreement. Any prior or contemporaneous oral or written statements to the contract may not be introduced to alter or contradict or add to the written contract.
- Exceptions. When the contract's express terms are unclear, the court may consider the course of performance, course of dealing, and usage of trade as outside sources to clarify the terms of the parties' agreement.

Refresh Your Memory

The following exercise will give you the opportunity to test your memory of the principles given in this chapter. Read the question twice and place your answer in the blank provided. Review the chapter material for any question that you are unable to answer or remember.

1. The _____ is a model act passed in 1949 that includes comprehensive laws that cover most aspects of commercial transactions.

2. A _____ is defined as the passing of title of goods from a seller to a buyer for a price.

3. A _____ is a transfer of the right to the possession and use of named goods for a set term in return for certain consideration.

4. A person who transfers the right of possession and use of goods under a lease is known as the _____.

5. The Article 2A of the Uniform Commercial Code governs _____.

6. Under the UCC, if the time, place, and manner of delivery of goods are not mentioned in a contract, _____.

7. According to the gap-filling rule, if a sales contract does not contain a specific price, _____.

8. The rule states that a merchant who offers to buy, sell, or lease goods and gives a written and signed assurance on a separate form that the offer will be held open cannot revoke the offer for the time stated or, if no time is stated, for a reasonable time is referred to as _____.

9. A contract is created when _____.

10. A shipment that is offered to a buyer as a replacement for the original shipment when the original shipment cannot be filled is referred to as a(n) _____.

11. The _____ requires all contracts for the sale of goods costing $500 or more and lease contracts involving payments of $1,000 or more to be in writing.

12. _____ is a rule that says that if a written contract is a complete and final statement of the parties' agreement, any prior or contemporaneous oral or written statements that alter, contradict, or are in addition to the terms of the written contract are inadmissible in court regarding a dispute over the contract.

13. A computer program or an electronic or other automated means used independently to initiate an action or respond to electronic records or performances in whole or in part, without review or action by an individual, is known as _____.

14. Article 5 of the UCC governs _____.

15. A _____ is a document that is issued by a bank on behalf of a buyer who purchases goods on credit from a seller that guarantees that if the buyer does not pay for the goods, then the bank will pay the seller.

Critical Thought Exercise

Apex Mattress Company, for whom you are the vice president of material acquisition, entered into an oral agreement with Davis Wool Ranch (DWR), a wool supplier, in which DWR agreed to sell Apex 800 bundles of wool, each weighing 350 pounds. Shortly after your conversation with Dan Davis of DWR, you sent Davis an e-mail confirming the terms of the oral contract. Davis did not respond to the e-mail or offer any objection to the terms stated in the e-mail. When the delivery date arrived four months later, you contacted DWR to finalize the delivery terms. DWR stated that there was no agreement and DWR had sold the 800 bundles to Fluffy-Air Mattress because the price of wool had doubled on the open market since the date of the oral agreement. The board of directors of Apex requests that you inform them of your position in regards to bringing suit against DWR and the likelihood that Apex will prevail.

Write a memo to the board setting forth your position and authority for your conclusion.

Please compose your answer to the Critical Thinking Exercise using a separate sheet of paper or your computer word processing program.

Practice Quiz

True/False

16. _____ Article 2 of the Uniform Commercial Code is also applied by federal courts to sales contracts governed by federal law.

17. _____ Article 2 of the UCC applies to sales contracts for the sale of intangible goods.

18. _____ Only movable goods come under the scope of Article 2 of the UCC.

19. _____ Contracts for the provision of services are not covered by Article 2 of the UCC.

20. _____ Article 2 of the UCC defines a merchant as a person who deals in the goods of the kind involved in the transaction.

21. _____ In a lease contract, the title of goods is passed from the lessor to the lessee.

22. _____ Revised Article 2A (Leases) includes provisions that recognize the importance of electronic lease contracts.

23. _____ A finance lease involves a lessor leasing money to a lessee.

24. _____ The UCC does not allow for open terms to be read into a sales or lease contract.

25. _____ The open price term requires for a contract to mention a specific price.

26. _____ The firm offer rule allows the offeror to revoke an offer at any point of time prior to the acceptance.

27. _____ Modification to a sales or lease contract is binding even if it is made under duress.

28. _____ As per the Statute of Frauds provisions, all contracts for the sale of goods costing $500 or more must be in writing.

29. _____ The common law of contract allows for gap-filling terms that are implied in the contract.

30. _____ Article 5 of the UCC governs letter of credit.

Multiple Choice

31. Which of the following articles in the UCC deals with the sale of goods?

A. Article 2
B. Article 4
C. Article 5
D. Article 8

32. Which of the following sales would be covered by Article 2 of the UCC?

A. the sale of intangible goods
B. the sale of tangible goods
C. the sale of real estate
D. the sale of stocks

33. Which of the following describes a mixed sale?

A. a sale that involves two or more intangible goods
B. a sale that involves the passing of title of goods from a seller to a buyer for a price
C. a sale that involves the possession and use of named goods for a set
D. a sale that involves the provision of a service and a good in the same transaction

34. Which of the following is true for goods under the purview of Article 2 of the UCC?

A. Goods can be replaced by money.
B. Intangible goods must be exchanged with other intangible goods.
C. Goods in the contract must be movable.
D. Immovable goods like real estate must have provisions of service attached to their contracts.

35. Which of the following is true of consideration for modifying a sales or lease contract under the UCC?

A. An agreement modifying a contract needs no consideration to be binding.
B. Modifying a contract requires consideration from the offeree's side.
C. An offeror who modifies a contract must do so by providing reasonable consideration.
D. The party providing the consideration must complete it within three months of acceptance.

36. In which of the following cases do additional terms contained in an acceptance become part of the contract as per the battle of the forms rule?

A. if the additional terms materially alter the original contract
B. if the sale is between two nonmerchants
C. if the additional terms expressly limit the acceptance to the terms of the offer
D. if the offeror notifies the offeree that he or she does not object to the additional terms

37. When is the parol rule evidence used in contracts?

A. when a written confirmation has not been sent for an oral contract
B. when the party against whom enforcement of an oral contract is sought has not admitted in pleadings of such a contract
C. when an oral modification is required in a written contract
D. when there is a written statement that contradicts an agreed written contract

38. What is "course of dealing" when interpreting the express terms of a written statement?

A. the previous conduct of the parties regarding the contract in question
B. the conduct of the parties in prior transactions and contracts
C. the conduct of contractual parties with parties not involved in the contract
D. any practice of dealing that is regularly observed or adhered to in an industry

39. Which of the following is true for terms to be expressed in a contract under the common law of contract?

A. Additional terms can be added during acceptance.
B. Additional terms can be added without consideration.
C. Gap-filling rules are permitted for time, delivery, and prices of goods.
D. Contract must contain all the material terms of the parties' agreement.

40. Which of the following acceptances is allowed for an offer under common law?

A. mirror image rule acceptance
B. open term acceptance
C. accommodation
D. additional terms acceptance

Short Answer

41. What is the most important point in the battle of the form?

_____

_____

42. If one or both parties to a sales contract are nonmerchants, what are any additional terms considered to be?

_____

_____

43. What does Article 5 of the Uniform Commercial Code governs?

_____

_____

44. When express terms are not clear and need interpretation, what three things will the court look at?

_____

_____

45. What was the common law rule with regard to revocation of an offer?

_____

_____

46. What is the comprehensive statutory scheme that includes laws that cover most aspects of contract transactions?

_____

_____

47. What is an accommodation shipment?

_____

_____

48. What do Article 2 and Article 2A of the Uniform Commercial Code govern?

_____

_____

49. How may an offer for a contract for the sale or lease of goods be formed?

_____

_____

50. If the post office loses an acceptance letter, what happens to the contract?

_____

_____

51. According to the Statute of Frauds, what types of sales and lease contracts need to be in writing?

_____

_____

52. What three situations involving a sales or lease contract will still warrant their enforcement despite the fact that they are not in writing as per the Statute of Frauds?

_____

_____

53. What is course of performance?

_____

_____

54. What is course of dealing?

_____

_____

55. What is usage of trade?

_____

_____

Answers to Refresh Your Memory

1. Uniform Commercial Code [p. 299]
2. sale [p. 300]
3. lease [p. 303]
4. lessor [p. 303]
5. leases [p. 303]
6. the place of delivery is the seller's place of business [p. 305]
7. the contract can be enforced by either party by fixing an open term price [p. 304]
8. firm-offer rule [p. 305]
9. the offeree dispatches the acceptance [p. 306]
10. accommodation [p. 307]
11. Statute of Frauds [p. 307]
12. Parol evidence rule [p. 309]
13. electronic agent [p. 310]
14. letters of credit [p. 310]
15. letter of credit [p. 310]

Critical Thought Exercise Model Answer

If both parties to an oral sales contract are merchants, the Statute of Frauds requirement can be met if one of the parties to the oral agreement sends a written confirmation of the sale within a reasonable time after making the agreement and the other merchant does not give written notice of an objection to the contract within 10 days after receiving confirmation. If both merchants are in the U.S., UCC section 2-201(2) will control. If one of the merchants is a foreign entity, then the 1980 United Nations Convention on Contracts for the International Sale of Goods (CISG) will apply. Under the CISG, Article 11, an international sales contract "need not be concluded in or even evidenced by writing and is not subject to any other requirements as to form."

When the confirming e-mail was sent to DWR, they did not respond within a ten-day period or voice any objections to the contents of our e-mail. Modernly, an e-mail can serve as a writing. Thus, Apex had a legally binding contract with DWR. The failure of DWR to tender delivery of the 800 bundles of wool on the delivery date put them in breach. The fact that DWR desired to sell the wool for a larger profit hurts their position and helps us because of the requirement that they deal with us in good faith.

Lastly, we will have to obtain the wool from another source and may be required to pay a premium for the wool because of the urgency that we face due to the actions of DWR. We should be able to recover damages in an amount equal to the difference between the contract price and market price at the time we enter into a new contract with a different wool supplier.

Answers to Practice Quiz

True/False

16. True. Article 2 is also applied by federal courts to sales contracts governed by federal law. [p. 300]

17. False. Certain items are not considered goods and are not subject to Article 2. They include money and intangible items are not tangible goods. [p. 301]

18. True. Goods are defined as tangible things that are movable at the time of their identification to a contract [UCC 2-105(1)]. [p. 301]

19. True. Contracts for the provision of services—including legal services, medical services, and dental services—are not covered by Article 2. [p. 301]

20. True. UCC 2-104(1) defines a merchant as (1) a person who deals in the goods of the kind involved in the transaction or (2) a person who by his or her occupation holds himself or herself out as having knowledge or skill peculiar to the goods involved in the transaction. [p. 302]

21. False. In a lease contract, the lessor is the person who transfers the right of possession and use of goods under the lease [UCC 2A-103(1)(p)]. [p. 303]

22. True. Revised Articles 2 and 2A contain many new provisions and rules that recognize the importance of electronic contracting for the sale and lease of goods. [p. 304]

23. False. A finance lease is a three-party transaction consisting of a lessor, a lessee, and a supplier (or vendor). The lessor does not select, manufacture, or supply the goods. Instead, the lessor acquires title to the goods or the right to their possession and use in connection with the terms of the lease [UCC 2A-103(1)(g)]. [p. 303]

24. False. The UCC is tolerant of open terms. Certain open terms are permitted to be "read into" a sales or lease contract. This rule is commonly referred to as the gap-filling rule. [p. 304]

25. False. In an open price term if a sales contract does not contain a specific price (open price term), a "reasonable price" is implied at the time of delivery. [p. 304]

26. False. The firm offer rule states that a merchant who (1) offers to buy, sell, or lease goods and (2) gives a written and signed assurance on a separate form that the offer will be held open cannot revoke the offer for the time stated or, if no time is stated, for a reasonable time. [p. 305]

27. False. As in the common law of contracts, modifications are not binding if they are obtained through fraud, duress, extortion, and such. [p. 306]

28. True. All contracts for the sale of goods costing $500 or more must be in writing [UCC 2-201(1)]. [p. 307]

29. False. Under the Common Law of Contract a contract must contain all the material terms of the parties' agreement. [p. 309]
30. True. Letters of credit are governed by Article 5 (Letters of Credit) of the Uniform Commercial Code (UCC). [p. 311]

Multiple Choice

31. A. Answer A is correct. Article 2, establishes rules that govern the sale of goods. [p. 300]

32. B. Answer B is correct. Goods are defined as tangible things that are movable at the time of their identification to a contract [UCC 2-105(1)]. Article 2 of the UCC applies to transactions in goods [UCC 2-102]. [p. 300-301]

33. D. Answer D is the correct answer. A mixed sale is a sale that involves the provision of a service and a good in the same transaction. [p. 301]

34. C. Answer C is correct. Goods are defined as tangible things that are movable at the time of their identification to a contract [UCC 2-105(1)]. Article 2 of the UCC applies to transactions in goods [UCC 2-102]. [p. 300-301]

35. A. Answer A is correct. An agreement modifying a sales or lease contract needs no consideration to be binding [UCC 2-209(1), 2A-208(1)]. [p. 306]

36. D. Answer D is correct. Under UCC 2-207(2), if both parties are merchants, any additional terms contained in an acceptance become part of the sales contract unless (1) the offer expressly limits acceptance to the terms of the offer, (2) the additional terms materially alter the terms of the original contract, or (3) the offeror notifies the offeree that he or she objects to the additional terms within a reasonable time after receiving the offeree's modified acceptance. [p. 307]

37. B. Answer B is correct. The parol evidence rule states that when a sales or lease contract is evidenced by a writing that is intended to be a final expression of the parties' agreement or a confirmatory memorandum, the terms of the writing may not be contradicted by evidence of (1) a prior oral or written agreement or (2) a contemporaneous oral agreement (i.e., parol evidence) [UCC 2-202, 2A-202]. This rule is intended to ensure certainty in written sales and lease contracts. [p. 310]

38. B. Answer B is correct. Course of dealing refers to the conduct of the parties in prior transactions and contracts. [p. 309]

39. D. Answer D is correct. Under the Common Law of Contract a Contract must contain all the material terms of the parties' agreement. [p. 309]

40. A. Answer A is correct. Under the Common Law of Contract Acceptance must be a mirror image of the offer. A counteroffer rejects and terminates the offeror's original offer. [p. 309]

Short Answer

41. There is no contract if the additional terms so materially alter the terms of the original offer that the parties cannot agree on the contract. [p. 307]

42. Additional terms in these circumstances are considered proposed additions. [p. 307]

43. Letters of credit. [p. 310]

44. Course of performance, course of dealing, usage of trade. [p. 309]

45. The offeror could revoke his/her offer any time before acceptance. [p. 305]

46. The Uniform Commercial Code. [p. 299]

47. A shipment that is offered to the buyer as a replacement for the original shipment when the original shipment cannot be filled. [p. 307]

48. These two articles govern personal property sales and leases. [p. 299]

49. A contract for the lease or sale of goods may be made in any manner adequate to show agreement. [p. 304]

50. The contract is still valid, regardless if the post office loses the letter. [p. 306]

51. Contracts for the sale of goods $500 or more and lease contracts involving payments of $1,000 or more must be in writing. [p. 307]

52. Specially manufactured goods, admissions in pleadings or court, part acceptance. [p. 308]

53. Course of performance is previous conduct of the parties during the contract in dispute. [p. 309]

54. Course of dealing is conduct of the parties in prior transactions and contracts. [p. 309]

55. Usage of trade is any practice or method of dealing that is regularly observed or adhered to in a place, a vocation, a trade, or an industry. [p. 309]

19 | TITLE TO GOODS AND RISK OF LOSS

Chapter Overview

This chapter discusses sales and destination contracts, as well as risk of loss and the passage of title to goods. Emphasis is placed on the identification of goods. It provides an understanding of the differences between a sale on approval and a sale or return. Emphasis is placed on insurable interest in goods, good faith purchasers for value, and sales by nonowners.

Objectives

Upon completion of the exercises in this chapter, you should be able to:
1. Identify when title to goods passes in shipment and destination contracts.
2. Define shipment and delivery terms.
3. Describe who bears the risk of loss when goods are lost or damaged in shipment.
4. Identify who bears the risk of loss when goods are stolen and resold.
5. Define good faith purchaser for value and buyer in the ordinary course of business.

Practical Application

You should be able to determine what type of contract has been formed as you analyze the shipping terms. You should be able to determine who bears the risk of loss in situations involving damaged, lost or stolen, and resold goods. You should gain a better familiarity with the laws involving consignments, as well as laws concerning good faith purchasers for value.

Helpful Hints

As you peruse the material in this chapter, it is helpful to keep in mind who is receiving the most benefit with regard to the type of contract into which the parties are entering. If you remember that the seller begins with the letter "s" and usually will want a shipment (also begins with the letter "s") contract as the carrier that the goods are placed on will then bear the risk of loss. A buyer will want the contract to be a destination contract as the seller will bear the risk of loss up until the time that the buyer receives the goods.

The remaining rules in this chapter are fairly easy to learn. One of the easiest ways to analyze facts in this area is to ask the following questions in the following order:
- Who are the parties?
- Have the goods been identified to the contract?
- Do the parties have a shipment or a destination contract?
- Who bears the risk of loss in light of the type of contract that exists?
- What if anything has happened to the goods?
- Are there any third parties involved?
- If so, what is their capacity or role in the facts?
- Are there any special rules of law that apply?

Study Tips

Title to Goods and Risk of Loss

The risk of loss under common law was placed on the party who held title to the goods. Article 2 of the UCC changes this and gives rules for risk of loss that are not tied to title. Article 2A of the UCC gives rules about title and risk of loss for leased goods. It also provides that the parties to sales contracts and lease contracts have the right to insure the goods against loss if they have an "insurable interest" in the goods.

Identification of Goods and Passage of Title

Identification of goods is to distinguish the goods named in a contract from the seller's or lessor's other goods. The risk of loss remains with the seller or lessor until the goods are identified to the contract.

Identification. Identification of the goods can occur at any time and in any manner. If no time is specified, then the UCC will state when it occurs.
- Already existing goods are identified at the contract's inception.
- Goods that are part of a bulk shipment are identified when specific merchandise is separated or tagged.
- Future goods are identified when the goods are shipped, marked, or otherwise designated.

Passage of Title. Title to goods passes from seller to buyer in any manner and on any conditions agreed on by the parties. If the parties have not agreed on a specific time for the passage of title, title will pass to the buyer when and where physical delivery is to be made by the seller.

Shipment and Destination Contracts.
- Shipment Contract. The seller must ship and deliver goods to the buyer via a common carrier. Proper shipping arrangements and delivery to the carrier are required.
    - Title passes to the buyer at the time and place of shipment.
    - Risk of loss passes to the buyer when conforming goods are delivered to the carrier.
- Destination Contract. The seller must deliver the goods to the buyer's place of business or another specified destination. The seller is required to replace any goods lost in transit.
    - Title passes when the seller tenders delivery of the goods at the specified destination.
    - Risk of loss does not pass until the goods are tendered at the specified destination.

Delivery of Goods Without Moving Them. Where goods are not required to be moved by the seller, passage of title is dependent upon whether or not document of title is required to be given to the buyer.
- If a document of title is required. Title passes when and where the seller delivers the document to the buyer [UCC 2-401(3)(a)].
- If no document of title is required. If the goods are identified at the time of contracting, title passes at the time and place of contracting [UCC 2-401(3)(b)].

Risk of Loss: No Breach of Sales Contract

If the parties to a sales contract have not designated who will risk the loss if the goods are lost or destroyed, and there has been no breach of the sales contract, the UCC mandates who bears the risk of loss.

Carrier Cases: Movement of Goods. Goods shipped via carrier are considered to be sent either by a shipment contract or a destination contract. Unless otherwise specified, sales contracts are presumed to be shipment contracts.
- Shipment Contract. The seller must ship and deliver goods to the buyer via a common carrier. The buyer bears the risk of loss during transportation. These contracts are created in one of two ways:
    - by using the term shipment contract or
    - using delivery terms such as F.O.B., F.A.S., C.I.F. or C.& F.
- Destination Contract. The seller must deliver the goods to the buyer's place of business or another specified destination. The seller bears the risk of loss during transportation. These contracts are created in one of two ways:
    - by using the term destination contract or
    - using delivery terms such as: F.O.B. *place of destination*, ex-ship, or no-arrival, no-sale contract

Noncarrier Cases: No Movement of Goods. A sales contract may specify that the buyer is to pick up the goods at the seller's place of business or other specified location.
- Merchant-Seller. Risk of loss does not pass until the goods are received.
- Nonmerchant-Seller. Risk of loss occurs when there is a tender of delivery of the goods.

Goods in the Possession of a Bailee. When goods are in the possession of a bailee and are to be delivered without moving them, the risk of loss passes to the buyer in three circumstances:
- The buyer receives a negotiable document of title covering the goods; or
- The bailee acknowledges the buyer's right to possession of the goods; or
- The buyer receives a nonnegotiable document of title or other written direction to deliver and has a reasonable time to present the document or direction to the bailee and demand the goods.
    - If the bailee refuses to honor the document or direction, the risk of loss remains on the seller [UCC 2-509(2)].

Risk of Loss: Conditional Sales

Sellers often entrust possession of goods to buyers on a trial basis. These transactions are classified as sales on approval, sales or returns, and consignment transactions [UCC 2-326].

Sale on Approval. A sale does not occur unless the buyer accepts the goods. The situation presents itself when a merchant allows a buyer to take the goods home for a specified period of time to determine if it meets the customer's needs.
- Acceptance is shown by
    - expressly accepting the goods,
    - failing to notify the seller of buyer's rejection, or
    - use of the goods inconsistently with the purpose of the trial.
- Risk of loss and title stay with the seller and do not pass until the buyer accepts the goods.
- Goods are not subject to buyer's creditor's claims until buyer accepts them.

Sale or Return. The seller delivers the goods to the buyer letting the buyer know that he or she may return them if they are not used or resold within a stated period of time.
- If the buyer doesn't return them within a reasonable time, the goods are considered sold.
- Risk of loss and title pass when the buyer takes possession of the goods.
- Buyer's creditors may make claims against the buyer while the goods are in the buyer's possession.

Consignment. The seller, or consignor, delivers goods to a buyer, or consignee, to sell. The consignee will be paid a fee if the goods are sold on behalf of the consignor.
- A consignment is treated as a sale or return under the UCC.
- Risk of loss and title pass to the consignee when the consignee takes possession of the goods.
- Seller's creditors may make claims against the goods if the seller files a financing statement.
- Buyer's creditors may make claims against the goods if the seller fails to file a financing statement.

Risk of Loss: Breach of Sales Contract

In situations where there has been a breach of the sales contract, the UCC specifies special risk of loss rules.

Seller in Breach of a Sales Contract. Breach occurs when the seller tenders nonconforming goods to the buyer.
- If the buyer has the right to reject the goods, the *risk of loss* stays with the seller until
    o the nonconformity or defect is cured or
    o the buyer accepts the nonconforming goods.

Buyer in Breach of a Sales Contract. Breach occurs where the buyer refuses to take delivery of conforming goods or if the buyer repudiates the contract or otherwise breaches the contract.
- The risk of loss rests on the buyer for a commercially reasonable time.
- Buyer is liable for any loss in excess of insurance covered by the seller.

Risk of Loss: Lease Contracts

The parties may agree who will bear the risk of loss if the goods are lost or destroyed. If there is no such provision, the UCC provides rules for risk of loss.
- Ordinary Lease. The risk of loss stays with the lessor.
- Finance Lease. The risk of loss passes to the lessee [UCC 2A-219].
- If tender of delivery of goods fails to conform to the lease contract, the risk of loss stays with the lessor or supplier until acceptance or cure [UCC 2A-220(1)(a)].

Sales by Nonowners

This category involves individuals who sell goods that they do not have good title to.

Stolen Goods: Void Title. Where the buyer purchases goods from a thief, title to the goods does not pass and the lessee does not require any leasehold interest in the goods.
- The real owner of the goods may reclaim the goods from the buyer or lessee.
- Title is void.

Sales or Lease of Goods to Good Faith Purchasers for Value: Voidable Title. A seller has voidable title to goods if the goods were obtained by fraud, dishonored check, or impersonation of another person.
- An individual with voidable title may transfer good title to goods to a good faith purchaser for value or a good faith subsequent lessee.
- A good faith purchaser for value is one who pays consideration or rent for the goods to one he or she honestly believes has good title to those goods.
    - The real owner cannot reclaim the goods from this type of purchaser.

Entrustment Rule. If an owner entrusts the possession of his or her goods to a merchant who deals in the particular type of goods, the merchant may transfer all rights to a buyer in the ordinary course of business.
- The real owner cannot reclaim the goods from this type of buyer.

Refresh Your Memory

The following exercise will give you the opportunity to test your memory of the principles given in this chapter. Read the question twice and place your answer in the blank provided. Review the chapter material for any question that you are unable to answer or remember.

1. In a finance lease contract, the title to goods is passed from _____.

2. The term _____ refers to the legal, tangible evidence of ownership of goods.

3. A(n) _____ is an actual piece of paper, such as a warehouse receipt or bill of lading, which is required in some transactions of pickup and delivery of sold goods.

4. _____ is a shipping term in a contract that requires the seller to bear the expense and risk of loss until the goods are unloaded from the ship at its port of destination.

5. In a shipping contract _____ bears the risk of loss of goods during transport.

6. The _____ bears the risk of loss during transportation in a destination contract.

7. A holder of goods who is not a seller or a buyer is referred to as a(n) _____.

8. A(n) _____ involves the seller entrusting possession of goods to a buyer on a trial basis.

9. The term _____ refers to a type of sale in which there is no actual sale unless and until the buyer accepts the goods.

10. _____ refers to an arrangement in which a seller delivers goods to a buyer to sell on his or her behalf.

11. A consignment deal would be an example of a(n) _____.

12. A title for goods obtained by a seller through fraud, impersonation, or a dishonored check is referred to as a _____.

13. _____ is a good faith purchaser.

14. _____ is a person to whom a lease interest can be transferred from a person with voidable title. The real owner cannot reclaim the goods from the subsequent lessee until the lease expires.

15. _____ is a model act for international sales contracts that provides legal rules that govern the formation, performance, and enforcement of international sales contracts entered into between international businesses.

Critical Thought Exercise

Bristol Physical Therapy (BPT) contracted with Summit Pools, Inc., for the purchase of a "fully installed portable therapy whirlpool" for the sum of $14,000. The price included all labor and parts but the order form was not itemized. The freight carrier hired by the manufacturer delivered the pool to the parking lot just outside the building occupied by BPT. A receptionist for BPT signed the delivery invoice and immediately called Summit Pools. When the installation crew for Summit Pools arrived five days later to install the whirlpool, it was gone.

In this situation, had the risk of loss of the whirlpool passed from Summit Pools to BPT?

Please compose your answer to the Critical Thinking Exercise using a separate sheet of paper or your computer word processing program.

Practice Quiz

True/False

16. _____ Article 2 of the Uniform Commercial Code establishes precise rules for determining the passage of title in sales contracts.

17. _____ Common law places the risk of loss of goods on the party to whom the title of goods were to be passed.

18. _____ Goods that are part of a larger mass of goods are identified when the specific merchandise is designated.

19. _____ A shipment contract requires the seller to deliver goods to a destination specified in the sales contract.

20. _____ In a destination contract, title passes to the buyer when the seller tenders delivery of the goods at the specified delivery address..

21. _____ A shipment contract requires the seller to ship the goods to the buyer via a common carrier

22. _____ In an F.O.B. point of shipment, the buyer bears the risk of loss while the goods are in transit.

23. _____ In an F.A.S. port of shipment, the buyer bears the shipping costs and the risk of loss during transport

24. _____ In a no-arrival, no-sale contract, the seller is not required to deliver replacement goods to the buyer.

25. _____ C.&F. is a pricing term that means that the price includes the cost of the goods and the costs of insurance and freight.

26. _____ In a destination contract, the seller is required to replace any goods lost in transit.

27. _____ The delivery term of "no-arrival, no-sale" can be added to a shipment contract.

28. _____ In a sale on approval, there is no sale unless and until the buyer accepts the goods.

29. _____ A consignment is treated as a sale or return contract under the UCC.

30. _____ A seller has voidable title interest to goods if he or she obtained the goods through fraud.

Multiple Choice

31. In which of the following does the title to the goods pass from the seller to the buyer?

A. option contract
B. rental agreement
C. lease
D. sale of goods

32. What kinds of goods are termed as future goods?

A. goods that exist but are to be sold at a future date
B. goods that are not yet in existence
C. goods that can be sold partly in the present and partly at a later date
D. goods that exist without a title

33. In a shipment contract, when is the title to the goods considered to have passed to the buyer?

A. when the seller makes the offer to the buyer
B. when the seller hands over the goods to the common carrier
C. when the seller tenders delivery of the goods at the specified destination
D. when the goods are at the time and place of the shipment

34. In a destination contract, when is the title to the goods considered to have passed to the buyer?

A. when the buyer specifies a specific destination in the sales contract
B. when the seller tenders delivery of the goods at the specified destination
C. when the seller makes the shipping arrangements
D. when the seller hands over the goods to the common carrier

35. Which of the following is true for the passage of title in a contract requiring a document of title?

A. The title passes when the shipping arrangements are made.
B. The title passes at the time and place of contracting.
C. The title passes when the destination of delivery is first mentioned in the contract.
D. The title passes when and where the seller delivers the document to the buyer.

36. Which of the following is true of a contract with the no-arrival, no-sale term?

A. The buyer bears shipping costs and the risk of loss during transport.
B. The seller does not have to deliver replacement goods to the buyer in case of damages.
C. The seller does not have to bear the expense and risk of loss of the goods during transportation.
D. The buyer has to arrange for the shipment to be handed over to a carrier.

37. Which of the following is true of a destination contract containing a "no-arrival, no-sale" clause?

A. The seller is required to bear the expense and risk during transportation.
B. The seller is required to replace any goods lost in transit.
C. The buyer does not have to pay for destroyed goods.
D. The risk of loss passes once the shipping has been arranged.

38. In which of the following cases is a buyer in breach of a sales contract?

A. if the buyer refuses to accept nonconforming goods
B. if the buyer accepts nonconforming goods
C. if the buyer refuses to accept conforming goods
D. if the buyer asks replacements for defective goods

39. What is the role of a financing statement in a consignment if the consignor files it?

A. It protects the consignor from bearing a risk of loss for the goods.
B. It protects the consignor from possible payment revocation by the consignee.
C. It gives the buyer's creditors claim over the goods.
D. It gives the seller's creditors claim over the goods.

40. Steve brings his watch to Knell Watches to be repaired. Knell Watches sells and repairs watches. Steve entrusts his watch at Knells' until it is repaired. The watch store repairs the watch, but then sells it to Kevin, who buys the watch with a fraudulent check that bounced. Kevin then resells the watch to his friend Jonathan, who is unaware of the stolen nature of the watch. What kind of title did Jonathan hold over the watch when he fraudulently bought the watch?

A. an unequivocal title
B. a conditional title
C. a voidable title
D. a void title

Short Answer

41. If Zeb has fifty acres of corn that he planted, when is the corn identified?

_____

_____

42. What does the shipping term ex-ship mean?

_____

_____

43. What types of terms signify a destination contract?

_____

44. Who bears the risk of loss if the goods are stolen or destroyed after the contract date and before the buyer picks up the goods from the seller who is a merchant?

_____

_____

45. What is meant by the terminology void title?

_____

_____

46. How long does the risk of loss rest on a buyer when he or she is in breach?

_____

_____

47. What does the shipping term F.O.B. Houghton, Michigan, require the seller to do?

_____

_____

48. Give an example of a document of title.

_____

_____

49. Where does the shipping term F.A.S. require the seller to deliver and tender the goods?

_____

_____

50. If the goods are so nonconforming that the buyer has the right to reject them, the risk of loss remains on the seller until when?

_____

_____

51. A buyer who breaches a sales contract before the risk of loss would normally pass to him or her bears the risk of loss as to which goods?

_____

_____

52. Who has title in a lease transaction?

_____

_____

53. What types of terms are needed for the creation of a shipment contract?

_____

_____

54. Who is a good faith purchaser for value?

_____

_____

55. What is the entrustment rule?

_____

_____

Answers to Refresh Your Memory

1. supplier to lessor [p. 321]
2. title [p. 316]
3. document of title [p. 316]
4. Ex-ship [p. 317]
5. the buyer [p. 318]
6. seller [p. 318]
7. bailee [p. 318]
8. conditional sale [p. 320]
9. sale on approval [p. 320]
10. Consignment [p. 320]
11. sale or return contract [p. 320]
12. voidable title [p. 322]
13. A person who buys goods from a person with a voidable title [p. 322]
14. A good faith subsequent lessee [p. 322]
15. United Nations Convention on Contracts for the International Sale of Goods (CISG) [p. 319]

Critical Thought Exercise Model Answer

The goods in this case, a whirlpool, had been delivered to the customer and a representative of BPT had signed for the shipment. The whirlpool had been placed on BPT's property by the common carrier. Normally, the risk of loss passes in a shipment contract when the goods are placed with the common carrier. In this case, however, the goods are being resold by Summit Pools to BPT. Thus, the risk of loss will not pass to BPT until they have been delivered to BPT as dictated by the agreement. In this agreement, the goods were to be fully installed as part of the contract and there was no separation of the goods from the installation services in the agreement.

In a mixed goods and services contract, a court will look to see whether the goods or services are the predominant item to be provided. The whirlpool being sold to BPT is considered a portable unit, so the installation services appear to be a secondary purpose in the sales contract. Risk of loss will therefore not pass to BPT until the whirlpool is fully installed as required by the agreement. The theft or loss of the whirlpool unit will fall upon Summit Pools.

Answers to Practice Quiz

True/False

16. True. Article 2 of the UCC establishes precise rules for determining the passage of title in sales contracts. [p. 316]

17. False. In the case of sales contracts, common law placed the risk of loss of goods on the party who had title to the goods. [p. 317]

18. True. Goods that are part of a larger mass of goods are identified when the specific merchandise is designated. [p. 315]

19. False. A shipment contract requires the seller to ship the goods to the buyer via a common carrier. The seller is required to (1) make proper shipping arrangements and (2) deliver the goods into the carrier's hands. [p. 316]

20. True. A destination contract requires the seller to deliver the goods either to the buyer's place of business or to another destination specified in the sales contract. Title passes to the buyer when the seller tenders delivery of the goods at the specified destination [UCC 2-401(2)(b)]. [p. 316]

21. True. A shipment contract requires the seller to ship the goods to the buyer via a common carrier. The seller is required to (1) make proper shipping arrangements and (2) deliver the goods into the carrier's hands. [p. 316]

22. True. F.O.B. (free on board) point of shipment requires the seller to arrange to ship the goods and put the goods in the carrier's possession. The buyer bears the shipping expense and risk of loss while the goods are in transit [UCC 2-319(1) (a)]. [p. 317]

23. True. F.A.S. (free alongside ship) or F.A.S. (vessel) port of shipment requires the seller to deliver and tender the goods alongside the named vessel or on the dock designated and provided by the buyer. The seller bears the expense and risk of loss until this is done. [p. 317]

24. True. No-arrival, no-sale contract requires the seller to bear the expense and risk of loss of the goods during transportation. However, the seller is under no duty to deliver replacement goods to the buyer because there is no contractual stipulation that the goods will arrive at the appointed destination. [p. 317]

25. False. C.&F. (cost and freight) is a pricing term that means that the price includes the cost of the goods and the cost of freight. [p. 317]

26. True.. A destination contract requires the seller to deliver conforming goods to a specific destination. The risk of loss in a destination contract is on the seller while the goods are in transport. Thus, except in the case of a no-arrival, no-sale contract, the seller is required to replace any goods lost in transit. The buyer does not have to pay for destroyed goods. [p. 318]

27. False. A shipment contract requires the seller to deliver goods conforming to the contract to a carrier. The risk of loss in a shipment contract passes to the buyer when the seller delivers the conforming goods to the carrier. The buyer bears the risk of loss of the goods during

transportation [UCC 2-509(1)(a)]. Shipment contracts are created in two ways. The first method requires the use of the term shipment contract. The second requires the use of one of the following delivery terms: F.O.B. point of shipment, F.A.S., C.I.F., or C.&F. [p. 318]

28. True. In a sale on approval, there is no sale unless and until the buyer accepts the goods. [p. 320]

29. True. A consignment is treated as a sale or return under the UCC; that is, title and risk of loss of the goods pass to the consignee when the consignee takes possession of the goods. [p. 320]

30. True. A seller or lessor has voidable title or voidable leasehold interest to goods if he obtained the goods through fraud, if his check for the payment of the goods or lease is dishonored, or if he impersonated another person. [p. 322]

Multiple Choice

31. D. Answer D is correct since once the goods that are the subject of a contract exist and have been identified, title to the goods may be transferred from the seller to the buyer. Article 2 of the UCC establishes precise rules for determining the passage of title in sales contracts. [p. 316]

32. B. Answer B is correct, as future goods are goods not yet in existence. [p. 316]

33. D. Answer D is correct, as. a shipment contract requires the seller to ship the goods to the buyer via a common carrier. The seller is required to (1) make proper shipping arrangements and (2) deliver the goods into the carrier's hands. Title passes to the buyer at the time and place of shipment [UCC 2-401(2)(a)]. [p. 316]

34. B. Answer B is correct, as a destination contract requires the seller to deliver the goods either to the buyer's place of business or to another destination specified in the sales contract. Title passes to the buyer when the seller tenders delivery of the goods at the specified destination [UCC 2-401(2)(b)]. [p. 316]

35. C. Answer C is correct. If a document of title is required, title passes when and where the seller delivers the document to the buyer [UCC 2-401(3)(a)]. [p. 316]

36. B. Answer B is correct, as. No-arrival, no-sale contract requires the seller to bear the expense and risk of loss of the goods during transportation. However, the seller is under no duty deliver replacement goods to the buyer because there is no contractual stipulation that the goods will arrive at the appointed destination [UCC 2-324(a),(b)]. [p. 317]

37. A. Answer A is correct. In a No-arrival, no-sale contract requires the seller to bear the expense and risk of loss of the goods during transportation. However, the seller is under no duty deliver replacement goods to the buyer because there is no contractual stipulation that the goods will arrive at the appointed destination [UCC 2-324(a),(b)]. [p. 317]

38. C. Answer C is correct. A buyer breaches a sales contract if he or she (1) refuses to take delivery of conforming goods, (2) repudiates the contract, or (3) otherwise breaches the contract. [p. 319]

39. D. Answer D is correct. Whether goods are subject to the claims of a buyer's creditors usually depends on whether the seller files a financing statement, as required by Article 9 of the UCC. If the seller files a financing statement, the goods are subject to the claims of the seller's creditors. If the seller fails to file such a statement, the goods are subject to the claims of the buyer's creditors [UCC 2-326(3)]. [p. 320]

40. C. Answer C is correct. In a case in which a buyer purchases goods or a lessee leases goods from a thief who has stolen them, the purchaser does not acquire title to the goods, and the lessee does not acquire any leasehold interest in the goods. The real owner can reclaim the goods from the purchaser or lessee [UCC 2-403(1)]. This is called void title or void leasehold interest. [p. 321]

Short Answer

41. When Zeb planted the corn, it became identified. [p. 316]

42. To bear the expense and risk of loss until the goods are loaded from the ship at its port of destination [UCC 2-322(1)(b)]. [p. 317]

43. F.O.B. place of destination, ex-ship, or no-arrival, no-sale contract. [p. 317]

44. A merchant-seller bears the risk of loss between the time of contracting and the time that the buyer picks up the goods. [p. 318]

45. A situation in which a thief acquires no title to the goods he or she steals. [p. 321]

46. For a commercially reasonable time. [p. 319]

47. It requires the seller to arrange to ship goods and put goods in the carrier's possession in Houghton, Michigan. [p. 317]

48. A warehouse receipt or bill of lading. [p. 318]

49. Alongside the named vessel or on the dock designated and provided by the buyer. [p. 317]

50. The defect or nonconformity is cured, or the buyer accepts the nonconforming goods. [p. 319]

51. Any goods identified to the contract. [p. 319]

52. Title to the leased goods remains with the lessor or a third party. [p. 315]

53. The term shipment and one of the delivery terms such as F.O.B., F.A.S., C.I.F, or C&F must be present. [p. 318]

54. A person to whom good title can be transferred from a person with voidable title. The real owner cannot reclaim goods from a good faith purchaser for value. [p. 322]

55. If an owner entrusts the possession of his or her goods to a merchant who deals in the particular type of goods, the merchant may transfer all rights to a buyer in the ordinary course of business. The real owner cannot reclaim the goods from this type of buyer. [p. 322]s

20 | REMEDIES FOR BREACH OF SALES AND LEASE CONTRACTS

Chapter Overview

The Uniform Commercial Code provides several remedies to an injured party based on a breach of a sales or lease contract. This chapter explores the prelitigation and litigation remedies available to an injured party. The performance of obligations and options of the remedies that are available for breach of sales and lease contracts are examined.

Objectives

Upon completion of the exercises in this chapter, you should be able to:
1. Describe the performance of sales and lease contracts.
2. List and describe the seller's remedies for the buyer's breach of a sales contract.
3. List and describe the buyer's remedies for the seller's breach of a sales contract.
4. List and describe the lessor's remedies for the lessee's breach of a lease contract.
5. List and describe the lessee's remedies for the lessor's breach of a lease contract.

Practical Application

This chapter should enable you to know what types of obligations are expected of you as a buyer or a seller. It will solidify the remedies that are available to you in the event of a breach of a sales or lease contract if you are a buyer and lessee or a seller and lessor.

Helpful Hints

As with many of the chapters involving the area of contracts, it is helpful to organize your studying around the parties and the concepts that pertain to those parties. In this chapter, you are studying obligations of the buyer and seller and the remedies available in the event of a breach by the buyer or seller. The study tips section has been created to help you learn what the obligations of each party are and what remedies are available to each of them in the event of a breach.

Study Tips

Remedies for Breach of Sales and Lease Contracts

The UCC provides several prelitigation and litigation remedies to the injured party in the event of breach of a sales or lease contract. These remedies are designed to put the injured party in as good of a position as if the contract had been performed.

Seller and Lessor's Performance

The seller must tender delivery in accordance with his or her contract terms with the buyer.
- Tender of delivery refers to conforming goods.
- Seller must give the buyer reasonable notice of the delivery and delivery must be at a reasonable hour and goods must be kept for a reasonable time.
- Goods must be delivered in one single delivery unless the parties agree to another arrangement.

Place of Delivery. The contract may state where delivery is to take place. The contract may state that the buyer will pick up the goods. If nothing is stated in the contract, the UCC will dictate this term.

Noncarrier Cases. If no carrier is involved, then delivery is at the seller's or lessor's business.
- If the parties know the goods are located in another location, then that is the place of delivery.
- If the goods are in the possession of a bailee, delivery is where the seller tenders to the buyer a negotiable document of title, produces acknowledgment from the bailee of the buyer's right of possession, or tenders a nonnegotiable document of title.

Carrier Cases. If a carrier is involved, it will depend on if the contract is a shipment or a destination contract.
- Shipment Contract. The seller must deliver the goods to the carrier, obtain proper contract documentation and give the buyer notice.
- Destination Contract. The seller is required to deliver the goods to the buyer's place of business or wherever is designated in the parties' contract. Delivery must be at a reasonable time and in a reasonable manner accompanied with proper notice and documents of title.

Perfect Tender Rule. The seller is under a duty to deliver conforming goods to the buyer.
- If tender is not perfect, the buyer may:
  - o reject the whole shipment
  - o accept the whole shipment
  - o reject part and accept part of the shipment

Exceptions to the Perfect Tender Rule.
- Agreement of the Parties. The parties may also agree to limit the application of the perfect tender rule by doing so in their written contract.
- Substitution of Carriers. If a carrier is involved, the UCC mandates a commercially reasonable substitute be used if the agreed-upon manner of delivery fails or becomes unavailable.
- Opportunity to Cure. If nonconforming goods are delivered, the UCC gives the seller the chance to cure the defective delivery if the time for performance has not expired or the lessor gives the buyer notice that he or she will make a conforming delivery within the time frame stated in the parties' contract.

Installment Contracts. One that requires or authorizes the goods to be accepted or delivered in separate lots.
- The UCC alters the perfect tender rule by allowing the buyer to reject the entire shipment if the nonconformity substantially impairs the entire contract.
- The court will view installment contracts on a case-by-case basis.

Destruction of Goods. If the destruction of goods is not the fault of either party and the goods have been identified to the contract, the contract will be void; but if the goods are partially destroyed, the buyer may then inspect and partially accept the goods or treat the contract as void. If the buyer opts to accept, compensation will be adjusted accordingly.

Good Faith and Reasonableness. These two principles rule the performance of lease and sales contracts. These principles apply to both the buyer and the seller.

Buyer and Lessee's Performance

If proper tender of delivery is made to the buyer (lessee), the buyer is then obligated to accept and pay for the goods as per the parties' contract or as mandated by the UCC in the event that there is no contract.

Right of Inspection. Buyer has the right to inspect goods that are tendered, delivered, or identified to the contract.
- If the goods are shipped, inspection will be at the time the goods arrive.
   - If the goods are nonconforming, buyer may reject the goods and not pay for them.
- Parties may agree as to time, place, and manner of inspection. If there is no agreement, then it must be at a reasonable time, place, and manner.
   - Reasonableness is determined by common usage of trade, prior course dealings, etc.
   - If the goods conform to the contract, buyer pays for the inspection.
- C.O.D. deliveries are not subject to buyer inspection until the buyer pays for the goods.

Payment of the Goods. Goods that are accepted must be paid for when the goods are delivered even if the delivery place is the same as the place where the goods are shipped.
- Goods paid for on credit have a credit period that begins to run from the time that the goods are shipped.
- Goods may be paid for using any acceptable method of payment unless the agreed-upon terms involve cash only.
   - If cash is all that a seller will accept from the buyer, then the buyer must be given extra time to procure the cash.
- Payment by check is conditioned on the check being honored.

Acceptance.
- Acceptance occurs when, after a reasonable chance to inspect the goods, the buyer or lessee either
   - shows the seller or lessor in words or actions that the goods are conforming or that the buyer will retain the nonconforming goods, or
   - fails to reject the goods after a reasonable time after tender of delivery.
- It can also occur if the buyer resells the goods.
- Buyers and lessees can only accept delivery of a commercial unit.
   - Acceptance of any part of a commercial unit is acceptance of the entire unit.

Revocation of Acceptance.
- A buyer or lessee, after accepting goods, can thereafter revoke this acceptance if
   - the goods are nonconforming
   - the nonconformity substantially impairs the value of the goods and

- one of the following can be shown
  - the seller's or lessor's promise to cure is not met
  - the nonconformity was difficult to discover and the goods were accepted prior to discovery
  - the goods were accepted prior to discovery of the defect and the seller or lessor had given assurances of conformity
- Revocation is not effective until the seller or lessor is notified.
  - It must be made within a reasonable time.
  - It must be made prior to a substantial change in the condition of the goods.

Seller's and Lessor's Remedies

The seller and lessors have several remedies available if the buyer or lessee breaches the contract. These remedies are as follows:

Right to Withhold Delivery. Delivery of the goods may be withheld if the seller is in possession of the goods when the buyer or lessee is in breach. If there has been a partial delivery of the goods when the breach occurs, then the seller or lessor may withhold delivery of the remaining part of the goods.
- A buyer's or lessee's insolvency will also justify a seller's or lessor's withholding of delivery of the goods under the contract.

Right to Stop Delivery of Goods in Transit. Goods are in transit when they are in the carrier's bailee's possession.
- If a buyer is discovered to be insolvent while the goods are in transit, the seller may stop the goods while in transit.
- If the buyer or lessee repudiates the contract, delivery can be withheld only if it is a carload, a planeload, or a truckload. Notice to the carrier or bailee is required.
- The seller must hold the goods for the buyer after the delivery has been stopped.

Right to Reclaim Goods. Reclamation refers to a seller or lessor's right to demand the return of goods from the buyer or lessee under certain situations.
- Where the buyer is insolvent, seller has 10 days to demand the return of the goods.
- Where the buyer has misrepresented his or her solvency in writing three months before delivery or presents a check that is later dishonored, reclamation may occur at any time.
- Requirements of reclamation include:
  - Written notice to the buyer or lessee.
  - Refraining from self-help if the buyer refuses.
    - Use of legal proceedings must be instituted.

Right to Dispose of Goods. If the buyer or lessee breaches or repudiates before the seller or lessor disposes of the goods, then the seller may release or resell goods and recover damages from the buyer or lessee.
- Damages incurred as a result of disposition are measured by the disposition price and the contract price.
- Incidental damages may also be recovered.
- Disposition of the goods must be in good faith and in a commercially reasonable manner.
- Disposition may be as a unit or in parcels and publicly or privately.
- Notice must be given.

Unfinished Goods. If a sales or lease contract is breached or repudiated before the goods are finished the seller can:

- stop manufacturing of the goods and resell them for scrap or salvage value or
- complete the goods and resell, release, or otherwise dispose of them or
- recover damages from the buyer or lessee.

Right to Recover the Purchase Price or Rent. The UCC allows a seller to sue the buyer for the purchase price or rent as provided in the parties sale or lease contract. This remedy is available when:

- The buyer or lessee accepts the goods but does not pay for them when the rent is due.
- The buyer or lessee breaches the contract after the goods have been identified to the contract and the seller or lessor cannot dispose of or sell the goods.
- The goods are damaged or lost after the risk of loss passes to the buyer or lessee.

Right to Recover Damages for Breach of Contract. A cause of action to recover damages caused by the breach of contract may be brought where the buyer or lessee repudiates a sales or lease contract or wrongfully rejects tendered goods.

- The measure of damages is the difference between the contract price and the market price at the time and place where the goods were delivered plus incidental damages.
    - If this does not place the seller in a position as though the contract was performed, the seller may recover lost profits that would have resulted from full performance plus an allowance for reasonable overhead and incidental damages.

Right to Cancel the Contract. The seller or lessor may cancel the contract if the buyer or lessee breaches the contract by revoking acceptance of the goods, rejects the contract, or fails to pay for the goods or repudiates all or any part of the contract.

- The cancellation may apply to the entire contract or to only the affected goods.
- The seller or lessor who notifies the buyer or lessee of the cancellation is discharged from any further obligations under the contract.
    - He or she may also seek damages against the buyer or lessee for the breach.

Buyer and Lessee's Remedies

The buyer or lessee also has many remedies available to him or her upon the breach of a sales or lease contract by the seller or lessor. These remedies are as follows:

Right to Reject Nonconforming Goods or Improperly Tendered Goods. If tender of delivery fails, the buyer may reject the whole, accept the whole or accept any commercial unit and reject the rest.

- A buyer who rejects nonconforming goods must identify the defects that are able to be determined by a reasonable inspection.
    - Rejection must be within a reasonable time after delivery and in a reasonable manner.
    - The buyer must also hold the goods for a reasonable period of time.

Right to Recover Goods from an Insolvent Seller or Lessor. If the buyer makes a partial payment to the seller and the seller or lessor becomes insolvent within ten days of the first payment, the buyer or lessee may recover the goods from the seller or lessor. This is called capture.

Right to Obtain Specific Performance. When the remedy at law is inadequate and the goods are unique, the buyer or lessee may ask for specific performance of the sales or lease contract.

Right to Cover. The buyer or lessee may cover if the seller or lessor fails to make delivery of goods or repudiates the contract or the buyer or lessee rightfully rejects the goods or justifiably revokes their acceptance. Renting or purchasing substitute goods accomplish covering.

Right to Replevy Goods. A buyer or lessee may recover scarce goods wrongfully withheld by a seller or lessor by demonstrating that he or she was unable to cover or the attempts to cover will not come to fruition. This is only available as to goods identified to the lease or sales contract.

Right to Cancel the Contract. Failure to deliver conforming goods, repudiation of the contract by the seller, rightful rejection of the goods, or justifiable revocation of goods that were accepted all may enable the buyer to cancel with respect to the affected goods or the whole contract if the breach is material in nature.

Right to Recover Damages for Non delivery or Repudiation. The buyer or lessee may recover damages that equate to the difference between the contract price and the market price, along with incidental and consequential damages, less expenses saved if a seller or lessor fails to deliver the goods or repudiates the sales or lease contract.

Right to Recover Damages for Accepted Nonconforming Goods. A buyer may seek to recover damages from any loss as a result of the nonconforming goods accepted from the seller. Incidental damages as well as consequential damages may also be recovered. The buyer must give notice of the nonconformity to the seller within a reasonable time of when the breach should have been discovered.

Additional Performance Issues

Assurance of Performance. If one party has reasonable grounds to believe that the other party either will not or cannot perform his or her contractual obligations, the other party may demand assurance for performance in writing.
- The aggrieved party may suspend his or her own performance if it is commercially practicable to do so until the assurance is forth-coming from the potential wrongdoer.

Statute of Limitations. Under the UCC, an action for breach of any written or oral sales or lease contract must be within four years. The parties can agree to a one-year statute of limitations.

Agreements Affecting Remedies. The parties may agree to limit buyer's or lessee's remedies to repair and replacement of defective goods or return and refund.
- The parties must expressly state that the agreed upon remedies are exclusive, or they are in addition to UCC remedies.
- If an exclusive remedy fails, any remedy may be had.

Liquidated Damages. These are pre-established damages, which act as a substitute for actual damages.

Refresh Your Memory

The following exercise will give you the opportunity to test your memory of the principles given in this chapter. Read the question twice and place your answer in the blank provided. Review the chapter material for any question that you are unable to answer or remember.

1. _____ is an action a party to a sales or lease contract is required by law to carry out.

2. Failure of a party to perform an obligation in a sales or lease contract is known as _____.

3. The obligation of a seller to transfer and deliver goods to the buyer or lessee in accordance with a sales or lease contract is known as _____.

4. A sales contract that requires the seller to send the goods to the buyer but not to a specifically named destination is known as a(n) _____.

5. A(n) _____ is a sales contract that requires the seller to deliver goods to the buyer's place of business or another specified location.

6. A person buying goods from the place where the goods are manufactured would be an example of _____ delivery.

7. In a destination contract, delivery is completed when the shipment _____.

8. A(n) _____ is a type of contract that requires or authorizes goods to be delivered and accepted in separate lots.

9. The right of a seller or lessor to refuse to send goods to a buyer or lessee upon breach of a sales or lease contract by the buyer or lessee or the insolvency of the buyer or lessee is known as the _____.

10. _____ is the right of a seller or lessor to demand the return of goods from the buyer or lessee under specified situations.

11. _____ is a right to remedy that a seller can claim while the goods are in possession of the buyer.

12. The term _____ refers to an action by a buyer or lessor to recover scarce goods wrongfully withheld by a seller or lessor.

13. A(n) _____ can be obtained in writing from the other party if there is an indication that a contract will be breached by that party.

14. _____ is a rule which provides that an action for breach of any written or oral sales or lease contract must commence within four years after the cause of action accrues.

15. Damages that will be paid upon a breach of contract, but that are established in advance are known as _____.

Critical Thought Exercise

Sanco Corporation agreed to sell two seven-ton diesel forklifts to Agro-Star, Inc., for $250,000, with an option to purchase four more at $500,000. The forklifts were to be installed in a produce cooling warehouse according to specific design and performance standards. Sanco did not deliver and Agro-Star covered by purchasing different forklifts from Power Arm Lifts for $200,000, plus an additional $300,000 for testing and development by Power Arm Lifts. Agro-Star also bought the four additional lifts that they needed from Power Arm Lifts for $350,000.

At trial, Agro-Star is awarded $250,000, the difference between Sanco's price for the first two forklifts and the cost of the first two Power Arm forklifts.

As an officer in Sanco Corporation, you must decide whether to pay the judgment or pay an additional $20,000 in attorney's fees and appeal the judgment. Will you authorize the appeal? Why? Is it fair for Sanco to receive the benefit of a bargain struck by Agro-Star when they covered?

Please compose your answer to the Critical Thinking Exercise using a separate sheet of paper or your computer word processing program.

Practice Quiz

True/False

1. _____ The seller's or lessor's general obligation is to transfer and deliver the goods to the buyer or lessee.

2. _____ Destination contracts are an example of noncarrier delivery.

3. _____ A sales contract requires the seller to send the goods to the buyer at a specifically named destination.

4. _____ In a shipment contract, delivery occurs when the shipment reaches the destination.

5. _____ Under the perfect render rule, the buyer can reject a whole shipment of nonconforming goods.

6. _____ The right to cure rule can be invoked by the seller.

7. _____ The right to cure rule allows buyers to claim replacements for nonconforming goods

8. _____ The UCC alters the perfect tender rule with regard to installment contracts.

9. _____ A buyer cannot revoke his acceptance if he or she has already accepted nonconforming goods.

10. _____ Revocation of acceptance is not effective until the seller or lessor is so notified.

11. _____ Goods in possession with bailees are considered to be in transit.

12. _____ Incidental charges can be claimed by the seller incurred on the disposition of goods.

13. _____ The measure of damages for nondelivery is the difference between the contract price and the market price at the time the breach is realized.

14. _____ Liquidated damages can be claimed in addition to actual damages.

15. _____ An unconscionable contract can be enforced if the unconscionable clause is removed.

Multiple Choice

16. Which of the following would be considered as a breach of contract?

A. acceptance of nonconforming goods by a buyer
B. nonacceptance of conforming goods by a buyer
C. delivery of conforming goods by a seller
D. non-delivery of goods to a buyer that has a document of title

17. Which of the following is true for a perfect tender rule delivery?

A. The seller can reject delivery of certain parts of the goods.
B. The buyer can only reject parts of the goods and not the whole shipment.
C. The buyer can seek remedies for accepting nonconforming goods.
D. The seller can seek remedies for nonconforming goods that were accepted by the buyer.

18. Which of the following is a recourse for sellers, under the UCC, in case of shipment of nonconforming or defective goods?

A. tender of delivery
B. right to cure
C. perfect tender rule
D. replevin

19. When is a delivery considered completed in a shipment contract?

A. when the buyer receives the shipment
B. when the seller hands over the shipment to the carrier
C. when the shipment reaches the destination that the buyer specified
D. when the seller notifies the buyer of the shipment in transit

20. Which of the following is true of a contract in which the goods were destroyed, of no fault of the buyer or seller, before the title to goods passed to the buyer?

A. The buyer has to still pay for the destroyed goods.
B. The seller and buyer are excused from contractual obligations.
C. The buyer can successfully claim for replacements from the seller.
D. The seller is obligated to make a new shipment as the previous contract.

21. Which of the following constitutes an acceptance by the buyer?

A. if the buyer asks for inspection of goods upon its arrival
B. if the buyer does not pass the title of the goods to another buyer
C. if the buyer fails to reject the goods within a reasonable time after delivery
D. if the buyer accepts nonconforming goods

22. Which of the following is grounds for revoking an acceptance?

A. if the seller makes a timely cure of nonconforming goods
B. if the goods were accepted after the nonconformity was discovered
C. if the buyer has accepted only one commercial unit from the entire unit
D. if the nonconformity substantially impairs the value of the goods to the buyer
23. Which of the following is a buyer's right to remedy?

A. right to recover damages for nondelivery
B. right to dispose of goods
C. right to replevy goods
D. right to obtain specific performance

24. Which of the following is true for a seller's right to dispose of goods from a breach of contract?

A. Any profit made on the resale or release of the goods has to be shared with the original buyer.
B. Incidental charges can be recovered from the original buyer.
C. The seller cannot resell the goods unless the original buyer agrees to it.
D. The buyer can only dispose of goods that have already been delivered.

25. Which one of the following is a remedy for buyers in cases where the seller or lessor tenders nonconforming goods, and the buyer or lessee accepts them?

A. cover and then recover damages
B. deduct damages from the unpaid purchase or rent price
C. replevy the goods
D. sue for specific performance

Short Answer

26. When a carrier is not involved, where is the place of delivery to where goods can be delivered?

_____

_____

27. If a contract does not specifically state where the delivery will take place, what is the first thing that is looked at in order to determine the place of delivery?

_____

_____

28. If the parties have no agreement respecting the time, place, and manner of delivery, how must tender of goods be made?

_____
_____

29. If a set of family room furniture to be delivered to the buyer was partially destroyed by fire, what may the buyer choose to do with regard to the goods?

_____
_____

30. When may a cure take place?

_____
_____

31. When is revocation of goods accepted by a buyer or lessee effective?

_____
_____

32. What sort of proof is necessary for the court to find that an unconscionable contract exists between two parties to a contract?

_____
_____

33. With regard to the statute of limitation for a breach of any written or oral sales or lease contract, what may the parties agree to do?

_____
_____

34. How are the terms good faith and reasonableness applied to a contractual setting?

_____
_____

35. What is specific performance?

_____
_____

36. List at two things that must occur in order for a revocation by the buyer to be effective.

_____
_____

37. When may an adequate assurance of due performance be demanded of one party by the other party?

_____
_____

38. What remedy is available to a seller when a buyer or lessor when the buyer or lessee repudiates or breaches his or her contract before the seller has delivered the goods?

_____
_____

39. Give examples of incidental damages.

_____

_____

40. What is a lost volume seller?

_____

_____

Answers to Refresh Your Memory

1. Obligation [p. 328]
2. breach [p. 328]
3. tender of delivery [p. 328]
4. shipment contract [p. 328]
5. destination contract [p. 329]
6. noncarrier case [p. 328]
7. reaches the destination specified in the contract [p. 329]
8. installment contract [p. 330]
9. right to withhold delivery [p. 332]
10. Right to reclaim goods [p. 332]
11. Right to reclaim goods [p. 332]
12. replevin [p. 336]
13. adequate assurance of performance [p. 337]
14. UCC statute of limitations [p. 337]
15. liquidated damages [p. 338]

Critical Thought Exercise Model Answer

Yes, I will authorize the appeal. Under UCC 2-715, the remedy of cover allows the buyer, on the seller's breach, to purchase the goods, in good faith and within a reasonable time, from another seller and substitute them for the goods due under the contract. If the cost of cover exceeds the cost of the contract goods, the breaching seller will be liable to the buyer for the difference, plus incidental and consequential damages.

In our case, the cost of the contracted forklifts was to be $750,000. Agro-Star had to pay only $550,000 for the forklifts, plus the incidental damages of $300,000 for further testing and development. By exercising their right of cover, Agro-Star only suffered damages of $100,000. The cost of the appeal is only $20,000 and we will likely have the award reduced by $150,000.

It is both fair and ethical for us to take advantage of the cover rule. The purpose of contract damages is to put the nonbreaching party in the same position they would have been if the breach had not occurred. Damages awarded after the nonbreaching party has covered make the buyer whole while avoiding a punitive result to the seller.

Answers to Practice Quiz

True/False

16. True. The seller's or lessor's general obligation is to transfer and deliver the goods to the buyer or lessee. The buyer's or lessee's general obligation is to accept and pay for the goods. [p. 328]

17. False. A sales contract that requires the seller to deliver goods to the buyer's place of business or another specified destination is a destination contract. It is not an example of a noncarrier delivery. [p. 329]

18. False. A sales contract that requires the seller to deliver goods to the buyer's place of business or another specified destination is a destination contract. [p. 329]

19. False. In a shipment contract delivery occurs when the seller puts the goods in the carrier's possession. [p. 328]

20. True. The perfect tender rule is a rule that says if the goods or tender of a delivery fail in any respect to conform to the contract, the buyer may opt (1) to reject the whole shipment, (2) to accept the whole shipment, or (3) to reject part and accept part of the shipment. [p. 329]

21. True. The UCC gives a seller or lessor who delivers nonconforming goods the right to cure the nonconformity. [p. 329]

22. False. The UCC gives a seller or lessor who delivers nonconforming goods the right to cure the nonconformity. Right to cure is an opportunity to repair or replace defective or nonconforming goods. [p. 329]

23. True. The UCC alters the perfect tender rule with regard to installment contracts. [p. 330]

24. False. A buyer or lessee who has accepted goods may subsequently revoke his or her acceptance if the goods are nonconforming, [p. 332]

25. True. Revocation of acceptance is not effective until the seller or lessor is so notified. [p. 332]

26. True. The goods are considered to be in transit while they are in possession of these carriers or bailees. [p. 332]

27. True. The seller or lessor may also recover any incidental damages (reasonable expenses incurred in stopping delivery, transportation charges, storage charges, sales commission, and the like [UCC 2-710, 2A-530]) incurred on the disposition of the goods [UCC 2-706(1), 2A-527(2)]. [p. 333]

28. True. The measure of damages is the difference between the contract price (or original rent) and the market price (or rent) at the time the buyer or lessee learned of the breach. [p. 336]

29. False. The UCC permits parties to a sales or lease contract to establish in advance in their contract the damages that will be paid upon a breach of the contract. Such preestablished damages, called liquidated damages, substitute for actual damages. [p. 338]

30. True. If a court finds that a contract or any clause in a contract is unconscionable, the court may refuse to enforce the contract, it may enforce the remainder of the contract without the unconscionable clause, or it may so limit the application of any unconscionable clause as to avoid any unconscionable result. [p. 338]

Multiple Choice

31. B. Answer B is the correct answer. Usually, the parties to a sales or lease contract owe a duty to perform the obligations specified in their agreement [UCC 2-301, 2A-301]. The seller's or lessor's general obligation is to transfer and deliver the goods to the buyer or lessee. The buyer's or lessee's general obligation is to accept and pay for the goods. [p. 328]

32. C. Answer C is the correct answer. If the goods or tender of delivery fail in any respect to conform to the contract, the buyer or lessee may opt (1) to reject the whole shipment, (2) to accept the whole shipment, or (3) to reject part and accept part of the shipment. This option is referred to as the perfect tender rule [UCC 2-601, 2A-509]. If a buyer accepts nonconforming goods, the buyer may seek remedies against the seller. [p. 329]

33. B. Answer B is the correct answer. The UCC gives a seller or lessor who delivers nonconforming goods the right to cure the nonconformity. [p. 329]

34. B. Answer B is the correct answer. Delivery occurs in shipment contracts when the seller puts the goods in the carrier's possession. [p. 329]

35. B. Answer B is correct. The UCC provides that if goods identified in a sales or lease contract are totally destroyed without the fault of either party before the risk of loss passes to the buyer or the lessee, the contract is void. Both parties are then excused from performing the contract. [p. 330]

36. C. Answer C is the correct answer. Acceptance occurs when the buyer or lessee takes either of the following actions after a reasonable opportunity to inspect the goods: (1) signifies to the seller or lessor in words or by conduct that the goods are conforming or that the buyer or lessee will take or retain the goods despite their nonconformity or (2) fails to effectively reject the goods within a reasonable time after their delivery or tender by the seller or lessor. [p. 331]

37. D. Answer D is the correct. A buyer or lessee who has accepted goods may subsequently revoke his or her acceptance if the nonconformity substantially impairs the value of the goods to the buyer or lessee. [p. 332]

38. B. Answer B is the correct answer. If a buyer or lessee breaches or repudiates a sales or lease contract before the seller or lessor has delivered the goods, the seller or lessor may resell or release the goods and recover damages from the buyer or lessee [UCC 2-703(d), 2-706(1), 2A-523(1)(e), 2A-527(1)]. The right to dispose of goods also arises if the seller or lessor has reacquired the goods after stopping them in transit. [p. 333]

39. B. Answer B is the correct answer. The seller or lessor may also recover any incidental damages (reasonable expenses incurred in stopping delivery, transportation charges, storage charges, sales commission, and the like [UCC 2-710, 2A-530]) incurred on the disposition of the goods. Incidental charges can be recovered from the original buyer. [p. 333]

40. B. Answer B is the correct answer. If the buyer or lessee accepts nonconforming goods, he or she may deduct all or any part of damages resulting from the breach from any part of the purchase price or rent still due under the contract. [p. 337]

Short Answer

41. The seller's or lessor's place of business. [p. 328]

42. Whether or not a carrier is involved. [p. 328]

43. Tender must be made at a reasonable hour and the goods must be kept available for a reasonable period of time. [p. 328]

44. Buyer or lessee may inspect the goods and then choose either to treat the contract as void or to accept the goods. [p. 330]

45. If the time for performance has not expired and the buyer is given notice. [p. 329]

46. When the seller or lessor is notified. [p. 332]

47. That the parties had substantially unequal bargaining power. [p. 338]

48. The parties may agree to reduce the limitations period to one year. [p. 337]

49. The concept of good faith and reasonableness also refers to the "spirit" of the contract with the underlying theory being that the parties are more apt to perform properly if their conduct is to be judged against these principles. [p. 330]

50. Specific performance is a decree of the court that orders a seller or lessor to perform his or her obligations under the contract; this usually occurs when the goods in question are unique, such as art or antiques. [p. 335]

51. It must be shown that the goods are nonconforming and the nonconformity substantially impairs the value of the goods to the buyer or lessee. [p. 332]

52. An adequate assurance of performance may be demanded of a party if one party to the contract has reasonable grounds to believe that the other party either will or cannot perform his or her contractual obligations. [p. 337]

53. The seller or lessor may resell or release the goods and recover damages from the buyer or lessee. [p. 334]

54. Incidental damages include reasonable expenses in stopping delivery, transportation charges, storage charges, sales commission, and the like. [p. 333]

55. A seller becomes a lost volume seller when a buyer defaults on a sale and the seller resells the item when the seller could have produced more of the item. The seller could have made the profit on the original sale as well as a profit on additional sales from the additional production. [p. 334]

21 | WARRANTIES

Chapter Overview

This chapter focuses on the different types of warranties, providing clear examples for each. Among the warranties that are discussed are the express warranty, implied warranty of merchantability, and the implied warranty of fitness for a particular purpose. It provides a concise understanding of the special warranties of title and possession, as well as the remedies that are available for breach of the various warranties. Disclaimers and their lawfulness are examined.

Objectives

Upon completion of the exercises in this chapter, you should be able to:
1. Identify and describe express warranties.
2. Describe the implied warranty of merchantability.
3. Describe the implied warranty of fitness for a particular purpose.
4. Identify warranty disclaimers and determine when they are unlawful.
5. Describe the warranties of good title and no infringements.

Practical Application

You should recognize the various types of warranties as they exist within a transaction. You will be able to assess whether or not a warranty has been breached. You should be able to recognize disclaimers and determine whether or not they are lawful.

Helpful Hints

It is helpful to understand that there are three categories of warranties: oral, express, and implied. As you study warranties, it is helpful to keep them organized according to the type of warranty it is, and to keep an example of each type in mind so that the material can be kept clear.

Study Tips

Sales and Lease Warranties

Consumers have often been taken advantage of in their daily transactions. Initially *Caveat Emptor*, which in Latin means "Buyer Beware," governed consumer transactions. However, various Uniform Commercial Code laws have been developed which establish certain warranties for the sales of goods and certain lease transactions. A warranty is like insurance to a consumer in that it is a way to make sure that goods meet certain standards.

Express Warranty

Express warranties are created when a seller or lessor affirms that the goods he or she is selling or leasing meet certain criteria of quality, performance, description, or condition. These warranties are found in brochures, ads, catalogs, diagrams, etc. Express warranties are created in the following circumstances:

- *Affirmations of fact or promise.* Promises made about the goods, such as "This aluminum siding will last for 25 years."
- *Description.* Descriptions of the goods, such as "Iowa Corn."
- *Model or sample.* Modes or samples of goods, such as a sample of fabric.

Statement of Opinion. Puffing or statements of opinion do not create an express warranty. In order to be an express warranty, it must qualify as an affirmation of fact.

- An affirmation of value does not create an express warranty.

Damages for Breach of Warranty. The buyer or lessee may sue the seller or lessor for compensatory damages.

- Compensatory damages are equal to the difference between the value of the goods as warranted and the actual value of the goods accepted at the time and place of acceptance.

Implied Warranty of Merchantability

This warranty is not expressly stated in a sales or lease contract. If a seller or lessor of a good is a merchant with respect to goods of that kind, this warranty will be implied, unless it is properly disclaimed.

- The goods must be fit for the ordinary purpose for which they are used.
- The goods must be adequately contained, packaged, and labeled.
- The goods must be of a kind, quality, and quantity with each unit.
- The goods must conform to any promise or affirmation of fact made on the container or label.
- The quality of the goods must pass without objection in the trade.
- Fungible goods must meet a fair average or middle range of quality.

Implied Warranty of Fitness for Human Consumption

The UCC includes this warranty within the implied warranty of merchantability. This warranty applies to food and drink consumed on or off the premises.

- *Foreign Substance Test.* Used to determine whether food products are unmerchantable. A food product is unmerchantable if a foreign object in a product causes injury to an individual.
- *Consumer Expectation Test.* Merchantability is tested based on what the average consumer would expect to find in his or her food products.

Implied Warranty of Fitness for a Particular Purpose

A warranty that comes about where a seller or lessor warrants that the goods will meet the buyer's or lessee's expressed needs and applies to both merchant and nonmerchant sellers and lessors.

- The seller or lessor has reason to know the particular purpose for which the buyer is purchasing the goods or the lessee is leasing the goods.
- The seller or lessor makes a statement that the goods will serve this purpose.
- The buyer or lessee relies on the seller's or lessor's skill and judgment and purchases or leases the goods. [UCC 2-315, 2A-213]

Warranty Disclaimers

Statements that negate implied and express warranties.

- *"As is" Disclaimer.* This is primarily good for used products and is accomplished by words such as *with all faults, as is, etc.*
- *Disclaimer of Implied Warranty of Merchantability.* This can be oral or written, but must use the term merchantability.
- *Disclaimer of Implied Warranty of Fitness for a Particular Purpose.* This can be achieved by using general language without using the word fitness, but it must be in writing.

Conspicuous Display of Disclaimer. The disclaimer must be conspicuous to a reasonable person.

Magnuson-Moss Warranty Act

This act involves written warranties as they pertain to consumer products. If the product exceeds ten dollars and an express warranty is made, then the warranty must be labeled as "full" or "limited."

- *Full Warranty.* The warrantor must guarantee free repair or replacement of the defective product as well as the time limit of the warranty. The warranty must be conspicuous and able to be understood.
- *Limited Warranty.* A limitation of the scope of the warranty is placed on the product. The warranty must be conspicuous and able to be understood.

Violations of the Magnuson-Moss Warranty Act. Under the act, a consumer may recover damages, attorney's fees, and costs. The consumer must go through the act's arbitration procedure first before taking legal action.

- The act modifies the state law of implied warranties by forbidding sellers or lessors who make express written warranties from disclaiming or modifying implied warranties of merchantability or fitness for a particular purpose.
    - Time limits may be placed on implied warranties but the time limits must correspond to that of the written warranties.

Special Warranties of Title and Possession

The UCC imposes special warranties on sellers and lessors of goods: a warranty of good title, a warranty of no security interests, a warranty against infringements, and a warranty of no interference.

Warranty of Good Title. Unless there is a proper disclaimer, sellers of goods warrant that they have valid title to the goods.

Warranty of No Security Interests. Unless specifically excluded or modified, sellers of goods automatically warrant that the goods they sell are delivered free of any encumbrances, liens, or third-party security interests.

Warranty Against Infringements. Unless the parties agree otherwise, a lessor or seller who is a merchant who regularly deals in goods of the kind leased or sold automatically warrants that the goods are delivered free of any third-party patent, copyright, or trademark claim.

Warranty of No Interference. In a lease transaction, the lessor warrants that no person holds a claim or interest in the goods that arose from an act or omission of the lessor that will interfere with the lessee's enjoyment of his or her leasehold interest.

Refresh Your Memory

The following exercise will give you the opportunity to test your memory of the principles given in this chapter. Read the question twice and place your answer in the blank provided. Review the chapter material for any question that you are unable to answer or remember.

1. The doctrine of _____ means "let the buyer beware"

2. _____ is a seller's or lessor's express or implied assurance to a buyer or lessee that the goods sold or leased meet certain quality standards.

3. _____ is created when a seller or lessor makes an affirmation that the goods he or she is selling or leasing meet certain standards of quality, description, performance, or condition.

4. _____, also known as puffing, is a commendation of goods made by a seller or lessor that does not create an express warranty.

5. An affirmation of the value of goods does not create a(n) _____.

6. _____ are generally equal to the difference between the value of the goods as warranted and the actual value of the goods accepted at the time and place of acceptance.

7. The _____ does not apply to sales or leases by nonmerchants or casual sales.

8. Under the _____ test, a food product is unmerchantable if a foreign object in that product causes injury to a person.

9. The _____ determines merchantability based on what the average consumer would expect to find in food products.

10. A _____ is a statement that negates express and implied warranties.

11. A(n) "_____" disclaimer is often included in sales contracts for used products.

12. In 1975, Congress enacted the Magnuson-Moss Warranty Act, which covers written warranties related to _____.

13. Persons who transfer goods without proper title breach the warranty of _____.

14. Warranty of _____ is a warranty in which sellers of goods warrant that the goods they sell are delivered free from any third-party security interests, liens, or encumbrances that are unknown to the buyer.

15. The warranty of no interference is also known as the warranty of _____.

Critical Thought Exercise

Bob French, an engineer with Worldwide Construction, travels to Accu-Steel Company in Pennsylvania for the purpose of buying steel cable made by Accu-Steel to help support the upper decks of a new football stadium that Worldwide is building in California. The representative of Accu-Steel reviews the plans for the stadium and sells its recommended cable to Worldwide. The stadium is built using the cable selected by Accu-Steel.

During an exciting football game, the upper deck collapses onto the lower deck due to the inability of the cable to support the weight load. Worldwide Construction now faces suit from thousands of plaintiffs injured or killed in the collapse. Assuming that the steel cable was not defective in either its design or manufacturing process, does Worldwide have a cause of action against Accu-Steel?

Please compose your answer to the Critical Thinking Exercise using a separate sheet of paper or your computer word processing program.

Practice Quiz

True/False:

16. _____ Only written express warranties are valid.

17. _____ Sellers and lessors are not required to make express warranties.

18. _____ A manufacturer is liable for express warranties made by wholesalers and retailers.

19. _____ A retailer is not liable for the express warranties made by manufacturers of goods it sells.

20. _____ A seller's or lessor's statement of opinion or commendation of the goods does not create an express warranty.

21. _____ Implied warranties are expressly stated in the sales or lease contract.

22. _____ Under the foreign substance test, the court asks what a consumer would expect to find or not find in food or drink that he or she consumes.

23. _____ An express warranty can only be limited if the warranty disclaimer and the warranty can be reasonably construed with each other.

24. _____ Disclaimer of the implied warranty of fitness for a particular purpose can be in oral.

25. _____ An "as is" disclaimer implies that all implied warranties are disclaimed.

26. _____ Written disclaimers must be conspicuously displayed to be valid.

27. _____ Persons who transfer goods without proper title breach the warranty of quiet possession.

28. _____ A person selling stolen property would be breaching the warranty of good title.

29. _____ The warranty against infringements protects trademarks and copyright claims.

30. _____ The warranty of no interference warrants that goods sold are free from any third-party security interests, or encumbrances that are unknown to the buyer.

Multiple Choice

31. What was the doctrine of caveat emptor in sales or lease contracts?

A. It was law balanced risk of loss between seller and buyer.
B. It was a law that gave more protection to the buyer in a sales contract.
C. It was a law that stated the risk of loss was completely on the buyer.
D. It was a law that stipulated the issue of warrants in sale or lease transactions.

32. Which of the following is true about express warranties?

A. A manufacturer is liable for express warranties made by wholesalers.
B. A retailer is not allowed to make warranties on manufacturer goods.
C. A retailer is liable for the express warranties made by manufacturers of goods it sells.
D. A manufacturer is obligated by law to make an express warranty on all its goods.

33. Which of the following would constitute the creation of an express warranty for goods?

A. commendation of the goods
B. description of the goods
C. prior experience with the goods
D. affirmation of the value of the goods

34. Which of the following is true of a statement of opinion?

A. It is an affirmation of the value of the goods.
B. It is a type of guarantee.
C. It is an implied assurance not expressly stated.
D. It is the explicit description of the goods.

35. Sam expressed interest in buying a painting from Jasper, who claimed that the painting was a family heirloom. Jasper's asking price was $15,000, but Sam was only willing to offer $13,000. Jasper told him that it was a very old painting worth a fortune and that others would gladly pay $20,000 for it. He also told him that he was only selling it under its market value because he needed the money immediately. He then implied that Sam could sell it for a higher rate if he wanted.

In legal terms, Jasper's words to Sam would be considered as _____.

A. an express warranty
B. an implied warranty of merchantability
C. an oral contract
D. a statement of opinion

36. Where there has been a breach of warranty, the buyer or lessee may sue the seller or lessor to recover _____ damages.

A. future
B. compensatory
C. punitive
D. liquidated

37. That "goods must be fit for the ordinary purposes for which they are used," would be an example for a(n) _____.

A. stamp of approval
B. explicit warranty
C. statement of opinion
D. implied warranty

38. A(n) _____ is a warranty that applies to food or drink consumed on or off the premises of restaurants, grocery stores, fast-food outlets, and vending machines.

A. implied warranty of fitness for human consumption
B. express warranty
C. stamp of approval
D. statement of opinion

39. Which of the following is a similarity between the foreign substance food test and the consumer expectation test?

A. They are both used to determine a buyer's knowledge of a particular food product.
B. They are both used to determine a buyer's interest in a particular food product.
C. They are both part of the express warranty an eatery provides.
D. They are both part of the implied warranty of fitness for human consumption.

40. A(n) _____ is a warranty that arises where a seller or lessor warrants that the goods will meet the buyer's or lessee's expressed needs.

A. disclaimer of the implied warranty of merchantability
B. implied warranty of fitness for human consumption
C. implied warranty of fitness for a particular purpose
D. warranty of good title

41. A statement that negates express and implied warranties is known as a _____.

A. limited warranty
B. warranty disclaimer
C. warranty infringement
D. warranty of no interference

42. What of the following is true of an "as is" disclaimer?

A. It disclaims all express warranties.
B. It disclaims all implied warranties.
C. It is a type of implied warranty.
D. It cannot be replaced by another warranty.

43. Which of the following is true for display of warranty disclaimers as ruled by the court?

A. It can be implied as an understanding between the buyer and seller.
B. It need only be present in the contract.
C. It should be conspicuous and noticeable.
D. It must be published in the local newspaper before actually being displayed.

44. What type of transaction is covered under the Magnuson-Moss Warranty Act?

A. governmental transactions
B. commercial transactions
C. industrial transactions
D. consumer transactions

45. A full warranty is an example of a(n) _____.

A. implied warranty of fitness for a particular purpose
B. disclaimer warranty
C. express warranty
D. implied warranty of fitness for human consumption

Short Answer

46. Give an account of express warranties.

_____

_____

47. What are the requirements for the creation of an express warranty?

_____

_____

48. What are the damages recoverable for a breach of warranty?

_____

_____

49. Explain the implied warranty of merchantability.

_____

_____

50. What is implied warranty of fitness for human consumption? Explain the tests used to determine a breach of this warranty.

_____

_____

51. Explain the implied warranty of fitness for a particular purpose.

_____

_____

52. Given an account of the different types of warranty disclaimers.

_____

_____

53. What is the difference between a full warranty and a limited warranty?

_____

_____

54. Explain the warranty of no security interests.

_____

_____

55. Explain warranty against infringements.

_____

_____

Answers to Refresh Your Memory

1. express [p. 326]
2. express [p. 326]
3. opinion [p. 327
4. merchantability [p. 328]
5. foreign substance [p. 330]
6. fitness, human consumption [p. 330]
7. foreign substance [p. 330]
8. merchantability [p. 332]
9. conspicuously [p. 332]
10. Magnuson-Moss Warranty [p. 333]

11. against infringements [p. 335]
12. good title [p. 335]
13. no security interests [p. 335]
14. against infringement [p. 335]
15. against interference [p. 335]

Critical Thought Exercise Model Answer

An implied warranty of fitness for a particular purpose arises under UCC 2-315 when the buyer's purpose or use for goods is expressly or impliedly known by the seller and the buyer purchases the goods in reliance on the seller's selection of the goods. Accu-Steel was informed of the express purpose for which the steel cable was being bought. Accu-Steel sold the cable to Worldwide that it recommended for the job. Accu-Steel may also be liable to Worldwide and the injured plaintiffs based upon a theory of product liability founded upon Accu-Steel's negligence. Due care must be used by the manufacturer in designing the product, selecting materials, using the appropriate manufacturing process, assembling and testing the product, and placing adequate warnings on the label or product. Accu-Steel selected the size of the cable to be produced. By failing to select a thicker and stronger cable, Accu-Steel was negligent and is liable to those persons who were foreseeable victims of its failure to perform its duties in a reasonable manner. Accu-Steel knew that the cable was going to be used in a stadium where spectators would be the end consumer.

Answers to Practice Quiz

True/False

16. False. The buyer or lessee relies on the seller's or lessor's skill and judgment and purchases or leases the goods. [UCC 2-315, 2A-213] [pp. 330-331]

17. False. Evan can recover against the thief for implied warranty of good title as the thief impliedly warranted that he or she had good title to the limousine and that the transfer of title to Evan was rightful. [p. 335]

18. False. The warranty of no security interest automatically warrants that they are delivered free from any third-party security interests, not that the goods have a third-party security interest. [p. 335]

19. False. Christopher may notify the home and garden retailer that they can no longer use the Weed-O-Rama without his permission except for a fee. The home and garden retailer may rescind its contract with Blake based on the no infringement warranty. [p. 335]

20. False. A statement of value is merely opinion and will not form the basis for an express warranty. [p. 327]

21. False. All prior, concurrent, and postsale statements are presumed to be part of the basis of the bargain unless there is something contradictory in nature. [p. 327]

22. True. The lessor or seller of goods is a merchant with respect to the goods of that kind, of which the goods must be adequately contained, packaged, and labeled accordingly. [p. 328]

23. False The foreign food substance test is used to determine whether food is unmerchantable based on objects that are found in the food. [p. 330]

24. True Disclaimers must be conspicuous and noticeable to the reasonable person. [p. 332]

25. True Such terms as with all faults or as is, or other language that makes it clear to the buyer that there are no implied warranties, may be considered expressions to connote a disclaimer. [p. 332]

26. True. When goods are leased, the lessor warrants that no person holds a claim or an interest in the goods that arose from an act or omission of the lessor that will interfere with the lessee's enjoyment of his or her leasehold interest. [p. 335]

27. False. Most software licenses do contain warranty disclaimer and limitation on liability clauses in their packaging. [p. 332]

28. True. An express warranty can be created when the seller or lessor indicates that the goods will conform to any description of them, such as Santa Maria style tri-tip refers to the special cut of meat that the seller claims will conform to that cut. [p. 326]

29. False. Disclaimers may be both written or oral. [p. 332]

30. False. The Magnuson-Moss Warranty Act covers written warranties. [p. 333]

Multiple Choice

31. C. Answer C is the correct answer, as the warranty of no security interests provides that the goods that are sold are free from any third-party security interest, liens, or encumbrances that are unknown to the buyer. Under this warranty, this is automatically done by the seller. Answer A is incorrect, as sellers of goods warrant that the title they possess is good and that the transfer of title is rightful. Answer B is incorrect, as the doctrine of caveat emptor simply means "Let the buyer beware." Answer D is incorrect, as this warranty involves a lessor who is a merchant dealing in the goods of the kind that are being leased or sold, which automatically warrants that the goods are delivered free of any third-party trademark, copyright, or patent claims. [p. 335]

32. D. Answer D is the correct answer, as answers A, B, and C all correctly state what the implied warranty of merchantbility does not apply to, that it does not apply to sales or leases by nonmerchants or casual sales. [p. 329]

33. B. Answer B is the correct answer, as the warranty of quiet possession is referred to as the warranty of no infringement. Answers A and C are incorrect, as they make no sense. Answer D is incorrect for the reasons given above. [p. 335]

34. A. Answer A is the correct answer, as express warranties can be made as an assurance of the fulfillment of a goods standards or quality by the seller or lessor to the buyer or lessee. Answer B is incorrect, as this would act more as a disclaimer if a seller or lessor affirmed that the goods do not meet certain criteria or quality. Answer C is incorrect, as this better describes implied warranties. Answer D is incorrect for the reasons stated above. [p. 326]

35. D. Answer D is the correct answer, as answers A, B, and C are all correct statements regarding the basis of the bargain. [p. 327]

36. A. Answer A is the correct answer, as it is an affirmation of value, which does not create any warranty under UCC 2-313(2). Answer B is incorrect, as statements that involve affirmation of value do not create an express warranty. Answer C is incorrect because, even though it is true, it does not specifically state what is created as answer A does. Answer D is a false statement and therefore not correct. [p. 327]

37. B. Answer B is the correct answer, as the statement is an affirmation of fact, which creates an express warranty. Answer A is incorrect, as it is not a statement of opinion as it is factual as opposed to puffing with regard to the quality of the product. Answer C is incorrect based on the reasoning given with regard to answer A. Answer D is incorrect, as there is no legal basis known as an affirmation of mileage. [p. 327]

38. B. Answer B is the correct answer, as nonmerchants are not included in the provisions related to the implied warranty of merchantability. Answer A is incorrect, as the implied warranty of merchantability does apply to merchants. Answer C is incorrect, as the implied warranty of merchantability also applies to leases by merchants. Answer D is incorrect, as a vacuum cleaner salesperson would be a merchant to whom the implied warranty of merchantability would apply based on his or her status of being a merchant. [p. 329]

39. A. Answer A is the correct answer, as the UCC incorporates the implied warranty of fitness for human consumption into the implied warranty of merchantability. Answer B is incorrect, as the warranty of good title stands on its own merit without being incorporated into another warranty. Answer C is incorrect, as this is an automatic warranty that also stands on its own merit. Answer D is incorrect, as this is also an automatic warranty that is not incorporated as a subcategory of another warranty. [p. 330]

40. B. Answer B is correct, as the implied warranty for fitness for a particular purpose fits the facts well since the hardware store manager sold rope to Josef after being told the purpose for which the rope would be used, and the rope failed in that purpose. Answer A is incorrect, as the warranty of fitness for human consumption is specifically for food. Answer C is incorrect, as the warranty of quiet enjoyment refers to the circumstances where a lessor warrants that the use of the leased property by the lessee will not be interfered with. Answer D is incorrect, as this warranty protects against the violation of an intellectual property right. [pp. 330-331]

Short Answer

41. They are made to entice consumers and others to buy or lease their products. [p. 326]

42. If the manufacturer authorizes or ratifies the warranty. [p. 327]

43. Buyers and lessors may recover for breach of express warranty if the warranty was a contributing factor that induced the buyer to purchase the product or to lease the product to the lessee. [p. 328]

44. The goods must be fit for the ordinary purpose for which they are used; The goods must be adequately contained, packaged, and labeled; The goods must be of a kind, quality, and quantity with each unit; The goods must conform to any promise or affirmation of fact made on the

container or label; The quality of the goods must pass without objection in the trade; Fungible goods must meet a fair average or middle range of quality. (answers will vary) [p. 328]

45. A consumer would expect that a food preparer would remove all foreign objects from the food. [p. 330]

46. It applies to both merchant and nonmerchant sellers and lessors. [p. 331]

47. Lydia may want to use the terminology "There are no warranties that extend beyond the description on the face hereof." (answers will vary) [p. 332]

48. Ben's placing a disclaimer on his motorcycle. [p. 332]

49. To limit the licensor's liability if the software malfunctions. [p. 332]

50. Brochures, illustrations, ads, blueprints (answers will vary) [p. 326]

51. This is sufficient to disclaim the warranty of fitness for a particular purpose. [p. 332]

52. The warranty of merchantability would not be applicable, as it does not apply to casual sales. [p. 329]

53. It would be considered merchantable because a reasonable consumer would expect to find an apple seed in an apple pie, as that is not be a foreign substance to the product. [p. 330]

54. The consumer expectation test. [p. 330]

55. The foreign substance test. [p. 330]

22 | CREATION OF NEGOTIABLE INSTRUMENTS

Chapter Overview

This chapter focuses on the creation of different types of negotiable instruments and their creation. Attention is given to prepayment, extension, and acceleration clauses, as well as nonnegotiable contracts.

Objectives

Upon completion of the exercises in this chapter, you should be able to:
1. Distinguish between negotiable and nonnegotiable instruments.
2. Describe drafts and checks and identify the parties to these instruments.
3. Describe promissory notes and certificates of deposit and identify the parties to these instruments.
4. List the formal requirements of a negotiable instrument.
5. Distinguish between instruments payable to order and instruments payable to bearer.

Practical Application

This chapter will enable you to have a better understanding of negotiable instruments and their importance in conducting your personal and business affairs. It will give you the tools that you need in the creation of a negotiable instrument.

Helpful Hints

This chapter involves several forms of negotiable instruments. The chance that you have used one or more of these instruments in your lifetime is great. If you remember that with which you are familiar in terms of commercial paper, this chapter will be very understandable for you. The best approach is to keep the parties separated on a sheet of paper to be able to view how they differ. The more you expose yourself to hypotheticals in this area, the easier the material becomes. If you imagine yourself in one or more of the party's positions, it becomes easier.

Study Tips

Creation of Negotiable Instruments

Commercial paper aids in conducting personal and business affairs. Modern commerce in the US could not occur without these instruments.

Negotiable Instruments

Article 3 of the UCC sets forth the requirements for a negotiable instrument. A transferee of such an instrument who qualifies as a holder in due course (HDC) is protected from many defenses to payment that could be asserted against the original payee.

- These instruments are considered ordinary contracts that are subject to contract law.
- These instruments must be freely transferable, or negotiable.

Functions of Negotiable Instruments.
- Negotiable instruments, such as a check, act as a substitute for money.
- Negotiable instruments may act as a credit device.
- Negotiable instruments may serve as a record-keeping device for preparing tax returns, etc.

Types of Negotiable Instruments

Revised Article 3 recognizes four kinds of negotiable instruments: drafts, checks, promissory notes, and certificates of deposit.

Draft. A three-party instrument that is an unconditional written order by one party that orders a second party to pay money to the third party.
- Parties:
  - *Drawer.* The customer who writes (draws) the check.
  - *Drawee.* The financial institution upon which the check is written.
  - *Payee.* The party to whom the check is written.
  - *Acceptor.* The drawee is also known as the acceptor because of his or her obligation to pay the payee instead of the drawer.
- The drawee must be obligated to pay the drawer money before the drawer can order the drawee to pay this money to a third party.
- For the drawee to be liable on a draft, the drawee must accept the drawer's written order to pay it.
- *Time Draft.* A draft payable at a designated future date.
- *Sight Draft.* A draft payable on sight.
- *Trade Acceptance.* A sight draft that arises when credit is extended with the sale of goods.
  - The seller is both the drawer and the payee.
  - The buyer to whom credit is extended is the drawee.
  - Even though only two actual parties are involved, it is considered a three-party instrument because three legal positions are involved.

Check. A three-party instrument that is a special kind of draft which is drawn on a financial institution and payable on demand. A check is an order to pay.
- *Drawer.* A customer who has a checking account and writes (draws) a check.
- *Drawee.* The financial institution upon which the check is written.
- *Payee.* The party to whom the check is written.

Promissory Note. An unconditional written promise by one party to pay money to another party.
- Parties:
  - *Maker.* This is the borrower who makes the promise to pay.

- o *Payee.* This is the lender to whom the promise is made.
- *Time Notes.* Notes payable at a specific time
- *Demand Notes.* Notes payable on demand.
- Notes can be made payable to a named payee or to "bearer."
- They can be payable in a single payment or in installments.
- Most notes require the borrower to pay interest on the principal.
- *Collateral.* Sometimes the lender needs security, known as collateral, when a promissory note is made.

Certificates of Deposit. A specially created note that is created upon a depositor depositing monies at a financial institution in exchange for the institution's promise to pay the deposited amount back with an agreed-upon amount of interest after a set period of time.
- *Maker.* The financial institution who is the borrower.
- *Payee.* The depositor who is the lender.

Creation of a Negotiable Instrument

In order to create a negotiable instrument in compliance with UCC 3-104(a), the following must be present and must appear on the face of the instrument:
- Be in writing.
- Be signed by the maker or drawer.
- Be an unconditional promise or order to pay.
- State a fixed amount of money.
- Not require any undertaking in addition to the payment of money.
- Be payable on demand or at a definite time.
- Be payable to order or to bearer.

Writing. The negotiable instrument must be in writing. This involves permanency and the writing must be portable.

Signed by the Maker or Drawer. The UCC is broad with this requirement. Symbols, typed, printed, lithographed, rubber-stamped, or other mechanical signatures are allowed.

Unconditional Promise or Order to Pay

Order to Pay. It must be an unconditional order to pay.
- It must be more than an authorization or a request to pay.
- The language of the order must be precise and contain the word *pay.*
- It can be directed to one or more parties jointly.
- It must identify the drawee, the financial institution, who is directed to make the payment

Promise to Pay. It must be an unconditional promise to pay.
- Mere debt acknowledgement is not sufficient for this requirement.
- CDs do not require an express promise to pay as the bank's acknowledgment of the payee's bank deposit and other terms show the bank's promise to repay the certificate holder.

Unconditional Promise or Order. A conditional promise or an order is not negotiable as the risk of the condition not occurring would fall on the person who held the instrument.

- A promise or an order remains unconditional even if it refers to a different writing for a description of rights to collateral, prepayment, or acceleration.
- A promise or an order may also stipulate that payment is limited to a particular fund or source [UCC 3-106(b)].

Payable to Order or to Bearer.
- *Order Instrument.* It is payable to the order of an identified person or to an identified person or order [UCC 3-109(b)].
- *Bearer Instrument.* It is payable to anyone in physical possession of it who presents it for payment when it is due.

Fixed Amount of Money

It must state a fixed amount of money. The principal amount of the instrument has to be on the face of the instrument.

Payable in Money. Money is a "medium of exchange authorized or adopted by a foreign or domestic government as part of its currency." [UCC 1-201(24)]
- Instruments fully or partially payable in a medium of exchange other than money are not negotiable.

Variable Interest Rate Loan. This type of loan ties interest to a set measure, such as a large bank's prime rate, so that the rate varies over the life of the loan.
- "Interest may be stated in an instrument as a fixed or variable amount of money or it may be expressed as a fixed or variable rate or rates." UCC 3-112(b)
- The amount or rate of interest may be determined by reference to information not contained in the instrument. UCC 3-112(b)

Not Require Any Undertaking in Addition to Money. It must not require any undertaking in addition to the payment of money.
- It may include authorization or power to protect collateral, dispose of collateral, and waive any law intended to protect the obligee.

Payable on Demand or at a Definite Time

The instrument must specify on its face that it is either payable on demand or payable at a certain time.

Payable on Demand. It must be payable on demand. Payable on demand instruments are created by language such as "payable on sight," or "payable on demand."
- Checks are an example of payable on demand instruments.

Payable at a Definite Time. Instruments payable at a definite time are called time instruments.
- Payable
    - at a fixed date OR
    - on or before a stated date OR
    - at a fixed period after sight OR
    - at a time readily ascertainable when the instrument is issued.
- Instruments payable on an uncertain act or event are not negotiable.

Prepayment, Acceleration, and Extension Clauses. Inclusion of these clauses in an instrument does not affect its negotiability.

- *Prepayment Clause.* Permits the maker to pay the amount due prior to the due date of the instrument.
- *Acceleration Clause.* Allows the payee or holder to accelerate payment of the principal amount of an instrument, plus accrued interest, upon the occurrence of an event (e.g., default).
- *Extension Clause.* Allows the date of maturity of an instrument to be extended to sometime in the future.

Negotiable Instruments Payable in Foreign Currency. The UCC provides that an instrument can be payable in foreign currency.

- Unless otherwise stated, an instrument payable in foreign currency can be paid by the equivalent in U.S. dollars as determined on the due date.
  - o The conversion rate is the current bank-offered spot rate at the place of payment on the due date.
- The instrument can expressly provide that it is payable only in the stated foreign currency.

Nonnegotiable Contract

If a promise or order to pay does not meet the requirements discussed under negotiable instruments, then it is a nonnegotiable contract.

- A nonnegotiable contract is enforceable under contract law.

Refresh Your Memory

The following exercise will give you the opportunity to test your memory of the principles given in this chapter. Read the question twice and place your answer in the blank provided. Review the chapter material for any question that you are unable to answer or remember.

1. Negotiable instruments are also known as _____.

2. The primary benefit of a negotiable instrument is that it can be used as a substitute for _____.

3. The term _____ is usually used to describe the transfer of negotiable instruments to subsequent transferees.

4. A _____ is a three-party instrument that is an unconditional written order by one party that orders a second party to pay money to a third party.

5. The _____ is called the acceptor of a draft because his or her obligation changes from having to pay the drawer to having to pay the payee.

6. A _____ draft is payable at a designated future date.

7. A _____, also known as a bill of exchange, is a sight draft that arises when credit is extended by the seller to the buyer with the sale of goods.

8. A _____ is a distinct form of draft drawn on a financial institution and payable on demand.

9. A _____ is a two-party negotiable instrument that is an unconditional written promise by one party to pay money to another party.

10. Notes that are secured by personal property are called _____ notes.

11. _____ is a requirement of negotiable instruments that says they must be able to be easily transported between areas.

12. _____ is a medium of exchange authorized or adopted by a domestic or foreign government.

13. A _____ permits the maker to pay the amount due prior to the due date of the instrument.

14. A(n) _____ allows the payee or holder to accelerate payment of the principal amount of an instrument, plus accrued interest, upon the occurrence of an event.

15. A _____ is a contract that fails to meet the requirements of a negotiable instrument and, therefore, is not subject to the provisions of UCC Article 3.

Critical Thought Exercise

The Gold Coast Investment Group (IG) is building a large office building that it is financing itself through its banking arm, Gold Coast Bank (GCB). When payments for the final phase of the building come due, GC issues checks to the contractors with a condition on the front of the check that states:

> *"This instrument valid only after a permit to occupy the building is granted by all governmental agencies from which a permit is mandatory."*

Ace Construction deposits the check with its bank, First City Bank. The occupancy permits are not issued by the city or county entities where the building is located. When presented with the checks by First City Bank, GCB refuses to honor them.

Ace Construction then brings suit against First City Bank, GCB, and IG.

Should GCB be compelled to pay the checks presented to it by First City Bank on behalf of Ace Construction? Was it ethical for IG to place a condition upon the negotiation of the instrument?

Please compose your answer to the Critical Thinking Exercise using a separate sheet of paper or your computer word processing program.

Practice Quiz

True/False

16. _____ The issuance of a negotiable instrument is known as negotiation.

17. _____ Negotiable instruments help in creating a credit economy.

18. _____ Acceptances for drafts can be done orally.

19. _____ A bill of exchange is a type of sight draft.

20. _____ A trade acceptance is a two-party transaction.

21. _____ A check is a type of promissory note.

22. _____ A promissory note is a two-party transaction.

23. _____ A certificate of deposit is an order to pay.

24. _____ In a certificate of deposit, the depositor is the payee.

25. _____ Trade names or assumed names cannot be used for signing negotiable instruments.

26. _____ A maker or drawer can appoint an agent to sign a negotiable instrument on his or her behalf.

27. _____ To be negotiable, a draft or check must contain the drawer's unconditional order to pay a payee.

28. _____ A promise or an order becomes conditional if it refers to a different writing for a description of rights to collateral, prepayment, or acceleration.

29. _____ Instruments that are payable on demand are called order instruments.

30. _____ An extension clause allows the date of maturity of an instrument to be extended to sometime in the future.

Multiple Choice

31. Which one of the following would be a three-party transaction?

A. a promissory note
B. a draft
C. an ordinary lease
D. a certificate of deposit

32. Who is the drawee in a draft transaction?

A. The party that demands the draft.
B. The party who receives the money from a draft.
C. The party who writes an order for a draft.
D. The party who pays the money stated in a draft.

33. Who is the acceptor of a draft in a draft transaction?

A. the drawee
B. the financee
C. the payee
D. the drawer

34. Which of the following is true about a trade acceptance?

A. The buyer is the payee.
B. The draft is countersigned by the drawee's bank.
C. The seller is both the drawer and payee.
D. The draft is only as good as the drawer's creditworthiness.

35. Who is the drawee of a check?

A. The drawer of the check is also its drawee.
B. The financial institute where the drawer has an account.
C. The party to whom a check is written.
D. The financee to whom the check is drawn.

36. Who is the drawee of a check?

A. The drawer of the check is also its drawee.
B. The financee to whom the check is drawn.
C. The party to whom a check is written.
D. The financial institute where the drawer has an account.

37. Which of the following is considered as a distinction of a check?

A. It is a two-party instrument.
B. It is created when credit is extended to a buyer by a seller.
C. It always draws its money from a financial institute.
D. It is an unconditional written promise to pay.

38. If a promissory note is secured by a piece of real estate, then the note is called a(n) _____.

A. mortgage note
B. collateral note
C. demand note
D. installment note

39. Which of the following is true about a certificate of deposit?

A. It is a three-party instrument.
B. It is used to extend credit to a buyer.
C. It is a promise to pay.
D. It can be made to pay on demand.

40. Which of the following statements is true for a negotiable instrument?

A. It should not require any undertaking other than the payment of money.
B. It need not state a fixed amount of money.
C. It should be signed by the payee.
D. It can be either written or oral.

41. The _____ requirement of negotiable instruments says that negotiable instruments must be able to be easily transported between areas.

A. signature
B. permanence
C. portability
D. transparency

42. Which of the following must a promissory note contain to make it negotiable?

A. an implied promise to pay
B. an unconditional affirmative to pay
C. an acknowledgement of debt
D. a promise to negotiate

43. A(n) _____ is type of instrument that is payable to anyone in physical possession of the instrument and presents it for payment when it is due.

A. certificate of deposit
B. order instrument
C. check
D. bearer instrument

44. A clause in an instrument that allows the date of maturity of the instrument to be prolonged to sometime in the future is referred to as the _____.

A. forestallment clause
B. extension clause
C. prepayment clause
D. acceleration clause

45. Roger, a certified lawyer, borrowed money from Jax to start a business. He gave a promissory note to Jax promising to pay the money back anytime within the next five years. But in order to accept the note Jax demanded a security deposit. Roger gave the gold that he owned as security. Roger in turn demanded that a specific clause be added to the promissory note to allow faster repayment of the lawn in case he inherited money within the next five years. But even after five years, Roger was unable to complete payment. He made a new promissory note promising to finish payment within the next year, and promised to provide free legal service to Jax for the next two years.

Which of the following is true for the validity of the new promissory note made by Roger?

A. It is a nonnegotiable instrument.
B. It must contain a specific date or time to be considered valid.
C. It must contain interest on the old principal to become a valid instrument.
D. It is a negotiable instrument if Jax accepts it.

Short Answer

46. What are the functions of negotiable instruments?

_____

_____

47. What is a draft?

_____

_____

48. What is a promissory note?

_____

_____

49. What are the requirements for creating a negotiable instrument?

_____

_____

50. Explain permanency and portability of negotiable instruments.

_____

_____

51. How does an authorized representative's signature work for negotiable instruments?

_____

_____

52. Differentiate between order to pay and promise to pay.

_____

_____

53. What is a bearer instrument?

_____

_____

54. Give an account of the requirement for a fixed amount in negotiable instruments?

_____

_____

55. What are nonnegotiable contracts?

_____

_____

Answers to Refresh Your Memory

1. commercial papers [p. 359]
2. money [p. 359]
3. negotiation [p. 359]
4. draft [p. 360]
5. drawee [p. 360]
6. time [p. 360]

Critical Thought Exercise Model Answer

The general rule is that the terms of the promise or order must be included in the writing on the face of a negotiable instrument. UCC 3-104(a) requires that the terms must also be unconditional. The terms cannot be conditioned on the occurrence or nonoccurrence of some other event or agreement.

By placing the condition on the face of the instrument, IG prevented the checks from being valid negotiable instruments. Both First City Bank and GCB would be within their rights to refuse to honor the checks. A promise to pay that is conditional on another event, such as the issuing of the occupancy permits, is not negotiable because the risk of the other event not occurring would fall on the person who held the instrument. A conditional promise like the one placed on the check by IG is subject to normal contract law.

IG will not have made payment on the required contractual installments and may now be in breach of contract. Ace Construction will be able to recover against IG for failure to meet its contractual obligations unless the occupancy permits were a condition of payment contained in the parties' original contract.

The placing of the condition upon the face of the check by IG appears to be unethical. If the condition were not part of its contract with Ace, it would be unethical to attempt to unilaterally modify the terms of their agreement. If the purpose of placing the condition on the check were to cause the checks to be dishonored and thus delay payment, this would also be unethical. IG would be employing a trick to avoid lawful payment, which may damage Ace Construction when it is unable to meet its financial obligations.

Answers to Practice Quiz

True/False

16. False. The term negotiation, however, is usually used to describe the transfer of negotiable instruments to subsequent transferees. [p. 359]

17. True. Some forms of negotiable instruments extend credit from one party to another. A seller may sell goods to a customer on a customer's promise to pay for the goods at a future time, or a bank may lend money to a buyer who signs a note promising to repay the money. [p. 359]

18. False. Acceptance is usually shown by the written word accepted on the face of the draft, along with the drawee's signature and the date. [p. 360]

19. True. A trade acceptance (bill of exchange) is a sight draft that arises when credit is extended by the seller to the buyer with the sale of goods. [p. 361]

20. False. Even though only two actual parties are involved, a trade acceptance is considered a three-party instrument because three legal positions are involved. [p. 361]

21. False. A check is a distinct form of draft. It is an order to pay. [p. 361]

22. True. A promissory note is an unconditional written promise by one party to pay money to another party. It is a two-party instrument, not an order to pay. [p. 362]

23. False. A certificate of deposit is a two-party instrument. It is a promise to pay, not an order to pay. [p. 363]

24. True. In a certificate of deposit, the financial institution is the borrower (the maker of a certificate of deposit), and the depositor is the lender (the payee of a certificate of deposit). [p. 363]

25. False. A signature is made by the use of any name, including a trade or an assumed name, or by any word or mark used in lieu of a written signature. [p. 364]

26. True. A maker or drawer can appoint an agent to sign a negotiable instrument on his or her behalf. In such circumstances, the representative's signature binds the maker or drawer. [p. 365]

27. True. To be negotiable, a draft or check must contain the drawer's unconditional order to pay a payee. An order is a direction for the drawee to pay and must be more than an authorization or a request to pay. [p. 366]

28. False. A promise or an order remains unconditional even if it refers to a different writing for a description of rights to collateral, prepayment, or acceleration. [p. 366]

29. False. Instruments that are payable on demand are called demand instruments. [p. 368]

30. True. An extension clause allows the date of maturity of an instrument to be extended to sometime in the future. An extension clause contains the terms for extension, such as setting the interest rate during the extension period. [p. 370]

Multiple Choice

31. B. A draft, which is a three-party instrument, is an unconditional written order by one party (the drawer of a draft) that orders a second party (the drawee of a draft) to pay money to a third party (the payee of a draft). [p. 360]

32. D. The drawee is obligated to pay the drawer money before the drawer can order the drawee to pay this money to a third party (the payee). [p. 360]

33. A. The drawee is called the acceptor of a draft because his or her obligation changes from having to pay the drawer to having to pay the payee. [p. 360]

34. C. A trade acceptance (bill of exchange) is a sight draft that arises when credit is extended by the seller to the buyer with the sale of goods. With this type of draft, the seller is both the drawer and the payee. [p. 361]

35. C. A sight draft is payable on sight. A sight draft is also called a demand draft. A trade acceptance (bill of exchange) is a sight draft that arises when credit is extended by the seller to the buyer with the sale of goods. [p. 360, 361]

36. D. The financial institution upon which the check is written is the drawee of a check. [p. 361]

37. C. A check is a distinct form of draft. It is unique in that it is drawn on a financial institution (the drawee) and is payable on demand. [p. 361]

38. A. Notes that are secured by real estate are called mortgage notes, and notes that are secured by personal property are called collateral notes. [p. 363]

39. C. A certificate of deposit is a two-party instrument. It is a promise to pay, not an order to pay. [p. 363]

40. A. According to UCC 3-104(a), a negotiable instrument must not require any undertaking in addition to the payment of money. [p. 364]

41. C. The portability requirement is intended to ensure free transfer of an instrument. [p. 365]

42. B. To be negotiable, a promissory note must contain the maker's unconditional and affirmative promise to pay. The mere acknowledgment of a debt is not sufficient to constitute a negotiable instrument. [p. 365]

43. D. A bearer instrument is payable to anyone in physical possession of the instrument who presents it for payment when it is due. Bearer paper results when the drawer or maker does not make the instrument payable to a specific payee. [p. 367]

44. B. An extension clause allows the date of maturity of an instrument to be extended to sometime in the future. An extension clause contains the terms for extension, such as setting the interest rate during the extension period. [p. 370]

45. A. If a promise or an order to pay does not meet one of the previously discussed requirements of negotiability, it is a nonnegotiable contract and is therefore not subject to the provisions of UCC Article 3. [p. 371]

Short Answer

46. Negotiable instruments serve the following functions:
1. Substitute for money – Merchants and consumers often do not carry cash for fear of loss or theft. Further, it would be almost impossible to carry enough cash for large purchases (e.g., a car, a house). Thus, certain forms of negotiable instruments—such as checks—serve as substitutes for money.
2. Act as credit devices – Some forms of negotiable instruments extend credit from one party to another. A seller may sell goods to a customer on a customer's promise to pay for the goods at a future time, or a bank may lend money to a buyer who signs a note promising to repay the money. Both of these examples represent extensions of credit.

3. Act as record-keeping devices – Negotiable instruments often serve as record-keeping devices. Banks may return canceled checks to checking account customers each month or allow customers to view them online. These act as a record-keeping device for the preparation of financial statements, tax returns, and the like. [p. 359]

47. A draft, which is a three-party instrument, is an unconditional written order by one party (the drawer of a draft) that orders a second party (the drawee of a draft) to pay money to a third party (the payee of a draft) [UCC 3-104(e)]. The drawee is obligated to pay the drawer money before the drawer can order the drawee to pay this money to a third party (the payee). For the drawee to be liable on a draft, the drawee must accept the drawer's written order to pay it. Acceptance is usually shown by the written word accepted on the face of the draft, along with the drawee's signature and the date. The drawee is called the acceptor of a draft because his or her obligation changes from having to pay the drawer to having to pay the payee. After the drawee accepts the draft, it is returned to the drawer or the payee. The drawer or the payee, in turn, can freely transfer it as a negotiable instrument to another party. [p. 360]

48. A promissory note (or note) is an unconditional written promise by one party to pay money to another party [UCC 3-104(e)]. It is a two-party instrument, not an order to pay. Promissory notes usually arise when one party borrows money from another. The note is evidence of (1) the extension of credit and (2) the borrower's promise to repay the debt. A party who makes a promise to pay is the maker of a note (i.e., the borrower). The party to whom the promise to pay is made is the payee of a note (i.e., the lender). A promissory note is a negotiable instrument that the payee can freely transfer to other parties. [p. 362]

49. According to UCC 3-104(a), a negotiable instrument must:
• Be in writing.
• Be signed by the maker or drawer.
• Be an unconditional promise or order to pay.
• State a fixed amount of money.
• Not require any undertaking in addition to the payment of money.
• Be payable on demand or at a definite time.
• Be payable to order or to bearer. [p. 364]

50. A negotiable instrument must be (1) in writing and (2) permanent and portable. Most writings on paper meet the permanency requirement. However, a writing that is on tissue paper would not meet this requirement because of its impermanence. The portability requirement is intended to ensure free transfer of an instrument. A promise to pay chiseled in a tree would not qualify as a negotiable instrument because the tree is not freely transferable in commerce. Writing the same promise or order to pay on a small block of wood could qualify as a negotiable instrument, however. [p. 364]

51. A maker or drawer can appoint an agent to sign a negotiable instrument on his or her behalf. In such circumstances, the representative's signature binds the maker or drawer. A maker or drawer is liable on a negotiable instrument signed by an authorized agent. The agent is not personally liable on the negotiable instrument if his or her signature properly unambiguously discloses his or her agency status and the identity of the maker or. In the case of an organization, the agent's signature is proper if the organization's name is preceded or followed by the name of the authorized agent. [p. 365]

52. To be negotiable, a draft or check must contain the drawer's unconditional order to pay a payee. An order is a direction for the drawee to pay and must be more than an authorization or a request to pay. The language of the order must be precise and contain the word pay.
To be negotiable, a promissory note must contain the maker's unconditional and affirmative promise to pay. The mere acknowledgment of a debt is not sufficient to constitute a negotiable instrument. In other words, an implied promise to pay is not negotiable, but an expressly stated promise to pay is negotiable. [p. 365]

53. A bearer instrument is payable to anyone in physical possession of the instrument who presents it for payment when it is due. The person in possession of the instrument is called the bearer. Bearer paper results when the drawer or maker does not make the instrument payable to a specific payee. In addition, any other indication that does not purport to designate a specific payee creates bearer paper [UCC 3-109(a)]. [p. 367]

54. To be negotiable, an instrument must contain a promise or an order to pay a fixed amount of money. The fixed amount requirement ensures that the value of the instrument can be determined with certainty. The principal amount of the instrument must appear on the face of the instrument. An instrument does not have to be payable with interest, but if it is, the amount of interest being charged may be expressed as either a fixed or variable rate. The amount or rate of interest may be stated or described in the instrument or may require reference to information not contained in the instrument. If an instrument provides for interest but the amount of interest cannot be determined from the description, interest is payable at the judgment rate (legal rate) in effect at the place of payment of the instrument. [p. 367]

55. If a promise or an order to pay does not meet one of the previously discussed requirements of negotiability, it is a nonnegotiable contract and is therefore not subject to the provisions of UCC Article 3. A promise or an order that conspicuously states that it is not negotiable or is not subject to Article 3 is not a negotiable instrument and is therefore a nonnegotiable contract. A nonnegotiable contract is not rendered either nontransferable or unenforceable. A nonnegotiable contract can be enforced under normal contract law. If the maker or drawer of a nonnegotiable contract fails to pay it, the holder of the contract can sue the nonperforming party for breach of contract. [p. 371]

23 | TRANSFERABILITY AND HOLDER IN DUE COURSE

Chapter Overview

In the previous chapter, you learned about the various types of negotiable instruments, as well as their creation and the ability to transfer them. This chapter expands the concept of commercial paper as a substitute for money by exploring the liability of parties on negotiable instruments and the requisites that must be satisfied to be deemed a holder in due course.

Objectives

Upon completion of the exercises in this chapter, you should be able to:
1. Describe how negotiable instruments are indorsed and transferred.
2. Describe how order and bearer paper are negotiated.
3. Distinguish between blank, special, qualified, and restrictive indorsements.
4. Define holder and holder in due course.
5. Identify and apply the requirements for becoming a holder in due course.

Helpful Hints

This chapter continues discussion of the concepts associated with negotiable instruments, with clear explanations concerning assignments, transfer by negotiation, and negotiating order and bearer paper. There is an emphasis on the types of indorsements and the necessary requirements for qualifying as a holder in due course. Since this chapter lays out a list of requirements that are necessary to be a holder in due course, as well as requirements for each of the elements contained within the basic definition, it is especially helpful to make use of lists. To facilitate your studies in this area, the study tips section has been organized so that you will be able to easily refer to the lists when analyzing the case studies or hypothetical problems presented to you.

Study Tips

Transferability and Holder in Due Course

After its creation, a negotiable instrument can be transferred through negotiation, which requires an indorsement on the instrument. Instruments held by a holder in due course are virtually the same as money, since there are limited claims and defenses that can be used against enforcement of the instrument.

Transfer by Assignment

An assignment is the transfer of rights under a contract. Assignments result when a nonnegotiable contract is transferred.
- The assignee (transferee) only acquires the rights that the assignor (transferor) possessed.

- All defenses that could be raised against the assignor can now be raised against the assignee.

Transfer by Negotiation

Negotiation is the transfer of a negotiable instrument by a person other than the issuer. The person to whom the instrument has been transferred is known as the holder.
- If the holder is found to be a holder in due course, he or she receives the rights of the transferor and may obtain even greater additional rights.
- A holder in due course (HDC) has greater rights as he or she is not subject to some of the defenses that may have been raised against the transferor.

Negotiating Order Paper. Order paper is described as an instrument that is negotiated by (1) delivery and (2) indorsement.

Negotiating Bearer Paper. Bearer paper is defined as an instrument that is negotiated by delivery; indorsement is not necessary.
- Bearer paper is not payable to a specific payee or indorsee.

Converting Order and Bearer Paper. An instrument can be converted from order paper to bearer paper and vice versa until eventually the instrument is paid. [UCC 3-109] The end result is dependent upon the indorsement placed on the instrument at the time of each subsequent transfer.

Indorsement

An indorsement is the signature of a signer that is placed on an instrument. The signer cannot be the maker, a drawer, or an acceptor. The indorsement can be (1) by itself, (2) name an individual to whom the instrument is to be paid, or (3) be accompanied by other words.
- Indorsements are usually placed on the back of the instrument.
- If there is a lack of space to indorse the instrument, the indorsement may be placed on a separate piece of paper (an allonge) affixed to the instrument.
- Indorsements are necessary to negotiate order paper, but they are not required to negotiate bearer paper [UCC 3-201 (b)].

Types of Indorsements

Blank Indorsement. No indorsee is given and may be a mere signature.
- A blank indorsement creates bearer paper.

Special Indorsement. It contains the indorser's signature and it indicates the person to whom the indorser intends the instrument to be payable to.
- Special indorsements create order paper, which are preferred over bearer paper.

Unqualified Indorsement. Where "the indorser promises to pay the holder or any subsequent indorser the amount of the instrument if the maker, drawer, or acceptor defaults on it."

Qualified Indorsement. "Indorsements that disclaim or limit liability on the instrument."
- There is no guaranteed payment of the instrument by the qualified indorser if the maker, drawer, or acceptor defaults on the instrument.

- These types of indorsements are often used by individuals signing instruments in the capacity as a representative.
- *A special qualified indorsement.* Creates order paper that can be negotiated by indorsement and delivery.
- *A blank qualified indorsement.* Creates bearer paper that can be further negotiated by delivery without indorsement

Nonrestrictive indorsement – This is an indorsement without conditions or instructions attached to the payment of the funds.

Restrictive indorsement – An indorsement with an instruction from the indorser.
There are two restrictive indorsements you should be familiar with as provided for under UCC 3-206.

- *Indorsement for Deposit or Collection.* This is an indorsement that establishes the indorsee, the indorser's collecting agent.
    - Example: "for deposit only."
- *Indorsement in Trust.* An indorsement for the benefit or use of the indorser or another individual.

Misspelled or Wrong Name. If the payee or indorsee name is misspelled, the payee or indorsee in the negotiable instrument may indorse the instrument in the misspelled name, the correct name or both.

Multiple Payees or Indorsees.

- If more two or more persons are listed as indorsees or payees on a negotiable instrument and are listed jointly, both indorsements are needed to negotiate the instrument.
    - *Example.* Payable to John and Sarah Smith requires both John's and Sarah's signature.
- If the instrument indicates that one or the other may negotiate the instrument, then each person's signature is sufficient to negotiate the instrument.
    - *Example.* Payable to Ann or Mark Jones would allow either Ann's or Mark's signature.
- If a *virgule* (which is a slash mark) is used, then the negotiable instrument may be paid in the alternative.
    - *Example.* Maile Price/Winnie Simms indicates that either person may individually negotiate the instrument.

Holder in Due Course (HDC)

Holder. A person in possession of an instrument that is payable to bearer or an identified person who is in possession of an instrument payable to that person.

Holder in Due Course (HDC). A holder who takes an instrument for value, in good faith, and without notice that it is defective or is overdue.

- An HDC can acquire greater rights than those of the transferor.
- Only universal defenses, and not personal defenses, can be used against an HDC.

Requirements for HDC Status

The person must be the holder of a negotiable instrument that was taken for value; in good faith; without notice that it is overdue, dishonored, or encumbered in any way; and bearing no apparent evidence of forgery, alterations, or irregularity [UCC 3-302].

Taking for Value Requirement. The holder must have given value for the instrument.
- The holder performs the agreed-upon promise.
- The holder acquires a security interest or lien on the instrument.
- The holder takes the instrument in payment of or as security for an antecedent claim.
- The holder gives a negotiable instrument as payment.
- The holder gives an irrevocable obligation as payment.

Taking in Good Faith Requirement. The holder must take the instrument in good faith.
- Good faith means honesty in fact.
  - Honesty is a subjective test as judged by the circumstances and only applies to the holder.

Taking Without Notice of Defect Requirement. The holder must take the instrument without notice of defect.
- A person cannot be a holder in due course if he or she knows that the instrument is defective in any way.
- *Overdue Instruments.* When a time instrument has not been paid on its expressed due date.
  - When a demand instrument has been presented or an unreasonable time after its issue.
- *Dishonored Instruments.* When an instrument has been presented for payment and has been refused.
- *Red Light Doctrine.* Notice than an instrument has an unauthorized signature or has been altered in any way or there is any adverse claim or defense against it.

No Evidence of Forgery, Alteration, or Irregularity Requirement. A holder may not be a holder in due course if at the time of negotiation to the holder it was forged or altered, casting doubt on its authentication.

Payee as an HDC Requirement. Payees usually are not considered to be holders in due course because of their knowledge of claims or defenses against the instrument.

Shelter Principle. The shelter principle involves a holder who does not qualify as a holder in due course in his or her own right but becomes a holder in due course if he or she obtains the instrument through a holder in due course. The rules that apply to being a holder in due course under the shelter principle are as follows:
- The holder does not have to qualify as a holder in due course in his or her own right.
- The holder must acquire the instrument from a holder in due course or be able to trace his or her title back to a holder in due course.
- The holder must not have been a party to a fraud or illegality affecting the instrument.
- The holder cannot have notice of a defense or claim against the payment of the instrument.

Refresh Your Memory

The following exercise will give you the opportunity to test your memory of the principles given in this chapter. Read the question twice and place your answer in the blank provided. Review the chapter material for any question that you are unable to answer or remember.

1. The transfer of rights under a nonnegotiable contract is called _____.

2. _____ is the transfer of a negotiable instrument by a person other than the issuer.

3. An instrument that is payable to a specific payee or indorsed to a specific indorsee is _____.

4. An instrument that is not payable to a specific payee or indorsee is _____.

5. The signature (and other directions) written by or on behalf of the holder somewhere on an instrument is called _____.

6. _____ is a separate piece of paper attached to an instrument on which an indorsement is written.

7. A _____ indorsement does not specify a particular indorsee.

8. A special indorsement creates _____ paper.

9. A _____ indorser does not guarantee payment of the instrument if the maker, drawer, or acceptor defaults on it.

10. An indorsement that contains some sort of instruction from the indorser is called _____ indorsement.

11. A _____ is a person in possession of an instrument that is payable to bearer or an identified person who is in possession of an instrument payable to that person.

12. The good faith test applies only to the _____.

13. A _____ instrument is an instrument with an express due date.

14. An instrument that is presented for payment and payment is refused is called _____ instrument.

15. _____ says that a holder who does not qualify as a holder in due course in his or her own right becomes a holder in due course if he or she acquires an instrument through a holder in due course.

Critical Thought Exercise

Betty Smith made out a check to George Bell of Bell Plumbing for $1,500 as a partial payment for plumbing renovation of her kitchen. When it was time for Bell to begin his work, he did not appear, nor could Ms. Smith locate him. Smith immediately ordered her bank to stop payment on the check. Bell had already cashed the check at Redi-Cash. When the check was returned to Redi-

Cash marked "payment stopped by account holder," Redi-Cash was contacted by an attorney for Smith who informed Redi-Cash that the plumber did not have a license and that engaging in a contracting trade without a license was a crime. Therefore the contract was void and his client would not honor the check.

As manager of Redi-Cash, will you commence suit against Smith to collect the amount of the check?

Please compose your answer to the Critical Thinking Exercise using a separate sheet of paper or your computer word processing program.

Practice Quiz

True/False

16. _____ An instrument that is payable to a specific payee or indorsed to a specific indorsee is called a bearer paper.

17. _____ For an order paper to be negotiated there must be delivery and indorsement.

18. _____ An instrument that is not payable to a specific payee or indorsee is called an order paper.

19. _____ Indorsements are required to negotiate bearer papers.

20. _____ An order paper that is indorsed in blank becomes bearer paper.

21. _____ A special indorsement does not specify to whom the indorser intends the instrument to be payable.

22. _____ A special indorsement is negotiable by indorsement and delivery.

23. _____ A holder can convert a blank indorsement into a special indorsement by adding his or signature on it.

24. _____ A qualified indorsement puts limited liability on the indorser.

25. _____ A qualified indorsement protects subsequent indorsers from liability.

26. _____ Nonrestrictive indorsements contain instructions from the indorser.

27. _____ An indorsement with just the indorsee's signature on it, and a specific payee would be an example of a nonrestrictive indorsement.

28. _____ An indorser is allowed to indorse an instrument so as to make the indorsee his collecting agent.

29. _____ Where the name of the payee is misspelled, the indorsement becomes invalid.

30. _____ If a virgule is used, both parties are necessary to negotiate the instrument.

Multiple Choice

31. Which of the following makes negotiable instruments transferable to a third party?

A. an indorsement
B. an insurance
C. a bill of exchange
D. a trade acceptance

32. The transfer of rights under a nonnegotiable contract is known as a(n) _____.

A. dishonored instrument
B. negotiation
C. indorsement
D. assignment

33. Which of the following would constitute the creation of an assignment?

A. if the indorsement falls under the shelter principle
B. if a transfer qualifies as a negotiation under Article 3
C. if a transferee qualifies as a holder in due course
D. if the transfer is of nonnegotiable instruments

34. A(n) _____ is an instrument that is payable to a specific payee or indorsed to a specific indorsee.

A. bearer bond
B. bearer paper
C. order paper
D. allonge

35. Which one of the following is a similarity between bearer paper and order paper?

A. both require a specific payee to be named
B. both require delivery to be considered negotiable
C. both require indorsements to be considered negotiable
D. both can be claimed by whoever presents the instrument for payment

36. Which of the following can be claimed by merely having possession of the instrument?

A. a certificate of deposit
B. an allonge
C. a bearer instrument
D. an order instrument

37. A(n) _____ is a signature and other directions written by or on behalf of the holder somewhere on an instrument.

A. recommendation
B. indorsement
C. assignment
D. reference

38. A separate piece of paper attached to an instrument on which an indorsement is written is known as a(n) _____.

A. allonge
B. bill of exchange
C. supplement
D. appendage

39. An indorsement that does not specify a particular indorsee is known as a(n) _____.

A. restrictive indorsement
B. special indorsement
C. qualified indorsement
D. blank indorsement

40. Which order paper when indorsed becomes a bearer paper?

A. blank indorsement
B. unqualified indorsement
C. special indorsement
D. special qualified indorsement

41. Which of the following is true for a special indorsement?

A. It requires the signature of the indorser to be valid.
B. It is only considered valid if it includes words of negotiation.
C. It can be negotiated just on delivery.
D. It is considered a bearer instrument.

42. A(n) _____ is an indorsement that includes the notation "without recourse" or similar language that disclaims liability of the indorser.

A. competent indorsement
B. unqualified indorsement
C. promissory indorsement
D. qualified indorsement

43. A(n) _____ is an indorsement that has no instructions or conditions attached to the payment of the funds.

A. indorsement in trust
B. nonrestrictive indorsement
C. indorsement for deposit
D. restrictive indorsement

44. Which of the following qualification renders a person as a holder in due course of a negotiable instrument?

A. if he is in possession of an instrument issued in his name
B. if he is subject to claims and defenses against the transferor
C. if he takes the negotiable instrument for value
D. if he is in possession of an instrument issued in another's name

45. An instrument that is refused payment when presented for payment is called a(n) _____.

A. dishonored instrument
B. restrictive instrument
C. demand instrument
D. blank instrument

Short Answer

46. Give an account of the transfer of nonnegotiable contracts by assignment.

_____

_____

47. What is the difference between negotiating order paper and negotiating bearer paper?

_____

_____

48. What is indorsement?

_____

_____

49. List the various types of indorsements.

_____

_____

50. What is the difference between blank indorsement and special indorsement?

_____

_____

51. Differentiate between restrictive and nonrestrictive indorsements.

_____

_____

52. What are the types of restrictive indorsements?

_____

_____

53. What happens if the payee's or indorsee's name is misspelled in a negotiable instrument?

_____

_____

54. What is the difference between a holder and holder in due course?

_____

_____

55. Explain the no evidence of forgery, alteration, or irregularity requirement for an HDC under the UCC.

_____

_____

Answers to Refresh Your Memory

1. assignment [p. 376]
2. Negotiation [p. 376]
3. order paper [p. 377]
4. bearer paper [p. 377]
5. indorsement [p. 379]
6. Allonge [p. 379]
7. blank [p. 380]
8. order [p. 380]
9. qualified [p. 381]
10. restrictive [p. 382]
11. holder [p. 385]
12. holder [p. 387]
13. time [p. 387]
14. dishonored [p. 387]
15. Shelter principle [p. 388]

Critical Thought Exercise Model Answer

A holder of a negotiable instrument is a holder in due course (HDC) pursuant to UCC 3-302 if he or she takes the instrument (1) for value; (2) in good faith; and (3) without notice that it is overdue, that it has been dishonored, that any person has a defense against it or claim to it, or that the instrument contains unauthorized signatures, alterations, or is so irregular or incomplete as to call into question its authenticity. Redi-Cash gave value for the instrument when they cashed it for Bell. The UCC defines good faith as "honesty in fact and the observance of reasonable commercial standards of fair dealing." UCC 3-103(4). It is immaterial whether the transferor acted in good faith. There is nothing in the facts to show that Redi-Cash did anything but act in good faith. There appears to have been nothing that would have put Redi-Cash on notice that Smith had a defense against the instrument. The fraud, deceit, or illegality of Bell's actions do not keep Redi-Cash from being an HDC.

Unless the instrument arising from a contract or transaction is, itself, made void by statute, the illegality defense under UCC 3-305 is not available to bar the claim of a holder in due course.

Therefore, Redi-Cash should be viewed as an HDC and actually has rights greater than Bell in regards to this negotiable instrument. Smith should be ordered to pay Redi-Cash the $1,500 that Redi-Cash paid for the instrument. Smith will have to seek recourse against Bell.

Answers to Practice Quiz

True/False

16. False. An instrument that is payable to a specific payee or indorsed to a specific indorsee is order paper. [p. 377]

17. True. Order paper is negotiated by delivery with the necessary indorsement. [p. 377]

18. False. An instrument that is not payable to a specific payee or indorsee is bearer paper. [p. 377]

19. False. Bearer paper is negotiated by delivery; indorsement is not necessary. [p. 377]

20. True. A blank indorsement does not specify a particular indorsee. It may consist of just a signature. Order paper that is indorsed in blank becomes bearer paper. [p. 381]

21. False. A special indorsement contains the signature of the indorser and specifies the person (indorsee) to whom the indorser intends the instrument to be payable. [p. 381]

22. True. A special indorsement creates order paper. Order paper is negotiated by indorsement and delivery. [p. 381]

23. False. A holder can convert a blank indorsement into a special indorsement by writing contract instructions over the signature of the indorser. [p. 381]

24. True. The UCC permits qualified indorsements—that is, indorsements that disclaim or limit liability on the instrument. [p. 381]

25. False. A qualified indorsement protects only the indorser who wrote an indorsement on the instrument. [p. 382]

26. False. Nonrestrictive indorsements do not have any instructions or conditions attached to the payment of the funds. [p. 382]

27. True. An indorsement is nonrestrictive if the indorsee merely signs his or her signature to the back of an instrument or includes a notation to pay a specific indorsee. [p. 382]

28. True. An indorser can indorse an instrument so as to make the indorsee his collecting agent. Such indorsement is often done when an indorser deposits a check or another instrument for collection at a bank. [p. 383]

29. False. Where the name of the payee or indorsee is misspelled in a negotiable instrument, the payee or indorsee can indorse the instrument using the misspelled name, the correct name, or both. [p. 384]

30. False. if a virgule is used, either person may individually negotiate the instrument. [p. 385]

Multiple Choice

31. A. Once created, a negotiable instrument can be transferred to subsequent parties by negotiation. This is accomplished by placing an indorsement on the instrument. [p. 376]

32. D. An assignment is the transfer of rights under a contract. It transfers the rights of the transferor (assignor) to the transferee (assignee). [p. 376]

33. D. A nonnegotiable contract is a contract that lacks one or more of the requirements to be a negotiable instrument. An assignment occurs when a nonnegotiable contract is transferred. [p. 376]

34. C. An instrument that is payable to a specific payee or indorsed to a specific indorsee is order paper. Order paper is negotiated by delivery with the necessary indorsement. [p. 377]

35. B. Order paper is negotiated by delivery with the necessary indorsement. Bearer paper is negotiated by delivery; indorsement is not necessary. [p. 377]

36. C. Bearer paper is an instrument that is not payable to a specific payee or indorsee. Bearer paper is negotiated by delivery; indorsement is not necessary. [p. 377]

37. B. An indorsement is the signature of a signer (other than as a maker, a drawer, or an acceptor) that is placed on an instrument to negotiate it to another person. [p. 379]

38. A. If there is no room on the instrument, the indorsement may be written on a separate piece of paper called an allonge. The allonge must be affixed (e.g., stapled, taped) to the instrument. [p. 379]

39. D. A blank indorsement does not specify a particular indorsee. It may consist of just a signature. [p. 380]

40. A. Order paper that is indorsed in blank becomes bearer paper. Bearer paper can be negotiated by delivery; indorsement is not required. [p. 381]

41. A. A special indorsement contains the signature of the indorser and specifies the person (indorsee) to whom the indorser intends the instrument to be payable. [p. 381]

42. D. The UCC permits qualified indorsements—that is, indorsements that disclaim or limit liability on the instrument. A qualified indorser does not guarantee payment of the instrument if the maker, drawer, or acceptor defaults on it. [p. 381]

43. B. Nonrestrictive indorsement is an indorsement that has no instructions or conditions attached to the payment of the funds. [p. 382]

44. C. A holder in due course (HDC) is a holder who takes an instrument for value, in good faith, and without notice that it is defective or overdue. [p. 285]

45. A. An instrument is dishonored when it is presented for payment and payment is refused. This is called a dishonored instrument. [p. 387]

Short Answer

46. An assignment is the transfer of rights under a contract. It transfers the rights of the transferor to the transferee. Because normal contract principles apply, the assignee acquires only the rights that the assignor possessed. Thus, any defenses to the enforcement of the contract that could have been raised against the assignor can also be raised against the assignee. A nonnegotiable contract is a contract that lacks one or more of the requirements to be a negotiable instrument. An assignment occurs when a nonnegotiable contract is transferred. In the case of a negotiable instrument, assignment occurs when the instrument is transferred but the transfer fails to qualify as a negotiation under Article 3 of the Uniform Commercial Code. In this case, the transferee is an assignee rather than a holder. [p. 376]

47. An instrument that is payable to a specific payee or indorsed to a specific indorsee is order paper. Order paper is negotiated by delivery with the necessary indorsement. Thus, for order paper to be negotiated, there must be delivery and indorsement. An instrument that is not payable to a specific payee or indorsee is bearer paper. Bearer paper is negotiated by delivery; indorsement is not necessary. Substantial risk is associated with the loss or theft of bearer paper. [p. 377]

48. An indorsement is the signature of a signer (other than as a maker, a drawer, or an acceptor) that is placed on an instrument to negotiate it to another person. The signature may (1) appear alone, (2) name an individual to whom the instrument is to be paid, or (3) be accompanied by other words. The person who indorses an instrument is called the indorser. If the indorsement names a payee, this person is called the indorsee. Indorsements are required to negotiate order paper, but they are not required to negotiate bearer paper. For identification purposes and to impose liability on the transferor, however, the transferee often requires the transferor to indorse bearer paper at negotiation. [p. 379]

49. There are four categories of indorsements:
1. Blank indorsement
2. Special indorsement
3. Qualified indorsement
4. Restrictive indorsement [p. 380]

50. A blank indorsement does not specify a particular indorsee. It may consist of just a signature. Order paper that is indorsed in blank becomes bearer paper. As mentioned earlier, bearer paper can be negotiated by delivery; indorsement is not required. Thus, a lost bearer paper can be presented for payment or negotiated to another holder.
A special indorsement contains the signature of the indorser and specifies the person (indorsee) to whom the indorser intends the instrument to be payable. A special indorsement creates order paper. As mentioned earlier, order paper is negotiated by indorsement and delivery. [p. 381]

51. Most indorsements are nonrestrictive. Nonrestrictive indorsements do not have any instructions or conditions attached to the payment of the funds. Occasionally, an indorser includes some form of instruction in an indorsement. This instruction is called a restrictive indorsement. A restrictive indorsement restricts the indorsee's rights in some manner. An indorsement that purports to prohibit further negotiation of an instrument does not destroy the negotiability of the instrument. [p. 382]

52. UCC 3-206 recognizes the following types of restrictive indorsements:
• Indorsement for deposit or collection. An indorser can indorse an instrument so as to make the indorsee his collecting agent. Such indorsement— called an indorsement for deposit or collection—is often done when an indorser deposits a check or another instrument for collection at a bank. Words such as for collection, for deposit only, and pay any bank create this type of indorsement. Banks use this type of indorsement in the collection process.
• Indorsement in trust. An indorsement can state that it is for the benefit or use of the indorser or another person. [p. 383]

53. Where the name of the payee or indorsee is misspelled in a negotiable instrument, the payee or indorsee can indorse the instrument using the misspelled name, the correct name, or both. For example, if Susan Worth receives a check payable to "Susan Wirth," she can indorse the check by signing "Susan Wirth" or "Susan Worth" or both. A person paying or taking the instrument for

value or collection may require a signature in both the misspelled and the correct versions. [p. 384]

54. A holder is a person in possession of an instrument that is payable to bearer or an identified person who is in possession of an instrument payable to that person. The holder of a negotiable instrument has the same rights as an assignee of an ordinary nonnegotiable contract. That is, the holder is subject to all the claims and defenses that can be asserted against the transferor. A holder in due course is a holder who takes an instrument for value, in good faith, and without notice that it is defective or overdue. An HDC takes a negotiable instrument free of all claims and most defenses that can be asserted against the transferor of the instrument. [p. 385]

55. The UCC has a no evidence of forgery, alteration, or irregularity requirement. Under this rule, a holder does not qualify as an HDC if at the time the instrument was issued or negotiated to the holder, it bore apparent evidence of forgery or alteration or was otherwise so irregular or incomplete as to call into question its authenticity. Clever and undetectable forgeries and alterations are not classified as obvious irregularities. Determining whether a forgery or an alteration is apparent and whether the instrument is so irregular or incomplete that its authenticity should be questioned are issues of fact that must be decided on a case-by-case basis. [p. 388]

24 | LIABILITY, DEFENSES AND DISCHARGE

Chapter Overview

In the previous chapter, you learned about the various types of negotiable instruments as well as their creation and the ability to transfer them. This chapter expands on the concept of commercial paper being a substitute for money by exploring warranty liability of the parties on negotiable instruments and defenses that can be raised against the imposition of such liability, as well as the requirements for discharging liability.

Objectives

Upon completion of the exercises in this chapter, you should be able to:
1. Describe the signature liability of makers, drawees, drawers, acceptors, and accommodation parties for negotiable instruments.
2. List the transfer and presentment warranties and describe the liability of parties for breaching them.
3. Identify universal (real) defenses that can be asserted against a holder in due course.
4. Describe the Federal Trade Commission rule that limits holder in due course status in consumer transactions.
5. Describe how parties are discharged from liability on negotiable instruments.

Practical Application

This chapter will provide you with the understanding that you need to determine whether you are a holder in due course of negotiable instruments. You will be aware of any defenses that you may be able to assert, as well as what is involved in discharging liability on these instruments.

Helpful Hints

This focus of this chapter is on signature, primary, and secondary liability, as well as the role of an accommodation party and agent. Forged instruments and warranty, transfer, and presentment liability are discussed, in addition to the universal and personal defenses that may arise from the underlying transaction. It is important to realize why certain parties are discharged from liability on negotiable instruments. To assist your studies in this area, the study tips section has been organized so that you will be able to easily refer to the lists when analyzing the case studies or hypothetical problems presented to you.

Study Tips

Liability, Defenses, and Discharge

A holder of a negotiable instrument may use the court system to enforce the instrument when payment is not made when due. Signors, non-signors, and accommodation parties may have either primary or secondary liability on the instrument. Various defenses may be asserted against holders and, to a lesser extent, holders in due course to the enforcement of the instrument.

Signature Liability

A person cannot be held contractually liable on a negotiable instrument unless his or her signature appears on it. A signature on an instrument identifies who is obligated to pay on it. If a signature cannot be identified, parol evidence may be used. Liability does not attach to bearer paper as no indorsement is needed.

- Signers of instruments may sign in various capacities:
  - makers of notes and certificates of deposit
  - drawers of drafts and checks
  - drawees who accept checks and drafts
  - indorsers who indorse instruments
  - agents who sign on behalf of others
  - accommodation parties
- Every party that signs a negotiable instrument (except qualified indorsers and agents) is either primarily or secondarily liable.

Signature defined. The signature on a negotiable instrument can be any name, word, or mark used in lieu of a written signature; any symbol that is handwritten, typed, printed, stamped, or made in almost any other manner; and executed or adopted by a party to authenticate the writing.

- The unauthorized signature of a person on an instrument is ineffective as that person's signature.
  - It is effective as the signature of the unauthorized signer in favor of an HDC.
  - An unauthorized signature may be ratified.

Primary Liability

Makers of certificates of deposits and promissory notes have what is known as primary liability. The maker unconditionally promises to render the amount stipulated in the note when it is due.

- No party is primarily liable when a draft or check is issued since these instruments are merely an order to pay.

Secondary Liability

Secondary liability attaches to the drawers of checks and drafts and unqualified indorsers of negotiable instruments.

- This is similar to a guarantor of a simple contract.
- The drawer is obligated to pay if it is an unaccepted draft or check that is dishonored by the drawee or acceptor.

Unqualified Indorser. This type of indorser has secondary liability on negotiable instruments and must pay any dishonored instrument to the holder or to any subsequent indorser according to its terms, when the instrument has been properly issued or completed.

Qualified Indorser. An indorser that indorses an instrument "without recourse", or with other language that disclaims liability, is not secondarily liable on the instrument.

- Indorsers cannot disclaim liability in this way on a check.

Requirements for Imposing Secondary Liability.
- The instrument must be properly presented for payment.
- The instrument is dishonored.
- Notice of the dishonor is given in a timely manner to the person who is to be secondarily liable on the instrument.

Accommodation Party. A party who signs an instrument and lends his or her credit (and name) to another party to the instrument.
- *Guarantee of Payment.* The accommodation party who signs an instrument is basically guaranteeing payment and is primarily liable on the instrument.
- *Guarantee of Collection.* This arises where the accommodation party guarantees collection rather than payment. Requirement of payment arises only if:
  o execution of judgment against the other party has been returned unsatisfied,
  o the other party is in an insolvency proceeding or is insolvent,
  o the other party is unable to be served with process, or
  o it is otherwise obvious that payment cannot be received from the other party. [UCC3-419(d)]

Agent's Signatures

A person may sign an instrument him- or herself or authorize a representative known as an agent to sign on his or her behalf. The representative is the agent and the represented person is the principal.

Authorized Signature. The authorized agent's signature binds the principal regardless if the agent signs the principal's name or the agent's own name. Personal liability of the agent is dependent on how much information is revealed in the signature.
- If there is no ambiguity with a signature on behalf of a principal, then the agent has no liability.
- If there is an ambiguity in an authorized agent's signature and the agent cannot demonstrate that the original parties to the contract had no intent of holding the agent liable, then the agent is liable.
  o *Exception*: If the agent signs his or her name as the drawer of a check without indicating the agent's representative status and the check is payable from the account of the principal who is identified on the check, the agent is not liable on the check. [UCC 3-402(c)]

Unauthorized Signature.
- A signature made by a purported agent without authority from a purported principal.
  o A person signs a negotiable instrument on behalf of a person for whom he or she is not an agent; or
  o An unauthorized agent exceeds the scope of his or her authority.
- The purported agent is liable to any person who in good faith pays the instrument or takes it for value.
  o The agent is not liable if the principal ratifies the unauthorized signature.

Forged Instrument

The forged signature of a payee or holder on a negotiable instrument is generally inoperative as the indorsement of the person whose name is signed.

- Where an indorsement on an instrument has been forged or is unauthorized, the general rule is that the loss falls on the party who first takes the forged instrument after the forgery.
  - *Exception.* Where a drawer or maker bears the loss
  - *Exception.* Where an indorsement is forged

Imposter Rule. If the imposter forges the indorsement of the named payee, the drawer or maker is liable on the instrument to any person who, in good faith, pays the instrument or takes it for value or for collection.

- The imposter rule is inapplicable if the wrongdoer poses as the agent of the drawer or maker.

Fictitious Payee Rule. If a person signs as or on behalf of a drawer or maker and intends the named payee to have no interest in the instrument, or when the person identified as the payee is a fictitious person, the drawer or maker is liable on the instrument.

- This rule applies if an agent or employee of the drawer or maker supplies the drawer or maker with the name of a fictitious payee.

Transfer and Presentment Warranties

Warranty liability is placed upon a transferor irrespective of whether the transferor signed the instrument or not. Transfer and presentment warranties shift the risk of loss to the party who was in the best position to prevent the loss.

Transfer Warranties. A transfer is, "Any passage of an instrument other than its issuance and presentment for payment".

- There are five warranties that are made when a person transfers a negotiable instrument for consideration:
  - The transfer of good title to the instrument or authorization to obtain acceptance or payment on behalf of one who does have good title.
  - All signatures are authentic or authorized.
  - The instrument has not been altered materially.
  - No defenses of any party are applicable against the transferor.
  - The transferor is unaware of any insolvency proceeding against the maker, the acceptor, or the drawer of an unaccepted instrument.
- Instruments other than checks may disclaim transfer warranties with the use of an indorsement such as "without recourse" [UCC3-416 (c)].

Presentment Warranties. "Any person who presents a draft or check for payment or acceptance makes the following warranties to a drawee or acceptor who pays or accepts the instrument in good faith [UCC 3-417(a)]:

- The presenter has good title to the instrument or is authorized to obtain payment or acceptance of the person who has good title.
- The material has not been materially altered.
- The presenter has no knowledge that the signature of the maker or drawer is unauthorized.

Defenses

There are universal (real) and personal defenses that arise from the underlying transaction concerning the creation of negotiable instruments.

Universal (real) defenses	Personal defenses
These can be raised against both holders and holders in due course. If one of these defenses is proven, neither holder nor holder in due course can recover on the instrument. Minority Extreme duress Mental incapacity Illegality Discharge in bankruptcy Fraud in the inception Forgery Material alteration	These can be raised against enforcement of a negotiable instrument by an ordinary holder. Breach of contract Fraud in the inducement Other personal defenses -mental illness -illegality of a contract -ordinary duress or undue Influence UCC3-305(a)(ii) -discharge of an instrument By payment or cancellation [UCC 3-602 and 3-604]

FTC Rule Limits HDC Status. The rule puts the holder of due course of a consumer credit contract on the same level as an assignee of a simple contract. The result is the holder of due course of a consumer credit instrument is subject to all of the defenses and claims of the consumer.

- This rule applies to consumer credit transactions that include a promissory note, the buyer signs an installment sales contract that contains a waiver of defenses clause, and the seller arranges consumer financing with a third-party lender.

Discharge

There are several rules that are specified by the UCC on when and how certain parties are discharged from liability on negotiable instruments. The three main ways that will relieve the parties from liability are:
- By payment of the instrument
- By cancellation
  - by any manner or
  - by destroying or mutilating a negotiable instrument with the intent of getting rid of the obligation.
- By impairment of the right of recourse which is accomplished by
  - releasing an obligor from liability or
  - surrendering collateral without the consent of the parties who would benefit by it.

Refresh Your Memory

The following exercise will give you the opportunity to test your memory of the principles given in this chapter. Read the question twice and place your answer in the blank provided. Review the chapter material for any question that you are unable to answer or remember.

1. Signature liability is also known as _____ liability.

2. Absolute liability to pay a negotiable instrument, subject to certain universal (real) defenses is called _____ liability.

3. _____ are those who are secondarily liable on negotiable instruments they endorse.

4. A demand for acceptance or payment of an instrument made upon the maker, acceptor, drawee, or other payer by or on behalf of the holder is called _____.

5. The _____ signs an instrument and lends his or her name (and credit) to another party to the instrument.

6. A(n) _____ is a person who has been authorized to sign a negotiable instrument on behalf of another person.

7. A signature made by a purported agent without authority from the purported principal is called a(n) _____.

8. _____ rule states that a drawer or maker is liable on a forged or unauthorized indorsement if the person signing as or on behalf of a drawer or maker intends the named payee to have no interest in the instrument or when the person identified as the payee is a fictitious person.

9. Any passage of an instrument other than its issuance and presentment for payment is called _____.

10. A defense that can be raised against both holders and HDCs is called a(n) _____, also known as real defense.

11. _____ consists of adding to any part of a signed instrument, removing any part of a signed instrument, making changes in the number or relations of the parties, or completing an incomplete instrument without having the authority to do so.

12. _____ can be raised against enforcement of a negotiable instrument by an ordinary holder but not against an HDC.

13. _____ occurs when a wrongdoer makes a false statement to another person to lead that person to enter into a contract with the wrongdoer.

14. The holder of a negotiable instrument can discharge the liability of any party to the instrument by _____.

15. Actions or events that relieve certain parties from liability on negotiable instruments are known as _____.

Critical Thought Exercise

Sally Knapp made out a check to Harold Dodd of Dodd Electrical for $1,000 as a partial payment for electrical work in her kitchen. When it was time for Dodd to begin his work, he did not appear, nor could Ms. Knapp locate him. Knapp immediately ordered her bank to stop payment on the check. Dodd had already cashed the check at Quik-Cash. When the check was returned to Quik-Cash marked "payment stopped by account holder," Quik-Cash was contacted by an attorney for Knapp who informed Quik-Cash that the plumber did not have a license and that engaging in a contracting trade without a license was a crime. Therefore the contract was void and his client would not honor the check.

As manager of Quik-Cash, will you commence suit against Knapp to collect the amount of the check?

Please compose your answer to the Critical Thinking Exercise using a separate sheet of paper or your computer word processing program.

Practice Quiz

True/False

16. _____ A person cannot be held contractually liable on a negotiable instrument unless his or her signature appears on it.

17. _____ Marks used in lieu of a written signature cannot be used on indorsements.

18. _____ The payee of a cashier's check is also primarily liable on the instrument.

19. _____ An unqualified indorser has secondary liability on negotiable instruments.

20. _____ A qualified indorser is only liable for secondary liability.

21. _____ A presentment is a demand for the acceptance of a dishonored instrument.

22. _____ The person represented by a representative agent is known as the principal.

23. _____ The imposter rule does not apply for the wrongdoer who poses as the agent of the payee.

24. _____ Implied warranties are made when the negotiable instrument is originally issued.

25. _____ Transfer warranties cannot be disclaimed with respect to checks.

26. _____ Presentment warranties are made by the drawer of a check or draft.

27. _____ Personal and universal defenses can be raised against an ordinary holder of a negotiable instrument.

28. _____ Extreme duress is considered a personal defense.

29. _____ Fraud in the inception is a type of personal defense.

30. _____ An instrument is not considered canceled if it is destroyed or mutilated by accident or by an unauthorized third party.

Multiple Choice

31. Liability in which a person cannot be held contractually liable on a negotiable instrument unless his or her signature appears on the instrument is referred to as _____.

A. warranty liability
B. unqualified liability
C. accommodation
D. contract liability

32. In which of the following conditions is a drawee primarily liable to a draft?

A. when the drawee is an acceptor to the instrument
B. when the instrument is dishonored
C. when the instrument s presented for payment
D. when the instrument is issued

33. Those who are secondarily liable on negotiable instruments they endorse are known as _____.

A. qualified indorsers
B. unqualified indorsers
C. accommodation parties
D. agents

34. Those who disclaim liability and are not secondarily liable on instruments they endorse are referred to as _____.

A. unqualified indorsers
B. agents
C. qualified indorsers
D. accommodation parties

35. _____ is a demand for acceptance or payment of an instrument made upon the maker, acceptor, drawee, or other payer by or on behalf of the holder.

A. Accommodation
B. Duress
C. Allonge
D. Presentment

36. In which of the following accommodations is an accommodation party primarily liable?

A. in a guarantee of collection
B. in a guarantee of payment
C. in a guarantee of demand
D. in a guarantee of promise

37. An accommodation party is secondarily liable in case the accommodation is in a _____.

A. guarantee of promise
B. guarantee of demand
C. guarantee of payment
D. guarantee of collection

38. A person who has been authorized to sign a negotiable instrument on behalf of another person is known as a(n) _____.

A. principal
B. accommodation party
C. agent
D. holder in due course

39. What is the similarity between the fictitious payee rule and the imposter rule?

A. Both hold the drawee liable to the instrument.
B. Both put the risk of loss on the forger.
C. Both hold the drawer liable to the instrument.
D. Both put the risk of loss on the indorsee.

40. What is transfer of an instrument?

A. the issuance of the instrument
B. the presentment for payment of the instrument
C. the cancellation of the instrument
D. the passage of the instrument other than issuance and presentment

41. To which of the following placements of a negotiable instrument are transfer warranties applicable?

A. issuance of the instrument
B. indorsement of the instrument
C. presentment of the instrument
D. accommodation of the instrument

42. A _____ defense is a type of defense that can be raised against both holders and HDCs.

A. personal
B. universal
C. fraud in the inducement
D. breach of contract

43. A(n) _____ defense is a type of defense that can be raised against enforcement of a negotiable instrument by an ordinary holder but not against an HDC.

A. discharge in bankruptcy
B. extreme duress
C. universal
D. personal

44. _____ is a type of personal defense where a wrongdoer makes a false statement or misrepresentation to another person to lead that person to enter into a contract with the wrongdoer.

A. Discharge in bankruptcy
B. Forgery
C. Fraud in the inducement
D. Extreme duress

45. A(n) _____ is an action or event that relieves certain parties from liability on negotiable instruments.

A. discharge
B. presentment
C. accommodation
D. breach of contract

Short Answer

46. Explain primary liability for negotiable instruments.

_____
_____

47. What is the difference between an unqualified and a qualified indorser?

_____
_____

48. What are the requirements for imposing secondary liability?

_____
_____

49. What are the types of liability of an accommodation party?

_____
_____

50. Who are agent and principal?

_____
_____

51. Explain the imposter rule and the fictitious payee rule.

_____
_____

52. What are presentment warranties?

_____
_____

53. List the various universal defenses?

_____
_____

54. What is material alteration as a universal defense?

_____

_____

55. What is the defense of fraud in the inducement?

_____

_____

Answers to Refresh Your Memory

1. contract [p. 393]
2. primary [p. 394]
3. Unqualified indorsers [p. 394]
4. presentment [p. 395]
5. accommodation party [p. 395]
6. agent [p. 396]
7. unauthorized signature [p. 397]
8. Fictitious payee [p. 398]
9. transfer [p. 399]
10. universal defense [p. 400]
11. Material alteration [p. 401]
12. Personal defense [p. 402]
13. Fraud in the inducement [p. 403]
14. cancellation [p. 404]
15. discharge [p. 405]

Critical Thought Exercise Model Answer

A holder of a negotiable instrument is a holder in due course (HDC) pursuant to UCC 3-302 if he or she takes the instrument (1) for value; (2) in good faith; and (3) without notice that it is overdue, that it has been dishonored, that any person has a defense against it or claim to it, or that the instrument contains unauthorized signatures, alterations, or is so irregular or incomplete as to call into question its authenticity. Quik-Cash gave value for the instrument when they cashed it for Dodd. The UCC defines good faith as "honesty in fact and the observance of reasonable commercial standards of fair dealing." UCC 3-103(4). It is immaterial whether the transferor acted in good faith. There is nothing in the facts to show that Quik-Cash did anything but act in good faith. There appears to have been nothing that would have put Quik-Cash on notice that Knapp had a defense against the instrument. The fraud, deceit, or illegality of Dodd's actions do not keep Quik-Cash from being an HDC.

Unless the instrument arising from a contract or transaction is, itself, made void by statute, the illegality defense under UCC 3-305 is not available to bar the claim of a holder in due course.

Therefore, Quik-Cash should be viewed as an HDC and actually has rights greater than Dodd in regards to this negotiable instrument. Knapp should be ordered to pay Quik-Cash the $1,000 that Quik-Cash paid for the instrument. Knapp will have to seek recourse against Dodd.

Answers to Practice Quiz

True/False

16. True. A person cannot be held contractually liable on a negotiable instrument unless his or her signature appears on it [UCC 3-401(a)]. Therefore, this type of liability is often referred to as signature liability, or contract liability. [p. 393]

17. False. A signature is any symbol that is (1) handwritten, typed, printed, stamped, or made in almost any other manner and (2) executed or adopted by a party to authenticate a writing [UCC 1-201(39)]. [p. 393]

18. False. The issuer of a cashier's check is also primarily liable on the instrument [UCC 3-411]. [p. 394]

19. True. An unqualified indorser has secondary liability on negotiable instruments. In other words, he or she must pay any dishonored instrument to the holder or to any subsequent indorser according to its terms, when issued or properly completed. [p. 394]

20. False. A qualified indorser is not secondarily liable on an instrument because he or she has expressly disclaimed liability. [p. 395]

21. False. Presentment is a demand for acceptance or payment of an instrument made upon the maker, acceptor, drawee, or other payer by or on behalf of the holder. [p. 395]

22. True. Principal is a person who authorizes an agent to sign a negotiable instrument on his or her behalf. [p. 396]

23. True. Imposter rule states that if an imposter forges the indorsement of the named payee, the drawer or maker is liable on the instrument to any person who, in good faith, pays the instrument or takes it for value or for collection. [p. 397]

24. False. Implied warranties are not made when a negotiable instrument is originally issued. [p. 398]

25. True. Transfer warranties cannot be disclaimed with respect to checks, but they can be disclaimed with respect to other instruments. An indorsement that states "without recourse" disclaims the transfer warranties. [p. 399]

26. False. Any person who presents a draft or check for payment or acceptance makes presentment warranties to a drawee or an acceptor who pays or accepts the instrument in good faith. [p. 399]

27. True. A holder in due course (HDC) (or a holder through an HDC) takes an instrument free from personal defenses but not universal defenses. Personal and universal defenses can be raised against a normal holder of a negotiable instrument. [p. 400]

28. False. Extreme duress is a universal defense against the enforcement of a negotiable instrument by a holder or an HDC. [p. 400]

29. False. Fraud in the inception (also called the fraud in the factum or fraud in the execution) is a universal defense against the enforcement of a negotiable instrument by a holder or an HDC. [p. 401]

30. True. An instrument is not canceled if it is destroyed or mutilated by accident or by an unauthorized third party. The holder can bring suit to enforce the destroyed or mutilated instrument. [p. 405]

Multiple Choice

31. D. A person cannot be held contractually liable on a negotiable instrument unless his or her signature appears on it [UCC 3-401(a)]. Therefore, this type of liability is often referred to as signature liability, or contract liability. [p. 393]

32. A. On occasion, a drawee is requested to accept a draft or check. Acceptance of a draft occurs when the drawee writes the word accepted across the face of the draft. The acceptor—that is, the drawee—is primarily liable on the instrument. [p. 394]

33. B. An unqualified indorser has secondary liability on negotiable instruments. In other words, he or she must pay any dishonored instrument to the holder or to any subsequent indorser according to its terms, when issued or properly completed. [p. 394]

34. C. A qualified indorser (i.e., an indorser who indorses instruments "without recourse" or similar language that disclaims liability) is not secondarily liable on an instrument because he or she has expressly disclaimed liability. [p. 395]

35. D. Presentment is a demand for acceptance or payment of an instrument made upon the maker, acceptor, drawee, or other payer by or on behalf of the holder. Presentment is effective when it is received by the person to whom presentment is made. [p. 395]

36. B. An accommodation party who signs an instrument guaranteeing payment is primarily liable on the instrument. [p. 396]

37. D. An accommodation party may sign an instrument guaranteeing collection rather than guaranteeing payment of an instrument. In this situation, the accommodation indorser is only secondarily liable on the instrument. [p. 396]

38. A. A person may either sign a negotiable instrument him- or herself or authorize a representative to sign the instrument on his or her behalf [UCC 3-401(a)]. The representative is the agent, and the represented person is the principal. [p. 396]

39. C. Imposter rule states that if an imposter forges the indorsement of the named payee, the drawer or maker is liable on the instrument to any person who, in good faith, pays the instrument or takes it for value or for collection. Fictitious payee rule states that a drawer or maker is liable on a forged or unauthorized indorsement if the person signing as or on behalf of a drawer or maker intends the named payee to have no interest in the instrument or when the person identified as the payee is a fictitious person. [p. 398, 397]

40. D. Any passage of an instrument other than its issuance and presentment for payment is considered a transfer. [p. 399]

41. B. Transfer warranties cannot be disclaimed with respect to checks, but they can be disclaimed with respect to other instruments. An indorsement that states "without recourse" disclaims the transfer warranties. [p. 399]

42. B. Universal defenses (also called real defenses) can be raised against both holders and HDCs [UCC 3-305(b)]. If a universal defense is proven, the holder or HDC cannot recover on the instrument. [p. 400]

43. D. Personal defenses cannot be raised against an HDC. Personal defenses can, however, be raised against enforcement of a negotiable instrument by an ordinary holder. [p. 402]

44. C. Fraud in the inducement occurs when a wrongdoer makes a false statement to another person to lead that person to enter into a contract with the wrongdoer. Fraud in the inducement is a personal defense that is not effective against HDCs. It is effective against ordinary holders, however. [p. 403]

45. A. The UCC specifies when and how certain parties are discharged (relieved) from liability on negotiable instruments. Generally, all parties to a negotiable instrument are discharged from liability if (1) the party primarily liable on the instrument pays it in full to the holder of the instrument or (2) a drawee in good faith pays an unaccepted draft or check in full to the holder. [p. 404]

Short Answer

46. Makers of promissory notes and certificates of deposit have primary liability for the instruments. Upon signing a promissory note, the maker unconditionally promises to pay the amount stipulated in the note when it is due. A maker is absolutely liable to pay the instrument, subject only to certain universal (real) defenses. The holder need not take any action to give rise to this obligation. Generally, the maker is obligated to pay a note according to its original terms. If the note was incomplete when it was issued, the maker is obligated to pay the note as completed, as long as he or she authorized the terms as they were filled in [UCC 3-412]. [p. 394]

47. An unqualified indorser has secondary liability on negotiable instruments. In other words, he or she must pay any dishonored instrument to the holder or to any subsequent indorser according to its terms, when issued or properly completed. Unless otherwise agreed, indorsers are liable to each other in the order in which they indorsed the instrument. A qualified indorser (i.e., an indorser who indorses instruments "without recourse" or similar language that disclaims liability) is not secondarily liable on an instrument because he or she has expressly disclaimed liability. [p. 394]

48. A party is secondarily liable on a negotiable instrument only if the following requirements are met: The instrument is properly presented for payment. Presentment is a demand for acceptance or payment of an instrument made upon the maker, acceptor, drawee, or other payer by or on behalf of the holder.
The instrument is dishonored. An instrument is a dishonored instrument when acceptance or payment of the instrument is refused or cannot be obtained from the party required to accept or pay the instrument within the prescribed time after presentment is duly made.
Notice of the dishonor is timely given to the person to be held secondarily liable on the instrument. A secondarily liable party cannot be compelled to accept or pay an instrument unless proper notice of dishonor has been given. [p. 395]

49. There are two types of liability of an accommodation party:
1. Guarantee of payment – An accommodation party who signs an instrument guaranteeing payment is primarily liable on the instrument. That is, the debtor can seek payment on the instrument directly from the accommodation maker without first seeking payment from the maker.
2. Guarantee of collection – An accommodation party may sign an instrument guaranteeing collection rather than guaranteeing payment of an instrument. In this situation, the accommodation indorser is only secondarily liable on the instrument. To reserve this type of liability, the signature of the accommodation party must be accompanied by words indicating that he or she is guaranteeing collection rather than payment of the obligation. [p. 396]

50. A person may either sign a negotiable instrument him- or herself or authorize a representative to sign the instrument on his or her behalf [UCC 3-401(a)]. The representative is the agent, and the represented person is the principal. The authority of an agent to sign an instrument is established under general agency law. No special form of appointment is necessary. If an authorized agent signs an instrument with either the principal's name or the agent's own name, the principal is bound as if the signature were made on a simple contract. It does not matter whether the principal is identified in the instrument. [p. 396]

51. An imposter is someone who impersonates a payee and induces the maker or drawer to issue an instrument in the payee's name and give the instrument to the imposter. If the imposter forges the indorsement of the named payee, the drawer or maker is liable on the instrument to any person who, in good faith, pays the instrument or takes it for value or for collection [UCC 3-404(a)]. This rule is called the imposter rule.
A drawer or maker is liable on a forged or unauthorized indorsement under the fictitious payee rule. This rule applies when a person signing as or on behalf of a drawer or maker intends the named payee to have no interest in the instrument or when the person identified as the payee is a fictitious person. [p. 398]

52. Any person who presents a draft or check for payment or acceptance makes the following presentment warranties to a drawee or an acceptor who pays or accepts the instrument in good faith [UCC 3-417(a)]:
1. The presenter has good title to the instrument or is authorized to obtain payment or acceptance of the person who has good title.
2. The instrument has not been materially altered.
3. The presenter has no knowledge that the signature of the maker or drawer is unauthorized. [p. 399]

53. The various universal defenses are as follows:
- Minority
- Extreme duress
- Mental incompetence
- Illegality
- Discharge in bankruptcy
- Fraud in the inception
- Forgery
- Material Alteration [p. 400, 401]

54. An instrument that has been fraudulently and materially altered cannot be enforced by an ordinary holder. Material alteration consists of adding to any part of a signed instrument,

removing any part of a signed instrument, making changes in the number or relations of the parties, or completing an incomplete instrument without having the authority to do so. Under the UCC rule that words control figures, correcting the figure on a check to correspond to the written amount on the check is not a material alteration. If an alteration is not material, the instrument can be enforced by a holder for the original amount in which the drawer wrote the check. [p. 401]

55. Fraud in the inducement occurs when a wrongdoer makes a false statement or misrepresentation to another person to lead that person to enter into a contract with the wrongdoer. Negotiable instruments often arise out of such transactions. Fraud in the inducement is a personal defense that is not effective against HDCs. It is effective against ordinary holders, however. [p. 403]

25 | CHECKS, THE BANKING SYSTEM, AND E-MONEY

Chapter Overview

This chapter is primarily concerned with checks, the most common form of negotiable instrument. In this chapter you will learn about several different kinds of checks, as well as the process involved regarding payment and collection of checks through the banking system. This chapter explores the duties and liabilities of banks and other parties in the collection process, as well as electronic fund transfers.

Objectives

Upon completion of the exercises in this chapter, you should be able to:
1. Describe the difference between certified and cashier's checks.
2. Describe the system of processing and collecting checks through the banking system.
3. Describe electronic banking and e-money.
4. Define commercial wire transfer and describe the use of wire transfers in commerce.
5. Describe the banking reform provisions of the Dodd-Frank Wall Street Reform and Consumer Protection Act.

Practical Application

Whether you are part of a large or small business, or personally transfer funds and pay bills by way of checks or electronic transfers, an understanding of checks and how they are processed is crucial. Since almost everyone will have the opportunity to either have a checking account or purchase one of the various types of checks, this chapter will prove to be an invaluable resource. It will provide insight into the banking procedures involving payment and collection of checks and assist you in knowing what the banks' duties and other parties' duties and liabilities are in the collection process. You will gain useful information concerning electronic fund transfers.

Helpful Hints

This chapter will be relatively easy for most individuals to learn, since much of what is presented has already been experienced in most individuals' everyday personal and business affairs. In addition to this basic knowledge is an examination of areas where a bank, business, or individual may be liable for improper use or processing of a check. There may be a few terms that you recognize by definition and other terms that you will want to review a little more carefully. Examples of these types of terms include, but are not limited to, such words as stale checks, incomplete checks, deferred posting, provisional posting, etc. This chapter's high applicability makes it a very interesting learning experience.

Study Tips

Checks, Banking System, and E-Money

Checks are both a substitute for money and a record-keeping device, but do not serve a credit function. There are special forms of check, such as cashier's checks. The banking system processes checks, and sometimes must deal with forged or altered checks.

The Bank-Customer Relationship

The customer is the creditor. The bank is the debtor.
- A principal-agent relationship may also be formed whereby the customer is the principal ordering the bank to collect or pay on the check.
  - The bank is the agent obligated to follow the customer as principal's order.

Uniform Commercial Code (UCC) Articles Related to Checks and Banking. Various articles of the UCC establish rules for creating, collecting, and enforcing checks and wire transfers.
- *Article 3 (Commercial Paper)*. Gives requirements for negotiable instruments.
- *Article 4 (Bank Deposits and Collections)*. Regulates deposit and collection procedures for checking accounts and check-like accounts.
- *Article 4A (Funds Transfers)*. Regulates the creation and collection of and liability for wire transfers.

Ordinary Checks

When a customer goes to a bank, fills out the proper forms along with a signature card, followed by a deposit, the bank issues checks to him or her. Thereafter, the customer uses the checks for his or her purchases.
- The checks are presented to the bank and paid provided the drawer's signature matches the signature card.

Parties to a Check.
- *Drawer*. This is the customer with a checking account.
- *Drawee*. This is the bank (or payer) at which the check is drawn.
- *Payee*. The one to whom the check is written.

Indorsement of a Check. This refers to the holder or payee signing the back of the check.
- The payee is the indorser and the person to whom the check is indorsed is the indorsee.

Special Types of Checks

Bank checks are special checks, which are usually considered "as good as cash."

Certified Checks. With this type of check, the bank agrees in advance to accept the check when it is presented for payment and pay the check out of funds set aside from the customer's account.
- These types of checks are payable at any time from when they are issued.
- The bank writes or stamps the word "certified" across the face of an ordinary check thereby certifying it.

- o The date, amount being certified, and the name of individual certifying the check also are placed on the check.
    - Payment may not be stopped on a certified check.

Cashier's Checks. This is a bank-issued check where the customer has paid the bank the amount of the check and a fee.
- The bank guarantees the payment of the check.
- The bank acts as the drawer and the drawee with the holder as payee.
- The bank debits its own account when the check is presented.

Honoring Checks

The customer of a bank agrees to keep sufficient funds in the account to cover any checks written. If the customer keeps his or her end of this implied agreement, the bank is under a duty to honor the check and charge the customer's (or drawer's) account for whatever amount(s) the check(s) were written.

Stale Checks. A stale check is one that has been outstanding for more than six months.
- Under UCC 4-404, the bank is not obligated to pay on a stale check.
- If the bank does pay it, it may also in good faith charge the drawer's account.

Incomplete Checks. If a drawer fails to provide information on a check, the holder may complete the information and the bank may charge the customer's account the amount of the completed amount.
- The exception to this is if the bank receives notice that the completion was improper.

Postdated Checks. If a drawer does not want a check to be cashed until sometime in the future, he or she can postdate the check.
- The bank must abide by the date on the check if
    - o The check is postdated to a future date, and
    - o The drawer provides separate written notice that identifies the postdated check and the date of postdate.
- If these requirements are met, the bank is liable for losses resulting from cashing the check prior to the postdate.

Stop Payment Orders. This is an order by a drawer of a check to the payer bank not to pay or certify a check. It may be accomplished orally or in writing.
- If the order is oral, the order is good for only fourteen days.
- If the order is in writing, the order is good for six months, and may be renewed in writing for additional six-month periods.

Overdrafts . If a customer does not have sufficient funds in his or her account to cover the amount, the payer bank may either dishonor the check or honor the check and create an overdraft in the drawer's account.
- In the event of a dishonor, the payer bank notifies the drawer of the dishonor and returns the check to the holder marked insufficient funds.
    - o If the holder resubmits the check and there still are insufficient funds in the customer's account, then the holder may seek recourse against the drawer.

Wrongful Dishonor. When the bank fails to honor a check where there are sufficient funds in the drawer's account to pay a properly payable check, it is liable for wrongful dishonor.
- The bank is liable to the drawer for damages proximately caused by the dishonor along with consequential damages and damages that may have resulted from criminal prosecution.

Forged Signatures and Altered Checks

The UCC provides rules for cases of forged signatures and alteration of negotiable instruments.

Forged Signature of the Drawer. The bank is under a duty to verify the drawer's signature by matching the signature on the check with that of the signature card on file at the bank.
- The instrument with a forged signature of the drawer is inoperative.
- The bank cannot charge the customer's account if it pays a check over a forged signature.
- The bank's recourse is against the party who presented the check, provided he or she was not aware of the unauthorized signature.
- The forger is liable on the check if he or she can be found.

Altered Checks. An unauthorized change in the check that modifies a legal obligation of a party is an altered check.
- The check may be dishonored by the bank if it discovers the alteration.
- If an altered check is paid by the bank, the bank may charge the drawer's account for the original tenor (amount) of the check, but not the altered amount.
- The warranty of presentment applies here, especially if there has been an alteration in a chain of collection.
  - Each party in the chain may collect from the preceding transferor based on a breach of this warranty.

One-Year Rule. The drawer of a check must report a forged or altered check within one year of receiving the bank statement containing the check or the bank is relieved of liability.

Series of Forgeries. If the same wrongdoer engages in a series of forgeries or alterations on the same account, the customer must report that to the payer bank within a reasonable period of time, not exceeding 30 days from the date that the bank statement was made available to the customer, or the bank is relieved of liability on all similar forgeries after this date and prior to notification.

The Collection Process

The collection process is ruled by Article 4 of the UCC. When an individual receives a check, he or she may go to the drawer's bank or to his or her own bank (known as the depository bank). The depository bank must present the check to the payer bank for collection.
- Banks not classified as payers or depository banks are intermediary banks.

The Federal Reserve System. The Federal Reserve System helps banks to collect on checks.
- Member banks may submit paid checks to the Federal Reserve Bank for payment.
- Member banks pay the federal reserve to debit and credit their accounts and to show collection and payment of checks.

Deferred Posting. Deferred posting applies to all banks. This refers to a daily cutoff for posting checks or deposits.

- Weekends and holidays do not count as business days unless all of the bank's functions are carried on as usual on those days.

Provisional Credits. When a collecting bank gives credit to a check in the collection process prior to its final settlement.

- Provisional credits may be reversed if the check does not "clear."

Final Settlement. A check is deemed finally settled if the payer bank pays the check in cash, settles for the check without having the right to revoke the settlement, or fails to dishonor the check within certain time periods. UCC 4-215(a)

"On Us" Checks. If the drawer and holder have accounts at the same bank, then the check is called an "on us" item.

- The check is considered paid if the bank fails to dishonor the check by business on the second banking day following the receipt of the check.

"On Them" Checks. If the drawer and holder have accounts at different banks, the check is an "on them" item.

- Each bank must take action prior to its midnight deadline following the banking day it received an "on them" check for collection. UCC 4-104(a)(10)

Deposit of Cash. A deposit of money becomes available for withdrawal at the opening of the next banking day following the deposit. UCC 4-215 (a)

Failure to Examine Bank Statements in a Timely Manner. Generally banks send monthly statements to their customers.

- If this does not occur, banks must provide adequate information to allow the customer to be aware of which checks were paid and when and for what amount.
- If the checks are not given back to the customer, then the bank must keep the checks or copies for seven years.
- *Customer's duty.* To examine the statements promptly and with reasonable care.
    o If an error or forgery is present, the customer must promptly notify the bank.

E-Banking and E-Money

Banks offer electronic payment and collection systems to bank customers using computers and electronic technology, collectively referred to as the electronic funds transfer system (EFTS).

Automated Teller Machine. An ATM is an electronic machine located on a bank's premises or at some other convenient location and is connected online to the bank's computers.

- Bank customers access accounts using a personal identification number (PIN)

Point-of-Sale Terminal. The customer's account is immediately debited for the amount of the purchase by using a bank issued debit card to make a purchase.

Direct Deposit and Withdrawal. The customer's bank and the payee's bank must belong to the same clearinghouse to provide the service of paying recurring payments and recurring deposits.

Online Banking. Customers may pay bills from their account using their PIN number and account number, the amount of the bill to be paid, and the account number of the payee.

Electronic Wire Transfers

A commercial wire transfer involves the transferring of money over one or both of the two main wire systems, the Federal Reserve wire transfer network and the New York Clearing House Interbank Payments System.

UCC Article 4A (Funds Transfers). This article governs wholesale wire transfers.
- It only applies to commercial electronic fund transfers.

Funds Transfer Procedures. Commercially reasonable security procedures should be established.

Refresh Your Memory

The following exercise will give you the opportunity to test your memory of the principles given in this chapter. Read the question twice and place your answer in the blank provided. Review the chapter material for any question that you are unable to answer or remember.

1. When a customer makes a deposit into a bank, a _____ relationship is formed.

2. The checking account holder and writer of a check is called the _____ of the check.

3. A payee's signing of the back of a check in order to turn it over to another party is called _____ of a check.

4. _____ is a check issued by a bank for which the customer has paid the bank the amount of the check and a fee.

5. A check that has been outstanding for more than six months is a _____ check.

6. _____ is the amount of money a drawer owes a bank after it has paid a check despite the drawer's account having insufficient funds.

7. _____ is a situation in which there are sufficient funds in a drawer's account to pay a properly payable check, but the bank does not do so.

8. A guarantee in which each prior transferor warrants that a check has not been altered is called _____.

9. _____ is the bank where the drawer has a checking account and on which a check is drawn.

10. A bank in the collection process that is not the depository bank or the payer bank is called the _____ bank.

11. The _____ rule allows banks to fix an afternoon hour of 2:00 p.m. or later as a cutoff hour for the purpose of processing items.

12. The check is called a(n) "_____" item if the drawer and the payee or holder have accounts at the same bank.

13. _____ is a government agency that insures deposits at most banks and savings institutions ("insured bank") in the United States.

14. Debit cards can be used at merchants that have _____ terminals at the checkout counters.

15. _____ is a federal statute that regulates consumer electronic funds transfers.

Critical Thought Exercise

Dave Austin of Austin Imports is an antique dealer who often makes purchases without sufficient funds in his account because he must often act quickly to purchase a one-of-a-kind item before another dealer can take advantage of a very profitable sale price. Austin often postdates checks for the purchases of furniture, art, rugs, and other items that he resells. Austin has a very good relationship with Everglades Bank in Miami, where his main studio is located. The operations officer of Everglades Bank knows that Austin uses postdated checks for purchases approximately 50-75 times per year out of a total of 1,200 checks written on his account.

When the operations officer at Everglades Bank took a position with another bank, four postdated checks totaling $58,000 were negotiated before the written date, causing 47 other checks to be dishonored.

If Austin sues Everglades Bank to recover incidental and consequential damages for wrongful dishonor, will he prevail?

Please compose your answer to the Critical Thinking Exercise using a separate sheet of paper or your computer word processing program.

Practice Quiz

True/False

16. _____ A creditor-debtor relationship between a customer and a bank is created if the customer writes a check against his or her account.

17. _____ Certified checks become stale after two years from the date of their issue.

18. _____ A cashier's check is a two-party check.

19. _____ It is not necessary to have a checking account at the issuing bank to purchase a cashier's check.

20. _____ A check that has been outstanding for more than three months is considered stale, and the bank is under no obligation to pay it.

21. _____ An oral order to stop payment on a check is binding on the payer bank for a period of 14 calendar days.

22. _____ A stop-payment order can be issued either by the drawer or the payee.

23. _____ The payer bank cannot charge the customer's account if it pays a check over the forged signature.

24. _____ A presentment warranty is a guarantee in which each prior transferor warrants that a check has not been altered.

25. _____ A check is finally paid when the payer bank fails to dishonor the check within certain statutory time periods.

26. _____ If the drawer and the payee of a check have accounts at the same bank, the check is called an "on them" item when it is presented for payment by the payee.

27. _____ Banks are obligated under the provisions of Article 4 of the UCC to send canceled checks along with the monthly statements of account to their checking account customers.

28. _____ Except for the collecting bank, each bank in the collection process, including the payer bank, must take proper action on an "on them" check prior to its midnight deadline.

29. _____ If a customer notifies the issuing bank within two days of learning that his or her debit card has been lost or stolen, the customer is liable for only $100 for unauthorized use.

30. _____ The Dodd-Frank Wall Street Reform and Consumer Protection Act grants powers to the Federal Reserve to monitor and regulate institutions it supervises, including bank holding companies, savings bank holding companies, and affiliates of holding companies.

Multiple Choice

31. In banking terminology, a creditor-debtor relationship is created when _____.

A. a customer fails to maintain adequate funds in his bank checking account
B. a customer writes a postdated check drawn on his bank
C. a customer writes a check against his account
D. a customer makes a deposit into a bank

32. Jill Scott is an accountant with Cameron and Associates, a law firm in downtown Seattle. The firm maintains a checking account with Southern Rock Bank for its operating expenses. On the 10th of every month, Jill gets an inventory report from the office manager listing the office supplies that are needed. Jill places the appropriate orders with Office Depot and writes them a check against the office's checking account.
Who is the drawee in this banking transaction?

A. Jill Scott
B. Southern Rock Bank
C. Cameron and Associates
D. Office Depot

33. Jill Scott is an accountant with Cameron and Associates, a law firm in downtown Seattle. The firm maintains a checking account with Southern Rock Bank for its operating expenses. On the 10th of every month, Jill gets an inventory report from the office manager listing the office supplies that are needed. Jill places the appropriate orders with Office Depot and writes them a check against the office's checking account.

In the above banking transaction, Cameron and Associates is the _____.

A. drawer
B. payee
C. indorser
D. holder

34. Ross receives a check for $100 from Sheldon. He signs the back of the check and turns it over to Leo to pay off the $100 he owed Leo. The check is now said to be _____.

A. certified
B. stale
C. drawn
D. indorsed

35. Which of the following is implied when a bank certifies a check?

A. The bank withholds payment on the check until the drawer authorizes payment.
B. The bank cashes the check only if the holder himself presents it for payment.
C. The bank agrees to accept the check when it is presented for payment.
D. The bank holds the check as guarantee for repayment of a loan taken by a customer.

36. How is a cashier's check different from an ordinary check?

A. Cashier's checks can be postdated, but ordinary checks cannot be postdated.
B. Cashier's checks are three-party checks, while ordinary checks involve only two parties.
C. Unlike ordinary checks, cashier's checks are cancellable negotiable instruments upon issue.
D. Unlike ordinary checks, cashier's checks do not require the purchaser to hold a checking account at that bank.

37. When a bank pays the holder of a properly drawn check, it is said to have _____ the check.

A. honored
B. indorsed
C. certified
D. collected

38. In which of the following cases is an overdraft created in a drawer's account?

A. when the bank pays the holder of a check in which the amount payable is altered to indicate a higher amount than was originally intended
B. when the drawer issues a stop-payment order for a check, but the bank still goes ahead and pays the holder of the check
C. when a properly payable check issued by the drawer is presented for payment, but the drawer's account does not have sufficient funds in it
D. when the payee presents the check after six months from the date of the check and the bank still pays the holder

39. A check that has been modified without authorization and thus modifies the legal obligation of a party is known as a(n) _____.

A. altered check
B. incomplete check
C. stale check
D. forged check

40. The bank where the payee or holder of a check has an account is known as the _____.

A. payer bank
B. private bank
C. intermediary bank
D. depository bank

41. Which of the following describes the "deferred posting rule"?

A. Banks have to mail their checking account customers monthly statements of their accounts and any canceled checks should accompany this statement.
B. When a customer deposits a check for collection, the depository bank does not have to pay the customer until the check clears.
C. Banks can fix an afternoon hour of 2:00 or later as a cutoff hour for the purpose of processing checks and deposits.
D. A customer is liable for payment to his bank if he fails to report any unauthorized transactions within 30 days from the receipt of the account statement.

42. Which of the following describes a situation in which a collecting bank gives credit to a check in the collection process prior to its final settlement?

A. presentment across a counter
B. provisional credit
C. certification of a check
D. indorsement of a check

43. A check is finally paid when _____.

A. the depository bank credits the customer's account with an option to reverse the credit in case of dishonoring of the check
B. the final bank in the collection process tentatively credits the account of the prior transferor
C. the drawer settles for the check while holding a right to revoke the settlement
D. the payer bank fails to dishonor the check within certain statutory time periods

44. Which of the following is one of the provisions of the Electronic Funds Transfer Act and Regulation E of the Federal Reserve Board?

A. A bank can send unsolicited EFTS debit cards to a consumer only if the cards are valid for use.
B. Other than for a telephone transaction, a bank must provide a customer with a written receipt of a transaction made through a computer terminal.
C. A bank must provide annual statements of electronic funds transfers to customers who conduct such transactions in a given financial year.
D. If a customer notifies the issuing bank of a stolen or lost debit card within two days of the loss, the customer's liability is limited to a maximum of $500.

45. Which of the following is one of the purposes of the Dodd-Frank Wall Street Reform and Consumer Protection Act of 2010?

A. regulating previously unregulated financial products and institutions
B. establishing the reporting requirements for financial transactions, including off-balance-sheet transactions
C. monitoring the legitimacy of consumer and commercial wire transfers
D. overseeing, inspecting, and disciplining accounting firms in their roles as auditors of public companies

Short Answer

46. What is an ordinary check? What are the three parties to an ordinary check?

_____

_____

47. Describe how a check can be indorsed.

_____

_____

48. What are the two special types of checks?

_____

_____

49. What is a stop-payment order?

_____

_____

50. When is a bank liable for wrongful dishonor?

_____

_____

51. What are altered checks? What are the actions that a bank can take when it encounters a case of check alteration?

_____

_____

52. Explain the one-year rule.

_____

_____

53. Explain the collection process.

_____

_____

54. What is a provisional credit?

_____

_____

55. What recommendations did the Dodd-Frank Wall Street Reform and Consumer Protection Act make to reform lending regulation?

_____

_____

Answers to Refresh Your Memory

1. creditor-debtor [p. 409]
2. drawer [p. 410]
3. indorsement [p. 411]
4. Cashier's check [p. 412]
5. stale [p. 413]
6. overdraft [p. 413]
7. wrongful dishonor [p. 414]
8. presentment warranty [p. 415]
9. Payer bank [p. 414]
10. intermediary [p. 417]
11. deferred posting [p. 418]
12. on us [p. 419]
13. Federal Deposit Insurance Corporation [p. 420]
14. point-of-sale [p. 421]
15. Electronic Funds Transfer Act [p. 422]

Critical Thought Exercise Model Answer

A bank may charge a postdated check against a customer's account as a demand instrument, unless the customer notifies the bank of the postdating in time to allow the bank to act on the notice before the bank commits itself to pay on the check. If the bank receives timely notice from the customer and nonetheless charges the customer's account before the date on the postdated check, the bank may be liable for any damages incurred by the customer as a result.

Everglades Bank had discussed the use of postdated checks with Austin and permitted his practice of postdating a significant number of checks each year. Everglades Bank will have a difficult time convincing a court that it was not on notice that postdated checks were being written by Austin. However, the UCC makes it clear that the customer must not only give notice that a postdated check has been issued, but must also describe the postdated check with reasonable certainty. Austin never contacted the bank to describe the checks with any certainty. He just relied upon the practice of a prior employee of the bank who examined his checks carefully before charging them to his account. Under the UCC, Everglades Bank has not received notice concerning the specific checks. Therefore, Austin should not prevail in a suit to recover damages caused by having the other 47 checks dishonored.

Answers to Practice Quiz

True/False

16. False. When a customer makes a deposit into a bank, a creditor–debtor relationship is formed. [p. 409]

17. False. Certified checks do not become stale. Thus, they are payable at any time from the date they are issued. [p. 411]

18. True. A cashier's check is a two-party check for which (1) the issuing bank serves as both the drawer and the drawee and (2) the holder serves as payee. [p. 412]

19. True. A person can purchase a cashier's check from a bank by paying the bank the amount of the check plus a fee for issuing the check. The purchaser does not have to have a checking account at the bank. [p. 412]

20. False. A check that has been outstanding for more than six months is considered stale, and the bank is under no obligation to pay it. [p. 413]

21. True. An oral order is binding on the bank for only 14 calendar days, unless confirmed in writing during this time. A written order is effective for six months. [p. 413]

22. False. A stop-payment order is an order by a drawer of a check to the payer bank not to pay or certify a check. [p. 413]

23. True. The payer bank cannot charge the customer's account if it pays a check over the forged signature. If the bank has charged the customer's account, it must recredit the account, and the forged check must be dishonored. [p. 415]

24. True. The presenter of the check for payment and each prior transferor warrant that the check has not been altered. This is called the presentment warranty. [p. 415]

25. True. A check is finally paid when the payer bank (1) pays the check in cash, (2) settles for the check without having a right to revoke the settlement, or (3) fails to dishonor the check within certain statutory time periods. [p. 418]

26. False. If the drawer and the payee or holder have accounts at the same bank, the depository bank is also the payer bank. The check is called an "on us" [p. 419]

27. False. Ordinarily, banks send their checking account customers monthly statements of account. The canceled checks usually accompany the statement, although banks are not required to send them. [p. 419]

28. True. Except for the collecting bank, each bank in the collection process, including the payer bank, must take proper action on an "on them" check prior to its midnight deadline. The midnight

deadline is the midnight of the next banking day following the banking day on which the bank received an "on them" check for collection. [p. 419]

29. False. If a customer notifies the issuing bank within two days of learning that his or her debit card has been lost or stolen, the customer is liable for only $50 for unauthorized use. [p. 422]

30. True. The Dodd-Frank Act reorganized and streamlined the federal government agencies that regulate the banking industry and increased the powers and strengthened bank regulatory oversight by federal agencies. The act grants additional powers to the Federal Reserve to monitor and regulate institutions it supervises, including bank holding companies, savings bank holding companies, and affiliates of holding companies. [p. 423]

Multiple Choice

31. D. When a customer makes a deposit into a bank, a creditor–debtor relationship is formed. The customer is the creditor and the bank is the debtor. [p. 409]

32. C. The drawee is the bank on which a check is drawn. [p. 410]

33. A. The drawer is the customer who maintains the checking account and writes (draws) checks against the account. [p. 410]

34. D. A payee's signing of the back of a check in order to turn it over to another party is called indorsement of a check. [p. 411]

35. C. When a bank certifies a check, it agrees in advance (1) to accept the check when it is presented for payment and (2) to pay the check out of funds set aside from the customer's account and either placed in a special certified check account or held in the customer's account. [p. 411]

36. D. A person can purchase a cashier's check from a bank by paying the bank the amount of the check plus a fee for issuing the check. The purchaser does not have to have a checking account at the bank. [p. 412]

37. A. When the drawee bank receives a properly drawn and payable check, the bank is under a duty to honor the check and charge (debit) the drawer's account the amount of the check if there are sufficient funds in the customer's checking account at the bank. [p. 412]

38. C. If the drawer does not have enough money in his or her account when a properly payable check is presented for payment, the payer bank can either (1) dishonor the check or (2) honor the check and create an overdraft in the drawer's account. [p. 413]

39. A. Sometimes a check is altered before it is presented for payment. This is an unauthorized change in the check that modifies the legal obligation of a party. [p. 415]

40. B. When a payee or holder receives a check, he or she can either go to the drawer's bank (the payer bank) and present the check for payment in cash or—as is more common—deposit the check into a bank account at his or her own bank, called the depository bank. [p. 417]

41. C. The deferred posting rule applies to all banks in the collection process. This rule allows banks to fix an afternoon hour of 2:00 p.m. or later as a cutoff hour for the purpose of processing checks and deposits. [p. 418]

42. B. When a customer deposits a check into a checking account for collection, the depository bank does not have to pay the customer the amount of the check until the check "clears"—that is, until final settlement occurs. The depository bank may provisionally credit the customer's account. [p. 418]

43. D. A check is finally paid when the payer bank (1) pays the check in cash, (2) settles for the check without having a right to revoke the settlement, or (3) fails to dishonor the check within certain statutory time periods. [p. 418]

44. B. Other than for a telephone transaction, a bank must provide a customer with a written receipt of a transaction made through a computer terminal. This receipt is prima facie evidence of the transaction. [p. 422]

45. A. The Act reorganizes federal government supervision of the banking system, regulates previous unregulated financial products and institutions, and adds a new consumer protection agency to protect consumers from abusive lending and banking practices. [p. 423]

Short Answer

46. Ordinary check is an order by a drawer to a drawee bank to pay a specified sum of money from the drawer's checking account to the named payee (or holder). There are three parties to an ordinary check:
1. Drawer. The drawer is the customer who maintains the checking account and writes (draws) checks against the account.
2. Drawee (or payer bank). The drawee is the bank on which a check is drawn.
3. Payee. The payee is the party to whom a check is written. [p. 410]

47. The payee is the holder of a check. As such, the payee has the right to either (1) demand payment of the check or (2) indorse the check to another party by signing the back of the check. This latter action is called indorsement of a check. The payee is the indorser, and the person to whom the check is indorsed is the indorsee. The indorsee in turn becomes a holder who can either demand payment of the check or indorse it to yet another party. Any subsequent holder can demand payment of the check or further transfer the check. [p. 411]

48. Certified Checks – When a bank certifies a check, it agrees in advance (1) to accept the check when it is presented for payment and (2) to pay the check out of funds set aside from the customer's account and either placed in a special certified check account or held in the customer's account. Certified checks do not become stale. Thus, they are payable at any time from the date they are issued.
Cashier's Checks – A person can purchase a cashier's check from a bank by paying the bank the amount of the check plus a fee for issuing the check. Usually, a specific payee is named. The purchaser does not have to have a checking account at the bank. The check is a noncancellable negotiable instrument upon issue. [p. 411, 412]

49. A stop-payment order is an order by a drawer of a check to the payer bank not to pay or certify a check. Only the drawer can order a stop-payment order. A stop-payment order can be given orally or in writing. An oral order is binding on the bank for only 14 calendar days, unless confirmed in writing during this time. A written order is effective for six months. It can be

renewed in writing for additional six-month periods [UCC 4-403]. If the payer bank fails to honor a valid stop-payment order, it must recredit the customer's account. [p. 413]

50. If a bank does not honor a check when there are sufficient funds in the drawer's account to pay a properly payable check, it is liable for wrongful dishonor. The payer bank is liable to the drawer for damages proximately caused by the wrongful dishonor as well as for consequential damages, damages caused by criminal prosecution, and such. A payee or holder cannot sue the bank for damages caused by the wrongful dishonor of a drawer's check. The only recourse for the payee or holder is to sue the drawer to recover the amount of the check [UCC 4-402]. [p. 414]

51. Sometimes a check is altered before it is presented for payment. This is an unauthorized change in the check that modifies the legal obligation of a party. The payer bank can dishonor an altered check if it discovers the alteration. If the payer bank pays the altered check, it can charge the drawer's account for the original tenor of the check but not the altered amount.
If the payer bank has paid the altered amount, it can recover the difference between the altered amount and the original tenor from the party who presented the altered check for payment. This is because the presenter of the check for payment and each prior transferor warrant that the check has not been altered. This is called the presentment warranty. If there has been an alteration, each party in the chain of collection can recover from the preceding transferor based on a breach of this warranty. The ultimate loss usually falls on the party that first paid the altered check because that party was in the best position to identify the alteration. The forger is liable for the difference between the original tenor and the altered amount—if he or she can be found and is not judgment proof. [p. 415]

52. The drawer's failure to report a forged or altered check to the bank within one year of receiving the bank statement and canceled checks containing it relieves the bank of any liability for paying the instrument [UCC 4-406(3)]. Thus, the payer bank is not required after this time to recredit the customer's account for the amount of the forged or altered check, even if the customer later discovers the forgery or alteration. This is called the one-year rule. [p. 415]

53. A bank is under a duty to accept deposits into a customer's account. This includes collecting checks that are drawn on other banks and made payable or indorsed to the depositor. The collection process, which may involve several banks, is governed by Article 4 of the UCC.
When a payee or holder receives a check, he or she can either go to the drawer's bank (the payer bank) and present the check for payment in cash or—as is more common—deposit the check into a bank account at his or her own bank, called the depository bank. (The depository bank may also serve as the payer bank if both parties have accounts at the same bank.)
The depository bank must present a check to the payer bank for collection. At this point in the process, the Federal Reserve System (discussed next) and other banks may be used in the collection of a check. The depository bank and these other banks are called collecting banks. Banks in the collection process that are not the depository or payer bank are called intermediary banks. A bank can have more than one role during the collection process [UCC 4-105]. [p. 417]

54. When a customer deposits a check into a checking account for collection, the depository bank does not have to pay the customer the amount of the check until the check "clears"—that is, until final settlement occurs. The depository bank may provisionally credit the customer's account. Each bank in the collection process provisionally credits the account of the prior transferor [UCC 4-201(a)]. If the check is dishonored by the payer bank (e.g., for insufficient funds, a stop payment order, or a closed account), the check is returned to the payee or holder, and the provisional credits are reversed. The collecting bank must either return the check to the prior

transferor or notify that party within a reasonable time that provisional credit is being revoked. If the collecting bank fails to do this, it is liable for any losses caused by its delay. [p. 418]

55. The financial crisis of 2008 was partially caused by banks making loans to home purchasers without verifying their ability to repay the loans. Many of these loans defaulted, leading to substantial foreclosures and causing a housing crisis. The Dodd-Frank Wall Street Reform and Consumer Protection Act requires mortgage lenders to make a reasonable and good-faith determination that a borrower has the ability to repay the loan. This must be based upon the verified and documented income and assets of the proposed borrower. In a foreclosure action brought by a lender, a borrower may assert a violation of this standard as a defense to the lender recovering money from the borrower. [p. 423]

26 | CREDIT, MORTGAGES, AND DEBTOR'S RIGHTS

Chapter Overview

We depend upon credit for our economy to function. Consumers and businesses alike use credit to obtain goods and services. This chapter examines the rights of creditors and debtors under federal and state consumer protection laws. You will explore the repercussions of noncompliance with the recording statutes and the foreclosure process in real estate. You will learn about deficiency judgments, lender liability, and the difference between a surety and a guaranty arrangement. This chapter gives a good explanation of attachment, garnishment, execution and the difference between a composition agreement and an assignment for the benefit of creditors.

Objectives

Upon completion of the exercises in this chapter, you should be able to:
1. Distinguish between unsecured and secured credit.
2. Describe security interests in real property, such as mortgages and deeds of trust.
3. Compare surety and guaranty arrangements.
4. Describe the provisions of the Consumer Financial Protection Act of 2010, Mortgage Reform and Anti-Predatory Lending Act of 2010, and Credit CARD Act of 2009.
5. Describe the Bureau of Consumer Financial Protection.

Practical Application

This chapter will provide you with greater insight into the various types of credit and security interests in real and personal property. You will gain a better understanding of the available remedies associated with personal property transactions. You will gain broader base of knowledge concerning surety and guaranty arrangements and remedies associated with the collection of debts.

Helpful Hints

Many items are purchased on credit. The best way to approach this chapter is by differentiating between the main terms, such as secured versus unsecured credit, real versus personal property, and surety arrangement versus a guaranty arrangement. Once you have a grasp of these main terms, the remedies that are available become easier to understand and learn. The exercises that follow, and the critical thinking exercises located at the end of the chapter in your main text, are very helpful in solidifying the concepts with which you should be familiar.

Study Tips

Creditor's and Debtor's Rights

The United States has a credit economy in which businesses and consumers use credit to make both daily and major purchases.
- Collateral. The property purchased or other property owned by the borrower in which lenders often take a security interest.
- Suretyship. A person who guarantees payment to a creditor on behalf of a debtor.

Credit

Credit can be extended as either secured or unsecured credit.

Debtor and Creditor.
- Debtor. The borrower in a credit transaction.
- Creditor. The lender in a credit transaction.

Unsecured Credit. Credit that does not need any collateral to protect the debt.
- Judgment Proof. A debtor who has little or no property or income to garnish.

Secured Credit. Credit that does need collateral to secure the payment of the loan.

Security Interest in Real Property

Mortgage. A property owner borrows money from a creditor who thereafter uses a deed as a means of security (collateral) to secure the repayment of the loan.
- Mortgagor. This is the owner-debtor in a mortgage transaction.
- Mortgagee. This is the creditor in a transaction involving a mortgage.

Note and Deed of Trust. Some states allow for the use of a note and deed of trust.
- Note. A legal instrument that is proof of the borrower's debt to the lender.
- Deed of Trust. A legal instrument that evinces the creditor's security interest in the debtor's property that is pledged as collateral.
  - Trustee. The entity with which legal title to the property is placed until the amount borrowed has been paid.
  - Trustor. The owner-debtor.
  - Beneficiary. The creditor.

Recording Statute. A law that requires the mortgage or deed of trust to be recorded in the county recorder's office of the county where the real property is located.
- Nonrecordation of a mortgage or deed of trust. Does not affect the legality of the instrument or the relationship between the parties.
  - An improperly recorded document is not effective against subsequent purchasers or other lienholders or mortgagors who have no notice of the document.

Foreclosure Sale. A legal procedure whereby the mortgagee can declare the entire debt due and payable if a debtor defaults on his or her loan.

- Power of Sale. This type of foreclosure must be expressly in the mortgage or deed of trust.

Deficiency Judgment. When a debtor has inadequate collateral to cover the debt, the court will issue an order letting the creditor recover other property or income from the defaulting debtor.

Antideficiency Statute. Many states prohibit deficiency judgments on mortgages, especially those involving residential property.

Right of Redemption. Many state laws follow the common law, which gives the mortgagor the right to redeem his or her real property after default and before foreclosure.
- The mortgagor must pay the entire debt including principal, interest, and other costs borne by the mortgagee as a result of the mortgagor's default.
- The mortgagor will obtain title free and clear upon redeeming the property.
- A majority of states allow any party holding an interest in the property may redeem the property during the redemption period.

Land Sales Contract. The transfer and sale of real property in accordance with a land sales contract whereby the owner of the real property agrees to sell the property to a buyer, who assents to pay the asking price to the owner-seller over a stated, agreed period of time.
- The loan is termed as *"carrying the paper."*
- If the purchaser defaults, the seller may claim a forfeiture and retake possession of the property.
- The right of redemption is allowed in many states.

Mechanic's Lien. When an individual provides contracting or a service toward improvement of real property, their investments are protected by statutory law that allow them to file a mechanic's lien (also referred to as a material person's lien) against the improved real property.

Surety and Guaranty Arrangements

Creditors sometimes require a third party to become liable for the debt of a borrower, thereby giving their credit as security for the loan.

Surety Arrangement. An arrangement where a third party promises to be liable for payment of another person's debt.
- Accommodation Party. The party who acts as the surety, also called a co-signor.
- The surety becomes primarily liable, along with the debtor, on the debt.

Guaranty Arrangement. An arrangement where a third party promises to be liable for payment of another person's debt if the debtor does not pay the debt when due.
- The guarantor becomes secondarily liable on the debt.

Defenses of a Surety or Guarantor. The defenses that the principal debtor can assert against the creditor can also be asserted by the surety or guarantor.

Debtor Protection Laws

The federal government has enacted various laws to protect consumers from abusive, deceptive, and unfair practices of creditors when dealing with consumer-debtors.

Truth in Lending Act (TILA). This 1968 act requires creditors to make certain disclosures to debtors in consumer transactions and on real estate loans on the debtor's principle dwelling.

- Regulation Z. A rule adopted by the Federal Reserve Board, regulatory agency regarding the TILA, which gives detailed rules for compliance with the TILA, including disclosure of such things as finance charges, annual percentage rates, and penalties for credit transactions.

Fair Credit Billing Act. This act requires creditors to promptly acknowledge customer complaints in writing and investigate billing errors.

- Prohibits adverse actions by the creditor before investigations are complete.
- Requires prompt posting of payments.
- Requires prompt refund or account credit for overpayments.

Consumer Leasing Act (CLA). This act extends the coverage of the TILA to consumer leases.

Fair Credit and Charge Card Disclosure Act. This 1988 act requires the disclosure of credit terms in solicitations and applications for credit and charge cards.

Equal Credit Opportunity Act (ECOA). This 1975 act prohibits discrimination in the extension of credit based on sex, marital status, race, color, national origin, religion, age, or receipt of income from public assistance programs.

- The creditor must notify the applicant for credit of the action taken within 30 days.
- If an adverse action is taken by the creditor, the applicant must be informed of the specific reasons for that action.

Fair Credit Reporting Act (FCRA). This act was enacted in 1970 as Title VII of the FILA and sets forth guidelines for consumer reporting agencies.

- A consumer may request at any time the information in their credit file, the source of that information, and names of recipients of their report.
- An agency may be compelled to investigate consumer challenges to information in their report.
- A consumer can, after a challenge has been investigated without an error being found, file a 100 word version of their side of the dispute to be included in their file.

Fair Debt Collection Practices Act (FDCPA). This 1977 act prohibits debt collectors from using certain practices that are harassing, abusive or intimidating, that are false or misleading misrepresentations, and that are unfair or unconscionable.

Collection Remedies

Attachment. A prejudgment order that allows a debtor's property to be seized while the lawsuit is pending.

Execution. A postjudgment order that allows a debtor's property in the debtor's possession to be seized.

- Writ of Execution. A court order directing the seizure and sale of a debtor's property by the sheriff or other government official.

Garnishment. A postjudgment order that allows a debtor's property in the possession of a third party to be seized.

- Writ of Garnishment. A court order directing the seizure of a debtor's property in the possession of third parties.
- Title III of the Consumer Credit Protection Act. Limits the amount of income that can be garnished from a debtor per pay period.

Refresh Your Memory

The following exercise will give you the opportunity to test your memory of the principles given in this chapter. Read the question twice and place your answer in the blank provided. Review the chapter material for any question that you are unable to answer or remember.

1. Credit that does not require any collateral to protect the payment of the debt is referred to as _____.

2. Credit that requires collateral that protects payment of the loan is referred to as _____.

3. An arrangement where an owner of real property borrows money from a lender and pledges the real property as collateral to secure the repayment of the loan is known as a(n) _____.

4. A _____ is an instrument that gives a creditor a security interest in the debtor's real property that is pledged as collateral for a loan.

5. A(n) _____ is an instrument that evidences a borrower's debt to the lender for a real property.

6. The _____ requires a mortgage or deed of trust to be recorded in the county recorder's office of the county in which the real property is located.

7. A legal procedure by which a secured creditor causes the judicial sale of the secured real estate to pay a defaulted loan is known as _____.

8. A power stated in a mortgage or deed that permits foreclosure without court proceedings and sale of the property through an auction is known as _____..

9. A _____ is a judgment of a court that permits a secured lender to recover other property or income from a defaulting debtor if the collateral is insufficient to repay the unpaid loan.

10. The _____ prohibits deficiency judgments regarding certain types of mortgages, such as those on residential property.

11. A right that allows the mortgagor to redeem real property after default and before foreclosure is known as _____.

12. An arrangement in which the owner of real property sells property to a purchaser and extends credit to the purchaser is known as _____.

13. The term _____ refers to a contractor's, laborer's, and material person's statutory lien that makes the real property to which services or materials have been provided security for the payment of the services and materials.

14. The term _____ refers to a written document signed by a contractor, subcontractor, laborer, or material person, waiving his or her statutory lien against real property.

15. An arrangement in which a third party promises to be primarily liable with the borrower for the payment of the borrower's debt is referred to as _____.

Critical Thought Exercise

Steve and Bonnie West purchased an old Victorian home outside St. Louis and planned on renovating it and selling it for a profit before moving onto another renovation project. Bonnie's brother, Doug Nixon, did most of the major work on the house and hired trades people to assist in areas that were beyond his expertise. Nixon hired Summit Roofing to replace the old shake roof with a fire resistant composite product that matched the house in color and style. The cost of the new roof is $17,400, including all labor and materials. Steve and Bonnie pay Doug $86,500 for the entire project. Doug failed to pay Summit Roofing and absconded with all the funds.

Steve and Bonnie West entered into a real estate purchase agreement with Lucy Rogers to purchase the home for $515,000. The contract between West and Rogers states that the property is free of all encumbrances and escrow will close in 30 days.

Summit Roofing filed a mechanic's lien against the property. The West's demanded that Summit Roofing seek payment from Doug Nixon. Summit Roofing gave notice that it was going to foreclose against the property to recover the $17,400 owed to it.

What action should Steve and Bonnie West take to ensure that the sale to Rogers will not be thwarted?

Please compose your answer to the Critical Thinking Exercise using a separate sheet of paper or your computer word processing program.

Practice Quiz

True/False

16. _____ The property on which a security interest is taken is called collateral.

17. _____ Unsecured credits require collateral to protect the payment of the debt.

18. _____ Legal action cannot be bought against a debtor who is judgment proof.

19. _____ The primary function of collateral is to secure payment of the loan.

20. _____ The creditor who has to rely on collateral to secure payment is known as an unsecured creditor.

21. _____ In a mortgage transaction, the creditor is known as the mortgagee.

22. _____ A deed of trust is a two-party instrument.

23. _____ The surety is primarily liable for paying the principal debtor's debt when it is due in a surety arrangement.

24. _____ The surety is primarily liable for paying the principal debtor's debt when it is due in a surety arrangement.

25. _____ The writ of attachment releases a property in the creditor's possession to the debtor.

26. _____ Execution is a postjudgment court order that permits the seizure of the debtor's property that is in the possession of the debtor.

27. _____ Garnishment is a court order that permits the seizure of a debtor's property that is in the debtor's possession.

28. _____ The Fair Credit Billing Act requires that creditors promptly acknowledge in writing consumer billing complaints and investigate billing errors.

29. _____ The Fair and Accurate Credit Transactions Act of 2003 permits credit reporting companies to place fraud alerts in their credit files.

30. _____ The Equal Credit Opportunity Act does not have provisions for consumers to recover damages against the creditor.

Multiple Choice

31. When is credit said to have occurred?

A. when a promissory note for payment is issued
B. when one party sells goods to another party
C. when one party gives a loan to another party
D. when one party pays back money that he owes to another party

32. When is a creditor referred to as a secured creditor?

A. when the creditor has been guaranteed payment by a trustee
B. when the creditor gives a loan without security
C. when the creditor has been paid back his debt
D. when the creditor has acquired collateral.

33. Which of the following is true of a deed of trust?

A. The legal right of the property is with the creditor until payment.
B. The legal rights to possession of real property lie with a trustee.
C. The trustor has legal rights to possession of the real property.
D. The deed of trust is a two-party instrument.

34. Which of the following real property transactions involves the use of transfer of legal title in real property to a trustee?

A. land sales contract
B. garnishment
C. deed of trust
D. mortgage

35. Who is the beneficiary in a deed of trust transaction?

A. the creditor
B. the debtor
C. the trustee
D. the trustor

36. To which of the following type of mortgages does the antideficiency statute apply?

A. foreign currency mortgages
B. home improvement mortgages
C. first purchase money mortgages
D. second purchase money mortgages

37. What is the statutory period of redemption?

A. The time limit that a trustee can claim legal title to the real property.
B. The time allotted to a mortgagor to keep the property even after foreclosure.
C. The time by which the mortgagor has to pay his debts.
D. The time allotted by which a mortgagee must start legal proceedings against a defaulter.

38. A prejudgment court order that permits the seizure of a debtor's property while a lawsuit is pending is known as the _____.

A. writ of exigent
B. writ of attachment
C. writ of execution
D. writ of garnishment

39. Which of the following Acts protects debtors who are subject to writ of garnishment from excessive action?

A. Fair Credit Billing Act
B. Consumer Leasing Act
C. Truth-in-Lending Act
D. Title III of the Consumer Credit Protection Act.

40. Which of the following writs is a prejudgment writ?

A. writ of garnishment
B. writ of execution
C. writ of attachment
D. writ of exigent

Short Answer

41. What is unsecured credit?

_____

_____

42. What is the use of collateral?

_____

_____

43. Cliff's Concrete contracts with Gus to remove an old driveway and install a new cement driveway and walkway on Gus's property. After Cliff's Concrete has completed the job, Gus refuses to pay for the work because he does not like the color of the concrete work. If Cliff's Concrete decides to place a material person's lien on Gus's home, what four requirements must be met?

_____

_____

44. What is the major difference between a mortgage and a deed of trust?

_____

_____

45. What is a right of redemption?

_____

_____

46. A land sales contract is normally used to sell what type of real estate?

_____

_____

47. Between a mortgagor and mortgagee, what happens if the mortgagee does not record the mortgage in compliance with the applicable recording statute?

_____

_____

48. What happens if a mortgagee is successful in a foreclosure action?

_____

_____

49. What is a writ of execution?

_____

_____

50. Who holds legal title to real property under a deed of trust?

_____

_____

51. How is a power of sale created?

_____

_____

52. What is a deficiency judgment?

_____

_____

53. To what kind of financing are antideficiency statutes directed?

_____

_____

54. What is the difference between a surety arrangement and a guaranty arrangement?

_____

_____

55. Give three examples of disclosure required of creditors under Regulation Z.

_____

_____

Answers to Refresh Your Memory

1. unsecured credit [p. 431]
2. secured credit [p. 432]
3. mortgage [p. 432]
4. deed of trust [p. 433]
5. note [p. 433]
6. recording statute ,loan [p. 433]
7. foreclosure sale [p. 434]
8. power of sale [p. 434]
9. deficiency judgment [p. 435]
10. antideficiency statute [p. 435]
11. right of redemption [p. 435]
12. land sales contract [p. 436]
13. mechanic's lien [p. 437]
14. lien release [p. 437]
15. surety arrangement [p. 438]

Critical Thought Exercise Model Answer

Contractors and laborers who expend time and money for materials that are used for improvements upon real property may protect themselves by filing a mechanic's lien against the real property upon which the improvement was made by the contractor or laborer. In order to obtain a mechanic's lien, the contractor will usually have to meet the following requirements to perfect their lien: (1) File a notice of lien with the county recorder's office in the county where the real property is located; (2) The notice must state the amount of the claim, a description of the real property, the name of the property owner, and the name of the claimant; (3) The notice must be filed within the statutory time as set forth in the statute (usually 30-120 days), and; (4) Notice of the lien must be transmitted to the owner of the real property.

Summit Roofing performed actual work on the West's house and is entitled to file a mechanic's lien if it is not paid. When Nixon absconded with the funds, the Wests may have been defrauded by Nixon, but this does nothing to prevent a proper filing of the lien. The lien will prevent the Wests from conveying clear title and is an encumbrance upon the property. The Wests will be in breach when the date for closing arrives and they are unable to convey clear title to Rogers. The only recourse that the Wests have in this case is to pay Summit Roofing and obtain a release of lien before the escrow closing date. The Wests should be careful to have all the contractors, laborers, and material persons who have worked on their home or supplied materials sign the lien release. The Wests can then proceed against Nixon to recover their $17,400.

Answers to Practice Quiz

True/False

16. True. Lenders are sometimes reluctant to lend large sums of money simply on the borrower's promise to repay, many of them take a security interest in the property purchased or some other property of the debtor. The property in which the security interest is taken is called collateral. [p. 431]

17. False. Unsecured credit does not require any security (collateral) to protect the payment of the debt. Instead, the creditor relies on the debtor's promise to repay the principal (plus any interest) when it is due. [p. 431]

18. True. If the debtor fails to make the payments, the creditor may bring legal action and obtain a judgment against him or her. If the debtor is judgment proof (i.e., has little or no property or no income that can be garnished), the creditor may never collect.. [p. 432]

19. True. To minimize the risk associated with extending unsecured credit, a creditor may require a security interest in the debtor's property (collateral). The collateral secures payment of the loan. This type of credit is called secured credit. [p. 432]

20. False. To minimize the risk associated with extending unsecured credit, a creditor may require a security interest in the debtor's property (collateral). The collateral secures payment of the loan. This type of credit is called secured credit. The creditor who has a security interest in collateral is called a secured creditor, or secured party. [p. 432]

21. True. The creditor in a mortgage transaction is the mortgagee. [p. 432]

22. False. A deed of trust is a three-party instrument. [p. 433]

23. True. In a strict surety arrangement, a third person—known as the surety, or co- debtor—promises to be liable for the payment of another person's debt. A person who acts as a surety is commonly called an accommodation party, or co-signer. Along with the principal debtor, the surety is primarily liable for paying the principal debtor's debt when it is due. [p. 438]

24. False. In a strict surety arrangement, a third person—known as the surety, or co- debtor—promises to be liable for the payment of another person's debt. A person who acts as a surety is commonly called an accommodation party, or co-signer. Along with the principal debtor, the surety is primarily liable for paying the principal debtor's debt when it is due. The principal debtor does not have to be in default on the debt, and the creditor does not have to have exhausted all its remedies against the principal debtor before seeking payment from the surety. [p. 438]

25. False. Attachment is a prejudgment court order that permits the seizure of a debtor's property that is in the debtor's possession while a lawsuit against the debtor is pending. [p. 439]

26. True. Execution is a postjudgment court order that permits the seizure of the debtor's property that is in the possession of the debtor. [p. 439]

27. False. Garnishment is a postjudgment court order that permits the seizure of a debtor's property that is in the possession of third parties. The creditor (also known as the garnishor) must go to court to seek a writ of garnishment. [p. 439]

28. True. The Fair Credit Billing Act (FCBA)5 is a federal statute that regulates billing errors involving consumer credit. The act requires that creditors promptly acknowledge in writing consumer billing complaints and investigate billing errors. [p. 442]

29. False. The Fair Credit Billing Act (FCBA)5 is a federal statute that regulates billing errors involving consumer credit. The act requires that creditors promptly acknowledge in writing consumer billing complaints and investigate billing errors. [p. 443]

30. False. If a creditor violates the Equal Credit Opportunity Act, the consumer may bring a civil action against the creditor and recover actual damages (including emotional distress and embarrassment). [p. 444]

Multiple Choice

31. C. Answer C is correct. Credit occurs when one party makes a loan to another party. [p. 431]

32. D. Answer D is the correct answer. Secured credit is credit that requires security (collateral) that secures payment of the loan. [p. 432]

33. B. Answer B is the correct answer. A deed of trust is a three-party instrument. Under it, legal title to the real property is placed with a trustee (usually a trust corporation) until the amount borrowed has been paid. [p. 433]

34. C. Answer C is correct. A deed of trust is a three-party instrument. Under it, legal title to the real property is placed with a trustee (usually a trust corporation) until the amount borrowed has been paid. [p. 433]

35. A. Answer A is correct. A deed of trust is a three-party instrument. Under it, legal title to the real property is placed with a trustee (usually a trust corporation) until the amount borrowed has been paid. The owner-debtor is called the trustor. The creditor is called the beneficiary. [p. 433]

36. C. Answer C is correct. Antideficiency statutes usually apply only to first purchase money mortgages (i.e., mortgages that are taken out to purchase houses). [p. 435]

37. B. Answer B is a correct statement. Some states allow the mortgagor to redeem real property for a specified period (usually six months or one year) after foreclosure. This is called the statutory period of redemption. [p. 436]

38. B. Answer B is correct. Writ of attachment is a prejudgment court order that permits the seizure of a debtor's property while a lawsuit is pending. [p. 439]

39. C. Answer C is correct. To protect debtors from abusive and excessive garnishment actions by creditors, Congress enacted Title III of the Consumer Credit Protection Act. [p. 440]

40. C. Answer C is correct. Writ of attachment is a prejudgment court order that permits the seizure of a debtor's property that is in the debtor's possession while a lawsuit against the debtor is pending. [p. 439]

Short Answer

41. Credit that does not require any security (collateral) to protect payment of the debt. [p. 431]

42. Collateral is used to secure payment of the loan. [p. 432]

43. Cliff's Concrete must: 1) File a notice of lien with the county recorder's office, 2) The notice must state the amount of the claim, the name of the claimant, the name of the owner, and a description of the real property, 3) The notice must be filed within the specified time period, and 4) Notice of the lien must be given to the owner of the property. [p. 437]

44. A mortgage is a two-party instrument having a collateral arrangement. A deed of trust is a three-party instrument with legal title being placed with the trustee. [p. 432-433]

45. A mortgagor has the option of exercising his or her right to redemption of the property by paying the full amount of the purchase price, plus interest and other costs. [p. 436]

46. Undeveloped property, farms, and similar types of property such as timberlands and wetlands. [p. 436]

47. Nonrecordation of a mortgage does not affect either the legality of the instrument between the mortgagor and mortgagee or the rights and obligations of the parties. [p. 433]

48. The court will issue a judgment that orders the real property to be sold at a judicial sale. The procedures are mandated by state statute and any surplus from the sale must be paid to the mortgagor. [p. 434]

49. Writ of execution is a postjudgment court order that permits the seizure of the debtor's property that is in the possession of the debtor. [p. 439]

50. A trustee holds legal title to the property subject to a deed of trust. This is usually a trust corporation. [p. 433]

51. The procedure for the sale must be contained in the mortgage or deed of trust itself. [p. 434]

52. A court judgment allowing a secured lender to recover other income or property from a defaulting debtor if the collateral is insufficient to repay the unpaid loan. [p. 435]

53. Antideficiency statutes generally apply to first purchase money mortgages. Second mortgages and subsequent mortgages are usually not covered. [p. 435-436]

54. In a surety arrangement, a third person promises to be responsible for the payment of another person's debt. In a guaranty arrangement, a third person promises to pay another person's debt if that person does not pay the debt when due. [p. 438]

55. (Answers will vary.) Creditors are required to make disclosures regarding the following: Cash price, down payment and trade allowance, unpaid cash price, finance charge, annual percentage rate, other charges, total financed, date charges begin accruing, number and amount and due dates of payments, description of security interest, penalties, and prepayment penalties. [p. 442]

27 | SECURED TRANSACTIONS AND E-FILING

Chapter Overview

This chapter elaborates on the concept of security interests as they pertain to the items that are purchased or to other personal property of the debtor. The security interest that is taken by a creditor is known as a secured transaction. You will learn about the creation of security interests and the ways these interests are perfected through rules presented by Article 9 of the Uniform Commercial Code.

Objectives

Upon completion of the exercises in this chapter, you should be able to:
1. Describe the scope of Revised Article 9 of the UCC.
2. Describe how a security interest in personal property is created.
3. Describe the perfection of a security interest through the filing of a financing statement.
4. Explain the UCC rule for determining priority among conflicting claims.
5. Describe the electronic filing of financing statements and records.

Practical Application

You will be able to apply the Uniform Commercial Code rules of Article 9 when creating and enforcing security interests you may have in personal property. You will become more familiar with the terminology associated with secured transactions. You should be able to determine the priority among conflicting claims of creditors and whether or not an exception to the perfection-priority rule applies. If you are a secured party, you will be more aware of the remedies that are available to you should a debtor default on a security agreement.

Helpful Hints

If you have been in a situation involving a secured transaction, this chapter will be like second nature to you. However, for the individual who is studying this material for the first time, it is advisable to understand the basic vocabulary first and then look upon the remaining materials like building blocks from which to gather and expand the information obtained from Article 9 of the UCC. The first building block that you should familiarize yourself with is that of creation of a security interest in personal property, followed by the floating lien concept. The third building block involves perfecting a secured interest, and then termination followed by the last two building blocks of priority of claims and remedies for the creditor. The following Study Tips section utilizes the building block approach to make your learning easier.

Study Tips

Secured Transactions and Electronic Filing

Article 9 of the Uniform Commercial Code governs secured transactions. When a creditor loans money to a debtor in exchange for the debtor's pledge of personal property as security (collateral), then a secured transaction is created.

- Debtor. The party owing payment or some other performance of the secured obligation.
- Personal Property. Tangible property such as furniture, automobiles, and jewelry, and intangible property such as intellectual property and securities
- Secured Party. The individual, albeit seller, lender, or other person who holds the security interest.
- Security Interest. A personal property interest that secures payment or performance of an obligation.
- Security Agreement. The agreement created by the secured party and the debtor that allows for a security interest in personal property.
- Collateral. Property, including chattel paper and accounts, which is subject to a security interest.

Secured Transactions

Various items of tangible and intangible personal property is purchased and leased by businesses and individuals, often through credit transactions. Particularly for large or expensive items, the purchase may be made through secured credit, where the borrower provides the creditor with an interest in the borrowers property as security for the loan.

Secured Transaction. A transaction where the creditor gives credit to a debtor in exchange for a security interest in personal property of the debtor.
- The creditor can foreclose on property given as security if the debtor fails to repay the loan.

Two-party Secured Transaction. Where a seller sells goods to a buyer on credit and keeps a security interest in the goods.

Three-party Secured Transaction. Where a seller sells goods to a buyer who has financed the goods through a third party.

Personal Property Subject to a Security Agreement. Collateral for a loan may consist of various types of personal property.
- Tangible Personal Property. All things that are movable when a security interest attaches.
- Intangible Personal Property. Nonphysical personal property, such as stocks.

Creating a Security Interest

Article 9 of the UCC governs the creation of security interests in personal property.

Security Agreement. In general, security interests must be in writing, unless the creditor is in possession of the collateral. The following lists what the writing must contain.
- The collateral must be clearly described so that it may be easily identified.

- The writing must state the debtor's promise to pay the creditor and the terms of repayment.
- The writing must state what the creditor's rights are in the event of a debtor's default.
- The debtor must sign the writing.

Attachment. If the writing, value, and debtor's rights in the collateral are met, then the rights of the secured party attach to the collateral and the creditor can satisfy the debt out of the collateral if need be.

- The debtor must have a present or future right in or the right to possession of the collateral in order to give a security interest in that property.
- The secured party must give any adequate consideration that will support a simple contract. The debtor must owe a debt to the creditor.

The Floating-Lien Concept. This concept deals with security agreements that refer to either property that is acquired after the security agreement is executed, sales proceeds, or future advances.

- After-Acquired Property. This refers to property that the debtor obtains after the execution of the security agreement.
- Sale Proceeds. This refers to property subject to the security agreement that the debtor sells, exchanges so that the secured party automatically has the right to receive the sale proceeds.
- Future Advances. As defined in your main text, this is "personal property of the debtor that is designated as collateral for future loans from a line of credit."

Perfecting a Security Interest

Perfection is a legal process that is accomplished by three main methods to establish a secured creditor's rights against the claims of other creditors.

Perfection by Filing a Financing Statement. This method is the most common way to perfect a creditor's interest.

- The financing statement must contain the debtor's name and address, the creditor's name and address, and a statement that reveals the types of collateral or a description of the items. [Revised UCC 9-502(a)]
- The secured party may file the security agreement as a financing statement.
- The financing statement must be filed with the appropriate state or county office. [Revised UCC 9-501].

Perfection by Possession of Collateral. This method does not require the secured party to file a financing statement if the creditor has possession of the collateral.

- The secured creditor is required to use reasonable care in the collateral's custody and preservation if he or she holds the debtor's property. [Revised UCC 9-310, 9-312(b), 9-313]

Perfection by a Purchase Money Security Interest in Consumer Goods. This is an interest that a creditor gets automatically when it gives credit to a consumer to purchase consumer goods.

- Since the creditor does not have to file a financing statement or take possession of the goods, this interest is termed perfection by attachment or the automatic perfection rule. [Revised UCC 9-309(1)]

- Examples of consumer goods include television sets, home appliances, furniture, and the like that are mainly used for family, personal, or household use.

Termination Statement. This should really be termed tumbling block #4, as once a secured consumer debt has been satisfied, a termination statement must be filed with the same state or county office that the financing statement was filed with.
- The termination statement must be filed within a month of the debt's satisfaction or within twenty days from receipt of the debtor's demand to do so. [Revised UCC 9-513(b)]
- If the termination statement is not filed, the creditor is liable to the debtor for any other losses suffered by the debtor.

Priority of Claims

In order to determine which creditor's claim on the same collateral or property takes priority over another, the UCC decides based on whether the claim is secured or unsecured and the time at which secured claims were perfected or attached.

UCC Rules for Determining Priority. The UCC provides rules for establishing the priority of creditor claims.
- Secured vs. Unsecured Claims. Secured creditors take priority over unsecured creditors.
- Competing Unperfected Secured Claims. If there are two or more secured yet unperfected claims to the same collateral exist, then the first to attach takes priority. [Revised UCC 9-322(a)(3)]
- Perfected vs. Unperfected. If two or more have a claim or interest in the same collateral, where one is perfected and the other is unperfected, the perfected claim will take priority. [Revised UCC 9-322(a)(2)]
- Competing Perfected Secured Claims. When two or more secured parties have perfected security interests in the same collateral, the first to perfect either by filing a financing statement or taking possession of the collateral has priority over the other. [Revised UCC 9-322(a)(1)]
- Perfected Secured Claims in Fungible, Commingled Goods. If goods that have a perfected security status associated with them become commingled with other goods that also have perfected security interests to the point where the goods have lost their identity, then security interests will be determined according to the ratio that cost of goods "to which each interest originally attached bears to the cost of the total product or mass." [Revised UCC 9-336]

Buyers in the Ordinary Course of Business. Article 9 of the UCC provides that "a buyer in the ordinary course of business who purchases goods from a merchant takes the goods free of any perfected or unperfected security interest in the merchant's inventory even if the buyer knows of the existence of the security interest." [Revised UCC 9-320(a), 1-201(9)].

Default and Remedies

Article 9 sets forth the rights, duties, and remedies of the secured party if the debtor defaults.
- The parties might define the term default in their security agreement.
- There are several remedies that a secured party may pursue upon default by the debtor.

Taking Possession of the Collateral. Many secured creditors repossess the goods from the defaulting debtor and then either keep the collateral or sell it and dispose of it to satisfy the debtor's debt.

- "The secured party must act in good faith and with commercial reasonableness, and with reasonable care to preserve the collateral in his or her possession." [Revised UCC 9-603, 9-610(a), 9-620].

Retention of Collateral. Notice of a secured creditor's intention to repossess and keep the debtor's collateral must be sent to the debtor unless there is a signed written statement renouncing this right.

- A secured creditor cannot keep the collateral and must dispose of it if he or she receives a written objection from a person entitled to receive notice within 21 days of the notice being sent or if the debt concerns consumer goods and the debtor has paid 60 percent of the cash price or loan.
  - The secured creditor must dispose of the goods within 90 days after taking possession of them.
- A consumer may renounce his or her rights under this section. [Revised UCC 9-620(e), 9-620(f)]

Disposition of Collateral. A secured creditor in possession of a debtor's collateral may sell, lease, or otherwise dispose of the collateral in a commercially reasonable manner if the debtor is in default.

- The proceeds from the sale must be applied in the order prescribed by Revised UCC 9-608.

Deficiency Judgment. If the proceeds from the disposition of the collateral are insufficient to satisfy the debt, then the secured party may bring a cause of action to recover a deficiency judgment against the debtor. [Revised UCC 9-608(a)(4)].

Redemption Rights. The debtor may redeem the collateral by paying all obligations secured by the collateral as well as expenses reasonably incurred by the secured party in retaking and holding the collateral along with any attorney's fees and legal expenses provided for in the security agreement and not prohibited by law. [Revised UCC 9-623].

Relinquishing the Security Interest and Proceeding to Judgment on the Underlying Debt. The secured creditor may proceed to judgment against the debtor to recover on the underlying debt instead of repossessing the collateral. [Revised UCC 9-601(a)].

Artisan's Lien. This lien occurs when a worker in the ordinary course of business provides materials or services for goods and receives a lien on the goods by statute.

- Super-priority Lien. This lien prevails over all other security interests in the goods, unless a statutory lien provides otherwise.
- Possessory Lien. The artisan must be in possession of the property.

Refresh Your Memory

The following exercise will give you the opportunity to test your memory of the principles given in this chapter. Read the question twice and place your answer in the blank provided. Review the chapter material for any question that you are unable to answer or remember.

1. A property in which a security interest is taken is called _____.

2. _____ is a situation in which a creditor agrees to extend credit only if the purchaser pledges some personal property as collateral for the loan.

3. When a creditor extends credit to a debtor and takes a security interest in some personal property of the debtor, it is called a _____.

4. A(n) _____ has an ownership or other interest in the collateral and owes payment of a secured obligation.

5. John buys a new car with the help of a loan. He permits the creditor to take possession of the car if he cannot repay the loan in time. Here, the car is the _____.

6. A business purchases an airplane from an airplane manufacturer. The business obtains a loan to purchase the airplane from a bank, which obtains a security interest in the airplane. The airplane manufacturer is paid for the airplane from of the proceeds of the loan. This is a _____ transaction.

7. When a buyer obtains a loan from a bank to pay the seller, the transaction is known as a(n) _____.

8. A _____ is a written document signed by a debtor that creates a security interest in personal property.

9. A(n) _____ is a situation in which a creditor has an enforceable security interest against a debtor and can satisfy the debt out of the designated collateral.

10. A(n) _____ refers to a security interest in property that was not in the possession of the debtor when the security agreement was executed.

11. A(n) _____ is property that a debtor acquires post the execution of a security agreement.

12. A(n) _____ is a record that evidences both a monetary obligation and a security interest in specific goods and software used in the goods.

13. _____ is a process that establishes the right of a secured creditor against other creditors who claim an interest in the collateral.

A(n) _____ refers to a document filed by a secured creditor with the appropriate government office that constructively notifies the world of his or her security interest in personal property.

15. _____ is a situation in which the creditor does not have to file a financing statement or take possession of the goods to perfect his or her security interest.

Critical Thought Exercise

Carl Rice and Carpet City Inc. signed a security agreement with Pacific Ocean Bank for $86,400, plus interest. The collateral for the loan was a commercial truck used for the business run by Rice. The truck had a large hydraulic lift attached to the truck that allowed Rice to load and offload heavy rolls of carpet. Rice and Carpet City defaulted, and the bank took possession of the truck. The bank solicited bids for the truck by word of mouth from other financial institutions, two local furniture stores, and some bank customers. Pacific Ocean Bank sold the truck to a local business for $69,000. The buyer did not need a truck equipped for transporting carpet so they did modifications and repairs totaling $17,000 and sold it two years later for $62,000. Pacific Ocean Bank sued Rice and Carpet City for the difference between the amount due on the loan and the proceeds from the sale. Pacific Ocean Bank did not advertise the truck nor did it contact any carpet stores that might desire to purchase a truck equipped with an integrated hydraulic lift. Rice does not contend that the sale price was wholly unreasonable, only that Pacific Ocean did not use all reasonable means to get the best price.

Should Pacific Ocean Bank be allowed to recover the deficiency from the sale or did it fail to sell the truck in a commercially unreasonable manner, which would preclude recovery by the bank?

Please compose your answer to the Critical Thinking Exercise using a separate sheet of paper or your computer word processing program.

Practice Quiz

True/False

16. _____ The property in which a security interest is taken is called collateral.

17. _____ A secured transaction is one in which the creditor and debtor carry out financial transaction in a secure medium, such as a private communication channel.

18. _____ Tangible personal property includes securities, patents, trademarks, and copyrights.

19. _____ If a lender extends unsecured credit to a debtor, the creditor takes no interest in any collateral to secure the loan.

20. _____ The extension of credit in a secured credit requires the purchaser's pledge to some personal property as collateral for the loan.

21. _____ Intangible personal properties cannot be used as collateral to a security agreement.

22. _____ In a secured transaction, the debtor is the secured party.

23. _____ A two-party secured transaction occurs when a seller sells goods to a buyer on credit and retains a security interest in the goods.

24. _____ To be valid, a security agreement must set forth the creditor's rights upon the debtor's default.

25. _____ Attachment is a situation in which the value of the creditor's collateral is insufficient to satisfy the debt it is collated for.

26. _____ A floating lien is a security interest in property that was not in the possession of the debtor when the security agreement was executed.

27. _____ Perfection of a security interest establishes the right of a secured creditor against other creditors who claim an interest in the collateral.

28. _____ A financing statement refers to a document filed by a secured creditor with the appropriate government office that constructively notifies the world of his or her security interest in personal property.

29. _____ Repossession refers to a right granted to a secured creditor to take possession of the collateral upon default by the debtor.

30. _____ For an artisan's lien to be effective, the artisan must be in possession of the property.

Multiple Choice

31. Which article of the Uniform Commercial Code governs secured transactions in personal property?

A. Article 8
B. Article 9
C. Article 18
D. Article 19

32. Which of the following transactions occurs when a seller sells goods to a buyer on credit and retains a security interest in the goods?

A. two-party secured
B. three-party secured
C. perfected
D. attached

33. Which of the following refers to the resulting assets from the exchange or disposal of collateral subject to a security agreement?

A. sale proceeds
B. future advances
C. floating lien
D. after-acquired property

34. Which of the following is true of financing statements?

A. They cannot be electronically filed.
B. They are effective for one year from the date of filing.
C. Expired financing statements cannot be extended.
D. They are available for review by the public.

35. What of the following is true of the rule of perfection by possession of collateral?

A. A creditor cannot take possession of the collateral until a financing statement is filed.
B. No financing statement has to be filed if the creditor has physical possession of the collateral.
C. A debtor cannot acquire security against the collateral without filing a financing statement.
D. A financing statement can be filed only against intangible personal property placed as collateral.

36. _____ is an interest a creditor automatically obtains when he or she extends credit to a consumer to purchase consumer goods.

A. Purchase money security interest
B. Cumulative security interest
C. Future advance monetary interest
D. Default interest

37. Which of the following is true of priority of claims?

A. If two or more secured parties claim an interest in the same collateral but only one has perfected his or her security interest, the perfected security interest has priority.
B. Although one of the parties to claim an interest in the collateral has perfected his or her security interest, all the parties are given fair and equal priority.
C. If two or more secured parties claim an interest in the same collateral but neither has a perfected claim, they are given equal priority irrespective of attachments.
D. If two or more secured parties claim an interest in the same collateral but neither has a perfected claim, the first to claim has priority.

38. Which of the following constitutes default?

A. repaying a debt before it is due
B. bankruptcy of the debtor
C. increase of rate of interest by the creditor midway through debt repayment
D. theft of the collateral

39. What is repossession?

A. a right granted to the debtor to take possession of the collateral after repayment of the debt
B. a right granted to the debtor to take possession of the collateral before repayment of the debt
C. a right granted to a secured creditor to take possession of the collateral upon default by the debtor
D. the act of possession of the collateral by the court owing to default by both debtor and creditor

40. Which of the following is true of disposition of collateral?

A. Disposition of collateral must be a public proceeding.
B. The debtor is entitled to receive any surplus collateral that remains after disposition.
C. The debtor need not be notified of the disposition as the creditor has complete claim on the collateral.
D. Disposition of collateral occurs when the default is by the creditor.

Short Answer

41. What is a security agreement?

_____

_____

42. What is attachment?

_____

_____

43. What does the perfection of a security interest accomplish for the creditor?

_____

_____

44. What is a financing statement?

_____

_____

45. If two or more secured parties claim an interest in the same collateral, but neither has perfected a claim, who has priority?

_____

_____

46. How is the right of redemption accomplished?

_____

_____

47. Name three types of goods that can become collateral for a loan.

_____

_____

48. If a debtor sells, disposes, or exchanges collateral that is subject to a security agreement, what right does the secured party have?

_____

_____

49. When does a secured creditor not have to file a financing statement?

_____

_____

50. Name three events or conditions that will cause the debtor to be in default under a security agreement.

_____

_____

51. What is a buyer in the ordinary course of business?

_____

_____

52. What is a deficiency judgment?

_____

_____

53. Why is an artisan's lien called a "super-priority lien"?

_____

_____

54. Under the revised Article 9 of the UCC, what is a "record"?

_____

_____

55. What is a fixture filing?

_____

_____

Answers to Refresh Your Memory

1. collateral [p. 449]
2. Secured credit [p. 449]
3. secured transaction [p. 449]
4. debtor [p. 450]
5. collateral [p. 449]
6. two-party secured [p. 450]
7. three-party secured transaction [p. 451]
8. security agreement [p. 451]
9. attachment [p. 452]
10. floating lien [p. 453]
11. after-acquired property [p. 453]
12. chattel paper [p. 457]
13. Perfection of a security interest [p. 453]
14. financing statement [p. 454]
15. Perfection by attachment [p. 456]

Critical Thought Exercise Model Answer

It is the secured party's duty to the debtor to use all fair and reasonable means to obtain the best price under the circumstances, but the creditor need not use extraordinary means. Under the circumstances of this particular case, the sale may be commercially reasonable even with a lack of advertising. One of the factors to be considered in determining whether the sale was commercially reasonable is the adequacy or insufficiency of the sale price after default. In this case, the truck was sold for far less than the purchaser had invested in its purchase and repair. Though Pacific Ocean may have been able to get a better price for the truck had it advertised the sale to carpet stores, there is no evidence that the sale was conducted in a commercially unreasonable manner. Therefore, Pacific Ocean should recover the full amount of the deficiency.

Answers to Practice Quiz

True/False

16. True. The property in which a security interest is taken is called collateral. [p. 449]

17. False. A secured transaction is a transaction that is created when a creditor makes a loan to a debtor in exchange for the debtor's pledge of personal property as security. [p. 450]

18. False. Tangible personal property includes equipment, vehicles, furniture, computers, clothing, jewelry, and such. [p. 449]

19. True. Sometimes a lender extends unsecured credit to a debtor to purchase personal property. In this case, the creditor takes no interest in any collateral to secure the loan but bases the decision to extend credit on the credit standing of the debtor. [p. 449]

20. True. Where personal property is used as collateral for a loan or the extension of credit, a resulting secured transaction is governed by Article 9 of the UCC. [p. 449]

21. False. Because lenders are reluctant to lend large sums of money simply on the borrower's promise to repay, many of them take a security interest in either the item purchased or some other personal property of the debtor. The property in which a security interest is taken is called collateral. Personal property includes tangible property such as equipment, vehicles, furniture, and jewelry, as well as intangible property such as securities, patents, trademarks, and copyrights. [p. 449]

22. True. In a secured transaction the secured party is the seller, lender, or other party in whose favor there is a security interest. [p. 450]

23. True. A two-party secured transaction occurs when a seller sells goods to a buyer on credit and retains a security interest in the goods. [p. 450]

24. True. To be valid, a security agreement must (1) clearly describe the collateral so that it can be readily identified, (2) contain the debtor's promise to repay the creditor, including terms of repayment (e.g., interest rate, time of payment), (3) set forth the creditor's rights upon the debtor's default, and (4) be signed by the debtor. [p. 451]

25. False. Attachment is a situation in which a creditor has an enforceable security interest against a debtor and can satisfy the debt out of the designated collateral. [p. 452]

26. True. Floating lien is a security interest in property that was not in the possession of the debtor when the security agreement was executed. [p. 453]

27. True. The concept of perfection of a security interest establishes the right of a secured creditor against other creditors who claim an interest in the collateral. [p. 453]

28. True. Financing statement is a document filed by a secured creditor with the appropriate government office that constructively notifies the world of his or her security interest in personal property. [p. 454]

29. True. Repossession is a right granted to a secured creditor to take possession of the collateral upon default by the debtor. [p. 458]

30. True. An artisan's lien is possessory; that is, the artisan must be in possession of the property in order to affect an artisan's lien. [p. 460]

Multiple Choice

31. B. Answer B is correct Article 9 (Secured Transactions) of the Uniform Commercial Code (UCC) governs secured transactions in personal property. [p. 449]

32. A. Answer A is correct. A two-party secured transaction occurs when a seller sells goods to a buyer on credit and retains a security interest in the goods. [p. 450]

33. A. Answer A is correct. Unless otherwise stated in a security agreement, if a debtor sells, exchanges, or disposes of collateral subject to such an agreement, the secured party automatically has the right to receive the sale proceeds of the sale, exchange, or disposition [Revised UCC 9-102(a)(64), 9-203(f), 9-315(a)]. [p. 453]

34. D. Answer D is correct. Financing statements are available for review by the public. They serve as constructive notice to the world that a creditor claims an interest in a property. [p. 454]

35. B. Answer B is correct. No financing statement has to be filed if the creditor has physical possession of the collateral; this is known as perfection by possession of collateral. The rationale behind this rule is that if someone other than the debtor is in possession of the property, a potential creditor is on notice that another may claim an interest in the debtor's property. [p. 455]

36. A. Answer A is correct. Purchase money security interest is an interest a creditor automatically obtains when he or she extends credit to a consumer to purchase consumer goods. [p. 456]

37. A. Answer A is correct. If two or more secured parties claim an interest in the same collateral but neither has a perfected claim, the first to attach has priority [Revised UCC 9-322(a)(3)]. [p. 456]

38. B. Answer B is correct. Bankruptcy of the debtor, breach of the warranty of ownership as to the collateral, and other such events are commonly defined in security agreements as default. [p. 458]

39. C. Answer C is correct. Repossession is a right granted to a secured creditor to take possession of the collateral upon default by the debtor. [p. 458]

40. B. Answer B is correct. In disposition of collateral the proceeds from a sale, a lease, or another disposition are applied to pay reasonable costs and expenses, satisfy the balance of the indebtedness, and pay subordinate (junior) security interests. The debtor is entitled to receive any surplus that remains [Revised UCC 9-608]. [p. 458-459]

Short Answer

41. A security agreement is the agreement between the debtor and the secured party that creates or provides for a security interest. [Revised UCC 9-102(a)(73)] [p. 451]

42. Attachment is a situation in which the creditor has an enforceable security interest against the debtor and can satisfy the debt out of the designated collateral. [p. 452]

43. Perfecting a security interest establishes the right of a secured creditor against other creditors who claim an interest in the collateral. [p. 453]

44. A document filed by a secured creditor with the appropriate government office that constructively notifies the world of his security interest in personal property. [p. 454]

45. The first party to attach has priority. [p. 456]

46. The right of redemption may be accomplished by payment of all obligations secured by the collateral, all expenses reasonably incurred by the secured property in retaking and holding the collateral, and any attorneys' fees and other legal expenses provided for in the security agreement. [p. 459]

47. (Answers will vary.)consumer goods, equipment used for business, farm products, inventory, fixtures. [p. 452]

48. The secured creditor automatically has the right to receive the proceeds of the disposition, exchange or sale. [p. 453]

49. The creditor does not have to file a financing statement if he or she has physical possession of the collateral. [p. 455]

50. (Answers will vary.) Bankruptcy of the debtor, failure to make regular payments when due, breach of the warranty of ownership as to the collateral. [p. 457-458]

51. A buyer in the ordinary course of business purchases goods in good faith and without knowledge that the sale violates the rights of another person in the goods. [p. 457]

52. A deficiency judgment occurs when the collateral for a loan does not satisfy the debt owed to a creditor and the creditor obtains a judgment against the debtor for the remaining debt to be satisfied from other property of the debtor. [p. 457]

53. An artisan's lien is a "super-priority lien" because it has priority overall other liens, even purchase money security interests, unless otherwise dictated by statute. [p. 460]

54. The Revised Article 9 defines a records as "information that is inscribed on a tangible medium or that is stored in an electronic or other medium and is retrievable in perceivable form" [Revised UCC 9-102(a)(69)]. [p. 457]

55. A fixture filing is a financing statement covering fixtures. [p. 454]

28 | BANKRUPTCY AND REORGANIZATION

Chapter Overview

The Bankruptcy Abuse Prevention and Consumer Protection Act of 2005 substantially amended federal bankruptcy law, making it much more difficult for debtors to escape unwanted debt through bankruptcy. This chapter explores Chapter 7 liquidation bankruptcy, as well as Chapter 13 consumer debt adjustment bankruptcy and Chapter 11 business reorganization bankruptcy. Individual debtors and businesses often find that they are unable to be responsible for the debts that they have incurred and, as such, must rely on the federal bankruptcy laws to free them from their obligations for past debts. You will become more familiar with the procedure involved in filing for bankruptcy, as well as creditors' rights, the order of priority for paying creditors, the meaning of an automatic stay in bankruptcy, and voidable transfers and preferential payments.

Objectives

Upon completion of the exercises contained in this chapter, you should be able to:
1. Identify and describe the major changes to federal bankruptcy law made by the Bankruptcy Abuse Prevention and Consumer Protection Act of 2005.
2. Describe how a bankruptcy estate is determined.
3. Describe a Chapter 7 liquidation bankruptcy and how the median and means tests are met for filing for Chapter 7 bankruptcy.
4. Describe a Chapter 13 adjustment of debts of an individual with regular income.
5. Describe how businesses are reorganized in Chapter 11 bankruptcy.

Practical Application

You should be able to understand the main purpose of bankruptcy law and be familiar with the different types of bankruptcies. You will have a clearer understanding of the impact of bankruptcy and which creditors take priority with regard to payment in bankruptcy.

Helpful Hints

The concepts in this chapter are easier to learn if you keep it simple by learning each of the three types of bankruptcies separately. The study tips section that follows gives you background information, procedures, and little nuances that may be important to know for each kind of bankruptcy. Each type of bankruptcy has main points with which you should become familiar.

Study Tips

Bankruptcy and Reorganization

The main purpose of bankruptcy is to balance the interests of debtors and creditors so as to free the debtor from cumbersome debts so that the debtor can make a "fresh start".

Bankruptcy Law

The law of bankruptcy is federally governed, as the US Constitution expressly gives the federal government the power to enact uniform bankruptcy laws.

The Bankruptcy Abuse Prevention and Consumer Protection Act. The 2005 act made filing for bankruptcy more difficult, especially for those wishing to file a Chapter 7, Liquidation.

Types of Bankruptcy. The Bankruptcy Code provides for several types of bankruptcy.
- Chapter 7. Liquidation.
- Chapter 11. Reorganization.
- Chapter 12. Adjustment of Debts of a Family Farmer or Fisherman with Regular Income.
- Chapter 13. Adjustment of Debts of an Individual with Regular Income.

Bankruptcy Courts. Congress has created a system of federal courts to hear bankruptcy proceedings, with a federal bankruptcy court being attached to each of the US District Courts.
- The US District Court to which each bankruptcy court is attached hears appeals of bankruptcy proceedings.
- Federal bankruptcy judges are appointed for 14 year terms.
- A US Trustee is an administrative official empowered to perform many of the services and duties formerly performed by bankruptcy judges.

Bankruptcy Procedure

The Bankruptcy Code requires that certain procedures be followed.

Pre-Petition and Post-Petition Counseling. The 2005 Act added a new provision that requires an individual filing for bankruptcy to receive pre-petition and post-petition credit and financial counseling.

Filing a Bankruptcy Petition. A petition must be filed with the bankruptcy court for a bankruptcy proceeding to commence.
- Voluntary Petition. The debtor files the petition.
  - This type of petition can be filed in a Chapter 7, 11, 12, or 13 bankruptcy.
- Involuntary Petition. A creditor or creditors file the petition.
  - This type of petition can be filed in a Chapter 7 or 11 bankruptcy.
  - This type of petition cannot be filed in a Chapter 12 or 13 bankruptcy.

Schedules. Several schedules must be submitted by an individual debtor, as well as a certificate that states that the debtor has received the required pre-petition credit counseling. All forms must be sworn to under oath and signed by the debtor.
- A list of secured and unsecured creditors.
- A list of all property owned.
- A statement of the financial affairs of the debtor.
- A statement of the debtor's monthly income.
- Current income and expenses.
- Evidence of payments received from employers within 60 days prior to filing.
- A copy of the debtor's most recent federal income tax return.

Attorney Certification. An attorney, under penalty of perjury and other penalties, must certify in writing that the schedules and information filed by the debtor are accurate.

Order for Relief. The filing of a voluntary petition, or an unchallenged involuntary petition, is such an order.

Meeting of the Creditors. A meeting with the creditors where the debtor is questioned by his or her creditors without a judge being present.
- The debtor may have his or her attorney present.

Proof of Claim and Proof of Interest. A proof of claim that states the amount of the claim against the debtor must be filed by a creditor. A proof of interest must be filed by an equity security holder.

Bankruptcy Trustee. A trustee must be appointed to be the legal representative of the debtor's estate in a Chapter 7, 12, or 13 bankruptcy.
- In cases showing fraud, dishonesty, incompetence, or gross mismanagement by current management, a trustee may be appointed in a Chapter 11 bankruptcy.

Automatic Stay. An automatic stay goes into effect upon the filing of an involuntary or voluntary petition.
- The effect of an automatic stay is that it suspends creditors' actions against the debtor or the debtor's property.

Discharge. If the requirements for a Chapter 7, 11, 12, or 13 bankruptcy are met, the court grants the debtor a discharge of some or all of his, her, or its debts.
- The debtor is no longer legally liable for discharged debts.
- Exceptions to Discharge. The following debts, whose dollar limits were established by the 2005 act, are not dischargeable in bankruptcy:
    - Taxes owed to federal, state, or local governments accrued within three years prior or for taxes for any period where the debtor engaged in tax fraud, evasion and property taxes accrued within one year prior to filing.
    - Certain fines and penalties payable to federal, state, and local governmental units.
    - Claims based on the debtor's liability for causing willful or malicious injury
    - Claims arising from fraud, larceny, or embezzlement as a fiduciary.
    - Domestic support obligations and alimony, maintenance, and child support payments.
    - Claims not included in the schedules.
    - Claims based on the purchase of luxury goods or services of more than $550 from a single creditor on or within 90 days of the order for relief.
    - Cash advances in excess of $825 obtained by use of a revolving line of credit or credit cards on or within 70 days of the order for relief.
    - Judgments and consent decrees against the debtor for liability incurred as a result of the operation of a motor vehicle, a vessel, or an aircraft while legally intoxicated.
    - A debt that benefits the debtor more than it is detrimental to a spouse, former spouse, or child of the debtor.
    - An amount owed to a pension, profit-sharing or stock bonus plan, and loans owed to employee retirement plans.

Reaffirmation Agreement. An agreement where the debtor agrees to pay a debt that is dischargeable in bankruptcy.

Bankruptcy Estate

The bankruptcy estate involves the entire debtor's legal and equitable interests in all types of property, including community property, from the onset of a bankruptcy proceeding. If the debtor obtains property after he or she files his or her petition, this property usually is not considered to be part of the estate.
- Inheritance, divorce settlements, and the like, if obtained within 180 days of the filing of the petition, will be included in the estate.
- In Chapter 11, 12, and 13 bankruptcies, a portion of post-petition earnings for up to five years can be included in the estate.

Exempt Property. Property not included in the bankruptcy estate that may be kept by the debtor.
- The Bankruptcy Code establishes a list of exempt property.

State Exemptions. Some state laws provide for exemptions which are broad in scope.
- Some states require that the debtor choose between federal or state exemptions or adhere to the state laws.

Homestead Exemption. The federal Bankruptcy Code provides for a limited exemption for the debtor's principal residence.
- If the debtor's equity exceeds this exemption, the trustee can sell the property to realize this excess value.

Fraudulent Transfers Prior to Bankruptcy. Bankruptcy courts will examine transfers of property prior to the filing of the petition to determine if there has been a preferential or fraudulent transfer of property by the debtor.
- The court may set aside transfers within two years of the petition if they are fraudulent.

Chapter 7 – Liquidation

This is the most common type of bankruptcy and is also referred to as a "straight bankruptcy".
- The debtor's nonexempt property is sold to obtain cash and then the money is distributed to the debtor's creditors.
- Debts that are not paid are then discharged.

The 2005 Act's Changes to Chapter 7. Major changes in the bankruptcy code provide that the debtor may not be allowed discharge for debts if he or she does not pass the "simple abuse rule". If the debtor does not meet the median income or means test, their petition may be dismissed or converted to a Chapter 13 repayment plan.
- Test 1: Median Income Test. If the family income exceeds the state's median income.
  - Any party in interest may move to have the petition dismissed.
- Test 2: The Means Test. Under the means test, if the debtor passes the Median Income Test, the court will look to see if the debtor has the ability to pay pre-petition debts out of post-petition income.
  - The formula for the means test is complicated.

Statutory Distribution of Property. Nonexempt property has to be distributed to the debtor's unsecured and secured creditors. The secured creditors take priority over the unsecured creditors.

- Oversecured Secured Creditor. A secured creditor with collateral value exceeding the amount of the claim.
    - The property is usually sold to satisfy the secured creditor's claim.
    - The excess is available to satisfy the claims of unsecured creditors.
- Undersecured Secured Creditor. A secured creditor with collateral value insufficient to cover the amount of the claim.
    - The property is usually awarded to the secured creditor.
    - The unsatisfied portion of the claim becomes an unsecured claim against the estate.
- Secured Personal Property. When personal property secures a claim or is subject to an unexpired lease and is not exempt property, the debtor must either
    - surrender the personal property or
    - redeem the property by paying the secured lien in full or
    - assume the unexpired lease.
- Unsecured Claims. The Bankruptcy Code sets out the priority of unsecured claims, as shown in Exhibit 28.3 on page 444.

Chapter 7 Discharge. After the property has been distributed to satisfy the claims that are allowed, then the debtor is no longer responsible for the remaining unpaid claims.

- Only individuals may be given a discharge.

Acts That Bar Discharge. Discharge of unsatisfied debts is denied if the debtor engaged in behavior such as making false representations of his or her financial position, failed to account for assets, or failed to complete the instructional course in personal financial management.

- Any party of interest may file an objection to the discharge of a debt.
- If a discharge is obtained through fraud of the debtor, any party of interest may bring a motion to have the bankruptcy revoked.
- The bankruptcy court may revoke a discharge within one year after it is granted.

Discharge of Student Loans. The debtor must show undue hardship to him- or herself and his or her dependents.

- The courts strictly construe undue hardship and it is difficult to prove without showing severe physical or mental disability or the inability to pay for basic necessities.
    - Cosigners must also meet this test.

Chapter 13 - Adjustment of Debts of an Individual with Regular Income

Under this plan, the court may oversee the debtor's plan for installment payments of his or her unpaid debts. Chapter 13 is beneficial to both the debtor as well as creditor.

- The debtor's costs are less under this type of proceeding, and he or she may keep more property than is exempt under Chapter 7.
- The creditors are able to elicit a greater payment for the debts that are owing to them.

Filing a Chapter 13 Petition. The debtor must file a petition claiming that he or she is insolvent or not able to pay his or her debts when they are due.

- A debtor may ask for more time (an extension) to pay his or her debts or ask for a composition which reduces his or her debts.

Limitations on Who Can File a Chapter 13 Bankruptcy. Only individuals, along with their spouses, with regular income may file this type of bankruptcy.
- The debtor, along with his or her spouse cannot owe more than the following:
    o noncontingent, liquidated, unsecured debts of up to $336,900 and
    o secured debts up to $1,010,650 may file a petition for Chapter 13 bankruptcy.
- Individuals who owe more do not qualify.
- Sole proprietorships, as they are owned by individuals, may file for Chapter 13 bankruptcy.

Property of a Chapter 13 Bankruptcy. The estate includes all nonexempt property of the debtor at the time the petition is filed and nonexempt property acquired after the petition is filed and before the case is closed.
- Earnings and future income after the case begins and before it ends are included.
- The debtor retains possession of estate property while completing the plan.

Chapter 13 Plan of Payment. The debtor must file a plan of payment no later than 90 days of filing his or her petition.
- The plan may not go beyond three years; the court may grant a five-year period plan.

Confirmation of a Chapter 13 Plan of Payment. If all requirements are met, the court can confirm the plan of payment if the following conditions are also met:
- the plan was proposed in good faith
- the plan passes the feasibility test
- the plan is in the best interests of the creditors
- the debtor has paid all domestic support obligations owed, and
- the debtor has filed all applicable federal, state, and local tax returns.

Chapter 13 Discharge. When the debtor has made all payments under the plan, the court may discharge the debtor from all unpaid debts.
- The debtor must certify that domestic support payments have been paid.

Chapter 11 – Reorganization

Under this type of bankruptcy, the court assists the debtor in reorganizing his/her financial affairs.
- Individuals, corporations, non-incorporated associations, railroads, and partnerships are able to utilize this type of bankruptcy.
- Corporations use Chapter 11 bankruptcies the most.

Debtor in Possession. A unique feature about this type of bankruptcy is that the debtor is left to run his or her business while the reorganization proceeding is taking place.
- The debtor is referred to as a debtor-in-possession.
    o Has the authority to enter into contracts and operate the business accordingly.
- A trustee will be appointed only on a showing of fraud, dishonesty, or gross mismanagement.

Creditors' Committees. The court appoints a creditors' committee after an order for relief is granted, composed of representatives of the class of unsecured creditors.

- The court may appoint a committee of secured creditors and a committee of equity holders.

Automatic Stay in Chapter 11. The automatic stay, which suspends certain legal actions against the debtor, is particularly important in Chapter 11 because the debtor needs to keep its assets in tact to stay in business.

Executory Contracts and Unexpired Leases in Chapter 11. The debtor is allowed to accept or reject certain contracts that have not yet been fully performed.
- The debtor will not be liable for damages for rejecting these contracts.

Labor Union and Retiree Benefits Contracts in Chapter 11. The debtor and the representatives of the union members and retirees can voluntarily agree to modify the union collective bargaining agreement and retiree benefits.
- Absent such an agreement, the debtor can petition the bankruptcy court to reject the collective bargaining agreement and to modify retiree benefits.

Chapter 11 Plan of Reorganization. The debtor has a right to file a plan of reorganization within 120 days of the order for relief.
- The reorganization plan describes the debtor's proposed new capital structure that indicates the different classes of claims and interests.
- The creditors and equity holders must be given a court approved disclosure statement.

Confirmation of the Chapter 11 Plan of Reorganization. The court must confirm the debtor's plan for reorganization in order for it to become effective.
- Confirmation may be accomplished by giving the different classes of creditors the chance to accept or reject the plan.
  - The court looks at whether the plan is in the best interests of each class of claims, if the plan is feasible, if at least one class has accepted the plan, and whether or not each class of claims and interests is nonimpaired.
- Confirmation may also be achieved using the cram-down method.
  - The plan has to be fair and equitable to the impaired class.
  - The impaired class can be forced to take part in the plan of reorganization.

Small Business Bankruptcy. Small businesses with debts less than $2,190,000 can use a simplified form of Chapter 11 Reorganization.

Chapter 12 – Family Farmer and Family Fisherman

This chapter of the Bankruptcy Code was temporary prior to 2005, but was made a permanent part of the code at that time. It establishes special definitions for farmers and fishermen.

Family Farmer and Family Fisherman.
- Family Farmer. "An individual or an individual and spouse whose total debt does not exceed $3,544,525 and is at least 50 percent related to farming operations and whose gross income for the preceding taxable year or each of the second and third preceding taxable years was at least 50 percent earned from farming operations," as defined by the Bankruptcy Code.

- Family Fisherman. "an individual or an individual and spouse whose total debt does not exceed $1,642,500 and is at least 80 percent related to a commercial fishing operation and whose gross income for the preceding taxable year was at least 50 percent earned from the commercial fishing operation," as defined by the Bankruptcy Code.

Chapter 12 Procedure and Estate. The debtor may file a voluntary petition.
- An automatic stay goes into effect on filing the petition.
- A trustee is appointed after the petition is filed.
- The family farmer or fisherman is a debtor-in-possession.

Chapter 12 Plan of Reorganization. A debtor must file a plan of reorganization within 90 days.
- The plan can provide for no more than three years of payments to creditors, though the court can increase the plan period to five years.
- A debtor's plan can be confirmed as to a secured creditor if
    - the holder of the claim has accepted the plan or
    - the debtor surrenders the property securing the claim to the secured creditor or
    - the plan provides that the secured creditor retains the mortgage or lien securing the claim and the plan distributes property to the secured creditor that is not less than the allowed amount of the claim.
- The debtor and an unsecured creditor can voluntarily agree to terms for settling the claim.
    - If such an agreement is not reached, the plan must provide that all projected disposable income will be paid to creditors.

Confirmation of Chapter 12 Plan. The bankruptcy court will confirm a plan if the plan has been proposed in good faith, the plan is in the best interests of the unsecured creditors, and the plan is feasible.
- If an unsecured creditor objects to the plan, the court can use the cram-down provision to force the plan onto the objecting creditors.

Chapter 12 Discharge. The debtor is given a discharge of all claims that were not a part of the plan of reorganization.

Refresh Your Memory

The following exercise will give you the opportunity to test your memory of the principles given in this chapter. Read the question twice and place your answer in the blank provided. Review the chapter material for any question that you are unable to answer or remember.

1. Chapter 7 of the Bankruptcy Code of the bankruptcy act of 2005 primarily deals with _____.

2. The filing of either a voluntary petition or an unchallenged involuntary petition constitutes a(n) _____.

3. A(n) _____ is a document required to be filed by an equity security holder that states the amount of his or her interest against the debtor.

4. A bankruptcy trustee is a _____.

5. The suspension of certain legal actions by creditors against a debtor or the debtor's property is known as a(n) _____.

6. A(n) _____ is an agreement entered into by the creditor and the debtor whereby the debtor agrees to pay the creditor for a debt that is dischargeable in bankruptcy.

7. _____ is a form of bankruptcy in which the debtor's nonexempt property is sold for cash, the cash is distributed to the creditors, and any unpaid debts are discharged.

8. The _____ is a bankruptcy rule that applies to a debtor who has a median family income that exceeds the state's median family income for families the same size as the debtor's family.

9. A means test is used to determine whether _____.

10. If the value of the secured interest is lesser than the collateral securing the secured loan, the secured creditor is a(n) _____.

11. Under the 2005 bankruptcy act, if non-exempt personal property of an individual debtor secures a claim or is subject to an unexpired lease, the debtor _____.

12. _____ is a rehabilitation form of bankruptcy that permits bankruptcy courts to supervise the debtor's plan for the payment of unpaid debts in installments over the plan period.

13. A(n) _____ provides for the reduction of a debtor's debts.

14. A person filing for bankruptcy under Chapter 11 and left in place to operate the business during the reorganization proceeding is known as the _____.

15. A(n) _____ provision is a provision whereby the court confirms a plan of reorganization over an objecting class of creditors if certain requirements are met.

Critical Thought Exercise

Nancy Mills attended two different institutions of higher learning. She received educational loans totaling $22,480. After graduation, Mills was employed, but her monthly take-home pay was less than $1,200. The monthly expenses for herself and her four children were approximately $1,650. Mill's husband had abandoned the family and provided no financial support. Mills received no public assistance and had no possibility to increase her income. A neighbor paid her telephone, water, and gas bills for the two months prior to filing a petition in bankruptcy. Mills also had substantial medical bills and had not been well for months. In her bankruptcy petition, Mills sought to discharge her educational loans.

Are the educational loans owed by Mills dischargeable in bankruptcy? Why was the Bankruptcy Code amended to generally prohibit the discharge of student loans?

Please compose your answer to the Critical Thinking Exercise using a separate sheet of paper or your computer word processing program.

Practice Quiz

True/False

16. _____ The Bankruptcy Reform Act of 1978 made it easier for debtors to file for bankruptcy and have their unpaid debts discharged.

17. _____ Bankruptcy Abuse Prevention and Consumer Protection Act of 2005 makes it more difficult for debtors to file for bankruptcy and have their unpaid debts discharged.

18. _____ There are separate state and federal bankruptcy laws.

19. _____ A U.S. Trustee is a federal government official who has responsibility for handling and supervising many of the administrative tasks associated with a bankruptcy case.

20. _____ The Bankruptcy Act of 2005 requires that before an individual debtor receives a discharge in a Chapter 7 or Chapter 13 bankruptcy, the debtor must attend a personal financial management course approved by the U.S. Trustee.

21. _____ A debtor filing for bankruptcy who is represented by an attorney need not be investigated or verified.

22. _____ An order of relief occurs upon the filing of either a voluntary petition or an unchallenged involuntary petition.

23. _____ A proof of claim is a document required to be filed by a creditor that states the amount of his or her claim against the debtor.

24. _____ A secured creditor whose claim exceeds the value of the collateral may submit a proof of claim and become an unsecured claimant as to the difference.

25. _____ A reaffirmation agreement is an agreement whereby a creditor agrees to discharge the debtor of certain debts that maybe included in the bankruptcy.

26. _____ If the value of the collateral securing the secured loan is less than the secured interest, the secured creditor is an oversecured creditor.

27. _____ Unpaid debts that the debtor incurred prior to the date of the order for relief are discharged under Chapter 7.

28. _____ The property of a Chapter 13 estate consists of nonexempt property acquired after the case is closed.

29. _____ A debtor-in-possession is a debtor who is left in place to operate the business during the reorganization proceeding.

30. _____ An executory contract refers to a contract or lease that has not been fully performed.

Multiple Choice

31. Which of the following federal acts substantially amended federal bankruptcy law in 2005?

A. Bankruptcy Reform Act
B. Bankruptcy Abuse Prevention and Consumer Protection Act
C. the Nelson Act
D. the Chandler Act

32. Which of the following is true of bankruptcy law in the United States?

A. The 1978 bankruptcy law made it easier for debtors to be relieved of much of their debt.
B. The 1978 bankruptcy law was deemed to be "creditor friendly."
C. The bankruptcy act of 2005 makes it easier debtors be relieved of their debts under federal bankruptcy law.
D. The 2005 bankruptcy act has been called "debtor friendly."

33. Which of the following best defines a proof of claim?

A. a statement by the debtor that states that he or she has debts
B. a document required to be filed by a debtor stating the property that is exempted from constituting the bankruptcy estate
C. a document required to be filed by a creditor that states the amount of his or her claim against the debtor
D. a statement by creditors alleging that the debtor is not paying his or her debts as they become due

34. Why is a discharge of debt granted?

A. to divide the bankruptcy estate equally among all creditors
B. to relieve the debtor of the responsibility to pay some of or all the debt
C. to divide the bankruptcy estate according to the debt owed to each creditor
D. to suspend certain legal actions by creditors against a debtor's property

35. What is a homestead exemption?

A. investment in realty that a debtor must forfeit
B. equity in a home that a debtor is permitted to retain
C. remainder of the debtor's interest in commercial property that is returned to him after fulfilling creditors' claims
D. all of the debtor's assets converted to cash

36. Which of the following is true of the median income test?

A. If a family has median family income equal to the state's median family income, the debtor does not qualify for Chapter 7 bankruptcy.
B. If a family has median family income below the state's median family income, the debtor is subject to the "means" test.
C. If a family has median family income below to the state's median family income, the debtor automatically qualifies for Chapter 7 bankruptcy.
D. A debtor's debts are not discharged if the family median income is more than the state's median family income.

37. What is Chapter 7 discharge?

A. The termination of the legal duty of an individual debtor to pay both secured and unsecured secured debts before he or she is granted a court trial.
B. The termination of the legal duty of an individual debtor to pay unsecured debts that remain unpaid upon the completion of a Chapter 7 proceeding.
C. The cancellation of all debts of a debtor that remain unpaid upon the completion of a Chapter 13 proceeding.
D. An instruction to the debtor to propose a plan to pay all or a portion of the debts he or she owes in installments.

38. Which of the following bankruptcy methods allows the reorganization of the debtor's financial affairs under the supervision of the bankruptcy court?

A. Chapter 11
B. Chapter 13
C. Chapter 7
D. Chapter 12

39. What is an executory contract?

A. a contract that cannot be discharged under Chapter 13
B. a contract that the debtor is obliged to perform despite filing for bankruptcy
C. an agreement between several creditors and a single debtor, dividing the debtor's property
D. a lease that has not been fully performed

40. Which of the following does a Chapter 11 automatic stay provide?

A. automatic discharge of secured debts
B. suspension of certain legal actions against the debtor
C. creditors' foreclosure on assets given as collateral for loans
D. automatic discharge of unsecured debts

Short Answer

41. What additional burden does an attorney have under the 2005 act that did not exist before?

_____
_____

42. What is a proof of interest?

_____
_____

43. Give three examples of property that is exempt from bankruptcy.

_____
_____

44. What is the bankruptcy estate?

_____
_____

45. What is an abusive filing?

_____

_____

46. What is the means test?

_____

_____

47. What does the debtor's plan of reorganization in a Chapter 11 bankruptcy usually contain?

_____

_____

48. What is a "cram down" provision?

_____

_____

49. What counseling provisions does the 2005 act contain?

_____

_____

50. What is a reaffirmation agreement?

_____

_____

51. Smith owns a principal residence worth $300,000 that is subject to a $100,000 mortgage, and Smith therefore owns $100,000 of equity in the property. Smith files a petition for Chapter 7 liquidation bankruptcy. How would the bankruptcy trustee deal with this issue?

_____

_____

52. What is a fraudulent transfer?

_____

_____

53. If a debtor has personal property that secures a claim or an unexpired lease which is not exempt property, what options does the debtor have under the 2005 act?

_____

_____

54. What are three acts that will bar discharge of debts through bankruptcy?

_____

_____

55. Generally, student loans cannot be discharged in bankruptcy unless a debtor can show "undue hardship." What does this require a debtor to show?

_____

_____

Answers to Refresh Your Memory

1. liquidation [p. 464]
2. order for relief [p. 467]
3. proof of interest [p. 467]
4. legal representative of a debtor's estate [p. 467]
5. automatic stay [p. 467]
6. reaffirmation agreement [p. 468]
7. Liquidation [p. 471]
8. means test [p. 472]
9. the debtor has the capability to pay prepetition debts out of postpetition income [p. 472]
10. an oversecured creditor [p. 473]
11. must surrender the property [p. 473]
12. Chapter 13 [p. 474]
13. composition [p. 475]
14. debtor-in-possession [p. 478]
15 cram-down [p. 480]

Critical Thought Exercise Model Answer

The restriction against discharge of student loans was designed to remedy an abuse by students, who, immediately upon graduation, would file bankruptcy to secure a discharge of student loans. These students often had no other indebtedness and could pay their debts out of future wages.

In this case, Mills has truly fallen on hard times. Her monthly income does not meet her usual expenses. The combination of no support from her husband, four in-home dependents, and no prospects for more income, give rise to a situation where a court could easily find that repayment of the educations loans would create an undue hardship. The restriction against discharge of educational loans was passed by Congress to stop an abuse and was never intended to prevent a deserving petitioner from getting protection and a fresh start from the bankruptcy court. Mills should be allowed to have all of her debts discharged in bankruptcy to avoid undue hardship.

Answers to Practice Quiz

True/False

16. True. The Bankruptcy Reform Act of 1978 law was structured to make it easier for debtors to be relieved of much of their debt by declaring bankruptcy; it was deemed "debtor friendly" because it allowed many debtors to escape their unsecured debts. [p. 464]

17. True. The Bankruptcy Abuse Prevention and Consumer Protection Act of 2005.The 2005 act makes it much more difficult for debtors to escape their debts under federal bankruptcy law. [p. 464]

18. False. Bankruptcy law is exclusively federal law; there are no state bankruptcy laws. [p. 464]

19. True. A U.S. Trustee is a federal government official who has responsibility for handling and supervising many of the administrative tasks associated with a bankruptcy case. [p. 465]

20. True. The 2005 act requires that before an individual debtor receives a discharge in a Chapter 7 or Chapter 13 bankruptcy, the debtor must attend a personal financial management course approved by the U.S. Trustee. [p. 466]

21. False. If an attorney represents a debtor in bankruptcy, the attorney has to conduct a thorough investigation of the debtor's financial position and schedules to determine the accuracy of the information contained in the petition and schedules. [p. 466]

22. True. An order for relief occurs upon the filing of either a voluntary petition or an unchallenged involuntary petition, or an order that is granted after a trial of a challenged involuntary petition. [p. 467]

23. True. A proof of claim is a document required to be filed by a creditor that states the amount of his or her claim against the debtor. [p. 467]

24. True. A secured creditor whose claim exceeds the value of the collateral may submit a proof of claim and become an unsecured claimant as to the difference. [p. 467]

25. False. A reaffirmation agreement is an agreement entered into by a debtor with a creditor prior to discharge, whereby the debtor agrees to pay the creditor a debt that would otherwise be discharged in bankruptcy. Certain requirements must be met for a reaffirmation agreement to be enforced. [p. 468]

26. False. If the value of the collateral securing the secured loan exceeds the secured interest, the secured creditor is an oversecured creditor. [p. 448]

27. True. Unpaid debts that the debtor incurred prior to the date of the order for relief are discharged under Chapter 7. [p. 473]

28. False. The property of a Chapter 13 estate consists of all nonexempt property of the debtor at the commencement of the case and nonexempt property acquired after the commencement of the case but before the case is closed. [p. 475]

29. True. A debtor-in-possession is a debtor who is left in place to operate the business during the reorganization proceeding. [p. 478]

30. True. An executory contract is a contract or lease that has fully not been performed.[p. 478]

Multiple Choice

31. B. Answer B is the correct answer. The Bankruptcy Abuse Prevention and Consumer Protection Act of 2005 A federal act that substantially amended federal bankruptcy law. [p. 464]

32. A. Answer A is the correct answer. The 1978 bankruptcy law was structured to make it easier for debtors to be relieved of much of their debt by declaring bankruptcy; it was deemed "debtor friendly" because it allowed many debtors to escape their unsecured debts. [p. 464]

33. C. Answer C is the correct answer. Proof of claim is a document required to be filed by a creditor that states the amount of his or her claim against the debtor. [p. 467]

34. B. Answer B is the correct answer. Discharge is a court order that relieves a debtor of the legal liability to pay his or her debts that were not paid in the bankruptcy proceeding. [p. 468]

35. B. Answer B is the correct answer. . Homestead exemption refers to equity in a debtor's home that the debtor is permitted to retain. [p. 470]

36. C. Answer C is the correct answer. If a family has median family income equal to or below the state's median family income, there is no presumption of abuse, and the debtor qualifies for Chapter 7 bankruptcy. [p. 472]

37. B. Answer B is the correct answer. Chapter 7 discharge refers to the termination of the legal duty of an individual debtor to pay unsecured debts that remain unpaid upon the completion of a Chapter 7 proceeding. [p. 473]

38. A. Answer A is the correct answer,. Chapter 11 Reorganization of the Bankruptcy Code provides a method for reorganizing a debtor's financial affairs under the supervision of the bankruptcy court. [p. 478]

39. D. Answer D is the correct answer. Executory contract or unexpired lease is a contract or lease that has not been fully performed. With the bankruptcy court's approval, a debtor may reject executory contracts and unexpired leases in bankruptcy.[p. 478]

40. B. Answer B is the correct answer. The filing of a Chapter 11 petition stays (suspends) actions by creditors to recover the debtor's property. This automatic stay suspends certain legal actions against the debtor or the debtor's property, including the ability of creditors to foreclose on assets given as collateral for their loans to the debtor. [p. 478]

Short Answer

41. The attorney must swear under penalty of perjury that he/she has certified the accuracy of the information contained in the bankruptcy petition and the schedules. The attorney is subject to monetary fines and sanctions if there are any factual discrepancies. [p. 466]

42. The document required to be filed by an equity security holder that states the amount of his or her interest against the debtor. [p. 467]

43. (Answers will vary.) Interest up to $3,225 in one motor vehicle; interest in jewelry up to $1,350 that is held for personal use; interest up to $2,025 in value in implements, tools, or professional books used in the debtor's trade. Complete list on page 441 of text. [p. 470]

44. Debtor's property and earnings comprising the estate of a bankruptcy proceeding. [p. 469]

45. A Chapter 7 filing found to be an abuse of Chapter 7 liquidation bankruptcy. [p. 471]

46. A new test added by the 2005 act that applies to debtors who have family incomes that exceed the state's median income for families of the same size. [p. 472]

47. The plan contains the debtor's proposed new capital structure wherein he or she designates the different classes of claims and interests. [p. 478]

48. A "cram down" provision is a provision whereby the court confirms a plan of reorganization over the objection of a certain class of creditors, so long as certain requirements are met. [p. 480]

49. The 2005 act added a new provision that requires an individual filing for bankruptcy to receive prepetition counseling and postpetition counseling. A debtor must receive prepetition credit counseling within 180 days prior to filing his or her petition for bankruptcy. [p. 466]

50. An agreement between the debtor and a creditor prior to discharge where the debtor agrees to pay a debt that would otherwise be discharged in bankruptcy. [p. 468]

51. The trustee may sell the home, pay off the mortgage, pay Smith $20,200 (applying the federal exemption), and use the remaining proceeds of $79,800 for distribution to the debtor's creditors. [p. 470]

52. The transfer of property or taking on an obligation by a debtor within 2 years of filing a petition for bankruptcy, where the debtor intended to hinder or defraud a creditor or received less than a reasonable amount in exchange when the debtor was insolvent or unable to pay at the time. [p. 469]

53. A debtor must surrender or redeem the property or assume the unexpired lease. [p. 473]

54. (Answers will vary.) False representations of financial position in obtaining credit, falsifying or destroying or concealing records, failure to account for assets, failure to complete required financial counseling. [p. 474]

55. Courts are strict in interpreting "undue hardship" and it is difficult for a debtor to show, unless severe physical or mental disability or the inability to pay for basic necessities can be shown. Additionally, cosigners must also meet this test. [p. 477]

29 | AGENCY FORMATION AND TERMINATION

Chapter Overview

This chapter will provide you with a thorough understanding of agency, including the important role that it plays in the business world, as well as the creation and termination of an agency relationship. You will become familiar with the three most common types of employment relationships and how to differentiate among them.

Objectives

Upon completion of the exercises in this chapter, you should be able to:
1. Define agency.
2. Identify and define a principal–independent contractor relationship.
3. Describe how express and implied agencies are created.
4. Define apparent agency.
5. Describe how an agency is terminated.

Practical Application

You will learn how the different types of agencies are created and terminated. You will also be able to recognize an irrevocable agency and whether or not there has been a wrongful termination of an agency contract. You will understand the differences among the three main types of employment relationships and the liabilities associated with each. This chapter will be especially useful to anyone in business, because agencies are an essential part of any successful business.

Helpful Hints

Since most of us have been, or will be, in some sort of employment relationship in our lifetime, this chapter is very easy to apply to either our past employment experiences or our future endeavors. Many of us have been agents and have not realized that fact. You will find this chapter easier to learn if you place yourself in the shoes of the person in the situation you are trying to learn about. If you familiarize yourself with the basic terminology given in the Study Tips section that follows, the concepts will become easier and clearer for you to understand.

Study Tips

Agency Formation and Termination

Without agents, the business world would be much more limited in its activities, as partnerships and corporations could not operate and sole proprietorships could not hire employees.

Agency

Section 1(1) of the Restatement (Second) of Agency defines agency as "a fiduciary relationship which results from the manifestation of consent by one person to another that the other shall act in his behalf and subject to his control, and consent by the other so to act."

- Principal. A party who employs another individual to act on his or her behalf.
- Agent. A party who agrees to act on behalf of another.

Persons Who Can Initiate an Agency Relationship. If an individual has the capacity to enter into a contract, then he or she can appoint an agent to act on his or her behalf.

- A court can appoint a representative for those who lack capacity who can enter into contracts and agency relationships on their behalf.
- The agency must be formed for a lawful purpose.

Principal-Agent Relationship. A relationship whereby an employee is hired and given the authority to act and enter into contracts on the employer's behalf.

Employer-Employee Relationship. An association that results when an employer hires an employee to perform some type of physical service but does not authorize the employee to enter into contracts on his behalf.

Principal-Independent Contractor Relationship. Persons and businesses who are hired to perform certain tasks on behalf of the principal, but are not employees of that person or business.

Formation of an Agency

There are various ways that an agency may be formed.

Express Agency. This is the most common type of agency wherein an agent and a principal expressly agree to enter into an agency agreement with one another. It may be oral or in writing.

- Exclusive Agency Contract. A distinct contract between the principal and agent whereby the principal agrees not to employ any agent other than the exclusive agent.
- Power of Attorney. An agency agreement that expressly gives an agent the authority to sign legal documents on the principal's behalf. The agent is referred to as an Attorney-in-fact.
  - General Power of Attorney. An express agency giving broad powers to the agent to act in any matters on the principal's behalf
  - Special Power of Attorney. An express agency giving limited powers as provided for in the parties' agreement

Implied Agency. An agency that is created by the parties' conduct.

- The implied authority of the agent may be given by custom in the industry, the agent's position, or the prior dealing between the parties.
- There cannot be a conflict between the express and implied authority.

Incidental Authority. The implied authority to act in emergency situations and other contingent circumstances in order to protect the principal's property and rights.

Agency by Ratification. An agency that is a result of a principal ratifying an unauthorized act by one who represents himself as another's agent when he is not actually the principal's agent.

Apparent Agency

An agency by estoppel, or apparent agency, is created when a principal gives the appearance of an agency that in reality does not exist.

- Upon creation of this type of agency, the principal is bound to contract entered into by the apparent agent while acting within the parameters of the apparent agency.

Principal's Duties

The principal's duties may be stated in the parties' contract or implied by law. An easy mnemonic to remember the principal's duties is: <u>C</u>onnie <u>R</u>emembers the <u>I</u>ndian <u>C</u>oin.

<u>C</u>ompensation
<u>R</u>eimbursement
<u>I</u>ndemnification
<u>C</u>ooperation

Principal's Duty to Compensate. The principal owes a duty to compensate an agent for the services he or she has provided.

- If the compensation is not stated in the parties' agreement, then compensation will be based on custom or what is the reasonable value for the agent's services.

Principal's Duty to Reimburse and Indemnify.

- Duty to Reimburse. The principal owes a duty to reimburse the agent for all expenses the agent has expended from his own money if the expenses were authorized and within the scope of the agency and necessary to discharge the agent's duties in carrying out the agency.
- Duty to Indemnify. The principal owes a duty to indemnify the agent for any losses that the agent may suffer due to the principal's misconduct.

Principal's Duty to Cooperate. The principal owes a duty to cooperate with and help the agent in the performance of the agent's duties and the goal of the agency.

Agent's Duties

Agent's Duty to Perform. The agent owes a duty to perform the lawful duties stated in the parties' contract. Additionally the agent must meet the standard of reasonable care, skill, and diligence that is implied in all contracts.

- An agent that presents himself or herself as having higher than average skills will be held to a higher standard of performance.
  - Example. A physician who contends that he or she is a plastic surgeon specialist will be held to a reasonable specialist in plastic surgery standard.

Agent's Duty to Notify. The agent owes a duty of notification to the principal if the agent learns information that is important to the principal.

- Imputed Knowledge. It is assumed the principal knows most information the agent knows.

Agent's Duty to Account. The agent owes a duty to keep an accurate accounting of all transactions performed on behalf of the principal.

- The agent must keep records of all money that has been spent and all money that has been received during the duration of the agency.
- The principal's separate account must be maintained by the agent and the principal's property must be used in an authorized manner.

Termination of an Agency by Acts of the Parties

An agency contract may be terminated by an act of the parties. Once terminated, the agent can no longer represent the principle.
- Mutual Agreement. The parties may mutually agree to terminate their agreement.
- Lapse of Time. The agency agreement will end after a certain period of time passes.
- Purpose Achieved. The agency ends when the purpose of the agreement is accomplished.
- Occurrence of a Specified Event. The agency ends when a specified event in the parties' agreement happens.

Notification Required at the Termination of an Agency. The principal has a duty to notify others of the termination of the agency when the agency is terminated by agreement.
- If the principal fails to give proper notice of termination of an agency, the agent has apparent authority to act on the principal's behalf and contracts can be enforced against the principal.
    - o Parties who dealt with the agent. Direct notice of termination must be given to all persons with whom the agent dealt.
    - o Parties who have knowledge of the agency. The principal must give direct or constructive notice to any third party who has knowledge of the agency but with whom the agent has not dealt.
    - o Parties who have no knowledge of the agency. The principal is not obligated to give notice of termination to strangers who have no knowledge of the agency.

Agency Coupled with an Interest. This type of agency is not ended by death or incapacity of either party and only terminates upon performance of the agent's obligations.
- It is irrevocable and created for the agent's benefit.

Termination by an Unusual Change in Circumstances
An agency terminates when there is an unusual change in circumstances that would lead the agent to believe that the principal's original instructions should no longer be valid.

Termination of an Agency by Operation of Law

There are five ways to terminate an agency relationship by operation of law.
- Death. The death of either the agent or principal ends the agency relationship.
- Insanity. Insanity of either party ends the agency relationship.
- Bankruptcy. If the principal is found bankrupt, the agency is terminated. However, an agent's bankruptcy usually does not end the agency.
- War. War between the agent's and principal's countries terminates the agency.

Termination by Impossibility. The agency ends if circumstances make the agency impossible. The following have been recognized under this method of termination:
- Loss or destruction of the subject matter of the agency.

- Loss of a required qualification.
  - Example. A private physician loses his or her license.
- A change in the law. If the agency contains a provision that becomes illegal, the agency contract will end.

Refresh Your Memory

The following exercise will give you the opportunity to test your memory of the principles given in this chapter. Read the question twice and place your answer in the blank provided. Review the chapter material for any question that you are unable to answer or remember.

1. A party who employs another person to act on his or her behalf is known as a _____.

2. A(n) _____ is a fiduciary relationship which results from the manifestation of consent by one person to another that the other shall act in his behalf and subject to his control, and consent by the other so to act.

3. A(n) _____ is a relationship formed when an employer hires an employee and gives that employee authority to act and enter into contracts on his or her behalf.

4. If a person employs an architect to design the layout of his or her own home, it would constitute a(n) _____ relationship.

5. An agency that occurs when a principal and an agent categorically agree to enter into an agency agreement with each other is known as a(n) _____.

6. A(n) _____ is a contract a principal and agent enter into that says the principal cannot employ another agent other than the one stated.

7. The agency of power of attorney is an example of a(n) _____ agreement.

8. An express agency agreement that is often used to give an agent the control to sign legal documents on behalf of the principal is known as a(n) _____.

9. A power of attorney where a principal confers powers on an agent to act in specified matters on the principal's behalf is referred to as _____.

10. An agency that occurs when a principal and an agent do not expressly create an agency, but it is inferred from the conduct of the parties is known as _____.

11. An agency by ratification occurs when the principal _____.

12. A duty that a principal owes to pay an agreed-upon amount to the agent either upon the completion of the agency or at some other mutually agreeable time is known as a principal's _____.

13. The _____ is principal's duty to cover the agent for any losses the agent suffers because of the principal's conduct.

14. _____ is a special type of agency that is created for the agent's benefit and that the principal cannot revoke.

15. The termination of an agency contract in violation of the terms of the agency contract is referred to as _____.

Critical Thought Exercise

Dave Polk was a self-employed handyman, doing business under the name Polk Speedy-Fix. From 2000-2007, Polk performed maintenance and repair work for numerous people in Sun City West, Arizona, including Frank and Martha Hamilton. Polk did landscape maintenance, cactus trimming, painting, plumbing, and carpentry. Polk completed a job in May 2007 for the Hamilton's wherein he replaced a toilet and vanity. Polk was then hired to trim a 30-foot-tall palm tree in the Hamilton's' side yard. Polk was paid $20 per hour for his previous jobs by the Hamilton's. Polk was to receive the same rate of pay for trimming the palm tree.

When Polk arrived to trim the palm tree, Mr. Hamilton told him he wanted it trimmed to a height that was approximately the same as the house, along with trimming back the fronds so that they were at least five feet from the homes of both the Hamilton's and their neighbors. Polk took out several saws and two ladders from his repair van. Polk also borrowed a tree trimming saw and a rope from the Hamilton's. When his ladder was unable to reach the top areas of the tree, Polk climbed the tree. Polk fell from the palm tree when the rope broke and he received severe injuries to his back, pelvis, and internal organs. At age 32, he was totally unable to work.

Polk sued the Hamilton's to recover for his injuries, claiming that he was working as an employee at the time of his injuries and was therefore entitled to workers' compensation protection from the Hamilton's. The Hamilton's argued that Polk was an independent contractor. Was Polk an employee of the Hamilton's or an independent contractor?

Please compose your answer to the Critical Thinking Exercise using a separate sheet of paper or your computer word processing program.

Practice Quiz

True/False

16. _____ Agency law is a mixture of tort and contract laws.

17. _____ The principal is obliged to perform the contract made with a third-party.

18. _____ The principal works on behalf of an agent.

19. _____ Minors can appoint an agent without court approval.

20. _____ An employer–employee relationship exists when an employer gives an employee authority to act and enter into contracts on his or her behalf.

21. _____ A principal can authorize an independent contractor to enter into contracts.

22. _____ An express agency contract cannot be orally agreed upon.

23. _____ An agent given a power of attorney is known as an attorney-in-fact.

24. _____ A durable power of attorney remains effective even if the principal is incapacitated.

25. _____ In a contingency-fee contract, the principal must pay the agent prior to completion of agency.

26. _____ A principal also owes a duty to indemnify the agent for any losses the agent suffers because of the principal's conduct.

27. _____ An agent who has negligently or intentionally failed to perform his express duties is also liable to tort laws.

28. _____ The legal rule of imputed knowledge means that the principal is assumed to know what the agent knows..

29. _____ Constructive notices are not valid against strangers who assert claims of apparent agency.

30. _____ If an agency terminates by operation of law, there is no duty to notify third parties about the termination.

Multiple Choice

31. Who is an agent?

A. a party who agrees to act on behalf of another
B. a party who employs another person to act on his or her behalf
C. a party that directs a worker under an express or implied contract of employment
D. a party who receives the services of another for remuneration

32. Which of the following constitutes an agency?

A. principal-agent relationship
B. agent-agent relationship
C. principal-principal relationship
D. agent-independent contractor relationship

33. Which of the following types of relationship exists when a person hires another person to perform some form of physical service but does not authorize that person to enter into contracts on behalf his or her behalf?

A. employer-employee relationship
B. employer-agent relationship
C. principal-third party relationship
D. principal-agent relationship

34. Which of the following is true of a principal-independent contractor relationship?

A. Principals are bound by the authorized contracts of their independent contractors.
B. Independent contractors cannot be authorized by principals.
C. Independent contractors are employees of the principals.
D. Principals cannot directly employ independent contractors.

35. Which of the following is true of an express agency?

A. The agency involved is allowed to have multiple agents if necessary.
B. The agency is implied from the conduct of the parties.
C. The agency comes to effect when the principal ratifies an unauthorized act.
D. The agency arises when a principal creates the appearance of an agency that does not exist.

36. Which of the following is true about a durable power of attorney?

A. It is only effective as long as the principal is able.
B. It remains effective even though the principal is incapacitated.
C. It is effective even when the agency is an oral agreement.
D. It is only effective if the agent is a certified lawyer.

37. Which of the following describes an agency by estoppel?

A. an agency that arises when a principal ratifies a contract created by an unauthorized agent
B. an agency created when a principal and an agent expressly agree to enter into an agency agreement
C. an agency that is not expressly stated but is implied and inferred in the conduct of the parties
D. an agency that arises when a principal creates the appearance of an agency that in actuality does not exist

38. Which of the following is true of an apparent agency?

A. The authority of an apparent agent is implied from the conduct of the parties.
B. The third-party is not bound to a contracted created by an apparent agent.
C. The principal is bound to the contracts entered into by an apparent agent.
D. The actions of an apparent agent create an apparent agency.

39. What is imputed knowledge?

A. information collected by a principal prior to engaging in an agency
B. information collected by a principal on an agency
C. information learned by an agent that is attributed to the principal
D. information learned by a principal that is attributed to an agent

40. Which of the following would lead to the termination of an agency by operation of law?

A. loss or destruction of the subject matter of the agency
B. death of either the principal or agent
C. loss of a required qualification
D. a change in the law

Short Answer

41. What effect do agency agreements that are formed for illegal purposes have?

_____

_____

42. What governs the extent of authority granted to an agent in a principal-agent relationship?

_____

_____

43. What is an exclusive agency contract?

_____

_____

44. What is the most common form of agency?

_____

_____

45. Whose actions create an apparent agency?

_____

_____

46. Give three ways that the parties may terminate an agency relationship.

_____

_____

47. Give at least two ways that an agency relationship may terminate where a situation presents itself and thereby makes its fulfillment impossible.

_____

_____

48. What is imputed knowledge?

_____

_____

49. What determines whether or not an employee is an agent?

_____

_____

50. What is wrongful termination?

_____

_____

51. If an insurance company hires ten bounty hunters to apprehend a wanted felon, when do the agencies terminate?

_____

_____

52. What type of notice must parties who dealt with an agent be given when the agency is terminated by agreement?

_____

_____

53. When an agency terminates by operation of law, what type of duty does the principal owe to third parties?

_____

_____

54. What is special power of attorney?

_____

_____

55. What type of notice is usually given by a newspaper announcement upon the termination of an agency?

_____

_____

Answers to Refresh Your Memory

1. principal [p. 487]
2. agency [p. 487]
3. principal-agent relationship [p. 488]
4. principal-independent contractor [p. 4689]
5. express agency [p. 489]
6. exclusive agency contract [p. 489]
7. express agency [p. 490]
8. power of attorney [p. 490]
9. special power of attorney [p. 490]
10. implied agency [p. 491]
11. accepts an unauthorized act created by an unauthorized agent [p. 491]
12. duty to compensate [p. 493]
13. duty to indemnify [p. 493]
14. Agency coupled with an interest [p. 496]
15. wrongful termination [p. 497]

Critical Thought Exercise Model Answer

A court would have to determine Polk's status as to employee versus independent contractor based upon answering several questions.

Did the Hamilton's exercise control over the details of Polk's work? Polk was instructed to trim the tree to an approximate size. The Hamilton's gave no other instructions concerning how the task was to be accomplished.

Was Polk engaged in an occupation or business distinct from that of the Hamilton's? Polk had an ongoing handyman business and accepted work from numerous people. The Hamilton's were not in the home repair or landscape maintenance business.

Is the type of work usually done under the employer's direction or by a specialist without supervision? Tree trimming is a job that requires skill and training. It is not the type of job a homeowner would supervise. The Hamilton's did not supervise Polk.

Does the employer supply the tools at the place of work? Polk had his own van with tools for his jobs. In this case, Polk did borrow a saw and a piece of rope, but this does not appear to be the usual way that Polk accomplishes his tasks.

For how long was Polk employed? Polk was only hired for a limited time until a specific job was completed. He was hired separately for the bathroom work and the tree trimming.

What was the method of payment—periodic or upon completion of the job? Polk was paid an hourly wage, but he was paid by the job instead of receiving a paycheck every week or month.

What degree of skill is required of the worker? Each of the jobs performed by Polk required skill and specialized knowledge. The average homeowner does not have the skill or ability to trim a large tree. A tree trimming service usually performs the cutting back of a large tree.

Polk's status as an independent contractor is borne out by the above analysis. Polk had his own handyman business with his own tools and possessed special skills for accomplishing tasks that are often handled by trades people and specialists. The fact that he was hired for more than one job does not change the fact that he acted as an independent contractor on each job. Therefore, the Hamilton's were under no obligation to purchase workers' compensation insurance for Polk.

Answers to Practice Quiz

True/False

16. True. Agency law is a large body of common law that governs agency; a mixture of contract law and tort law. [p. 487]

17. True. Principal's obligation to perform the contract. [p. 487]

18. False. A principal–agent relationship is formed when an employer hires an employee and gives that employee authority to act and enter into contracts on his or her behalf.. [p. 488]

19. False. Generally, persons who lack contractual capacity, such as insane persons and minors, cannot appoint agents. However, the court can appoint legal guardians or other representatives to handle the affairs of insane persons, minors, and others who lack capacity to contract. With court approval, these representatives can enter into enforceable contracts on behalf of the persons they represent. [p. 487-488]

20. False. An employer–employee relationship exists when an employer hires an employee to perform some form of physical service.. [p. 488]

21. True. A principal can authorize an independent contractor to enter into contracts. Principals are bound by the authorized contracts of their independent contractors. [p. 489]

22. False. Express agency contracts can be either oral or written unless the Statute of Frauds stipulates that they must be written. [p. 489]

23. True. The agent is called an attorney-in-fact even though he or she does not have to be a lawyer. Powers of attorney must be written. [p. 490]

24. True. A durable power of attorney remains effective even though the principal is incapacitated. [p. 490]

25. False. Under a contingency-fee contract the principal owes a duty to pay the agent the agreed-upon contingency fee only if the agency is completed. [p. 493]

26. True. A principal also owes a duty to indemnify the agent for any losses the agent suffers because of the principal's conduct. This duty usually arises where an agent is held liable for the principal's misconduct. [p. 493]

27. True. An agent who does not perform his or her express duties or fails to use the standard degree of care, skill, or diligence is liable to the principal for breach of contract. An agent who has negligently or intentionally failed to perform properly is also liable in tort. [p. 494]

28. True. The legal rule of imputed knowledge means that the principal is assumed to know what the agent knows. This is so even if the agent does not tell the principal certain relevant information.. [p. 494]

29. False. Constructive notice is valid against strangers who assert claims of apparent agency. [p. 496]

30. True. If an agency terminates by operation of law, there is no duty to notify third parties about the termination. [p. 497]

Multiple Choice

31. A. Answer A is correct. An agent is a party who agrees to act on behalf of another. [p. 487]

32. A. Answer A is correct. The principal–agent relationship is commonly referred to as an agency [p. 487]

33. A. Answer A is the correct answer. An employer–employee relationship is a relationship that results when an employer hires an employee to perform some task or service but the employee has not been authorized to enter into contracts on behalf of his employer. [p. 488]

34. A. Answer A is the correct answer. A principal can authorize an independent contractor to enter into contracts. Principals are bound by the authorized contracts of their independent contractors. [p. 489]

35. A. Answer A is the correct answer. If an agency is not an exclusive agency, the principal can employ more than one agent to try to accomplish a stated purpose. When multiple agents are employed, the agencies with all the agents terminate when any one of the agents accomplishes the stated purpose. [p. 489]

36. B. Answer B is the correct answer. A durable power of attorney remains effective even though the principal is incapacitated. [p. 490]

37. D. Answer D is the correct answer. Apparent agency (or agency by estoppel) arises when a principal creates the appearance of an agency that in actuality does not exist. [p. 492]

38. C. Answer C is the correct answer. Where an apparent agency is established, the principal is estopped (stopped) from denying the agency relationship and is bound to contracts entered into by the apparent agent while acting within the scope of the apparent agency. [p. 492]

39. C. Answer C is the correct answer. Imputed knowledge refers to information that is learned by an agent that is attributed to the principal. [p. 494]

40. B. Answer B is the correct answer. An agency contract is terminated by operation of law in the following circumstances- the death of either the principal or agent, the insanity of either the principal or the agent, the bankruptcy of the principal, the outbreak of a war between the principal's country and the agent's country [p. 497]

Short Answer

41. They are against public policy, thus void and unenforceable. [p. 488]

42. This authority is governed by any express agreement between the parties and implied from the circumstances of the agency. [p. 488]

43. Exclusive agency contract is a contract a principal and agent enter into that says the principal cannot employ any agent other than the exclusive agent. [p. 489]

44. An express agency. [p. 489]

45. The principal's actions create an apparent agency. [p. 492]

46. Lapse of time, mutual agreement, occurrence of a specified event, and purpose achieved are three ways that the parties may terminate an agency relationship. [p. 496]

47. The loss or destruction of the subject matter of the agency, loss of a required qualification, and a change in law are ways that an agency relationship may terminate if a situation presents itself that makes the agency purpose impossible to fulfill. [p. 497]

48. Information that is learned by an agent that is attributed to the principal imputed knowledge. [p. 494]

49. If an employee is given the authority to enter into contracts on behalf of the principal-employer, then the employee is an agent. [p. 488]

50. Wrongful termination is the termination of an agency contract in violation of the terms of the agency contract. [p. 497]

51. The agencies with all of the agents end when any one of the agents fulfills the stated purpose. Here, when one of the bounty hunters captures the wanted felon. [p. 496]

52. These parties must be given direct notice of termination when the agency is terminated by agreement of the parties. [p. 496]

53. There's no duty to notify third parties if an agency terminates by operation of law. [p. 497]

54. Special power of attorney is a power of attorney where a principal confers powers on an agent to act in specified matters on the principal's behalf. [p. 491]

55. Constructive notice usually involves placing a notice of the termination of the agency in a newspaper that is distributed throughout the community. [p. 496]

30 | LIABILITY OF PRINCIPALS, AGENTS, AND INDEPENDENT CONTRACTORS

Chapter Overview

The previous chapter gave you an overview of the creation and termination of an agency, as well as the various types of agencies. This chapter expands on what you have learned about agency by discussing the duties of principals and agents, as well as liability for the breach of these duties.

Objectives

Upon completion of the exercises in this chapter, you should be able to:
1. Describe the duty of loyalty owed by an agent to a principal.
2. Identify and describe the principal's liability for the tortious conduct of an agent.
3. Describe the principal's and agent's liability on third-party contracts.
4. Describe how independent contractor status is created.
5. Describe the principal's liability for torts of an independent contractor.

Practical Application

You will become aware of the duties of both the agent as well and the principal, as one day you may be in a position of fulfilling either of these roles. You will be more cognizant of the liabilities that both the agent and principal face for breach of their respective duties, thereby giving you more insight into what is expected of an agent and a principal.

Helpful Hints

Many of the concepts that you will learn in this chapter are filled with common sense. However, in order to remember the duties of the principal and agent and the liabilities for breach of these duties, it is much easier to not only list them separately, but to commit them to memory by using the suggested mnemonics given in the Study Tips section that follows. Since this chapter is an expansion of the previous chapter, the concepts are easily learned.

Study Tips

Liability of Principals, Agents, and Independent Contractors

Under agency law, principals and agents are liable to each other for breach of specific duties, and principals, agents, and independent contractors are liable to third parties for contracts and tortious conduct.

Agent's Duty of Loyalty to the Principal

The agent owes a duty to be faithful to the principal.

Self-Dealing. An agent is prohibited from undisclosed self-dealing with the principal.

Usurping an Opportunity. An agent may not usurp an opportunity that belongs to the principal unless upon consideration the principal has rejected it.

Competing with the Principal. An agent may not compete with the principal during the agency relationship.

Misuse of Confidential Information. An agent may not misuse confidential information regarding the principal' affairs.

Dual Agency. An agent may not act for two or more different principals in the same transaction as this is a dual agency.
- The parties may agree to a dual agency.

Tort Liability to Third Parties

The principal and agent are personally responsible for their own tortious conduct.
- The principal is liable for the agent's conduct if he or she was acting within the scope of his or her authority.
- The agent is only liable for the torts of the principal if he or she directly or indirectly participates in or abets and aids the conduct of the principal.
- The factors that are examined in determining whether an agent's conduct was within the scope of his or her employment include:
  - Did the principal request or authorize the agent's act?
  - Was the principal's purpose being advanced by the agent when the act occurred?
  - Was the agent employed to perform the act that he or she completed?
  - Was the act accomplished during the time that the time of employment authorized by the principal?

Negligence. Liability for negligence is based on the doctrine of *respondeat superior*, which assesses liability based on the employment relationship between the principal and agent not on any fault of the principal. There are some situations where liability is not clear.
  - Frolic and Detour. This refers to the situation where an agent performs a personal errand while performing a job for the principal.
    - Negligent acts in this situation are viewed on a case-by-case basis.
    - The court will examine if the detour is minor or substantial.
  - The Coming and Going Rule. Under common law, a principal is not held liable for injuries caused by employees and agents who are on their way to or from work.
    - This rule holds true regardless if the principal provided the transportation.
  - Dual-Purpose Mission. This situation refers to when the agent is doing something for him or herself and for the principal.
    - The majority rule holds that both the principal and agent are liable if an injury occurs while the agent is on this sort of mission.

Intentional Tort. If the intentional tort occurs outside of the principal's scope of business, the principal is not liable.
- The doctrine of vicarious liability applies in the situation where the agent or employee commits an intentional tort in the scope of his or her employment.
  - The Motivation Test. If the agent's motivation in performing the intentional tort was the principal's business, then the principal is liable for any injury caused by the tort.
  - The Work-Related Test. If the intentional tort was performed during a work-related time or space, the principle is liable for any injuries caused by the intentional torts.
    - The motivation of the agent is not considered in the use of this test.

Misrepresentation. This tort is also referred to as fraud or deceit.
- The principal is liable for the misrepresentation of the agent if it is made during the scope of his or her employment.
- The third party may rescind the contract with the principal and recover any consideration paid or affirm the contract and recover damages.

Contract Liability to Third Parties

If an agent is authorized by the principal to enter into a contract with a third party, then the principal is liable on the contract.

Fully Disclosed Agency. The third party knows for whom the agent is acting.
- The principal is liable in a fully disclosed agency situation.
- The agent will also be held liable if he or she guarantees that the principal will perform the contract.

Partially Disclosed Agency. The agent's status is disclosed but the principal's identity is undisclosed.
- Both the principal and agent are liable on a third-party contract.
- If the agent is made to pay, he or she may seek indemnification from the principal.

Undisclosed Agency. If a third party does not know about the agency or the principal's identity, then an undisclosed agency exists.
- The principal and the agent are liable on a contract with a third party, as the agent's nondisclosure makes him a principal to the contract.
- The agent may seek indemnification from the principal if he or she is made to pay on the contract.

Agent Exceeding the Scope of Authority. An agent who enters into a contract with a third party has, in essence, warranted that he or she has the authority to do so.
- The principal will not be liable on the contract where the agent has exceeded his or her authority on the contract, unless the principal ratifies the contract.

Independent Contractor

The degree of control that an employer has over an agent is the most important factor in determining whether someone is an employee or an independent contractor.

Factors for Determining Independent Contractors. Factors considered in determining independent contractor status include but are not limited to:

- The amount of skill needed to finish the task.
- Whether the principal provides the equipment and tools used in the job.
- Whether payment is by time or by the job.
- Whether the employer controls the means and manner of completing the job.

Liability for Independent Contractor's Contracts. A principal can authorize an independent contractor to enter into contracts and will be liable on those contracts.

Liability for Independent Contractor's Torts. The general rule is that a principal is not liable for the torts of its independent contractors. However, there are some exceptions:

Exceptions in Which a Principal Is Liable for the Torts of an Independent Contractor. The law imposes liability on the principal for the tortious acts of an independent contractor in certain circumstances.

Inherently Dangerous Activities. Principals may not avoid strict liability for dangerous activities by assigning them to independent contractors.

Negligence in the Selection of an Independent Contractor. The hiring of an unqualified or knowingly dangerous person who injures someone while on the job will cause the principal to be held liable for such negligent selection of this type of independent contractor.

Refresh Your Memory

The following exercise will give you the opportunity to test your memory of the principles given in this chapter. Read the question twice and place your answer in the blank provided. Review the chapter material for any question that you are unable to answer or remember.

1. Harrison hires an agent to look for a three-bedroom house in Atlanta. Elaine, the agent, finds a three-bedroom house in Harrison's budget but buys it herself without informing Harrison. This is an instance of the agent's _____.

2. If a casting agent works for two Hollywood actors, the agent is liable for _____.

3. _____ is a rule that says an employer is liable for the tortuous conduct of its employees or agents while they are acting within the scope of the employer's authority.

4. _____ occurs where a principal is liable for an agent's tortious conduct because of the employment contract between the principal and agent, not because the principal was personally at fault.

5. Gem's principal asked her to pick up his dry-cleaning on her way to work. After she had picked up the dry-cleaning and while driving to work, Gem knocked over an old man crossing the street as she did not apply the brakes in time. Under the theory of _____, Gem's principal is liable to the injured man.

6. _____ is a situation in which an agent does something during the course of his or her employment to further his or her own interests rather than the principal's.

7. Dan asks his agent Jude to drop off some medicines at his mother's house. On his way back, Jude decides to have lunch at a diner two blocks away from his workplace. While walking back to work, he jaywalks at a green signal on the road, causing a motorcyclist to hit the kerb and injure himself while attempting to avoid hitting Jude. Under the concept of _____, Dan is liable for the injuries caused to the motorcyclist.

8. A dual-purpose mission is a situation that occurs when _____.

9. An actor asks an agent to place an order for a couch on the agent's way back to work. This is an instance of _____.

10. Most jurisdictions hold the _____ liable for injuries caused on a dual-purpose mission.

11. Under the _____ test, if the agent committed an intentional tort to promote the principal's business, the principal is liable for any injury caused by the tort.

12. Under the _____ test, the principal is liable for any intentional torts committed by an agent during working hours on the principal's premises.

13. An employee motivated by jealousy injures a colleague who dated her boyfriend, on work premises and during work hours. Based on the _____ test, the principal is liable.

14. A _____ is a deceit in which an agent makes an untrue statement that he or she knows is not true.

15. In a fully-disclosed agency, the contract is between _____.

Critical Thought Exercise

Earl West works for Dubyah International, an Illinois corporation that sells commercial fixtures and lighting to cities, developers, mall owners, and the government. West is mostly responsible for making sales calls for light poles, light standards, and lighting towers. West is on the road 40 or more weeks per year and often does not come back to his home or office for three or more months at a time. Over the course of his 17 years of employment with Dubyah, West has had several stretches on the road that last six months or more. When West is traveling for Dubyah, he often has to shop for food, toiletries, clothing, gifts, and business-related items, such as computer accessories for his laptop computer.

During a sales trip to Indianapolis, Indiana, in March 2006, West found it necessary to wash his laundry and buy an anniversary present for his wife. West went to the mall and then to Suds Town Laundromat to wash his clothes. While wrapping the present on a laundry-folding table, another patron of the Suds Town, Mike, spilled fabric softener on the wrapping paper. West then overloaded a dryer with flammable items, in direct violation of the warnings and rules posted directly above the dryer. This caused a dryer fire. When Mike verbally attacked West for starting the dryer fire, West punched Mike in the eye, causing severe eye damage. Suds Town then burned to the ground due to the dryer fire started by West.

Mike and Suds Town sue Dubyah for the damage caused by West. Dubyah argues that when the events at Suds Town occurred, West was not acting within the scope of his employment, relieving it of all liability.

If you were the judge in this case, what law would you apply and which party would prevail?

Please compose your answer to the Critical Thinking Exercise using a separate sheet of paper or your computer word processing program.

Practice Quiz

True/False

16. _____ The duty of loyalty is a fiduciary duty owned by an agent not to act adversely to the interests of the principal.

17. _____ A third-party offer to an agent must be conveyed to the principal.

18. _____ Agents can compete with the principal during the course of the agency if the principal agrees.

19. _____ An agent does not violate his or her duty of loyalty by serving two parties with the same interest.

20. _____ Middlemen and finders are not considered dual agents.

21. _____ Dual agency is permitted if all parties to a transaction agree to it.

22. _____ Battery committed by an agent in the principal's premises and during the scope of employment is considered an unintentional tort.

23. _____ Principals are liable for negligence caused by an agent during substantial frolic and detour.

24. _____ The agent is compulsorily liable for any intentional or innocent misrepresentation made by the principal in a transaction.

25. _____ The principal is liable for the innocent misrepresentation made by an agent acting within the scope of employment.

26. _____ A fully disclosed agency results if a third party entering into a contract knows the actual identity of the principal.

27. _____ A partially disclosed agency can be created by mistake.

28. _____ If an agent exceeds his or her scope of authority, a principal is bound on the contract only if he or she ratifies the contract.

29. _____ Ratification of a contract is a situation in which a principal accepts an agent's unauthorized contract.

30. _____ An independent contractor cannot represent more than one principal at a time.

Multiple Choice

31. Which of the following is a fiduciary duty owed by an agent not to act adversely to the interests of the principal?

A. duty of loyalty
B. duty of undertaking
C. duty of discharge
D. duty of resolution

32. Which of the following is true of an agent's undisclosed self-dealing?

A. It does not violate the duty of loyalty.
B. The principal cannot rescind purchases made.
C. The principal can ratify the purchase.
D. The principal must accept liability.

33. Which of the following is an instance of misuse of confidential information?

A. An agent gives the seller the principal's name and phone number in a fully disclosed transaction.
B. A principal gives the contact details of an agent to a third-party without the agent's knowledge.
C. An agent withholds critical information from the principal about the agency.
D. An agent divulges details of his past employer to his principal.

34. What is vicarious liability?

A. non-liability
B. liability for multiple torts
C. liability without knowledge
D. liability without fault

35. According to the coming and going rule, what is the liability of the principal for injuries caused by its agents and employees while they are on their way to or from work?

A. complete liability
B. vicarious liability
C. limited liability
D. no liability

36. Which of the following is considered an intentional tort?

A. negligence
B. innocent misrepresentation
C. fraud
D. dual-purpose mission

37. In which of the following cases is a motivation test used to establish the employee's motive?

A. An employee commits a tort to promote the principal's business, outside work premises.
B. An employee commits an intentional tort against another employee at work premises.
C. An employee commits an unintentional tort that helps promote the principal's business.
D. An employee assaults another employee due to personal reasons.

38. Which of the following is true of misrepresentation?

A. An intentional misrepresentation by an agent is not considered fraud or deceit.
B. The principal is not liable for an agent's intentional misrepresentation.
C. A third party cannot recover damages from the principal due to an agent's intentional misrepresentation.
D. The principal is liable for an agent's innocent misrepresentation.

39. Which of the following best describes a partially disclosed agency?

A. an agent with multiple principals who do not know each other's identities
B. a transaction in which the third party does not know the identity of the agent
C. a transaction in which the third party knows the agent, not the principal
D. an agent who discloses only the name of his or her principal in a transaction

40. Which of the following is true of an undisclosed agency?

A. The third party has no knowledge of the agency.
B. The third party knows the agent, not the principal.
C. All transactions with the third party are made by the principal without involving the agent.
D. Transactions under such an agency are considered unlawful.

Short Answer

41. What is a fully disclosed agency?

_____

_____

42. What are the three classifications of agencies that establish contract liability to third parties?

_____

_____

43. Give at least two examples of what is considered an agent's breach of loyalty.

_____

_____

44. If an agent exceeds the scope of his or her authority, the principal is not liable on the contract unless?

_____

_____

45. What is the doctrine of *respondeat superior*?

_____

_____

46. Under the doctrine of *respondeat superior*, employer liability is based upon what legal theory?

_____

_____

46. If Carl stops at a gas station for a drink while making deliveries and injures a motorist while pulling out of the gas station, who is liable for the motorist's injuries caused by Carl's tortious conduct during this frolic and detour?

_____

_____

47. What is the rationale used in applying the "coming and going rule"?

_____

_____

48. Why aren't principals generally liable for the torts of independent contractors?

_____

_____

50. Acme Air Service hires Fuel Transport to haul jet fuel to its airport facility, and the truck explodes and kills six people because the driver of the truck drove too fast. Is the principal liable for the negligence of the independent contractor?

_____

_____

51. What is a dual purpose mission?

_____

_____

52. What is a work-related test?

_____

_____

53. What is intentional misrepresentation?

_____

_____

54. What is a partially disclosed agency?

_____

_____

55. What is ratification of a contract?

_____

_____

Answers to Refresh Your Memory

1. usurping an opportunity [p. 501]
2. dual agency [p. 502]
3. Respondeat superior [p. 503]

4. Vicarious liability [p. 503]
5. vicarious liability [p. 503]
6. Frolic and detour [p. 503]
7. frolic and detour [p. 503]
8. frolic and detour [p. 503]
9. a principal requests an agent to run an errand when the agent is on his or her own personal business [p. 504]
10. dual-purpose mission [p. 504]
11. principal and the agent [p. 504]
12. motivation [p. 505]
13. work-related [p. 505]
14. work-related [p. 505]
15. misrepresentation [p. 506]

Critical Thought Exercise Model Answer

An employer may be liable for the torts of its employee under the doctrine or respondeat superior. This doctrine imposes vicarious, or indirect, liability on the employer without regard to the fault of the employer for torts committed by an employee in the course or scope of employment. There are several factors that a court will usually consider in deciding whether or not a particular act occurred within the course or scope of employment.

Whether the act was authorized by the employer. West was expected to be on the road making sales calls for long periods of time. Dubyah knew that West had to conduct personal business during sales trips for his employer.

The time, place, and purpose of the act. West was on a sales trip to a city where he was conducting Dubyah's business. The purpose of the act was to clean his laundry so that he could remain on the sales trip for a prolonged period. The overall purpose still favors the employer and would be within the scope of employment, especially when the past employment history and prior lengthy trips are taken into account.

Whether the act was one commonly performed by employees on behalf of their employers. Doing laundry and buying a gift may seem to be very personal tasks unless they are viewed from the broader perspective of the traveling salesperson. It is more economical for Dubyah and allows more sales calls to be made if West says on the road and performs his personal tasks on the road. The overall task or act is that of a sales trip and is clearly within the normal scope of West's duties that he usually performs for Dubyah.

The extent to which the employer's interest was advanced. The reasoning for this factor is the same. Dubyah benefits by having its sales representatives remain on prolonged trips. It is therefore expected that personal business will have to be conducted, allowing the employer to benefit from numerous sales calls to sell its products.

There was no instrumentality (such as an automobile) used for the act in this case, so the fact that an employer did or did not supply the instrumentality that caused an injury is not relevant to this analysis.

Whether the employer had reason to know that the employee would do the act in question and whether the employee had ever done it before. This factor is the most import one for deciding the liability issue. The act of conducting personal business while on the employer's sales trip was obviously an act that had been repeated innumerable times by West over 17 years of employment with Dubyah. Dubyah knew about the long sales trips and apparently was active in creating the situation where personal business had to be conducted while on company trips.

Whether the act involved a serious crime. This factor is the one that draws a distinction between the negligent act of overloading the dryer and causing a fire and the act of striking Mike and severely injuring Mike's eye. The employer is not liable for the intentional torts of employees committed outside the employer's scope of business. However, an employer is liable under the doctrine of vicarious liability for intentional torts of employees committed within the employee's scope of employment. The court will apply either the motivation test or the work-related test. Under the motivation test, if the employee's motivation in committing the intentional tort is to promote the employer's business, the employer is liable. However, if the employee's motivation in committing the tort was personal, the employer is not liable. Under this rule, Dubyah would not be liable to Mike because West was motivated to conduct personal business, not company business. Under the work-related test, however, the result would be different. If the tort is committed within a work-related time or space, the employer is liable. Since West is working around the clock while on a sales trip, some states would hold the employer, Dubyah, liable for both the damage to Suds Town and the damage to Mike's eye.

Answers to Practice Quiz

True/False

16. True. Duty of loyalty is a fiduciary duty owed by an agent not to act adversely to the interests of the principal. [p. 501]

17. True. A third-party offer to an agent must be conveyed to the principal. [p. 501]

18. True. Agents are prohibited from competing with the principal during the course of an agency unless the principal agrees. [p. 502]

19. False. An agent cannot meet a duty of loyalty to two parties with conflicting interests. Dual agency occurs when an agent acts for two or more different principals in the same transaction. This practice is generally prohibited unless all the parties involved in the transaction agree to it. If an agent acts as an undisclosed dual agent, he or she must forfeit all compensation received in the transaction. [p. 502]

20. True. Some agents, such as middlemen and finders, are not considered dual agents. This is because they only bring interested parties together; they do not take part in any negotiations. [p. 502]

21. True. Dual agency occurs when an agent acts for two or more different principals in the same transaction. This practice is generally prohibited unless all the parties involved in the transaction agree to it. [p. 502]

22. False. Intentional torts include acts such as assault, battery, false imprisonment, and other intentional conduct that causes injury to another person. A principal is not liable for the intentional torts of agents and employees that are committed outside the principal's scope of business. [p. 504]

23. False. Principals are generally relieved of liability if the agent's frolic and detour is substantial. [pp. 503-504]

24. False. A principal is liable for the intentional and innocent misrepresentations made by an agent acting within the scope of employment. [p. 506]

25. True. A principal is liable for the intentional and innocent misrepresentations made by an agent acting within the scope of employment. [p. 506]

26. True. A fully disclosed agency is an agency in which a contracting third party knows (1) that the agent is acting for a principal and (2) the identity of the principal. [p. 507]

27. True. A partially disclosed agency can be created either expressly or by mistake. [p. 507]

28. True. If the agent exceeds the scope of his or her authority, he principal is not liable on the contract. A principal is bound on the contract only if she ratifies the contract. [p. 508]

29. True. Ratification of a contract is a situation in which a principal accepts an agent's unauthorized contract. [p. 508]

30. False. Independent contractors usually work for a number of clients, have their own offices, hire employees, and control the performance of their work. [p. 509]

Multiple Choice

31. A. Answer A is correct. Duty of loyalty is a fiduciary duty owed by an agent not to act adversely to the interests of the principal.[p. 501]

32. C. Answer C is correct. Agents are generally prohibited from undisclosed self-dealing with the principal. An agent who engages in undisclosed self-dealing with the principal has violated his duty of loyalty to the principal. If there has been undisclosed dealing by an agent, the principal can rescind the purchase and recover the money paid to the agent. As an alternative, the principal can ratify the purchase. [p. 501]

33. D. Answer D is the correct answer. In the course of an agency, the agent often acquires confidential information about the principal's affairs (e.g., business plans, technological innovations, customer lists, and trade secrets). The agent is under a legal duty not to disclose or misuse confidential information either during or after the course of the agency. [p. 502]

34. D. Answer D is the correct answer. Vicarious liability is liability without fault. Vicarious liability occurs where a principal is liable for an agent's tortious conduct because of the employment contract between the principal and agent, not because the principal was personally at fault. [p. 503]

35. D. Answer D is the correct answer. Under the common law, a principal is generally not liable for injuries caused by its agents and employees while they are on their way to or from work. This so-called coming and going rule, which is sometimes referred to as the going and coming rule, applies even if the principal supplies the agent's automobile or other transportation or pays for gasoline, repairs, and other automobile operating expenses. [p. 504]

36. C. Answer C is the correct answer. Intentional torts include acts such as assault, battery, false imprisonment, and other intentional conduct that causes injury to another person. [p. 504]

37. A. Answer A is the correct answer. Under the motivation test, if the agent's motivation in committing an intentional tort is to promote the principal's business, the principal is liable for any injury caused by the tort. [p. 505]

38. D. Answer B is the correct answer. A principal is liable for the intentional and innocent misrepresentations made by an agent acting within the scope of employment. [p. 506]

39. C. Answer C is the correct answer. Partially disclosed agency is an agency in which the contracting third party knows that the agent is acting for the principal but does not know the identity of the principal. [p. 507]

40. A. Answer A is the correct answer,. An undisclosed agency occurs when a third party is unaware of the existence of an agency. [p. 508]

Short Answer

41. An agency in which a contracting third party knows that the agent is acting for a principal and the third party knows the identity of the principal. [p. 507]

42. Fully disclosed agency, partially disclosed agency, undisclosed agency. [p. 507]

43. Usurping an opportunity that belongs to the principal and the misuse of confidential information about the principal's affairs are two examples of an agent's breach of loyalty. [p. 501-502]

44. The principal ratifies it. [p. 508]

45. It is a rule that says an employer is liable for the tortious conduct of its employees or agents while they are acting within the scope of its authority. [p. 503]

46. The doctrine of *respondeat superior* is based on the legal premise of vicarious liability, meaning the principal is liable because of his or her employment contract with the agent not due to any fault on his or her part. [p. 503]

47. Under the frolic and detour rule, if the deviation is minor, the principal is liable for injuries caused by the agent's torts. Stopping to get a drink while making deliveries would either be a minor frolic and detour or an expected part of Carl's job, keeping the act within the scope of employment. [p. 503-504]

48. Since principals do not control where their employees and agents live, they should not be held liable for tortious conduct of agents on their way to and from work. [p. 504]

49. The rationale behind this rule is that principals do not control the means by which the results are accomplished. [p. 510]

50. Principals cannot avoid strict liability for inherently dangerous activities assigned to independent contractors. Hauling jet fuel is a dangerous activity, so Acme Air Service will be liable for the negligence of Fuel Transport. [p. 510]

51. A dual-purpose mission is a situation that occurs when a principal requests an employee or agent to run an errand or do another act for the principal while the agent is on his or her own personal business. [p. 504]

52. A work-related test is a test that determines whether an agent committed an intentional tort within a work-related time or space; if so, the principal is liable for any injury caused by the agent's intentional tort. [p. 505]

53. Intentional misrepresentation is a deceit in which an agent makes an untrue statement that he or she knows is not true. [p. 506]

54. A partially disclosed agency is an agency in which a contracting third party knows that the agent is acting for a principal but does not know the identity of the principal. [p. 507]

55. Ratification of a contract is a situation in which a principal accepts an agent's unauthorized contract. [p. 508]

31 | EMPLOYMENT, WORKER PROTECTION, AND IMMIGRATION LAWS

Chapter Overview

This chapter examines the statutes that have been enacted to protect workers, including workers' compensation, minimum wage and overtime pay, occupational safety, pension, immigration, unemployment, Social Security, and other laws that protect employees from unfair treatment.

Objectives

Upon completion of the exercises in this chapter, you should be able to:
1. Explain how state workers' compensation programs work and describe the benefits available.
2. Describe employers' duty to provide safe working conditions under the Occupational Safety and Health Act.
3. Describe the minimum wage and overtime pay rules of the Fair Labor Standards Act.
4. Describe the protections afforded by the Family and Medical Leave Act.
5. Describe immigration laws and how they apply to the employment relationship.

Practical Applications

Upon mastering the material in this chapter, you should be able to recognize the situations where employee rights and protections are applicable and the specific laws that cover a dispute or loss of income. You will understand the limits of the protections and the employee's requirements that must be met to gain protection under the various statutes.

Helpful Hints

Both the employee and employer benefit by a clear understanding of how various employment protection statutes function. The requirements of some laws apply only to specific employers, based upon the qualifying language of the statute. Employees often have requirements of notice and cooperation built into the statute with which they must comply to gain enforcement of their rights. Employers must understand and adhere to government regulation in the workplace or they may be subject to the high costs of law suits and lost production in the workplace.

Study Tips

It is just as important to understand when the employment laws may apply as it is to understand the technical requirements built into the individual statutes. You should develop your understanding of employment laws by organizing the material into general areas.

Employment, Worker Protection and Immigration Law

Prior to the industrial Revolution, employment was subject to the common law of contracts and agency law. Industrialization brought unequal bargaining power of employers compared to employees, and the legislation of statutes that protect workers. Today, employment law is a mixture of contract and agency law and government regulation, with immigration law providing regulation of non-citizen workers.

Workers' Compensation

These acts were enacted to compensate employees for injuries that occurred on the job regardless of fault.

- The amount of compensation payable to the employee is set by statute.
- Payment under the workers' compensation statute is the employee's exclusive remedy, meaning that an employee cannot sue his/her employer when he/she is injured on the job.

Workers' Compensation Insurance. States generally require employers to purchase insurance from private insurance companies or state funds to cover workers' compensation claims.

Employment-Related Injury. A claimant must demonstrate that the injury arose out of and in the course of his or her employment before an injury is compensable under workers' compensation.

- Work-related injuries include those that happen while an employee is actively working, or at a company cafeteria, or while on a business-related lunch.
- Stress has often been found to be a work-related injury worthy of compensation.
- Accidents that occur at an off-premises restaurant for a personal lunch are not covered.

Exclusive Remedy. Because workers' compensation is an exclusive remedy, a lawsuit against an employer is not an option for an employee.

- The exception to this rule exists where an injury occurs to a worker as a result of an employer's intentional act to injure which allows a worker to sue his or her employer.

Occupational Safety

The Occupational Safety and Health Act was enacted to promote safety in the workplace and imposes record-keeping and reporting requirements upon the employer.

- The enforcement arm created by the act is the Occupational Safety and Health Administration (OSHA).
  - o OSHA has adopted regulations to enforce the safety standards created by the act.
  - o OSHA may inspect places of employment and cite the employer for violations.
  - o OSHA violations carry both civil and criminal penalties.

Specific Duty Standards. OSHA establishes standards regarding specific duties, such as setting the maximum exposure levels for hazardous materials.

General Duty Standards. OSHA imposes a general duty on employers to provide a working environment free from recognized hazards.

Fair Labor Standards Act (FSLA)

The FSLA prohibits child labor and establishes minimum wage and overtime pay requirements.

Child Labor. The FSLA forbids the use of oppressive child labor and makes it unlawful to ship goods produced by businesses that use oppressive child labor.

- Children under age 14 cannot work except as newspaper deliverers.
- Children ages 14 and 15 may work limited hours in nonhazardous jobs approved by the Department of Labor (examples: restaurants, gas stations).
- Children ages 16 and 17 may work unlimited hours in nonhazardous jobs.
- Persons 18 years and older may work at any job regardless if it is hazardous or not.
- *Exception.* Children who are exempt from the above rules include children who work in agricultural employment, child actors, and performers.

Minimum Wage. The FSLA establishes minimum wage and overtime pay requirements. Covered workers are to receive the minimum wage for their regular work hours.

- Managerial, administrative, and professional employees are exempt from the act's wage and hours provisions.
- Students and apprentices may be paid less than minimum wage as per the Department of Labor.

Overtime Pay. The FSLA requires that covered workers receive overtime pay for those hours worked beyond the regular work hours.

- Overtime pay is provided to nonexempt employees who work more than 40 hours per week.
    - They receive one and a half times their regular pay for hours in excess of the 40 hours.
    - Each week is treated separately.

Exemptions from Minimum Wage and Overtime Pay Requirements

- *Executive exemption.* Executives compensated by salary, engaged in management, with authority to hire employees, and regularly supervise two or more employees.
- *Administrative employee exemption.* Employees compensated by salary or fee, primarily performing office or non-manual work, required to exercise discretion and independent judgment.
- *Learned professional exemption.* Employees compensated by salary or fee, performing work of intellectual nature, possessed of advanced knowledge in a field of science or learning acquired through intellectual instruction.
- *Highly compensated employee exemption.* Highly compensated employees performing office or non-manual work, being paid $100,000 or more, and regularly performing at least one duty of an exempt executive, administrative, or professional employee.
- *Computer employee exemption.* Employees compensated by salary or fee, employed as a systems analyst, programmer, software engineer or similar, and are engaged in the design, development, documentation, analysis, creation, testing, or modification of computer systems or programs.
- *Outside sales representative exemption.* Employees making sales or obtaining orders or contracts for services, paid by the client or customer, and engaged away from employer's place of business.

Other Worker Protection Laws

Consolidated Omnibus Budget Reconciliation Act (COBRA). Provides that employee or his beneficiaries must have the opportunity to maintain group health coverage upon dismissal or death due to certain events.

- Government employees are covered by the Public Health Service Act.

Family and Medical Leave Act. The act guarantees workers unpaid time off for medical emergencies.
- Applies to employers with 50 or more employees.
- Employee must have worked for at least one year and performed at least 1,250 hours of work during the previous 12-month period.
- Covers time off for birth or care of child, serious health condition, and care for spouse, parent, or child with a serious health problem.
- Employee must be restored to their same or a similar position upon their return.
- An employer may deny restoration to a salaried employee who is among the highest-paid 10 percent of that employer's employees if the denial is necessary to prevent "substantial and grievous economic injury" to the employer's operations.

Employee Retirement Income Security Act (ERISA). ERISA is designed to prevent fraud and abuses associated with private pension funds.
- Requires that the pension plan be in writing and name a pension fund manager.
- ERISA dictates how the pension funds can be invested and sets time limits for when pension rights must vest.

Government Programs

Unemployment Compensation. Employers must pay unemployment taxes to compensate employees during periods of unemployment.
- Employee does not receive benefits if they are discharged for misconduct or quit without cause.

Social Security. Under the Federal Insurance Contributions Act (FICA) employees and employers make contributions to the Social Security Fund.
- The funds are used to pay current recipients of Social Security.

Immigration Laws

The Immigration Reform and Control Act forbids employers from hiring illegal immigrants.
- Employers must examine documents to determine employee's right to work in the country.

H-1B Foreign Guest Worker Visa. This is a non-immigrant visa that allows individuals with special skills to work in the US.
- The foreign guest worker must be sponsored by a US employer.
- The number of these visas is limited.

Refresh Your Memory

The following exercise will give you the opportunity to test your memory of the principles given in this chapter. Read the question twice and place your answer in the blank provided. Review the chapter material for any question that you are unable to answer or remember.

1. Insurance that employers obtain and pay for from private insurance companies or from government-sponsored programs is called the _____.

2. Workers cannot both receive workers' compensation and sue their employers in court for damages. This is called _____.

3. An OSHA standard that requires an employer to provide a work environment free from recognized hazards that are causing or are likely to cause death or serious physical harm to employees is called the _____ standard.

4. Children under the age of 14 cannot work except as _____.

5. Some cities have enacted minimum wage requirements, usually called _____ laws, which set higher minimum wage rates than the federal level.

6. The _____ exemption applies to employees who are compensated on a salary or fee basis, whose primary duty is the performance of office or nonmanual work, and whose work includes the exercise of discretion and independent judgment with respect to matters of significance.

7. The _____ exemption applies to employees compensated on a salary or fee basis that perform work that is predominantly intellectual in character, who possess advanced knowledge in a field of science or learning, and whose advanced knowledge was acquired through a prolonged course of specialized intellectual instruction.

8. _____ guarantees workers unpaid time off from work for family and medical emergencies and other specified situations.

9. ERISA is administered by the _____.

10. _____ occurs when an employee has a nonforfeitable right to receive pension benefits.

11. _____ is a federal system that provides limited retirement and death benefits to covered employees and their dependents.

12. _____ is a visa that allows U.S. employers to employ in the United States foreign nationals who are skilled in specialty occupations.

13. A(n) _____ visa holder is not eligible to work in the United States.

14. Issuance of _____ to an H-1B holder permits the foreign national to eventually obtain U.S. citizenship.

15. A(n) _____ is a visa that allows U.S. employers to employ in the United States foreign nationals who possess extraordinary ability for certain types of employment.

Critical Thought Exercise

Sid Frost worked as a merchandising supervisor for Global-Mart, Inc., a large discount store employing over 26,000 people. When Frost suffered his third stroke in April 1999, he took leave from work, which was covered by the Family and Medical Leave Act (FMLA) of 1993. The vice president of personnel for Global-Mart approved the leave. Mike Allen, who had been hired only two months after Frost in 1984, temporarily filled Frost's position. When Frost returned to work, he discovered that Allen had been promoted to senior supervisor and given a $7,000 raise. The senior supervisor position is filled from the supervisor classification based upon seniority. Global-Mart refused to allow Frost to return to his position as a supervisor and demoted him to a senior salesman position that required travel away from home on a weekly basis. Six weeks later Global-Mart fired Frost because he was unable to keep up the schedule required by his position and because his expense account was not timely filed by the end of the month.

Frost sues Global-Mart for violation of the FMLA based upon Global-Mart's failure to promote him to senior supervisor or return him to his prior position. Did Global-Mart violate the FMLA?

Please compose your answer to the Critical Thinking Exercise using a separate sheet of paper or your computer word processing program.

Practice Quiz

True/False

16. _____ Employees are required to purchase workers' compensation insurance from private insurance companies or state funds.

17. _____ For an injury to be compensable under workers' compensation, the claimant must prove that he or she was harmed by an employment-related injury.

18. _____ Workers' compensation insurance does not cover stress and mental illness that are employment related.

19. _____ Workers cannot both receive workers' compensation and sue their employers in court for damages.

20. _____ If an employer intentionally injures a worker, the worker cannot collect workers' compensation benefits.

21. _____ The general duty standard requires an employer to provide a work environment that does not result in its employees' mental stress.

22. _____ Only private employers, and not governmental bodies, come under the purview of the FSLA.

23. _____ The FLSA makes it unlawful to ship goods produced by businesses that use oppressive child labor.

24. _____ The Department of Labor permits employers to pay less than the minimum wage to students and apprentices.

25. _____ Overtime pay must always be set at twice the regular pay of an employee.

26. _____ Senior professors and physicists in research laboratories are entitled to federal overtime pay.

27. _____ Software developers and other computer professionals cannot claim overtime pay.

28. _____ The COBRA is an act designed to prevent fraud and other abuses associated with private pension funds.

29. _____ Workers who quit work without just cause can claim unemployment benefits.

30. _____ An H4 visa holder is eligible to work in the United States for minimum wages or higher.

Multiple Choice

31. Before the Industrial Revolution, the doctrine of _____ governed the employment relationship in the United States.

A. *respondeat superior*
B. *laissez-faire*
C. *scienter*
D. *voir dire*

32. Which of the following is true of workers' compensation?

A. Families of workers cannot claim workers' compensation despite the death of the worker.
B. The claim for workers' compensation must be filed with the employer.
C. Workers' compensation is only awarded for injuries resulting from the job.
D. Workers' compensation is a fixed amount throughout the country.

33. Workers' compensation is a(n) _____ remedy.

A. cumulative
B. exclusive
C. provisional
D. equitable

34. What is the employer's advantage in offering workers' compensation?

A. The employer need not pay for workers' compensation insurance.
B. The employer is exempt from having to offer paid medical leave.
C. The employer can offer lower basic pay to workers.
D. The employer can avoid a lawsuit by an injured worker.

35. In which of these situations can an employee sue an employer to recover employment-related injuries?

A. The employer intentionally injures a worker covered under workers' compensation.
B. The employer unintentionally injures a worker covered under workers' compensation.
C. The employee suffers an injury at work premises that is not related to work.
D. The employer is self-insured.

36. The OSHA guidelines that set safety rules for specific equipment, procedures, types of work, unique work conditions, and the like are known as _____.

A. standard of wellness
B. code of direction
C. specific duty standards
D. general standard of work

37. Which of the following is true of OSHA's general duty standard?

A. The standard needs to be established with each safety regulation.
B. It requires an employer to provide a working environment that does not result in mental stress of the employee.
C. OSHA has no say in safety violations of an employer as it is just a model act.
D. An employer is obliged to provide a work environment that is free from recognized hazards.

38. The FLSA applies to _____.

A. employees in government organizations
B. employees earning less than minimum wages
C. self-employed US citizens
D. employees engaged in the production of goods for interstate commerce

39. Which of the following is true of child labor regulations adopted by the Department of Labor?

A. Children employed in agriculture have no time or work restriction.
B. Children between the ages of 16 and 17 may work limited hours in hazardous jobs.
C. Children under the age of 14 may work limited hours in nonhazardous jobs.
D. Children between the ages of 14 and 15 may work unlimited hours in nonhazardous jobs.

40. Which of the following is true of the federal minimum wage?

A. An employer may not reduce minimum wage although he or she provides other benefits like food to the employees.
B. Apprentices cannot be paid less than minimum wages.
C. Managerial employees are not subject to minimum wage requirements.
D. Employees who earn tips, such as waiters and valets, are not entitled to minimum wage.

41. Who among the following is exempt from federal minimum wage requirement?

A. Kelly, a sales executive at a pharmacy
B. John, a waiter by day and a guitar teacher by night
C. Orlando, a telemarketer
D. Tsun, a software applications developer

42. To be covered by the FMLA, an employee must _____.

A. have worked for the employer for at least six months
B. not have claimed maternity leave in the past
C. have performed more than 1,250 hours of service
D. be suffering from a serious injury or ailment

43. _____ occurs when an employee has a nonforfeitable right to receive pension benefits.

A. Easement
B. Vesting
C. Anti-lapse
D. Reconciliation

44. Which of the following benefits is a component of Social Security benefits?

A. disability benefits
B. legal assistance
C. unemployment compensation
D. workers' compensation

45. Cliff Thomas, a cardiologist, emigrates from the U.K. to the U.S. Under which of the following visa categories can his wife live in the U.S. as Mr. Thomas' dependent?

A. H1
B. H-1C
C. H4
D. H-1B

Short Answer

46. "Workers' compensation is an exclusive remedy." Elaborate on this statement with the help of an example.

_____
_____

47. Explain the purpose of enacting the Occupational Safety and Health Act.

_____
_____

48. What is the general duty standard?

_____
_____

49. Describe the measures taken by the U.S. Department of Labor against oppressive child labor.

_____
_____

50. Outline the minimum wage requirement established by the FLSA. How are wages given to a tipped employee?

_____
_____

51. List the various exemptions from minimum wage and overtime pay requirements.

_____

_____

52. Explain COBRA and ERISA.

_____

_____

53. How is Social Security awarded in the U.S.A.?

_____

_____

54. What is an EB-1 visa? Who qualifies for it?

_____

_____

55. Explain the act that governs undocumented workers in the United States.

_____

_____

Answers To Refresh Your Memory

1. workers' compensation insurance [p. 516]
2. exclusive remedy [p. 517]
3. general duty [p. 519]
4. newspaper deliverers [p. 519]
5. living wage [p. 520]
6. administrative employee [p. 521]
7. learned professional [p. 521]
8. Family and Medical Leave Act [p. 522]
9. Department of Labor [p. 522]
10. vesting [p. 523]
11. Social Security [p. 523]
12. H1-B visa [p. 524]
13. H4 [p. 524]
14. green card [p. 525]
15. EB-1 [p. 525]

Critical Thought Exercise Model Answer

The FMLA guarantees workers unpaid time off work for medical emergencies. There is little doubt that a stroke is a medical emergency and Global-Mart had approved the leave for Frost. The FMLA will apply to Global-Mart because it has over 50 employees. Under the FMLA, the employer must guarantee employment in the same position or a comparable position when the employee returns to work. Employers who violate the FMLA may be held liable for damages to compensate employees for unpaid wages, lost benefits, denied compensation, and actual monetary losses up to an amount equivalent to the employee's wages for twelve weeks. The employer may also be required to grant a promotion that has been denied. The restored employee is not entitled to the accrual of seniority during the leave period, however.

Frost was not returned to his former position when he returned. He was forced to take a demotion, which required travel. Global-Mart violated the FMLA by demoting Frost. The failure to promote Frost may not be a violation because the promotion was based upon seniority and Frost had less seniority than Allen at the time of the promotion. Therefore, Global-Mart should be ordered to return Frost to his prior supervisor position but will not be required to promote him to senior supervisor. Global-Mart will also be required to pay damages for lost wages during the time Frost was not working due to his firing.

Answers to Practice Quiz

True/False

16. False. States usually require employers to purchase workers' compensation insurance from private insurance companies or state funds to cover workers' compensation claims. [p. 516]

17. True. For an injury to be compensable under workers' compensation, the claimant must prove that he or she was harmed by an employment-related injury. Thus, injuries that arise out of and in the course of employment are compensable. [p. 516]

18. False. In addition to covering physical injuries, workers' compensation insurance covers stress and mental illness that are employment related. [p. 517]

19. True. Workers' compensation is an exclusive remedy. Thus, workers cannot both receive workers' compensation and sue their employers in court for damages. [p. 517]

20. False. If an employer intentionally injures a worker, the worker can collect workers' compensation benefits and can also sue the employer. [p. 517]

21. False. The Occupational Safety and Health Act contains a general duty standard that imposes on an employer a duty to provide employment and a work environment that is free from recognized hazards that are causing or are likely to cause death or serious physical harm to its employees. [p. 519]

22. True. The FLSA applies to private employers and employees engaged in the production of goods for interstate commerce. [p. 519]

23. True. The FLSA forbids the use of oppressive child labor and makes it unlawful to ship goods produced by businesses that use oppressive child labor. [p. 519]

24. True. The Department of Labor permits employers to pay less than the minimum wage to students and apprentices. An employer may reduce the minimum wage by an amount equal to the reasonable cost of food and lodging provided to employees. [p. 519]

25. False. Under the FLSA, an employer cannot require nonexempt employees to work more than 40 hours per week unless they are paid overtime pay of one-and-a-half times their regular pay for each hour worked in excess of 40 hours that week. [p. 520]

26. False. The learned professional exemption applies to employees compensated on a salary or fee basis that perform work that is predominantly intellectual in character, who possess advanced

knowledge in a field of science or learning, and whose advanced knowledge was acquired through a prolonged course of specialized intellectual instruction. [p. 521]

27. True. The computer employee exemption applies to employees who are compensated either on a salary or fee basis; who are employed as computer systems analysts, computer programmers, software engineers, or other similarly skilled workers in the computer field. [p. 521]

28. False. Consolidated Omnibus Budget Reconciliation Act (COBRA) is a federal law that permits employees and their beneficiaries to continue their group health insurance after an employee's employment has ended. [p. 520]

29. False. Workers who have been let go because of bad conduct (e.g., illegal activity, drug use on the job) or who voluntarily quit work without just cause are not eligible to receive unemployment benefits. [p. 523]

30. False. An H4 visa holder is not eligible to work in the United States. [p. 524]

Multiple Choice

31. B. Before the Industrial Revolution, the doctrine of laissez-faire governed the employment relationship in this country. Generally, this meant that employment was subject to the common law of contracts and agency law. [p. 516]

32. C. For an injury to be compensable under workers' compensation, the claimant must prove that he or she was harmed by an employment-related injury. [p. 516]

33. B. Workers' compensation is an exclusive remedy. Thus, workers cannot both receive workers' compensation and sue their employers in court for damages. [p. 517]

34. D. Workers can sue an employer in court to recover damages for employment-related injuries if the employer does not carry workers' compensation insurance or does not self-insure if permitted to do so. [p. 517]

35. A. If an employer intentionally injures a worker, the worker can collect workers' compensation benefits and can also sue the employer. [p. 517]

36. C. Many of the OSHA standards are specific duty standards. That is, these rules are developed and apply to specific equipment, procedures, type of work, individual industry, unique work conditions, and the like. [p. 518]

37. D. General duty standard is an OSHA standard that requires an employer to provide a work environment free from recognized hazards that are causing or are likely to cause death or serious physical harm to employees. [p. 519]

38. D. The FLSA applies to private employers and employees engaged in the production of goods for interstate commerce. [p. 519]

39. A. Children who work in agricultural employment and child actors and performers are exempt from FLSA restrictions. [p. 519]

40. C. The executive exemption applies to executives who are compensated on a salary basis, who engage in management, who have authority to hire employees, and who regularly direct two or more employees. [p. 521]

41. D. The computer employee exemption applies to employees who are compensated either on a salary or fee basis; who are employed as computer systems analysts, computer programmers, software engineers, or other similarly skilled workers in the computer field. [p. 521]

42. C. To be covered by the act, an employee must have worked for the employer for at least one year and must have performed more than 1,250 hours of service during the previous twelve-month period. [p. 522]

43. B. Vesting occurs when an employee has a nonforfeitable right to receive pension benefits. First, ERISA provides for immediate vesting of each employee's own contributions to the plan. Second, it requires employers' contributions to be either (1) totally vested after five years (cliff vesting) or (2) gradually vested over a seven-year period and completely vested after that time. [p. 523]

44. A. Social Security benefits include (1) retirement benefits, (2) survivors' benefits to family members of deceased workers, (3) disability benefits, and (4) medical and hospitalization benefits (Medicare). [p. 523]

45. C. H-1B visa holders are allowed to bring their immediate family members (i.e., spouse and children under 21) to the United States under the H4 visa category as dependents. [p. 524]

Short Answer

46. Workers' compensation is an exclusive remedy. Thus, workers cannot both receive workers' compensation and sue their employers in court for damages. Workers' compensation laws make a trade-off: An injured worker qualifies for workers' compensation benefits and does not have to spend time and money to sue his employer, with a possible risk of not winning. The employer has to pay for workers' compensation insurance but does not have to incur the expense and risk of a lawsuit.
Example: A professor is covered by her university's workers' compensation insurance.
While teaching her class, the professor is injured when she trips over a power cord that was lying on the floor in the classroom. In this case, the professor's sole remedy is to recover workers' compensation. The worker cannot sue the university to recover damages. [p. 517]

47. In 1970, Congress enacted the Occupational Safety and Health Act1 to promote safety in the workplace. Virtually all private employers are within the scope of the act, but federal, state, and local governments are exempt. Industries regulated by other federal safety legislation are also exempt.2 The act also established the Occupational Safety and Health Administration (OSHA), a federal administrative agency within the Department of Labor that is empowered to enforce the act. The act imposes record-keeping and reporting requirements on employers and requires them to post notices in the workplace, informing employees of their rights under the act. OSHA is empowered to adopt rules and regulations to interpret and enforce the Occupational Safety and Health Act. OSHA has adopted thousands of regulations to enforce the safety standards established by the act. [p. 518]

48. The Occupational Safety and Health Act contains a general duty standard that imposes on an employer a duty to provide employment and a work environment that is free from recognized hazards that are causing or are likely to cause death or serious physical harm to its employees. This general duty standard is a catchall provision that applies even if no specific workplace safety regulation addresses the situation. OSHA is empowered to inspect places of employment for health hazards and safety violations. If a violation is found, OSHA can issue a written citation that requires the employer to abate or correct the situation. Contested citations are reviewed by the Occupational Safety and Health Review Commission. Its decision is appealable to the Court of Appeals for the Federal Circuit. Employers who violate the act, OSHA rules and regulations, or OSHA citations are subject to both civil and criminal penalties. [p. 519]

49. The FLSA forbids the use of oppressive child labor and makes it unlawful to ship goods produced by businesses that use oppressive child labor. The Department of Labor has adopted the following regulations that define lawful child labor: (1) Children under the age of 14 cannot work except as newspaper deliverers; (2) children ages 14 and 15 may work limited hours in nonhazardous jobs approved by the Department of Labor (e.g., restaurants, gasoline stations); and (3) children ages 16 and 17 may work unlimited hours in nonhazardous jobs. The Department of Labor determines which occupations are hazardous (e.g., mining, roofing, working with explosives). Children who work in agricultural employment and child actors and performers are exempt from these restrictions. [p. 519]

50. The FLSA establishes minimum wage and overtime pay requirements for workers. Managerial, administrative, and professional employees are exempt from the act's wage and hour provisions. The FLSA requires that most employees in the United
States be paid at least the federal minimum wage for all hours worked. The federal minimum wage is set by Congress and can be changed. The Department of Labor permits employers to pay less than the minimum wage to students and apprentices. An employer may reduce the minimum wage by an amount equal to the reasonable cost of food and lodging provided to employees. There is a special minimum wage rule for tipped employees. An employee who earns tips can be paid $2.13 an hour by an employer if that amount plus the tips received equals at least the minimum wage. If an employee's tips and direct employer payment does not equal the minimum wage, the employer must make up the difference. [p. 519]

51. The FLSA establishes the following categories of exemptions from federal minimum wage and overtime pay requirements:
• Executive exemption
• Administrative employee exemption
• Learned professional exemption
• Highly compensated employee exemption
• Computer employee exemption
• Outside sales representative exemption [p. 521]

52. The Consolidated Omnibus Budget Reconciliation Act (COBRA) of 19855 provides that an employee of a private employer or the employee's beneficiaries must be offered the opportunity to continue his or her group health insurance after the voluntary or involuntary termination of a worker's employment or the loss of coverage due to certain qualifying events defined in the law. The employer must notify covered employees and their beneficiaries of their rights under COBRA.
Employee Retirement Income Security Act (Erisa) – Employers are not required to establish pension plans for their employees. If they do, however, they are subject to the record-keeping, disclosure, and other requirements of the Employee Retirement Income Security Act (ERISA).

ERISA is a complex act designed to prevent fraud and other abuses associated with private pension funds. Federal, state, and local government pension funds are exempt from its coverage. ERISA is administered by the Department of Labor. [p. 522]

53. The federal Social Security system provides limited retirement and death benefits to certain employees and their dependents. The Social Security system is administered by the Social Security Administration. Social Security benefits include (1) retirement benefits, (2) survivors' benefits to family members of deceased workers, (3) disability benefits, and (4) medical and hospitalization benefits. Under the Federal Insurance Contributions Act (FICA), employees must make contributions (i.e., pay taxes) into the Social Security fund. An employee's employer must pay a matching amount. Social Security does not operate like a savings account. Instead, current contributions are used to fund current claims. The employer is responsible for deducting employees' portions from their wages and remitting the entire payment to the Internal Revenue Service (IRS). Under the Self-Employment Contributions Act, self-employed individuals must pay Social Security contributions, too. The amount of tax self-employed individuals must pay is equal to the combined employer–employee amount. [p. 523]

54. An EB-1 visa is a visa that allows U.S. employers to employ in the United States foreign nationals who possess extraordinary ability for certain types of employment. The three categories of workers who can qualify for an EB-1 visa are (1) persons who can demonstrate extraordinary ability in the sciences, arts, education, business, or athletics through sustained national or international acclaim; (2) outstanding professors and researchers who can demonstrate international recognition for outstanding achievements in a particular academic field; and (3) multinational managers or executives employed by a firm outside the United States who seek to continue to work for that firm in the United States. [p. 525]

55. Many persons enter the United States without permission, and once in the country, many of these persons seek employment in the United States. The Immigration Reform and Control Act (IRCA) of 1986, which is administered by the USCIS, requires employers to verify whether prospective employees are either U.S. citizens or otherwise authorized to work in the country (e.g., have proper work visas).
Employers are required to have prospective employees complete Form I-9 Employment Eligibility Verification. Employers must obtain a completed Form I-9 for every employee, regardless of citizenship or national origin. Employers must examine evidence of prospective employee's identity and employment eligibility. A state issued driver's license is not sufficient. Employers must review other documents to establish eligibility, such as social security cards, birth certificates, and such.
Employers must maintain records and post in the workplace notices of the contents of the law. The IRCA imposes criminal and financial penalties on employers who knowingly hire undocumented workers. [p. 525]

32 | LABOR LAW AND COLLECTIVE BARGAINING

Chapter Overview

When the U.S. became industrialized in the late 1800s, large corporate employers assumed much greater power than their employees. It was not until the 1930s, during the Great Depression, that state and federal governments began to regulate employment relationships. Legislation granted employees the right to form labor unions and bargain with management for improved working conditions, better pay, and benefits. Further legislation guaranteed the right to strike and picket. This chapter discusses the creation of labor unions and regulation of labor relations.

Objectives

Upon completion of the exercises in this chapter, you should be able to
1. Describe how a union is organized.
2. Explain the consequences of an employer's illegal interference with a union election.
3. Describe the process of collective bargaining.
4. Describe employees' rights to strike and picket.
5. Explain labor's bill of rights.

Practical Application

Upon mastering the concepts in this chapter, you should be able to recognize when the conduct involved in a particular labor relationship is legal or illegal. You should be able to recognize the general legal principle that applies to a dispute and understand the likely outcome.

Helpful Hints

When there is a labor dispute, emotions are often frayed and the parties are likely to react impulsively. It is helpful to realize that both state and federal governments and the courts have created a large amount of statutory and case law that will dictate the proper conduct of the parties and the consequences of illegal activity. Examine each statute and case closely for the precise conduct that was either condoned or forbidden. By understanding what conduct triggers which rule of law, you will be more effective in your labor relationships.

Study Tips

Labor Law and Collective Bargaining

Following the industrialization of the U.S., the balance of power between employers and employees changed to heavily favor employers. In response to this shift, federal legislation provided for the formation of labor unions and the protection of the right to do so.

Labor Law

During the 1880's, workers reacted to abuses by employers by forming labor unions to improve their bargaining power.
- *The American Federation of Labor (AFL)*. Formed in 1886 and only allowed skilled craft workers to join.
- *The Congress of Industrial Organizations (CIO)*. Formed in 1935 and permitted semiskilled and unskilled workers to join.
- The AFL and CIO. Formed in 1955 when the AFL and CIO combined.
- Approximately 10 percent of private-sector wage and salary workers belong to labor unions.

Federal Labor Union Statutes. It is crucial for you to understand the following rules of law and mandates that must be followed when you are involved in a labor action or negotiations.
- *Norris-LaGuardia Act*. Made it legal for employees to organize.
- *National Labor Relations Act*. Established the right of employees to form, join, and participate in unions.
    - o Placed a duty on employers to bargain and deal in good faith with unions.
- *Labor-Management Relations Act*. Expanded the activities that unions were allowed to engage in.
    - o Gave employers the right to speak out against the unions.
    - o Gave the president the right to enjoin a strike for up to 80 days if the strike would create a national emergency.
- *Labor-Management Reporting and Disclosure Act*. This act regulates internal union affairs related to union elections, who can hold office, and makes union officials accountable for union funds.
- *Railway Labor Act*. This act allows railroad and airline employees to organize and created a mechanism for the adjudication of grievances.

National Labor Relations Board (NLRB). Appointed by the president, the five members of the NLRB oversee union elections, prevent unfair labor practices, and enforce federal labor laws.

Organizing a Union

Section 7 of the NLRA gives employees the right to join together to form a union. Section 7 states that employees shall have the right
- to self-organization;
- to form, join, or assist labor organizations;
- to bargain collectively through representatives of their own choosing; and
- to engage in other concerted activities for the purpose of collective bargaining or other mutual aid protection.

Types of Union Elections.
- *Contested Election*. Most union elections are contested by the employer.
    - o The NLRB must supervise all contested elections.
- *Consent Election*. If management does not contest the election, a consent election may be held without NLRB supervision.
- *Decertification Election*. If employees no longer want to be represented by a union, a decertification election will be held.

o Such elections must be supervised by the NLRB.

Union Solicitation on Company Property. Employers may restrict solicitation activities to the employees' free time.
- Areas of solicitation activities may be limited to nonworking areas.
- Off-duty employees may be barred from union solicitation on company premises and nonemployees may be prohibited altogether from soliciting on behalf of the union anywhere on company property.
- Employers may dismiss those employees in violation of the rules.

Lechmere v. NLRB (1992). Labor organizers have no right to trespass onto the employer's property to organize the employees when they can have access to the employees via nontrespassory means.
- Even if it is difficult to contact employees away from work, this does not give the organizers the right to trespass onto the employer's property to pass out leaflets.

Illegal Interference with an Election.
- *Section 8 of the NLRA.* Makes it an unfair labor practice for an employer to interfere with, coerce, or restrain employees from exercising their statutory right to form and join unions.
  - o Threats of union closure by employers are considered to be an unfair labor practice.
- *Section 8(b) of the NLRA.* Prohibits unions from engaging in unfair labor practices that interfere with a union election.
  - o If an unfair labor practice is found, the courts or the NLRB may issue a cease-and-desist order or an injunction to restrain unfair labor practices and may set aside an election and order a new election.

Collective Bargaining

The act of negotiating is called collective bargaining. Negotiation between the employer and union must be done in good faith. Subjects of collective bargaining include:
- *compulsory subjects* (wages, hours, fringe benefits, health benefits, retirement plans, safety rules, etc.);
- *illegal subjects* (closed shops and discrimination) cannot be negotiated; and
- *permissive subjects* (size and composition of the supervisory force, location of plants, and corporate reorganizations).

Union Security Agreements. There are two types of security agreements:
- *The Union Shop.* An employee must join the union within a certain time period after being hired.
  - o Those who don't join must be discharged by the employer once notice is given.
- *The Agency Shop.* Employees do not have to become union members, but they do have to pay an agency fee to the union.
  - o Once the union has been notified, employers are required to deduct union dues and agency fees from employees' wages and forward the same to the union.

State Right-to-Work Laws. In 1947 Congress amended the Taft-Hartley Act to allow states to enact laws forbidding union and agency shops.

- Individual employees cannot be forced to join a union or to pay union dues or agency fees.

Strikes

If a collective bargaining agreement cannot be reached, union management has the right to recommend that the union call a strike.

Cooling-Off Period. The union must give the employer 60 days' notice that the union intends to strike.

Illegal Strikes. The following strikes are illegal and not protected by federal labor law:
- violent strike
- sit-down strikes
- partial or intermittent strikes
- wildcat strikes
- strikes during the 60-day cooling-off period
- strikes in violation of a no-strike clause

No-Strike Clause. The employer and the union can agree that the union will not strike during a specified period of time.

Crossover and Replacement Workers. Workers can elect not to strike or return to work after joining strikers for a period of either. If either of these two options is chosen, the workers are called crossover workers.
- Once the strike has begun, temporary or permanent replacement workers may be hired.
  - If the new employees are permanent, they do not have to be dismissed when the strike is through.

Employer Lockout. When an employer reasonably anticipates a strike by some of its employees, it may prevent those employees from entering the plant or premises.

Picketing

Picketing usually takes the form of striking employees and union representatives walking in front of the employer's premises carrying signs announcing their strike.
- Picketing is not lawful if it is accompanied by violence, obstructs customers from entering the employer's place of business, prevents nonstriking employees from entering the employer's premises, or prevents pickups and deliveries at the employer's place of business.
- An injunction may be sought by the employer if unlawful picketing takes place.

Secondary Boycott Picketing. Picketing an employer's suppliers or customers sometimes pressures an employer.
- This type of picketing is lawful only if the picketing is against the primary employer's products.

Internal Union Affairs

A union may be operated by internal union rules that are adopted by the union.

- Title I of the Landrum Griffin Act gives each union member equal rights and privileges to nominate candidates for union office, vote in elections, and participate in membership meetings.
- Union members are also permitted to initiate judicial and administrative action.
- Union members may be disciplined for participating in activities like walking off the job in a nonsanctioned strike, working for wages below union scale, spying for an employer, or any other activity that is adverse to employer.

Plant Closing Act

This act covers employers with 100 or more employees and requires employers to give their employees 60 days' notice before taking part in plant closings or layoffs. It addresses plant closings and mass layoffs. Employers are exempt from the notice requirement of this act if:

- the closing or layoff was as a result of business circumstances that were not reasonably foreseeable as of the time that the notice would have been required.
- the business was actively seeking capital or business that, if obtained, would have avoided or postponed the shutdown and the employer in good faith believed that giving notice would have precluded it from obtaining the needed capital or business.

Refresh Your Memory

The following exercise will give you the opportunity to test your memory of the principles given in this chapter. Read the question twice and place your answer in the blank provided. Review the chapter material for any question that you are unable to answer or remember.

1. National Labor Relations Act is also known as _____.

2. _____ is also known as the Taft-Hartley Act.

3. _____ is a group of employees that a union is seeking to represent.

4. If management does not contest an election, a(n) _____ election may be held without NLRB supervision.

5. _____ is a rule that permits employees and union officials to engage in union solicitation on company property if the employees are beyond reach of reasonable union efforts to communicate with them.

6. The act of negotiating contract terms between an employer and the members of a union is called _____.

7. Subjects that are not compulsory or illegal are _____ subjects of collective bargaining.

8. A _____ is a cessation of work by union members in order to obtain economic benefits or correct an unfair labor practice.

9. A mandatory sixty days' notice before a strike can commence is called the _____.

10. In _____ strikes, individual union members go on strike without proper authorization from the union.

11. _____ is an act of an employer to prevent employees from entering the work premises when the employer reasonably anticipates a strike.

12. _____ is the action of strikers walking in front of an employer's premises, carrying signs announcing their strike.

13. _____ is a type of picketing in which a union tries to bring pressure against an employer by picketing the employer's suppliers or customers.

14. A _____ is a permanent or temporary shutdown of a single site that results in a loss of employment for fifty or more employees during any thirty-day period.

15. A _____ is a reduction of 33 percent of the employees or at least fifty employees during any thirty-day period.

Critical Thought Exercise

When the collective bargaining agreement between the United Pickle and Catsup Makers (Union) and Good Foods Company (Good) expired, the Union called for a strike. Picketers were used to walk in front of 27 grocery stores in the greater Cleveland, Ohio, area and distribute literature. Some of the picket signs said, "Boycott Pickles and Catsup," and "Don't buy Good pickles here, make them at home." Most signs were pre-printed by the Union and stated, "Boycott All Good Products." The majority of pickles and catsup sold by People's Grocery Store and Larry's Supermarket are made by Good. Though customers never saw anyone spray them with catsup, they found their clothing squirted with catsup if they entered People's Grocery Store. Customers refused to enter People's Grocery and Larry's Supermarket because they felt intimidated and were afraid of the unknown catsup squirter. People's and Larry's file suit in federal court seeking injunctions and damages against the Union. Were the activities by the Union illegal?

Please compose your answer to the Critical Thinking Exercise using a separate sheet of paper or your computer word processing program.

Practice Quiz

True/False

16. _____ Labor unions have the right to engage in picketing in support of their positions.

17. _____ The NLRB is an administrative body that oversees and prevents union members from engaging in illegal labor practices.

18. _____ Individual unions are not allowed to join AFL-CIO; the members need to be individual employees.

19. _____ The Taft-Hartley Act gives the president of the United States the right to seek an injunction against a strike that would create a national emergency.

20. _____ The NLRB oversees union elections, prevents employers and unions from engaging in illegal and unfair labor practices.

21. _____ An appropriate bargaining unit must consist of employees from a single company.

22. _____ Most union elections are contested by the employer.

23. _____ A decertification election is held when an employer does not want the presence of multiple unions in the organization.

24. _____ The act of negotiating contract terms between an employer and the members of a union is known as mediation.

25. _____ Wages, hours, and other terms and conditions of employment are permissive subjects of collective bargaining.

26. _____ Under a closed shop agreement, an employer agrees to hire only employees who are already members of a union.

27. _____ Under an agency shop agreement, an employer may hire anyone whether she belongs to a union or not.

28. _____ It is legal for a union to begin a strike thirty days after it has informed the employer about the strike.

29. _____ Employees who choose not to return to work after joining the strikers are known as crossover workers.

30. _____ Picketing that prevents customers from entering the employer's place of business is illegal.

Multiple Choice

31. Only _____ were allowed to belong to the American Federation of Labor.

A. illiterate workers
B. unskilled workers
C. literate workers
D. skilled craft workers

32. Which of the following is provided by the National Labor Relations Act of 1935?

A. to regulate internal affairs of each union
B. to bargain collectively with employers
C. to represent employees according to their sectors of employment
D. to equally represent every union member

33. Which of the following is true of the Taft-Hartley Act?

A. It gives employers the right to engage in free-speech efforts against unions.
B. It establishes the right of employees to bargain collectively with employers.
C. It provides for the equal representation of skilled and unskilled workforce.
D. It gives the president of the United States the right to seek an injunction against a strike.

34. Which of the following federal statutes that regulate labor-management relationships cover airline carriers?

A. Norris-LaGuardia Act
B. Railway Labor Act
C. National Labor Relations Act
D. Landrum-Griffin Act

35. A group of employees that a union is seeking to represent is known as a(n) _____.

A. combined conciliation unit
B. appropriate mediation unit
C. appropriate bargaining unit
D. collective negotiation unit

36. A(n) _____ election can be held without NLRB supervision.

A. consent
B. employer-contested
C. decertification
D. management-contested

37. Which of the following is a provision of Section 8(a) of the NLRA?

A. makes it an unfair labor practice for an employer to restrain employees from forming and joining unions
B. prohibits unions from engaging in unfair labor practices that interfere with a union election
C. enables employees to opt out of unions by organizing a decertification election
D. permits employees and union officials to engage in union solicitation on company property

38. Which of the following is a compulsory subject during collective bargaining?

A. location of workplace
B. discrimination
C. corporate reorganization
D. health benefits

39. Which of the following is true of a union shop agreement while hiring an employee?

A. The employee must be represented by more than one union.
B. The employee does not join the union but pays an agency fee.
C. The employee must be a skilled worker represented by more than one union.
D. The employee must join the union within a certain time after employment.

40. A _____ is a cessation of work by union members in order to obtain economic benefits or correct an unfair labor practice.

A. strike
B. collective bargain
C. crossover
D. persuasion

41. Which of the following best describes a wild-cat strike?

A. Union members occupy the employer's premises while striking.
B. Individual union members go on strike without proper union authorization.
C. Union members strike part of the day or workweek and work the other part.
D. The union declares indefinite cessation of work.

42. Employees who choose not to strike or return to work after joining the strikers for a period of time are known as _____ workers.

A. locked-out
B. wildcat
C. crossover
D. borderline

43. Once a strike begins, the employer may continue operations by _____ to take the place of the striking employees.

A. acquiring wildcat strikers
B. temporarily demoting supervisors
C. acquiring crossover workers
D. hiring replacement workers

44. In which of the following circumstances is picketing unlawful?

A. when picketing is carried out against the neutral employer
B. when picketing is carried out against the struck employer's product
C. when picketing obstructs customers from entering the employer's place of business
D. when the employer carries out a "lockout" against the picketers at work premises

45. Secondary boycott picketing is lawful only if it is directed at _____.

A. the neutral employer
B. the primary employer's product
C. customers who purchase the product
D. employees not part of the union

Short Answer

46. List the major federal statutes that regulate the labor-management relationship along with their respective provisions.

_____

_____

47. What are the types of union elections?

_____

_____

48. Explain the inaccessibility exception.

_____

_____

49. What are the prohibitions stated in the Section 8 of the NLRA?

_____

_____

50. Outline the act of collective bargaining.

_____

_____

51. What are the types of security agreements?

_____

_____

52. What are the strikes that have been held to be illegal?

_____

_____

53. What are crossover and replacement workers?

_____

_____

54. Distinguish between strikes and picketing. When is picketing lawful?

_____

_____

55. How does the Landrum-Griffin Act regulate internal affairs of unions? Can unions discipline their members? Elaborate.

_____

_____

Answers to Refresh Your Memory

1. Wagner Act [p. 530]
2. Labor Management Relations Act [p. 530]
3. Appropriate bargaining unit [p. 531]
4. consent [p. 531]
5. Inaccessibility exception [p. 532]
6. collective bargaining [p. 533]
7. permissive [p. 533]
8. strike [p. 535]
9. cooling-off period [p. 535]
10. wildcat [p. 535]
11. Employer lockout [p. 536]
12. Picketing [p. 536]
13. Secondary boycott picketing [p. 536]
14. plant closing [p. 538]
15. mass layoff [p. 538]

Critical Thought Exercise Model Answer

Picketing is a form of lawful protest that can be undertaken by unions during a strike. The picketing is lawful unless it (1) is accompanied by violence, (2) obstructs customers from entering the employer's business, (3) prevents replacement or nonstriking employees from entering the premises, or (4) prevents shipments or deliveries from entering or exiting the premises. If the picketing is unlawful for any of these reasons, the employer may seek an injunction to stop the activity. Picketing of the employer's customers or suppliers is known as secondary boycott picketing. Secondary picketing is lawful only if the union pickets the product or service of the employer. The picketing is illegal if it is directed against the business of the customer or supplier who is not involved in the strike. Good Foods can be lawfully struck by picketing the suppliers and customers of Good Foods. Though the Union may picket both People's Grocery and Larry's Supermarket, the picketers cannot ask customers to not enter the stores or refrain from buying goods in the store that are not produced by Good Foods. The picket signs that are being used are legal for the most part. The only sign that creates a problem is the one that says, "Boycott Pickles and Catsup." This sign is not calling for an exclusive boycott of Good pickles and catsup. Both stores could be selling pickles and catsup made by several manufacturers. This would be asking for a general boycott and would be illegal. The other signs are referring to Good Food products and are a proper form of secondary boycott. The squirting of catsup upon the clothing of customers at People's would allow People's to sue the Union for the tort of intentional interference with a contractual relationship. An injunction could also be issued to stop this from happening again. Failure to honor the injunction would subject the Union to damages for illegal strike activities.

Answers to Practice Quiz

True/False

16. True. Labor unions have the right to strike and to engage in picketing in support of their positions. However, there are some limits on these activities. [p. 530]

17. False. National Labor Relations Board (NLRB) is a federal administrative agency that oversees union elections, prevents employers and unions from engaging in illegal and unfair labor practices, and enforces and interprets certain federal labor laws. [p. 531]

18. False. Individual unions (e.g., United Auto Workers, United Steel Workers) may choose to belong to the AFL-CIO, but not all unions opt to join. [p. 530]

19. True. In 1947, Congress enacted the Labor Management Relations Act, also known as the Taft-Hartley Act.3 This act gives the president of the United States the right to seek an injunction (for up to eighty days) against a strike that would create a national emergency. [p. 530]

20. True. The NLRB oversees union elections, prevents employers and unions from engaging in illegal and unfair labor practices, and enforces and interprets certain federal labor laws. The decisions of the NLRB are enforceable in court. [p. 531]

21. False. An appropriate bargaining unit can be the employees of a single company or plant, a group within a single company (e.g., maintenance workers at all of a company's plants), or an entire industry (e.g., nurses at all hospitals in the country). [p. 531]

22. True. Most union elections are contested by the employer. The NLRB is required to supervise all contested elections. [p. 531]

23. False. If employees no longer want to be represented by a union, a decertification election will be held. [p. 531]

24. False. The act of negotiating contract terms between an employer and the members of a union is called collective bargaining. [p. 533]

25. False. Wages, hours, and other terms and conditions of employment are compulsory subjects of collective bargaining. [p. 533]

26. True. Under a closed shop agreement, an employer agrees to hire only employees who are already members of a union. Closed shops are illegal in the United States. [p. 534]

27. True. Under an agency shop agreement, an employer may hire anyone whether she belongs to a union or not. After an employee has been hired, she does not have to join the union, but if she does not join the union, she must pay an agency fee to the union. [p. 534]

28. False. Before a strike, a union must give sixty-day notice to the employer that the union intends to strike. It is illegal for a strike to begin during the mandatory sixty-day cooling-off period. [p. 535]

29. False. Individual members of a union do not have to honor a strike. They may (1) choose not to strike or (2) return to work after joining the strikers for a time. Employees who choose either of these options are known as crossover workers. [p. 535]

30. True. Picketing is lawful unless it (1) is accompanied by violence, (2) obstructs customers from entering the employer's place of business, (3) prevents nonstriking employees from entering the employer's premises, or (4) prevents pickups and deliveries at the employer's place of business. [p. 536]

Multiple Choice

31. D. The American Federation of Labor (AFL) was formed in 1886, under the leadership of Samuel Gompers. Only skilled craft workers such as silversmiths and artisans were allowed to belong. [p. 530]

32. B. The National Labor Relations Act (NLRA), also known as the Wagner Act, was enacted in 1935. The NLRA establishes the right of employees to form and join labor organizations, to bargain collectively with employers, and to engage in concerted activity to promote these rights. [p. 530]

33. A. In 1947, Congress enacted the Labor Management Relations Act, also known as the Taft-Hartley Act. This act gives employers the right to engage in free-speech efforts against unions prior to a union election. [p. 530]

34. B. The Railway Labor Act of 1926, as amended in 1934, covers employees of railroad and airline carriers. [p. 531]

35. C. The group that a union is seeking to represent—which is called the appropriate bargaining unit, or bargaining unit—must be defined before the union can petition for an election. [p. 531]

36. A. If management does not contest an election, a consent election may be held without NLRB supervision. [p. 531]

37. A. Section 8(a) of the NLRA makes it an unfair labor practice for an employer to interfere with, coerce, or restrain employees from exercising their statutory right to form and join unions. [p. 533]

38. D. Wages, hours, and other terms and conditions of employment are compulsory subjects of collective bargaining. [p. 533]

39. D. Under a union shop agreement, an employer may hire anyone whether he belongs to a union or not. However, an employee must join the union within a certain time period (e.g., thirty days) after being hired. Union shops are lawful. [p. 534]

40. A. The NLRA gives union management the right to recommend that a union call a strike if a collective bargaining agreement cannot be reached. In a strike, union members refuse to work. Strikes are permitted by federal labor law. [p. 535]

41. B. In wildcat strikes, individual union members go on strike without proper authorization from the union. The courts have recognized that a wildcat strike becomes lawful if it is quickly ratified by the union. [p. 535]

42. C. Individual members of a union do not have to honor a strike. They may (1) choose not to strike or (2) return to work after joining the strikers for a time. Employees who choose either of these options are known as crossover workers. [p. 535]

43. D. Once a strike begins, the employer may continue operations by using management personnel and hiring replacement workers to take the place of the striking employees. Replacement workers can be hired on either a temporary or permanent basis. [p. 535]

44. C. Picketing is lawful unless it (1) is accompanied by violence, (2) obstructs customers from entering the employer's place of business, (3) prevents nonstriking employees from entering the employer's premises, or (4) prevents pickups and deliveries at the employer's place of business. [p. 536]

45. B. Unions sometimes try to bring pressure against an employer by picketing the employer's suppliers or customers. The picketing is illegal if it is directed against the neutral employer instead of the struck employer's product. [p. 536]

Short Answer

46. The following are the major federal statutes that regulate labor-management relationships:
1. Norris-LaGuardia Act- Enacted in 1932, the Norris-LaGuardia Act stipulates that it is legal for employees to organize.
2. National Labor Relations Act (NLRA) - The NLRA establishes the right of employees to form and join labor organizations, to bargain collectively with employers, and to engage in concerted activity to promote these rights.
3. Labor Management Relations Act - This act (1) expands the activities that labor unions can engage in, (2) gives employers the right to engage in free-speech efforts against unions prior to a union election, and (3) gives the president of the United States the right to seek an injunction (for up to eighty days) against a strike that would create a national emergency.

4. Labor Management Reporting and Disclosure Act - This act regulates internal union affairs and establishes the rights of union members.
5. Railway Labor Act. The Railway Labor Act covers employees of railroad and airline carriers. [p. 530]

47. The following types of elections are possible:
• Contested election. Most union elections are contested by the employer. The NLRB is required to supervise all contested elections. A simple majority vote (more than 50 percent) wins the election. Example If 51 of 100 employees vote for the union, the union is certified as the bargaining agent for all 100 employees.
• Consent election. If management does not contest an election, a consent election may be held without NLRB supervision.
• Decertification election. If employees no longer want to be represented by a union, a decertification election will be held. Decertification elections must be supervised by the NLRB. [p. 531]

48. If union solicitation is being conducted by employees, an employer may restrict solicitation activities to the employees' free time (e.g., coffee breaks, lunch breaks, before and after work). The activities may also be limited to nonworking areas, such as the cafeteria, rest room, or parking lot. Off-duty employees may be barred from union solicitation on company premises, and nonemployees (e.g., union management) may be prohibited from soliciting on behalf of the union anywhere on company property. Employers may dismiss employees who violate these rules.
An exception to this rule applies if the location of the business and the living quarters of the employees place the employees beyond the reach of reasonable union efforts to communicate with them. This exception, called the inaccessibility exception, applies to logging camps, mining towns, company towns, and the like. [p. 532]

49. Section 8(a) of the NLRA makes it an unfair labor practice for an employer to interfere with, coerce, or restrain employees from exercising their statutory right to form and join unions. Threats of loss of benefits for joining the union, statements such as "I'll close this plant if a union comes in here," and the like are unfair labor practices. Also, an employer may not form a company union.
Section 8(b) of the NLRA prohibits unions from engaging in unfair labor practices that interfere with a union election. Coercion, physical threats, and such are unfair labor practices. Where an unfair labor practice has been found, the NLRB or the courts may issue a cease-and-desist order or an injunction to restrain unfair labor practices and may set aside an election and order a new election. [p. 533]

50. Once a union has been elected, the employer and the union discuss the terms of employment of union members and try to negotiate a contract that embodies these terms. The act of negotiating is called collective bargaining, and the resulting contract is called a collective bargaining agreement. The employer and the union must negotiate with each other in good faith. Among other things, this prohibits making take-it-or-leave-it proposals. The subjects of collective bargaining are classified as follows:
1. Compulsory subjects: Wages, hours, and other terms and conditions of employment are compulsory subjects of collective bargaining.
2. Permissive subjects: Subjects that are not compulsory or illegal are permissive subjects of collective bargaining. These subjects may be bargained for if the company and union agree to do so.
3. Illegal subjects: Certain topics are illegal subjects of collective bargaining and therefore cannot be subjects of negotiation or agreement. [p. 533]

51. There are several types of security agreements:
• Closed shop. Under a closed shop agreement, an employer agrees to hire only employees who are already members of a union. The employer cannot hire employees who are not members of a union. Closed shops are illegal in the United States.
• Union shop. Under a union shop agreement, an employer may hire anyone whether he belongs to a union or not. However, an employee must join the union within a certain time period (e.g., thirty days) after being hired. Union shops are lawful.
• Agency shop. Under an agency shop agreement, an employer may hire anyone whether she belongs to a union or not. After an employee has been hired, she does not have to join the union, but if she does not join the union, she must pay an agency fee to the union. This fee will include an amount to help pay for the costs of collective bargaining. [p. 534]

52. The following are illegal strikes:
• Violent strikes. In violent strikes, striking employees cause substantial damage to property of the employer or a third party. Courts usually tolerate a certain amount of isolated violence before finding that an entire strike is illegal.
• Sit-down strikes. In sit-down strikes, striking employees continue to occupy the employer's premises. Such strikes are illegal because they deny the employer's statutory right to continue its operations during the strike.
• Partial or intermittent strikes. In partial strikes, or intermittent strikes, employees strike part of the day or workweek and work the other part. This type of strike is illegal because it interferes with the employer's right to operate its facilities at full operation.
• Wildcat strikes. In wildcat strikes, individual union members go on strike without proper authorization from the union. The courts have recognized that a wildcat strike becomes lawful if it is quickly ratified by the union. [p. 535]

53. Individual members of a union do not have to honor a strike. They may (1) choose not to strike or (2) return to work after joining the strikers for a time. Employees who choose either of these options are known as crossover workers.
Once a strike begins, the employer may continue operations by using management personnel and hiring replacement workers to take the place of the striking employees. Replacement workers can be hired on either a temporary or permanent basis. If replacement workers are given permanent status, they do not have to be dismissed when the strike is over. [p. 535]

54. A strike is a cessation of work by union members in order to obtain economic benefits or correct an unfair labor practice. Picketing is the action of strikers walking in front of an employer's premises, carrying signs announcing their strike. Picketing is lawful unless it (1) is accompanied by violence, (2) obstructs customers from entering the employer's place of business, (3) prevents nonstriking employees from entering the employer's premises, or (4) prevents pickups and deliveries at the employer's place of business. [p. 536]

55. Title I of the Landrum-Griffin Act gives each union member equal rights and privileges to nominate candidates for union office, vote in elections, and participate in membership meetings. It further guarantees union members the rights of free speech and assembly, provides for due process (notice and hearing), and permits union members to initiate judicial or administrative action. A union may discipline members for participating in certain activities, including (1) walking off the job in a nonsanctioned strike, (2) working for wages below union scale, (3) spying for an employer, and (4) any other unauthorized activity that has an adverse economic impact on the union. A union may not punish a union member for participating in a civic duty, such as testifying in court against the union. [p. 537]

33 | EQUAL OPPORTUNITY IN EMPLOYMENT

Chapter Overview

Prior to the 1960s there was little that an employee could do to address discrimination by the employer in regards to hiring, discharge, promotion, pay, and work assignments. Congress addressed discrimination by passing a comprehensive set of laws that made it actionable to discriminate against a person because of race, sex, religion, national origin, age, or disability. The interpretation of these federal statutes has created a large body of law that has created a much more level playing field in the workplace. The chapter examines the major legislation and the application of these laws by the courts.

Objectives

Upon completion of the exercises in this chapter, you should be able to:
1. Describe the scope of coverage of Title VII of the Civil Rights Act of 1964.
2. Identify race, color, and national origin discrimination that violate Title VII.
3. Identify and describe gender discrimination, sexual harassment, and genetic information discrimination.
4. Describe the scope of coverage of the Age Discrimination in Employment Act.
5. Describe the protections afforded by the Americans with Disabilities Act.

Practical Application

Antidiscrimination laws set forth mandates for employers and protection for employees that alter the course of conduct of people in the business environment. You should be able to recognize the situations where discrimination is unlawful and instances where a defense to discrimination may apply so that you can make decisions that stay within the requirements of federal laws.

Helpful Hints

Since most of this chapter concentrates on specific laws and cases that interpret the laws, it is beneficial to know the basic definition or content of each law and understand the examples of how they are applied in the real world. You should focus on the type of conduct that is involved in a situation to determine which area of law is applicable and what actions must be taken to correct the action, if at all possible.

Study Tips

Equal Opportunity in Employment

Employees could be terminated at any time and for any reason, and employers could hire and promote as they saw fit, at common law. In the 1960s, Congress began enacting laws protecting workers from employment discrimination. Many state and local governments have similar laws.

Title VII of the Civil Rights Act of 1964

Overall, Title VII is the most important piece of legislation ever passed to address discrimination. It provides the authority for the largest number of cases brought to rectify discrimination.
- Prohibits actions based upon a person's race, color, religion, sex, or national origin; or
- Prohibits actions where the employee is limited in any way that deprives them of an opportunity based upon race, color, religion, sex, or national origin,

Scope of Coverage of Title VII.
- Title VII applies to:
    - employers with 15 or more employees
    - employment agencies
    - labor union with 15 or more employees
    - state and local governments
    - most federal employees
    - undocumented aliens
- Title VII does not apply to:
    - Indian tribes
    - tax-exempt private clubs
- The conduct that will trigger a Title VII action will be within the areas of:
    - Hiring
    - Discharge
    - Compensation (rate of pay and classification that affects pay)
    - Terms of employment (work schedule, fringe benefits)
    - Conditions of the employment (rules, policies, and procedures)
    - Privileges granted as part of employment (honorary positions, use of company assets)
    - Promotion (not promoted when qualified)
    - Work assignment (given less desirable assignments that prevent growth)
- There are two types of discrimination that Title VII addresses:
    - *Disparate treatment.* When an employer discriminates against the individual.
    - *Disparate impact.* When an employer discriminates against entire protected class

Intentional Discrimination. Aggrieved parties can recover compensatory damages.
- Punitive damages can be awarded for an employer showing malice or reckless indifference
- Damages are capped according to the size of the employer

Equal Employment Opportunity Commission (EEOC). The Equal Employment Opportunity Commission (EEOC) is appointed by the president and is responsible for enforcing the provisions of all the federal laws that address areas of discrimination in the workplace.
- The EEOC is empowered to not only investigate, but also to issue opinions and directives to offending employers, bring suit against the violator, and even seek injunctive relief to stop the actual conduct that violated a particular law.
- The procedure for bringing Title VII action requires that
    - Private complainant must file complaint with EEOC within 180 or 300 days
    - EEOC given opportunity to sue on behalf of complainant
    - If EEOC chooses not to sue, issues right to sue letter
    - Complainant now has right to sue employer

Remedies for Violations of Title VII. Remedies include back pay and attorney's fees.
- Courts can award equitable remedies, such as reinstatement, seniority rights, and injunctions.

Race, Color, and National Origin Discrimination

Title VII was enacted to bar employment discrimination based on race, color, or national origin.

Race Discrimination. Discrimination based on racial categories.

Color Discrimination. Discrimination based on the color of a person's skin.

National Origin or Heritage Discrimination. Discrimination based on the individual's country of ancestors, cultural characteristics, or heritage.

Sex Discrimination and Sexual Harassment

Title VII, EEOC rules, and court decisions prohibit discrimination in employment based on gender, sexual harassment, pregnancy, and sexual orientation.

Sex Discrimination. Discrimination based on gender is prohibited and cases have been brought for direct sex discrimination and for quid pro quo discrimination.

Pregnancy Discrimination. The Pregnancy Discrimination Act was added to Title VII in 1978 to forbid discrimination because of pregnancy, birth, or related medical conditions.

Sexual Harassment. In evaluating sexual harassment claims, the courts look at the circumstances to determine whether the workplace is permeated with discriminatory intimidation, ridicule, and insult, that is sufficiently severe or pervasive to alter the conditions of the victim's employment and create an abusive working environment.
- Lewd remarks, touching, intimidation, posting pinups, and other verbal of physical conduct of a sexual nature that occur on the job
- Requesting that an employee has sex with the employer to get hired, receive a promotion, or prevent discharge

Same-Sex Discrimination. In 1998, in *Omcale v. Sundowner Offshore Services, Incorporated*, the U.S. Supreme Court held that same-sex harassment violated Title VII.

Employer's Defense to a Charge of Sexual Harassment. An employer may raise an affirmative defense against liability or damages for sexual harassment by proving that:
- The employer exercised reasonable care to prevent and correct promptly any sexually-harassing behavior, and
- The plaintiff employee unreasonably failed to take advantage of any preventive of coercive opportunities by the employer or to otherwise avoid harm

Religious Discrimination

Under Title VII, the employer is under a duty to reasonably accommodate religious observances, practices, or beliefs of its employees if it does not cause undue hardship on the employer.

- Religious organizations are permitted to give preference in employment to individuals of a particular religion.

Defenses to a Title VII Action

Merit. Employers can select or promote employees based on merit.
- A promotion can lawfully be based upon experience, skill, education, and ability tests.
- A test or condition that has no relevance to the position may not be used to prevent a protected class or individual from qualifying for employment.

Seniority. An employer may maintain a seniority system that rewards long-term employees.
- o The system is lawful unless persons in a position of seniority achieved their position through intentional discrimination in the past.

Bona Fide Occupational Qualification. Employment discrimination based on a protected class (such as sex, but other than race or color), is lawful if it is job related and a business necessity.
- o Hiring only women to work in a women's health spa would be legal but hiring only women for a women's clothing store in the mall would be a violation of Title VII.

Civil Rights Act of 1866

Section 1981 of this act gives all persons equal contract rights. Section 1981 also prohibits racial discrimination and discrimination based upon national origin. Though most discrimination cases are brought under Title VII, there are two good reasons to bring an action under Section 1981:
- A private plaintiff need not go through the procedural requirements of Title VII, and
- There is no limitation period on the recovery of back pay (claimant can only go back two years under Title VII) and no cap on the recovery of compensatory or punitive damages.

Equal Pay Act of 1963

Protects both sexes from pay discrimination based on sex. The act prohibits disparity in pay for jobs that require equal skill, equal effort, equal responsibility, or similar working conditions.
- If two jobs are determined to be equal and similar, an employer cannot pay disparate wages to members of different sexes.

Criteria That Justify a Differential in Wages. The employer bears the burden of proving the following criteria.
- Seniority
- Merit
- Quantity of quality of product (commissions)
- A differential based on any factor other than sex (shift differential)

Age Discrimination in Employment Act

The ADEA prohibits age discrimination in all employment decisions, including hiring, promotions, compensation, and other terms and conditions of employment.
- The ADEA covers
  - o nonfederal employers with at least 20 employees
  - o labor unions with at least 25 members

- o all employment agencies
- o State and local government employees except those in policy-making positions
- o employees of certain sectors of the federal government
- The Older Worker Benefit Protection Act prohibits age discrimination in employee benefits.

Protected Age Categories. The ADEA applies to all employees over age 40, is administered by the EEOC, and allows private plaintiffs to sue.
- A successful plaintiff can recover back wages, attorneys' fees, and equitable relief.
- An employer found to be in violation of the ADEA must raise the wages of the discriminated-against employee, but cannot lower the wages of other employees.

The Americans with Disabilities Act of 1990

The ADA imposes obligations on employers and providers of public transportation, telecommunications, and public accommodations to accommodate individuals with disabilities.
- Title I bars employment discrimination against qualified individuals with disabilities in job application procedures, hiring, compensation, training, promotion, and termination.
- Title I requires an employer to make reasonable accommodations to individuals with disabilities that do not cause hardship to the employer.

Qualified Individual with a Disability. A qualified individual with a disability is a person who, with or without reasonable accommodation, can perform the essential functions of the job that the person desires or holds.
- A disabled person is someone who
  - o has a physical or mental impairment that substantially limits one or more of his or her major life activities
  - o has a record of such impairment, or
  - o is regarded as having such impairment
- See pages 522 through 523 of your text for conditions that are covered under the ADA.
  - o Recovering alcoholics and former users of illegal drugs are protected, but current users of illegal drugs or an alcoholic using alcohol or those under the influence of alcohol at the workplace is not covered.

Forbidden Conduct. Employers may not inquire into the existence, nature, or severity of a disability during the application process.
- An employer may inquire about the applicant's ability to perform job-related functions.
- Pre-employment medical examinations are forbidden before a job offer.
- Once a job offer is made, an employer may require a medical examination and may condition the offer on the results, as long as all entering employees are subject to such an examination.

Procedure and Remedies. Complaints under the ADA must be filed with the EEOC, which may decide to sue on behalf of the aggrieved or permit the aggrieved to sue.
- Remedies include
  - o compensatory and punitive damages
  - o hiring or reinstatement with back pay
  - o injunctions
  - o attorneys' fees

Affirmative Action

This is a policy that provides that certain job preferences will be given to minority or other protected class applicants when an employer makes an employment decision.

Affirmative Action Plans. Affirmative action plans will not be upheld when they discriminate against a majority after past discriminatory practices have already been rectified.
- The courts will not allow employers to give a preference to a minority when another employee is far better qualified for a position.

Reverse Discrimination. Reverse discrimination is also protected under Title VII. Though the courts have held that "this effect is not actionable by members of the majority class who are affected," there is an exception of sorts.
- If an affirmative action plan is based on pre-established numbers or percentage quotas for hiring or promoting minority applicants, then reverse discrimination is the result whereby the members of the majority may sue under Title VII and recover damages as well as other remedies for the same.

Retaliation

Retaliatory actions by employers are forbidden under Title VII and Section 1981.
- Retaliatory actions include dismissing, demoting, and harassing.

Refresh Your Memory

The following exercise will give you the opportunity to test your memory of the principles given in this chapter. Read the question twice and place your answer in the blank provided. Review the chapter material for any question that you are unable to answer or remember.

1. A plaintiff can file a claim against an employer within _____ days of the most recent paycheck violation.

2. _____ occurs when an employer treats a specific individual less favorably than others because of that person's race, color, national origin, sex, or religion.

3. _____ occurs when an employer discriminates against an entire protected class.

4. Employment discrimination against a person because of his or her heritage, cultural characteristics, or the country of the person's ancestors is called _____.

5. Gender discrimination where sexual favors are requested in order to obtain a job or be promoted is called _____.

6. _____ includes lewd remarks, touching, intimidation, posting of indecent materials, and other verbal or physical conduct of a sexual nature that occurs on the job.

7. _____ decisions are often based on work, educational experience, and professionally developed ability tests.

8. Discrimination based on protected classes other than race or color is permitted if it is shown to be a _____.

9. A broad class of individuals with common characteristics is called a _____.

10. The _____ Act of 1963 protects both sexes from pay discrimination based on sex.

11. The _____ protects employees who are 40 and older from job discrimination based on their age.

12. The _____ imposes obligations on employers and providers of public transportation, telecommunications, and public accommodations to accommodate physically challenged individuals.

13. A _____ is a person who has a physiological or psychological impairment that substantially limits a major life activity who, with or without reasonable accommodation, can perform the essential functions of the job that person desires or holds.

14. Employers are not obligated to provide accommodations that would impose a(n) _____— that is, actions that would require significant difficulty or expense.

15. _____ is based on information from which it is possible to determine a person's propensity to be stricken by diseases.

Critical Thought Exercise

Carol Jones was employed with Richmond Components, Inc. (RCI), an electrical engineering and manufacturing company that supplied parts and guidance system development for the United States Air Force. Jones was a public relations and communications manager for RCI at their facility located on Davis Air Force Base for over nine years. Of the 135 employees at the RCI facility at Davis AFB, only 9 women were in professional positions. Employees in the office where Jones worked used e-mail as the major form of communication between employees. Jones was sent sexually explicit material via e-mail, including pictures that had been downloaded from the Internet. Two male engineers in her work area used semi-nude swimsuit pictures as the screensaver on their computer. Pictures of nude women from magazines were cut out and put in her mailbox with notes, such as, "Will you pose like this for us?" When Jones requested that information for press releases be given to her by a stated deadline, she was told to "Go have sex and chill out," along with other sexually demeaning comments about her anatomy. When Jones complained to the vice president in charge of personnel, she was told that she worked in a high-stress 'boys' club" and she had better learn to accept the "give-and-take" environment at RCI. Jones quit her job and filed an action under Title VII. Will she prevail?

Please compose your answer to the Critical Thinking Exercise using a separate sheet of paper or your computer word processing program.

Practice Quiz

True/False

16. _____ If a person believes that he or she has been discriminated against in the workplace, he or she cannot immediately file a lawsuit against the employer.

17. _____ The EEOC and a complainant can jointly sue an employer who discriminated against the complainant.

18. _____ A plaintiff can file a claim against an employer within 180 days of the most recent paycheck violation.

19. _____ Disparate-treatment discrimination occurs when an employer treats a specific individual less favorably than others because of that person's race, color, national origin, sex, or religion.

20. _____ If an employer refuses to promote all persons of the Asian race, the company has engaged in disparate-impact discrimination.

21. _____ If a light-skinned member of a race refuses to hire a dark-skinned member of the same race, it constitutes racial discrimination.

22. _____ Denying employment to a woman because she is pregnant is a form of quid pro quo sex discrimination.

23. _____ Employers are not strictly liable to any of their employees who might have suffered sexual harassment at the workplace.

24. _____ Federal workers are not covered under the Equal Pay Act.

25. _____ If an employer denies a salary hike to an employee because she is a woman, the employer is liable for sexual harassment.

26. _____ Employers are obligated to provide reasonable accommodations to physically challenged employee if they do not incur significant difficulty or expense for the employers.

27. _____ Employees stricken with cancer, diabetes, or epilepsy are considered qualified individuals with a disability under ADA provisions.

28. _____ The ADAAA is a federal statute that makes it illegal for an employer to discriminate against job applicants and employees based on genetic information.

29. _____ An affirmative action plan provides that certain job preferences will be given to members of minority racial and ethnic groups, females, and other protected-class applicants when making employment decisions.

30. _____ Federal antidiscrimination laws prohibit employers from engaging in retaliation against an employee for filing a charge of discrimination.

Multiple Choice

31. If the EEOC chooses not to bring suit, it issues a(n) _____ to the complainant.

A. affirmative defense
B. filing date
C. right to sue letter
D. document of claim

32. The _____ is a federal statute that permits a complainant to file an employment discrimination claim against an employer within 180 days of the most recent paycheck violation.

A. Lilly Ledbetter Fair Pay Act
B. Title II of GINA
C. Civil Rights Act of 1964
D. Civil Rights Act of 1968

33. The _____ was intended to eliminate job discrimination based on race, color, national origin, sex, and religion.

A. Lilly Ledbetter Fair Pay Act
B. Title II of GINA
C. Fair Employment Practices Act
D. Title I of the ADA

34. _____ discrimination occurs when an employer treats a specific individual less favorably than others because of that person's race, color, national origin, sex, or religion.

A. Disparate-impact
B. Disparate-treatment
C. Favored-treatment
D. Unfair-impact

35. _____ discrimination occurs when an employer discriminates against an entire protected class.

A. Disparate-treatment
B. Favored-treatment
C. Disparate-impact
D. Unfair-impact

36. Which of the following is an instance of disparate-treatment discrimination?

A. An employer does not promote Kelly as she is about take maternity leave.
B. An employer refuses to install a wooden ramp to accommodate Lin who is restricted to a wheelchair.
C. Ghalib, who is fluent in English, is not hired as a writer due to his Iraqi heritage.
D. A factory hires 22-year old Jerry over 46-year old Barry, citing age as the reason.

37. Which of the following types of employment discrimination is carried out against a person because of his or her heritage or cultural characteristics?

A. race discrimination
B. color discrimination
C. genetic information discrimination
D. national origin discrimination

38. Which of the following is true of sex discrimination?

A. It is not the same as gender discrimination.
B. Employment discrimination because of pregnancy is sex discrimination.
C. Prohibition against sex discrimination applies only to women, not men.
D. Sex discrimination is covered by Title II of GINA.

39. Which of the following best describes quid pro quo sex discrimination?

A. discrimination where sexual favors are requested in order to obtain a job or be promoted
B. employment discrimination because of pregnancy, childbirth or related medical conditions
C. discrimination in hiring or promotion based on the gender of the employee under consideration
D. selective or partial treatment offered to an employee or a group of employees based on their gender

40. Lila Miller who works for a large software firm is four-months pregnant and is due for a promotion. However, her employer offers the promotion to Harry Oswald, a less-experienced candidate, as Lila would go on maternity leave soon and would be unable to perform her duties. Which of the following is true of this scenario?

A. Lila's employer has violated Title VII of the Civil Rights Act of 1964.
B. Lila's employer is liable for disparate-impact discrimination.
C. The employer was lawful in denying Lila the promotion.
D. Lila's employer is liable for disparate-treatment discrimination.

41. Using a sexually explicit picture or screensaver to mock an employee constitutes _____.

A. gender discrimination
B. quid pro quo sex discrimination
C. physical abuse
D. sexual harassment

42. Jason Smith is a Hispanic scriptwriter from Brazil who works for a television show on an American cable network. He was fired after the producer came to know that Smith was a scientologist by faith. The producer's official reason for this termination was that as Smith was based in Brazil, communication was a problem. This is an example of _____ discrimination that violates Title VII of the Civil Rights Act.

A. racial
B. national origin
C. religious
D. disparate-impact

43. Why is proving a bona fide occupational qualification essential?

A. to establish the employer's violation of Title VII
B. for discrimination to be legal
C. to establish the employee's claim is fraudulent
D. for an employee to claim being discriminated against by the employer

44. Which of the following is true of the Equal Pay Act?

A. An employer who has violated the Equal Pay Act must lower the wages of employees whose wages had been increased.
B. Federal workers are covered under the Equal Pay Act.
C. Employees cannot bring a private cause of action against an employer for violating the Equal Pay Act.
D. It protects both sexes from pay discrimination based on gender.

45. A(n) _____ provides that certain job preferences will be given to members of minority racial and ethnic groups, females, and other protected-class applicants when making employment decisions.

A. retaliation
B. affirmative action plan
C. affirmative defense
D. reasonable accommodation plan

Short Answer

46. An employee feels discriminated against by his employer, based on his religion. Who must he approach before filing a lawsuit against the employer? Describe the process.

_____
_____

47. Explain the Lilly Ledbetter Fair Pay Act of 2009.

_____
_____

48. Explain the scope and provisions of Title VII of the Civil Rights Act.

_____
_____

49. Distinguish between disparate-treatment and disparate-impact discrimination.

_____
_____

50. Explain gender discrimination.

_____
_____

51. Outline an Employer's defense to a charge of sexual harassment.

_____
_____

52. What are the defenses to a Title VII action?

_____

_____

53. When is an employer required to prove a bona fide occupational qualification? Explain with an example.

_____

_____

54. What are the Criteria that justify a differential in wages?

_____

_____

55. Explain the concept of reasonable accommodation of physically challenged employees. When is an employer not obligated to provide such accommodation?

_____

_____

Answers To Refresh Your Memory

1. 180 [p. 544]
2. Disparate-treatment discrimination [p. 546]
3. Disparate-impact discrimination [p. 546]
4. national origin discrimination [p. 547]
5. quid pro quo sex discrimination [p. 549]
6. Sexual harassment [p. 550]
7. Merit [p. 552]
8. bona fide occupational qualification [p. 552]
9. race [p. 553]
10. Equal Pay [p. 553]
11. Age Discrimination in Employment Act [p. 554]
12. Americans with Disabilities Act [p. 555]
13. qualified individual with a disability [p. 555]
14. undue hardship [p. 556]
15. Genetic information discrimination [p. 557]

Critical Thought Exercise Model Answer

Title VII applies to employers with 15 or more employees. With 135 employees at this facility alone, RCI will be covered by Title VII. Title VII prohibits harassment based upon gender in the workplace. Sexual harassment may be based upon lewd remarks, touching, intimidation, posting of sexually explicit pictures, and other unwanted verbal or physical conduct that is sexual in nature. Jones will argue that the activities of her coworkers have created a hostile work environment. To determine if the environment at RCI is hostile, a court will look at all the circumstances. These will include the frequency of the discriminatory conduct; its severity; whether it is physically threatening or humiliating, or a mere offensive utterance, and whether it unreasonably interferes with an employee's work performance.

The conduct of the male employees at RCI has created a hostile work environment. The acts are frequent and quite severe. Pictures are deliberately put in Jones's mailbox with notes that ask her to pose nude for fellow employees. Jones is berated verbally with sexual statements when she tries to do her job and get information for press releases. She is subjected to the sexually explicit pictures on computers on a daily basis because they have been installed as screensavers. Finally, there was no effort by RCI to stop or correct the harassment. Jones was told to accept it and no action was taken against the offending employees. Jones should prevail on a claim brought under Title VII for sexual harassment.

Answers to Practice Quiz

True/False

16. True. If a person believes that he or she has been discriminated against in the workplace, he or she cannot immediately file a lawsuit against the employer. The complainant must first file a complaint with the EEOC. [p. 544]

17. False. If the EEOC sues the employer, the complainant cannot sue the employer. In this case, the EEOC represents the complainant. [p. 544]

18. True. The Lilly Ledbetter Fair Pay Act of 2009 provides that each discriminatory pay decision restarts the statutory 180-day clock. Thus, a plaintiff can file a claim against an employer within 180 days of the most recent paycheck violation. [p. 544]

19. True. Disparate-treatment discrimination is a form of discrimination that occurs when an employer discriminates against a specific individual because of his or her race, color, national origin, sex, or religion. [p. 546]

20. False. If an employer refuses to promote all persons of the Asian race, the company has engaged in racial discrimination. [p. 547]

21. False. If a light-skinned member of a race refuses to hire a dark-skinned member of the same race, this constitutes color discrimination, in violation of Title VII. [p. 549]

22. False. Title VII also prohibits any form of gender discrimination where sexual favors are requested in order to obtain a job or be promoted. This is called quid pro quo sex discrimination. [p. 549]

23. True. An employer may raise an affirmative defense against liability by proving two elements: 1. The employer exercised reasonable care to prevent, and promptly correct, any sexual harassing behavior. 2. The plaintiff-employee unreasonably failed to take advantage of any preventive or corrective opportunities provided by the employer or to otherwise avoid harm. [p. 550]

24. True. The Equal Pay Act of 1963 protects both sexes from pay discrimination based on sex. This act covers all levels of private-sector employees and state and local government employees. Federal workers are not covered, however. [p. 553]

25. False. The Equal Pay Act of 1963 protects both sexes from pay discrimination based on sex. [p. 553]

26. True. Under Title I, an employer is under the obligation to make a reasonable accommodation to accommodate the individual's disability as long as such accommodation does not cause an undue hardship on the employer. [p. 556]

27. False. The ADA does not consider some impairments or illnesses or certain conditions to be disabilities. [p. 556]

28. False. Genetic Information Nondiscrimination Act (GINA) is a federal statute that makes it illegal for an employer to discriminate against job applicants and employees based on genetic information. [p. 557]

29. True. Employers often adopt an affirmative action plan, which provides that certain job preferences will be given to members of minority racial and ethnic groups, females, and other protected-class applicants when making employment decisions. [p. 558]

30. True. Federal antidiscrimination laws prohibit employers from engaging in retaliation against an employee for filing a charge of discrimination or participating in a discrimination proceeding concerning race, color, national origin, gender, religion, age, disability, genetic information, and other forms of discrimination. [p. 558]

Multiple Choice

31. C. If the EEOC finds a violation and chooses not to bring suit, or does not find a violation, the EEOC will issue a right to sue letter to the complainant. This gives the complainant the right to sue his or her employer. [p. 544]

32. A. The Lilly Ledbetter Fair Pay Act of 2009 provides that each discriminatory pay decision restarts the statutory 180-day clock. Thus, a plaintiff can file a claim against an employer within 180 days of the most recent paycheck violation. [p. 544]

33. C. Title VII of the Civil Rights Act, also called the Fair Employment Practices Act, was intended to eliminate job discrimination based on the following protected classes: race, color, national origin, sex, and religion. [p. 545]

34. B. Disparate-treatment discrimination is a form of discrimination that occurs when an employer discriminates against a specific individual because of his or her race, color, national origin, sex, or religion. [p. 546]

35. C. Disparate-impact discrimination is a form of discrimination that occurs when an employer discriminates against an entire protected class. An example is discrimination in which a racially neutral employment practice or rule causes an adverse impact on a protected class. [p. 546]

36. C. Disparate-treatment discrimination occurs when an employer treats a specific individual less favorably than others because of that person's race, color, national origin, sex, or religion. [p. 546]

37. D. National origin discrimination would include discrimination against persons of a particular nationality (e.g., persons of Irish descent), against persons who come from a certain place (e.g., Iran), against persons of a certain culture (e.g., Hispanics), or against persons because of their accents. [p. 547]

38. B. Title VII of the Civil Rights Act of 1964 prohibits job discrimination based on gender. The act, as amended, the EEOC's rules, and court decisions prohibit employment discrimination based on gender, pregnancy, and sexual orientation. [p. 549]

39. A. Title VII prohibits any form of gender discrimination where sexual favors are requested in order to obtain a job or be promoted. This is called quid pro quo sex discrimination. [p. 549]

40. A. In 1978, the Pregnancy Discrimination Act was enacted as an amendment to Title VII. This amendment forbids employment discrimination because of "pregnancy, childbirth, or related medical conditions." [p. 549]

41. D. Sexual harassment includes lewd remarks, offensive or sexually oriented jokes; name-calling, slurs, intimidation, ridicule, mockery, and insults or put-downs; offensive or sexually explicit objects, pictures, cartoons, posters, and screen savers; physical threats; touching; and other verbal or physical conduct of a sexual nature. [p. 550]

42. C. Title VII prohibits employment discrimination based on a person's religion. Religions include traditional religions, other religions that recognize a supreme being, and religions based on ethical or spiritual tenets. [p. 551]

43. B. Discrimination based on protected classes other than race or color is permitted if it is shown to be a bona fide occupational qualification (BFOQ). [p. 552]

44. D. Discrimination often takes the form of different pay scales for men and women performing the same job. The Equal Pay Act of 1963 protects both sexes from pay discrimination based on sex. [p. 553]

45. B. Employers often adopt an affirmative action plan, which provides that certain job preferences will be given to members of minority racial and ethnic groups, females, and other protected-class applicants when making employment decisions. [p. 558]

Short Answer

46. If a person believes that he or she has been discriminated against in the workplace, he or she cannot immediately file a lawsuit against the employer. The complainant must first file a complaint with the EEOC. The EEOC often requests that the parties try to resolve their dispute through mediation. If mediation does not work, the EEOC will investigate the charge. If the EEOC finds a violation, it will decide whether to sue the employer. If the EEOC sues the employer, the complainant cannot sue the employer. In this case, the EEOC represents the complainant. If the EEOC finds a violation and chooses not to bring suit, or does not find a violation, the EEOC will issue a right to sue letter to the complainant. This gives the complainant the right to sue his or her employer. If a state has a Fair Employment Practices Agency (FEPA), the complainant may file his or her claim with the FEPA instead of the EEOC. Often a complainant will file a complaint with an FEPA if state law provides protection from discrimination not covered by federal laws or if the FEPA's procedure permits a filing date that is longer than that of the EEOC. The FEPA complaint process is similar to that of the EEOC. [p. 544]

47. The Civil Rights Act provided that a rejected applicant for a job or an employee who suffers pay discrimination must file a discrimination lawsuit within 180 days of the employer's act that causes the discrimination. In Ledbetter v. Goodyear Tire & Rubber Co., Inc.,1 the U.S. Supreme

Court held that the 180-day statute of limitations began to run on the date the pay was agreed upon, not when the most recent paycheck violation occurred. Thus, a victim who had been subject to pay discrimination for more than 180 days and had failed to report the claim within 180 days of the first violation was denied his or her claim.

Congress responded by enacting the Lilly Ledbetter Fair Pay Act of 2009, which overruled the U.S. Supreme Court's decision. The act provides that each discriminatory pay decision restarts the statutory 180-day clock. Thus, a plaintiff can file a claim against an employer within 180 days of the most recent paycheck violation. The act provides that a court can award back pay for up to two years preceding the filing of the claim if similar violations occurred during the prior two-year time period. [p. 544]

48. Title VII of the Civil Rights Act of 1964 applies to (1) employers with fifteen or more employees, (2) all employment agencies, (3) labor unions with fifteen or more members, (4) state and local governments and their agencies, and (5) most federal government employment. Native American tribes and tax-exempt private clubs are expressly excluded from coverage. Other portions of the Civil Rights Act of 1964 prohibit discrimination in housing, education, and other facets of life. Title VII prohibits discrimination in hiring, decisions regarding promotion or demotion, payment of compensation and fringe benefits, availability of job training and apprenticeship opportunities, referral systems for employment, decisions regarding dismissal, work rules, and any other "term, condition, or privilege" of employment. Any employee of a covered employer, including undocumented aliens, may bring actions for employment discrimination under Title VII. U.S. citizens employed by U.S.-controlled companies in foreign countries are covered by Title VII. Foreign nationals employed in foreign countries by U.S. controlled companies are not covered by Title VII. [p. 545]

49. Disparate-treatment discrimination occurs when an employer treats a specific individual less favorably than others because of that person's race, color, national origin, sex, or religion. In such situations, the complainant must prove that (1) he or she belongs to a Title VII protected class, (2) he or she applied for and was qualified for the employment position, (3) he or she was rejected despite this, and (4) the employer kept the position open and sought applications from persons with the complainant's qualifications. Disparate-impact discrimination occurs when an employer discriminates against an entire protected class. Often, this type of discrimination is proven through statistical data about an employer's employment practices. The plaintiff must demonstrate a causal link between the challenged practice and the statistical imbalance. Showing a statistical disparity between the percentages of protected class employees and the percentage of the population that the protected class makes within the surrounding community is not enough, by itself, to prove discrimination. Disparate-impact discrimination can occur when an employer adopts a work rule that is neutral on its face but is shown to cause an adverse impact on a protected class. [p. 546]

50. Title VII prohibits employment discrimination based on gender. Although the prohibition against gender discrimination, also known as sex discrimination, applies equally to men and women, the overwhelming majority of Title VII sex discrimination cases are brought by women. Sex discrimination cases are brought where there is direct sex discrimination.

Title VII also prohibits any form of gender discrimination where sexual favors are requested in order to obtain a job or be promoted. This is called quid pro quo sex discrimination.

In 1978, the Pregnancy Discrimination Act was enacted as an amendment to Title VII.10 This amendment forbids employment discrimination because of "pregnancy, childbirth, or related medical conditions." [p. 549]

51. Employers are not strictly liable for the sexual harassment of their employees. An employer may raise an affirmative defense against liability by proving two elements:
1. The employer exercised reasonable care to prevent, and promptly correct, any sexual harassing behavior.
2. The plaintiff-employee unreasonably failed to take advantage of any preventive or corrective opportunities provided by the employer or to otherwise avoid harm.
The defendant-employer has the burden of proving this affirmative defense.
In determining whether the defense has been proven, a court must consider (1) whether the employer has an anti-harassment policy, (2) whether the employer had a complaint mechanism in place, (3) whether employees were informed of the anti-harassment policy and complaint procedure, and (4) other factors that the court deems relevant. [p. 550]

52. Title VII and case law recognize several defenses to a charge of discrimination under Title VII. Employers can select or promote employees based on merit. Merit decisions are often based on work, educational experience, and professionally developed ability tests. To be lawful under Title VII, such a requirement must be job related. Many employers maintain seniority systems that reward long-term employees. Higher wages, fringe benefits, and other preferential treatment (e.g., choice of working hours, choice of vacation schedule) are examples of such rewards. Seniority systems provide an incentive for employees to stay with the company. Such systems are lawful if they are not the result of intentional discrimination. [p. 552]

53. Discrimination based on protected classes other than race or color is permitted if it is shown to be a bona fide occupational qualification (BFOQ). Thus, an employer can justify discrimination based on gender in some circumstances. To be legal, a BFOQ must be both job related and a business necessity.
Example: Allowing only women to be locker room attendants in a women's gym is a valid BFOQ. Prohibiting males from being managers or instructors at the same gym would not be a BFOQ. [p. 552]

54. The Equal Pay Act expressly provides four criteria that justify a differential in wages. These defenses include payment systems that are based on:
• Seniority.
• Merit (as long as there is some identifiable measurement standard).
• Quantity or quality of product (i.e., commission, piecework, or quality control– based payment systems are permitted).
• "Any factor other than sex" (including shift differentials, such as night versus day shifts). [p. 554]

55. Under Title I of ADA, an employer is under the obligation to make a reasonable accommodation to accommodate an individual's disability as long as such accommodation does not cause an undue hardship on the employer. If an employer makes a reasonable accommodation to accommodate an individual's disability, there is no violation of the ADA. However, if an employer does not make a reasonable accommodation that could be made without causing an undue hardship on the employer, the employer has violated the ADA. Employers are not obligated to provide accommodations that would impose an undue hardship—that is, actions that would require significant difficulty or expense. [p. 556]

34 | SMALL BUSINESSES, ENTREPRENEURS, AND GENERAL PARTNERSHIPS

Chapter Overview

This chapter focuses on the role of the entrepreneur, sole proprietorship, and general partnership in business. You will learn the advantages and disadvantages of operating a business as a sole proprietorship, and become aware of the liabilities that a sole proprietor may face. You will learn about general partnerships, their formation, and the rights and duties among the partners. You will learn that the right to participate in the partnership's management is as important as the right to share in the partnership's profits and losses. You will gain familiarity with the duty of loyalty and its violation among partners. The duty of care, the liabilities in contract and tort, and the incoming and outgoing responsibilities of partners are discussed. You will become aware of how a partnership is terminated and how partners may continue a partnership after termination.

Objectives

Upon completion of the exercises in this chapter, you should be able to:
1. Define entrepreneurship and describe the types of businesses that an entrepreneur can use to operate a business.
2. Define sole proprietorship and describe the liability of a sole proprietor.
3. Define general partnership and describe how general partnerships are formed and operated.
4. Explain the contract and tort liability of general partners.
5. Describe how a general partnership is dissolved and terminated.

Practical Application

This chapter will enable you to be more aware of the positive and concerning aspects of operating a business as a sole proprietorship. You will have a greater understanding of the magnitude of the liability associated with conducting business in this manner. You will have valuable knowledge that will enable you to make informed decisions regarding the possibility of conducting business as a partnership. It will give you insight into the legal duties and ramifications of failing to adhere to the duties expected of a partner under the law.

Helpful Hints

Since the information contained in this chapter focuses on the topics of entrepreneurs and sole proprietorship, as well as general partnerships, the principles are quickly committed to memory. The Study Tips section has been organized in much the same way as the chapter in your text has been presented. Since the information is so concisely written, the concepts will be easy to grasp.

Study Tips

When studying this chapter, it is best to commit the definition of an entrepreneur to memory, as well as be familiar with the fact that there are various choices in which to operate an entrepreneur's business organization. If you make a mental check list with duties of partners on one side and rights on the other, the principles associated with general partnerships will readily come to you. This chapter provides an excellent insight into the types of businesses into which many individuals enter and gives a good basis for learning about some of the more complicated businesses that are discussed in the chapters that follow.

Small Businesses, Entrepreneurs, and General Partnerships

When starting a business, one can choose to operate as any one of several major forms.
- The choice depends on many factors, including the ease and cost of formation, the capital requirements of the business, the flexibility of management decisions, government restrictions, personal liability, and tax considerations.

Entrepreneurship

An entrepreneur is an individual who creates and operates a new business, either by him- or herself or with others.

Entrepreneurial Forms of Conducting Business. There are several choices of organizational form available, each of which has advantages and disadvantages.
- sole proprietorship
- general partnership
- limited partnership
- limited liability partnership
- limited liability company
- corporation

Sole Proprietorship

Sole proprietorships are the simplest form of business organization as well as most common form in the United States. A sole proprietorship is not a distinct legal entity.
- *Advantages.*
  - Easy to form and relatively inexpensive.
  - The owner can make all management decisions, including hiring and firing.
  - The owner has the right to all profits of the business.
  - It is easily transferred or sold without anyone else's approval.
- *Disadvantages.*
  - Access to capital is limited to personal funds plus any loans the proprietor can obtain.
  - The sole proprietor is held responsible for the business's contracts and torts he/she or any of his or her employees commit in the course of employment.

Creation of a Sole Proprietorship. No state or federal formalities are required.
- Some local governments may require that a sole proprietor obtain a license to do business.
- If no other business form is chosen, it is by default a sole proprietorship.

"d.b.a." – Doing Business As. A sole proprietorship may conduct itself under the name of the sole proprietor or a trade name, commonly referred to as d.b.a. (*doing business as*).
- Most states require the filing of a fictitious business name statement, which gives the name and address of the applicant, address of the business, and the trade name.
    - Publication of the notice of the trade name is often required.

Personal Liability of Sole Proprietors. If the sole proprietorship fails, the owner will lose his or her entire contribution of capital.
- He or she has unlimited personal liability, subjecting personal assets to creditors' claims.

Taxation of a Sole Proprietorship. A sole proprietorship is not a separate legal entity, thus all earnings and losses are reported on the sole proprietor's personal income tax filing.

General Partnership

A general partnership is "a voluntary association of two or more persons for carrying on a business as co-owners for profit."
- General partners personally liable for the debts and obligations of the partnership

Uniform Partnership Act (UPA). The UPA requirements are like the building code requirements of a house in that it is codified partnership law that has been adopted by 48 states.
- The UPA details laws concerning formation, operation, and dissolution of basic partnerships.
- The UPA adopted the entity theory of partnership which considers partnerships as separate legal entities that are able to hold title to both real and personal property, and transact business in the partnership name.

General Partnership Name. The name of an ordinary partnership can be the name of any one or more of the partners or a fictitious business name.
- A fictitious business name statement must be filed with the proper governmental agency.
    - Notice of the fictitious name must be published.
- The name cannot indicate that it is a corporation.
- The name cannot be similar to the name used by an existing business.

Formation of a General Partnership.
- There are four requirements in order to be considered a general partnership.
    - It must be an association of two or more persons.
        - All partners must be in agreement of each participating co-partner.
        - Person includes natural persons, partnerships, associations, and corporations.
    - These persons must be carrying on a business.
        - Co-ownership such as joint tenancy, tenancy by the entireties, and tenancy in common qualify.
        - A series of transactions conducted over a period of time.
    - These individuals must be operating as co-owners.
        - Essential to form a partnership.
        - Co-ownership is evaluated based on the sharing of business profits and management responsibility.
    - The business must be for profit or have a profit motive.
- Receipt of a share of profits is prima facie evidence of a partnership.
- An agreement to share losses of a business is strong evidence of a partnership.

- The right to participate in the management of a business is important, but not conclusive, evidence for determining a partnership exists.
- It is compelling evidence a partnership exists if a person is given the right to share in profits, losses, and management of a business.

The General Partnership Agreement. Partnerships may be expressly formed or impliedly formed, either verbally or in writing.
- There is no necessity to file a partnership's agreement in most states.
  - A select few require a general partnership to file certificates of partnership with the proper government agency.
- Partnerships are viewed as separate legal entities that can hold title to real and personal property.

Taxation of Partnerships. Partnerships, though they do not pay federal income taxes, must file an information return with the government.
- Income and losses of the partnership "flow through" to the partners and are reported on the personal income tax returns of the partners.

Rights of General Partners

Right to Participate in Management. All partners have equal rights in the conduct and management of the partnership business, unless otherwise agreed.
- Each partner has one vote regardless of the proportional size of his or her capital contribution or share in the partnership profits.
- A simple majority decides most partnership matters.

Right to Share in Profits. Unless otherwise agreed, each partner has the right to share in partnership profits and losses.

Right to Compensation and Reimbursement. Unless otherwise agreed, no partner is entitled to remuneration for his or her performance in the partnership's business.
- Unless otherwise agreed, income earned by partners from providing services elsewhere belongs to the partnership.
- A partner is entitled to indemnification for expenditures if they are reasonably incurred in the ordinary and proper conduct of the business.

Right to Return of Loans and Capital. Partners are entitled to the repayment of loans, with interest, made to the partnership, subordinated to the claims of other creditors.
- Partners are entitled to the return of capital contributions on the termination of the partnership, subordinated to the claims of other creditors.

Right to Information. Partners have the right to true and full information from any other partners regarding all things affecting the partnership.
- Each partner has a duty to provide other partners with such information on demand.

Duties of General Partners

The Duty of Loyalty. Partners have the fiduciary duty of loyalty that cannot be waived. If there is a conflict between partnership interests and personal interests, the partner must choose the partnership interests. Breaches of loyalty include the following:

- The duty not to self-deal.
- The duty not to usurp a partnership opportunity.
- The duty not to compete with the partnership.
- The duty not to make a secret profit from the partnership.
- The duty to keep partnership information confidential.
- The duty not to use partnership property for personal use.

The Duty of Care. The duty of care encompasses the duty to use the same level of care and skill a reasonable businessperson would use in the same circumstances.
- Breach of the duty of care is equivalent to negligence.

The Duty to Inform. Partners must inform their co-partners of all information they possess that concerns the partnership affairs.

The Duty of Obedience. This refers to the partners' duties to act in accordance with the partnership agreement.

Right to an Accounting. Instead of being allowed to sue one another, partners may bring an action for an accounting against the other partners.

Liability of General Partners

"General partners are personally liable for contracts entered into on the partnership's behalf."

Tort Liability. The liability of the partnership for the torts of its partners, employees, or agents depends on whether or not the person was acting within the ordinary course of the partnership business or with the authority of his or her co-partners. UPA Sections 13 and 14.
- *Joint and Several Liability of Partners.* Partners are jointly and severally liable for torts and breaches of trust regardless of a partner's participation in the act.
  - A third party can sue one or more of the partners separately.
    - Judgment can be collected only against the partners who are sued.

Contract Liability. Contracts entered into with suppliers, customers, lenders, or others on the partnership's behalf are binding on the partnership.
- *Joint Liability of Partners.* Partners are jointly liable for the contracts and debts of the partnership, so that a third party who sues to recover on a partnership contract or debt must name all the partners in the lawsuit.
  - If successful, the plaintiff can collect the entire amount of the judgment against any or all of the partners.
  - If the suit does not name all the partners, the judgment cannot be collected against any of the partners or the partnership assets.

Liability of Incoming Partners. A new partner is liable for existing debts and obligations only to the extent of his capital contributions.
- He is liable for obligations and debts obtained by the partnership after becoming a partner.

Dissolution of a General Partnership

The duration of a partnership can be for a specified time, until a specified purpose has been accomplished, or for an unspecified time.

- *Dissolution.* "The change in the relation of the partners caused by any partner ceasing to be associated in the carrying on of the business."
  - *Partnership for a term.* A partnership with a fixed duration, where the partnership ends on the specified date or at the completion of the specified task.
  - *Partnership at will.* A partnership with no fixed duration, where the partnership ends at the behest of one or more of the partners.
- *Winding up.* The process of liquidating partnership assets and distributing the proceeds to satisfy claims against the partnership.

Wrongful Dissolution. A partner may wrongfully attempt to dissolve the partnership by withdrawing before the expiration of the stated term.

- If a partner's actions constitute wrongful dissolution of the partnership, he or she is liable for damages caused by the wrongful dissolution.

Notice of Dissolution. Third parties must be given notice of the dissolution. If proper notice is not given to third parties and a partner enters into a contract with the third party, previous partners may be held liable on the grounds of apparent authority.

- *Third Parties with Actual Dealings with the Partnership.* If the third party has had actual dealing with the partnership, then actual notice, oral or in writing must be given, or the third party must have obtained notice of the dissolution from another source.
- *Third Parties with Knowledge of the Partnership.* If the third party has not dealt with the partnership, but has knowledge of it, constructive or actual notice must be given.
  - Publication of the notice in a local newspaper where the partnership business was normally conducted is sufficient to satisfy the constructive notice requirements.
- *Third Parties without Knowledge of the Partnership.* Third parties without knowledge of the partnership or who have not dealt with the partnership do not need to be given any notice of the dissolution.

Distribution of Assets. After dissolution, the partnership goes through winding up.

- The debts of a partnership are satisfied in the following order:
  - creditors (except partners who are creditors)
  - creditor-partners
  - capital contributions
  - profits
- Partners may agree to alter the order of distribution of the assets.
- If the partnership does not have sufficient means to satisfy the creditors' claims, the partners are personally liable for the obligations and debts of the partnership.

Continuation of a General Partnership after Dissolution. The remaining or surviving partners have the right to continue a partnership after it is dissolved.

- It is wise for the partners to enter into a continuation agreement detailing the partnership's continuation, amount to be paid to outgoing partners, etc.
- The creditors of the old partnership become creditors of the new partnership and have equal status with the creditors of the new partnership.

Liability of Outgoing Partners. If a partnership is dissolved because a partner leaves the partnership and the partnership is continued by the remaining partners, the outgoing partner is personally liable for the debts and obligations of the partnership at the time of dissolution.

- The outgoing partner is not liable for any new debts and obligations incurred by the partnership after the dissolution, as long as proper notification of his or her withdrawal from the partnership has been given to the creditor.

Right of Survivorship. Upon the death of a partner, the deceased partner's right in specific partnership property vests in the remaining partner or partners—it does not vest in his or her heirs or next of kin.

- The value of the deceased partner's interest in the partnership passes to his or her beneficiaries or heirs upon his or her death.
- Upon the death of the last surviving partner, the rights in specific partnership property vest in the deceased partner's legal representative.

Refresh Your Memory

The following exercise will give you the opportunity to test your memory of the principles given in this chapter. Read the question twice and place your answer in the blank provided. Review the chapter material for any question that you are unable to answer or remember.

1. A _____ is a person who forms and operates a new business either by himself or herself or with others.

2. _____ is a form of business in which the owner is actually the business; the business is not a separate legal entity.

3. _____ statement is a document that is filed with the state that designates a trade name of a business, the name and address of the applicant, and the address of the business.

4. _____ is an association of two or more persons to carry on as co-owners of a business for profit.

5. The income and losses of partnership flow onto and have to be reported on the individual partners' personal income tax returns. This is called _____.

6. The right of a partner to be reimbursed for expenditures incurred on behalf of the partnership is called _____.

7. A duty that a partner owes not to act adversely to the interests of the partnership is called _____.

8. _____ is the obligation partners owe to use the same level of care and skill that a reasonable person in the same position would use in the same circumstances.

9. A breach of the duty of care is _____.

10. The _____ requires general partners to adhere to the provisions of the partnership agreement and the decisions of the partnership.

11. The partnership and partners who are made to pay _____ may seek indemnification from the partner who committed the wrongful act.

12. A partnership with a fixed duration is called _____.

13. The _____ of a partnership is the change in the relation of the partners caused by any partner ceasing to be associated in the carrying on of the business.

14. If proper notice is not given to a required third party after the dissolution of a partnership, and a partner enters into a contract with the third party, liability may be imposed on the previous partners on the grounds of _____.

15. _____ is a rule which provides that upon the death of a general partner, the deceased partner's right in specific partnership property vests in the remaining partner or partners; the value of the deceased general partner's interest in the partnership passes to his or her beneficiaries or heirs.

Critical Thought Exercise

Larry and Diane Ortiz own and operate Maria's Restaurant in Houston, Texas. As husband and wife, they operate the restaurant as a sole proprietorship. As part of the advertising plan for Maria's, they participate in several 2-for-1 dinner coupon books and school fundraiser sticker books. An average of 15 2-for-1 coupons are redeemed each week. After Larry Ortiz is struck with a serious illness, the restaurant is sold to Bob Nelson. Nelson files the proper fictitious business name statement with the county and city clerk. The sale of the restaurant did not include the assignment of any contracts entered into prior to the sale by Larry and Diane Ortiz.

After Nelson remodels the restaurant, he reopens it with a Grand Reopening advertising campaign. Signs stating "New Owners" are posted at the restaurant and the same notice is in each advertisement. When Nelson refuses to honor the 2-for-1 coupons, 24 plaintiffs file suit against Maria's Restaurant and Bob Nelson for breach of contract and fraud. Is Bob Nelson liable because he failed to honor coupons for Maria's Restaurant?

Please compose your answer to the Critical Thinking Exercise using a separate sheet of paper or your computer word processing program.

Practice Quiz

True/False

16. _____ A sole proprietorship cannot be easily transferred when the owner desires to do so.

17. _____ The designation of d.b.a. refers to the description for a business that is operating under a trade name.

18. _____ No federal or state government approval is required for creating a sole proprietorship.

19. _____ The UPA is a model act that codifies sole proprietorship law.

20. _____ A general partnership is valid only if it is carried out for profit.

21. _____ A general partnership cannot operate under the name of any one of the partners; the name has to represent all the partners if a fictitious name is not being adopted.

22. _____ A general partnership agreement must always be in writing to be considered legal.

23. _____ General partnerships do not pay federal income taxes.

24. _____ The UPA provides that all general partners are entitled to remuneration for their performance in the partnership's business.

25. _____ Self-dealing—although fully disclosed—is not permitted in a general partnership.

26. _____ General partners owe a duty to inform their co-partners of all information they possess that is relevant to the affairs of the partnership

27. _____ No monetary damages can be claimed between partners for breach of duty of obedience in a general partnership.

28. _____ General partners are not permitted to sue other partners at law.

29. _____ General partners have unlimited personal liability for the debts and obligations of the partnership.

30. _____ The dissolution of a general partnership discharges the liability of an outgoing partner for existing partnership debts and obligations.

Multiple Choice

31. _____ are the most common form of business organization in the United States.

A. General partnerships
B. Limited partnerships
C. Limited liability companies
D. Sole proprietorships

32. Which of the following is true of a sole proprietorship?

A. A business operated under sole proprietorship cannot be transferred.
B. Creditors can recover claims against the business from the sole proprietor's personal assets.
C. A business operated under sole proprietorship should be owned by one or more people of the same family.
D. Large businesses cannot be operated under sole proprietorship.

33. A _____ is a document that is filed with the state that designates a trade name of a business.

A. fictitious business name statement
B. partnership agreement
C. proprietorship statement
D. nomenclature affidavit

34. Which of the following is true of a business operating under sole proprietorship?

A. It requires governmental approval when being transferred.
B. It cannot be sold when the owner decides to do so.
C. It is not considered a separate legal entity.
D. It has access to unrestricted capital by means of investments.

35. The earnings and losses from a sole proprietorship are reported on _____.

A. the proprietor's personal income tax filing
B. the business license that is renewed each year
C. the federal income tax filing document
D. the state income tax filing document

36. An ordinary partnership is also known as a _____.

A. sole proprietorship
B. limited liability company
C. limited partnership
D. general partnership

37. Which of the following is true of general partnership?

A. General partnerships can be either oral or implied from the conduct of the parties.
B. The general partners need not be the co-owners of the business.
C. A business should make a profit in order to qualify as a general partnership.
D. Charity organizations and schools are mostly formed from general partnerships.

38. Which of the following is true in the creation of a general partnership?

A. The business name has to have the names of all the partners.
B. The name selected by the partnership cannot indicate that it is a corporation.
C. The business name cannot be a fictitious name.
D. The business cannot operate under a trade name.

39. How long should a general partnership have existed for it to be in writing under the Statute of Frauds?

A. six months
B. one year
C. five years
D. 180 days

40. Which of the following is true of profits and losses in a general partnership?

A. The proportion of profit shared is equal to the general partner's initial investment.
B. The proportion of investment governs only the proportion of loss shared and not profit obtained.
C. The general partner who proposed the idea of the business gets most profit.
D. Losses are shared equally by all general partners.

41. Which of the following is a right to which every general partner is entitled?

A. right to return of capital
B. right to free and open speech
C. right to remuneration
D. right to legal action

42. Competing with the partnership without the permission of other partners violates a general partner's _____.

A. duty to inform
B. duty of obedience
C. duty of care
D. duty of loyalty

43. Which of the following is true of the liability of an incoming partner?

A. An incoming partner is liable for the debts of the partnership only to the extent of his or her capital contribution.
B. An incoming partner is equally liable for all existing debts of the partnership.
C. An incoming partner is liable for the previous debts of the partnership.
D. An incoming partner is not liable for the future debts of the partnership.

44. A(n) _____ is a partnership created with no fixed duration.

A. partnership for a term
B. ordinary partnership
C. partnership at will
D. limited partnership

45. _____ is a situation in which a partner withdraws from a partnership without having the right to do so at that time.

A. Winding up
B. Indemnification
C. Proliferation
D. Wrongful dissolution

Short Answer

46. List the advantages and disadvantages of a sole proprietorship.

_____

47. Explain the taxation levied on a sole proprietorship.

_____

_____

48. Outline the Uniform Partnership Act.

_____

_____

49. Briefly explain the formation of a general partnership.

_____

_____

50. Explain the general partnership agreement.

_____

51. What is flow-through taxation?

_____

_____

52. How are profits and losses shared in a partnership?

_____

_____

53. List a few basic forms of breach of loyalty.

_____

_____

54. Explain with an example the duty of care owed by a general partner.

_____

_____

55. How are assets distributed after the dissolution of a general partnership?

_____

_____

Answers to Refresh Your Memory

1. entrepreneur [p. 565]
2. Sole proprietorship [p. 565]
3. Fictitious business name [p. 566]
4. General partnership [p. 568]
5. flow-through taxation [p. 570]
6. indemnification [p. 571]
7. duty of loyalty [p. 572]
8. Duty of care [p. 573]
9. negligence [p. 573]
10. duty of obedience [p. 573]
11. tort liability [p. 574]
12. partnership for a term [p. 575]
13. dissolution [p. 575]
14. apparent authority [p. 576]
15. Right of survivorship [p. 577

Critical Thought Exercise Model Answer

A sole proprietorship has no legal identity separate from that of the individual who owns it. In this case, the 2-for-1 offers were made by Larry and Diane Ortiz. Only Larry and Diane Ortiz can be held liable for not honoring the coupons and fundraiser stickers unless Nelson assumes the liability as part of an assignment and delegation. Bob Nelson did not assume any of the liabilities or assume any of the contracts that had been made with Maria's Restaurant when it was owned by Larry and Diane Ortiz. Bob Nelson did not assume liability for the coupons simply because he chose to use the same name for his restaurant. The sole proprietor who does business under one or several names remains one person. There is no continuity of existence for Maria's Restaurant because, upon the sale of the restaurant, the sole proprietorship of Larry and Diane Ortiz ended.

In this case, "Maria's Restaurant" has no legal existence. Bob Nelson did not continue the previous sole proprietorship. He began a new sole proprietorship, that of Bob Nelson, doing business as Maria's Restaurant.

Answers to Practice Quiz

True/False

16. False. A sole proprietorship can be easily transferred or sold if and when the owner desires to do so; no other approval (e.g., from partners or shareholders) is necessary. [p. 566]

17. True. The designation of d.b.a. is for a business that is operating under a trade name; it means "doing business as." [p. 566]

18. True. There are no formalities, and no federal or state government approval is required. Some local governments require all businesses, including sole proprietorships, to obtain licenses to do business within the city. [p. 566]

19. False. The UPA is a model act that codifies general partnership law. [p. 568]

20. True. A business must meet four criteria to qualify as a general partnership under the UPA [UPA Section 6(1)]. It must be (1) an association of two or more persons (2) carrying on a business (3) as co-owners (4) for profit. [p. 569]

21. False. A general partnership can operate under the names of any one or more of the partners or under a fictitious business name. [p. 570]

22. False. The agreement to form a general partnership may be oral, written, or implied from the conduct of the parties. [p. 570]

23. True. General partnerships do not pay federal income taxes. Instead, the income and losses of partnership flow onto and have to be reported on the individual partners' personal income tax returns. This is called flow-through taxation. [p. 570]

24. False. Unless otherwise agreed, the UPA provides that no general partner is entitled to remuneration for his or her performance in the partnership's business [UPA Section 18(f)]. [p. 571]

25. False. Self-dealing occurs when a partner deals personally with the general partnership, such as buying or selling goods or property to the partnership. Such actions are permitted only if full disclosure is made and consent of the other partners is obtained. [p. 572]

26. True. General partners owe a duty to inform their co-partners of all information they possess that is relevant to the affairs of the partnership [UPA Section 20]. [p. 573]

27. False. A partner who breaches the duty of obedience is liable to the partnership for any damages caused by the breach. [p. 573]

28. True. General partners are not permitted to sue the partnership or other partners at law. Instead, they are given the right to bring an action for an accounting against other partners. [p. 574]

29. True. Unlimited personal liability of a general partner is a general partner's personal liability for the debts and obligations of the general partnership. [p. 574]

30. False. The dissolution of a general partnership does not of itself discharge the liability of an outgoing partner for existing partnership debts and obligations. If a general partnership is dissolved, each general partner is personally liable for debts and obligations of the partnership that exist at the time of dissolution. [p. 575]

Multiple Choice

31. D. There is only one owner of the business, who is called the sole proprietor. Sole proprietorships are the most common form of business organization in the United States. [p. 565]

32. B. The sole proprietor has unlimited personal liability. Therefore, creditors may recover claims against the business from the sole proprietors' personal assets (e.g., home, automobile, bank accounts). [p. 566]

33. A. Fictitious business name statement is a document that is filed with the state that designates a trade name of a business, the name and address of the applicant, and the address of the business. [p. 566]

34. C. A sole proprietorship is not a separate legal entity, so it does not pay taxes at the business level. [p. 568]

35. A. A sole proprietorship is not a separate legal entity, so it does not pay taxes at the business level. Instead, the earnings and losses from a sole proprietorship are reported on each sole proprietor's personal income tax filing. [p. 568]

36. D. A general partnership, also known as ordinary partnership, is a voluntary association of two or more persons for carrying on a business as co-owners for profit. [p. 568]

37. A. The agreement to form a general partnership may be oral, written, or implied from the conduct of the parties. It may even be created inadvertently. [p. 570]

38. B. The name selected by the partnership cannot indicate that it is a corporation (e.g., it cannot contain the term Inc.) and cannot be similar to the name used by any existing business entity. [p. 570]

39. B. General partnerships that exist for more than one year or are authorized to deal in real estate must be in writing under the Statute of Frauds. [p. 570]

40. D. Unless otherwise agreed, the UPA mandates that a general partner has the right to an equal share in the partnership's profits and losses [UPA Section 18(a)]. [p. 571]

41. A. Upon termination of a general partnership, the partners are entitled to have their capital contributions returned to them [UPA Section 18(a)]. [p. 571]

42. D. General partners are in a fiduciary relationship with one another. As such, they owe each other a duty of loyalty. A general partner may not compete with the partnership without the permission of the other partners. [p. 572]

43. A. A new partner who is admitted to a general partnership is liable for the existing debts and obligations (antecedent debts) of the partnership only to the extent of his or her capital contribution. [p. 575]

44. C. The duration of a partnership can be a fixed term (e.g., five years) or until a particular undertaking is accomplished (e.g., until a real estate development is completed), or it can be an unspecified term. A partnership with no fixed duration is called a partnership at will. [p. 575]

45. D. A partner who withdraws from a partnership for a term prior to the expiration of the term does not have the right to dissolve the partnership. The partner's action causes a wrongful dissolution of the partnership. [p. 576]

Short Answer

46. There are several major advantages to operating a business as a sole proprietorship. They include the following:
a) Forming a sole proprietorship is easy and does not cost a lot.
b) The owner has the right to make all management decisions concerning the business, including those involving hiring and firing employees.
c) The sole proprietor owns all of the business and has the right to receive all of the business's profits.
d) A sole proprietorship can be easily transferred or sold if and when the owner desires to do so; no other approval is necessary.
There are important disadvantages to this business form, too. For example, a sole proprietor's access to the capital is limited to personal funds plus any loans he or she can obtain, and a sole proprietor is legally responsible for the business's contracts and the torts he or she or any of his or her employees commit in the course of employment. [p. 566]

47. A sole proprietorship is not a separate legal entity, so it does not pay taxes at the business level. Instead, the earnings and losses from a sole proprietorship are reported on each sole proprietor's personal income tax filing. A sole proprietorship business earns income and pays expenses during the course of operating the business. A sole proprietor has to file tax returns and pay taxes to state and federal governments. For federal income tax purposes, a sole proprietor must prepare a personal income tax Form 1040 U.S. Individual Income Tax Return and report the income or loss from the sole proprietorship on his or her personal income tax form. The income or loss from the sole proprietorship is reported on Schedule C (Profit or Loss from Business), which must be attached to the taxpayer's Form 1040. [p. 568]

48. In 1914, the National Conference of Commissioners on Uniform State Laws, which is a group of lawyers, judges, and legal scholars, promulgated the Uniform Partnership Act (UPA). The UPA is a model act that codifies general partnership law. Its goal was to establish consistent partnership law that was uniform throughout the Unites States. The UPA has been adopted in whole or in part by most states, the District of Columbia, Guam, and the Virgin Islands. A Revised Uniform Partnership Act (RUPA) has been issued by the National Conference of Commissioners on Uniform State Laws, but it has not been adopted by many states. [p. 568]

49. A business must meet four criteria to qualify as a general partnership under the UPA. It must be (1) an association of two or more persons, (2) carrying on a business, (3) as co-owners, (4) for profit. A general partnership is a voluntary association of two or more persons. All partners must agree to the participation of each co-partner. A business—a trade, an occupation, or a profession—must be carried on. The organization or venture must have a profit motive in order to qualify as a partnership, even though the business does not actually have to make a profit. Receipt of a share of business profits is prima facie evidence of a general partnership because nonpartners usually are not given the right to share in a business's profits. [p. 569]

50. The agreement to form a general partnership may be oral, written, or implied from the conduct of the parties. It may even be created inadvertently. No formalities are necessary, although a few states require general partnerships to file certificates of partnership with an appropriate government agency. General partnerships that exist for more than one year or are authorized to deal in real estate must be in writing under the Statute of Frauds.
A written agreement is called a general partnership agreement, or articles of general partnership, or articles of partnership. The parties can agree to almost any terms in their partnership agreement, except terms that are illegal. The articles of partnership can be short and simple or

long and complex. If an agreement fails to provide for an essential term or contingency, the provisions of the UPA apply. Thus, the UPA acts as a gap-filling device to the partners' agreement. [p. 570]

51. General partnerships do not pay federal income taxes. Instead, the income and losses of partnership flow onto and have to be reported on the individual partners' personal income tax returns. This is called flow-through taxation. A general partnership has to file an information return with the government, telling the government how much income was earned or the amount of losses incurred by the partnership. This way, the government tax authorities can trace whether partners are correctly reporting their income or losses. [p. 570]

52. Unless otherwise agreed, the UPA mandates that a general partner has the right to an equal share in the partnership's profits and losses [UPA Section 18(a)]. The right to share in the profits of the partnership is considered to be the right to share in the earnings from the investment of capital. Where a partnership agreement provides for the sharing of profits but is silent as to how losses are to be shared, losses are shared in the same proportion as profits. The reverse is not true, however. If a partnership agreement provides for the sharing of losses but is silent as to how profits are to be shared, profits are shared equally. Partnership agreements can provide that profits and losses are to be allocated in proportion to the partners' capital contributions or in any other manner. [p. 571]

53. Some basic forms of breach of loyalty involve:
- Self-dealing
- Usurping a partnership opportunity
- Competing with the partnership
- Making secret profits
- Breach of confidentiality
- Misuse of partnership property [p. 572]

54. A general partner must use reasonable care and skill in transacting partnership business. The duty of care calls for the partners to use the same level of care and skill that a reasonable business manager in the same position would use in the same circumstances. Breach of the duty of care is negligence. A general partner is liable to the partnership for any damages caused by his or her negligence. The partners are not liable for honest errors in judgment.
Example: Tina, Eric, and Brian form a general partnership to sell automobiles. Tina, who is in charge of inventory management, orders large and expensive sport-utility vehicles that consume large amounts of gasoline. A war breaks out in the Middle East that interrupts the supply of oil to the United States. The demand for large SUVs drops substantially, and the partnership cannot sell its inventory. Tina is not liable because the duty of care was not breached. [p. 573]

55. After partnership assets have been liquidated and reduced to cash, the proceeds are distributed to satisfy claims against the partnership. The debts are satisfied in the following order:
a) Creditors (except partners who are creditors)
b) Creditor-partners
c) Capital contributions
d) Profits
The partners can agree to change the priority of distributions among themselves. If the partnership cannot satisfy its creditors' claims, the partners are personally liable for the partnership's debts and obligations. After the proceeds are distributed, the partnership automatically terminates. Termination ends the legal existence of the partnership. [p. 575]

35 | LIMITED PARTNERSHIPS AND LIMITED LIABILITY LIMITED PARTNERSHIPS

Chapter Overview

This chapter provides a further exploration of partnerships, with an emphasis on limited partnerships and their formation, as well as the differentiation between limited and general partners. This chapter discusses the limited liability limited partnership and the partners' liability. The process of dissolution and winding-up of limited partnerships is explained.

Objectives

Upon completion of the exercises in this chapter, you should be able to:
1. Define limited partnership.
2. Describe the process of forming a limited partnership.
3. Identify and describe the liability of general and limited partners.
4. Describe the process of dissolution and winding up of a limited partnership.
5. Define a limited liability limited partnership.

Practical Application

This chapter will provide you with information that will enable you to differentiate between the various types of limited partnerships and give you the necessary knowledge of the liability involved in the partnerships discussed herein. For the student who wants to operate a business, the basic partnership explanations will be an invaluable tool in determining the type of business operation that would be best in light of an individual's circumstances.

Helpful Hints

Before beginning this chapter, it is helpful to review the previous study guide chapter on general partnerships, as it provides a solid foundation for this chapter to build upon. It is best to study this material methodically in order for the information that is given to be of maximum benefit.

Study Tips

It is important that you learn the difference between a limited partnership and a limited liability limited partnership.

Limited Partnerships and Limited Liability Limited Partnerships

Limited partnerships are statutory creations which include both general and limited partners. Generally, the formation, operation, and termination of limited partnerships are regulated by the Revised Uniform Limited Partnership Act (RULPA). Master limited partnerships, a specific type of limited partnership, are traded publicly. Many states now permit the formation of limited liability limited partnerships.

Limited Partnership

A limited partnership involves general partners who conduct the business and limited partners who invest in the partnership but who do not participate in the management.

- A corporation may act as a general partner, but is liable only to the extent of its assets.

Revised Uniform Limited Partnership Act (RULPA). A modern, comprehensive law for the formation, operation, and dissolution of limited partnerships. This law supersedes the ULPA in states that have adopted it.

Certificate of Limited Partnership. The creation of a limited partnership is formal and requires public disclosure.

- Two or more persons must execute and sign a certificate of limited partnership.
- The certificate must contain general information:
  - partnership name
  - business type
  - address of business
  - each partner's address
  - latest date of partnership dissolution
  - partner contributions
  - any other matters
- The certificate of limited partnership must be filed with the secretary of state and, if required, the county recorder where the business is being conducted.
- The limited partnership is formed upon the filing of the certificate of limited partnership.

Amendments to the Certificate of Limited Partnership. A limited partnership must be kept current by way of certificates of amendment, which must be filed within 30 days of the happening of certain events.

- A partner's capital contribution changes.
- A new partner's admission.
- A partner's withdrawal.
- A business's continuation after a judicial dissolution to dissolve the partnership.

Name of the Limited Partnership. A limited partnership may not include the surname of a limited partner unless it is also the surname of the general partner or the business was carried on under that name before the limited partner was admitted to the firm.

- The name may not be deceptively similar to other corporations' names or other limited partnerships' names.
- The name must contain, without abbreviations, the words "limited partnership".

Capital Contributions. General and limited partners' capital contributions may be made in cash, property, services rendered, or a promissory note.

Defective Formation. If there is a substantial defect, persons who thought they were limited partners are then in the position of finding themselves as general partners. Defective formation occurs when

- a certificate of limited partnership is not properly filed
- there are defects in a certificate that is filed or
- some other statutory requirement for the creation of a limited partnership is not met.

Limited Partnership Agreement. This agreement drafted by the partners describes the rights and duties of the general and limited partners and the conditions concerning operation, termination, and dissolution.

Share of Profits and Losses. The limited partnership agreement may state how profits and losses from the limited partnership are to be distributed among the general and limited partners.
- If the agreement does not state how the profits and losses are to be shared, then they will be shared based on the value of the partner's capital contribution.
- A limited partner is not liable for losses beyond his or her capital contribution.

Right to Information. Each limited partner has a right to information regarding the financial condition of the limited partnership.

Admission of a new partner. The addition of a partner to an existing limited partnership can only be accomplished by the written consent of all partners.
- Admission of a new partner is effective on filing of the amendment of the certificate of limited partnership.
- Withdrawal of a partner can be accomplished as per the certificate of limited partnership, upon the happening of an event, or upon six months' prior notice to each general partner.

Foreign Limited Partnerships. A foreign limited partnership must file an application for registration with the secretary of state before it conducts business with a foreign country.
- If the application is all in order, a certificate of registration will be issued so that it may transact business.
- The limited partner's status is not affected by whether the foreign limited partnership is registered or unregistered.

Master Limited Partnership (MLP). A limited partnership whose limited partnership interests are traded on organized securities exchanges.
- The tax benefits in owning an MLP are that MLPs do not pay any income tax, and partnership income and losses go directly onto the individual partner's income tax return.
- Double taxation is also avoided with an MLP.

Liability of General and Limited Partners

- General partners generally have unlimited liability for partnership debts and obligations.
- Limited partners generally have limited liability, up to the amount of their capital contributions.

Participation in Management. General partners have the right to manage the affairs of the limited partnership.
- Limited partners relinquish their right to participate in the control and management of the limited partnership in exchange for limited liability.
  - There is no right to bind the partnership to contracts or other obligations.

- Limited partners that participate in substantially the same manner as a general partner may be held liable as a general partner.

Permissible Activities of Limited Partners. The types of activities a limited partner may participate in without losing his or her limited liability status include:
- being an agent, employee, contractor of the limited partnership or a general partner, being a consultant or an advisor to a general partner regarding the partnership, or acting as a surety for the limited partnership.
- an individual may approve or disapprove an amendment to the limited partnership and vote on partnership matters.

Liability on a Personal Guarantee. If a limited partner personally guarantees a loan made to the limited partnership and the limited partnership defaults, the creditor may enforce the personal guarantee and recover payment from the limited partner guarantor.

Dissolution of a Limited Partnership

The affairs of a limited partnership may be dissolved and wound up just like an ordinary partnership.
- A certificate of cancellation must be filed with the secretary of state that the limited partnership is organized.

Causes of Dissolution. The end of the limited partnership's life, the written consent of limited and general partners, the withdrawal of a general partner, and the entry of a decree of judicial dissolution are the events that can cause dissolution of a limited partnership.
- A limited partnership is not dissolved upon the withdrawal of a general partner if
  - the certificate of limited partnership allows the business to be carried on or
  - within 90 days of the withdrawal, all partners agree in writing to continue.

Winding Up. A limited partnership's general partners must wind up its affairs once it dissolves itself.

Distribution of Assets. RULPA established the order of distribution of partnership assets:
- creditors
- partners
  - unpaid distributions
  - capital contributions
  - remainder of the proceeds.

Limited Liability Limited Partnership

The 2001 amendments to RULPA allow limited liability limited partnerships (LLLPs).
- organized under state law by filing articles of limited liability limited partnership with the secretary of state's office.
- An existing limited partnership may convert to being a LLLP.
- In most states, an LLLP must identify itself by using "L.L.L.P." or "LLLP" after the name.
- An LLLP requires at least one general partner and at least one limited partner.

- o Neither the general partners nor the limited partners have personal liability for the debts and obligations of the LLLP.
- o The debts of an LLLP are the sole responsibility of the partnership.

Refresh Your Memory

The following exercise will give you the opportunity to test your memory of the principles given in this chapter. Read the question twice and place your answer in the blank provided. Review the chapter material for any question that you are unable to answer or remember.

1. Limited partnership has two types of partners: _____ and limited partners.

2. Partners in a limited partnership who invest capital, manage the business, and are personally liable for partnership debts are called _____.

3. Limited partnership is also known as _____ partnership.

4. _____ invest capital but do not participate in management and are not personally liable for partnership debts beyond their capital contributions.

5. _____ is a modern, comprehensive law for the formation, operation, and dissolution of limited partnerships.

6. _____ is a document that two or more persons must execute and sign that makes a limited partnership legal and binding.

7. A limited partnership in all other states besides the one in which it was formed is called a _____.

8. _____ occurs when (1) a certificate of limited partnership is not properly filed, (2) there are defects in a certificate that is filed, or (3) some other statutory requirement for the creation of a limited partnership is not met.

9. _____ is a document that sets forth the rights and duties of general and limited partners; the terms and conditions regarding the operation, termination, and dissolution of a partnership; and so on.

10. _____ is a type of limited partnership that is listed on a stock exchange and is publicly traded to provide liquidity to investors.

11. The general partners of a limited partnership have _____ liability for the debts and obligations of the limited partnerships.

12. A document that is filed with the secretary of state upon the dissolution of a limited partnership is called the _____.

13. The end of the life of the limited partnership, as specified in the certificate of limited partnership is a cause of _____ of the limited partnership.

14. In a _____, neither the general partners nor the limited partners have personal liability for the debts and obligations of the LLLP.

15. An LLLP is a _____ in the state in which it is formed.

Critical Thought Exercise

Harris, Nix, and Lewis form a limited partnership for the purpose of hiring and booking motivational speakers for corporate and government training seminars. Harris was a former boxing promoter and will act as the general partner. Nix and Harris contribute $35,000 each and Harris contributes all the furniture and supplies from his current office. A certificate of limited partnership is prepared in a proper and complete manner and filed with the secretary of state. The partnership begins to hire and book motivational speakers and is very successful.

Fifteen months later, Harris has a heart attack and is unable to work for several months. Instead of hiring a temporary manager to run the business, Nix completely takes over the day-to-day running of the business. Nix wants to build the business and hire famous speakers. He signs a contract with a famous football coach to give two speeches at a rate of $200,000 each. Harris then returns to work and takes over management duties. Due to poor decisions made by Nix, the partnership is unable to pay the coach after he makes the two speeches. In his suit, the coach alleges that both Harris and Nix are personally liable for the damages caused by the partnerships breach of contract if the damages cannot be satisfied out of partnership assets.

Is Nix personally liable for damages to the coach even though he is only a limited partner?

Please compose your answer to the Critical Thinking Exercise using a separate sheet of paper or your computer word processing program.

Practice Quiz

True/False

16. _____ A limited partnership cannot have general partners.

17. _____ Master limited partnerships are traded publicly.

18. _____ A limited liability limited partnership limits the liability of general partners.

19. _____ General partners are not personally liable for partnership debts beyond their capital contributions.

20. _____ The ULPA supersedes the RULPA in the states that have adopted it.

21. _____ The name of a limited partnership can include any or all of the limited partners' surnames.

22. _____ Defective formation of a limited partnership occurs when a certificate of limited partnership is not properly filed.

23. _____ In the absence of a partnership agreement, profits and losses from a limited partnership are shared on the basis of the value of each partner's capital contribution.

24. _____ New partners cannot be added to a limited partnership once it is formed.

25. _____ A limited partner may engage in voting on the dissolution of the limited partnership without losing his or her limited liability.

26. _____ The retirement of a general partner does not dissolve a limited partnership.

27. _____ Upon dissolution, a limited partnership's affairs must be wound up by partners who have acted wrongfully in actions that resulted in the dissolution.

28. _____ Any partner may petition the court to wind up the affairs of a limited partnership.

29. _____ An existing limited partnership cannot be converted to a limited liability limited partnership.

30. _____ Limited partners of an LLLP are involved in the management functions of the partnership.

Multiple Choice

31. A limited partnership has two types of partners, _____.

A. general partners and sole proprietors
B. ordinary partners and liable partners
C. general partners and limited partners
D. special partners and sole proprietors

32. Which of the following partners in a limited partnership invest capital, manage the business, and are personally liable for partnership debts?

A. specific partners
B. limited partners
C. sole proprietors
D. general partners

33. Which of the following is true of general and limited partners in a limited partnership?

A. Limited partners are not personally liable for partnership debts beyond their capital contributions.
B. General partners are not personally liable for partnership debts.
C. General partners are required to invest capital and refrain from managerial activities.
D. Limited partners are exempt from annual capital investment and need only participate in management functions.

34. Which of the following is true of a limited partnership?

A. Other limited partnerships cannot become limited partners in an existing limited partnership.
B. A limited partner is personally liable for the debts of the partnership.
C. A limited partnership can have only one general partner but multiple limited partners.
D. Corporations are allowed to become partners in a limited partnership.

35. Which of the following information should a certificate of limited partnership contain?

A. a clause to not accept new general partners
B. the latest date of dissolution of the partnership
C. the name of the party who becomes a general partner in the event of transfer
D. the scope of potential business opportunities and related investment

36. A limited partnership is formed when the _____ is filed.

A. certificate of limited partnership
B. articles of limited partnership
C. limited trade affidavit
D. certificate of cancellation

37. A limited partnership is a _____ in the state in which it is organized.

A. sole proprietorship
B. domestic limited partnership
C. limited liability corporation
D. general partnership

38. A limited partnership that was organized in Alabama and operating in Texas with no operations outside the U.S. is considered a _____ in Texas.

A. limited liability corporation
B. foreign limited partnership
C. domestic limited partnership
D. general partnership

39. In which of the following cases can the name of a limited partnership include the surname of a limited partner?

A. the limited partner has stayed longer than all other partners
B. the limited partner has invested more than the general partner
C. the name is also the surname of a general partner
D. the name is unanimously voted for by other limited partners

40. _____ is said to have occurred if a certificate of limited partnership was not properly filed.

A. Voidable association
B. Illegitimate partnership
C. Void partnership
D. Defective formation

41. Which of the following is true of a limited partnership agreement?

A. It sets forth the terms and conditions regarding the termination of the partnership.
B. It does not contain information about dissolution of the partnership as it an agreement of formation.
C. It provides that general and limited partners have equal voting rights.
D. It provides that all transactions must be approved by all partners.

42. How are profits and losses shared in the absence of a limited partnership agreement?

A. Both profits and losses are shared on the basis of the value of each partner's capital contribution.
B. Profits and losses are shared equally among general partners and unequally among limited partners.
C. Profits are shared equally among all partners, losses are shared based on the value of each partner's capital contribution.
D. Profits and losses are shared equally among all partners.

43. New general partners can be admitted only with the _____.

A. approval of at least two-thirds of the partners
B. merger with another limited partnership
C. specific consent of each partner
D. death of or transfer by a general partner

44. Which of the following types of liability do limited partners of a limited partnership have for the debts and obligations of the limited partnerships?

A. unlimited personal liability
B. liability of termination as partner
C. liability restricted to debts up to their capital contributions
D. unlimited organizational capital liability

45. In which of the following circumstances is a decree of judicial dissolution granted to a partner?

A. It is not reasonably practical to carry on the business in conformity with the limited partnership agreement.
B. the partners do not have sufficient funds to repay debts.
C. A partner is rendered incapacitated to perform his or her duties.
D. All limited partners have withdrawn but the general partners want to continue with the partnership.

Short Answer

46. Explain the constitution of partners in a limited partnership. What are their liabilities? Who is permitted to join as a partner to such a partnership?

_____

_____

47. Explain the Revised Uniform Limited Partnership Act.

_____

_____

48. What are the constraints levied upon the name of a limited partnership? How do they influence a limited partner?

_____

_____

49. When does defective formation occur?

_____

_____

50. Explain with an example the share of profits and losses in a limited partnership.

_____

_____

51. What are the requirements for the admission of a new partner in a limited partnership?

_____

_____

52. Explain in brief the liabilities of general and limited partners in a limited partnership.

_____

_____

53. Explain liability on a personal guarantee.

_____

_____

54. What are the permissible activities of a limited person?

_____

_____

55. Explain the events that cause the dissolution of a limited partnership under RULPA.

_____

_____

Answers to Refresh Your Memory

1. general partners [p. 582]
2. general partners [p. 582]
3. special [p. 582]
4. Limited partners [p. 582]
5. Revised Uniform Limited Partnership Act [p. 583]
6. Certificate of limited partnership [p. 583]
7. foreign limited partnership [p. 583]
8. Defective formation [p. 584]
9. Limited partnership agreement [p. 584]
10. Master limited partnership [p. 585]
11. unlimited [p. 586]

12. certificate of cancellation [p. 588]
13. dissolution [p. 588]
14. limited liability limited partnership [p. 590]
15. domestic limited liability limited partnership [p. 590]

Critical Thought Exercise Model Answer

General partners are personally liable to the partnership's creditors. The liability of a limited partner is limited to the capital that he or she contributes to the partnership. A limited partner gains this protection if the requirements for signing and filing the limited partnership certificate are met. In this case the certificate was properly filed. When the partnership began business, both Nix and Lewis had the protection afforded a limited partner.

However, under the Revised Uniform Limited Partnership Act (RULPA), section 303, limited partners only enjoy limited liability as long as they do not participate in management. A limited partner who undertakes management of the partnership's business will be just as liable as a general partner to any creditor who transacts business with the limited partnership and believes, based upon the acts of the limited partner, that the limited partner is a general partner [RULPA, section 303]. In this case, Nix took over complete management and was running the daily affairs of the partnership. With Harris not working at all during the time the contract was signed with the coach, Nix would have appeared to be the general manager and thus, a general partner. Therefore, Nix should be personally liable to the coach for damages for breach of contract. Harris, even though he was not working at the time, will also be personally liable because he is listed as the general partner on the partnership certificate. Lewis is the only partner whose liability to the coach will be limited to his investment in the partnership.

Answers to Practice Quiz

True/False

16. False. Limited partnership is a type of partnership that has two types of partners: general partners and limited partners. [p. 582]

17. True. Some limited partnerships qualify as master limited partnerships that are traded publicly. [p. 582]

18. True. Some states permit the formation of a special form of partnership called a limited liability limited partnership that limits the liability of general partners. [p. 582]

19. False. General partners invest capital, manage the business, and are personally liable for partnership debts. [p. 582]

20. False. The Revised Uniform Limited Partnership Act (RULPA) provides a more modern, comprehensive law for the formation, operation, and dissolution of limited partnerships. This law supersedes the ULPA in the states that have adopted it. [p. 583]

21. False. The name of a limited partnership may not include the surname of a limited partner unless (1) it is also the surname of a general partner or (2) the business was carried on under that name before the admission of the limited partner [RULPA Section 102(2)]. [p. 584]

22. True. Defective formation occurs when (1) a certificate of limited partnership is not properly filed, (2) there are defects in a certificate that is filed, or (3) some other statutory requirement for the creation of a limited partnership is not met. [p. 584]

23. True. If there is no agreement, the RULPA provides that profits and losses from a limited partnership are shared on the basis of the value of each partner's capital contribution [RULPA Section 503]. [p. 585]

24. False. Once a limited partnership has been formed, a new limited partner can be added only upon the written consent of all partners, unless the limited partnership agreement provides otherwise. [p. 585]

25. True. The RULPA clarifies that voting on the dissolution and winding up of the limited partnership is a type of activity that a limited partner may engage in without losing his or her limited liability. [p. 587]

26. False. The withdrawal of a general partner causes the dissolution of a limited partnership. Withdrawal includes the retirement, death, bankruptcy, adjudged insanity, or removal of a general partner or the assignment by a general partner of his or her partnership interest. [p. 589]

27. False. Unless otherwise provided in the limited partnership agreement, the partnership's affairs may be wound up by the general partners who have not acted wrongfully or, if there are none, the limited partners. [p. 589]

28. True. A limited partnership must wind up its affairs upon dissolution. Any partner may petition the court to wind up the affairs of a limited partnership [RULPA Section 803]. [p. 589]

29. False. An existing limited partnership may convert to being a limited liability limited partnership. [p. 589]

30. False. Typically, the general partners of an LLLP manage the partnership, and the limited partners are investors who only have a financial interest in the LLLP. [p. 590]

Multiple Choice

31. C. Limited partnership (special partnership) is a type of partnership that has two types of partners: general partners and limited partners. [p. 582]

32. D. General partners are partners in a limited partnership who invest capital, manage the business, and are personally liable for partnership debts. [p. 582]

33. A. Limited partners invest capital but do not participate in management and are not personally liable for partnership debts beyond their capital contributions. [p. 582]

34. D. Any person—including natural persons, partnerships, limited partnerships, trusts, estates, associations, and corporations—may be a general or limited partner. [p. 583]

35. B. Certificate of limited partnership is a document that two or more persons must execute and sign that makes a limited partnership legal and binding. The certificate must contain the latest date on which the limited partnership is to dissolve. [p. 583]

36. A. Partners who erroneously but in good faith believe they have become limited partners can escape liability as general partners by causing the appropriate certificate of limited partnership (or certificate of amendment) to be filed. [p. 584]

37. B. A limited partnership is a domestic limited partnership in the state in which it is organized. It is a foreign limited partnership in all other states. [p. 583]

38. B. A limited partnership is a foreign limited partnership in all other states other than the one in which it is organized. [p. 583]

39. C. The name of a limited partnership may not include the surname of a limited partner unless (1) it is also the surname of a general partner or (2) the business was carried on under that name before the admission of the limited partner [RULPA Section 102(2)]. [p. 584]

40. D. Defective formation occurs when (1) a certificate of limited partnership is not properly filed, (2) there are defects in a certificate that is filed, or (3) some other statutory requirement for the creation of a limited partnership is not met. [p. 584]

41. A. A limited partnership agreement sets forth the rights and duties of the general and limited partners; the terms and conditions regarding the operations, termination, and dissolution of the partnership; and so on. [p. 584]

42. A. In the absence of a limited partnership agreement, profits and losses from a limited partnership are shared on the basis of the value of each partner's capital contribution [RULPA Section 503]. [p. 585]

43. C. New general partners can be admitted only with the specific written consent of each partner [RULPA Section 401]. A limited partnership agreement cannot waive the right of partners to approve the admission of new general partners. [p. 585]

44. C. Limited partners are liable only for the debts and obligations of the limited partnership up to their capital contributions, and they are not personally liable for the debts and obligations of the limited partnership. [p. 586]

45. A. The entry of a decree of judicial dissolution, which may be granted to a partner whenever it is not reasonably practical to carry on the business in conformity with the limited partnership agreement [RULPA Section 802] (e.g., if the general partners are deadlocked over important decisions affecting the limited partnership). [p. 589]

Short Answer

46. A limited partnership has two types of partners: (1) general partners, who invest capital, manage the business, and are personally liable for partnership debts, and (2) limited partners, who invest capital but do not participate in management and are not personally liable for partnership debts beyond their capital contributions. A limited partnership must have one or more general partners and one or more limited partners. There are no upper limits on the number of general or limited partners allowed in a limited partnership. Any person—including natural persons, partnerships, limited partnerships, trusts, estates, associations, and corporations—may be a general or limited partner. A person may be both a general partner and a limited partner in the same limited partnership. [p. 582]

47. In 1976, the National Conference of Commissioners on Uniform State Laws promulgated the Revised Uniform Limited Partnership Act (RULPA), which provides a more modern, comprehensive law for the formation, operation, and dissolution of limited partnerships. This law supersedes the ULPA in the states that have adopted it. The RULPA provides the basic foundation for the discussion of limited partnership law in the following text. In 2001, certain amendments were made to the RULPA. [p. 583]

48. The name of a limited partnership may not include the surname of a limited partner unless (1) it is also the surname of a general partner or (2) the business was carried on under that name before the admission of the limited partner. A limited partner who knowingly permits his or her name to be used in violation of this provision becomes liable as a general partner to any creditors who extend credit to the partnership without actual knowledge of his or her true status. Other restrictions on the name of a limited partnership are that (1) the name cannot be the same as or deceptively similar to the names of corporations or other limited partnerships, (2) states can designate words that cannot be used in limited partnership names, and (3) the name must contain, without abbreviation, the words limited partnership. [p. 584]

49. Defective formation occurs when (1) a certificate of limited partnership is not properly filed, (2) there are defects in a certificate that is filed, or (3) some other statutory requirement for the creation of a limited partnership is not met. If there is a substantial defect in the creation of a limited partnership, persons who thought they were limited partners can find themselves liable as general partners.
Partners who erroneously but in good faith believe they have become limited partners can escape liability as general partners by either (1) causing the appropriate certificate of limited partnership (or certificate of amendment) to be filed or (2) withdrawing from any future equity participation in the enterprise and causing a certificate showing this withdrawal to be filed. [p. 584]

50. A limited partnership agreement may specify how profits and losses from the limited partnership are to be allocated among the general and limited partners. If there is no such agreement, the RULPA provides that profits and losses from a limited partnership are shared on the basis of the value of each partner's capital contribution [RULPA Section 503].
Example – There are four general partners, each of whom contributes $50,000 in capital to the limited partnership, and four limited partners, each of whom contributes $200,000 capital. The total amount of contributed capital is $1 million. The limited partnership agreement does not stipulate how profits and losses are to be allocated. Assume that the limited partnership makes $3 million in profits. Under the RULPA, each general partner would receive $150,000 in profit, and each limited partner would receive $600,000 in profit. [p. 585]

51. Once a limited partnership has been formed, a new limited partner can be added only upon the written consent of all partners, unless the limited partnership agreement provides otherwise. New general partners can be admitted only with the specific written consent of each partner [RULPA Section 401]. A limited partnership agreement cannot waive the right of partners to approve the admission of new general partners. The admission is effective when an amendment of the certificate of limited partnership reflecting that fact is filed [RULPA Section 301]. [p. 585]

52. The general partners of a limited partnership have unlimited liability for the debts and obligations of the limited partnerships. Thus, general partners have unlimited personal liability for the debts and obligations of the limited partnership. This liability extends to debts that cannot be satisfied with the existing capital of the limited partnership. Generally, limited partners have limited liability for the debts and obligations of the limited partnership. Limited partners are liable only for the debts and obligations of the limited partnership up to their capital

contributions, and they are not personally liable for the debts and obligations of the limited partnership. [p. 586]

53. On some occasions, when limited partnerships apply for an extension of credit from a bank, a supplier, or another creditor, the creditor will not make the loan based on the limited partnership's credit history or ability to repay the credit. The creditor may require a limited partner to personally guarantee the repayment of the loan in order to extend credit to the limited partnership. If a limited partner personally guarantees a loan made by a creditor to the limited partnership and the limited partnership defaults on the loan, the creditor may enforce the personal guarantee and recover payment from the limited partner who personally guaranteed the repayment of the loan. [p. 586]

54. The RULPA clarifies the types of activities that a limited partner may engage in without losing his or her limited liability. These activities include [RULPA Sections 303(b), 303(c)]:
• Being an agent, an employee, or a contractor of the limited partnership.
• Being a consultant or an advisor to a general partner regarding the limited partnership.
• Acting as a surety for the limited partnership.
• Approving or disapproving an amendment to the limited partnership agreement.
• Voting on the following partnership matters:
a. The dissolution and winding up of the limited partnership.
b. The sale, transfer, exchange, lease, or mortgage of substantially all of the assets of the limited partnership.
c. The incurrence of indebtedness by the limited partnership other than in the ordinary course of business.
d. A change in the nature of the business of the limited partnership.
e. The removal of a general partner. [p. 587]

55. The end of the life of the limited partnership, as specified in the certificate of limited partnership.
b) The written consent of all general and limited partners.
c) The withdrawal of a general partner. Withdrawal includes the retirement, death, bankruptcy, adjudged insanity, or removal of a general partner or the assignment by a general partner of his or her partnership interest. If a corporation or partnership is a general partner, the dissolution of the corporation or partnership is considered withdrawal.
d) The entry of a decree of judicial dissolution, which may be granted to a partner whenever it is not reasonably practical to carry on the business in conformity with the limited partnership. [p. 588]

CORPORATE FORMATION AND FINANCING

Chapter Overview

This chapter explores the formation and financing of corporations. It explains the difference between publicly held and closely held corporations. It examines the various types of stock issues and the preferences associated with preferred stock. Other topics that are covered include promoters' liability, S corporations, various issuances of stock and preferences that accompany preferred stock, rights of debenture and bondholders, and the organization and operation of multinational corporations. Though a corporation is an unnatural being, it is one of the strongest and most important forms of business organization forms in business today.

Objectives

Upon completion of the exercises in this chapter, you should be able to:
1. Define corporation and list the major characteristics of a corporation.
2. Describe the process of forming a corporation.
3. Define common stock and preferred stock.
4. Define S corporation and describe the tax benefits of this form of corporation.
5. Describe the importance of Delaware corporation law.

Practical Application

You will better understand how a corporation is formed and operates. You will be more aware of the benefits and concerns of operating a business as a corporation. You will better appreciate the impact corporations have on business, the world and our everyday lives.

Helpful Hints

Since there is a vast amount of information to learn in this chapter, organization is key to learning the various topics. A corporation is similar to raising a child, in that it starts out small without a name and eventually grows with the help of its family members into a fully functioning being. If you keep in mind that the different aspects of operating a business as a corporation all depend on one another, you will begin to see how the entire picture fits together.

Study Tips

Corporate Formation and Financing

Shareholders are the owners of corporations, which are the dominate form of business in the U.S. They have been known since medieval times, and states began to enact legislation specifically permitting their formation without separate approval of legislatures in the 1700s. Today, most corporations are formed using general corporation laws of states.

Nature of the Corporation

Corporations are created according to the state laws where they are incorporated. These laws are vital to a corporation's success, as they regulate formation, operation, and the dissolution of corporations.

The Corporation as a "Legal Person". A corporation is considered to be a legal person or legal entity that is separate and distinct which include the following many interesting characteristics:
- A corporation is an artificial person that is state created.
- A corporation may bring a lawsuit or be sued.
- A corporation may enter into and enforce contracts, hold title to and transfer property.
- A corporation may be found civilly and criminally liable and may have fines assessed or its license revoked.

Limited Liability of Shareholders. The shareholders have limited liability to the extent of their contributions.

Free Transferability of Shares. Corporate shares are freely transferable by the shareholder.

Perpetual Existence. Corporations have a perpetual existence if there is no duration stated in the corporation's articles of incorporation.
- Shareholders may voluntarily terminate the corporation's existence.
- Death, insanity, or bankruptcy of a shareholder has no effect on a corporation's existence.

Revised Model Business Corporation Act (RMBCA). This act was promulgated in 1984, wherein it arranged the provisions of the 1950 act more logically and made substantial changes in provisions of the model act.

Centralized Management. The shareholders elect the directors who in turn appoint corporate officers to conduct the corporation's daily business.

Public and Private Corporations.
- Public Corporations. Government-owned corporations are formed with a governmental or political reason in mind.
- Private Corporations. Private corporations are created to carry on a privately owned business.

Profit and Not-for-Profit Corporations. Private corporations may be for profit or nonprofit.
- Profit Corporations. These corporations are created to conduct a business for profit.
  - They can distribute profits to shareholders in the form of dividends.
- Not-for-Profit Corporations. Nonprofit corporations are created for charitable, educational, scientific, or religious reasons.
  - They may not distribute any profit to their members, directors, or officers.
  - The Model Nonprofit Corporation Act governs nonprofit corporations.

Publicly Held and Closely Held Corporations.
- Publicly Held Corporations. These are generally large corporations with hundreds and even thousands of shareholders whose shares are traded on organized securities markets.
  - Shareholders seldom participate in this type of corporation's management.
  - Coca-Cola and Bristol-Myers are examples of publicly held corporations.

- Closely Held Corporations. These are relatively small corporations whose shares are held by a few shareholders, mostly comprised of family, friends, and relatives.
  - Shareholders do participate in a closely held corporation's management.
  - Shareholders sometimes try to stop outsiders from becoming shareholders.

Professional Corporations. These are formed by professionals, such as dentists, doctors, lawyers, and accountants.

- The initials give a clue that it is a professional corporation: P.C. for Professional Corporation or S.C. for service corporation.
- This type of corporation is formed like other corporations and has many of the same traits.
- Its professional members are generally not liable for the torts committed by its agents or employees.

Domestic, Foreign, and Alien Corporations.

- Domestic Corporation. A corporation in the state in which it was formed.
- Foreign Corporation. A corporation in any state or jurisdiction other than the one in which it was formed.
- Alien Corporation. A corporation that is incorporated in another country.

Incorporation Procedure

The organizers of a corporation must follow the state's corporations code, which varies from state to state, to form a corporation.

Selecting a State for Incorporating a Corporation. Incorporation may only be in one state, even though a corporation may conduct its business in many states.

- When choosing where to incorporate, the law of the state being considered should be examined.
- Large corporations look for the state with the most favorable corporate law (e.g., Delaware).

Selecting a Corporate Name. The organizers must choose a name for the corporation.

- The name must contain the words corporation, company, incorporated, limited, or an abbreviation of any one of these.
- The name cannot contain a word or phrase that states or implies that the corporation is organized for a purpose different than that in the articles of incorporation.
- A trademark search should be conducted to make sure that the name is available for use.
- A domain name search for purposes of Internet use should also be performed.

Incorporators. An incorporator is the person or persons, partnerships, or corporations that are responsible for the incorporation of the corporation.

- Incorporators often become shareholders, directors, or officers of the corporation.

Promoter's Liability. A promoter is an individual or individuals who organizes and starts the corporations. He/she or they enter into contracts before the corporation is formed, find investors, and sometimes subject themselves to liability as a result of all that is done.

- Promoters enter into contracts such as leases, sales contracts, property contracts, etc. Liability depends on the corporation, keeping the following instances in mind.

      o   If the corporation never comes into existence, then the promoter is solely liable on the contract unless the third party exempts the promoter.

      o   If the corporation is formed, it is liable on the promoter's contract if it agrees to be bound to the contract as per a board of director's resolution.

      o   The promoter remains liable on the contract unless a novation is entered into.

            ■   A novation is a three-party agreement wherein the corporation assumes the promoter's contract liability with the third party's consent.

            ■   A novation has the effect of leaving the corporation solely liable on the promoter's contract.

Articles of Incorporation. The articles of incorporation, also known as the corporate charter, are the basic documents that must be filed with and approved by the state in order to be officially incorporated. The articles must contain:

- the name of the corporation
- number of shares the corporation is authorized to issue
- address of the corporation's registered office
- agent for the corporation
- name and address of each incorporator
- duration, regulation of powers, and corporate affairs
- the corporate purpose

Amending the Articles of Incorporation. Amendments to the articles of incorporation must be filed with the secretary of state after the shareholders approve them.

Corporate Status. Corporate status begins when the articles of incorporation are filed.

- Upon the secretary of state's filing of the articles of incorporation, it is conclusive proof that the incorporators have satisfied all conditions of the incorporation.
- Failure to file the articles of incorporation is conclusive proof that the corporation does not exist.

Purpose of the Corporation. A general purpose clause should be in a corporation's articles.

- Some corporations insert a limited purpose clause.

Registered Agent. A registered agent must be identified along with a registered office.

- The purpose of the agent is to have someone be able to accept service of process on behalf of the corporation.

Corporate Bylaws. Corporate bylaws are a more exacting set of rules adopted by the board of directors.

- It contains provisions for managing the business and the affairs of the corporation.
- The bylaws may also be amended.

Corporate Seal. A corporate seal is a design affixed by a metal stamp containing the name and date of incorporation.

Organizational Meeting. An organizational meeting of the first corporate directors must be held upon the filing of the articles of incorporation.

- The bylaws are adopted, officers elected, and other business transacted at this initial meeting.

- Additional matters such as ratification of promoter's contracts, approving the form of stock certificates, etc., are also discussed.

Close Corporation Election Under State Corporation Law. The Model Statutory Close Corporation Supplement (Supplement) was added to the RMBCA to allow entrepreneurial corporations to choose to be close corporations under state law.
- Only those with 50 or fewer shareholders may elect statutory close corporation (SCC) status.
- Two-thirds of the shares of each class of shares of the corporation must approve the election.
- The articles of incorporation must contain a statement that the corporation is a SCC.
- The share certificates must conspicuously state that the shares have been issued by a SCC.

S Corporation Election for Federal Tax Purposes. Corporations that meet the following criteria can elect to be taxed as S corporations:
- The corporation must be a domestic corporation.
- The corporation cannot be a member of an affiliated group of corporations.
- The corporation can have no more than 100 shareholders.
- Shareholders must be individuals, estates, or certain trusts.
  - Corporations and partnerships cannot be shareholders.
- Shareholders must be citizens or residents of the United States.
  - Nonresident aliens cannot be shareholders.
- The corporation cannot have more than one class of stock.
- Shareholders do not have to have equal voting rights.

Financing the Corporation: Stock

The sale of equity and debt securities is the simplest way to finance the operation of a corporation.
- Equity securities are stocks which represent the ownership rights in the corporation in the form of common stock or preferred stock.

Common Stock. A kind of equity security that represents the residual value of the corporation.
- The creditors and preferred shareholders receive their interest first.
- There is no fixed maturity date.
- Common stockholders may vote on mergers, elect directors, and receive dividends.

Preferred Stock. This is a kind of equity security that is given preferences and rights over common stock.
- Holders of this type of stock are issued preferred stock certificates.
- The general rule with regard to voting is that this class of stock may not do so, unless there has been a merger or there has been a failure to pay a dividend.
- Preferences of preferred stock include dividend preference, liquidation preference, cumulative dividend right, cumulative preferred stock, the right to participate in profits with participating preferred stock and convertible preferred stock.

Redeemable Preferred Stock. Redeemable preferred stock (also termed callable preferred stock) allows the corporation to buy back the preferred stock at a future date.

Authorized, Issued, and Outstanding Shares.

- Authorized Shares. Number of shares that are provided for in the articles of incorporation.
- Issued Shares. Authorized shares that have been sold.
- Treasury Shares. Repurchased shares.
- Outstanding Shares. Shares of stock that are in the shareholder hands.

Consideration to be Paid for Shares. Consideration to be paid for shares may include any property or benefit to the corporation as determined by the board of directors.

Financing the Corporation: Debt Securities

Debt Securities are securities that establish a debtor-creditor relationship in which the corporation borrows money from the investor to whom the debt security is issued.

Debenture. A long-term unsecured debt instrument that is based on the corporation's general credit standing.

Bond. A long-term debt security that is secured by some form of collateral.

Note. A debt security with a maturity of five years or less.

Indenture Agreement. A contract between the corporation and the holder that contains the terms of the debt security.

Corporate Powers

Essentially, a corporation can perform acts and enter into contracts as a physical person.

Express Powers. Express powers may be found in the U.S. Constitution, state constitutions, federal statutes, articles of incorporations, bylaws, and resolutions by the board of directors.

- Corporations may purchase, own, and lease real as well as personal property, borrow money, incur liability, make donations, and perform various other financial functions.

Implied Powers. The implied powers of a corporation are those that go beyond the express powers and that allow a corporation to accomplish its corporate purpose.

Ultra Vires Act. This refers to a corporate act that goes beyond its express and implied powers.

- An action for damages or an action to enjoin the act or an action to dissolve the corporation are some the remedies available for the commission of an ultra vires act.

Dissolution and Termination of Corporations

Voluntary Dissolution. This occurs upon recommendation of the board of directors and a majority vote of the shares entitled to vote.

Administrative Dissolution. This is an involuntary dissolution of a corporation that is order by the secretary of state to comply with certain procedures required by law.

Judicial Dissolution. This occurs when a corporation is dissolved by a court proceeding initiated by the state.

Winding Up, Liquidation, and Termination.
- Winding-up and liquidation refers to the method by which a dissolved corporation's assets are gathered, liquidated, and then distributed to creditors, shareholders, and other claimants.
- Termination is the ending of the corporation that happens only after the winding up of the corporate affairs, the liquidation of its assets, and the distribution of the proceeds to the claimants.

Refresh Your Memory

The following exercise will give you the opportunity to test your memory of the principles given in this chapter. Read the question twice and place your answer in the blank provided. Review the chapter material for any question that you are unable to answer or remember.

1. Owners of a corporation who elect the board of directors and vote on fundamental changes in the corporation are known as _____.

2. A(n) _____ is a fictitious legal entity that is created according to statutory requirements.

3. A panel of persons who are elected by the shareholders that make policy decisions concerning the operation of a corporation is known as _____.

4. _____ is a general rule of corporate law that provides that generally shareholders are liable only to the extent of their capital contributions for the debts and obligations of their corporation and are not personally liable for the debts and obligations of the corporation.

5. A corporation in the state in which it was formed is referred to as a(n) _____.

6. A corporation that is incorporated in another country is known as a(n) _____.

7. _____ are corporations that have many shareholders and whose securities are often traded on national stock exchanges.

8. A corporation is a(n) _____ corporation in the state in which it is incorporated.

9. A corporation in the United States that has been incorporated in another country is referred to as a(n) _____ corporation.

10. The person or persons, partnerships, or corporations that are responsible for incorporation of a corporation is known as a(n) _____.

11. A(n) _____ is a person or persons who organize and start a corporation, negotiate and enter into contracts in advance of its formation, find the initial investors to finance the corporation, and so forth.

12. A(n) _____ is the basic governing documents of a corporation which must be filed with the secretary of state of the state of incorporation._____

13. A(n) _____ is a clause that can be included in the articles of incorporation that permits the corporation to engage in any activity permitted by law.

14. A(n) _____ is a clause that can be included in the articles of incorporation that stipulates the activities that the corporation can engage in. The corporation can engage in no other purposes or activities.

15. A person or corporation that is empowered to accept service of process on behalf of a corporation is referred to as a(n) _____.

Critical Thought Exercise

Gus Hill runs a successful sole proprietorship under the name "Custom Rides." Hill makes custom motorcycles that often sell for over $40,000 each. Hill decides to expand the business and make motorcycles that are more of a standard production. In order to do this, Hill decides to form a corporation and solicit investors through the sale of company stock. Hill contacts an attorney and requests that all of the paperwork necessary for the incorporation be prepared. To prepare for the expanded business that will be done by the corporation, Hill leases a large manufacturing building from LandCo for one year at $12,000 per month. Hill also signs a $175,000 contract with VanTolker Tool Co. for the purchase of equipment and an employment contract with Dirk Dodds, who was hired to serve as plant manager and chief financial officer. Dodds's contract stated that he understood that his $130,000 yearly salary would come from corporate income and that Hill had no ability to pay his salary.

The corporation is formed and all legal filings are complete. Custom Rides immediately begins making payments on all three contracts. Custom Rides, Inc., operates for eight months before poor sales make it unable to meet its financial obligations. LandCo, Dodds, and VanTolker all file suit against Custom Rides, Inc., and Gus Hill personally to recover their contract damages.

Is Gus Hill personally liable for the contracts he signed on behalf of Custom Rides, Inc.?

Please compose your answer to the Critical Thinking Exercise using a separate sheet of paper or your computer word processing program.

Practice Quiz

True/False

16. _____ Corporation codes regulate the formation, operation, and dissolution of corporations.

17. _____ Corporations are not allowed to enter into contracts in their own name.

18. _____ The board of directors makes policy decisions concerning the operation of a corporation.

19. _____ Shareholders of a closely held corporation play a minor role in its management.

20. _____ Publicly held corporations are corporations run by the government.

21. _____ Shareholders are liable for the debt and obligations of a corporation.

22. _____ A foreign corporation can conduct intrastate commerce if it obtains a certificate of authority from the state.

23. _____ A corporation is a foreign corporation in states other than the one in which it is incorporated.

24. _____ The articles of incorporation must contain the name and address of every incorporator.

25. _____ Amendments to the articles of incorporation must be filed with the secretary of state of the state of incorporation.

26. _____ The RMBCA provides that corporate existence begins when the articles of incorporation are filed.

27. _____ According to the RMBCA, only corporations with 50 or fewer shareholders may elect statutory close corporation status.

28. _____ Bylaws of a corporation must be filed with a government official.

29. _____ Secured bondholders can foreclose on the collateral in the event of nonpayment of interest.

30. _____ A corporation is dissolved upon the effective date of the articles of dissolution.

Multiple Choice

31. Which of the following can dismiss the existence of a corporation?

A. voluntary termination by shareholder
B. death of a shareholder
C. bankruptcy of a shareholder
D. voluntary termination by the corporation's creditors

32. Which of the following elects members of the board of directors for a corporation?

A. the CEO
B. corporate officers
C. shareholders
D. employees

33. Which of the following is a definition of a foreign corporation?

A. A corporation with incorporations in multiple states.
B. A corporation in the state in which it is incorporated.
C. A corporation in states other than the one in which it is incorporated.
D. A corporation in the United States which has been incorporated in another country.

34. Which of the following is true for a corporation's incorporation in a state?

A. Domestic corporations can incorporate into only one state.
B. Domestic corporations can incorporate into all states that it conducts business in.
C. Alien corporations can only incorporate into one state.
D. Foreign corporations can incorporate into more than one state.

35. Which of the following must be included in an article of incorporation?

A. The minutes of the first organizational meeting of the board of directors.
B. The number of shares the corporation is authorized to issue.
C. The dissolution terms of the incorporation.
D. The corporate seal must be used in the articles of incorporation.

36. Which of the following acts is seen as conclusive proof for the existence of a corporation?

A. creation of the promoter's contracts
B. filing of the articles of incorporation
C. acquiring the domain name for the corporation
D. selecting a state for incorporation

37. Which of the following must necessarily be met for a corporation to elect as a statutory close corporation?

A. The corporation must have 100 or more shareholders.
B. The corporation must have 50 or fewer shareholders.
C. The corporation must contain a board of directors.
D. The corporation must have a set of bylaws.

38. Which of the following is true of corporate bylaws?

A. They only contain rules on how the corporation can deal with the government.
B. They are only adopted by the shareholders of the corporation.
C. They are not binding on the directors, or shareholders of the corporation.
D. They do not have to be filed with any government official.

39. Which of the following shares have the right to vote?

A. unissued shares
B. treasury shares
C. outstanding shares
D. liquidated shares

40. Which of the following has a fixed maturity date?

A. bonds
B. common stock
C. cumulative preferred stock
D. participating preferred stock

Short Answer

41. What is the only way that corporations may be created?

_____

_____

42. What are the basic governing documents of a corporation called?

_____

_____

43. Before the articles of incorporation can be amended, what must the board of directors adopt?

_____

_____

44. Who do the bylaws of a corporation bind?

_____

_____

45. What is a registered agent?

_____

_____

46. What is a corporate seal?

_____

_____

47. What type of voting rights do common stockholders have?

_____

_____

48. What is meant by the terminology "issued shares"?

_____

_____

49. What are repurchased shares called?

_____

_____

50. Why is it a benefit to hold participating preferred stock?

_____

_____

51. Define what a corporation is by elaborating on what it can or cannot do based upon its status as an artificial person. List at least two things.

_____

_____

52. What are the differences between the first drafted MBCA and the revised Model Business Corporation Act?

_____

_____

53. Which act allows some corporations and their shareholders to avoid double taxation by electing to be an S corporation?

_____

_____

54. What are the articles of incorporation?

_____

_____

55. What function do the corporate bylaws serve?

_____

_____

Answers to Refresh Your Memory

1. shareholders [p. 594]
2. corporation [p. 594]
3. board of directors [p. 595]
4. Limited liability of shareholders [p. 595]
5. domestic corporation [p. 598]
6. alien corporation [p. 598]
7. Publicly held corporations [p. 597]
8. domestic [p. 598]
9. alien [p. 598]
10. incorporator [p. 600]
11. promoter [p. 600]
12. articles of incorporation [p. 601]
13. general-purpose clause [p. 602]
14. limited-purpose clause [p. 602]
15. registered agent [p. 602]

Critical Thought Exercise Model Answer

Before a corporation is formed, a promoter takes the preliminary steps in organizing the corporation. The promoter makes contracts with investors and third parties. A promoter may purchase or lease property and goods with the intent that it will be sold or transferred to the corporation when the corporation is formed. The promoter may also enter into contracts with professionals whose services are needed. As a general rule, a promoter is held personally liable on preincorporation contracts. A promoter is not an agent when the corporation does not yet exist. If, however, the promoter secures a contracting party's agreement to only hold the corporation liable, then the promoter will not he held liable for any breach. Additionally, the promoter's personal liability continues even after the corporation is formed unless the promoter gains a release of liability from the third party. It does not matter whether or not the contract was made in the name of, or on behalf of, the named corporation.

Hill was acting as a promoter when he entered into contracts with LandCo, VanTolker, and Dodds. The fact that he signed the contracts as a purported agent of Custom Rides, Inc., will have no effect because the corporation had yet to be incorporated. The employment with Dodds is different than the others because Dodds agreed to seek payment only from Custom Rides, Inc., effectively releasing Hill from any personal liability. Even though Custom Rides, Inc., adopted the contracts executed with LandCo and VanTolker, the lack of a formal novation meant that Hill remained personally liable after incorporation. There could not have been a ratification of the preincorporation contracts because there was no principal to ratify the agent's acts at the time the contract was executed. Therefore, Hill will be personally liable to both LandCo and VanTolker.

Answers to Practice Quiz

True/False

16. True. Corporations codes are state statutes that regulate the formation, operation, and dissolution of corporations. [p. 594]

17. False. Corporations are treated, in effect, as artificial persons created by the state that can sue or be sued in their own names, enter into and enforce contracts, hold title to and transfer property, and be found civilly and criminally liable for violations of law. [p. 594]

18. True. The board of directors makes policy decisions concerning the operation of a corporation. [p. 595]

19. False. A closely held corporation is one whose shares are owned by a few shareholders who are often family members, relatives, or friends. Frequently, the shareholders are involved in the management of the corporation. [p. 597]

20. False. A publicly held corporation is a corporation that has many shareholders and whose securities are often traded on national stock exchanges. [p. 597]

21. False. As separate legal entities, corporations are liable for their own debts and obligations. Generally, the shareholders have only limited liability. That is, they are liable only to the extent of their capital contributions and do not have personal liability for the corporation's debts and obligations [p. 595]

22. True. Where a foreign corporation is required to qualify to conduct intrastate commerce in a state, it must obtain a certificate of authority from the state [RMBCA Section 15.01(a)]. [p. 598]

23. True. A corporation is a domestic corporation in the state in which it is incorporated. It is a foreign corporation in all other states and jurisdictions. [p. 598]

24. True. Under the RMBCA, the articles of incorporation must include the name and address of each incorporator. [p. 601]

25. True. After the shareholders approve an amendment, the corporation must file articles of amendment with the secretary of state of the state of incorporation. [p. 601]

26. True. The RMBCA provides that corporate existence begins when the articles of incorporation are filed. [p. 601]

27. True. Only corporations with 50 or fewer shareholders may elect statutory close corporation (SCC) status. [p. 603]

28. False. Bylaws do not have to be filed with any government official. [p. 603]

29. True. Secured bondholders can foreclose on the collateral in the event of nonpayment of interest, principal, or other specified events. [p. 611]

30. True. A corporation is dissolved upon the effective date of the articles of dissolution.[p. 612]

Multiple Choice

31. A. Answer A is the correct answer. The existence of a corporation can be voluntarily terminated by the shareholders. [p. 595]

32. C. Answer C is the correct answer. The members of the board of directors are elected by the shareholders. [p. 595]

33. C. Answer C is the correct answer. A foreign corporation is a corporation in any state or jurisdiction other than the one in which it was formed. [p. 598]

34. A. Answer A is the correct answer. A domestic corporation is a corporation in the state in which it was formed. [p. 598]

35. B. Answer B is the correct answer. Under the RMBCA, the articles of incorporation must include the number of shares the corporation is authorized to issue. [p. 601]

36. B. Answer B is the correct answer. The RMBCA provides that corporate existence begins when the articles of incorporation are filed. [p. 601]

37. B. Answer B is the correct answer. Only corporations with 50 or fewer shareholders may elect statutory close corporation (SCC) status. [p. 603]

38. D. Answer D is the correct answer. Bylaws do not have to be filed with any government official. [p. 603]

39. C. Answer C is the correct answer. Only outstanding shares have the right to vote. [p. 611]

40. A. Answer A is the correct answer. Debt securities (also called fixed income securities) establish a debtor– creditor relationship in which the corporation borrows money from the investor to whom the debt security is issued. The corporation promises to pay interest on the amount borrowed and to repay the principal at some stated maturity date in the future. The three classifications of debt securities are, debentures, bonds and notes. [p. 611]

Short Answer

41. Corporations can only be created according to the laws of the state of incorporation. [p. 594]

42. Articles of incorporation. [p. 601]

43. A resolution recommending the amendment. [p. 601]

44. Bylaws are binding on directors, officers, and shareholders of a corporation. [p. 603]

45. An individual or corporation that has the authority to accept service of process on behalf of the corporation. [p. 603]

46. It is a design that contains the name and date of incorporation. [p. 604]

47. The right to vote on mergers and other important matters. [p. 609]

48. It means shares are sold by the corporation. [p. 610]

49. Treasury shares. [p. 610]

50. It is beneficial as it allows the stockholder to participate in the profits of the corporation. [p. 610]

51. A corporation is a legal entity that may sue or be sued in its own name, and enter into and enforce contracts as well as hold title to and transfer property. (Answers will vary.) [p. 594]

52. The RMBCA arranges provisions of the act more logically and there are substantial changes in the provisions of the revised act. [p. 599]

53. Subchapter S Revision Act. [p. 606]

54. The articles of incorporation are the basic ruling documents of the corporation that must be drafted, filed, and approved by the secretary of state. [p. 601]

55. The bylaws regulate the internal management structure of the corporation. [p. 603]

37 | CORPORATE GOVERNANCE AND THE SARBANES-OXLEY ACT

Chapter Overview

The previous chapter explored the formation of corporations, the various types of corporations, and the characteristics associated with corporations. In this chapter, the rights, duties and liabilities of corporate shareholders, officers, and directors are examined, with an emphasis on the differences in the roles and responsibilities of each. Changes to the corporate environment made by the Sarbanes-Oxley Act are examined.

Objectives

Upon completion of the exercises in this chapter, you should be able to:
1. Describe the functions of shareholders, directors, and officers in managing the affairs of a corporation.
2. Describe a director's and an officer's duty of care and the business judgment rule.
3. Describe a director's and an officer's duty of loyalty and how this duty is breached.
4. Define piercing the corporate veil, or alter ego doctrine.
5. Describe how the Sarbanes-Oxley Act affects corporate governance.

Practical Application

Whether you are a shareholder, a director, officer, or a corporate observer, this chapter will provide you with practical information regarding the internal management structure and its direct impact on one another. This knowledge will provide you with the ability to make educated decisions as may pertain to the basic decisions associated with the management of corporations.

Helpful Hints

Just as it takes a village to raise a child, it takes an entire management structure to mold and develop a corporation. If you follow this analogy as you study the key players in the corporate infrastructure, your understanding will be rewarding and insightful. If you view shareholders, directors, and officers as a pyramid, with each having different responsibilities impacting the other tiers, you will better understand their importance in keeping the corporate pyramid intact.

Study Tips

Corporate Governance and the Sarbanes-Oxley Act

Directors are elected by the shareholders, who also vote on other important issues affecting the corporation. The responsibility for policy decisions and employing officers rests with the directors. The officers carry out the day-to-day operations of the corporation.
- The corporation, as a legal entity, can be held liable for the acts of directors and officers.
- Directors and officers own certain duties to the corporation and its shareholders.

      ○   Breach of these duties can result in personal liability of the director or officer.
- Sarbanes-Oxley rules to improve corporate governance, prevent fraud, improve transparency.

Shareholders

Shareholders hold a significant position in the corporate pyramid, as they own the corporation.
- They vote on the directors and other important actions to be taken by the corporation, but cannot bind the corporation to any contract.

Shareholders' Meetings. Annual shareholder meetings are held to take actions such as the election of director and independent auditors.
- Special Shareholder Meetings. May be conducted to evaluate and vote on significant or emergency issues, such as potential mergers, or amendments to the articles of incorporation.

Notice of Shareholders' Meetings. A corporation must give the shareholders written notice of the place, day, and time of annual and special meetings.
- For a special meeting, the purpose of the meeting must be stated.
- Only matters stated in the notice of a meeting can be considered at the meeting.

Proxies. Shareholders who do not attend the shareholder's meeting to vote may vote by proxy by appointing another person as their agent to vote at the meeting.
- The proxy may be directed how to vote or may be given discretion on how to vote the shares.
- The proxy card is the written document, which is valid for 11 months.

Voting Requirements. At least one class of stock must have voting rights and only those shareholders who own stock on the record date may vote at the shareholders' meeting.
- The corporation must prepare a shareholders' list containing names and addresses of the shareholders as of the record date, the class and number of shares owned by each shareholder.
- This list must be available for inspection at the corporation's main office [RMBCA §7.20].

Quorum and Voting Required. A quorum is the number of directors required to hold a board of directors' meeting or conduct business of the board.
- An affirmative vote for elections other than the board of directors is required.

Straight (Non-Cumulative) Voting. The election of the directors may be by straight voting.
- Each shareholder votes the number of shares he or she owns on candidates for the directors positions that are open.

Cumulative Voting. The method of cumulative voting may be used in voting for the directors.
- This method entails a shareholder accumulating all of his or her votes and voting them all for one candidate or dividing his or her votes among many candidates.
- A shareholder may multiply the number of shares he or she owns by the number of directors to be elected, then vote the entire amount on a single candidate or apportion the product among contenders.

Supramajority Voting Requirement. This requirement can be made, thereby requiring a greater than majority of shares to comprise a quorum of the shareholders' vote.

Voting Trust. Shareholders transfer stock certificates to a trustee with authority to vote shares.

Shareholder Voting Agreements. Two or more shareholders agree on how to vote their shares.

Right of First Refusal. The right of first refusal is an agreement that shareholders enter into which grants one another the right of first refusal to purchase shares they are going to sell.

Buy-and-Sell Agreement. In a buy-and sell agreement, the shareholders are required to sell their shares to the other shareholders or the corporation at a price set in the agreement.

Preemptive Rights. Preemptive rights give existing shareholders the option of subscribing to new shares being issued in proportion to their current ownership interest.

Right to Receive Information and Inspect Books and Records. Shareholders have a right to be current on financial affairs of the corporation and must be given an annual financial statement.
- Shareholders have an absolute right to inspect the articles of incorporation, bylaws, minutes, and so on within the past three years.

Dividends. Dividends are paid at the discretion of the board of directors.
- The date that is set prior to the actual payment of a dividend is called a record date.
- Shareholders on that date are entitled to receive a dividend, even if they sell their shares before the payment date.

Stock Dividends. Corporations may choose to provide dividends in stock, which are distributed in proportion to existing ownership interests.

Derivative Lawsuits. In this lawsuit, the directors can bring suit on behalf of the corporation but fail to do so, so that shareholders have the right to bring it on the corporation's behalf.

Piercing the Corporate Veil. Generally shareholders are liable for the debts and obligations of the corporation to the extent of their capital contribution.
- If the corporation is dominated or misused by the shareholder(s) for improper purposes, the court can disregard the corporate entity theory and hold the shareholders of a corporation personally liable for the corporation's debts and obligations. Called the alter ego doctrine.
- Reasons to pierce the corporate veil include: the corporation not being formed with sufficient capital and lack of separateness between the corporation and its shareholders.

Board of Directors

The board of directors makes policy decisions as well as employs the major officers for the corporation. They also make suggestions concerning actions implemented by the shareholders.

Compensating Directors. Directors are often paid a retainer fee and an attendance fee for attending meetings.

Selecting Directors. The number of directors is stated in the articles of incorporation, but may be as little as only one individual. There are two types of directors:
- Inside Director. A member of the board of directors who is also an officer of the corporation.
- Outside Director. A member of the board who is not an officer of the corporation.

Term of Office. A director's term expires at the next annual shareholders' meeting following his or her election unless the terms are staggered so that only a part of the board of directors is up for election each year.

Meetings of the Board. The directors of a corporation can act only as a board, not individually.
- Every director has the right to participate in any meeting of the board, each has one vote, and cannot vote by proxy.
- Regular Meetings. These meetings are held at the times and places established in the bylaws.
- Special Meetings. These meetings are usually convened for such reasons as issuing new shares, considering proposals to merge, defending against hostile takeover attempts, etc.

Quorum and Voting Requirement. A simple majority of the number of directors stated in the articles of incorporation or bylaws usually constitutes a quorum for transacting business.

Sarbanes-Oxley Act Imposes Duties on Audit Committee. An audit committee is required of all public companies and all public companies must establish adequate internal controls.
- Members must be members of the board and must be independent.
  - At least one member must be a financial expert.
- The committee is responsible for appointment of, payment to, and oversight of auditors.
  - The committee must pre-approve all audit and non-audit services of accounting firms.
  - The committee has authority to employ independent legal and other advisors.

Corporate Officers

Officers have the responsibility of managing the day-to-day operation of the corporation.
- They act as agents and hire other officers and employees.
- The following officers exist in many corporations: president, one or more vice presidents, a secretary, and a treasurer.

Agency Authority of Officers. Officers have the express, implied, and apparent authority to bind the corporation to contract.

Duty of Obedience. Directors and officers owe the fiduciary duty of obedience and must not intentionally or negligently act outside of their authority.
- If he or she does, he or she is personally responsible for any resulting damages caused to the corporation or its shareholders.

Fiduciary Duty: Duty of Care

The duty of due care involves an officer's or director's obligation to discharge his or her duties in good faith and with the care of an ordinary prudent person in a like position would use, and in a manner that is in the best interests of the corporation.

- Examples of breaches: A director or officer will be held personally liable for failure to make reasonable investigation in a corporate matter, or failure to regularly attend board meetings, or properly supervise a subordinate, or failure to be sufficiently informed of corporate affairs.

The Business Judgment Rule. A director's or officer's duty of care is measured as of the time that he or she makes a decision.
- Honest mistakes of judgment do not render the director or officer liable.

Fiduciary Duty: Duty of Loyalty

Officers and directors are to place their personal interest below that of the corporation and its shareholders.
- Breaches of this duty include the usurping of a corporate opportunity, self-dealing, competing with the corporation, and disgorgement of secret profits.

Usurping a Corporate Opportunity. Directors and officers may not personally usurp, or steal, a corporate opportunity for themselves.
- If usurpation is proven, the corporation can acquire the opportunity or recover the profits.
- If the opportunity was fully disclosed and presented to the corporation, and then rejected, the director or officer is free to take advantage of the opportunity.

Self-Dealing. A contract by a corporation with a director or officer is voidable if it is deemed to be unfair to the corporation.

Competing with the Corporation. Unless full disclosure is made and the activity is approved by a majority of the disinterested directors or shareholders, directors and officers cannot compete with the corporation.

Making a Secret Profit. The corporation can sue a director or officer to recover the secret profit if a director or an officer breaches his duty of loyalty and makes a secret profit on a transaction.

Sarbanes-Oxley Act

The Sarbanes-Oxley Act of 2002 establishes far-reaching rules regarding corporate governance with an aim to improve corporate governance rules, eliminate conflicts of interest, and instill confidence in investors and the public in the management of public companies.

Sarbanes-Oxley Act Improves Corporate Governance.
- CEO and CFO Certification. The CEO and CFO of a public company must certify
  - that each annual and quarterly report has been reviewed,
  - that the report does not contain any untrue statement of a material fact or omit to state a material fact that would make the statement misleading, and
  - that financial statement and disclosures fairly present the condition of the company.
    - Knowing and willful violations subject to 20 years in prison, $5 million fine.
- Reimbursement of Bonuses and Incentive Pay. The CEO and CFO must reimburse the company for any bonuses, incentive pay, or securities trading profits made because of the noncompliance that required restatement of the financial statements.

- **Prohibition on Personal Loans.** Public companies are forbidden from making personal loans to their directors or executive officers.
- **Tampering with Evidence.** Criminalizes knowingly altering, destroying, mutilating, concealing, or creating any document to impair, impede, influence, or obstruct any federal investigation.
  - Violations are punishable by up to 20 years in prison and a monetary fine.
- **Bar from Acting as an Officer or a Director.** The Securities and Exchange Commission (SEC) may prohibit any person who has committed securities fraud from acting as an officer or a director of a public company.
- Private companies and nonprofit organizations are influenced by the act's accounting and corporate governance rules.

Refresh Your Memory

The following exercise will give you the opportunity to test your memory of the principles given in this chapter. Read the question twice and place your answer in the blank provided. Review the chapter material for any question that you are unable to answer or remember.

1. The _____ Act of 2002 is a federal statute enacted by Congress to improve corporate governance.

2. Owners of a corporation who elect the board of directors and vote on fundamental changes in the corporation are known as _____.

3. A shareholder's authorization of another person to vote the shareholder's shares at the shareholders' meetings in the event of the shareholder's absence is called a(n) _____.

4. The written document submitted by a person who has been authorized by a shareholder to vote the shareholder's shares at the shareholders' meetings in the event of the shareholder's absence is known as _____.

5. A _____ is a date specified in corporate bylaws that determine whether a shareholder may vote at a shareholders' meeting.

6. _____ is a system in which each shareholder votes the number of shares he or she owns on candidates for each of the positions open.

7. A system in which a shareholder can accumulate all of his or her votes and vote them for one candidate or split them among several candidates is known as _____.

8. The _____ is a requirement that a greater than majority of shares constitutes a quorum of the vote of the shareholders.

9. An arrangement in which the shareholders transfer their stock certificates to a trustee who is empowered to vote the shares is known as _____.

10. A _____ is an agreement that requires a selling shareholder to offer his or her shares for sale to the other parties to the agreement before selling them to anyone else.

11. An agreement that requires selling shareholders to sell their shares to the other shareholders or to the corporation at the price specified in the agreement is referred to as _____.

12. _____ are rights that give existing shareholders the option of subscribing to new shares being issued in proportion to their current ownership interests.

13. A lawsuit a shareholder brings against an offending party on behalf of a corporation when the corporation itself fails to bring the lawsuit is known as a _____.

14. _____ is a doctrine that says if a shareholder dominates a corporation and uses it for improper purposes, a court of equity can disregard the corporate entity and hold the shareholder personally liable for the corporation's debts and obligations.

15. _____ are a panel of decision makers who are elected by the shareholders.

Critical Thought Exercise

Ned West was the sole shareholder and president of Westward Co., a corporation that ran truck stops along interstate highways. The corporation did not have its own bank accounts. All business was conducted through West's personal account. All supplies, payroll, debts, and purchases were handled through this one checking account. West also paid all of his personal expenses out of this account. All receipts from the truck stops were deposited into the same account. While the corporation was in business, no directors meetings were ever held. All decisions for the corporation were made solely by West.

For a four-year period, Westward Co. accumulated $187,455 in federal tax liabilities. The government is now seeking to collect the overdue tax payments directly from West. West argues that the government is ignoring his corporate entity. Can the government pierce the corporate veil in this case and force West to incur personal liability for the taxes owed by Westward Co.?

Please compose your answer to the Critical Thinking Exercise using a separate sheet of paper or your computer word processing program.

Practice Quiz

True/False

16. _____ One of the powers of a shareholder is his or her right to elect the board of directors.

17. _____ Shareholders of a corporation act as agents of the corporation.

18. _____ Shareholders do not have to attend a shareholders' meeting to vote.

19. _____ A system in which each shareholder votes the number of shares he or she owns on candidates for each of the positions open is known as cumulative voting.

20. _____ According to the right of first refusal, a selling shareholder must offer to sell his or her shares to the other parties to the agreement before selling them to anyone else.

21. _____ The buy-and-sell agreement allows shareholders to sell their shares to people other than fellow shareholders or the corporation.

22. _____ The shareholders are responsible for determining how much will be paid in dividends.

23. _____ Persons who are shareholders on the record date are entitled to receive the dividend, even if they sell their shares before the payment date.

24. _____ Once declared, a cash or property dividend cannot be revoked.

25. _____ The election of directors of the corporation can be held by electronic transmission.

26. _____ The board of director's right to inspection can be limited by bylaws.

27. _____ The business judgment rule protects shareholders for honest mistakes of judgment.

28. _____ A director's failure to properly supervise a subordinate who causes a loss to the corporation would be considered a breach of duty of care.

29. _____ The Sarbanes-Oxley Act contains provisions for prosecuting U.S. firms that bribe foreign officials.

30. _____ The Sarbanes-Oxley Act applies only to public companies.

Multiple Choice

31. Which of the following is true of shareholders?

A. They cannot enter into contracts that bind the corporation.
B. They cannot vote to elect the board of directors.
C. They cannot take active charge in deciding fundamental changes in the corporation.
D. They are considered as agents of the corporation.

32. When is the annual shareholder's meeting held?

A. according to the dates fixed in the bylaws
B. at the whim of the board of directors
C. only if and when there is a crisis
D. only at the time of electing a new board of members

33. Derrick has 2,000 shares of the Unistone Corporation which is planning to vote for two new directors. Through a special voting provision in the corporation's articles of incorporation, Derrick was able to vote for both his preferred candidates with 2,000 shares, giving him a virtual voting count of 4,000 shares. What voting rule in the articles of incorporation allows Derrick to achieve this?

A. supramajority voting
B. noncumulative voting
C. cumulative voting
D. preemptive voting

34. According to the RMBCA, what establishes a quorum to hold a meeting of the shareholders?

A. a majority of outstanding shares
B. a majority of unissued shares
C. a majority of treasury shares
D. a majority of liquidated shares

35. Which of the following is true of a shareholder voting agreement?

A. It's an agreement between the board of directors and a shareholder.
B. It has a limited duration of 10 months.
C. It does not have to be filed with the corporation.
D. It is always revocable.

36. Which of the following is true about dividends?

A. Dividends are paid at the discretion of the shareholders.
B. Dividends cannot be used for corporate purposes.
C. Dividends will be paid to shareholders who have sold their shares prior to the record date.
D. Dividends once declared, cannot be revoked.

37. Which of the following is true of stock dividends?

A. They are the redistribution of corporate assets as shares.
B. They increase an existing shareholder's proportionate ownership interest.
C. They are additional stocks distributed as dividends.
D. They are distributed according to existing ownership interest of the board of members.

38. Which of the following policies helps a corporate officer from being sued for honest mistakes made on behalf of a corporation?

A. duty of loyalty
B. duty of obedience
C. business judgment rule
D. self-dealing

39. Which of the following would be seen as a breach of the duty of loyalty by a corporate officer?

A. straight voting
B. cumulative voting
C. piercing the corporate veil
D. self-dealing

40. The _____ Act prohibits public companies from making personal loans to their directors or executive officers.

A. Foreign Corrupt Practices
B. Deregulation and Monetary Control
C. Sarbanes-Oxley
D. Commodity Futures Modernization

Short Answer

41. What is the right of first refusal as it pertains to stock?

_____

_____

42. What is a buy-and-sell agreement?

_____

_____

43. What is negligence?

_____

_____

44. What is duty of obedience?

_____

_____

45. For what is a corporation's audit committee responsible under Sarbanes-Oxley?

_____

_____

46. Who can fill a vacancy on the board of directors?

_____

_____

47. How many people are needed to comprise a board of directors?

_____

_____

48. Define the meaning of fiduciary duty.

_____

_____

49. When does a director's term of office usually expire?

_____

_____

50. As a legal entity, for what can a corporation be held liable?

_____

_____

51. In the structure of a corporation, who owns it?

_____

_____

52. Why are annual shareholders' meetings held?

_____

_____

53. What is meant by a proxy?

_____

_____

54. To what does the record date refer?

_____

_____

55. What is the main responsibility of the corporations' officers?

_____

_____

Answers to Refresh Your Memory

1. Sarbanes-Oxley [p. 618]
2. shareholders [p. 618]
3. proxy . [p. 619]
4. proxy card [p. 619]
5. record date . [p. 619]
6. Straight voting [p. 620]
7. cumulative voting [p. 620]
8. supramajority voting [p. 620]
9. voting trust [p. 620]
10. right of first refusal [p. 621]
11. buy-and-sell agreement [p. 621]
12. Preemptive rights [p. 621]
13. derivative action [p. 622]
14. Piercing the corporate veil [p. 623]
15. Board of directors [p. 624]

Critical Thought Exercise Model Answer

In corporate law, if personal and company interests are commingled to the extent that the corporation has no separate identity, a court may "pierce the corporate veil" and expose the shareholders to personal liability. West mixed all aspects of his personal business with corporate business. All purchases and payroll checks were made from his personal account. There is no way to separate corporate receipts from West's personal funds. In order to prevent a creditor from "piercing the corporate veil" a sole stockholder needs to be careful to preserve the corporate identity. Maintaining separate accounts and detailed records are imperative if corporate identity is to be preserved. West did not attempt to preserve the identity of Westward Co.

Another key factor that favors the government in this case is the failure of Westward Co. to hold directors meetings. The failure of the sole shareholder to comply with statutory corporate formalities demonstrates that the corporate form may be a sham. West never consulted with his directors and made all decisions for Westward Co. by himself. When the corporate business is treated in such a careless and flippant manner, the corporation and the shareholder in control are no longer separate entities, requiring the sole shareholder to assume personal liability to creditors of the corporation. West ignored the corporate identity and now the government will be allowed to "pierce the corporate veil." West will be personally liable for the corporation's tax debt.

Answers to Practice Quiz

True/False

16. True. The shareholders elect the directors and vote on other important issues affecting the corporation. [p. 618]

17. False. A corporation's shareholders own the corporation. Nevertheless, they are not agents of the corporation (i.e., they cannot bind the corporation to contracts), and the only management duty they have is the right to vote on matters such as the election of directors and the approval of fundamental changes in the corporation. [p. 618]

18. True. Any act that can be taken at a shareholders' meeting can be taken without a meeting if all the corporate shareholders sign a written consent approving the action [RMBCA Section 7.04]. [p. 619]

19. False. Cumulative voting is a system in which a shareholder can accumulate all of his or her votes and vote them all for one candidate or split them among several candidates. [p. 620]

20. True. Right of first refusal is an agreement that requires a selling shareholder to offer his or her shares for sale to the other parties to the agreement before selling them to anyone else. [p. 621]

21. False. Buy-and-sell agreement is an agreement that requires selling shareholders to sell their shares to the other shareholders or to the corporation at the price specified in the agreement. [p. 621]

22. False. The directors are responsible for determining when, where, how, and how much will be paid in dividends. [p. 622]

23. True. When a corporation declares a dividend, it sets a date, usually a few weeks prior to the actual payment, that is called the record date. Persons who are shareholders on that date are entitled to receive the dividend, even if they sell their shares before the payment date. [p. 622]

24. True. Once declared, a cash or property dividend cannot be revoked. [p. 622]

25. True. The election of directors of the corporation may be held by electronic transmission. [p. 624]

26. False. Corporate directors are required to have access to the corporation's books and records, facilities, and premises, as well as any other information that affects the operation of the corporation. This right of inspection is absolute. It cannot be limited by the articles of incorporation, the bylaws, or board resolution. [p. 625]

27. False. Business judgment rule is a rule that says directors and officers are not liable to the corporation or its shareholders for honest mistakes of judgment. [p. 629]

28. True. A director or an officer who breaches the duty of care is personally liable to the corporation and its shareholders for any damages caused by the breach. Such breaches, which are normally caused by negligence, often involve a director's or an officer's failure to (1) make a

reasonable investigation of a corporate matter, (2) attend board meetings on a regular basis, (3) properly supervise a subordinate who causes a loss to the corporation through embezzlement and such, or (4) keep adequately informed about corporate affairs. [p. 629]

29. False. Foreign Corrupt Practices Act is a federal statute that makes it a crime for U.S. companies, or their officers, directors, agents, or employees, to bribe a foreign official, a foreign political party official, or a candidate for foreign political office, where the bribe is paid to influence the awarding of new business or the retention of a continuing business activity. [p. 633]

30. True. The goals of the Sarbanes-Oxley Act are to improve corporate governance rules, eliminate conflicts of interest, and instill confidence in investors and the public that management will run public companies in the best interests of all constituents. [p. 633]

Multiple Choice

31. A. Answer A is the correct answer. A corporation's shareholders own the corporation Nevertheless, they are not agents of the corporation (i.e., they cannot bind the corporation to contracts), and the only management duty they have is the right to vote on matters such as the election of directors and the approval of fundamental changes in the corporation. [p. 618]

32. A. Answer A is correct. Annual shareholders' meetings are held to elect directors, choose an independent auditor, and take other actions. These meetings must be held at the times fixed in the bylaws. [p. 619]

33. C. Answer C is the correct answer. Cumulative voting is a system in which a shareholder can accumulate all of his or her votes and vote them all for one candidate or split them among several candidates. [p. 620]

34. A. Answer A is correct. The RMBCA establishes a majority of outstanding shares as a quorum to hold a meeting of the shareholders. [p. 619]

35. C. Answer C is the correct answer. A voting trust agreement must be in writing and cannot exceed 10 years. It must be filed with the corporation and is open to inspection by shareholders of the corporation [RMBCA Section 7.30]. [p. 621]

36. D. Answer D is correct. Once declared, a cash or property dividend cannot be revoked. Shareholders can sue to recover declared but unpaid dividends. [p. 622]

37. C. Answer C is correct. Stock dividends are additional shares of stock distributed as a dividend. [p. 622]

38. C. Answer C is correct. Business judgment rule is a rule that says directors and officers are not liable to the corporation or its shareholders for honest mistakes of judgment. [p. 629]

39. D. Answer D is correct. Under the RMBCA, a contract or transaction with a corporate director or officer is voidable by the corporation if it is unfair to the corporation [RMBCA Section 8.31]. Contracts of a corporation to purchase property from, sell property to, or make loans to corporate directors or officers where the directors or officers have not disclosed their interest in the transaction are often voided under this standard. In the alternative, the corporation can affirm the contract and recover any profits from the self-dealing employee. [p. 630]

40. C. Answer C is correct The Sarbanes-Oxley Act prohibits public companies from making personal loans to their directors or executive officers. [p. 634]

Short Answer

41. An agreement entered into by shareholders that grant one another the right of first refusal to purchase shares that they are going to sell. [p. 621]

42. An agreement entered into by shareholders that requires selling shareholders to sell their shares to other shareholders of the corporation at the price in the agreement. [p. 621]

43. It is failure of a corporate director or officer to exercise the duty of care while conducting the corporation's business. [p. 629]

44. It is a duty that directors and officers of a corporation have to act within the authority conferred upon them by state corporation codes, the articles of incorporation, the corporate bylaws, and the resolutions adopted by the board of directors. [p. 628]

45. The appointment, payment of compensation, and oversight of public accounting firms employed to audit the company. [p. 627]

46. Shareholders or the remaining directors. [p. 626]

47. A board of directors can consist of one or more individuals. [p. 626]

48. The duty of loyalty, integrity, honesty, trust, and confidence owed by directors and officers to their corporate employers is what is known as their fiduciary duty. [p. 629]

49. A director's term of office expires at the next annual shareholder's meeting following his or her election, unless the terms are staggered. [p. 626]

50. A corporation can be held liable for the acts of the directors and officers and for authorized contracts entered into on its behalf. [p. 618]

51. The corporation's shareholders own the corporation. [p. 618]

52. Annual shareholders' meetings are held to elect directors, to choose an independent auditor, or to take other actions. [p. 619]

53. A proxy is a written document that a shareholder signs authorizing another person to vote his shares at the shareholders' meetings in the event of the shareholder's absence. [p. 619]

54. The record date is date specified in corporate bylaws that determines whether a shareholder may vote at a shareholders' meeting. [p. 619]

55. The main responsibility of the corporation's officers is to manage the day-to-day operations of the corporation. [p. 628]

38 | CORPORATE ACQUISITIONS AND MULTINATIONAL CORPORATIONS

Chapter Overview

Corporate change is found by controlling stockholder votes. Shareholder votes are solicited and voted by proxy. Persons who desire fundamental change in the direction or control of a company often engage in a proxy contest to win over shareholder votes. Another fundamental change may be made by acquiring another company. This may be through a friendly merger of consolidation or by a hostile tender offer. The target company may mount a defense to the takeover. This chapter focuses on all these possible fundamental changes that a corporation may go through.

Objectives

Upon completion of the exercises in this chapter, you should be able to:
1. Describe the process of soliciting proxies from shareholders and engaging in proxy contests.
2. Define shareholder resolution and identify when a shareholder can include a resolution in proxy materials.
3. Describe the process for approving a merger or share exchange.
4. Define tender offer and describe poison pills, greenmail, and other defensive maneuvers to prevent hostile takeover.
5. Examine the use of multinational corporations in conducting international business.

Practical Application

For those businesspersons that obtain ownership interests incorporations or choose the corporation as their business form, obtaining or maintaining control of the company is often imperative. It is wise to understand how control of the company may be lost and what efforts can lawfully be made to thwart a proxy battle or hostile takeover.

Helpful Hints

In the corporate environment, mergers, acquisitions, proxy fights, and tender offers are realities that are effectuated only be adhering to the laws and regulations related to these processes and changes. The individual has a greater ability to control his/her financial stake in a corporation if he/she understands his/her rights and duties under the applicable laws. The exercises in this chapter will help you advance your understanding of this area of corporate law.

Study Tips

Before an individual can participate in corporate change and defend his/her investment, he/she must understand the major guiding principles and law that controls the areas of proxy fights, mergers, acquisitions, tender offers, and defenses to corporate takeovers. Understanding the following terms and principles is essential to meaningful participation in any of these corporate events. This short outline and glossary of terms is divided into subject areas.

Corporate Acquisitions and Multinational Corporations

Proxy contests often occur in efforts to win over shareholder votes to take over management of a corporation. Corporations often seek to acquire other businesses. Multinational corporations conduct business using different business arrangements, like branch offices and subsidiaries.

Proxy Solicitation and Proxy Contest

Shareholders can exercise their power to vote on corporate matters in person, or by proxy.
- Proxy. A proxy is a means by which a shareholder authorizes another person to represent him or her and vote his or her shares at a shareholders' meeting.
- Proxy Card. A written document signed by a shareholder that authorizes another person to vote the shareholder's shares.

Federal Proxy Rules. Section 14(a) of the Securities Exchange Act of 1934 gives the SEC the authority to regulate the solicitation of proxies.
- Proxy Statement. One soliciting proxies must prepare a proxy statement that fully describes
  - the matter for which the proxy is being solicited,
  - who is soliciting the proxy, and
  - any other pertinent information.

Antifraud Provision. Section 14(a) prohibits misrepresentations or omissions of a material fact in proxy materials.

Proxy Contest. When shareholders oppose the actions of incumbent directors and management, they may challenge the management in a proxy contest in which both sides solicit proxies.

Shareholder Resolution

Shareholders who own less than $5 million in stock of a company may communicate with other shareholders without filing proxy solicitation materials with the SEC.
- Companies seeking proxies must unbundle the propositions so that the shareholders can vote on each separate issue.
  - Performance charts must be included in annual reports.
  - Companies must provide tables in their annual reports that summarize executive compensation.
- Because proxy contests can be very expensive, the incumbent management can obtain reimbursement from the corporation if the contest concerns an issue of corporate policy.
  - The dissenting group can get reimbursed only if it wins the proxy contest.

Mergers and Acquisitions

Mergers, consolidations, share exchanges, and sale of assets are friendly in nature, as both corporations have agreed to the combination of corporations or acquisition of assets.

Merger. When one corporation is absorbed into another corporation and ceases to exist.
- The corporation that continues is the surviving corporation.
- The other is the merged corporation.

      o   Shareholders of the merged corporation receive stock or securities of the surviving corporation.

Share Exchange. When one corporation (parent corporation) acquires all the shares of another corporation (subsidiary corporation) and both corporations retain their separate legal existence.

Required Approvals for a Merger or Share Exchange. A merger or share exchange requires:
- the recommendation of the board of directors of each corporation and
- an affirmative vote of the majority of shares of each corporation that is entitled to vote.
- Articles of Merger or Share Exchange. Must be filed with the secretary of state.
  - o The secretary of state will then issue a certificate of merger or share exchange to the surviving corporation.

Short-Form Merger. If the parent corporation owns 90 percent of the subsidiary corporation, a short-form merger procedure may be followed.
- Approval of shareholders of neither corporation is required for short-form merger.
- All that is required is approval of the board of directors of the parent corporation.

Sale or Lease of Assets. A corporation may sell, lease, or otherwise dispose of all or substantially all of its property. Such a sale requires
- the recommendation of the board of directors and
- an affirmative vote of the majority of the shares of the selling corporation entitled to vote.

Dissenting Shareholder Appraisal Rights. Shareholders who object to a proposed merger, share exchange, or sale or lease of all or substantially all of the property of a corporation have a right to have their shares valued by a court and receive cash payment of this value from the corporation.

Tender Offer

A tender offer is an offer that an acquirer (tender offeror) makes directly to a target corporation's shareholders in an effort to acquire the target corporation.
- The shareholders of the target make an individual decision about whether to sell to the tender offeror.

Williams Act. This act regulates tender offers whether they are made with securities, cash, or other consideration, and establishes certain disclosure requirements and antifraud provisions.

Tender offer rules. The tender offeror is not required to notify the target company or the SEC until after the offer is made.
- Offer cannot be closed before 20 days after the commencement of the tender offer.
- Offer must be extended for 10 days if the tender offer increases the number of shares that it will take or the price it will pay.
- Fair price rule. Stipulates that any increase in price paid for shares must be offered to all shareholders, even those who have already tendered their shares.
- Pro rata rule. Requires that shares must be purchased on a pro rata basis if too many. shares are tendered.

Antifraud Provision. Section 14(e) of the Williams Act prohibits fraudulent, deceptive, or manipulative practices in connection with tender offers.

Fighting a Tender Offer. The incumbent management of a target corporation may desire to oppose a tender offer. Management may engage in a variety of activities to impede or defeat the tender offer. Some of these include:

- Persuasion of shareholders. Media campaigns used to oppose the tender offer.
- Delaying lawsuits. Suits filed alleging antitrust or securities violations to buy time.
- Selling a crown jewel. Selling an asset that makes the target corporation less attractive.
- White knight merger. Merger with friendly party that will leave target intact.
- Pac-Man tender offer. Target makes tender offer for the tender offeror.
- Adopting a poison pill. Strategy built into articles of incorporation, bylaws, contracts, or leases whereby large payouts or termination of contracts become effective if the corporation changes hands.
- Issuing additional stock. Issuing more stock makes tender offeror buy more shares.
- Creating Employee Stock Ownership Plan (ESOP). Block of stock owned by employees is used to oppose acquirer in proxy fight.
- Flip-over and flip-in rights plans. Allows stockholders to buy twice the value in stock to make company too expensive to buy.
- Greenmail and standstill agreements. Target pays premium to get back shares from tender offeror.

Business Judgment Rule. A rule that protects the decisions of the board of directors, who act on an informed basis, in good faith, and in the honest belief that the action taken was in the best interests of the corporation and its shareholders.

State Antitakeover Statutes

These are statutes that enacted by state legislatures that protect corporations incorporated in or doing business in the state from hostile takeovers.

- They are often challenged as being unconstitutional because they violate the Williams Act and the Commerce and Supremacy Clauses of the U.S. Constitution.

Multinational Corporations

Transnational corporations operate across borders through the use of branch offices, subsidiaries, and other agents, business alliances, strategic partnerships, franchising, and other arrangements.

Branch Office. A branch office is merely an office of the corporation, not a separate legal entity.

- The corporation is liable for the contracts of the branch office and is also liable for the torts committed by personnel of the branch office.
- There is no liability shield between the corporation and the branch office.

Subsidiary Corporation. A subsidiary corporation is organized under the laws of the foreign country.

- The parent corporation usually owns all or the majority of the subsidiary corporation.
- A subsidiary corporation is a separate legal entity.
- The parent corporation is not liable for the contracts of or torts committed by the subsidiary.
- There is a liability shield between the parent corporation and the subsidiary corporation.

The Exon-Florio Law. The Exon-Florio Law of 1988, as amended by the Byrd-Exon Amendment of 1992, mandates the president of the United States to suspend, prohibit, or dismantle the acquisition of U.S. businesses by foreign investors if there is credible evidence that the foreign investor might take action that threatens to impair the national security.

Refresh Your Memory

The following exercise will give you the opportunity to test your memory of the principles given in this chapter. Read the question twice and place your answer in the blank provided. Review the chapter material for any question that you are unable to answer or remember.

1. A(n) _____ refers to a written document signed by a shareholder that authorizes another person to vote the shareholder's shares.

2. The federal proxy rules promote _____ during proxy solicitation.

3. Section 14(a) of the Securities Exchange Act of 1934 is a(n) _____.

4. _____ shareholders are shareholders who propose a slate of directors to replace the incumbent directors.

5. A(n) _____ is a situation in which one corporation is absorbed into another corporation and ceases to exist.

6. A _____ is a situation in which one corporation acquires all the shares of another corporation, and both corporations retain their separate legal existence.

7. The corporation that owns the shares of the subsidiary corporation in a share exchange is known as the _____.

8. A _____ is a merger between a parent corporation and a subsidiary corporation that does not require the approval of the board of directors of the subsidiary corporation.

9. _____ are the rights of shareholders who object to a proposed merger to have their shares valued by the court and receive cash payment of this value from the corporation.

10. The _____ is a federal law that mandates the president of the United States to suspend, prohibit, or dismantle the acquisition of U.S. businesses by foreign investors if there is credible evidence that the foreign investor might take action that threatens to impair the "national security."

11. _____ are made without the permission of the target company's management.

12. Instaworks Inc. wants to acquire IOK Corp. Instaworks makes a tender offer to the shareholders of IOK to acquire their shares of IOK without the permission of the latter corporation's board of directors. This is a _____ tender offer.

13. The _____ is an amendment to the Securities Exchange Act of 1934 that specifically regulates tender offers.

14. The _____ states that any increase in price paid for shares tendered must be offered to all shareholders, even those who have previously tendered their shares.

15. A _____ is a defensive strategy built into the target corporation's articles of incorporation, corporate bylaws, or contracts and leases that can be adopted to defeat a tender offer.

Critical Thought Exercise

Blue Cab Co. was merged into Atlantic Cab Corp., with Atlantic being the surviving corporation in the merger. Atlantic did not take over any of the cabs owned by Blue because they were old and in disrepair. Blue Cab was poorly run and owed over $600,000 to Valley Bank for cab purchases. Blue Cab also owed over $60,700 to Fleet Gas Co. for fuel purchased by its employees. Blue Cab is owed $43,000 by Broadway Actors Transportation, Inc. (BAT) for limousine services rendered pursuant to a contract. Blue Cab has already commenced suit against BAT for breach of contract. Valley Bank and Fleet Gas brought a suit against Atlantic for payment of the debts. The board of directors of Atlantic refused to honor the debts of Blue Cab because the purpose in taking over Blue Cab was to eliminate a competitor. Atlantic had no desire to acquire the assets of Blue Cab Co. Atlantic argued that it had never agreed to assume any debt owed by Blue Cab.

What is the effect of the merger and will Valley Bank and Fleet Gas be able to recover breach of contract damages from Atlantic? Can Atlantic maintain the suit against BAT?

Please compose your answer to the Critical Thinking Exercise using a separate sheet of paper or your computer word processing program.

Practice Quiz

True/False

16. _____ Section 14(a) of the Securities Exchange Act prohibits the solicitation of proxies.

17. _____ A friendly merger of two corporations is not considered an acquisition.

18. _____ A proxy card authorizes another person to vote the shareholder's shares.

19. _____ Section 14(a) of the Securities Exchange Act of 1934 requires the disclosure of the identities of the parties involved in a tender offer.

20. _____ Section 14(a) of the Securities Exchange Act prohibits omissions of material facts in proxy materials.

21. _____ Courts are permitted to order a new election in case of fraudulent proxy solicitation.

22. _____ Incumbent directors are the former directors of a corporation.

23. _____ Shareholders are permitted to submit issues for a vote of other shareholders.

24. _____ Shareholder resolutions cannot be made when a corporation is soliciting proxies from its shareholders.

25. _____ A merged corporation ceases to exist after the merger.

26. _____ An ordinary merger or share exchange requires the recommendation of the board of directors of each corporation.

27. _____ A tender offer targets the board of directors of the target corporation.

28. _____ The pro rata rule states that any increase in price paid for shares tendered must be offered to all shareholders, even those who have previously tendered their shares.

29. _____ Section 14(e) protects shareholders from fraud committed in connection with a tender offer.

30. _____ Greenmail refers to a target corporation's purchase of its stock from an actual or perceived tender offeror at a premium

Multiple Choice

31. Which of the following is true of proxies?

A. Proxies are not permitted to be submitted electronically.
B. Proxies are signed by a corporation and sent to shareholders.
C. Directors or officers of the corporation cannot hold proxies.
D. Corporations are permitted to solicit proxies from shareholders.

32. Section 14(a) of the Securities Exchange Act gives the SEC the authority to regulate _____.

A. the formation of the board of directors of a corporation
B. mergers between two or more corporations
C. the issue of shares by a corporation
D. the solicitation of proxies by a corporation

33. Which of the following defines a proxy contest?

A. an instance of proxies being awarded to the shareholder with the highest bid
B. an event in which insurgent shareholders and incumbent directors solicit proxies from other shareholders
C. an event in which proxies are chosen by voting between different factions of shareholders
D. an event in which a corporation seeks affirmative majority from its shareholders in the event of a hostile tender

34. Which of the following best defines a shareholder resolution?

A. a document submitted by insurgent shareholders formally announcing forfeiture of shares
B. an issue submitted by the board of directors requiring the reorganization of shares held by shareholders
C. an issue submitted by a shareholder for a vote of other shareholders
D. a document that authorizes another person to vote the shareholder's shares

35. Which of the following best defines a merged corporation?

A. the corporation that is absorbed in the merger and ceases to exist after the merger
B. the corporation that is absorbed in the merger and continues to exist after the merger
C. the corporation that is not absorbed in the merger but gains stake in the surviving corporation
D. the corporation that is not absorbed in the merger but is owned by a parent company

36. Which of the following best defines a subsidiary corporation?

A. the corporation that is absorbed into the merger
B. the corporation that continues to exist after a merger
C. the corporation that has brought all the shares of another corporation
D. the corporation that is owned by the parent corporation in a share exchange

37. Which of the following is a valid tender offer rule?

A. The offer cannot be closed after 20 business days after the commencement of the tender offer.
B. The offer cannot be extended if the tender offeror increases the number of shares it will take or the price it will pay for the shares.
C. Any increase in price paid for shares tendered must be offered to all shareholders, including those who have previously tendered their shares.
D. A shareholder who tenders his or her shares loses the right to withdraw them prior to the closing of the tender offer.

38. State antitakeover statutes apply to _____.

A. corporations that are incorporated in the state
B. foreign corporations that operate in the state
C. U.S. corporations incorporated in other states operating in the state
D. corporations which export to the state

39. Which of the following is provided by the Delaware Antitakeover Statute?

A. An acquirer of a Delaware corporation cannot complete a merger with the acquired corporation unless it receives affirmative vote from at least 35 percent shareholders of the acquired corporation.
B. An acquirer of a Delaware corporation located outside Delaware cannot complete a merger with the acquired corporation until it has operated in Delaware for three years.
C. An acquirer of a Delaware corporation must be incorporated in the state of Delaware or have its principal office in the state of Delaware.
D. An acquirer of a Delaware corporation cannot complete a merger with the acquired corporation for three years after purchasing 15 percent or more of the Delaware corporation's shares.

40. Which of the following is true of a subsidiary of a multinational corporation present in a foreign country?

A. The subsidiary corporation is organized under the laws of the foreign country.
B. There is no liability shield between the parent company and the subsidiary.
C. The parent company is wholly responsible for torts committed by the subsidiary.
D. The subsidiary corporation is not considered as a separate legal entity.

Short Answer

41. Give two examples of tactics used by incumbent management in defending against hostile tender offers.

42. When media campaigns are organized to convince shareholders that a tender offer is not in their best interest, this is known as

43. What is an ESOP?

44. What is a merger?

45. Describe what happens in a share exchange.

46. What approvals are required for a regular merger?

47. What is a short-form merger?

48. When too many shares are tendered, what rule applies?

49. What are dissenting shareholder appraisal rights?

50. Describe a tender offer.

_____

_____

51. What is meant by greenmail?

_____

_____

52. What is required by the pro rata rule?

_____

_____

53. What is prohibited by Section 14(e) of the Williams Act?

_____

_____

54. What is the business judgment rule?

_____

_____

55. If a corporation places additional stock on the market, how does this impact a tender offer?

_____

_____

Answers to Refresh Your Memory

1. proxy [p. 639]
2. full disclosure of the proxy [p. 639]
3. antifraud provision [p. 640]
4. Insurgent [p. 640]
5. merger [p. 642]
6. share exchange [p. 643]
7. parent corporation [p. 643]
8. short-form merger [p. 643]
9. Appraisal rights [p. 644]
10. Exon-Florio Foreign Investment Provision [p. 644]
11. Hostile tender offers [p. 645]
12. hostile [p. 645]
13. Williams Act [p. 646]
14. fair price rule [p. 646]
15. poison pill [p. 647]

Critical Thought Exercise Model Answer

A merger involves the legal combination of two or more corporations in a manner that only one of the corporations continues to exist. When Blue Cab merged into Atlantic, Atlantic continued as the surviving corporation while Blue Cab ceased to exist as an entity. After the merger, Atlantic would be recognized as a single corporation, possessing all the rights, privileges, and powers of itself and Blue Cab Co. Atlantic automatically acquired all the assets and property of Blue Cab without the necessity of formality or deeds. The shareholders of Blue Cab receive stock or securities of Atlantic or other consideration as provided in the plan of merger. Additionally, Atlantic becomes liable for all of Blue Cab's debts and obligations. Lastly, Atlantic's articles of incorporation are deemed amended to include any changes that are stated in the articles of merger.

In a merger, the surviving corporation obtains the absorbed corporation's preexisting obligations and legal rights. If the merging corporation had a right of action against a third party, the surviving corporation can bring or maintain a suit after the merger to recover the merging corporation's damages. Atlantic will inherit Blue Cab's right to sue BAT and will be entitled to recover whatever damages Blue Cab was entitled to collect.

Answers to Practice Quiz

True/False

16. False. Section 14(a) of the Securities Exchange Act of 1934 gives the Securities and Exchange Commission (SEC) the authority to regulate the solicitation of proxies. [p. 639]

17. False. Corporations often engage in acquisitions of other corporations or businesses. This may occur by friendly merger or by hostile tender offer. [p. 639]

18. True. A proxy card is a written document signed by a shareholder that authorizes another person to vote the shareholder's shares. [p. 639]

19. True. Section 14(a) of the Securities Exchange Act of 1934 gives the Securities and Exchange Commission (SEC) the authority to regulate the solicitation of proxies. The federal proxy rules promote full disclosure. [p. 639]

20. True. Section 14(a) of the Securities Exchange Act of 1934 gives the Securities and Exchange Commission (SEC) the authority to regulate the solicitation of proxies.1 The federal proxy rules promote full disclosure. The management or any other party soliciting proxies from shareholders must prepare a proxy statement that fully describes (1) the matter for which the proxy is being solicited, (2) who is soliciting the proxy, and (3) any other pertinent information. [p. 639]

21. True. Shareholders who are injured by a material misrepresentation or omission in proxy materials can sue the wrongdoer and recover damages. The court can also order a new election if a violation is found. [p. 640]

22. False. Incumbent directors are the current directors of a corporation. [p. 640]

23. True. Shareholders submit issues for a vote of other shareholders. [p. 640]

24. True. Exchange Act of 1934 and SEC rules permit a shareholder to submit a resolution to be considered by other shareholders if (1) the shareholder has owned at least $2,000 worth of shares of the company's stock or 1 percent of all shares of the company (2) for at least one year prior to submitting the proposal. The resolution cannot exceed 500 words. Such shareholder resolutions are usually made when the corporation is soliciting proxies from its shareholders. [p. 640]

25. True. A merged corporation is the corporation that is absorbed in the merger and ceases to exist after the merger. [p. 642]

26. True. An ordinary merger or share exchange requires (1) the recommendation of the board of directors of each corporation and (2) an affirmative vote of the majority of shares of each corporation that are entitled to vote [RMBCA Section 11.03]. [p. 643]

27. False. A tender offer is an offer that an acquirer makes directly to a target corporation's shareholders in an effort to acquire the target corporation. [p. 645]

28. False. The pro rata rule holds that the shares must be purchased on a pro rata basis if too many shares are tendered. [p. 646]

29. True. Section 14(e) of the Williams Act prohibits fraudulent, deceptive, and manipulative practices in connection with a tender offer. Therefore, a shareholder who has been injured by a violation of Section.14 (e) can sue the wrongdoer for damages. [p. 646]

30. False. Greenmail is the purchase by a target corporation of its stock from an actual or perceived tender offeror at a premium. [p. 647]

Multiple Choice

31. B. Answer B is the correct answer. Corporate shareholders have the right to vote on the election of directors, mergers, charter amendments, and the like. They can exercise their power to vote either in person or by proxy [RMBCA Section 7.22]. Voting by proxy is common in large corporations that have thousands of shareholders located across the country and around the world. [p. 639]

32. D. Answer D is the correct answer. Section 14(a) of the Securities Exchange Act of 1934 gives the Securities and Exchange Commission (SEC) the authority to regulate the solicitation of proxies. [p. 639]

33. B. Answer B is the correct answer. The insurgent shareholders can challenge the incumbent directors in a proxy contest, in which both sides solicit proxies from the other shareholders. [p. 640]

34. C. Answer C is the correct answer. A shareholder resolution is a resolution that a shareholder who meets certain ownership requirements may submit to other shareholders for a vote. [p. 640]

35. A. Answer A is the correct answer. A merged corporation is the corporation that is absorbed in the merger and ceases to exist after the merger. [p. 642]

36. D. Answer D is the correct answer. A subsidiary corporation is the corporation that is owned by the parent corporation in a share exchange. [p. 643]

37. C. Answer C is correct as answers. The fair price rule stipulates that any increase in price paid for shares tendered must be offered to all shareholders, even those who have previously tendered their shares. [p. 646]

38. A. Answer A is the correct answer. State antitakeover statutes apply to corporations that are incorporated in the state. [p. 648]

39. D. Answer D is the correct answer. The Delaware antitakeover statute provides that an acquirer of a Delaware corporation cannot complete a merger with the acquired corporation for three years after purchasing 15 percent or more of the Delaware corporation's shares. [p. 648]

40. A. Answer A is the correct answer. A multinational corporation can conduct business in another country by using a subsidiary corporation. The subsidiary corporation is organized under the laws of the foreign country. [p. 649]

Short Answer

41. Adopting a poison pill and issuing additional stock (answers will vary). [p. 646-647]

42. persuasion of shareholders [p. 646]

43. ESOP is an Employee Stock Option Plan which helps keep the corporation intact as the employees have a vested interest. [p. 647]

44. A merger occurs when one corporation is absorbed into another corporation and ceases to exist. Title to all assets of the merged corporation passes to the surviving corporation without formality or deeds. [p. 642]

45. In a share exchange, both corporations retain their separate legal existence. The parent corporation owns all the shares of the subsidiary corporation. [p. 643]

46. A merger requires the recommendation of the board of directors of each corporation and an affirmative vote of the majority of shares of each corporation entitled to vote. [p. 643]

47. The short-form procedure can be used if the parent corporation owns 90 percent or more of the outstanding stock of the subsidiary corporation. It is a simple procedure because the only approval needed is from the board of directors of the parent corporation. [p. 643]

48. The pro rata rule applies. [p. 646]

49. Shareholders who object to a proposed merger, for example, have a right to have their shares valued by a court and receive cash payment of this value from the corporation. [p. 644]

50. A tender offer is an offer that an acquirer makes during a hostile takeover directly to a target corporation's shareholders in an effort to acquire the target corporation. The shareholders each make an individual decision about whether to sell their shares to the tender offeror. [p. 645]

51. Greenmail is the purchase by a target corporation of its stock from an actual or perceived tender offeror at a premium. [p. 647]

52. The pro rata rule requires that shares must be purchased on a pro rata basis if too many shares are tendered. [p. 646]

53. Section 14(e) prohibits fraudulent, deceptive, or manipulative practices in connection with tender offers. [p. 646]

54. It is a rule that protects the decisions of the board of directors, who act on an informed basis, in good faith, and in the honest belief that the action taken was in the best interests of the corporation and its shareholders. [p. 647]

55. It impacts the tender offer, as the placing of additional stock on the market increases the number of outstanding shares that the tender offeror must purchase in order to gain control of the target corporation. [p. 647]

39 | LIMITED LIABILITY COMPANIES AND LIMITED LIABILITY PARTNERSHIPS

Chapter Overview

The main focus of this chapter is the formation, operation, and thorough explanation of the business entity called a limited liability company (LLC). A limited liability company is a hybrid company of sorts in that it has some of the desirable characteristics of general partnerships, corporations, and limited corporations. The interesting fact about the LLC is that the owners are allowed to manage the business and yet have limited liability. It is allowed to be taxed as a partnership. Since it does offer so many advantages, it is a very favorable way for new business entrepreneurs to begin their ventures. This chapter provides a further exploration of partnerships, with an emphasis on limited partnerships and their formation, as well as the differentiation between limited and general partners. This chapter discusses the limited liability partnership and the partners' liability if involved in the same.

Objectives

Upon completion of the exercises in this chapter, you should be able to:
1. Define limited liability company (LLC*)* and limited liability partnership (LLP*)*.
2. Describe the process of organizing LLCs and LLPs.
3. Describe the limited liability shield provided by LLCs and LLPs.
4. Compare member-managed LLCs and manager-managed LLCs.
5. Determine when members and managers owe fiduciary duties of loyalty and care to an LLC.

Practical Application

You should be able to recognize the benefits from conducting a newly organized business in the form of a limited liability company. Your previous studies of partnerships will aid you in reaching a decision as to the form you may want your own business to take. If you are not planning on operating a business, not only is this chapter useful for general information but it will give you insight on the choices available and why a company may choose to function in this manner from a tax, liability, and management perspective. For the student who wants to operate a business, the basic partnership explanations will be an invaluable tool in determining the type of business operation that would be best in light of an individual's circumstances.

Helpful Hints

It is important to keep in mind that the Uniform Limited Liability Company Act is responsible for codifying the limited liability company law. Its primary goal is to establish a comprehensive limited liability company law that is uniform throughout the U.S. Since it is vital to this type of business, it is crucial to realize that it is your foundation toward learning this area of the law.

A limited liability company is much like a work of unique art that begins much like an ordinary piece of work, but develops into a creation that others would like to have, too. As you go through the study tips section, keep in mind that, as with all forms of business, a limited liability company will need to be organized with articles of organization, time limits set, capital contributions noted, its management set in place, and, of course, the duties of those operating under the company umbrella. Using your imagination to compare the characteristics of the limited liability company to an artistic endeavor will help to make the material enjoyable and manageable to learn.

It is helpful to review the previous study guide chapter on general partnerships, as it provides a solid foundation for this chapter to build upon. It is best to study this material in a methodical fashion in order for the information that is given to be of maximum benefit.

Study Tips

Limited Liability Companies and Limited Liability Partnerships

An LLC is an unincorporated business form that combines the best components of general partnerships, limited partnerships, and corporations. It is taxed as a partnership and the owners enjoy limited liability. An LLP is generally limited in use to certain professionals, such as accountants and doctors, and allows these professionals to enjoy limited liability.

Limited Liability Companies (LLC)

Limited liability companies are created by state law. A large number of states have adopted the Uniform Limited Liability Company Act, which sets forth the laws concerning formation, operation, and termination of the LCC.
- An LLC is a separate legal entity, separate from its members.

Taxation of LLCs. An LLC is taxed as a partnership, unless it elects to be taxed as a corporation, so that its income or losses "flow through" to the members' individual income tax returns.

Powers of an LLC. Limited liability companies can sue or be sued, enter into or enforce contracts, transfer and hold title to property, and be civilly as well as criminally liable under the law.

Formation of an LLC

A limited liability company may be organized for any lawful purpose. An example would be a real estate development company.
- An LLC cannot operate the practice of certain professions, such as doctors or lawyers.
    - These professionals can conduct business as a limited liability partnership.
- An LLC can conduct business in all states, but may only be registered in one.
    - An LLC is usually organized in the state in which it will be transacting most of its business.
- There is an important requirement to keep in mind when choosing a name for the LLC.
    - The name must have the words "limited liability company" or limited company or the abbreviations L.L.C. or LLC or LC.

Articles of Organization. Articles of organization must be delivered to the secretary of state's office for filing.

- If the articles are in proper form, the articles will be filed.
- The articles must contain
    - the name and address of the initial LLC office,
    - the name and address of the initial agent for service of process,
    - the name and address of each organizer, and
    - whether the LLC is a term LLC and, if yes,
    - then the specifics of the term must be stated.
    - Additionally, the articles must state
        - whether the LLC is to be manager-managed and
        - the identity and address(es) of the manager(s) given.
    - Finally, the articles must indicate whether the members will be personally liable for the debts and obligations of the LLC.

Duration of an LLC. An LLC is either an at-will LLC or a term LLC.

- The term LLC states how long the LLC will exist.
- An at-will LLC does not state a term of duration.

Capital Contribution to an LLC. A member's capital may consist of money, real property, personal property, intangible property, services performed, and so on.

- A member's death will not excuse a member's obligation to contribute, nor will disability or the inability to perform.

Certificate of Interest. This acts like a stock certificate, as it indicates a member's ownership interest in the LLC.

Operating Agreement. Members of an LLC may enter into an operating agreement to regulate the affairs of the company and the conduct of its business.

Conversion of an Existing Business to an LLC. Many businesses convert to operate as a limited liability company. They do so to obtain tax benefits as well as utilize the limited liability benefit. In order to convert, ULLCA at section 902 requires

- that there be a statement of terms contained in an agreement of conversion,
- that the agreement be approved by all parties and owners concerned, and
- that the articles of organization be filed with the secretary of state indicating the prior business name and form of operation.

Dividing an LLC's Profits and Losses. Generally speaking, a member has the right to an equal share in the LLC's profits and losses will be divided equally.

- The members of the LLC may agree otherwise.

Distributional Interest. The ownership share of a member is called the distributional interest, and that interest may be transferred.

Liability of an LLC

An LLC is liable for any loss or injury caused to anyone as a result of a wrongful act or omission by a member, a manager, an agent, or an employee of the LLC who commits the wrongful act while acting within the ordinary course of business of the LLC or with authority of the LLC [ULLCA Section 302].

Liability of Managers. Managers of LLCs are not personally liable for the debts, obligations, and liabilities of the LLC they manage [ULLCA Section 303(a)].

Members' Limited Liability

Owners are called members and members usually are not personally liable to third parties for debts obligations and liabilities of an LLC beyond their capital contribution.
- Debts and obligations of the LLC are entirely those of the LLC.

Liability of Tortfeasors. A member or manger of an LLC who negligently causes injury or death to another person, is a tortfeasor, he or she is personally liable to the injured person or the heirs of the deceased person.

Management of an LLC

An LLC is considered member-managed, unless it is deemed manager-managed in the articles of organization.
- In a member-managed LLC, all of the LLC member have agency authority to enter into contracts and bind the LLC.
- In a manager-managed LLC, only designated managers have agency authority to enter into contracts and bind the LLC and they also have equal rights in the management of the LLC business.
- Contracts must be in the ordinary course of business or ones in which the LLC has authorized.

Member-Managed LLC. Each member has equal rights in the management of the business.
- Business matters are decided by a majority vote of the members.

Manager-Managed LLC. Designated managers control the management of the LLC and non-manager members have no rights to manage the business.
- Business matters are decided by a majority vote of the managers.
- Members cannot delegate to managers the following:
  - amending the articles of organization,
  - amending the operating agreement,
  - admitting new members,
  - consenting to dissolve the LLC,
  - consenting to merge the LLC with another entity, and
  - selling, leasing, or disposing of all or substantially all of the LLC's property.

Compensation and Reimbursement. An LLC is required to reimburse members and managers for payments made on behalf of the LLC and to indemnify managers and members for liabilities incurred.

Agency Authority to Bind an LLC to Contracts. An LLC is bound to contracts that members or managers have properly entered into on its behalf in the ordinary course of business [ULLCA Section 301].

- Member-managed LLC. In a member-managed LLC, all members have agency authority to bind the LLC to contracts.
- Manager-managed LLC. In a manager-managed LLC, the managers have authority to bind the LLC to contracts, but nonmanager members cannot bind the LLC to contracts.

Duty of Loyalty Owed to an LLC. The duty of loyalty means that the parties must act honestly which means no usurping of LLC opportunities, no self-dealing, no competition with the LLC, and no making of secret profits.

Limited Duty of Care Owed to an LLC. There is a limited duty of care owed to the LLC which means that a manager or member must not engage in a known violation of the law, grossly negligent conduct, reckless conduct, a known violation of the law, etc.
- Liability for ordinary negligence will not be assessed against a member or manager of an LLC.

No Fiduciary Duty Owed by a Nonmanager Member. A member of a manager-managed LLC who is not a manager owes no fiduciary duty of loyalty or care to the LLC or its other members [ULLCA Section 409(h)(1)].

Dissolution of an LLC

A member may disassociate him or herself from the LLC by withdrawing from both a term and an at-will LLC.
- Wrongful disassociation from an at-will LLC occurs if the power to withdraw is absent from the operating agreement.
- Once a member is disassociated, he or she may not participate in the management of the LLC.
- The member's duties of loyalty and care to the LLC end upon disassociation.

Payment of Distributional Interest. Rightful disassociation from an at-will LLC requires the LLC's purchase of the disassociated member's distributional interest.
- Rightful disassociation from a term LLC, the LLC must only purchase the disassociating member's distributional interest on the expiration of the specified term of the LLC.

Notice of Disassociation. An LLC may give constructive notice of a disassociating member by filing a statement of disassociation with the secretary of state.

Continuation of an LLC. An LLC may be continued in two instances.
- The first situation is where the members unanimously vote prior to the expiration of the current LLC.
- The second situation is where there is a simple majority vote of the at-will LLC members.

Winding Up an LLC's Business. Winding up is "the process of preserving and selling the assets of the LLC and distributing the money and property to creditors and members."
- Assets of the LLC must be used to pay the creditors first, followed by any surplus left over to be distributed to the members in equal shares unless the operating agreement provides otherwise.
- After dissolution and winding up, articles of termination may be filed with the secretary of state.

Limited Liability Partnership (LLP)

Professionals commonly use this type of partnership.
- All partners are given limited liability.
- There is no tax paid at the partnership level.

Articles of Partnership. Limited liability partnerships must be created formally by filing articles of partnership with the secretary of state in which the LLP is organized.
- The LLP is a domestic LLP in the state in which it is organized.
- If an LLP does business in other states, it must register as a foreign LLP in the state(s) it wants to conduct business.

LLP Liability Insurance. The use of an LLP as a means of conducting business is restricted in many states to certain types of professionals such as lawyers and accountants.
- Most state laws mandate that LLPs carry a minimum of one million dollars of liability insurance to cover negligence, wrongful acts, and other misconduct by employees and partners of the company.

Refresh Your Memory

The following exercise will give you the opportunity to test your memory of the principles given in this chapter. Read the question twice and place your answer in the blank provided. Review the chapter material for any question that you are unable to answer or remember.

1. An LLC is a(n) _____.

2. The _____ is a model act that provides comprehensive and uniform laws for the formation, operation, and dissolution of LLCs.

3. A(n) _____ is an owner of an LLC.

4. In states where an LLC may be organized by only one member, _____ can obtain the benefit of the limited liability shield of an LLC.

5. _____ refers to the formal documents that must be filed at the secretary of state's office of the state of organization of an LLC to form the LLC.

6. An LLC is a _____ in the state in which it is organized.

7. A(n) _____ LLC has no specified term of duration.

8. A(n) _____ LLC has a specified term of duration.

9. A(n) _____ refers to a document that evidences a member's ownership interest in an LLC.

10. The certificate of interest acts the same as a(n) _____ issued by a corporation.

11. A(n) _____ refers to an agreement entered into among members that governs the affairs and business of the LLC and the relations among members, managers, and the LLC.

12. A(n) _____ refers a document that states the terms for converting an existing business to an LLC.

13. A member's distributional interest in an LLC is _____ and may be transferred in whole or in part.

14. A(n) _____ is a person who intentionally or unintentionally causes injury or death to another person.

15. _____ refer to the formal documents that must be filed at the secretary of state's office of the state of organization of an LLP to form the LLP.

Critical Thought Exercise

Hal, Mike, Sue, and Gail are college friends and have talents in the areas of e-commerce, marketing, product development, and business management. The four meet with a fifth friend, Karl, who is a second–year law student. They explain to Karl their idea for an Internet business that sends local cuisine from participating restaurants and caterers to students and military personnel who are away from home and miss their favorite food. Karl draws up the articles of organization as his contribution to being brought in as a member of the new limited liability company, "GoodGrub.com, LLC." Karl then decides that he does not have the time or energy to devote to the business. Karl declines the offer to join the LLC. Sue files the articles of organization with the secretary of state, but there is no mention of whether GoodGrub.com will be a manager-managed or member-managed LLC. It was originally anticipated that Hal would be the manager of the LLC but all four members begin to manage Good Grub.com and it is very successful. To keep up with demand and to expand their business into new markets, Hal and Gail secure a $200,000 loan from Jefferson Bank. When Hal is dividing up yearly profits, he gives each member 15 percent of the profits and invests the other 40 percent in the expansion efforts.

The resulting dispute over profits and quick expansion of the business leads to turmoil. GoodGrub.com is unable to meet its financial obligations. Mike, Sue, and Gail sue Hal for a full distribution of profits. Jefferson Bank sues GoodGrub.com, Hal, Mike, Sue, and Gail to recover the $200,000 loan.

Did Hal have the authority to withhold distribution of profits? Who is liable to Jefferson Bank?

Please compose your answer to the Critical Thinking Exercise using a separate sheet of paper or your computer word processing program.

Practice Quiz

True/False

16. _____ A limited liability company is an incorporated business entity.

17. _____ Limited liability companies are created by federal law.

18. _____ LLCs are treated as artificial persons who can sue or be sued, enter into and enforce contracts.

19. _____ A member or a shareholder is the owner of an LLC.

20. _____ Uniform Limited Liability Company Act is a model act that provides comprehensive and uniform laws for the formation, operation, and dissolution of LLCs.

21. _____ An LLC is taxed at the entity level.

22. _____ An LLC can be organized in only one state.

23. _____ A limited liability company cannot be abbreviated as LC.

24. _____ The existence of an LLC begins when the articles of organization are filed.

25. _____ The existence of an LLC begins when the articles of organization are filed.

26. _____ A member's obligation to contribute capital is excused by the member's death.

27. _____ An operating agreement can be amended orally.

28. _____ The United States does not permit an LLC to be member-managed.

29. _____ A nonmember is permitted to become a manager of an LLC.

30. _____ A manager does not owe a duty of loyalty to the LLC as he or she is not a member of the LLC.

Multiple Choice

31. Which of the following is true of an LLC?

A. An LLC is a creature of federal law.
B. An LLC is regarded a separate legal entity.
C. An LLC cannot hold title to property.
D. The owners of LLC are called general partners or specific partners.

32. Which of the following is true of the ULLCA?

A. It provides comprehensive laws for the formation of corporations.
B. It provides uniform laws for the dissolution of LLCs.
C. It is federal law that is uniform across the United States.
D. It governs the operation of proprietorships and LLPs.

33. Which of the following is true of capital contribution to an LLC?

A. Capital contribution can only be in the form of money or tangible property.
B. Promissory notes are not considered capital contribution.
C. A member's obligation to contribute capital is excused by the member's disability or other inability to perform.
D. A member's obligation to contribute capital is not excused by the member's death.

34. In which of the following cases does the conversion of an existing business to an LLC take effect?

A. the articles of organization are filed with the secretary of state
B. the members enter into an agreement of conversion
C. an operating agreement is finalized by members
D. the first certificate of interest is issued

35. Which of the following best define the term distribution interest?

A. the ratio in which profit is distributed among members of an LLC
B. the process of distributing profits or losses according the capital investment of the member
C. the constitution of management of the LLC based on the extent of each member's financial investment
D. a member's ownership interest in an LLC that entitles the member to receive distributions of money and property from the LLC

36. Members of an LLC have _____ liability.

A. limited
B. unlimited personal
C. unlimited capital
D. strict

37. Which of the following is true of the liability of LLCs?

A. Members of the LLC are personally liable for the debts, obligations, and liabilities of the LLC.
B. Managers of LLCs are not personally liable for the debts, obligations, and liabilities of the LLC.
C. LLCs are not liable for any loss or injury caused by their employees.
D. LLCs are not liable for losses caused due to negligence of their managers during the ordinary course of business.

38. Which of the following is true of the management of an LLC?

A. Members cannot become managers of an LLC.
B. A manager-managed LLC shares management powers between members and managers.
C. A nonmember can become a manager of an LLC.
D. An LLC can be both member-managed and manager-managed.

39. Which of the following methods are used to appoint a manager of a manager-managed LLC?

A. appointed by the secretary of state
B. vote of majority of the members
C. unanimous vote of members
D. unanimous vote of shareholders

40. Which of the following actions requires voting of all members in a manager-managed LLC?

A. issuing certificate of interest
B. admitting new members
C. converting an existing business into an LLC
D. expanding operations in another country

Short Answer

41. How is an LLC formed?

_____
_____

42. What types of capital contribution can members give to an LLC?

_____
_____

43. If a company wants to change its existing business to an LLC, what type of agreement must it file in satisfying part of the requirements set forth in ULLCA Section 902?

_____
_____

44. In what part of the profits does a member of an LLC have a right to share?

_____
_____

45. What does the duty of loyalty owed to an LLC encompass?

_____
_____

46. What effect does a member's disassociation from an LLC have on the member with respect to the LLC?

_____
_____

47. How may an LLC terminate its existence after it has dissolved or wound up its operations?

_____
_____

48. When does the existence of an LLC begin?

_____
_____

49. How may the articles of organization be amended in an LLC?

_____
_____

50. What is an agreement of conversion?

_____
_____

51. What is distributional interest?

_____

_____

52. Who is a tortfeasor?

_____

_____

53. What is a manager-managed LLC?

_____

_____

54. In a member-managed LLC who has the authority to bind the LLC to contracts?

_____

_____

55. What is a statement of disassociation?

_____

_____

Answers to Refresh Your Memory

1. unincorporated business entity [p. 655]
2. ULLCA [p. 655]
3. member [p. 655]
4. sole proprietors [p. 656]
5. Articles of organization [p. 656]
6. domestic LLC [p. 657]
7. at-will [p. 657]
8. term [p. 657]
9. certificate of interest [p. 658]
10. stock certificate [p. 658]
11. operating agreement [p. 658]
12. agreement of conversion [p. 658]
13. personal property [p. 659]
14. tortfeasor [p. 662]
15. Articles of LLP [p. 667]

Critical Thought Exercise Model Answer

GoodGrub.com could be either a member-managed or manager-managed LLC depending upon the wishes of its members. An LLC is a member-managed LLC unless it is designated as a manager-managed LLC in its articles of organization. The articles of organization do not specify whether the members named any member as a manager. Therefore, GoodGrub.com will be deemed a member-managed LLC. As a member-managed LLC, all members have agency authority to bind the LLC to contractual obligations. An LLC is only bound to contracts that are in the ordinary course of business or that have been authorized. As members, Hal and Gail have full authority to enter into the loan agreement with Jefferson Bank. Their action will legally obligate GoodGrub.com to repay the loan from GoodGrub.com assets.

The failure of GoodGrub.com to observe company formalities does not create personal liability for the members for the debts of the LLC. There is no mention of how the four members were running the company, but nothing in the facts would allow Jefferson Bank to seek repayment of the loan from the individual members.

Though an LLC will usually have a written operating agreement that regulates the affairs of the company and how the members will run the company, the agreement may be oral. Though Hal was the anticipated manager of GoodGrub.com, the facts state that all four members assumed a management role and the articles of organization did not specify a manager-managed LLC. All four members have the right to determine how the profits will be divided or reinvested. Any matter relating to the business of the LLC is decided by a majority vote of the members. Hal is obligated to acquiesce in the desires of the other three members as to how the profits should be divided.

Answers to Practice Quiz

True/False

16. False. A limited liability company (LLC) is an unincorporated business entity that combines the most favorable attributes of general partnerships, limited partnerships, and corporations. [p. 655]

17. False. Limited liability companies (LLCs) are creatures of state law, not federal law. An LLC can only be created pursuant to the laws of the state in which the LLC is being organized. [p. 655]

18. True. LLCs are treated as artificial persons who can sue or be sued, enter into and enforce contracts, hold title to and transfer property, and be found civilly and criminally liable for violations of law. [p. 655]

19. True. The owners of LLCs are usually called members (some states refer to owners of LLCs as shareholders). [p. 655]

20. True. Limited liability companies (LLCs) are creatures of state law, not federal law. An LLC can only be created pursuant to the laws of the state in which the LLC is being organized. These statutes, commonly referred to as limited liability company codes, regulate the formation, operation, and dissolution of LLCs. The owners of LLCs are usually called members (some states refer to owners of LLCs as shareholders). [p. 620]

21. False. An LLC is not taxed at the entity level, but its income or losses "flow through" to the members' individual income tax returns. [p. 656]

22. True. An LLC can be organized in only one state, even though it can conduct business in all other states. [p. 656]

23. False. When starting a new LLC, the organizers must choose a name for the entity. The name must contain the words limited liability company or limited company or the abbreviation L.L.C., LLC, L.C., or LC. Limited may be abbreviated as Ltd., and company may be abbreviated as Co. [ULLCA Section 105(a)]. [p. 656]

24. True. The existence of an LLC begins when the articles of organization are filed. [p. 656]

25. False. A member's obligation to contribute capital is not excused by the member's death, disability, or other inability to perform. [p. 658]

26. True. The operating agreement and amendments may be oral but are usually written. [p. 658]

27. False. An LLC can be either a member-managed LLC or a manager-managed LLC. [p. 662]

28. True. A manager may be a member of an LLC or a nonmember. [p. 662]

29. False. A member of a member-managed LLC and a manager of a manager-managed LLC owe a fiduciary duty of loyalty to the LLC. [p. 664]

30. True. A limited liability partnership (LLP) is a special form of partnership in which all partners are limited partners, and there are no general partners. [p. 667]

Multiple Choice

31. B. Answer B is the correct answer. An LLC is a separate legal entity (or legal person) distinct from its members [ULLCA Section 201]. LLCs are treated as artificial persons who can sue or be sued, enter into and enforce contracts, hold title to and transfer property, and be found civilly and criminally liable for violations of law.[p. 655]

32. C. Answer C is the correct answer. Uniform Limited Liability Company Act (ULLCA) is a model act that provides comprehensive and uniform laws for the formation, operation, and dissolution of LLCs. [p. 655]

33. D. Answer D is the correct answer. Member's obligation to contribute capital is not excused by the member's death, disability, or other inability to perform. [p. 658]

34. A. Answer A is the correct answer. The conversion takes effect when the articles of organization are filed with the secretary of state or at any later date specified in the articles of organization. [p. 658]

35. D. Answer D is the correct answer. Distributional interest A member's ownership interest in an LLC that entitles the member to receive distributions of money and property from the LLC. [p. 659]

36. D. Answer D is the correct answer. The general rule is that members of an LLC are not personally liable to third parties for the debts, obligations, and liabilities of an LLC beyond their capital contribution. Members have limited liability. [p. 660]

37. B. Answer B is the correct answer. Managers of LLCs are not personally liable for the debts, obligations, and liabilities of the LLC they manage. [p. 662]

38. C. Answer C is the correct answer. A manager may be a member of an LLC or a nonmember. [p. 662]

39. B. Answer B is the correct answer. In a manager-managed LLC, each manager has equal rights in the management and conduct of the company's business. Any matter related to the

business of the LLC may be exclusively decided by the managers by a majority vote of the managers. [p. 663]

40. B. Answer B is the correct answer. Certain actions cannot be delegated to managers but must be voted on by all members of the LLC. These include (1) amending the articles of organization, (2) amending the operating agreement, (3) admitting new members, (4) consenting to dissolve the LLC, (5) consenting to merge the LLC with another entity, and (6) selling, leasing, or disposing of all or substantially all of the LLC's property. [p. 663]

Short Answer

41. An LLC is formed by delivering articles of organization to the office of the secretary of state of organization for filing [p. 656]

42. A member's capital contribution may take the form of personal or real property, money, tangible or intangible property, etc. (Answers will vary.) [p. 658]

43. Agreement of conversion [p. 658]

44. Unless otherwise agreed, the ULLCA mandates that a member has the right to an equal share in the LLC's profits [ULLCA Section 405(a)]. [p. 658]

45. A member of a member-managed LLC and a manager of a manager-managed LLC must act honestly in their dealings with the LLC. [p. 664]

46. A member's disassociation terminates that member's right to take part in the management of the LLC, act as an agent of the LLC, or conduct any of the LLC's business. [p. 666]

47. It may terminate its existence by filing articles of termination with the secretary of state. [p. 667]

48. It begins when the articles of organization are filed. [p. 656]

49. The articles may be amended by filing articles of amendment with the secretary of state. [p. 657]

50. It is a document that states the terms of converting an existing business to an LLC. [p. 658]

51. Distributional interest is a member's ownership interest in an LLC that entitles the member to receive distributions of money and property from the LLC. [p. 659]

52. A tortfeasor is a person who intentionally or unintentionally (negligently) causes injury or death to another person. [p. 662]

53. A manager-managed LLC is an LLC that has designated in its articles of organization that it is a manager-managed LLC and whose nonmanager members give their management rights over to designated managers. [p. 663]

54. In a member-managed LLC, all members have agency authority to bind the LLC to contracts. [p. 663]

55. Statement of disassociation is a document filed with the secretary of state that gives constructive notice that a member has disassociated from an LLC. [p. 666]

40 | FRANCHISES AND SPECIAL FORMS OF BUSINESS

Chapter Overview

Franchising has become an extremely important method of distributing goods and services to the public. Franchises account for 25 percent of all retail sales. This method of doing business can have risks for the franchisee, especially when the franchise contract is drafted solely by the franchisor. The bulk of law controlling the area of franchises and franchise agreements comes from contract law, sales law, and intellectual property law. This chapter discusses the creation of a franchise, the rights and duties that arise in a franchise relationship, and the termination of a franchise.

Objectives

Upon completion of the exercises in this chapter, you should be able to:
1. Define franchise and describe the various forms of franchises.
2. Describe the rights and duties of the parties to a franchise agreement.
3. Identify the contract tort liability of franchisors and franchisees.
4. Define licensing and describe how trademarks and intellectual property are licensed.
5. Describe how international franchising, joint ventures, and strategic alliances are used in global commerce.

Practical Application

You should be able to understand and analyze the problem areas in franchise formation. This will entail applying contract law principles to the special issues created in a franchise arrangement. You will be able to comprehend the rights and liabilities associated with use of trademarks, service marks, patents, copyrights, trade name, and trade dress as they apply to franchises.

Helpful Hints

The biggest problem areas concerning franchises are in the areas of genuineness of assent, discharge, remedies, and intellectual property. It will be very helpful to review the pertinent chapters presented earlier in this test as part of the overall understanding of franchises.

Study Tips

Franchises and Special Forms of Business

Franchising is an important method for distributing goods and services to the public. Licensing allows one business to use the trademarks, service marks, trade names, and other intellectual property another business in selling goods or services. Two or more businesses may combine their resources to pursue a single project or transaction as a joint venture. Companies may use strategic alliances to enter foreign markets.

Franchise

A business arrangement that is established when one party licenses another party to use the franchisor's trade name, trademarks, patents, copyrights, and other property in the distribution and selling of goods and services.

Types of Franchises.
- Distributorship Franchise. The franchisor manufactures a product and licenses a retail franchisee to distribute the product to the public.
- Processing Plant Franchise. The franchisor provides a secret formula or process to the franchisee and the franchisee manufactures the product and distributes it to retail dealers.
- Chain-style Franchises. The franchisor licenses the franchisee to make and sell its products or distribute services to the public from a retail outlet serving an exclusive territory.
- Area Franchise. The franchisor grants the franchisee a franchise for an agreed-upon geographical area within which the franchisee may determine the location of outlets.

State Disclosure Laws. State laws require a franchisor to make specific presale disclosures to prospective franchisees and state franchise administrators developed a uniform disclosure form.
- Uniform Franchise Offering Circular (UFOC). A uniform disclosure document that requires the franchisor to make specific presale disclosures to prospective franchisees.

FTC Franchise Rule. A rule set out by the FTC that requires franchisors to make full presale disclosures to prospective franchisees.
- Disclosure of Sales or Earnings Projections Based on Actual Data
- Disclosure of Sales or Earnings Projections Based on Hypothetical Data

Franchise Agreement

A prospective franchisee must apply to the franchisor for a franchise. If the application is approved, the parties enter into a franchise agreement, which specifies the terms and conditions of the franchise.

Topics Covered in a Franchise Agreement. Franchise agreements are generally standardized form contracts with little room for negotiation, covering a variety of topics.
- Quality control standards. Standards or performance and product quality set forth in the franchise agreement to preserve the franchisor's market name and reputation.
- Training requirements. Employee standards that meet the franchisor's specifications.
- Covenant not to compete. An agreement by the franchisee to not compete with the franchisor for a period of time in a specified area after the termination of the franchise.
- Arbitration clause. A clause which provides that any claim or controversy arising from the franchise agreement or an alleged breach is subject to arbitration.
- Other terms and conditions. Capital requirements and other terms and conditions.

Franchise Fees. Fees payable by the franchisee as set forth in the franchise agreement.
- Initial license fee. A lump-sum payment to obtain a franchise.
- Royalty fees. Fees for use of franchisor's trade name, property, and assistance that is computed as a percentage of the franchisee's gross sales.

- Assessment fee. A fee for advertising and administrative costs.
- Lease fees. Payments for land or equipment leased from the franchisor.
- Cost of supplies. Payment for supplies purchased from the franchisor.
- Consulting fees and other expenses. A monthly or annual fee for having experts from the franchisor help the franchisee to better conduct business.

Trademarks. A distinctive mark, symbol, name, word, motto, or device that identifies the goods or products of the trademark owner.
- Service mark. Mark, symbol, name, word, motto, or device that identifies the service provided by the service mark owner.

Trade Secrets. Ideas that make a franchise successful but that do not qualify for trademark, patent, or copyright protection.

Liability of Franchisor and Franchisee

The franchisee is an independent contractor, preventing the franchisor from being liable for the franchisee's torts and contracts.
- Franchisors and franchisees are liable for their own contracts and torts.

Apparent Agency. An agency that arises when a franchisor creates the appearance that a franchisee is its agent when in fact an actual agency does not exist.
- The franchisor is responsible for the torts and contracts the franchisee committed or entered into within the scope of the apparent agency.

Termination of a Franchise

The franchise agreement usually states reasons or conditions that allow the franchisor or franchisee to terminate the franchise agreement.
- Termination "for cause". Termination of franchise agreement for failure to fulfill the duties imposed by the agreement.
- Wrongful termination. Termination of the franchise agreement when cause for such action does not exist.
- Termination-at-will. Termination-at-will clauses in franchise agreements are generally held to be void as unconscionable because the franchisee has spent time, money, and effort developing the franchise.

Breach of Franchise Agreement. An aggrieved party can sue the breaching party for rescission of the agreement, restitution, and damages.

Licensing

When one the franchisor, who owns trademarks, service marks, trade names, and other intellectual property, contracts with a franchisee to allow the franchisee to use the franchisor's intellectual property in the distribution of goods, services, software, and digital information.

Joint Venture

An arrangement where two or more businesses combine their resources in pursuit of a project or transaction is known as a joint venture.

- Joint venturers have equal management rights.
- Joint venturers owe each other the fiduciary duties of loyalty and care.

Joint Venture Partnership. If a joint venture is operated as a partnership, each joint venturer is liable for the debts and obligations of the joint venture partnership.

Joint Venture Corporation. Joint venturers often form a corporation to operate a joint venture.
- A joint venture corporation is liable for its debts and obligations.
- The joint venturers are liable for the debts and obligations of the joint venture corporation only up to their capital contributions.

Strategic Alliance

Arrangements between companies in the same industry where they agree to become allies to accomplish specific objectives, or strategic alliances, provide opportunities to reduce risks, share costs, combine technologies, and extend markets.
- Consideration must be given to the fact that a strategic alliance partner is always a potential competitor.

Refresh Your Memory

The following exercise will give you the opportunity to test your memory of the principles given in this chapter. Read the question twice and place your answer in the blank provided. Review the chapter material for any question that you are unable to answer or remember.

1. A(n) _____ is established when one party licenses another party to use the first party's trade name, trademarks, commercial symbols, patents, copyrights, and other property in the distribution and selling of goods and services.

2. In a _____ franchise, the franchisor manufactures a product and licenses a retail dealer to sell the product to the public.

3. In a _____ franchise, the franchisor licenses the franchisee to make and sell its products or services to the public from a retail outlet serving an exclusive geographical territory.

4. In a(n) _____ franchise, the franchisor authorizes the franchisee to negotiate and sell franchises on behalf of the franchisor.

5. The area franchisee is called a _____.

6. The _____ is a uniform disclosure document that requires a franchisor to make specific presale disclosures to prospective franchisees.

7. A(n) _____ refers to an agency that arises when a franchisor creates the image that a franchisee is its agent when in fact an actual agency does not exist.

8. Most franchise agreements permit a franchisor to terminate the franchise _____.

9. _____ is a business arrangement that occurs when the owner of intellectual property contracts to permit another party to use the intellectual property.

10. The party who grants a license is known as the _____.

11. The party to whom a license is granted is known as the _____.

12. A(n) _____ is an arrangement in which two or more business entities combine their resources to pursue a single project or transaction.

13. The parties to a joint venture are called _____.

14. A(n) _____ is a corporation owned by two or more joint venturers that is created to operate a joint venture.

15. A(n) _____ refers to an arrangement between two or more companies whereby they agree to ally themselves and work together to accomplish a designated objective.

Critical Thought Exercise

Federal Foods, Inc., runs company stores and sells franchises for its restaurants, known as Yum-Me's. Under the franchise agreement with Federal, each franchisee agrees to hire and train all employees and staff in strict compliance with Yum-Me's standards and policies. Federal employs area supervisors who are responsible for reviewing and approving all personnel actions at any restaurant within the four restaurant chains owned by Federal. This includes comprehensive policies relating to employee hiring, training, discipline, and work performance. As part of the franchise agreement, Federal retains the right to terminate any franchise that violates the rules or policies of the franchisor. In practice, the area managers approve the hiring of whatever employees the franchisee desires and the policies that the franchisee desires to create and implement. The area managers inspect each franchise, dictate the food production method, and enforce customer relations policies that were created by Federal.

Ned, a crew leader at a Yum-Me's restaurant, has repeatedly harassed female employees and customers by making rude and explicit sexual remarks. The franchisee and the on-site manager have done nothing to correct Ned's behavior. Two female employees and three customers have filed suit in federal court against Federal based upon Ned's acts. Federal argues that a franchisor cannot be held liable for harassment by franchise employees. Who should prevail?

Please compose your answer to the Critical Thinking Exercise using a separate sheet of paper or your computer word processing program.

Practice Quiz

True/False

16. _____ A general partnership is established when one party licenses another party to use the first party's trade name, trademarks, commercial symbols, patents, copyrights, and other property in the distribution and selling of goods and services.

17. _____ In an area franchise, the franchisor authorizes the franchisee to negotiate and sell franchises on behalf of the franchisor.

18. _____ FTC franchise rule is a rule that requires franchisors to make full presale disclosures to prospective franchisees.

19. _____ A franchisor that makes sales or earnings projections based on hypothetical examples need not disclose the assumptions underlying the estimates.

20. _____ Uniform Franchise Offering Circular refers to a uniform disclosure document that requires a franchisor to make specific presale disclosures to prospective franchisees.

21. _____ A service mark can only be a name: symbols are not classified as service marks.

22. _____ If a franchise is properly organized and operated, the franchisor and franchisee are separate legal entities.

23. _____ A franchisor is liable for the torts of its franchisee.

24. _____ An apparent agency is created when a franchisor and franchisee who use the same trade name and trademarks make no effort to inform the public of their separate legal status.

25. _____ Termination-at-will clauses in franchise agreements are generally held to be void on the grounds that they are unconscionable.

26. _____ A lawful franchise agreement is treated as an enforceable contract.

27. _____ Joint venturers generally have equal rights to manage a joint venture.

28. _____ Joint venturers are permitted to create a corporation that operates the joint venture.

29. _____ A strategic alliance is an arrangement between two or more companies whereby they agree to ally themselves and work together to accomplish a designated objective.

30. _____ Partners to a strategic alliance can be potential competitors.

Multiple Choice

31. Which of the following is true of a franchise?

A. The franchisor and franchisee are established as separate corporations.
B. A franchisee does not need a license to use the franchisor's trademark.
C. The franchisee does not have access to the franchisor's knowledge.
D. A franchise is also known as a joint venture.

32. In which of the following types of franchise does a franchisor provide a secret formula or process to the franchisee?

A. chain-style
B. area
C. distributorship
D. processing plant

33. Which of the following federal agencies is empowered to enforce federal franchising rules?

A. FTC
B. SEC
C. UCC
D. SCE

34. Which of the following does the FTC franchise rule require from franchisors?

A. registration of the disclosure of the document with the FTC
B. full presale disclosures nationwide to prospective franchisees
C. statement to fully finance the infrastructure necessary to bring the franchisee to the franchisor's standard
D. disclosure of license agreement made with franchisee that lets the franchisee use the franchisor's service mark.

35. If a franchisor makes sales or earnings projections based on hypothetical examples, the franchisor must _____ .

A. display a cautionary statement that states some franchises have earned this amount
B. disclose the assumptions underlying the estimates
C. register the disclosure document with the FTC prior to its use
D. state that all data disclosed is only hypothetical and that actual data will be made available at the earliest

36. Where should the FTC franchise notice appear?

A. in the licensing agreement between the franchisor and franchise
B. as a separate clause in the franchise agreement
C. on the cover of a franchisor's required disclosure statement
D. on the cover of a franchisee's required disclosure statement

37. Which of the following documents sets forth the terms and conditions of a franchise?

A. FTC disclosure
B. franchise agreement
C. UFOC
D. articles of organization

38. Which of the following is true of intellectual property of a franchisor?

A. Trademarks do not qualify for patents.
B. A word or motto that identifies a franchisor does not qualify for trademark protection.
C. A service mark is exclusive to the franchisor and cannot be licensed to franchisees.
D. Trade secrets of a franchisor do not qualify for patent protection.

39. Which of the following is true of the liabilities of a franchisor and a franchisee?

A. The franchisee has the legal identity of the franchisor.
B. A franchisor deals with the franchisee as an independent contractor.
C. Franchisees are liable on their own contracts.
D. Franchisors are liable for the torts of the franchisees.

40. Which of the following is true of a joint venture corporation?

A. The joint venturers are personally liable for debts of the joint venture corporation.
B. Joint venturers do not owe each other fiduciary duties as a venture is a single business transaction.
C. The management rights of joint venturers in a joint venture are divided in the ratio of their capital investment.
D. Each joint venture is liable for the debts and obligations of the joint venture.

Short Answer

41. A corporation owned by two or more joint ventures that is created to operate a joint venture is known as what?

_____
_____

42. How is franchise fees paid?

_____
_____

43. How does a prospective franchisee obtain a franchise?

_____
_____

44. What is wrongful termination?

_____
_____

45. Why are quality control standards important to the franchisor?

_____
_____

46. Why are termination-at-will clauses in franchise agreements generally held to be void?

_____
_____

47. What is the purpose of an assessment fee and what does it cover?

_____
_____

48. What is a joint venture?

_____
_____

49. If Bob's Baked Goods, a franchise, holds a trade secret regarding its bountiful bagel recipe and Betty's Bagels uses the recipe to attract business, for what may Bob's Baked Goods sue?

_____
_____

50. What is a trade secret?

_____

_____

51. List two examples of information that must be disclosed in the Uniform Franchise Offering Circular.

_____

_____

52. Why is a franchisor normally not liable for the torts of a franchisee?

_____

_____

53. What is an apparent agency?

_____

_____

54. If the Walt Disney Corporation allows McDonald's to sell plastic figurines from its movies in McDonald's Happy Meals, this would be known as what?

_____

_____

55. Who is liable for the debts and obligations of a joint venture partnership?

_____

_____

Answers to Refresh Your Memory

1. franchise [p. 673]
2. distributorship [p. 674]
3. chain-style [p. 674]
4. area [p. 674]
5. subfranchisor [p. 674]
6. UFOC [p. 676]
7. apparent agency [p. 681]
8. for cause [p. 682]
9. Licensing [p. 683]
10. licensor [p. 683]
11. licensee [p. 683]
12. joint venture [p. 683]
13. joint venturers [p. 683]
14. joint venture corporation [p. 683]
15. strategic alliance [p. 685]

Critical Thought Exercise Model Answer

Liability for Ned's acts may be imputed to Federal because of an agency relationship that exists between Federal and the employees of the franchisee. An agency results from the manifestation of consent by one person to another so that the other will act on his or her behalf and subject to the control of the principal, and consent by the agent to so act. An agency agreement may be evidenced by an express agreement between the parties, or it may be implied from the circumstances and conduct of the parties. The principal's consent and right to control the agent are the essential elements of an agency relationship.

The franchise agreement in this case required adherence to comprehensive policies and rules for the operation of the restaurant. Federal enforces these rules and policies by sending area managers to inspect each franchisee. The area managers also approve the hiring and training of each employee. Federal controls the franchisee and the employees of Yum-Me's Restaurant by retaining the right to terminate the franchise agreement. Most importantly, the franchise agreement gave Federal the right to control the franchisees in the very parts of the franchisee's business that resulted in the injuries to the plaintiffs, these parts being the areas of employee training and discipline. Federal, the franchisor, may be held liable under an agency theory for the intentional acts of sexual discrimination by the employee of its franchisee.

Answers to Practice Quiz

True/False

16. False. A franchise is established when one party (the franchisor, or licensor) licenses another party (the franchisee, or licensee) to use the franchisor's trade name, trademarks, commercial symbols, patents, copyrights, and other property in the distribution and selling of goods and services. [p. 673]

17. True. In an area franchise, the franchisor authorizes the franchisee to negotiate and sell franchises on behalf of the franchisor. [p. 674]

18. True. The FTC rule requires franchisors to make full presale disclosures nationwide to prospective franchisees. [p. 675]

19. True. The FTC franchise rule states that if a franchisor makes sales or earnings projections based on hypothetical examples, the franchisor must disclose the assumptions underlying the estimates. [p. 675]

20. True. An Uniform Franchise Offering Circular (UFOC) is an uniform disclosure document that requires a franchisor to make specific presale disclosures to prospective franchisees.[p. 676]

21. False. A service mark is a distinctive mark, symbol, name, word, motto, or device that identifies the goods or services of a particular franchisor. [p. 676]

22. True. If a franchise is properly organized and operated, the franchisor and franchisee are separate legal entities.[p. 678]

23. False. Franchisees are liable on their own contracts and are liable for their own torts. [p. 678]

24. True. An apparent agency is an agency that arises when a franchisor creates the appearance that a franchisee is its agent when in fact an actual agency does not exist. [p. 681]

25. True. Termination-at-will clauses in franchise agreements are generally held to be void on the grounds that they are unconscionable. [p. 682]

26. True. A lawful franchise agreement is an enforceable contract. [p. 682]

27. True. Unless otherwise agreed, joint venturers have equal rights to manage a joint venture. [p. 683]

28. True. In pursuing a joint venture, joint venturers often form a corporation to operate the joint venture. This is called a joint venture corporation. [p. 684]

29. True. A strategic alliance is an arrangement between two or more companies whereby they agree to ally themselves and work together to accomplish a designated objective. [p. 685]

30. True. A strategic alliance partner is also a potential competitor. [p. 685]

Multiple Choice

31. A. Answer A is the correct answer. The franchisor and the franchisee are established as separate corporations. [p. 673]

32. C. Answer C is the correct answer. In a processing plant franchise, the franchisor provides a secret formula or the like to the franchisee.[p. 674]

33. A. Answer A is the correct answer. The Federal Trade Commission (FTC), a federal administrative agency empowered
to regulate franchising, has adopted the FTC franchise rule. [p. 675]

34. B. Answer B is correct. The FTC rule requires franchisors to make full presale disclosures nationwide to prospective franchisees. [p. 675]

35. B. Answer B is correct. The FTC franchise rule states that if a franchisor makes sales or earnings projections based on hypothetical examples, the franchisor must disclose the assumptions underlying the estimates. [p. 675]

36. C. Answer C is correct. The FTC requires that the following statement, called the FTC franchise notice, appear in at least 12-point boldface type on the cover of a franchisor's required disclosure statement to prospective franchisees. [p. 676]

37. B. Answer B is correct. A franchise agreement is an agreement that a franchisor and franchisee enter into that sets forth the terms and conditions of a franchise. [p. 676]

38. D. Answer D is correct. Trade secrets Ideas that make a franchise successful but that do not qualify for trademark, patent, or copyright protection. [p. 676]

39. C. Answer C is correct. Franchisees are liable on their own contracts and are liable for their own torts (e.g., negligence). [p. 678]

40. D. Answer D is correct. In a joint venture partnership, each joint venturer is liable for the debts and obligations of the joint venture partnership. [p. 683]

Short Answer

41. It is known as a joint venture corporation. [p. 683]

42. Franchise fees and are usually stipulated in the franchise agreement. [p. 677]

43. The prospective franchisee must apply to the franchisor for a franchise. [p. 676]

44. Termination of a franchise without just cause. [p. 682]

45. The franchisor's most important assets are its name and reputation. The quality control standards set out in a franchise agreement are intended to protect those assets. [p. 678]

46. The termination-at-will clauses are found to be unconscionable and void based on the money and effort the franchisee has spent on the franchise. [p. 682]

47. An assessment fee pays for advertising and promotional campaigns and administrative costs. It is billed either as a flat monthly fee or a percentage of gross sales. [p. 677]

48. A joint venture is an arrangement in which two or more business entities combine their resources to pursue a single project or transaction. [p. 683]

49. Damages and to obtain an injunction to prohibit further unauthorized use of the trade secret. [p. 676]

50. Trade secrets are ideas that make a franchise successful but that do not qualify for trademark, patent, or copyright protection. [p. 676]

51. Description of the franchisor's business and balance sheets (answers will vary). [p. 676]

52. A franchisee is usually set up as an independent contractor in the franchise agreement. Because there is no agency relationship, the franchisor is not liable for the torts committed by the franchisee. [p. 678]

53. An agency that results when a franchisor creates the appearance that a franchisee is its agent when in fact an actual agency does not exist. [p. 681]

54. This would be known as licensing. [p. 683]

55. Each venturer is liable. for the debts and obligations of the joint venture partnership. [p. 683]

41 | INVESTOR PROTECTION AND ONLINE SECURITIES TRANSACTIONS

Chapter Overview

The stock market crash of 1929 motivated Congress to make investor security a priority. Up to this time, fraud and dealing on inside information was rampant. Congress passed two key pieces of legislation in an attempt to remedy the problem. The Securities Act of 1933 requires public disclosure of material information by companies and others who issue securities to the public. The Securities Exchange Act of 1934 was enacted to prevent fraud in the trading of securities, especially insider trading. Additional statutes have been passed by the states. These federal and state statutes are still the cornerstone that forms the protection for investors in securities. This chapter examines these protections.

Chapter Objectives

Upon completion of the exercises in this chapter, you should be able to:
1. Describe the procedure for going public and how securities are registered with the Securities and Exchange Commission.
2. Describe the requirements for qualifying for private placement, intrastate, and small offering exemptions from registration.
3. Describe insider trading that violates Section 10(b) of the Securities Exchange Act of 1934.
4. Describe e-securities transactions.
5. Describe how provisions of the Sarbanes- Oxley Act and the Dodd-Frank Wall Street Reform and Consumer Protection Act increase investor protection.

Practical Application

This chapter has application from several viewpoints. The investor, which includes individuals, employee groups, and businesses, needs to know the protections that are available under federal and state law that prevent fraudulent loss of their investment. Those persons and businesses that issue securities, and the people who work for them, need to know the standards to which the federal government will hold them. Lastly, the unsuspecting investor needs to know what acts may make them part of a fraudulent or criminal transaction so that liability can be avoided. Unless each person familiarizes himself with federal securities law, there is an increased risk of financial loss, damage to his business, and exposure to criminal prosecution.

Helpful Hints

The securities laws are geared to regulating transactions involving the issuance and trading of securities. They focus on the individual transaction or related transactions and the information that was exchanged or withheld as to the particular transaction. It is the improper release or suppression of material information and trading upon that information that triggers the application of the securities laws.

Study Tips

Investor Protection and Online Securities Transactions

Federal and state securities regulations were designed to require disclosure of information to investors and to prevent fraud.

Securities Law

Securities Act of 1933. A federal statute that primarily regulates the issuance of securities by a corporation, a general or limited partnership, an unincorporated association, or an individual.

Securities Exchange Act of 1934. A federal statute that primarily regulates the trading in securities.

Definition of Security

A security is defined as
- an interest or instrument that is common stock, preferred stock, a bond, a debenture, or a warrant;
- an interest or instrument that is expressly mentioned in securities acts; and
- an investment contract.

The Securities and Exchange Commission (SEC)

The Securities and Exchange Commission is a federal administrative agency that is empowered to administer federal securities laws.
- The SEC can adopt rules and regulations to interpret and implement federal securities laws.
- Violations of these rules carry civil and criminal penalties.

Private Transactions Exempt from Registration

Exempt securities transactions are transactions that are exempt from registration but must still comply with antifraud provisions of the federal securities laws.

Nonissuer Exemption. An exemption from registration that permits average investors from registering the resale of their securities because they are not the issuer, an underwriter, or a dealer in securities.

Intrastate Offerings Exemption. An exemption from registration that permits local businesses to raise capital from local investors to be used in the local economy without the need to register with the SEC.
- The issuer must be a resident of the state for which the exemption is claimed.
- The issuer must be doing business in that state.
- The purchasers of all securities must be residents of that state.
- *Rule 147.* Securities sold pursuant to an intrastate offering exemption cannot be sold to nonresidents for a period of nine months.

Private Placement Exemption. An exemption from registration that permits issuers to raise capital from an unlimited number of accredited investors and no more than 35 nonaccredited investors without having to register the offering with the SEC. An accredited investor may be:

- Any natural person with a net worth that exceeds $1 million.
- A natural person with income exceeding $200,000 in each of the two most recent years or joint income with a spouse exceeding $300,000 for those years and a reasonable expectation of the same income level in the current year.
- A charitable organization, a corporation, a partnership, a trust, or an employee benefit plan with assets exceeding $5 million.
- A bank, an insurance company, a registered investment company, a business development company, or a small business investment company.
- Insiders of the issuers, such as directors, executive officers, or general partner of the company selling the securities.
- A business in which all the equity owners are accredited investors.

Small Offerings Exemption. An exemption from registration for the sale of securities not exceeding $1 million during a 12-month period.

- *Rule 144.* Provides that securities sold pursuant to the private placement or small offering exemptions must be held for one year from the date when the securities are last sold by the issuer.

Securities Exempt from Registration. Certain securities are exempt from registration, no matter how many time they are transferred.

- Securities issued by any government in the United States.
- Short-term notes and drafts.
- Securities issued by nonprofit issuers.
- Securities of financial institutions.
- Securities issued by common carriers.
- Insurance and annuity contracts issued by insurance companies.
- Stock dividends and stock splits.
- Securities issued in a corporate reorganization.

The Securities Act of 1933: Going Public

This act primarily regulates the issuing of securities by corporations, limited partnerships, other types of businesses, and individuals. Section 5 requires the registration of securities being offered to the public with the SEC.

- *Issuer.* The business or party selling securities to the public.
- *Investment Bankers.* Independent securities companies employed to sell securities to the public

Registration . Document that an issuer of securities files with the SEC that contains required information about the issuer, the securities to be issued, and other relevant information.

Prospectus. A written disclosure document that must be submitted to the SEC along with the registration statement and given to prospective purchasers of the securities.

Conditioning the Market.
- *Prefiling Period.* A period of time that begins when the issuer first contemplates issuing securities and ends when the registration statement is filed.
- *Waiting Period.* A period of time that begins when the registration statement is filed with the SEC and continues until the registration statement is declared effective.
- The issuer may not condition the market by engaging in a public relation campaign during this period.

Sale of Unregistered Securities. For securities that should have been registered, but were not, investors can rescind their purchase and recover damages and the government can impose criminal penalties.

Regulation A Offering. Regulation A allows the sale of up to $5 million in securities to the public during a 12-month period in a simplified registration process.
- Offering exceeding $100,000 must file an offering statement with the SEC, which requires less disclosure than a registration statement.
- *Small Corporate Offering Registration (SCOR) Form.* The form is a question-and-answer disclosure form that small businesses can complete and file with the SEC if they plan on raising $1 million or less from the public issue of securities.

Private Actions. The Securities Act of 1933 allows private parties to have recourse for injuries caused by violations of the act.
- *Section 11.* A provision of the Securities Act of 1933 that imposes civil liability on persons who intentionally defraud investors by making misrepresentations or omissions of material facts in the registration statement or who are negligent for not discovering the fraud.
- *Section 12.* Imposes civil liability against those who violate Section 5 of the act. Under Section 12, a purchaser may rescind the purchase or sue for damages.

SEC Actions. For violations of the 1933 act, the SEC may:
- issue a consent order
- bring an action seeking an injunction
- request disgorgement of profits by the court

Criminal Liability. Section 24 of the Securities Act of 1933 imposes criminal liability of up to five years in prison for violating the act or the rules and regulations adopted thereunder.

Sarbanes-Oxley Act Erects a Wall Between Investment Bankers and Securities Analysts. In Section 501 of the act, rules are established for separating the investment banking and securities advice functions of securities firms.
- Securities firms must establish structural and institutional "walls" between their investment banking and securities analysis areas, which must protect analysts from review, pressure, and oversight by the investment banking area.
- Securities analysts must disclose in each research report or public appearance any conflicts of interest that are known or should have been known at the time of publication.

The Securities Exchange Act of 1934: Trading in Securities

This act primarily regulates the trading of securities subsequent to the initial issuance, including the registration of certain companies with the SEC, the continuous filing of periodic reports by these companies to the SEC, and the regulation of securities exchanges, brokers, and dealers.

Section 10(b) and Rule 10b-5.
- *Section 10(b).* A provision of the Securities Exchange Act of 1934 that prohibits the use of manipulative and deceptive devices in the purchase or sale of securities in contravention of the rules and regulations prescribed by the SEC.
- *Rule 10b-5.* A rule adopted by the SEC to clarify the reach of Section 10(b) against deceptive and fraudulent activities in the purchase and sale of securities.
  - Only conduct showing scienter, or intentional conduct, is a violation of 10b-5.

Private Right of Action. A private right of action for violations of Section 10(b) and Rule 10b-5 have been implied by the courts.

SEC Action. The SEC may enter into consent orders, seek injunctions, or seek disgorgement of profits by court order.
- *Insider Trading Sanctions Act.* Permits the SEC to obtain civil penalty of up to three times the illegal profits gained or losses avoided by insider trading.
- *Sarbanes-Oxley Act.* The SEC may issue an order prohibiting any person who has committed securities fraud from acting as an officer or a director of a public company.

Criminal Liability. Section 32 of the Securities Exchange Act of 1934 makes it a criminal offense to willfully violate the act or the rules or regulations adopted thereunder.
- Sarbanes-Oxley imposes additional penalties.

Insider Trading. When an insider makes a profit by personally purchasing shares of the corporation prior to public release of favorable information or by selling shares of the corporation prior to the public disclosure of unfavorable information.
- Insiders are:
  - officers, directors, and employees at all levels of the company
  - lawyers, accountants, consultants, and other agents hired by the company to provide services or work to the company
  - others who owe a fiduciary duty to the company

Tipper-Tippee Liability. A tipper is a person who discloses material nonpublic information to another person. A tippee is the person who receives material nonpublic information from a tipper.
- A tippee is liable for acting on material information that he or she knew or should have known was not public.
- The tipper is liable for the profits made by the tippee.

Misappropriation Theory. An outsider's misappropriation of information in violation of his or her fiduciary duty violates Section 10(b) and Rule 10b-5.

Aiders and Abettors. The SEC can bring civil cases, the US government can bring criminal charges, and private parties can bring civil actions for monetary damages against aiders and abettors.

Short-Swing Profits

Section 16(a) of the Securities Exchange Act of 1934 defines any person who is an executive officer, a director, or a 10 percent shareholder or an equity security of a reporting company as a statutory insider for Section 16 purposes.

Section 16(b). Requires that any profits made by a statutory insider on transactions involving short-swing profits belong to the corporation.
- *Short-Swing Profits.* Trades involving equity securities occurring within six months of each other.

SEC Section 16 Rules.
- *Officer.* Includes only executive officers who perform policy-making functions
- Relieves insiders of liability for transactions that occur within six months before becoming an insider.
- Continues the rule that insiders are liable for transactions that occur within six months of the last transaction engaged in while an insider.

State Securities Laws

State securities laws are usually apply to smaller companies issuing securities within the state. These laws, often called "blue sky laws" are designed to prevent investors from purchasing a piece of the blue sky. Many states have adopted the Uniform Securities Act to coordinate the state laws with federal laws.

Refresh Your Memory

The following exercise will give you the opportunity to test your memory of the principles given in this chapter. Read the question twice and place your answer in the blank provided. Review the chapter material for any question that you are unable to answer or remember.

1. _____ is the federal administrative agency that is empowered to administer federal securities laws.

2. Common stock, preferred stock, bonds, debentures, and warrants are examples of _____.

3. Interests or instruments that are expressly mentioned in securities acts are _____.

4. The courts apply the _____ test in determining whether an arrangement is an investment contract and therefore a security.

5. A business or party selling securities to the public is called a(n) _____.

6. The issuance of securities by an issuer is called a(n) _____.

7. A _____ is a written disclosure document that must be submitted to the SEC along with the registration statement.

8. The New York Stock Exchange (NYSE) is operated by _____.

9. _____ is the electronic data and record system of the Securities and Exchange Commission (SEC).

10. Stock dividends and stock splits are examples of _____.

11. _____ is an exemption from registration that permits local businesses to raise capital from local investors to be used in the local economy without the need to register with the SEC.

12. The law permits no more than thirty-five _____ to purchase securities pursuant to a private placement exemption.

13. _____ is a section of a federal statute that eliminates conflicts of interest by establishing rules for the separation of the investment banking and securities advice functions of securities firms.

14. _____ is a person who discloses material nonpublic information to another person.

15. State securities laws are often referred to as _____ laws.

Critical Thought Exercise

Jerry Dallas is a corporate officer for CompuGames (CG), the leading manufacturer of hand-held computer games. The profit margin of CG is greatly impacted by the cost of the microprocessor it purchases for its games from Mini-Micro. Dallas tells his girlfriend, Julie Profit, that she should watch for any announcement of a price increase of 20 percent or more by Mini-Micro and sell her stock in CG if there is such a large price increase. Profit has a friend, Louis Nooze, who works in the public relations department at Mini-Micro. She asks Nooze to tell her if he hears of an announcement of price increases by Mini-Micro. Two days before a 33 percent price increase is to be announced by Mini-Micro, Nooze gives the news to Profit. Profit calls her stockbroker and sells all her stock in CG. When the price increase is announced, CG stock falls from $38 per share to $22 per share. By selling her stock before the announcement by Mini-Micro, Profit realizes a profit of $800,000.

If a stockholder initiates a suit against Dallas, Profit, and Nooze, will any of these people be liable for realizing illegal profits based upon insider trading or misappropriation?

Please compose your answer to the Critical Thinking Exercise using a separate sheet of paper or your computer word processing program.

Practice Quiz

True/False

16. _____ Every U.S. state has an independent Securities Exchange Commission that regulates the issue and subsequent trading of securities in that state.

17. _____ An investment contract is a flexible standard for defining a security.

18. _____ The sale of securities by an issuer to the public is known an initial public offering.

19. _____ Only an established company is permitted to sell new securities to the public.

20. _____ A prospectus is provided to prospective investors to enable them to evaluate the financial risk of an investment.

21. _____ An offering statement requires more disclosure than a registration statement, including all speculated risks by the issuer.

22. _____ There are no resale restrictions on securities.

23. _____ If due diligence defense is proven, the defendant is liable for violation of securities.

24. _____ EDGAR is an electronic stock market and is the world's largest electronic securities exchange.

25. _____ The nonissuer exemption permits local businesses to raise capital from local investors to be used in the local economy without the need to register with the SEC.

26. _____ Negligent conduct that violates Section 10(b) and Rule 10b-5 of the SEC is not considered a violation.

27. _____ It is legal for a company employee to make a profit by personally purchasing shares of the corporation prior to public release of favorable information.

28. _____ A tipper cannot be held liable for the profits made by the tippee.

29. _____ A 10-percent shareholder of an equity security of a reporting company is considered a statutory insider.

30. _____ Blue-sky laws are state laws that regulate the issuance and trading of securities.

Multiple Choice

31. Which of the following is under the jurisdiction of the Securities and Exchange Commission (SEC)?

A. recommending criminal prosecution against violators of federal securities statutes
B. making investors aware of all possible risk factors of securities before purchase
C. providing an interface between investors and issuers of securities
D. regulating the use of funds by a public company that issues and sells securities

32. Which of the following is classified under "common securities"?

A. debenture
B. bullion
C. real estate
D. bank deposit

33. Interests or instruments that are expressly mentioned in securities acts are known as _____.

A. common securities
B. statutorily defined securities
C. investment contracts
D. implicit securities

34. A(n) _____ is a flexible standard for defining a security.

A. red herring prospectus
B. debenture
C. certificate of interest
D. investment contract

35. The courts apply the _____ in determining whether an arrangement is an investment contract.

A. strict scrutiny test
B. rational basis review
C. Howey test
D. intermediate test

36. Which of the following best defines an initial public offering?

A. subsequent trading of securities post issue
B. the sale of securities by an issuer to the
C. the disclosure document released for public scrutiny
D. public the filing of a registration statement by an issuer

37. Which of the following must be included in the registration statement?

A. names of investors who have purchased a company's shares
B. maximum number of times a share can be sold post issue
C. date of termination of the initial public offering
D. how proceeds from the offering will be used

38. Which of the following is true of a Regulation A offering?

A. Regulation A imposes resale restrictions on the securities.
B. It permits issuers to sell up to $5 million of securities to the public during a 12-month period.
C. An offering statement requires more disclosure than a registration statement.
D. It is more expensive to prepare an offering statement than a registration statement.

39. Which of the following is true of Section 11 of the Securities Act of 1933?

A. It permits criminal action to be brought against fraudulent registration statement filed by an issuer.
B. Negligent omission of a material fact in a registration statement is not actionable under Section 11.
C. It permits an issuer to assert a due diligence defense against the imposition of Section 11 liability.
D. It imposes liability on those who are negligent in not discovering the fraud.

40. Which of the following has the largest trading volume of any securities exchange in the world?

A. NASDAQ
B. Euronext
C. NYSE
D. London Stock Exchange

41. The electronic data and record system of the Securities and Exchange Commission is known as _____.

A. MICEX
B. NASDAQ
C. EDGAR
D. SPSE

42. Which of the following is true of exempt securities?

A. Exempt securities are those whose investors are exempt from taxation.
B. Exempt securities cannot be traded publicly.
C. An exemption must be made every time a security is transferred.
D. Once a security is exempt, it is exempt forever.

43. _____ is an exemption from registration that permits local businesses to raise capital from local investors to be used in the local economy without the need to register with the SEC.

A. Regulation A
B. SEC Rule 506
C. Intrastate offering exemption
D. Nonissuer exemption

44. Which of the following constitutes insider trading?

A. a director purchases enough shares of a public company to gain a majority stake in its management
B. an employee makes a profit by personally purchasing shares of the corporation prior to public release of favorable information
C. a manager purchases all shares of a corporation available to the public
D. an employee tips a potential investor with information that is confidential to the company

45. The Dodd-Frank Wall Street Reform and Consumer Protection Act imposes regulations on _____.

A. restricted securities
B. stock dividends and splits
C. interests in realty
D. hedge funds and derivatives

Short Answer

46. What are the major responsibilities of SEC?

_____

_____

47. What are the different types of securities?

_____

_____

48. How does a company sell its shares to the public for the first time? Explain the contents of a registration statement.

_____

_____

49. Explain NASDAQ and EDGAR.

_____

_____

50. List the securities exempt from registration with the SEC.

_____

_____

51. Distinguish between nonissuer exemption, intrastate offering exemption, and private placement exemption.

_____

_____

52. Who is an accredited investor?

_____

_____

53. Explain Sarbanes-Oxley Act.

_____

_____

54. What is insider trading? How is it regulated in the U.S.A?

_____

_____

55. How does Section 16(b) of the Securities Exchange Act of 1934 protect the interests of a corporation? Explain with an example.

_____

_____

Answers to Refresh Your Memory

1. Securities and Exchange Commission [p. 691]
2. common securities [p. 691]
3. statutorily defined securities [p. 691]

Critical Thought Exercise Model Answer

Under section 10(b) of the Securities Exchange Act of 1934 and SEC Rule 10b-5, persons may be sued and prosecuted for the commission of fraud in connection with the sale or purchase of any security. The 1934 Act prohibits officers and directors from taking advantage of inside information they obtain as a result of their position to gain a trading advantage over the general public. Section 10(b) of the 1934 act and SEC Rule 10b-5 cover not only corporate officers, directors, and majority shareholders but also any persons having access to or receiving information of a nonpublic nature on which trading is based. The key to liability under Section 10(b) and Rule 10b-5 is whether the insider's information is material. A significant change in a company's financial condition would be material information. The cost of an essential part from a supplier would create that significant change.

Jerry Dallas did not act upon inside information in this case, nor did he act as a tipper. The information he gave was general advice as to the strength of his company and the market factors that affected the price of its main product. All he did was advise Profit to watch for any announcements of a price increase from Mini-Micro. He did not provide any insider information regarding CG. Therefore, Dallas will not be liable for the profit realized by Profit.

To find liability for Nooze, his level of knowledge must be established. Though it appears that he is acting as a tipper, the information that he provided is not being used to trade on Mini-Micro stock. There is no information as to whether Profit told him the purpose of wanting to know when a price increase would occur. Under the tipper theory, however, liability is established when the inside information is obtained as a result of someone's breach of a fiduciary duty to the corporation whose shares are involved in the trading. In this case, Nooze owes no fiduciary duty to CG. There is no proof that his information leak hurt Mini-Micro in any way.

Under a theory of misappropriation, both Nooze and Profit may be liable. The misappropriation theory holds that if an individual wrongfully obtains inside information and trades on it for his or her own personal gain, then the person should be held liable because the individual stole information rightfully belonging to another. Profit and Nooze both knew that they were taking information that was material and belonged to Mini-Micro. Liability should be imposed upon Profit because she traded upon this stolen information. Though Nooze also misappropriated the information, there is a lack of evidence as to his knowledge that it would be used for making a trade of CG stock.

Answers to Practice Quiz

True/False

16. False. The Securities Exchange Act of 1934 created the Securities and Exchange Commission (SEC) and empowered it to administer federal securities laws. [p. 691]

17. True. An investment contract is a flexible standard for defining a security. Under the Howey test, a security exists if an investor invests money in a common enterprise and expects to make a profit from the significant efforts of others. [p. 692]

18. True. A business or party selling securities to the public is called an issuer. The issuance of securities by an issuer is called an initial public offering (IPO). [p. 692]

19. False. An issuer may be a new company that is selling securities to the public for the first time. This is referred to as going public. [p. 692]

20. True. A prospectus is a written disclosure document that must be submitted to the SEC along with the registration statement. It is provided to prospective investors to enable them to evaluate the financial risk of an investment. [p. 693]

21. False. An offering statement requires less disclosure than a registration statement and is less costly to prepare. [p. 693]

22. True. The issuer can advertise the sale of the security. There are no resale restrictions on the securities. [p. 693]

23. False. All defendants except the issuer may assert a due diligence defense against the imposition of Section 11 liability. If this defense is proven, the defendant is not liable. [p. 694]

24. False. The National Association of Securities Dealers Automated Quotation System (NASDAQ) is an electronic stock market. NASDAQ has the largest trading volume of any securities exchange in the world. [p. 696]

25. False. Nonissuers, such as average investors, do not have to file a registration statement prior to reselling securities they have purchased. This nonissuer exemption exists because the Securities Act of 1933 exempts from registration securities transactions not made by an issuer, an underwriter, or a dealer. [p. 697]

26. True. The U.S. Supreme Court has held that only conduct involving scienter (intentional conduct) violates Section 10(b) and Rule 10b-5. Negligent conduct is not a violation. [p. 700]

27. False. Insider trading occurs when a company employee or company advisor uses material nonpublic information to make a profit by trading in the securities of the company. This practice is considered illegal because it allows insiders to take advantage of the investing public. [p. 701]

28. False. A person who discloses material nonpublic information to another person is called a tipper. The tipper is liable for the profits made by the tippee. [p. 701]

29. True. Section 16(a) of the Securities Exchange Act of 1934 defines any person who is an executive officer, a director, or a 10 percent shareholder of an equity security of a reporting company as a statutory insider for Section 16 purposes. [p. 703]

30. True. State securities laws are often referred to as "blue-sky" laws because they help prevent investors from purchasing a piece of the blue sky. [p. 705]

Multiple Choice

31. A. One of the major responsibilities of the SEC is to investigating alleged securities violations and bringing enforcement actions against suspected violators. This may include recommendations of criminal prosecution. [p. 691]

32. A. Interests or instruments that are commonly known as securities are common securities. Examples – Common stock, preferred stock, bonds, debentures, and warrants are common securities. [p. 691]

33. B. Interests or instruments that are expressly mentioned in securities acts are statutorily defined securities. Examples – The securities acts specifically define preorganization subscription agreements; interests in oil, gas, and mineral rights; and deposit receipts for foreign securities as securities. [p. 691]

34. D. An investment contract is a flexible standard for defining a security. Under the Howey test, a security exists if an investor invests money in a common enterprise and expects to make a profit from the significant efforts of others. [p. 692]

35. C. Howey test is a test which states that an arrangement is an investment contract if there is an investment of money by an investor in a common enterprise and the investor expects to make profits based on the sole or substantial efforts of the promoter or others. [p. 692]

36. B. The issuance of securities by an issuer is called an initial public offering (IPO). [p. 692]

37. D. A covered issuer must file a written registration statement with the SEC. A registration statement must contain descriptions of how the proceeds from the offering will be used. [p. 692]

38. B. Regulation A permits issuers to sell up to $5 million of securities to the public during a 12-month period, pursuant to a simplified registration process. Such offerings may have an unlimited number of purchasers who do not have to be accredited investors. [p. 693]

39. D. Liability under Section 11 of the Securities Act of 1933 is imposed on those who are negligent in not discovering the fraud. [p. 694]

40. A. The National Association of Securities Dealers Automated Quotation System (NASDAQ) is an electronic stock market. NASDAQ has the largest trading volume of any securities exchange in the world. [p. 696]

41. C. The SEC requires both foreign and domestic companies to file registration statements, periodic reports, and other forms on its electronic filing and forms system, EDGAR, the SEC electronic data and records system. [p. 696]

42. D. Certain securities are exempt from registration with the SEC. Once a security is exempt, it is exempt forever. [p. 696]

43. C. The Securities Act of 1933 provides an intrastate offering exemption that permits local businesses to obtain from local investors capital to be used in the local economy without the need to register with the SEC. [p. 697]

44. B. Insider trading occurs when a company employee or company advisor uses material nonpublic information to make a profit by trading in the securities of the company. This practice is considered illegal because it allows insiders to take advantage of the investing public. [p. 701]

45. D. In 2010, Congress enacted the Dodd-Frank Wall Street Reform and Consumer Protection Act, a federal statute. This act imposes regulation on hedge funds and derivatives and other speculative investment devices. [p. 705]

Short Answer

46. The major responsibilities of the SEC are:
• Adopting rules (also called regulations) that further the purpose of the federal securities statutes. These rules have the force of law.
• Investigating alleged securities violations and bringing enforcement actions against suspected violators. This may include recommendations of criminal prosecution. Criminal prosecutions of violations of federal securities laws are brought by the U.S. Department of Justice.
• The SEC may bring a civil action to recover monetary damages from violators of securities laws. A "whistleblower bounty program" allows a person who provides information that leads to a successful SEC action to recover 10 percent to 30 percent of the monetary sanctions over $1 million recovered by the SEC.
• Regulating the activities of securities brokers and advisors. This includes registering brokers and advisors and taking enforcement action against those who violate securities laws. [p. 691]

47. The different types of securities are as follows:
• Common securities. Interests or instruments that are commonly known as securities are common securities.
• Statutorily defined securities. Interests or instruments that are expressly mentioned in securities acts are statutorily defined securities.
• Investment contracts. A statutory term that permits courts to define investment contracts as securities. The courts apply the Howey test in determining whether an arrangement is an investment contract and therefore a security. Under this test, an arrangement is considered an investment contract if there is an investment of money by an investor in a common enterprise and the investor expects to make profits based on the sole or substantial efforts of the promoter or others. [p. 692]

48. The issuance of securities by an issuer is called an initial public offering (IPO). A business or party selling securities to the public is called an issuer. An issuer may be a new company that is selling securities to the public for the first time. This is referred to as going public. Or the issuer may be an established company that sells a new security to the public. Many issuers of securities employ investment bankers, which are independent securities companies, to sell their securities to the public. A registration statement must contain descriptions of (a) the securities being offered for sale; (b) the registrant's business; (c) the management of the registrant, including compensation, stock options and benefits, and material transactions with the registrant; (d)

pending litigation; (e) how the proceeds from the offering will be used; (f) government regulation; (g) the degree of competition in the industry; and (h) any special risk factors. [p. 692]

49. The National Association of Securities Dealers Automated Quotation System (NASDAQ) is an electronic stock market. NASDAQ has the largest trading volume of any securities exchange in the world. More than three thousand companies are traded on NASDAQ, including companies such as Microsoft Corporation, Yahoo! Inc., Starbucks Corporation, Amazon.com, Inc., and eBay Inc., as well as companies from China, India, and other countries from around the world. NASDAQ, which is located in New York City, owns interests in electronic stock exchanges around the world.

Most public company documents—such as annual and quarterly reports—are now available online. The SEC requires both foreign and domestic companies to file registration statements, periodic reports, and other forms on its electronic filing and forms system, EDGAR, the SEC electronic data and records system. Anyone can access and download this information for free. [p. 696]

50. The securities exempt from registration with the SEC are:
a) Securities issued by any government in the United States.
b) Short-term notes and drafts that have a maturity date that does not exceed nine months.
c) Securities issued by nonprofit issuers, such as religious institutions, charitable institutions, and colleges and universities.
d) Securities of financial institutions that are regulated by the appropriate banking authorities.
e) Insurance and annuity contracts issued by insurance companies.
f) Stock dividends and stock splits.
g) Securities issued in a corporate reorganization in which one security is exchanged for another security. [p. 696-697]

51. Nonissuer exemption refers to an exemption from registration which states that securities transactions not made by an issuer, an underwriter, or a dealer do not have to be registered with the SEC. Intrastate offering exemption An exemption from registration that permits local businesses to raise capital from local investors to be used in the local economy without the need to register with the SEC. Private placement exemption is an exemption from registration that permits issuers to raise capital from an unlimited number of accredited investors and no more than thirty-five nonaccredited investors without having to register the offering with the SEC. [p. 697]

52. An accredited investor is:
• Any natural person who has individual net worth or joint net worth with a spouse that exceeds $1 million, to be calculated by excluding the value of the person's primary residence.
• A natural person with income exceeding $200,000 in each of the two most recent years or joint income with a spouse exceeding $300,000 for those years and a reasonable expectation of the same income level in the current year.
• A charitable organization, a corporation, a partnership, a trust, or an employee benefit plan with assets exceeding $5 million.
• A bank, an insurance company, a registered investment company, a business development company, or a small business investment company.
• Insiders of the issuers, such as directors, executive officers, or general partners of the company selling the securities.
• A business in which all the equity owners are accredited investors. [p. 698]

53. Investment banking is a service provided by many securities firms, whereby they assist companies in going public when issuing shares to the public and otherwise selling securities. The securities firms are paid lucrative fees for providing investment banking services in assisting companies to sell their securities and finding customers to purchase these securities. These same securities firms often provide securities analysis—providing investment advice and recommending securities listed on the stock exchanges and other securities to be purchased by the public.

In the late 1990s and early 2000s, many conflicts of interest were uncovered. Investment bankers and securities analysts of the same firm shared information, and the analysts were paid or pressured by the securities firms to write glowing reports of companies from which the investment bankers of the firm were earning fees. [p. 699]

54. Insider trading occurs when a company employee or company advisor uses material nonpublic information to make a profit by trading in the securities of the company. This practice is considered illegal because it allows insiders to take advantage of the investing public. In 1984, Congress enacted the Insider Trading Sanctions Act which permits the SEC to obtain a civil penalty of up to three times the illegal profits gained or losses avoided on insider trading. The fine is payable to the U.S. Treasury. Under the Sarbanes-Oxley Act, the SEC may issue an order prohibiting any person who has committed securities fraud from acting as an officer or a director of a public company. [p. 701]

55. Section 16(b) of the Securities Exchange Act of 1934 requires that any profits made by a statutory insider on transactions involving short-swing profits—that is, trades involving equity securities occurring within six months of each other— belong to the corporation. The corporation may bring a legal action to recover these profits. Involuntary transactions, such as forced redemption of securities by the corporation or an exchange of securities in a bankruptcy proceeding, are exempt. Section 16(b) is a strict liability provision. Generally, no defenses are recognized. Neither intent nor the possession of inside information need be shown.

Example—Rosanne is the president of a corporation and a statutory insider who does not possess any inside information. On February 1, she purchases one thousand shares of her employer's stock at $10 per share. On June 1, she sells the stock for $14 per share. The corporation can recover the $4,000 profit because the trades occurred within six months of each other. [p. 703]

ETHICS AND SOCIAL RESPONSIBILITY OF BUSINESS

Chapter Overview

This chapter provides a clear understanding of the moral principles that determine the conduct of individuals or a group. The five main theories of ethics are discussed, with case law providing an excellent example of each. Four theories of social responsibility of business are examined.

Objectives

Upon completion of the exercises in this chapter, you should be able to:
1. Describe how law and ethics intertwine.
2. Describe the moral theories of business ethics.
3. Describe the theories of the social responsibility of business.
4. Examine the provisions of the Sarbanes-Oxley Act.
5. Describe corporate social audits.

Practical Application

You should be able to recognize the types of ethical behavior being utilized in business based upon your knowledge of the various ethical principles. You will have a greater appreciation for the history of this area of the law.

Helpful Hints

It is important to become familiar with the key terms and phrases associated with ethics. It is helpful to be familiar with a case example for the theory you are trying to remember. The study tips given below have been organized similarly to how they are presented in the text.

Study Tips

Ethics and Social Responsibility of Business

The law specifies a minimum level of acceptable behavior, where ethics expects something more. Businesses organized in and operating in the U.S. are subject to its laws. They are also expected to act in an ethical manner in the conduct of their affairs.

Ethics and the Law

Ethics is a set of moral principles or values that governs the conduct of an individual or a group.
- Legal and ethical expectations are sometimes the same.
- Legal expectations sometimes permit something that ethical expectations will not permit.
- Ethical expectations sometimes permit something that legal expectations will not permit.

Business Ethics

There appear to be some universal rules about what conduct is and is not ethical.

Ethical Fundamentalism. A theory of ethics that says a person looks to an outside source for ethical rules or commands.

Utilitarianism. The concept behind this theory is that people have to choose or follow the rule that provides the greatest good to society.

Kantian Ethics. This theory of ethics is also referred to as duty ethics, or "do unto others as you would have them do unto you."
  • An obligated party must keep his or her part of the bargain as he or she has a moral duty to do so, regardless of any detriment that the party may suffer.

Rawl's Social Justice Theory. Under this theory, each person in society is presumed to have entered into a social contract with society in an effort to promote peace and harmony.
  • Those following this theory agree to abide by the rules as long as everyone else also keeps to the rules.

Ethical Relativism. Under this moral theory, individuals have to determine what is ethical using their own intuition or feelings as to what is right or wrong.
  • Due to the subjectivity of what the moral standard is, an individual who adopts ethical relativism cannot be criticized for the way he or she feels.
  • Most philosophers do not find this theory satisfactory when it comes to applying it to morals.

Social Responsibility of Business

More than ever we are looking at the impact of their actions, as well as the social responsibility owed to society, of businesses. Traditionally all that was viewed was a cost-benefit analysis and how a business's actions affected profits. Modernly, corporations are held responsible for their actions. The four theories of social responsibility are maximization of profits, moral minimum, stakeholder's interest, and corporate citizenship.

Maximizing Profits. The traditional rule regarding a business and its social responsibility was that it should maximize its profits for the shareholders.
  • Proponents of this theory affirm this philosophy by adding that a business should participate in activities that will increase its profits, as long as it is without any fraud or deception.

Moral Minimum. This theory states that a business's social responsibility is met as long as it either avoids or corrects any social injury it causes.
A corporation may make a profit, if it does not cause harm to others while doing so.

Sarbanes-Oxley Act Prompts Public Companies to Adopt Codes of Ethics. The Sarbanes-Oxley Act of 2002 makes certain conduct illegal and establishes criminal penalties for violations.
  • Section 406 of the act requires a public company to disclose whether it has adopted a code of ethics for senior financial officers, including its principal financial officer and principal accounting officer.

- Many companies have included all officers as well as employees in the coverage of their code of ethics.

Stakeholder Interest. Businesses have to consider the impact their actions will have on their stockholders, employees, suppliers, customers, creditors, and the community as a whole.
- All of these individuals have a stake in the business.

Corporate Citizenship. This theory maintains that a business has a responsibility to do well.
- Businesses are under a duty to help solve social problems that they had minimum or no association with.
  - The rationale behind this theory is because of the social power given to businesses.
- Opponents of this theory tend to lean toward moderation as society will always have some sort of social problem that needs to be solved.
  - Businesses have limits too.
- *Example.* Corporations owe a duty to fund a cure for a local child suffering from a rare disease.

The Corporate Social Audit. This audit examines how well employees have followed the company's code of ethics and how well the company has fulfilled its duty of social responsibility.

Refresh Your Memory

The following exercise will give you the opportunity to test your memory of the principles given in this chapter. Read the question twice and place your answer in the blank provided. Review the chapter material for any question that you are unable to answer or remember.

1. _____ is a set of moral principles or values that governs the conduct of an individual or a group.

2. _____ is a theory of ethics that says a person looks to an outside source for ethical rules or commands.

3. _____ dictates that people must choose the action or follow the rule that provides the greatest good to society.

4. If an action would increase the good of twenty-five people by one unit each and an alternative action would increase the good of one person by twenty-six units, then, according to _____, the latter action should be taken.

5. _____ is the best-known proponent of duty ethics.

6. Kantian ethics is also known as _____ ethics.

7. Under _____ theory, the principle of equal opportunity in employment would be promulgated by people who would not yet know if they were in a favored class.

8. _____ is a moral theory which holds that individuals must decide what is ethical based on their own feelings about what is right and wrong.

9. _____ requires corporations and businesses to act with awareness of the consequences and impact that their decisions will have on others.

10. The theory of _____, which dominated business and the law during the 19th century, holds that the interests of other constituencies are not important in and of themselves.

11. Some proponents of corporate social responsibility argue that a corporation's duty is to make a profit while avoiding causing harm to others. This theory of social responsibility is called the _____.

12. A corporation that pollutes a body of water and then compensates those whom the pollution has injured has met its _____ duty of social responsibility.

13. Section 406 of the _____ Act requires a public company to disclose whether it has adopted a code of ethics for senior financial officers.

14. _____ is a theory of social responsibility which says that a corporation must consider the effects its actions have on persons other than its shareholders.

15. A theory of social responsibility which says that a business has a responsibility to do good is called _____.

Critical Thought Exercise

You are an employee in the public relations department of Preciso, the luxury European automobile manufacturer. Preciso's sales have skyrocketed since the handcrafted vehicles were introduced to the United States ten years ago. Preciso's president has announced that Preciso will stop buying wood products from endangered forests following the example last year of Challenger Motor Company. Preciso will immediately stop buying wood from Canada's Great Bear Forest in British Columbia and phase out purchases of other wood from endangered forests. Instead, Preciso would like to use a "manmade wood-like product" for the interior parts (steering wheels, door panels, shifter knobs, etc.) of the autos it designs and builds.

There is no law against using wood from endangered forests and it is highly profitable to include these rare woods as part of the interiors of Preciso's cars. Shareholders are furious with the decision and are considering suing the board of directors and the officers for wasting profits.

You are asked by the president of Preciso to draft a speech that she will deliver to the annual shareholders meeting which will explain the ethical business decision that was made and persuade the shareholders to not pursue a suit against the company.

Please compose your answer to the Critical Thinking Exercise using a separate sheet of paper or your computer word processing program.

Practice Quiz

True/False

16. _____ All laws are framed to meet the highest ethical standards.

17. _____ Under ethical fundamentalism, a person looks to an outside source for ethical rules or commands.

18. _____ The False Claims Act permits private parties to sue the government on behalf of a corporation.

19. _____ The main criticism for ethical fundamentalism is that it does not allow people to decide what is right or wrong for themselves.

20. _____ Utilitarianism postulates doing the greatest good for the greatest number of people.

21. _____ One of the advantages of utilitarianism is that it is easy to apply in most real-life situations.

22. _____ Kantian ethics is also known as duty ethics.

23. _____ Kant believed that people owe moral duties that are based on universal rules.

24. _____ Relativism is one of principles of Kantian ethics that states that the actor must abide by the rule he or she uses to judge the morality of someone else's conduct.

25. _____ Under the theory of ethical relativism, fairness is considered the essence of justice.

26. _____ Ethical relativism holds that moral standards ought to be based on an individual's feelings of what is right or wrong.

27. _____ The traditional view of social responsibility of business emphasized maximizing profits for employees rather than shareholders.

28. _____ The theory of moral minimum stresses on making profit even while causing harm to others.

29. _____ In accordance to the stakeholder interest theory, a corporation must view employees solely as a means of maximizing shareholder wealth.

30. _____ The theory of corporate citizenship contends that corporations owe a duty to promote the same social goals as individual members of society

Multiple Choice

31. Which of the following cases describes an agreement of ethics and laws?

A. A person being penalized for bribing a judge to rule a case in the person's favor.
B. A company outsourcing its jobs to a foreign country.
C. A company not spending more money to keep its emission rates below the legal standard.
D. A person hiring an illegal alien worker whose family is in destitute.

32. Jules Renton, a financial accountant at Valkyrie Aviations, deals with the accounts Valkyrie has with the government. Valkyrie Aviations are in contract with the government to deliver a new bomber plane called Spearhead. While reviewing the Spearhead account, Renton noticed that Valkyrie has been falsely billing the government for Spearhead's production. If Renton chooses to be a whistleblower and expose the scam to the government, what Congress enacted statute must he invoke?

A. False Claims Act
B. Business Norms Act
C. Sarbanes-Oxley Act
D. Glass-Steagall Act

33. Which of the following statements describes the moral theory of utilitarianism?

A. People must follow actions based on moral duties imparted from one's community.
B. People must follow actions that are in accordance with a specific moral rule or principle from a religious text.
C. People must choose to follow actions of a virtuous person.
D. People must choose the action or follow the rule that provides the greatest good to society.

34. Which of the following is an apparent disadvantage of utilitarianism?

A. It does not allow people to have subjective notions of right and wrong.
B. It is based on moral duties derived from universal rules.
C. It treats morality as if it were an impersonal mathematical calculation.
D. It puts too much emphasis on one book or theory.

35. Which of the following moral theories lays emphasis on morality based on one's moral duties?

A. moral relativism
B. Kantian ethics
C. utilitarianism
D. ethical fundamentalism

36. Which of the following moral theories would closely follow the categorical imperative "Do unto others as you would have them do unto you?"

A. Rawls's social justice theory
B. moral relativism
C. utilitarianism
D. Kantian ethics

37. Consistency is one of the two important principles of _____ upon which its universal laws are based.

A. utilitarianism
B. Rawls's social justice theory
C. Kantian ethics
D. moral relativism

38. _____ is a moral theory which asserts that fairness is the essence of justice.

A. Rawls's social justice theory
B. moral relativism
C. utilitarianism
D. Kantian ethics

39. Which of the following theories of morality is Rawls's Social Justice Theory fundamentally derived from?

A. the theory of utilitarianism
B. the social contract theory
C. the theory of ethical fundamentalism
D. the theory of moral relativism

40. According to ethical relativism, _____.

A. ethics rely on duties based around universal rules which one is morally bound to follow
B. there are no universal ethical rules to guide a person's conduct
C. each person is presumed to have entered into a social contract with all others in society to obey moral rules
D. people must choose an action or follow a rule that provides the greatest good to society

41. What is "maximizing profits" as a social responsibility theory in business?

A. The theory that a corporation must consider the effects its actions have on persons other than its shareholders.
B. The theory that a corporation's duty is to make a profit while avoiding causing harm to others.
C. The theory that a business has a responsibility solely to its stakeholders that other than shareholders.
D. The theory that a corporation owes a duty to take actions that increases profits for shareholders.

42. A social responsibility theory of business which says that a corporation's duty is to make a profit while avoiding causing harm to others is referred to as _____.

A. stakeholder interest
B. corporate citizenship
C. moral minimum
D. maximizing profits

43. Under the theory of _____, if a business corrects the social injury it causes, it has met its duty of social responsibility.

A. stakeholder interest
B. maximizing profits
C. corporate citizenship
D. moral minimum

44. The _____ Act enacted by Congress in 2002, requires public companies to adopt codes of ethics, and establishes criminal penalties for companies that partake in violations.

A. Sarbanes-Oxley
B. Glass-Steagall
C. False Claims
D. Business Norms

45. What is "corporate citizenship" as a social responsibility theory in business?

A. Businesses have a responsibility solely to its stakeholders, and should strive to maximize their well-being.
B. Businesses owe a duty to take actions that increase profits for shareholders.
C. Businesses are responsible to even helping solve social problems that it did not cause.
D. Businesses are obliged to consider the effects its actions have on persons other than its shareholders.

Short Answer

46. Give an account of the relationship between ethics and law.

_____

_____

47. Explain utilitarianism with an example. Why has it been criticized?

_____

_____

48. Explain the two principles used to derive the universal rules of Kantian ethics?

_____

_____

49. What is Rawls's social justice theory?

_____

_____

50. What is ethical relativism?

_____

_____

51. Explain social responsibilities. What are the four social responsibilities of a business?

_____

_____

52. Explain the theory of maximizing profits.

_____

_____

53. What is theory of moral minimum in social responsibility for businesses?

_____

_____

54. Explain the stakeholder interest theory of social responsibility.

_____

_____

55. What is the corporate citizenship theory of social responsibility?

_____

_____

Answers to Refresh Your Memory

1. Ethics [p. 711]
2. Ethical fundamentalism [p. 712]
3. Utilitarianism [p. 714]
4. utilitarianism [p. 714]
5. Immanuel Kant [p. 714]
6. duty [p. 714]
7. Rawls's social justice [p. 715]
8. ethical relativism [p. 715]
9. Social responsibility [p. 716]
10. maximizing profits [p. 716]
11. moral minimum [p. 718]
12. moral minimum [p. 718]
13. Sarbanes-Oxley [p. 718]
14. Stakeholder interest [p. 718]
15. corporate citizenship [p. 720]

Critical Thought Exercise Model Answer

Traditionally, it was perceived that the duty to shareholders took precedence over all other duties owed by the corporation and that the primary duty and goal of a company was to maximize profits. However, as corporations have developed global markets and society has changed, corporations have come to realize that they have several other duties that must be fulfilled. Employers have an ethical duty to employees to provide a safe workplace, to pay a decent wage, and to provide employment opportunities to present and future employees. As society has changed, the corporation has had to take into account ethical concerns such as equal pay for equal work and the prevention of sexual harassment. The company has had to change its policies to comply with laws such as the Family and Medical Leave Act and the Americans with Disabilities Act. A corporation also has a duty to the persons who use its products. We must make a safe product that is economical and gives good value to consumers for their investment and faith in us. We have a duty to our suppliers to maintain good business relations and use good faith and fair dealing in our contracts with them. We have a duty to the community where our facilities and offices are located. What we do as a corporation affects the tax base of the community and the quality of the schools, services, and collateral businesses in the area. Lastly, we have a duty to society at large to be the most ethical citizen possible. This means complying with environmental protection laws, preservation of scarce natural resources, and being part of the solution to very big problems instead of a cause.

This corporation is in a unique position because of our wealth and power. We have a responsibility to society to use that wealth and power in socially beneficial ways. We should promote human rights, strive for equal treatment of minorities and women in the workplace, preserve and protect the environment, and not seek profits at the expense of ethics. If a corporation fails to conduct its operation ethically or respond quickly to an ethical crisis, its goodwill and reputation, along with profits, will suffer. Instead of aiming for maximum profits, we should aim for optimum profits—profits that can be realized while staying within legal and ethical limits set by government and society. For all these reasons, we have a duty to refrain from using wood from endangered forests to decorate our product. The manmade products we will substitute are more economical and will not detract from the overall look. Conversely, if we are known as the company that abuses scarce resources, consumers will support our competitors who are concerned about their corporate ethics.

Answers to Practice Quiz

True/False

16. False. In some situations, the law may permit an act that is ethically wrong. [p. 711]

17. True. Under ethical fundamentalism, a person looks to an outside source for ethical rules or commands. This may be a book (e.g., the Bible, the Koran) or a person (e.g., Karl Marx). [p. 712]

18. False. False Claims Act—also known as the Whistleblower Statute—permits private parties to sue companies for fraud on behalf of the government. [p. 714]

19. True. Critics argue that ethical fundamentalism does not permit people to determine right and wrong for themselves. Taken to an extreme, the result could be considered unethical under most other moral theories. [p. 713]

20. False. Utilitarianism dictates that people must choose the action or follow the rule that provides the greatest good to society. This does not mean the greatest good for the greatest number of people. [p. 714]

21. False. Utilitarianism has been criticized because it is difficult to estimate the "good" that will result from different actions, it is difficult to apply in an imperfect world, and it treats morality as if it were an impersonal mathematical calculation. [p. 714]

22. True. Immanuel Kant (1724–1804) is the best-known proponent of duty ethics, also called Kantian ethics. [p. 714]

23. True. Kant believed that people owe moral duties that are based on universal rules. Kant's philosophy is based on the premise that people can use reasoning to reach ethical decisions. [p. 714]

24. False. Reversibility is one of principles of Kantian ethics that states that the actor must abide by the rule he or she uses to judge the morality of someone else's conduct. [p. 714]

25. False. Under Rawls's social justice theory, fairness is considered the essence of justice. [p.715]

26. True. Ethical relativism holds that individuals must decide what is ethical based on their own feelings about what is right and wrong. Under this moral theory, if a person meets his or her own moral standard in making a decision, no one can criticize him or her for it. [p. 715]

27. False. The traditional view of the social responsibility of business is that business should maximize profits for shareholders. [p. 716]

28. False. Some proponents of corporate social responsibility argue that a corporation's duty is to make a profit while avoiding causing harm to others. This theory of social responsibility is called the moral minimum. [p. 718]

29. False. Under the stakeholder interest theory of social responsibility, a corporation must consider the effects its actions have on these other stakeholders. For example, a corporation would violate the stakeholder interest theory if it viewed employees solely as a means of maximizing shareholder wealth. [p. 718]

30. True. The corporate citizenship theory of social responsibility argues that business has a responsibility to do well. That is, business is responsible for helping to solve social problems that it did little, if anything, to cause. [p. 720]

Multiple Choice

31. A. Ethics is a set of moral principles or values that govern the conduct of an individual or a group. Ethics and the law are intertwined. Sometimes the rule of law and the rule of ethics demand the same response by a person confronted with a problem. [p. 711]

32. A. False Claims Act—also known as the Whistleblower Statute—permits private parties to sue companies for fraud on behalf of the government. [p. 714]

33. D. Utilitarianism is a moral theory with origins in the works of Jeremy Bentham (1748–1832) and John Stuart (1806–1873). This moral theory dictates that people must choose the action or follow the rule that provides the greatest good to society. [p. 714]

34. C. Utilitarianism has been criticized because it is difficult to estimate the "good" that will result from different actions, it is difficult to apply in an imperfect world, and it treats morality as if it were an impersonal mathematical calculation. [p. 714]

35. B. Immanuel Kant (1724–1804) is the best-known proponent of duty ethics, also called Kantian ethics. Kant believed that people owe moral duties that are based on universal rules. [p. 714]

36. D. Kant's philosophy is based on the premise that people can use reasoning to reach ethical decisions. His ethical theory would have people behave according to the categorical imperative "Do unto others as you would have them do unto you." [p. 714]

37. C. The universal rules of Kantian ethics are based on two important principles: (1) consistency— that is, all cases are treated alike, with no exceptions—and (2) reversibility—that is, the actor must abide by the rule he or she uses to judge the morality of someone else's conduct. [p. 714]

38. A. The leading proponent of the modern justice theory was John Rawls (1921– 2002), a philosopher at Harvard University. Under Rawls's social justice theory, fairness is considered the essence of justice. [p. 715]

39. B. John Locke (1632–1704) and Jean-Jacques Rousseau (1712–1778) proposed a social contract theory of morality. Under this theory, each person is presumed to have entered into a social contract with all others in society to obey moral rules that are necessary for people to live in peace and harmony. [p. 715]

40. B. Ethical relativism holds that individuals must decide what is ethical based on their own feelings about what is right and wrong. Thus, there are no universal ethical rules to guide a person's conduct. [p. 715]

41. D. The traditional view of the social responsibility of business is that business should maximize profits for shareholders. This view, which dominated business and the law during the 19th century, holds that the interests of other constituencies are not important in and of themselves. [p. 716]

42. C. Some proponents of corporate social responsibility argue that a corporation's duty is to make a profit while avoiding causing harm to others. This theory of social responsibility is called the moral minimum. [p. 718]

43. D. Moral minimum is a theory of social responsibility which says that a corporation's duty is to make a profit while avoiding causing harm to others. Under this theory, as long as business avoids or corrects the social injury it causes, it has met its duty of social responsibility. [p. 718]

44. A. Section 406 of the Sarbanes-Oxley Act is a section that requires a public company to disclose whether it has adopted a code of ethics for senior financial officers. [p. 718]

45. C. The corporate citizenship theory of social responsibility argues that business has a responsibility to do well. That is, business is responsible for helping to solve social problems that it did little, if anything, to cause. [p. 720]

Short Answer

46. Ethics and the law are intertwined. Although much of the law is based on ethical standards, not all ethical standards have been enacted as law. The law establishes a minimum degree of conduct expected by persons and businesses in society. Ethics demands more. Sometimes the rule of law and the rule of ethics demand the same response by a person confronted with a problem. However, in some situations, the law may permit an act that is ethically wrong. Another situation occurs where the law demands certain conduct but a person's ethical standards are contrary. [p. 711]

47. Utilitarianism is a moral theory with origins in the works of Jeremy Bentham (1748–1832) and John Stuart (1806–1873). This moral theory dictates that people must choose the action or

follow the rule that provides the greatest good to society. This does not mean the greatest good for the greatest number of people.

Example – If an action would increase the good of twenty-five people by one unit each and an alternative action would increase the good of one person by twenty-six units, then, according to utilitarianism, the latter action should be taken. Utilitarianism has been criticized because it is difficult to estimate the "good" that will result from different actions, it is difficult to apply in an imperfect world, and it treats morality as if it were an impersonal mathematical calculation. [p. 714]

48. The universal rules of Kantian ethics are based on two important principles:
(1) Consistency—that is, all cases are treated alike, with no exceptions—and
(2) Reversibility—that is, the actor must abide by the rule he or she uses to judge the morality of someone else's conduct. Thus, if you are going to make an Exception for yourself, that exception becomes a universal rule that applies to all others. [p. 714]

49. John Locke (1632–1704) and Jean-Jacques Rousseau (1712–1778) proposed a social contract theory of morality. Under this theory, each person is presumed to have entered into a social contract with all others in society to obey moral rules that are necessary for people to live in peace and harmony. This implied contract states, "I will keep the rules if everyone else does." These moral rules are then used to solve conflicting interests in society.

The leading proponent of the modern justice theory was John Rawls (1921– 2002), a philosopher at Harvard University. Under Rawls's social justice theory, fairness is considered the essence of justice. The principles of justice should be chosen by persons who do not yet know their station in society—thus, their "veil of ignorance" would permit the fairest possible principles to be selected. Example – Under Rawls's social justice theory, the principle of equal opportunity in employment would be promulgated by people who would not yet know if they were in a favored class. [p. 715]

50. Ethical relativism holds that individuals must decide what is ethical based on their own feelings about what is right and wrong. Under this moral theory, if a person meets his or her own moral standard in making a decision, no one can criticize him or her for it. Thus, there are no universal ethical rules to guide a person's conduct. This theory has been criticized because action that is usually thought to be unethical would not be unethical if the perpetrator thought it was in fact ethical. Few philosophers advocate ethical relativism as an acceptable moral theory. [p. 715]

51. Social responsibility requires corporations and businesses to act with awareness of the consequences and impact that their decisions will have on others. Thus, corporations and businesses are considered to owe some degree of responsibility for their actions.
Four theories of the social responsibility of business are discussed in the following paragraphs: (1) maximize profits, (2) moral minimum, (3) stakeholder interest, and (4) corporate citizenship. [p. 716]

52. The traditional view of the social responsibility of business is that business should maximize profits for shareholders. This view, which dominated business and the law during the 19th century, holds that the interests of other constituencies (e.g., employees, suppliers, residents of the communities in which businesses are located) are not important in and of themselves.
Milton Friedman, who won the Nobel Prize in economics when he taught at the University of Chicago, advocated the theory of maximizing profits for shareholders. Friedman asserted that in a free society, "there is one and only one social responsibility of business—to use its resources and engage in activities designed to increase its profits as long as it stays within the rules of the game, which is to say, engages in open and free competition without deception and fraud." [p. 716]

53. Some proponents of corporate social responsibility argue that a corporation's duty is to make a profit while avoiding causing harm to others. This theory of social responsibility is called the moral minimum. Under this theory, as long as business avoids or corrects the social injury it causes, it has met its duty of social responsibility. The legislative and judicial branches of government have established laws that enforce the moral minimum of social responsibility on corporations. [p. 718]

54. Businesses have relationships with all sorts of people besides their shareholders, including employees, suppliers, customers, creditors, and the local community. Under the stakeholder interest theory of social responsibility, a corporation must consider the effects its actions have on these other stakeholders. For example, a corporation would violate the stakeholder interest theory if it viewed employees solely as a means of maximizing shareholder wealth. The stakeholder interest theory is criticized because it is difficult to harmonize the conflicting interests of stakeholders.
Example – In deciding to close an unprofitable manufacturing plant, certain stakeholders would benefit (e.g., shareholders and creditors), whereas other stakeholders would not (e.g., current employees and the local community). [p. 718]

55. The corporate citizenship theory of social responsibility argues that business has a responsibility to do well. That is, business is responsible for helping to solve social problems that it did little, if anything, to cause.
Example – Under the corporate citizenship theory of social responsibility, corporations owe a duty to subsidize schools and help educate children. This theory contends that corporations owe a duty to promote the same social goals as individual members of society. Proponents of this "do good" theory argue that corporations owe a debt to society to make it a better place and that this duty arises because of the social power bestowed on them. That is, this social power is a gift from society and should be used to good ends. [p. 720]

43 | ADMINISTRATIVE LAW AND REGULATORY AGENCIES

Chapter Overview

Administrative agencies that have been established to administer the law have a large and direct impact on the operation of the government, the economy, and businesses. Modernly, we have administrative rules and regulations that cover almost every aspect of a business' operation. The growth in the size of administrative agencies and the rules they create have been staggering. Administrative law functions at the federal, state, and local levels. Understanding the sources and effects of administrative law and being able to function in the administrative law environment are essential for a business if it is going to succeed.

Chapter Objectives

Upon completion of the exercises in this chapter, you should be able to:
1. Describe the types of government regulation of business.
2. Define administrative law.
3. List and explain the functions of administrative agencies.
4. Describe the provisions of the Administrative Procedure Act.
5. Explain the procedure for judicial review of administrative agency decision.

Practical Application

Upon mastering the concepts in this chapter, you should understand the basis for the power of administrative agencies, the legality of administrative actions, procedures for challenging administrative action, and the effect of an administrative agency decision. The frontline contact between a business and the government is most often an administrative agency. The regulations and rules that control business behavior are generated and enforced by administrative agencies. The information in this chapter will make it easier for you to enforce your rights and meet your obligations under the law.

Helpful Hints

Administrative agencies only have the power granted to them by the branch of government that they serve. Administrative agencies are designed to implement the policy of the law as dictated by statute and the Constitution. The administrative agency must be in compliance with law before it can dictate the conduct of a business or individual. Focus on the parameters of administrative powers to understand when it is necessary to comply with an administrative agency rule or directive and when it is possible to challenge the authority of the agency to act.

Study Tips

It is wise to develop an understanding of the various powers possessed by agencies and the procedural steps that the agency and persons who come before the agency must adhere to. You should then look at the enforceability of agency decisions and a person's right to seek review of an agency decision. Lastly, you need to understand the rules and laws that govern access to agency controlled information.

Administrative Law and Regulatory Agencies

The legislative and executive branches of government – at the federal, state, and local levels – have created many administrative agencies to help in implementing and enforcing laws regulating business.

- The operation of these administrative agencies is governed by a body of administrative law.
- Administrative agencies are often referred to as the "fourth branch of government."

Sources of Administrative Agencies

The theory behind the creation of agencies is that they create a source of expertise in a particular field. Congress and the executive branch are unable to regulate the hundreds of individual industries and specialty areas that are part of our commerce and society. By delegating authority to the experts, the industries and commerce are regulated more efficiently.

General Government Regulation. Business is subject to general government regulation that applies to many businesses and industries collectively.

- Occupational Health and Safety Administration (OSHA) regulates workplace health and safety standards that apply to varied businesses, industries, and occupations.
- National Labor Relations Board (NLRB) regulates formation and operation of labor unions.
- Consumer Product Safety Commission (CPSC) establishes safety standards for products sold in this country, whether it is a toy for a child or a microwave oven.

Specific Government Regulation. Administrative agencies have been created by Congress and the executive branch to monitor specific industries.

- Federal Aviation Administration (FAA) regulates only air travel and the airline industry.
- Federal Communication Commission (FCC) is responsible for regulating only federal communications such as radio, television, and telecommunications.
- Office of the Comptroller of the Currency (OCC) regulates national banks.

Federal Administrative Agencies. The most regulation comes from federal administrative agencies that are either part of the executive branch or independent agencies created by Congress.

State Administrative Agencies. State agencies enforce state laws and regulations, such as corporations law, fish and game regulations, and workers' compensation law. Local (county and city) agencies closely regulate business, from redevelopment agencies to planning and zoning commissions.

Administrative Law

Administrative law is a combination of substantive and procedural law.

Administrative Procedure Act (APA). This act controls federal administrative procedure and sets up procedures that federal administrative agencies must follow.

- Some rules provide for hearings, rules for conducting adjudicative actions, and procedures for rule making.

Administrative Law Judge (ALJ). These are employees of the agency, who preside over administrative hearings and proceedings.

- An administrative law judge (ALJ) presides and makes rulings on fact and law without the use of a jury.
- Both sides have the right to be represented by an attorney, cross-examine witnesses, and produce their own evidence.
- The ALJ's decision is called an order, which may be reviewed by the agency.
- Any further appeal is to the appropriate federal or state court.

Delegation of Powers. The power of the agency is restricted to those powers that are delegated to it by either the legislative or executive branch under the delegation doctrine.

- The agency has powers from all three branches as it can adopt a rule, prosecute a violation of the rule, and adjudicate any dispute.
- *Rule Making.* Agencies are delegated legislative powers that include the following rule making and licensing powers:
  - Substantive rule making. An agency can issue a substantive rule that is like a statute.
    - The rule must be followed and carries civil and criminal sanctions, depending upon the purpose of the rule.
  - Interpretive rule making. An agency can issue interpretive rules that interpret existing statutes.
    - These give notice of how the agency will apply a statute.
  - Statements of policy. These statements announce a proposed course of action that the agency intends to follow.
- *Licensing Power.* Statutes often require the issuance of a government license before a person can take action of enter certain business markets.
  - Most agencies have the power to determine whether an applicant will receive a license.
- *Judicial Power.* Many administrative agencies have the judicial authority to adjudicate cases in administrative proceedings.
  - The administrative proceeding is initiated by serving a complaint on a respondent, who is the party that is accused by the agency of violating a statute or rule.
  - The respondent must be accorded procedural due process, which requires that the respondent be given
    - proper and timely notice of the allegations or charges, and
    - an opportunity to present evidence in the matter.
- *Executive Power.* The power that administrative agencies are granted, such as the investigation and prosecution of possible violations of statutes, administrative rules, and administrative orders. These powers are often exercised through the use of:
  - Administrative subpoenas. An order that directs the subject of the subpoena to disclose the requested information.
    - Failure to comply with the subpoena may lead to a judicial order for compliance.
    - Further failure to comply with the subpoena may cause the party to be held in contempt of court.
  - Administrative searches. Are physical inspection of business premises,

Administrative Searches. These inspections of business premises are considered searches and must comply with the Fourth Amendment, which forbids an unreasonable search and seizure. An administrative search will satisfy the requirements of the Fourth Amendment if

- The party voluntarily agrees to the search.
- The search is conducted pursuant to a validly issued search warrant.
- A warrantless search is conducted in an emergency situation.
- The business is part of a special industry where warrantless searches are automatically considered valid.
- The business is part of a hazardous industry and a statute expressly provides for nonarbitrary warrantless searches.

Judicial Review of Administrative Agency Actions

Most federal and state statutes provide for judicial review of administrative agency actions.

- If the statute does not contain authorization for judicial review, a party may rely upon the Administrative Procedure Act, which authorizes judicial review for federal administrative agency decisions.

Disclosure of Agency Administrative Actions

Congress has passed several statutes to make administrative agencies more accountable by subjecting them to increased public scrutiny. These statutes aim to make agency actions and procedures more public in nature and protect people and businesses from overzealous actions by agencies.

Freedom of Information Act. Requires that federal administrative agencies disclose certain records and documents to any person upon request.

- No reason for the request need be given.
- There are exceptions to the act, such as documents that must remain confidential to preserve national security.

Government in the Sunshine Act. Requires that every portion of every meeting of an agency be open to the public.

- The public must be given notice of the meeting and informed of the agenda.
- There are narrowly construed exceptions, such as meetings concerning future litigation and those where criminal acts of an agency target will be discussed.

Equal Access to Justice Act. Enacted to protect persons from harassment by federal administrative agencies.

- A private person can sue to recover attorneys' fees and costs associated with repelling an unjustified agency action.

Privacy Act. Requires that a federal agency maintain only that information about an individual that is relevant and necessary to accomplish a legitimate agency purpose.

- An individual has the right to inspect and correct the records.

Refresh Your Memory

The following exercise will give you the opportunity to test your memory of the principles given in this chapter. Read the question twice and place your answer in the blank provided. Review the chapter material for any question that you are unable to answer or remember.

1. _____ law is law enacted by governments that regulate industries and businesses and professionals.

2. Administrative laws are often referred to as _____ statutes.

3. _____ consists of laws that regulate businesses and industries collectively.

4. _____ are federal agencies that advise the president and are responsible for enforcing specific administrative statutes enacted by Congress.

5. Congress creates other federal administrative agencies called _____ that have broad regulatory powers over key areas of the national economy.

6. _____ law is law that an administrative agency enforces—federal statutes enacted by Congress or state statutes enacted by state legislatures.

7. Administrative law is a combination of substantive and _____ law.

8. A(n) _____ is a decision issued by an administrative law judge.

9. _____ is a rule issued by an administrative agency that has the force of law and to which covered persons and businesses must adhere.

10. Administrative agencies may issue a _____ that announces a proposed course of action that an agency intends to follow in the future.

11. _____ is a permission that an administrative agency grants to persons or businesses to conduct certain types of commerce or professions.

12. _____ requires the respondent to be given proper and timely notice of the allegations or charges against him or her and an opportunity to present evidence on the matter.

13. Administrative agencies are usually granted _____, such as the power to investigate and prosecute possible violations of statutes, administrative rules, and administrative orders.

14. _____ is a federal act that opens most federal administrative agency meetings to the public.

15. _____ is a federal act which states that federal administrative agencies can maintain only information about an individual that is relevant and necessary to accomplish a legitimate agency purpose.

Critical Thought Exercise

Macey Resources runs a hazardous waste facility where large quantities of industrial waste are stored, neutralized, and packaged for burial once it is dehydrated. A state statute provides that any business that handles more than 5 gallons of hazardous materials in a calendar month is subject to inspection without notice or warrant. Macey's operation includes 300 acres of ponds and transfer machinery. If a pond is not properly maintained, the seepage into the ground water could contaminate a large area with a radius over 15 miles. Within this radius there are numerous housing developments, schools, hospitals, and recreational facilities, including a small lake that is used for fishing, water skiing, and swimming. Inspectors from the state and federal environmental protection agencies enter Macey's property without a warrant or any advance notice to inspect the facility and test for hazardous waste seepage outside the drying ponds. The inspectors find numerous violations of state and federal law, including falsification of documents pertaining to disposal of potentially lethal chemicals from a military base. Macey is cited for the violations and is prosecuted by the U.S. Attorney for criminal charges. Macey files motions in the appropriate courts to have the evidence seized by the inspectors suppressed based upon a violation of the Fourth Amendment and failure to procure an administrative search warrant. What is the likely result of such a motion by Macey?

Please compose your answer to the Critical Thinking Exercise using a separate sheet of paper or your computer word processing program.

Practice Quiz

True/False

16. _____ Regulatory statutes can be termed as administrative laws.

17. _____ General government regulation consists of laws that regulate the operation of the three branches of the federal government.

18. _____ All federal administrative agencies answer directly to the president.

19. _____ The Department of Homeland Security is an example of a federal administrative agency.

20. _____ All state regulatory laws are drafted by the federal government and then adopted by the state.

21. _____ Local administrative agencies are agencies created by cities, municipalities, and counties to administer local regulatory law.

22. _____ Procedural administrative law establishes the procedure that must be followed by the federal or state legislatures in creating an administrative agency.

23. _____ The Administrative Procedure Act establishes procedures that industries and businesses must follow when conducting their affairs.

24. _____ The decisions issued by an administrative law judge are in the form of administrative orders.

25. _____ The delegation doctrine only allows executive and legislative powers to administrative agency, and not judicial.

26. _____ All substantive rules are subject to judicial review.

27. _____ Administrative agencies do not have to comply with the Due Process Clause of the U.S. Constitution when adjudicating cases of violation.

28. _____ Administrative subpoena refers to an order that directs the subject of the subpoena to disclose the requested information.

29. _____ Even in an emergency situation, a warrantless search conducted by an administrative agency constitutes a violation of the Fourth Amendment.

30. _____ The Privacy Act provides that documents in the possession of federal administrative agencies are confidential to the respective agencies and cannot be accessed by the public.

Multiple Choice

31. Which of the following is true of administrative agencies?

A. All administrative agencies directly answer to the president.
B. An existing administrative agency cannot administer a new law.
C. Administrative agencies can be created by federal, state, and local governments.
D. A separate administrative agency must be created to enforce every law.

32. General government regulation consists of laws that regulate _____.

A. businesses and industries
B. government-aided organizations
C. the executive branch of the federal government
D. the legislative branch of the federal government

33. _____ consists of laws that regulate particular industries.

A. Independent federal administration
B. General government regulation
C. Statements of policy
D. Specific government regulation

34. Federal administrative agencies are created by _____.

A. the U.S. President
B. general public elections
C. the U.S. Congress
D. the U.S. judiciary

35. Which of the following are responsible for enforcing specific administrative statutes enacted by Congress?

A. Cabinet-level federal departments
B. State administrative agencies
C. Law enforcement agencies
D. Independent federal administrative agencies

36. The Federal Trade Commission which enforces federal antitrust and consumer protection laws is an example of a(n) _____.

A. government-aided organizations
B. independent federal administrative agency
C. law enforcement agency
D. cabinet-level federal departments

37. Which of the following is the Department of Homeland Security's foremost responsibility?

A. to enforce laws to prevent and control civil unrest in the country
B. to enforce laws to prevent domestic terrorist attacks and related criminal activities
C. to enforce laws to prevent the possibility of the United States going to war
D. to enforce laws to prevent and control economic recession in the country

38. Which of the following is true of state administrative agencies?

A. They are created by federal administrative agencies.
B. They act as advisory boards for the president.
C. They are not empowered to enforce statutes.
D. Their decisions can be appealed to a state court.

39. _____ establishes the protocol that must be followed by an administrative agency while enforcing substantive laws.

A. Formal ruling
B. Substantive administrative law
C. Informal ruling
D. Procedural administrative law

40. Which of the following is true of the Administrative Procedure Act?

A. It establishes how rules and regulations can be adopted by federal administrative agencies.
B. It was enacted following the September 11, 2001 terrorist attacks.
C. It provides for a uniform legal and justice system across the United States.
D. It divides administrative power between the federal legislative branch and state legislatures.

41. Which of the following powers allow administrative agencies to issue substantive rules?

A. executive power
B. rule making
C. judicial authority
D. licensing

42. Which of the following is true of a substantive rule?

A. Violators can be held criminally liable.
B. It does not have the force of law and is only issued as a guideline.
C. Substantive rules are exempt from judicial review.
D. It interprets existing statutory language.

43. A(n) _____ announces a proposed course of action that an agency intends to follow in the future.

A. interpretive rule
B. operational code
C. statement of policy
D. substantive rule

44. Which of the following is a provision of the Freedom of Information Act?

A. It gives the public access to documents in the possession of federal administrative agencies.
B. It protects persons from harassment by federal administrative agencies.
C. It opens most federal administrative agency meetings to the public.
D. It allows public admission to the day-to-day workings of an administrative agency.

45. Which of the following acts protects persons from harassment by federal administrative agencies?

A. Freedom of Information Act
B. Equal Access to Justice Act
C. Government in the Sunshine Act
D. Privacy Act

Short Answer

46. Distinguish between general government regulation and specific government regulation.
_____
_____

47. What are federal administrative agencies?
_____
_____

48. Explain the administrative procedure.
_____
_____

49. Distinguish between substantive rules and interpretive rules. What is a statement of policy?
_____
_____

50. Explain the licensing power of administrative agencies.
_____
_____

51. What are the executive powers of the administrative agencies?

_____

_____

52. When are searches by administrative agencies considered reasonable?

_____

_____

53. Explain the Freedom of Information Act.

_____

_____

54. Why was the Government in the Sunshine Act enacted?

_____

_____

55. How is the general public protected from harassment by administrative agencies?

_____

_____

Answers to Refresh Your Memory

1. Administrative [p. 727]
2. regulatory [p. 727]
3. General government regulation [p. 728]
4. Cabinet-level federal departments [p. 728]
5. independent federal administrative agencies [p. 728]
6. Substantive administrative [p. 730]
7. procedural [p. 730]
8. order [p. 730]
9. Substantive rule [p. 731]
10. statement of policy [p. 731]
11. license [p. 731]
12. Procedural due process [p. 732]
13. executive power [p. 732]
14. Government in the Sunshine Act [p. 735]
15. Privacy Act [p. 736]

Critical Thought Exercise Model Answer

Physical inspection of the premises of a business is often crucial to the implementation of lawful administrative regulation by the agency entrusted with monitoring certain commercial activity. Searches by administrative agencies are generally deemed to be reasonable within the meaning of the Fourth Amendment if the business is part of a highly regulated industry where searches are automatically considered to be valid (liquor), or where the business is engages in hazardous activity and a statute expressly provides for nonarbitrary warrantless searches (mines, nuclear power). Evidence from an unreasonable search and seizure may be inadmissible in court depending upon the reasonableness of the search in the particular case. An expectation of privacy in commercial premises is different from, and is less than, expectation in an individual's home. This expectation is made much less if commercial property employed in "closely regulated" industries. Because the owner of the highly regulated business has less of an expectation of privacy, searches that are conducted pursuant to a regulatory scheme do not require a search warrant. The expectation is removed almost totally when the activity is ultra-hazardous and highly regulated. Macey, as an operator of a hazardous waste site, would be on notice that a search could take place at any time. He has impliedly waived his Fourth Amendment rights by engaging in this type of business.

Answers to Practice Quiz

True/False

16. True. Administrative law is law enacted by governments that regulate industries and businesses and professionals. Administrative laws are often referred to as regulatory statutes. [p. 727]

17. False. General government regulation consists of laws that regulate businesses and industries collectively. [p. 728]

18. False. Some agencies, such as the president's cabinet-level federal departments, answer directly to the president. [p. 728]

19. True. The Departments of State, Defense, Homeland Security, Commerce, Agriculture, and Education are cabinet-level federal administrative agencies. [p. 728]

20. False. All states have created administrative agencies to enforce and interpret state regulatory law. [p. 729]

21. True. Local governments such as cities, municipalities, and counties create local administrative agencies to administer local regulatory law. [p. 730]

22. False. Procedural administrative law establishes the procedures that must be followed by an administrative agency while enforcing substantive laws. [p. 730]

23. False. Administrative Procedure Act (APA) is a federal statute that establishes procedures to be followed by federal administrative agencies while conducting their affairs. [p. 730]

24. True. An order is a decision issued by an administrative law judge. [p. 730]

25. False. Delegation doctrine says that when an administrative agency is created, it is delegated certain powers; the agency can use only the legislative, judicial, and executive powers that are delegated to it. [p. 731]

26. True. A substantive rule is much like a statute: It has the force of law, and covered persons and businesses must adhere to it. All substantive rules are subject to judicial review. [p. 731]

27. False. In adjudicating cases, an administrative agency must comply with the Due Process Clause of the U.S. Constitution. [p. 732]

28. True. An administrative agency can issue an administrative subpoena to a business or person subject to its jurisdiction. The subpoena directs the party to disclose the requested information to the administrative agency. [p. 732]

29. False. Searches by administrative agencies are generally considered to be reasonable within the meaning of the Fourth Amendment if a warrantless search is conducted in an emergency situation. [p. 733]

30. False. Privacy Act is a federal act which states that federal administrative agencies can maintain only information about an individual that is relevant and necessary to accomplish a legitimate agency purpose. [p. 736]

Multiple Choice

31. C. Administrative agencies are agencies that governments create to enforce regulatory statutes. Administrative agencies are created by federal, state, and local governments to enforce regulatory statutes. [p. 727]

32. A. General government regulation consists of laws that regulate businesses and industries collectively. [p. 728]

33. D. Specific government regulation consists of laws that regulate specific industries. That is, an industry is subject to administrative laws that are specifically adopted to regulate that industry. [p. 728]

34. C. Federal administrative agencies are created by the U.S. Congress. Some agencies, such as the president's cabinet-level federal departments, answer directly to the president. [p. 728]

35. A. Cabinet-level departments advise the president and are responsible for enforcing specific laws enacted by Congress. [p. 728]

36. B. The Federal Trade Commission (FTC), which enforces federal antitrust and consumer protection laws, is an example of independent federal administrative agencies that have broad regulatory powers over key areas of the national economy. [p. 728]

37. B. The mission of the Department of Homeland Security is to enforce laws to prevent domestic terrorist attacks and related criminal activities, reduce vulnerability to terrorist attacks, minimize the harm caused by such attacks, and assist in recovery in the event of a terrorist attack. [p. 729]

38. D. An appeal consists of a review by the administrative agency. Further appeal can be made to the appropriate federal court (in federal agency actions) or state court (in state agency actions). [p. 730]

39. D. Procedural administrative law establishes the procedures that must be followed by an administrative agency while enforcing substantive laws. [p. 730]

40. A. The Administrative Procedure Act (APA) establishes procedures that federal administrative agencies must follow in conducting their affairs. [p. 730]

41. B. Many federal statutes expressly authorize an administrative agency to issue substantive rules. A substantive rule is much like a statute: It has the force of law, and covered persons and businesses must adhere to it. [p. 731]

42. A. A substantive rule is much like a statute: It has the force of law, and covered persons and businesses must adhere to it. Violators may be held civilly or criminally liable, depending on the rule. [p. 731]

43. C. Administrative agencies may issue a statement of policy. Such a statement announces a proposed course of action that an agency intends to follow in the future. [p. 731]

44. A. The Freedom of Information Act5 was enacted to give the public access to most documents in the possession of federal administrative agencies. The act requires federal administrative agencies to publish agency procedures, rules, regulations, interpretations, and other such information in the Federal Register. [p. 734]

45. C. Government in the Sunshine Act is a federal act that opens most federal administrative agency meetings to the public. [p. 735]

Short Answer

46. General government regulation consists of laws that regulate businesses and industries collectively. Most of the industries and businesses in the United States are subject to these laws. These laws do not regulate a specific industry but apply to all industries and businesses except those that are specifically exempt from certain regulations. On the contrary, specific government regulation consists of laws that regulate specific industries. That is, an industry is subject to administrative laws that are specifically adopted to regulate that industry. Administrative agencies, which are industry specific, are created to administer those specific laws. [p. 728]

47. Federal administrative agencies are created by the U.S. Congress. Some agencies, such as the president's cabinet-level federal departments, answer directly to the president. The president appoints cabinet members subject to confirmation by a majority vote of the U.S. Senate. Cabinet-level departments advise the president and are responsible for enforcing specific laws enacted by Congress. Examples – The Departments of State, Defense, Homeland Security, Commerce, Agriculture, and Education are cabinet-level federal administrative agencies. Congress creates other federal administrative agencies called independent federal administrative agencies that have broad regulatory powers over key areas of the national economy. Examples – The Securities and Exchange Commission (SEC), which regulates the issuance and trading of securities; the Federal Trade Commission (FTC), which enforces federal antitrust and consumer protection laws; and the Federal
Communications Commission (FCC), which regulates radio and television broadcasting and telecommunications, are examples of federal independent agencies. [p. 728]

48. Administrative law is a combination of substantive and procedural law. Substantive administrative law is law that an administrative agency enforces—federal statutes enacted by Congress or state statutes enacted by state legislatures. Procedural administrative law establishes the procedures that must be followed by an administrative agency while enforcing substantive laws.
Examples – Congress created the federal Environmental Protection Agency (EPA) to enforce federal environmental laws that protect the environment. This is an example of substantive law—

laws to protect the environment. In enforcing these laws, the EPA must follow certain established procedural rules (e.g., notice, hearing). These are examples of procedural law. [p. 730]

49. A substantive rule is much like a statute that has the force of law, and covered persons and businesses must adhere to it. Violators may be held civilly or criminally liable, depending on the rule. All substantive rules are subject to judicial review. An interpretive rule interprets existing statutory language. Such rules do not establish new laws. Neither public notice nor public participation is required. A statement of policy announces a proposed course of action that an agency intends to follow in the future. Statements of policy do not have the force of law. Public notice and participation are not required. [p. 731]

50. Statutes often require the issuance of a government license before a person can enter certain types of industries (e.g., banks, television and radio stations, commercial airlines) or professions (e.g., doctors, lawyers, dentists, certified public accountants, contractors). The administrative agency that regulates the specific area involved is granted licensing power to determine whether to grant a license to an applicant.
Applicants must usually submit detailed applications to the appropriate administrative agency. In addition, the agency usually accepts written comments from interested parties and holds hearings on the matter. Courts generally defer to the expertise of administrative agencies in licensing matters. [p. 731]

51. Administrative agencies are usually granted executive powers, such as the power to investigate and prosecute possible violations of statutes, administrative rules, and administrative orders. To perform these functions successfully, an agency must often obtain information from the persons and businesses under investigation as well as from other sources. If the required information is not supplied voluntarily, the agency may issue an administrative subpoena to search the business premises; this is called an administrative search. An administrative agency can issue an administrative subpoena to a business or person subject to its jurisdiction. The subpoena directs the party to disclose the requested information to the administrative agency. The administrative agency can seek judicial enforcement of the subpoena if the party does not comply with the subpoena. [p. 732]

52. Searches by administrative agencies are generally considered to be reasonable within the meaning of the Fourth Amendment if:
a. the party voluntarily agrees to the search.
b. the search is conducted pursuant to a validly issued search warrant.
c. warrantless search is conducted in an emergency situation.
d. the business is part of a special industry where warrantless searches are automatically considered valid.
e. the business is part of a hazardous industry and a statute expressly provides for nonarbitrary warrantless searches. [p. 733]

53. The Freedom of Information Act5 was enacted to give the public access to most documents in the possession of federal administrative agencies. The act requires federal administrative agencies to publish agency procedures, rules, regulations, interpretations, and other such information in the Federal Register. The act also requires agencies to publish quarterly indexes of certain documents. In addition, the act specifies time limits for agencies to respond to requests for information, sets limits on copying charges, and provides for disciplinary action against agency employees who refuse to honor proper requests for information. [p. 734]

54. The Government in the Sunshine Act6 was enacted to open most federal administrative agency meetings to the public. There are some exceptions to this rule. These include meetings (1) where a person is accused of a crime, (2) concerning an agency's issuance of a subpoena, (3) where attendance of the public would significantly frustrate the implementation of a proposed agency action, and (4) concerning day-to- day operations. Decisions by federal administrative agencies to close meetings to the public are subject to judicial review in the proper U.S. District Court. [p. 735]

55. Congress enacted the Equal Access to Justice Act to protect persons from harassment by federal administrative agencies. Under this act, a private party who is the subject of an unjustified federal administrative agency action can sue to recover attorneys' fees and other costs. The courts have generally held that the agency's conduct must be extremely outrageous before an award will be made under the act. A number of states have similar statutes. [p. 735]

44 | CONSUMER PROTECTION AND PRODUCT SAFETY

Chapter Overview

Federal and state governments have enacted numerous statutes in order to regulate the behavior of businesses that deal with consumers. The goal of the legislation was to promote product safety and prohibit abusive, unfair, and deceptive selling practices. This was a drastic change from earlier days when sales to consumers were governed by the principle of *caveat emptor*, which means "let the buyer beware."

This chapter presents the statutes, rules, and cases that allow consumers greater protection and have increased the ability of consumers to sue businesses for damages caused by their dangerous, fraudulent, and deceptive methods. Government mandates and regulation by administrative agencies have mushroomed in the area of consumer protection. These laws and regulations form the consumer protection laws that are examined in this chapter.

Objectives

Upon completion of the exercises in this chapter, you should be able to:
1. Describe government regulation of food and food additives.
2. Describe government regulation of drugs, cosmetics, and medicinal devices.
3. Explain the coverage of Consumer Product Safety Acts.
4. Describe the United Nations Biosafety Protocol concerning genetically altered foods.
5. Identify and describe unfair and deceptive business practices.

Practical Application

Upon learning the main legislative protections for consumers in this chapter, you will understand the duties, obligations, and requirements placed upon businesses when they deal in the manufacture, sale, or distribution of consumer goods or services. This information will allow you to determine your specific rights and obligations, whether you are a business that must comply with the law or a consumer who is seeking to enforce a protected right.

Helpful Hints

As with all law, your analysis of a situation must begin with the basic definitions and requirements as contained in the statutes. Once you have that foundation, your focus should turn to the act or nature of the product. By determining where the act or product fits in the legislative scheme of consumer protection, you can alleviate the illegality or enforce the mandates contained in a consumer law.

Study Tips

Consumer Protection and Product Safety

Federal and state governments have enacted statutes that regulate the behavior of businesses that deal with consumers, in order to promote the safety of foods, cosmetics, drugs, products, and services, and to prohibit abusive, unfair, and deceptive selling practices.

U.S. Department of Agriculture

The United States Department of Agriculture (USDA) is a federal administrative agency which regulates meat, poultry, and other food products.
- It inspects food processing and storage facilities and can initiate legal proceedings against those violating regulations.

Food, Drug, and Cosmetic Act (FDCA)

This act regulates much of the testing, manufacture, distribution, and sale of foods, drugs, cosmetics, and medical products and devices in the United States.
- The Food and Drug Administration (FDA) administers the act.

Regulation of Food. The FDCA prohibits the shipment, distribution, or sale of adulterated food, which is any food that consists in whole or in part of any "filthy, putrid, or decomposed substance" that is unfit for consumption.
- The FDA allows certain amounts of contaminants up to the amount set by their "action levels."
- For example, tomato juice is allowed to have 10 fly eggs per 3 ½ ounces. Anything below the action level is considered safe to eat.

Food Labeling. The Nutritional Labeling and Education Act (NLEA) requires food manufacturers and processors to provide more nutritional information on virtually all foods and forbids them from making scientifically unsubstantiated heath claims.
- The law requires labels on food items with information on calories, fat, fiber, cholesterol, and other substances.
- The FDA regulations adopted to implement the act required information on serving size and nutrients.
- Definitions were developed for light, low fat, and natural.

United Nations Biosafety Protocol for Genetically Altered Foods. The Biosafety Protocol was passed to resolve a dispute between exporters of genetically modified agricultural products and countries that desired to keep the products out of their country.
- As a compromise, the 138 countries that signed the protocol agreed to allow the importation of genetically engineered foods as long as they were clearly labeled with the phrase "May contain living modified organisms."
  - o This allows consumers to decide for themselves whether to purchase altered food products.
  - o Boxes and containers used in shipping such goods must also be clearly marked as containing genetically altered food products.

Regulation of Drugs. The FDA regulates the testing, licensing, manufacturing, distribution, and sale of drugs.
- The licensing process is long and thorough.
- Users of drugs must be provided with a copy of detailed directions that include any warnings and list possible side effects.

Regulation of Cosmetics. The FDA regulations require cosmetics to be labeled, to disclose ingredients, and to contain warnings as to any carcinogenic ingredients.
- The FDA may remove from the market any product that makes a false claim of preserving youth, increasing virility, or growing hair.

Regulation of Medicinal Devices. The FDA has authority under the Medicinal Device Amendment to the FDCA to regulate medicinal devices, such as heart pacemakers, surgical equipment, and other diagnostic, therapeutic, and health devices.
- The FDA is empowered to remove quack devices from the market.

Product Safety

The Consumer Product Safety Act (CPSA) regulates potentially dangerous consumer products and created the Consumer Product Safety Commission (CPSC).
- The CPSC is an independent federal agency that is not attached to any department. It interprets the CPSA, conducts research on the safety of products, and collects data regarding injuries caused by products.
- The CPSC sets safety standards for consumer products and has the power to compel a manufacturer to recall, repair, or replace a hazardous product.
  - Alternatively, the CPSC can seek injunctions and seize hazardous products.
  - It can also seek civil and criminal penalties.

Unfair and Deceptive Practices

When sellers engage in unfair, deceptive, or abusive techniques, the Federal Trade Commission (FTC), under the authority of the Federal Trade Commission Act (FTC Act), is authorized to bring an administrative proceeding to attack the unfair or deceptive practice.
- If the FTC finds a violation under Section 5 of the FTC Act, it may order a cease-and-desist order, an affirmative disclosure to consumers, or corrective advertising.
- The FTC may sue for damages on behalf of consumers in either state or federal court. Improper acts by sellers that are addressed by the FTC include:

False and Deceptive Advertising. Such advertising is prohibited under Section 5 when advertising
- contains misinformation or omits important information that is likely to mislead a "reasonable consumer" or
- makes an unsubstantiated claim (e.g., "This pain reliever works 50 percent faster on your headache than our competitors.").

Bait and Switch. This is a type of deceptive advertising that occurs when a seller advertises the availability of a low-cost discounted item but then pressures the buyer into purchasing more expensive merchandise. Bait and switch occurs when the seller
- refuses to show consumers the advertised merchandise

- discourages employees from selling the advertised merchandise or
- fails to have adequate quantities of the merchandise available.

Door-to Door Sales. These type of sales may entail overaggressive or abusive practices.
- These tactics are handled on a state level where laws give consumers a certain number of days to rescind door-to-door sales, usually three.

Do-Not-Call Registry. In 2003, the Federal Trade Commission (FTC) and the Federal Communications Commission (FCC), issued rules that created the "Do-Not-Call" Registry, on which consumers can place their names to prevent most unsolicited commercial telephone calls.
- Telemarketers have three months to remove the customer's phone number from their sales call list.
- Customer registration remains valid for five years and can be renewed.
- Charitable and political organizations are exempt.
- There is an "established business relationship" exception.
- Consumers can designate specific companies not to call them.

Refresh Your Memory

The following exercise will give you the opportunity to test your memory of the principles given in this chapter. Read the question twice and place your answer in the blank provided. Review the chapter material for any question that you are unable to answer or remember.

1. The principle of _____ means "let the buyer beware."

2. Federal and state statutes and regulations that promote product safety and prohibit abusive, unfair, and deceptive business practices are called _____.

3. The _____ is a federal administrative agency that is responsible for regulating the safety of meat, poultry, and other food products.

4. The FDCA prohibits the shipment, distribution, or sale of _____.

5. _____ is a United Nations–sponsored protocol that requires signatory countries to place the label "May contain living modified organisms" on all genetically engineered foods.

6. _____ is a 2010 federal statute that increases the number of persons who have health care insurance in the United States and provides new protections for insured persons from abusive practices of insurance companies.

7. _____ occurs when a seller advertises the availability of a low-cost discounted item to attract customers to its store and once the customers are in the store, the seller pressures them to purchase more expensive merchandise.

8. _____ is a register created by federal law on which consumers can place their names and free themselves from most unsolicited commercial telephone calls.

Critical Thought Exercise

James is a freshman biology student at LostLand University. One of his professors has given an assignment for each student to bring in a commercially prepared food item to class. James brings in a 3.5 ounce can of mushrooms and proceeds to follow the professor's instructions to identify all foreign materials in his food item. He carefully looks at the mushrooms under the microscope and identifies a total of 20 maggots from his 3.5 ounces of canned mushrooms. James is sickened and appalled to find maggots in his mushrooms, as he has always loved eating mushrooms.

James would like to complain about finding maggots in his commercially canned mushrooms. To whom should he complain and does he have a legitimate complaint?

Please compose your answer to the Critical Thinking Exercise using a separate sheet of paper or your computer word processing program.

Practice Quiz

True/False

9. _____ The U.S. Food and Drug Administration promotes the principle of caveat emptor in sale transactions involving food and drugs.

10. _____ The U.S. Department of Agriculture is the federal administrative agency that is primarily responsible for regulating meat, poultry, and other food products.

11. _____ The Consumer Product Safety Commission is the federal administrative agency empowered to enforce the FDCA.

12. _____ A manufacturer can be held liable for deceptive labeling or packaging under the Health Care Reform Act.

13. _____ Sellers of raw fruits and vegetables can adopt a voluntary approach when it comes to labeling requirements.

14. _____ The Biosafety Protocol label is used to identify certain food products that have been genetically modified.

15. _____ The FDA cannot withdraw approval of any previously licensed drug.

16. _____ The FDA cannot recall any cosmetics that contain unsubstantiated claims of preserving youth or increasing virility from the market.

17. _____ The FDA mandates a label of "NOT TESTED ON ANIMALS" on all cosmetic products.

18. _____ The CPSC is an independent federal administrative agency empowered to regulate potentially dangerous consumer products and issue product safety standards.

19. _____ Under the Consumer Product Safety Act, a private party can sue for an injunction to prevent violations of the act or of CPSC rules and regulations.

20. _____ Firearms represent an example of consumer products which do not come under the CPSC rules.

21. _____ The Family Smoking Prevention and Tobacco Control Act, which requires mandatory warnings to be placed on cigarette packages, is enforced by the Health Care Reform Act.

22. _____ Under the Health Care Reform Act, persons who do not obtain health coverage will be provided free health insurance by the government.

23. _____ The FTC can sue in either the state or federal courts to obtain compensation on behalf of consumers.

24. _____ Proof of actual deception is required for an advertising to be considered false under Section 5 of the FTC.

25. _____ In the bait and switch advertising model, the bait involves pressuring customers in a store into buying unadvertised or more expensive products.

26. _____ The consumer must send a required notice of cancellation to the seller of a door-to-door sales contract within three days to rescind an order.

Multiple Choice

27. The _____ is a federal administrative agency that is primarily responsible for regulating the safety of meat, poultry, and other food products.

A. Food and Drug Administration
B. Consumer Product Safety Commission
C. U.S. Department of Agriculture
D. Federal Trade Commission

28. In which of the following cases of consumer safety violations will the U.S. Department of Agriculture be required to take action?

A. A batch of sausages and cold cuts from a particular vendor was found to have high levels of salmonella and other pathogenic organisms.
B. A brand of soft toys for infants was produced with low grade foam and fabrics that are harmful for children when ingested.
C. A new drug was released into the market without adequate testing and this lead to adverse side effects among users.
D. A fleet of cars released into the market by famous company was found to have a defective braking system which could prove fatal for owners.

29. Ajax, a pharmaceutical company, has designed a new medicine for morning sickness among pregnant women. Testing at their R&D center showed the drug to be highly reliable. Ajax has to approach a U.S. federal administrative agency called _____ for the drug to be deemed legal for sale to the public.

A. Medicines and Healthcare products Regulatory Agency
B. Food and Drug Administration
C. Federal Trade Commission
D. Consumer Product Safety Commission

30. The Food and Drug Administration is empowered to _____.

A. recall unsafe toys, appliances, and other consumer products which are harmful to users
B. obtain orders for the seizure, recall, and condemnation of harmful products
C. prosecute violators directly by imposing fines and pronouncing sentences
D. regulate the safety of meat, poultry, and other food products

31. Which of the following is true of the Nutrition Labeling and Education Act?

A. The NLEA is a state law and its implementation is not federally regulated.
B. The NLEA specifically eliminates the practice of providing point-of-purchase nutrition information by sellers.
C. The NLEA mandates compulsory labeling for all kinds of raw and processed food with any exceptions.
D. The NLEA applies to packaged foods and other foods regulated by the Food and Drug Administration.

32. At the food processing company where Mika works, his primary job responsibility is to review the quality of preservatives that are used in the food products being made. A new and highly recommended preservative that has the potential to preserve food longer without refrigeration was approved by Mika. However, Mika failed to identify that the substance used to make the particular preservative was banned. If the food product is released with this new preservative, which of the following provisions of the NLEA would help consumers identify the banned preservative prior to consumption?

A. condemnation of unfit food products
B. initiating legal proceedings against violators
C. inspection of the storage facilities
D. disclosure of information on food labels

33. The _____ requires food manufacturers and processors to disclosure uniform information about serving sizes and nutrients, and establishes standard definitions for the various terms like "low fat," "lean" or "organic" which are indiscriminately used by food processors.

A. Nutrition Labeling and Education Act
B. Consumer Product Safety Act
C. Patient Protection and Affordable Care Act
D. Health Care Reform Act

34. The new line of fairness-enhancing products marketed by Radiance has allegedly been developed after using large-scale animal testing procedures. Insiders revealed that the high levels of lead present in the cosmetics have proven to be fatal for many of the animals used in the laboratories. Radiance is likely to be inspected for suspected criminal violations of the _____.

A. Federal Trade Commission Act
B. Consumer Product Safety Act
C. Health Care Reform Act
D. Food, Drug, and Cosmetic Act

35. Biosafety Protocol is a United Nations–sponsored protocol that requires signatory countries to place the label _____ on all genetically engineered foods.

A. "Warning—unnatural food particles"
B. "FDA tested and approved food"
C. "May contain living modified organisms"
D. "WHO tested and approved food"

36. The _____ is a federal law that gives the FDA broad powers to license new drugs in the United States.

A. Health Care Reform Act
B. Food Labeling and Education Act
C. Drug Amendment of the FDCA
D. Patient Protection and Affordable Health Care Act

37. Which of the following statements is true with regard to the FDA?
A. It places a complete ban on animal testing.
B. It recommends animal testing only if it increases product safety.
C. It provides tax exemptions to companies that avoid animal testing.
D. It allows animal testing for only certain kinds of cosmetics like household soaps.

38. Which of the following would come under the purview of the Medicinal Device Amendment to the FDCA?

A. a new and compact heart pacemaker
B. a new range of cosmetics to reduce signs of aging
C. a new oral medication for depression
D. a revolutionary drug therapy for cancer

39. The Consumer Product Safety Commission is _____.

A. an independent federal administrative agency that regulates potentially dangerous consumer products
B. a federal body created to ensure the safety of few consumer products like motor vehicles, boats, aircraft, and firearms
C. a communion of two state-funded regulatory bodies working together to ensure consumer safety
D. a federal agency working to ensure product safety standards for food, poultry, medicines, and medical devices

40. Which of the following is true of seeking injunctions on consumer products under the CPSC?

A. The CPSC can only seek an injunction once a private party has lodged a complaint with it.
B. A private party can sue for an injunction to prevent violations of the act or of CPSC rules and regulations.
C. Only the CPSC can sue for an injunction when CPSC rules are violated.
D. Injunctions cannot be pursued on products that have not yet been sold or marketed.

41. Which of the following is a requirement of the Family Smoking Prevention and Tobacco Control Act?

A. A 2 percent increase in excise tax per cigarette package
B. A hotline number to the FDA for apparent violations of the provisions of this Act
C. A tax exemption for companies that voluntarily display warning labels on their packages
D. A warning on the top 50 percent of both the front and back of each cigarette package

42. Which of the following is true of the Health Care Reform Act?

A. Excise taxes for pharmaceuticals are reduced.
B. Persons who do not obtain coverage will be required to pay a tax penalty to the federal government.
C. All employers are mandatorily required to provide health insurance coverage to their employees.
D. Employers of big corporations are given subsidies for providing health insurance to their employees.

43. The _____ prohibits health insurance companies from terminating health insurance coverage when a person gets sick.

A. Food, Drug, and Cosmetic Act
B. Drug Amendment of the FDCA Act
C. Medical Device Amendment Act
D. Health Care Reform Act

44. Which of the following would constitute a false advertising according to the Federal Trade Commission?

A. unsubstantiated claims
B. sales talk
C. minimal commercial speech
D. statements of opinion

45. Which of the following is true of the FTC?

A. The FTC can sue to obtain compensation on behalf of the consumer.
B. The FTC's decision can be appealed in a state court.
C. The FTC can only sue in state courts.
D. The FTC is not allowed to directly disclose its findings to the public.

Short Answer

46. Why was the consumer protection laws enacted?

_____

_____

47. Why was Food and Drug Administration formed?

_____

_____

48. Which is the law that applies to food labeling?

_____

_____

49. What is the United Nation's Biosafety Protocol for genetically altered food?

_____

_____

50. Give an account of the regulation of medicinal devices in the United States?

_____

_____

51. Explain the Consumer Product Safety Act.

_____

_____

52. What are the new protections provided to insured persons by the Health Care Reform Act?

_____

_____

53. What is false and deceptive advertising?

_____

_____

54. What is the bait and switch advertising model?

_____

_____

55. Explain the functions of Federal Communications Commission and Federal Trade Commission.

_____

_____

Answers to Refresh Your Memory

1. caveat emptor [p. 740]
2. consumer protection laws [p. 740]
3. U.S. Department of Agriculture [p. 740]
4. adulterated food [p. 742]
5. Biosafety Protocol [p. 743]

6. Health Care Reform Act [p. 746]
7. Bait and switch [p. 747]
8. Do-Not-Call Registry [p. 748]

Critical Thought Exercise Model Answer

James should file his complaint with the Food and Drug Administration (FDA), as it is responsible for enforcing the Food, Drug, and Cosmetic Act (FDCA), which regulates the testing, manufacture, distribution, and sale of foods, drugs, cosmetics, and medicinal products and devices in the US. Under this Act, the shipment, distribution, or sale of adulterated food is prohibited. Food is deemed adulterated if it consists in whole or in part of any "filthy, putrid, or decomposed substance" or if it is otherwise "unfit for food."

However, food may contain contaminants and still be lawfully distributed or sold, it just has to be unadulterated. The FDA has set ceilings, or "action levels," for contaminants for various foods. The courts have upheld the presence of some contamination in food as lawful. The FDA can mount inspections and raids to enforce its action levels. If it finds that the federal tolerance system has been violated, it can seize the offending food and destroy it at the owner's expense.

Under the FDA guidelines, canned mushrooms can contain up to 20 maggots per 3.5 ounces before they are sufficiently defective to warrant FDA investigation. James found 20 maggots in his sample of 3.5 ounces of canned mushrooms. This would seem to indicate that the canned mushrooms were not adulterated, as they contained the allowable level of maggots in 3.5 ounces.

Answers to Practice Quiz

True/False

9. False. Caveat emptor led to abusive practices by businesses that sold adulterated food products and other unsafe products. In response, federal and state governments have enacted a variety of statutes that regulate the safety of food and other products. [p. 740]

10. True. In the United States, the U.S. Department of Agriculture (USDA) is the federal administrative agency that is primarily responsible for regulating meat, poultry, and other food products. [p. 740]

11. False. The Food and Drug Administration (FDA) is the federal administrative agency empowered to enforce the FDCA. [p. 742]

12. False. A manufacturer may be held liable for deceptive labeling or packaging under the Food, Drug, and Cosmetic Act. [p. 742]

13. True. Nutrition labeling for raw fruits and vegetables and raw seafood is voluntary. [p. 742]

14. True. Biosafety Protocol is a United Nations–sponsored protocol that requires signatory countries to place the label "May contain living modified organisms" on all genetically engineered foods. [p. 743]

15. False. The FDA may withdraw approval of any previously licensed drug. [p. 744]

16. False. The FDA may remove from commerce any cosmetics that contain unsubstantiated claims of preserving youth, increasing virility, growing hair, and such. [p. 744]

17. False. The Food and Drug Administration advises cosmetics manufacturers to employ whatever testing is appropriate and effective for substantiating the safety of their products, which may include animal testing. [p. 744]

18. True. Consumer Product Safety Commission (CPSC) is a federal administrative agency empowered to adopt rules and regulations to interpret and enforce the Consumer Product Safety Act. [p. 745]

19. True. The CPSC can seek injunctions, bring actions to seize hazardous consumer products, seek civil penalties for knowing violations of the act or of CPSC rules, and seek criminal penalties for knowing and willful violations of the act or of CPSC rules. [p. 745]

20. True. Certain consumer products, including motor vehicles, boats, aircraft, and firearms, are regulated by other government agencies. [p. 745]

21. False. In 2009, the U.S. Congress enacted the Family Smoking Prevention and Tobacco Control Act. This act requires nine new larger and noticeable warnings to be placed on cigarette packages. [p. 745]

22. False. Health Care Reform Act is a 2010 federal statute that increases the number of persons who have health care insurance in the United States and provides new protections for insured persons from abusive practices of insurance companies. [p. 746]

23. True. The FTC may sue in state or federal court to obtain compensation on behalf of consumers. A decision of the FTC may be appealed to federal court. [p. 747]

24. False. Proof of actual deception is not required for an advertising to be considered false under Section 5 of the FTC. [p. 747]

25. False. Bait occurs when a seller advertises the availability of a low-cost discounted item to attract customers to its store. [p. 747]

26. True. To protect consumers from ill-advised decisions, many states have enacted laws that give the consumer a certain number of days to rescind (i.e., cancel) a door-to-door sales contract. The usual period is three days. [p. 748]

Multiple Choice

27. C. In the United States, the U.S. Department of Agriculture (USDA) is the federal administrative agency that is primarily responsible for regulating meat, poultry, and other food products. [p. 740]

28. A. The U.S. Department of Agriculture (USDA) is a federal administrative agency that is responsible for regulating the safety of meat, poultry, and other food products. [p. 740]

29. B. Food and Drug Administration (FDA) is a federal administrative agency that administers and enforces the federal Food, Drug, and Cosmetic Act and other federal consumer protection laws. [p. 742]

30. B. The FDA can seek search warrants and conduct inspections; obtain orders for the seizure, recall, and condemnation of products; seek injunctions; and turn over suspected criminal violations to the U.S. Department of Justice for prosecution. [p. 742]

31. D. The NLEA applies to packaged foods and other foods regulated by the Food and Drug Administration. The law requires food labels to disclose the number of calories derived from fat and the amount of dietary fiber, saturated fat, trans fat, cholesterol, and a variety of other substances contained in the food. [p. 742]

32. D. The law requires food labels to disclose the number of calories derived from fat and the amount of dietary fiber, saturated fat, trans fat, cholesterol, and a variety of other substances contained in the food. [p. 742]

33. A. In 1990, Congress passed a sweeping truth-in-labeling law called the Nutrition Labeling and Education Act (NLEA). The law requires the disclosure of uniform information about serving sizes and nutrients, and it establishes standard definitions for light (or lite), low fat, fat free, cholesterol free, lean, natural, organic, and other terms routinely bandied about by food processors. [p. 742]

34. D. Food, Drug, and Cosmetic Act is a federal statute that provides the basis for the regulation of much of the testing, manufacture, distribution, and sale of foods, drugs, cosmetics, and medicinal products. [p. 742]

35. C. Biosafety Protocol is a United Nations–sponsored protocol that requires signatory countries to place the label "May contain living modified organisms" on all genetically engineered foods. [p. 743]

36. C. Drug Amendment to the FDCA is a federal law that gives the FDA broad powers to license new drugs in the United States. [p. 743]

37. B. The Food and Drug Administration (FDA), which is responsible for ensuring that cosmetics are safe, does not specifically require that animals be used to test the safety of cosmetics. However, the agency advises cosmetics manufacturers to employ whatever testing is appropriate and effective for substantiating the safety of their products, which may include animal testing. [p. 744]

38. A. In 1976, Congress enacted the Medicinal Device Amendment to the FDCA. This amendment gives the FDA authority to regulate medicinal devices, such as heart pacemakers, kidney dialysis machines, defibrillators, surgical equipment, and other diagnostic, therapeutic, and health devices. [p. 744]

39. A. The Consumer Product Safety Commission (CPSC) is an independent federal administrative agency empowered to (1) adopt rules and regulations to interpret and enforce the CPSA, (2) conduct research on the safety of consumer products, and (3) collect data regarding injuries caused by consumer products. [p. 745]

40. B. Consumer Product Safety Commission (CPSC) is a federal administrative agency empowered to adopt rules and regulations to interpret and enforce the Consumer Product Safety Act. A private party can sue for an injunction to prevent violations of the act or of CPSC rules and regulations. [p. 745]

41. D. In 2009, the U.S. Congress enacted the Family Smoking Prevention and Tobacco Control Act that requires a warning to appear on the top 50 percent of both the front and back of each cigarette package. [p. 745]

42. B. The 2010 Health Care Reform Act mandates that most U.S. citizens and legal residents purchase "minimal essential" health care insurance coverage. Persons who do not obtain coverage will be required to pay a tax penalty to the federal government. [p. 746]

43. D. In addition to requiring and helping fund health care coverage, the Health Care Reform Act provides a number of new protections for insured persons. This includes prohibiting health insurance companies from terminating health insurance coverage when a person gets sick. [p. 747]

44. A. Advertising is false and deceptive under Section 5 of the FTC Act if it (1) contains misinformation or omits important information that is likely to mislead a "reasonable consumer" or (2) makes an unsubstantiated claim. [p. 747]

45. A. The Federal Trade Commission (FTC) was created to enforce the FTC Act as well as other federal consumer protection statutes. The FTC may sue in state or federal court to obtain compensation on behalf of consumers. [p. 747]

Short Answer

46. Consumer protection laws are federal and state statutes and regulations that promote product safety and prohibit abusive, unfair, and deceptive business practices. Originally, sales transactions in this country were guided by the principle of caveat emptor ("let the buyer beware"). This led to abusive practices by businesses that sold adulterated food products and other unsafe products. In response, federal and state governments have enacted a variety of statutes that regulate the safety of food and other products. These laws are collectively referred to as consumer protection laws. [p. 740]

47. The Food, Drug, and Cosmetic Act (FDCA or FDC Act) was enacted in 1938. This federal statute, as amended, regulates the testing, manufacture, distribution, and sale of foods, drugs, cosmetics, and medicinal devices in the United States. The Food and Drug Administration (FDA) is the federal administrative agency empowered to enforce the FDCA.
Before certain food additives, drugs, cosmetics, and medicinal devices can be sold to the public, they must receive FDA approval. An applicant must submit to the FDA an application that contains relevant information about the safety and uses of the product. The FDA, after considering the evidence, will either approve or deny the application. [p. 742]

48. In 1990, Congress passed a sweeping truth-in-labeling law called the Nutrition Labeling and Education Act (NLEA). This statute requires food manufacturers and processors to provide nutrition information on many foods and prohibits them from making scientifically unsubstantiated health claims. The NLEA applies to packaged foods and other foods regulated by the Food and Drug Administration. The law requires food labels to disclose the number of calories derived from fat and the amount of dietary fiber, saturated fat, trans fat, cholesterol, and a variety of other substances contained in the food. The law also requires the disclosure of uniform information about serving sizes and nutrients, and it establishes standard definitions for light (or lite), low fat, fat free, cholesterol free, lean, natural, organic, and other terms routinely bandied about by food processors. [p. 742]

49. In many countries, the food is not genetically altered. However, many food processors in the United States and elsewhere around the world genetically modify some foods by adding genes from other organisms to help crops grow faster or ward off pests. Although the companies insist that genetically altered foods are safe, consumers and many countries began to demand that such foods be clearly labeled so that buyers could decide for themselves. In 2000, more than 150 countries, including the United States, agreed to the United Nations–sponsored Biosafety Protocol for genetically altered foods. The countries agreed that all genetically engineered foods would be clearly labeled with the phrase "May contain living modified organisms." This allows consumers to decide on their own whether to purchase such altered food products. [p. 743]

50. In 1976, Congress enacted the Medicinal Device Amendment to the FDCA. This amendment gives the FDA authority to regulate medicinal devices, such as heart pacemakers, kidney dialysis machines, defibrillators, surgical equipment, and other diagnostic, therapeutic, and health devices. The mislabeling of such devices is prohibited. The FDA is empowered to remove "quack" devices from the market. [p. 744]

51. In 1972, Congress enacted the Consumer Product Safety Act (CPSA) and created the Consumer Product Safety Commission (CPSC). The CPSC is an independent federal administrative agency empowered to (1) adopt rules and regulations to interpret and enforce the CPSA, (2) conduct research on the safety of consumer products, and (3) collect data regarding injuries caused by consumer products.
Because the CPSC regulates potentially dangerous consumer products, it issues product safety standards for consumer products that pose unreasonable risk of injury. If a consumer product is found to be imminently hazardous—that is, if its use causes an unreasonable risk of death or serious injury or illness—the manufacturer can be required to recall, repair, or replace the product or take other corrective action. Alternatively, the CPSC can seek injunctions, bring actions to seize hazardous consumer products, seek civil penalties for knowing violations of the act or of CPSC rules, and seek criminal penalties for knowing and willful violations of the act or of CPSC rules. A private party can sue for an injunction to prevent violations of the act or of CPSC rules and regulations. [p. 745]

52. In addition to requiring and helping fund health care coverage, the Health Care Reform Act provides a number of new protections for insured persons. These protections do the following:
• Prevent insurance companies from denying health care insurance to individuals with preexisting health conditions
• Prohibit health insurance companies from terminating health insurance coverage when a person gets sick
• Prohibit insurers from establishing an annual spending cap for benefit payments
• Prohibit insurers from imposing lifetime limits on benefit payments
• Require health plans that provide dependent coverage to continue coverage for a dependent child until the child turns 26 years of age [p. 747]

53. Advertising is false and deceptive under Section 5 of the FTC Act if it (1) contains misinformation or omits important information that is likely to mislead a "reasonable consumer" or (2) makes an unsubstantiated claim (e.g., "This product is 33 percent better than our competitor's"). Proof of actual deception is not required. Statements of opinion and "sales talk" (e.g., "This is a great car") do not constitute false and deceptive advertising.
Example Kentucky Fried Chicken entered into an agreement with the FTC whereby KFC withdrew television commercials in which it claimed that its "fried chicken can, in fact, be part of a healthy diet." [p. 747]

54. Bait and switch is a type of deceptive advertising under Section 5 of the FTC Act. It occurs when a seller advertises the availability of a low-cost discounted item (the "bait") to attract customers to its store. Once the customers are in the store, however, the seller pressures them to purchase more expensive merchandise (the "switch"). The FTC states that a bait and switch occurs if the seller refuses to show consumers the advertised merchandise, discourages employees from selling the advertised merchandise, or fails to have adequate quantities of the advertised merchandise available. [p. 747]

55. The Federal Communications Commission (FCC) is a federal administrative agency that regulates communications by radio, television, cable, wire, and satellite. In 2003, the FCC and the Federal Trade Commission (FTC) promulgated administrative rules that created the Do-Not-Call Registry. Consumers can place their names on this registry and free themselves from most unsolicited commercial telephone calls. The FTC and FCC were given authority to adopt their coordinated do-not-call rules in several federal statutes. Both wire-connected phones and wireless phones can be registered. Telemarketers have three months from the date on which a consumer signs up for the registry to remove the customer's phone number from their sales call list. Customer registration remains valid for five years and can be renewed. Charitable and political organizations are exempt from the registry. Also, an "established business relationship" exception allows businesses to call a customer for ten months after they sell or lease goods or services to that person or conduct a financial transaction with that person. The Do-Not-Call Registry allows consumers to designate specific companies not to call them, including those that otherwise qualify for the established business relationship exemption. [p. 748]

45 | ENVIRONMENTAL PROTECTION

Chapter Overview

With the great increases in population growth, urbanization, and all forms of industry, our desire for higher profits, more products, and technological advancement lead to damage to the environment on a worldwide basis. In an effort to curtail the damaging effects of pollution, the federal government and states have created environmental protection laws that apply to all businesses and individuals. This chapter examines the efforts of the government to contain the levels of pollution that is still being made, while cleaning up huge amounts of pollution and hazardous waste that have been dumped into the environment.

Objectives

Upon completion of the exercises in this chapter, you should be able to
1. Describe an environmental impact statement and identify when one is needed.
2. Describe the Clean Air Act and national ambient air quality standards.
3. Describe the Clean Water Act and effluent water standards.
4. Explain how environmental laws regulate the use of toxic substances and the disposal of hazardous wastes.
5. Describe how the Endangered Species Act protects endangered and threatened species and their habitats.

Practical Application

Upon mastering the concepts in this chapter, you will understand the theory and application of environmental protections laws. You will recognize when an action violates one of the laws and the remedies for the violation.

Helpful Hints

With all of the different regulations that have been enacted to curtail pollution and its effects upon the environment, it is helpful if you organize your analysis of any situation based upon the type of damage done or the segment of the environment that is at risk. This will lead you to the correct statute or regulation for guidance as to how the situation will be handled by the appropriate agency or the courts.

Study Tips

You should organize your study of environmental protection by looking at the areas of the environment that are protected. Examine the laws and cases within the areas of air, water, toxic and hazardous substances, nuclear waste, and endangered species.

Environmental Protection and Global Warming

Pollution causes significant harm to humans and various forms of wildlife by contaminating water, air, and the environment. Because voluntary pollution control was not successful, the government took on the regulation and control of pollution.

Environmental Protection

In an effort to protect the environment from pollution, the federal government began enacting protective statutes in the 1970s to regulate air and water quality, hazardous wastes, and to protect wildlife. State statutes have been enacted to work with federal law and both provide civil and criminal penalties.

Environmental Protection Agency. With the creation of the Environmental Protection Agency (EPA) by Congress in 1970, the federal government had a vehicle for implementing and enforcing federal environmental protection laws.
- The EPA can make rules, adopt regulations, hold hearings, make decisions, and order remedies for violation of federal environmental laws.
- The EPA can also initiate judicial proceedings against violators.

Environmental Impact Statement (EIS). The National Environmental Policy Act became effective in January 1970, which requires that an environmental impact statement must be prepared to assess the adverse impact that any legislation or federal action will have upon the environment.
- The EIS must:
  - describe the affected environment,
  - describe the impact of the proposed federal action on the environment,
  - identify and discuss alternatives to the proposed action,
  - list the resources that will be committed to the action, and
  - contain a cost–benefit analysis of the proposed action and alternative actions.
- This study is required before the project or legislation can be approved.
- Each state has a similar statute.

Air Pollution

The Clean Air Act provides comprehensive regulation of air quality in the United States.

Sources of Air Pollution.
- *Stationary Sources.* Sources of pollution that do not move, such as industrial plants.
- *Mobile Sources.* Sources of pollution that move from place to place, such as automobiles.

National Ambient Air Quality Standards (NAAQS). The Clean Air Act directs the EPA to establish standards for certain pollutants.
- *Primary Levels.* Protect humans.
- *Secondary Levels.* Protect vegetation, climate, visibility, and economic values.
- The states are responsible for enforcing these levels.

Nonattainment Areas. Regions that do not meet air quality standards, classified as marginal, moderate, serious, severe or extreme.
- Deadlines are established for areas to meet attainment levels.

- States must submit compliance plans that
    - identify major sources of air pollution and require installation of pollution control equipment
    - institute permit systems for new stationary courses
    - implement inspection programs to monitor mobile sources.
- States that fail to develop and implement a plan are subject to the following sanctions:
    - loss of federal highway funds
    - limitations on new sources of emissions (prohibits new construction of industrial plants in the nonattainment area).

Indoor Air Pollution. This is a serious problem that is not regulated.
- Some buildings have air that is 100 times more polluted than the outdoor air.
- This is caused mainly by tightly sealed buildings and exposure to indoor chemicals and construction materials.

Water Pollution

The Clean Water Act has been updated and amended several times from 1948 to 1987. Pursuant to the act, the EPA has established water quality standards that define which bodies of water can be used for drinking water, recreation, wildlife, and agricultural and industrial uses.

Point Sources of Water Pollution. The Clean Water Act authorizes the EPA to establish water pollution standards for point sources of water pollution, which are stationary sources of pollution such as paper mills, manufacturing plants, electric utility plants, and sewage plants.
- The EPA sets standards for technology that must be used and requires dischargers of pollution to keep records, maintain monitoring equipment, and keep samples of discharges.

Thermal Pollution. The Clean Water Act prohibits thermal pollution because it damages the ecological balance and decreases oxygen in a waterway.

Wetlands. The Clean Water Act forbids the filling or dredging of wetlands unless a permit has been obtained from the Army Corps of Engineers.
- Wetlands include swamps, bogs, marshes, and similar areas that support birds, animals, and vegetative life.

The Safe Drinking Water Act. The Safe Drinking Water Act authorizes the EPA to establish national primary drinking water standards.
- The act prohibits dumping of waste into wells.

Ocean Protection. The Marine Protection, Research, and Sanctuaries Act requires a permit for dumping waste and foreign material into ocean waters and establishes marine sanctuaries as far seaward as the Continental Shelf and in the Great Lakes and their connecting waters.
- The Clean Water Act authorizes the U.S. government to clean up oil spills within 12 miles of shore and on the Continental Shelf and to recover the cleanup costs from responsible parties.
- The Oil Pollution Act of 1990, which is administered by the Coast Guard, requires the oil industry to adopt procedures that can more readily respond to oil spills.

Toxic Substances and Hazardous Waste

Many of the chemicals used for agriculture, mining, and industry contain toxic substances that cause birth defects, cancer, and other health-related problems. Wastes from agriculture, mining, and industry may contain hazardous substances that can cause or significantly contribute to an increase in mortality or serious illness or pose a hazard to human health or the environment if it is not handled properly.

Toxic Substances Control. The Toxic Substances Control Act requires manufacturers and processors to test new chemicals to determine their effect on human health and the environment before the EPA will allow them to be marketed.
- The EPA requires special labeling for toxic substances and may limit or prohibit their manufacture and sale.
- A toxic substance that poses an imminent hazard may be removed from commerce.

Insecticides, Fungicides, and Rodenticides. The Insecticide, Fungicide, and Rodenticide Act requires pesticides, herbicides, fungicides, and rodenticides to be registered with the EPA.
- The EPA may deny, suspend, or cancel the registration if it finds that the chemical poses an imminent danger.
- The EPA sets standards for the amount of residue that is permitted on crops sold for human and animal consumption.

Hazardous Waste. Congress enacted the Resource Conservation and Recovery Act to regulate the disposal of new hazardous waste.
- The act authorizes the EPA to regulate facilities that generate, treat, store, transport, and dispose of hazardous wastes.
- Any substance that is toxic, radioactive, or corrosive or can ignite is a hazardous material.
- Hazardous wastes are tracked and regulated from the moment they are created to the time of their final disposal or storage.

Superfund. The Comprehensive Environmental Response, Compensation, and Liability Act, which is known as the "Superfund," gave the federal government a mandate to deal with years of abuse and neglect in the disposal of hazardous waste. The EPA is required by the Superfund to:
- identify sites in the United States where hazardous wastes have been disposed, stored, abandoned, or spilled, and
- rank these sites regarding the severity of the risk they pose.
  - The sites with the highest ranking are put on a National Priority List.
    - The sites on this list receive first priority for cleanup.
  - Studies are conducted to determine the best method for cleaning up the site.
  - The Superfund provides for the creation of a fund to finance cleanup of sites.
- The EPA can order a responsible party to clean up a hazardous waste site.
  - If the party fails to do so, the EPA can clean up the site and recover the cost from any responsible party under a theory of strict liability.
  - The cost of cleanup can be recovered from:
    - the generator who deposited the wastes
    - the transporter of the wastes to the site
    - the owner of the site at the time of disposal
    - the current owner and operator of the site.

Nuclear Waste

Nuclear power plants create radioactive waste that maintains a high level of radioactivity for a very long period of time.
- The Nuclear Regulatory Commission (NRC) regulates the construction and opening of commercial nuclear power plants.
  - The NRC monitors the plants and may close an unsafe plant.
- The EPA sets standards for allowable levels of radioactivity in the environment and regulates the disposal of radioactive waste.
  - The EPA also regulates thermal pollution caused by the nuclear power plants and emissions and uranium production.
- The Nuclear Waste Policy Act of 1982 mandates that the federal government select and develop a permanent site for the disposal of nuclear wastes.

Global Warming

Scientists have been concerned for decades about global warming and its effect on the earth's protective ozone layer.
- Sea levels are rising because ice sheets are melting.
- Increasing global temperatures will cause extreme weather events, changes in agriculture yields, increased disease, and species extinctions.

Endangered Species

The Endangered Species Act protects endangered species and threatened species of animals.
- The EPA and the Department of Commerce designate critical habitats for each endangered and threatened species.
- Real estate or other development in these habitats is prohibited or severely limited.
- In addition to the Endangered Species Act, there are numerous other acts that protect migratory birds, eagles, horses, burros, marine mammals, and fish.

State Environmental Protection Laws

Many state and local governments have adopted laws to protect the environment and often require that an EIS be prepared before any proposed action by both governmental and private parties.
- States often enact laws to protect specific, unique areas within their boundaries.

Refresh Your Memory

The following exercise will give you the opportunity to test your memory of the principles given in this chapter. Read the question twice and place your answer in the blank provided. Review the chapter material for any question that you are unable to answer or remember.

1. _____ is a document that must be prepared for any proposed legislation or major federal action that significantly affects the quality of the human environment.

2. The _____ is a federal statute which mandates that the federal government consider the adverse impact a federal government action would have on the environment before the action is implemented.

3. The _____ was enacted in 1963 to assist states in dealing with air pollution.

4. _____ are certain standards for pollutants set by the EPA that protect (1) human beings (primary level) and (2) vegetation, matter, climate, visibility, and economic values (secondary level).

5. The EPA has divided each state into _____ to monitor and ensure compliance.

6. Regions that do not meet air quality standards are designated _____.

7. Heated water or material discharged into waterways that upsets the ecological balance and decreases the oxygen content is called _____.

8. _____ are defined as areas that are inundated or saturated by surface water or ground water that support vegetation typically adapted for life in saturated soil conditions.

9. The _____ is authorized to enforce this statute and to issue permits for discharge of dredged or fill material into navigable waters and qualified wetlands in the United States.

10. _____ is a federal statute that extends limited environmental protection to the oceans.

11. _____ are chemicals used by agriculture, industry, business, mining, and households that cause injury to humans, birds, animals, fish, and vegetation.

12. _____ is a federal statute that authorizes the EPA to regulate facilities that generate, treat, store, transport, and dispose of hazardous wastes.

13. _____ is a federal statute that authorizes the federal government to deal with hazardous wastes.

14. Emissions from radioactive wastes that can cause injury and death to humans and other life and can cause severe damage to the environment is called _____.

15. _____ is a federal agency that licenses the construction and opening of commercial nuclear power plants.

Critical Thought Exercise

The citizens of Marzville, Ohio, became concerned when they started noticing very high rates of death and birth defects in the community. The Friends of Marzville (FOM), an environmental group, investigated the situation and it was discovered that a hazardous waste disposal site in Marzville had polluted the ground water with very high levels of carcinogenic chemicals. Fast Dump, who had purchased the land from Wow Chemical Company, runs the disposal site. Wow Chemical had operated a chemical manufacturing facility at the site from 1951 to 1982. Wow Chemical dumped hundreds of thousands of gallons of chemicals and contaminated water into open pits and into a drainage pipe that emptied into the Marzville Creek, which in turn emptied into Marzville Lake. Fast Dump takes in solid and liquid waste from numerous sources, including Tripp Trucking, a hazardous waste transportation company who has the exclusive contract to haul all the hazardous waste for the huge, multinational petro-chemical corporation, Chemkill.

What relief can FOM seek for the citizens of Marzville? Who may be liable for the horrible situation in Marzville and the massive cleanup that is needed?

Please compose your answer to the Critical Thinking Exercise using a separate sheet of paper or your computer word processing program.

Practice Quiz

True/False

16. _____ The Environmental Protection Agency lacks adjudicative powers to hold hearings and order remedies for violation of environmental laws.

17. _____ An EIS must contain a cost–benefit analysis of the proposed action and alternative actions.

18. _____ An EIS can be challenged in court by environmentalists and other interested parties.

19. _____ The Clean Air Act does not apply to stationary sources of pollution.

20. _____ The pollutant standards under the NAAQS are set in two levels.

21. _____ The right to enforce air pollution standards is an exclusive prerogative of the federal government.

22. _____ Regions that do not meet air quality standards are designated as air quality control regions.

23. _____ The third category of the nonattainment areas is labeled "serious."

24. _____ Indoor air pollution is primarily caused by toxic fumes from industrial plants located in cities.

25. _____ The federal government is primarily responsible for the implementation of the Clear Water Act in all states.

26. _____ Point sources are sources of pollution that are fixed and stationary.

27. _____ The Marine Protection, Research, and Sanctuaries Act, enacted in 1972, extends environmental protection to the oceans.

28. _____ The Oil Pollution Act authorizes the U.S. government to clean up oil spills and spills of other hazardous substances in ocean waters within 12 miles of the shore.

29. _____ The Superfund is financed through taxes on products that contain hazardous substances.

30. _____ The Endangered Species Act applies only to private parties.

Multiple Choice

31. The National Environmental Policy Act is a federal statute which mandates that the federal government must _____.

A. consider focusing on air and water pollution to the exclusion of other sources of pollution as these two modes of pollution have the greatest impact on human lives
B. execute a complete ban on the commercial usage of the two hundred toxic substances identified as being harmful and polluting
C. consider the adverse impact a federal government action would have on the environment before the action is implemented
D. implement a zero-tolerance policy for all business activities that discharge waste products into water bodies

32. Which of the following is a document required by the NEPA that must be prepared for any proposed legislation or major federal action that significantly affects the quality of the human environment?

A. environmental impact statement
B. environmental impact abstract
C. environmental impact design
D. strategic environmental assessment

33. Which of the following would be considered a stationary source of air pollution?

A. oil rigs
B. aircrafts
C. cargo ships
D. automobiles

34. Which of the following is true of the Clean Air Act?

A. It is the only major state law regulating air pollution in the United States.
B. It fails to include the air pollution caused by fuel and fuel additives in its purview.
C. It requires air pollution controls to be installed on motor vehicles.
D. It is only concerned with stationary sources of air pollution.

35. The primary level of the NAAQS protects _____.

A. flora
B. climate
C. water bodies
D. human beings

36. Which of the following is true of the NAAQS?

A. Only standards for oxides of elements and particulate matter are evaluated under the NAAQS.
B. The state governments are responsible for setting standards for air quality in their respective state.
C. Human beings are protected under the secondary level of the NAAQS.
D. The federal government has the right to enforce these air pollution standards if the states fail to do so.

37. A geographical area that does not meet established air quality standards is designated as a(n)
_____.

A. limited pollution area
B. zoned ordinance area
C. nonattainment area
D. federal regulation area

38. Which of the following measures is likely to reduce indoor air pollution?

A. complete air conditioning with sealed windows
B. heavy insulation
C. no-fragrance policy
D. closure of all air ducts

39. Which of the following is primarily responsible for enforcing the provisions of the Clean Water Act regulations?

A. the federal government
B. the state government
C. independent agencies
D. non-profit organizations

40. Areas that are inundated or saturated by surface water or ground water that support vegetation typically adapted for life in such conditions are called _____.

A. marine reefs
B. wetlands
C. gullies
D. reservoirs

41. The Clean Water Act forbids the filling or dredging of navigable waters and qualified wetlands unless a permit has been obtained from the _____.

A. Ministry of Environmental Protection
B. Environmental Protection Agency
C. U.S. Army Corps of Engineers
D. Nuclear Regulatory Commission

42. The _____ is a federal statute that authorizes the EPA to establish national primary potable water standards.

A. Comprehensive Environmental Response, Compensation, and Liability Act
B. Federal Water Pollution Control Act
C. Safe Drinking Water Act
D. Clean Water Act

43. The U.S. Coast Guard administers the Oil Pollution Act which requires the oil industry to _____.

A. obtain a permit for dumping wastes and other foreign materials into ocean waters
B. adopt procedures and contingency plans to readily respond to and clean up oil spills
C. implement measures to avoid dumping of wastes into wells used for drinking water
D. establish marine sanctuaries in ocean waters as far seaward as the edge of the continental shelf

44. The Superfund Act, administered by the EPA, gives the federal government a mandate to _____.

A. establish marine sanctuaries in ocean waters as far seaward as the edge of the continental shelf
B. cleanup hazardous wastes that have been spilled, stored, or abandoned
C. impose fines on buildings and office that cause harm to their occupants due to indoor air pollution
D. set standards on the toxic substances that can be used or sold

45. Which of the following is true of the Endangered Species Act?

A. It empowers the secretary of the interior to declare a form of wildlife as endangered.
B. It is the only federal law that protects wildlife at present.
C. It does not include marine species and amphibian life forms.
D. It applies only to the government taking of any endangered species.

Short Answer

46. Describe the purpose and requirements of an EIS?

_____
_____

47. What are the sources of air pollution?

_____
_____

48. Explain the nature and enforcement of the NAAQS?

_____
_____

49. What are nonattainment areas?

_____
_____

50. What are the effects of water pollution? What steps has the Congress taken to control it?

_____
_____

51. What is thermal pollution?

_____
_____

52. What are the measures taken to protect wetlands in the United States?

_____

_____

53. Describe any two legislations that have been implemented to minimize the damage caused by oil spills.

_____

_____

54. How are endangered species protected in the United States? Name three laws that protect wildlife species.

_____

_____

55. Give an account of the state environmental protection laws.

_____

_____

Answers to Refresh Your Memory

1. Environmental impact statement [p. 752]
2. National Environmental Policy Act [p. 752]
3. Clean Air Act [p. 753]
4. National ambient air quality standards [p. 753]
5. air quality control regions [p. 753]
6. nonattainment areas [p. 754]
7. thermal pollution [p. 756]
8. Wetlands [p. 756]
9. U.S. Army Corps of Engineers [p. 756]
10. Marine Protection, Research, and Sanctuaries Act [p. 757]
11. Toxic substances [p. 758]
12. Resource Conservation and Recovery Act [p. 759]
13. Comprehensive Environmental Response, Compensation, and Liability Act [p. 759]
14. radiation pollution [p. 760]
15. Nuclear Regulatory Commission [p. 760]

Critical Thought Exercise Model Answer

Congress enacted the Comprehensive Environmental Response, Compensation, and Liability Act, known as the "Superfund," which gave the federal government the authority and duty to deal with hazardous wastes dumped, spilled, or abandoned in such a manner that a serious risk to public health has been created. The EPA is responsible for identifying hazardous waste sites in need of cleanup and coordinating studies to determine the best way to handle the situation. The EPA has authority to clean up hazardous sites quickly to prevent explosion, contamination of drinking water, or other imminent danger. Because Marzville's drinking water is contaminated, the city will be entitled to priority over other cleanup sites. The EPA can order a responsible party to clean up a hazardous waste site. If the party fails to do so, the EPA can clean up the site and recover the cost of cleanup. The Superfund imposes strict liability for all those involved in use of the site. The EPA can recover costs from the generator who deposited the waste, the transporter of the waste to the site, the owner of the site at the time of the disposal, and the current owner or operator of the site. Liability is joint and several, so that any party who is at fault even to the slightest degree will be responsible for the entire cleanup.

In the Marzville situation, Wow Chemical is liable as the original owner at the time the chemicals were dumped. Chemkill is liable as a generator of waste, and Tripp Trucking is liable as the transporter of the waste to the facility. Fast Dump is liable as the current operator. Superfund law applies retroactively, so acts of dumping at the Marzville site prior to 1980 are still covered. The application of the Superfund law only applies to the cost of cleanup. Any party damaged by the hazardous waste dumping can still pursue his/her own suit under applicable tort theories.

Answers to Practice Quiz

True/False

16. False. The EPA has broad rule-making powers to adopt regulations to advance the laws that it is empowered to administer. The agency also has adjudicative powers to hold hearings, make decisions, and order remedies for violations of federal environmental laws. [p. 752]

17. True. The environmental impact statement (EIS) is a document that must be prepared for any proposed legislation or major federal action that significantly affects the quality of the human environment. It contains a cost–benefit analysis of the proposed action and alternative actions. [p. 752]

18. True. Most states and many local governments have enacted laws that require an EIS to be prepared regarding proposed state and local government action as well as private development. These projects can be challenged in state court. [p. 753]

19. False. The Clean Air Act requires states to identify major stationary sources and develop plans to reduce air pollution from these sources. [p. 753]

20. True. The Clean Air Act directs the EPA to establish national ambient air quality standards (NAAQS) for certain pollutants. These standards are set at two different levels: primary (to protect human beings) and secondary (to protect vegetation, matter, climate, visibility, and economic values). [p. 753]

21. False. Although the EPA establishes air quality standards, the states are responsible for their enforcement. The federal government has the right to enforce these air pollution standards if the states fail to do so. [p. 753]

22. False. The EPA has divided each state into air quality control regions (AQCRs). Each region is monitored to ensure compliance. [p. 753]

23. True. A nonattainment area is classified into one of five categories—marginal, moderate, serious, severe, or extreme—based on the degree to which it exceeds the ozone standard. [p. 754]

24. False. Indoor air pollution has two primary causes. In an effort to reduce dependence on foreign oil, many recently constructed office buildings have been overly insulated and built with sealed windows and no outside air ducts. As a result, no fresh air enters many workplaces. [p. 754]

25. False. States are primarily responsible for enforcing the provisions of the Clean Water Act and EPA regulations adopted thereunder. If a state fails to do so, the federal government may enforce the act. [p. 754]

26. True. The Clean Water Act authorizes the EPA to establish water pollution control standards for point sources of water pollution. Point sources are sources of pollution that are fixed and stationary. [p. 755]

27. True. The Marine Protection, Research, and Sanctuaries Act is a federal statute that extends limited environmental protection to the oceans. [p. 757]

28. False. The Oil Pollution Act is a federal statute that requires the oil industry to take measures to prevent oil spills and to readily respond to and clean up oil spills. [p. 757]

29. True. In 1980, Congress enacted the Comprehensive Environmental Response, Compensation, and Liability Act (CERCLA), which is commonly called the Superfund. The fund is financed through taxes on chemicals, feedstock, motor fuels, and other products that contain hazardous substances. [p. 759]

30. False. The Endangered Species Act, which applies to both government and private persons, prohibits the taking of any endangered species. [p. 760]

Multiple Choice

31. C. The National Environmental Policy Act (NEPA) became effective January 1, 1970.1 The NEPA mandates that the federal government consider the "adverse impact" of proposed legislation, rulemaking, or other federal government action on the environment before the action is implemented. [p. 752]

32. A. The NEPA and EPA regulations require that an environmental impact statement (EIS) be prepared by the federal government for any proposed legislation or major federal action that significantly affects the quality of the natural and human environment. [p. 752]

33. A. Substantial amounts of air pollution are emitted by stationary sources of air pollution (e.g., industrial plants, oil refineries, public utilities). [p. 753]

34. C. In an effort to control emissions from these mobile sources of air pollution, the Clean Air Act requires air pollution controls to be installed on motor vehicles. [p. 753]

35. D. The Clean Air Act directs the EPA to establish national ambient air quality standards (NAAQS) for certain pollutants. These standards are set at two different levels: primary (to protect human beings) and secondary (to protect vegetation, matter, climate, visibility, and economic values). [p. 753]

36. D. Although the EPA establishes air quality standards, the states are responsible for their enforcement. The federal government has the right to enforce these air pollution standards if the states fail to do so. [p. 753]

37. C. Regions that do not meet air quality standards are designated nonattainment areas. A nonattainment area is classified into one of five categories—marginal, moderate, serious, severe, or extreme—based on the degree to which it exceeds the ozone standard. [p. 754]

38. C. Indoor air pollution has two primary causes. In an effort to reduce dependence on foreign oil, many recently constructed office buildings have been overly insulated and built with sealed windows and no outside air ducts. As a result, no fresh air enters many workplaces. [p. 754]

39. B. States are primarily responsible for enforcing the provisions of the Clean Water Act and EPA regulations adopted thereunder. If a state fails to do so, the federal government may enforce the act. [p. 754]

40. B. Wetlands are defined as areas that are inundated or saturated by surface water or ground water that support vegetation typically adapted for life in saturated soil conditions. Wetlands include swamps, marshes, bogs, and similar areas that support birds, animals, and vegetative life. [p. 756]

41. C. The U.S. Army Corps of Engineers (USACE) is authorized to enforce this statute and to issue permits for discharge of dredged or fill material into navigable waters and qualified wetlands in the United States. [p. 756]

42. C. The Safe Drinking Water Act, enacted in 1974 and amended in 1986, authorizes the EPA to establish national primary drinking water standards (setting the minimum quality of water for human consumption). The act prohibits the dumping of wastes into wells used for drinking water. [p. 756]

43. B. In response, in 1990, Congress enacted the federal Oil Pollution Act, which is administered by the U.S. Coast Guard. This act requires the oil industry to adopt procedures and contingency plans to readily respond to and clean up oil spills. [p. 757]

44. B. The Superfund requires the EPA to (1) identify sites in the United States where hazardous wastes have been disposed of, stored, abandoned, or spilled and (2) rank these sites regarding the severity of the risk. The hazardous waste sites with the highest ranking receive first consideration for cleanup. [p. 759]

45. A. The Endangered Species Act was enacted in 1973. The act, as amended, protects endangered and threatened species of wildlife. The secretary of the interior is empowered to declare a form of wildlife as endangered or threatened. [p. 760]

Short Answer

46. The purpose of an EIS is to provide enough information about the environment to enable the federal government to determine the feasibility of the project. An EIS must (1) describe the affected environment, (2) describe the impact of the proposed federal action on the environment, (3) identify and discuss alternatives to the proposed action, (4) list the resources that will be committed to the action, and (5) contain a cost–benefit analysis of the proposed action and alternative actions. [p. 752]

47. Substantial amounts of air pollution are emitted by stationary sources of air pollution (e.g., industrial plants, oil refineries, public utilities). The Clean Air Act requires states to identify major stationary sources and develop plans to reduce air pollution from these sources. Automobile and other vehicle emissions are a major source of air pollution in this country. In an effort to control emissions from these mobile sources of air pollution, the Clean Air Act requires air pollution controls to be installed on motor vehicles. Emission standards have been set for

automobiles, trucks, buses, motorcycles, and airplanes. In addition, the Clean Air Act authorizes the EPA to regulate air pollution caused by fuel and fuel additives. [p. 753]

48. The Clean Air Act directs the EPA to establish national ambient air quality standards (NAAQS) for certain pollutants. These standards are set at two different levels: primary, which is to protect human beings, and secondary, which is to protect vegetation, matter, climate, visibility, and economic values. Specific standards have been established for carbon monoxide, nitrogen oxide, sulfur oxide, ozone, lead, and particulate matter.
Although the EPA establishes air quality standards, the states are responsible for their enforcement. The federal government has the right to enforce these air pollution standards if the states fail to do so. Each state is required to prepare a state implementation plan (SIP) that specifies the state plans to meet the federal standards. The EPA has divided each state into air quality control regions (AQCRs). [p. 753]

49. Regions that do not meet air quality standards are designated nonattainment areas. A nonattainment area is classified into one of five categories—marginal, moderate, serious, severe, or extreme—based on the degree to which it exceeds the ozone standard. Deadlines are established for areas to meet the attainment level.
States must submit compliance plans that (1) identify major sources of air pollution and require them to install pollution-control equipment, (2) institute permit systems for new stationary sources, and (3) implement inspection programs to monitor mobile sources. States that fail to develop or implement approved plans are subject to the following sanctions: loss of federal highway funds and limitations on new sources of emissions (e.g., the EPA can prohibit the construction of a new pollution-causing industrial plant in a nonattainment area). [p. 754]

50. Water pollution affects human health, recreation, agriculture, and business. Pollution of waterways by industry and humans has caused severe ecological and environmental problems, including making water sources unsafe for human consumption, fish, birds, and animals. The federal government has enacted a comprehensive scheme of statutes and regulations to prevent and control water pollution.
In 1948, Congress enacted the Federal Water Pollution Control Act (FWPCA) to regulate water pollution. This act has been amended several times. As amended, it is simply referred to as the Clean Water Act.5 This act is administered by the EPA. [p. 754]

51. The Clean Water Act expressly forbids thermal pollution because the discharge of heated water or materials into the nation's waterways can upset the ecological balance; decrease the oxygen content of water; and harm fish, birds, and other animals that use the waterways.8
Sources of thermal pollution (e.g., electric utility companies, manufacturing plants) are subject to the provisions of the Clean Water Act and regulations adopted by the EPA.
Examples – Electric utility plants and manufacturing plants often cause thermal pollution by discharging heated water or materials into the water. This heated water or material could harm fish in the water as well as birds and other animals that use the water. [p. 756]

52. Wetlands are defined as areas that are inundated or saturated by surface water or ground water that support vegetation typically adapted for life in saturated soil conditions. Wetlands include swamps, marshes, bogs, and similar areas that support birds, animals, and vegetative life. The federal Clean Water Act regulates the discharge of dredged or fill material into navigable water and wetlands that have a significant nexus to navigable waters. The U.S. Army Corps of Engineers (USACE) is authorized to enforce this statute and to issue permits for discharge of dredged or fill material into navigable waters and qualified wetlands in the United States. The

Clean Water Act forbids the filling or dredging of navigable waters and qualified wetlands unless a permit has been obtained from the Army Corps of Engineers. [p. 756]

53. There have been several major oil spills from oil tankers and oil drilling facilities in ocean waters off the coast of the United States. These oil spills have caused significant damage to plant, animal, and human life, as well as to their habitats. Two legislations that have been implemented to minimize the damage caused by oil spills are described below.

The Clean Water Act authorizes the U.S. government to clean up oil spills and spills of other hazardous substances in ocean waters within 12 miles of the shore and on the continental shelf and to recover the cleanup costs from responsible parties.

The federal Oil Pollution Act is administered by the U.S. Coast Guard. This act requires the oil industry to adopt procedures and contingency plans to readily respond to and clean up oil spills. A tanker owner-operator must prove that it is fully insured to cover any liability that may occur from an oil spill. The act also requires oil tankers to have double hulls by 2015. [p. 754, 757]

54. In the United States, endangered species are protected under the Endangered Species Act that was enacted in 1973. The secretary of the interior is empowered to declare a form of wildlife as endangered or threatened. The act requires the EPA and the Department of Commerce to designate critical habitats for each endangered and threatened species. Real estate and other development in these areas is prohibited or severely limited. The secretary of commerce is empowered to enforce the provisions of the act as to marine species. In addition, the Endangered Species Act, which applies to both government and private persons, prohibits the taking of any endangered species. Taking is defined as an act intended to "harass, harm, pursue, hunt, shoot, wound, kill, trap, capture, or collect" an endangered animal. [p. 760]

55. Many state and local governments have enacted statutes and ordinances to protect the environment. Most states require that an EIS or a report be prepared for any proposed state action. In addition, under their police power to protect the "health, safety, and welfare" of their residents, many states require private industry to prepare EISs for proposed developments. Some states have enacted special environmental statutes to protect unique areas within their boundaries. [p. 761]

46 | ANTITRUST LAW AND UNFAIR TRADE PRACTICES

Chapter Overview

Post-Civil War, America changed from an agricultural to an industrialized nation. Freedom of competition took a huge blow with the formation of powerful business trusts that monopolized large segments of the country's economy. The anticompetitive practices of these large corporate enterprises resulted in monopolies in the oil, gas, sugar, cotton, and whiskey industries. Congress then passed antitrust laws to limit the anticompetitive behavior of powerful trusts. The laws were written in general language, much like the Constitution, so that they could be applied to a broad range of activity and have the ability to respond to economic, business, and technological changes. This chapter examines antitrust laws that strive to preserve freedom in the marketplace.

Objectives

Upon completion of the exercises in this chapter you should be able to
1. Describe the enforcement of federal antitrust laws.
2. Describe the horizontal and vertical restraints of trade that violate Section 1 of the Sherman Act.
3. Identify acts of monopolization that violate Section 2 of the Sherman Act.
4. Explain how the lawfulness of mergers is examined under Section 7 of the Clayton Act.
5. Apply Section 5 of the Federal Trade
Commission Act to antitrust cases.

Practical Application

As seen in the application of antitrust laws in the case of United States v Microsoft Corp., antitrust laws remain a vital part of the federal government's enforcement of freedom of competition. Whether it is the small investor, consumer, or business partners of large corporations, anticompetitive behavior can still damage many economic interests. When corporations are allowed to dominate large segments of the economy, their failure is more devastating because there is a void that is unfilled by an able competitor. The government will continue to examine each merger, acquisition, and anticompetitive contract through the scope of the federal antitrust laws. Our economy depends upon their existence and enforcement.

Helpful Hints

There can be no meaningful discussion of antitrust law until you understand the mandates of the major federal antitrust laws and the activities that trigger their application to the conduct of an individual, small business, or corporation. Examine each act individually and pay close attention to the type of conduct that it prohibits. Then focus on the types of activity that have triggered federal intervention in the past. This will make you better able to predict what type of behavior will be called into question in the future.

Study Tips

An organized examination of the individual antitrust laws and acts forbidden by the important sections is key to your understanding antitrust law. You must understand the general proposition or prohibition of each section and the specific practice or activity that violates the section.

Antitrust Law and Unfair Trade Practices

Where common law proved inadequate, Congress enacted antitrust legislation to limit anticompetitive activity by businesses.

Federal Antitrust Law

Federal antitrust law is an amalgamation of several major statutes that prohibit or limit anticompetitive and monopolistic behavior.
- Antitrust laws provide for both government and private suits.

Federal Antitrust Statutes.
- The Sherman Act. A federal statute, enacted in 1890, that makes certain restraints of trade and monopolistic acts illegal.
- The Clayton Act. A federal statute, enacted in 1914, that regulates mergers and prohibits certain exclusive dealing arrangements.
- The Federal Trade Commission Act (FTC Act). A federal statute enacted in 1914, prohibits unfair methods of competition.
- The Robinson-Patman Act. A federal statute, enacted in 1930, that prohibits price discrimination.

Government Actions. Enforcement of antitrust laws is divided between the Antitrust Division of the Justice Department and the Bureau of Competition of the Federal Trade Commission (FTC).
- The Sherman Act is the only major act with criminal sanctions.
- The government may seek civil damages, including treble damages for antitrust violations.
- The courts can also order divestiture of assets, cancellation of contracts, liquidation of businesses, or any other reasonable remedy that will effectuate freedom of competition.

Private Actions. Any private person who suffers antitrust injury to his or her business or property can bring a private civil action against the offenders.
- They may recover treble damages, costs of suit, and attorneys' fees.

Effect of a Government Judgment. A judgment against a defendant for a violation of antitrust law is *prima facie* evidence of liability in a private civil treble-damages action.
- Defendants often opt to settle a government action by entering a plea of *nolo contendere* in a criminal action or a consent decree in a civil action, as the defendant does not admit guilt.
- Section 16 of the Clayton Act allows the government or a private plaintiff an injunction against anticompetitive behavior that violates antitrust laws.
  - Only the FTC can obtain an injunction under the FTC Act.

Restraints of Trade: Section 1 of the Sherman Antitrust Act

Section 1 outlaws restraints of trade. To determine the lawfulness of a restraint, the court applies the rule of reason and the *per se* rule.

Rule of Reason. The Supreme Court held that only unreasonable restraints of trade violate Section 1. The courts examine the following factors when trying to apply the rule of reason:
- The pro- and anticompetitive effects of the challenged restraint
- The competitive structure of the industry
- The firm's market share and power
- The history and duration of the restraint
- Other relevant factors

Per Se **Rule.** Some restraints are automatically a violation of Section 1 and no balancing of pro- and anticompetitive effects is necessary.
- Once a restraint is characterized as a *per se* violation, there is no defense or justifications for the restraint.
- If a restraint is not a *per se* violation, it is examined under the rule of reason.

Horizontal Restraints of Trade. A horizontal restraint of trade occurs when two or more competitors at the same level of distribution enter into a contract, combination, or conspiracy to restrain trade. These horizontal restraints include:
- Price-Fixing. Occurs where competitors in the same line of business agree to set the price of the goods or services they sell: raising, depressing, fixing, pegging, or stabilizing the price of a commodity or service.
  - Price-fixing is a *per se* violation.
- Division of Markets. Occurs when competitors agree that each will serve only a designated portion of the market.
  - It is a *per se* violation to enter into a market-sharing arrangement that divides customers, geographical area, or products.
- Group Boycotts. Occurs when two or more competitors at one level of distribution agree not to deal with others at another level of distribution.
- Other Horizontal Agreements. Some agreements at the same level are lawful, such as trade association rules, exchanging nonprice information, and participating in joint ventures.
  - These horizontal restraints are examined using the rule of reason.

Vertical Restraints of Trade. A vertical restraint of trade occurs when two or more parties on different levels of distribution enter into a contract, combination, or conspiracy to restrain trade. The Supreme Court has applied both the *per se* rule and the rule of reason in determining the legality of vertical restraints of trade under Section 1. These vertical restraints include:
- Resale Price Maintenance. Occurs when a party at one level of distribution enters into an agreement with a party at another level to adhere to a price schedule that either sets or stabilizes prices.
- Nonprice Vertical Restraints. These restraints are examined using the rule of reason.
  - They are unlawful if their anticompetitive effects outweigh their procompetitive effects.
  - Nonprice vertical restraints occur when a manufacturer assigns exclusive territories to retail dealers or limits the number of dealers in a geographical area.

Unilateral Refusal to Deal. A unilateral choice by one party to refuse to deal with another party does not violate Section 1 as long as there was no action by two or more parties in concert.
- This rule is known as the Colgate doctrine.

Conscious Parallelism. This defense applies if two or more firms act the same but no concerted action is shown.

Noerr **Doctrine.** Under this doctrine two or more persons may petition the executive, legislative, or judicial branch of the government or administrative agencies to enact laws or take other action without violating antitrust laws.

Monopolization: Section 2 of the Sherman Act

Section 2 prohibits the act of monopolization and attempts or conspiracies to monopolize trade.
- To prove a violation of Section 2, the act requires showing that the defendant possesses monopoly power in the relevant market and is engaged in a willful act of monopolization to acquire or maintain the power.

Defining the Relevant Market. This requires defining the relevant product or service market and geographical market.
- The relevant market generally includes substitute products or services that are reasonably interchangeable with the defendant's products or services.
- The relevant geographical market is defined as the area in which the defendant and its competitors sell the product or service.

Monopoly Power. This is the power to control prices or exclude competition measured by the market share the defendant possesses in the relevant market.

Willful Act of Monopolizing. A required act for there to be a violation of Section 2.
- Possession of monopoly power without such act does not violate Section 2.

Attempts and Conspiracies to Monopolize. A single firm may attempt to monopolize.
- Two or more firms are required for a conspiracy to monopolize.

Defenses to Monopolization. Only two defenses to a charge of monopolization have been recognized:
- Innocent Acquisition. Acquisition because of superior business acumen, skill, foresight, or industry.
- Natural Monopoly. A small market that can only support one competitor.

Mergers: Section 7 of the Clayton Act

Section 7 provides that it is unlawful for a person or business to acquire stock or assets of another where, in any line of commerce or in any activity affecting commerce in any section of the country, the effect of such acquisition may be substantially to lessen competition or to tend to create a monopoly.

Line of Commerce. Determining the line of commerce that will be affected by the merger involves defining the relevant product or service market.
- It includes products or services that consumers use as substitutes.

- If an increase in the price of one product or service leads consumers to purchase another product or service, the two products are substitutes for each other.
- The two products are part of the same line of commerce because they are interchangeable.

Section of the Country. Defining the relevant section of the country consists of defining the relevant geographical market that will feel the direct and immediate effects of the merger.

Probability of a Substantial Lessening of Competition. If there is a probability that a merger will substantially lessen competition or create a monopoly, the court may prevent the merger under Section 7.

Types of Mergers.
- Horizontal Merger. A merger between two or more companies that compete in the same business and geographical market.
    - The court uses the presumptive illegality test for determining the lawfulness of horizontal mergers.
    - Under this test the merger is illegal under Section 7 if:
        - the merged firm would have a 30 percent or more market share in the relevant market and
        - the merger would cause an increase in concentration of 33 percent or more in the relevant market.
    - Other factors are also considered such as the past history of the firms involved, the aggressiveness of the merged firms, the economic efficiency of the proposed merger, and consumer welfare.
- Vertical Mergers. A vertical merger is a merger that integrates the operations of a supplier and a customer.
    - In a backward vertical merger, the customer acquires the supplier.
    - In a forward vertical merger, the supplier acquires the customer.
    - Vertical mergers do not increase market share, but may cause anticompetitive effects.
- Market Extension Mergers. A merger between two companies in similar fields whose sales do not overlap.
    - They are treated like conglomerate mergers under Section 7.
- Conglomerate Mergers. Are mergers between firms in totally unrelated businesses. Section 7 examines the lawfulness of such mergers under the following theories:
    - The Unfair Advantage Theory holds that a merger may not give the acquiring firm an unfair advantage over its competitors in finance, marketing, or expertise.

Defenses to Section 7 Actions.
- The Failing Company Doctrine. Under this defense, a competitor may merge with a failing company if:
    - there is no other reasonable alternative for the failing company
    - no other purchaser is available
    - the assets of the failing company would disappear from the market if the merger did not proceed.
- The Small Company Doctrine. Two small companies are permitted to merge if it would make them more competitive with a large company.

Premerger Notification. The Hart-Scott-Rodino Antitrust Improvement Act requires certain firms to notify the FTC and the Justice Department in advance of a proposed merger.
- Unless the government challenges the proposed merger within 30 days, the merger may proceed.

Tying Arrangements: Section 3 of the Clayton Act

Section 3 prohibits tying arrangements involving sales and leases of goods.
- Tying arrangements are vertical restraints where a seller refuses to sell one product to a customer unless the customer agrees to purchase a second product from the seller.
- The defendant must be shown to have sufficient economic power in the tying product market to restrain competition.

Price Discrimination: Section 2 of the Clayton Act

Section 2(a) prohibits direct and indirect price discrimination by sellers of a commodity of a like grade and quality where the effect of such discrimination may be to substantially lessen competition or to tend to create a monopoly in any line of commerce.

Direct Price Discrimination. To prove a violation of Section 2(a), the plaintiff must show sales to two or more purchasers involving goods of like grade and quality that results in actual injury.

Indirect Price Discrimination. This is a form of price discrimination (favorable credit terms, reduced shipping charges) that is less readily apparent than direct forms of price discrimination.

Defenses to Section 2(a) Actions.
- Cost Justification. A seller's price discrimination is not unlawful if the price differential is due to "differences in the cost of manufacture, sale, or delivery" of the product.
  - Quantity or volume discounts are lawful to the extent they are supported by cost savings.
- Changing Conditions. Price discrimination is not unlawful if it is in response to "changing conditions in the market for or the marketability of the goods."
  - Reduction in price of winter coats would be lawful when the spring line of clothing comes out.
- Meeting the Competition. A seller may engage in price discrimination to meet a competitor's price.

Federal Trade Commission Act

Section 5 prohibits unfair methods of competition and unfair or deceptive acts or practices in or affecting commerce. Section 5 covers conduct that
- violates any provision of the Sherman Act or the Clayton Act,
- violates the spirit of those acts,
- fills the gaps of those acts, and
- offends public policy, or is immoral, oppressive, unscrupulous, or unethical, or causes substantial injury to competition or consumers.

Exemptions from Antitrust Laws

Statutory Exemptions. These include labor unions, agricultural cooperatives, export activities of American companies, and insurance business that is regulated by a state.
- Other statutes exempt railroad, shipping, utility, and securities industries from most of the reach of antitrust law.

Implied Exceptions. These are given by federal court decision.
- Two such exemptions include professional baseball and the airline industry.

State Action Exemptions. These are economic regulations, such as utility rates, mandated by state law.
- Though it is a form or price-fixing, the states and utilities are not liable for antitrust violations.

State Antitrust Laws

States often enact antitrust laws that are patterned after federal statutes and are used to attack anticompetitive activity that occurs in intrastate commerce.
- Plaintiffs often bring lawsuits under state antitrust laws when federal antitrust laws are laxly applied.

Refresh Your Memory

The following exercise will give you the opportunity to test your memory of the principles given in this chapter. Read the question twice and place your answer in the blank provided. Review the chapter material for any question that you are unable to answer or remember.

1. _____ are a series of laws enacted to specifically limit anticompetitive behavior and monopolistic practices in almost all industries, businesses, and professions operating in the United States.

2. The _____ is a federal statute, enacted in 1914, that regulates mergers and prohibits certain exclusive dealing arrangements.

3. The _____ is a federal statute, enacted in 1930, that prohibits price discrimination.

4. The _____ is a federal statute, enacted in 1890, that makes certain restraints of trade and monopolistic acts illegal.

5. _____ damages are the only damages that may be recovered for violations of the FTC Act.

6. A private plaintiff has _____ years from the date on which an antitrust injury occurred to bring a private civil treble-damages action because only damages incurred during this period are recoverable.1.

7. A(n) _____ is a type of plea where the defendant pays a penalty without admission of guilt.

8. The two tests the U.S. Supreme Court has developed for determining the lawfulness of a restraint are the rule of reason and the _____.

9. Under the _____, the court must examine the pro- and anticompetitive effects of a challenged restraint.

10. The _____ is a rule that is applicable to restraints of trade considered inherently anticompetitive.

11. _____ is a restraint of trade in which competitors agree that each will serve only a designated portion of the market.

12. The legality of nonprice vertical restraints of trade under Section 1 of the Sherman Act is examined by applying the _____.

13. _____ is seen when an independent choice is made by one party not to deal with another party.

14. _____ is an antitrust principle which says that two or more persons can petition the executive, legislative, or judicial branch of the government or administrative agencies to enact laws or take other action without violating antitrust laws.

15. A merger between two or more companies that compete in the same business and geographical market is known as _____.

Critical Thought Exercise

When the partners of The Four Brothers Pizza Shoppe terminated the partnership, they divided the greater Chicago area into four parts and agreed to restrict the geographical area within which each would advertise and deliver pizzas. Two years later one partner filed suit against the other three alleging in part that the restriction on advertising and delivery area was a *per se* violation of the Sherman Act. Was the agreement made as part of a breakup of a partnership that divided a city into geographical areas for advertising and delivery a violation of antitrust law?

Please compose your answer to the Critical Thinking Exercise using a separate sheet of paper or your computer word processing program.

Practice Quiz

True/False

16. _____ The antitrust laws were enacted to promote anticompetitive behavior in commerce and industry.

17. _____ Antitrust laws are constant across changes in governmental administration.

18. _____ The Clayton Act, enacted in 1914, regulates mergers and prohibits certain exclusive dealing arrangements.

19. _____ Private parties cannot intervene in public antitrust actions brought by the government.

20. _____ Antitrust defendants often opt to settle government-brought antitrust actions by entering a plea of nolo contendere.

21. _____ The per se rule is applicable to restraints of trade that are considered inherently anticompetitive.

22. _____ Restraints that are not characterized as per se violations are not further examined using the rule of reason.

23. _____ Price fixing is a rule of reason violation of Section 1 of the Sherman Act.

24. _____ Group boycotts can be either a per se violation or rule of reason violation.

25. _____ Division of markets is considered to be a type of horizontal restraint of trade._

26. _____ Noerr doctrine is indirectly protected and guaranteed by the Bill of Rights.

27. _____ The unfair advantage theory is intended to prevent wealthy companies from overwhelming the competition in a given market.

28. _____ It is necessary to prove actual injury in order for a plaintiff to recover in a price discrimination lawsuit.

29. _____ The insurance business enjoys a statutory exemption from antitrust laws.

30. _____ For conscious parallelism to be proven, each manufacturer should be found to have acted on its own.

Multiple Choice

31. Which of the following is true of antitrust laws?

A. Antitrust laws are fixed and unchangeable.
B. Each new administration adopts a different policy for enforcing antitrust laws.
C. Federal antitrust laws provide for government lawsuits and exclude private lawsuits from their purview.
D. Treble damages cannot be sought in antitrust lawsuits.

32. Which of the following is the only act that includes criminal sanctions for the usage of unfair trade practices?

A. the Clayton Act
B. the Sherman Act
C. the Robinson-Patman Act
D. the Federal Trade Commission Act

33. Which of the following is considered an invalid antitrust injury?

A. lost profits
B. an increase in the cost of doing business
C. injury resulting from higher prices being "passed on"
D. a decrease in the value of tangible or intangible property caused by the antitrust violation

34. Which of the following is true of the *per se* rule in restraint of trade?

A. fails to permit any defenses and justifications to save the restraint of trade
B. applies only to restraints that are found to be unreasonable with certain evidentiary standards being met
C. applies to restraints that are based primarily on the firm's market share and power
D. requires a balancing of the positive and negative effects of the challenged restraint

35. The rule of reason is characterized by _____.

A. an automatic violation of Section 1 of the Sherman Act
B. an inherently anticompetitive nature
C. a lack of need for any evidence to deem the restraint unreasonable
D. an evaluation of the company's market share, power, and other facets

36. Which of the following is true with regard to price fixing?

A. Price fixing is a reasonable violation of Section 1 of the Sherman Act.
B. Price fixing is a process seen exclusively among sellers of goods and services.
C. Price fixing is permissible as it helps consumers or protects competitors from ruinous competition.
D. Price fixing also involves fixing the quantity of a product or service to be produced or provided.

37. Which of the following horizontal restraints of trade has the element of monopoly in it?

A. conscious parallelism
B. market sharing
C. group boycott
D. exchange of nonprice information

38. Which of the following is true of the Colgate doctrine?

A. It is not a violation of Section 1 of the Sherman Act.
B. It is an example of a horizontal restraint of trade.
C. It is a *per se* violation of Section 1 of the Sherman Act
D. It is a rule of reason violation of Section 1 of the Sherman Act.

39. Conscious parallelism is seen when _____.

A. parties at different levels enter into an agreement to adhere to a price schedule that stabilizes prices
B. one party makes an independent choice not to deal with another
C. two or more firms act the same but no concerted action is shown
D. a party's anticompetitive effects outweigh their procompetitive effects

40. Which of the following businesses and activities enjoys an implied exemption from antitrust laws?

A. railroads
B. agricultural cooperatives
C. airlines
D. labor unions

Short Answer

41. How is government enforcement of federal antitrust laws divided?

42. What factors does the court examine when applying the rule of reason?

43. What is the *per se* rule?

44. Explain the meaning of price-fixing.

45. What are the two defenses to a charge of monopolizing that have actually been recognized?

46. Unreasonable restraints on trade violate which act?

47. Describe an example of a nonprice vertical restraint.

48. Pepsi and Coca-Cola decide not to deal with Foodman grocery store, a retailer. Why wouldn't this situation be considered a violation of Section 1 of the Sherman Act?

49. For the purpose of analyzing a Section 2 violation of the Sherman Act, what is a relevant geographical market?

50. How is monopoly power defined by the courts?

51. What guidelines do the courts use in determining whether a defendant possesses monopoly power?

_____

_____

52. What is predatory pricing?

_____

_____

53. Which test is used to determine the relevant product or service market?

_____

_____

54. If two companies are proposing a merger, what must they do to comply with the Hart-Scott-Rodino Antitrust Improvement Act?

_____

_____

55. If a doctor charges one patient $200 for the same procedure as she charges another patient only $55, is this price discrimination a violation of the Robinson-Patman Act?

_____

_____

Answers to Refresh Your Memory

1. Antitrust laws [p. 766]
2. Clayton Act [p. 767]
3. Robinson-Patman Act [p. 767]
4. Sherman Act [p. 766]
5. Actual [p. 767]
6. four [p. 767]
7. *nolo contendere* [p. 767]
8. *per se* rule [p. 768]
9. rule of reason [p. 768]
10. *per se* rule [p. 768]
11. Market sharing [p. 769]
12. rule of reason [p. 771]
13. Unilateral refusal to deal [p. 773]
14. *Noerr* doctrine [p. 773]
15. horizontal merger [p. 777]

Critical Thought Exercise Model Answer

Society's welfare is harmed if rival businesses are permitted to join in an agreement that consolidates their market power or otherwise restrains competition. The types of trade restraints that Section 1 of the Sherman Act prohibits are generally divided into horizontal and vertical restraints. A horizontal restraint is any agreement that in some way restrains competition between rival businesses competing in the same market. These agreements include price fixing, group boycotts, and horizontal market division. It is a *per se* violation of Section 1 of the Sherman Act for competitors to divide up territories or customers. The effect of the agreement between the four former partners is to say, "That will be your market and this will be mine." The agreement to limit advertising and delivery to different geographical areas was intended to be, and was in practice, an agreement to allocate markets so that the *per se* rule of illegality applies.

Answers to Practice Quiz

True/False

16. False. Antitrust laws are a series of laws enacted to limit anticompetitive behavior in almost all industries, businesses, and professions operating in the United States. [p. 766]

17. False. Each administration that occupies the White House adopts a policy for the enforcement of antitrust laws. These policies differ from one administration to another. [p. 766]

18. True. The Clayton Act3 is a federal statute, enacted in 1914, that regulates mergers and prohibits certain exclusive dealing arrangements. [p. 767]

19. True. Private parties cannot intervene in public antitrust actions brought by the government.[p. 767]

20. True. Antitrust defendants often opt to settle government-brought antitrust actions by entering a plea of *nolo contendere* in a criminal action or a consent decree in a government civil action. [p. 767]

21. True. The Supreme Court adopted the *per se* rule, which is applicable to restraints of trade that are considered inherently anticompetitive. [p. 768]

22. False. Restraints that are not characterized as *per se* violations are examined using the rule of reason. [p. 768]

23. False. Price fixing is a *per se* violation of Section 1 of the Sherman Act.. [p. 769]

24. True. In the past, the U.S. Supreme Court held that all group boycotts were *per se* illegal. However, the Supreme Court changed this rule and now holds that only certain group boycotts are *per se* illegal; others are to be examined under the rule of reason. [p. 770]

25. True. Division of markets is considered to be a type of horizontal restraint of trade. [p. 769]

26. True. The Noerr doctrine holds that two or more persons may petition the executive, legislative, or judicial branch of the government or administrative agencies to enact laws or to take other action without violating antitrust laws. The rationale behind this doctrine is that the right to petition the government has precedence because it is guaranteed by the Bill of Rights. [p. 773]

27. True. The unfair advantage theory holds that a conglomerate merger may not give the acquiring firm an unfair advantage over its competitors in finance, marketing, or expertise. This rule is intended to prevent wealthy companies from overwhelming the competition in a given market. [p. 778]

28. True. A plaintiff who has not suffered injury because of price discrimination cannot recover. [p. 780]

29. True. Statutory exemptions include labor unions, agricultural cooperatives, export activities of American companies, and insurance business that is regulated by a state. [p. 781]

30. True. Sometimes two or more firms act the same, but they have done so individually. If two or more firms act the same but no concerted action is shown, there is no violation of Section 1 of the Sherman Act. This doctrine is often referred to as conscious parallelism. Thus, if two competing manufacturers of a similar product both separately reach an independent decision not to deal with a retailer, there is no violation of Section 1 of the Sherman Act. The key is that each of the manufacturers acted on its own. [p. 773]

Multiple Choice

31. B. Answer B is correct. Each administration that occupies the White House adopts a policy for the enforcement of antitrust laws. These policies differ from one administration to another. [p. 766]

32. B. Answer B is correct. The Sherman Act is the only major antitrust act that includes criminal sanctions. [p. 767]

33. C. Answer C is correct. The courts have required that consumers must have dealt directly with the alleged violators to have standing to sue; indirect injury resulting from higher prices being "passed on" is insufficient. [p. 767]

34. A. Answer A is correct. When a restraint is characterized as a *per se* violation, no defenses or justifications for the restraint will save it, and no further evidence need be considered.[p. 768]

35. D. Answer D is the correct answer. The courts examine the following factors in applying the rule of reason to a particular case: the pro- and anticompetitive effects of the challenged restraint, the competitive structure of the industry, the firm's market share and power, the history and duration of the restraint, and other relevant factors. [p. 768]]

36. D. Answer D is the correct answer. Horizontal price fixing occurs when competitors in the same line of business agree to set the price of goods or services they sell. Price fixing is defined as raising, depressing, fixing, pegging, or stabilizing the price of a commodity or service. Illegal price fixing includes setting minimum or maximum prices or fixing the quantity of a product or service to be produced or provided. [p. 769]

37. B. Answer B is correct. Competitors who agree that each will serve only a designated portion of the market are engaging in market sharing, which is a *per se* violation of Section 1 of the Sherman Act. Each market segment is considered a small monopoly served only by its designated "owner." [p. 769]

38. A. Answer A is correct. The U.S. Supreme Court has held that a firm can unilaterally choose not to deal with another party without being liable under Section 1 of the Sherman Act. A unilateral refusal to deal is not a violation of Section 1 because there is no concerted action with others. This rule was announced in United States v. Colgate & Co. and is therefore often referred to as the Colgate doctrine. [p. 773]

39. C. Answers C is correct. Conscious parallelism is a doctrine which states that if two or more firms act the same but no concerted action is shown, there is no violation of Section 1 of the Sherman Act. [p. 773]

40. C. Answer C is correct. The federal courts have implied several exemptions from antitrust laws. Examples of implied exemptions include professional baseball (but not other professional sports) and airlines. [p. 781]

Short Answer

41. It is divided between the Antitrust Division of the Department of Justice and the Bureau of Competition of the FTC. [p. 767]

42. The court will examine the following factors: The pro- and anticompetitive effects, the competitive structure of the industry, the firm's market share and power, the history and duration of the restraint, and other relevant factors. [p. 768]

43. A rule that is applicable to those restraints of trade considered inherently anticompetitive. [p. 768]

44. Price-fixing occurs when competitors in the same line of business agree to set the price of the goods or services they sell. It is accomplished by raising, depressing, fixing, pegging, or stabilizing the price of a commodity or service. [p. 769]

45. Innocent acquisition and natural monopoly. [p. 775]

46. Section 1 of the Sherman Act. [p. 771]

47. It includes a situation where a manufacturer assigns exclusive territories to retail dealers or limits the number of dealers that may be located in a certain territory. [p. 771]

48. There is no violation of Section 1 because each of the manufacturers acted on its own. [p. 773]

49. It is the area in which the defendant and its competitors sell the product or service. This may be a national, regional, state, or local area, depending on the circumstances. [p. 774]

50. Monopoly power is the power to control prices or exclude competition, measured by the market share the defendant possesses in the relevant market. [p. 774]

51. Market share above 70 percent is monopoly power. Market share under 20 percent is not monopoly power. [p. 774]
52. Predatory pricing is pricing below normal or average cost. [p. 774]

53. The functional interchangeability test. [p. 776]

54. They are required to notify the FTC and the Justice Department in advance of a proposed merger. [p. 778]

55. No, because Section 2 of the Clayton Act does not apply to the sale of services. [p. 779]

47 | PERSONAL PROPERTY AND BAILMENT

Chapter Overview

Property would have little if any value if the law did not protect the rights of owners to use, sell, dispose of, control, and prevent others from trespassing upon their property. Property may be either real property (buildings and land) or personal property. In this chapter we examine the types of personal property, the methods of acquiring ownership in personal property, and property rights in mislaid, lost, and abandoned property. The chapter then discusses bailment of property, situations where possession of (but not title to) property is delivered to another party for transfer, safekeeping, or use. The typical rental of equipment is a bailment.

Objectives

Upon completion of the exercises in this chapter, you should be able to
1. Define personal property.
2. Describe the methods for acquiring and transferring ownership in personal property.
3. Describe and apply rules regarding ownership rights in mislaid, lost, and abandoned property.
4. List and describe the elements for creating a bailment.
5. Explain the liability of bailees for lost, damaged, or destroyed goods.

Practical Application

Businesses are constantly transferring ownership of personal property or creating personal property for sale. Temporary use of property, whether by borrowing or renting, is a common commercial practice. The material in this chapter has valuable application to everyday business practices. Knowledge of the rights and duties relating to ownership and bailment of personal property helps one to make informed and reasoned choices when deciding how to deal with a personal property issue.

Helpful Hints

Once it is determined that something is personal property, it is wise to focus on the treatment of the property to determine who has rights in it and what duties may have arisen in regards to the property. The circumstances under which possession of property is transferred from person to person or business to business will determine who may ultimately be responsible for damage to or loss of the property. The law differentiates the rights of people depending upon how they came into possession of the property and the circumstances surrounding the acquisition of possession.
As you study this material, look at the status of the property as it changes possession. This will guide you in applying the correct law to solve a personal property issue.

Study Tips

In order to answer questions or resolve disputes relating to personal property, it is wise to examine personal property from the perspective of creation and acquisition, transfer by gift, temporary or permanent loss, and rights and duties associated with bailments.

Personal Property and Bailment

The law protects rights of property owners to use, sell, dispose of, control, and prevent others from trespassing on their property rights.

Personal Property

There are two kinds of property, real and personal property.
- Real Property. Includes land and property that is permanently attached to it.
- Personal Property. Consists of everything that is not real property; called goods or chattels.
- Fixture. Personal property that is permanently affixed to land or buildings.
- Tangible Property. Includes physically defined property, like goods, animals, and minerals.
- Intangible Property. Represents rights that cannot be reduced to physical form, such as stock certificates, certificates of deposit, bonds, and copyrights.

Acquiring Ownership in Personal Property

The acquisition of personal property is done with little formality.

Possession or Capture. Property can be acquired by capturing it.

Purchase. The most common way to obtain property is to purchase it.

Production. Production is another common method.
- A manufacturer who turns raw materials into a product acquires ownership of the product.

Gift. A gift is a voluntary transfer of property without consideration.
- The person making the gift is the donor.
- The person receiving the gift is the donee.
- The three elements of a valid gift are:
    - Donative intent. For a gift to be effective, a donor must have intended to make a gift.
    - Delivery. Delivery must occur for there to be a valid gift. Delivery can either be physical or constructive (giving title documents to a car).
    - Acceptance. This is usually not a problem unless the gift is refused.
- Gift *Inter Vivos* and Gift *Causa Mortis*. Gifts *inter vivos* are made during a person's lifetime while a gift *causa mortis* is made in contemplation of death.
    - Gifts *causa mortis* can be revoked up until the time of death.

Uniform Gift to Minor Act and Uniform Transfers to Minors Act. These acts allow adults to make irrevocable gifts to minors.
- The custodian of the gift has broad discretionary powers to invest the money or securities for the benefit of the minor.

Will or Inheritance. If a person who dies has a valid will, the property is distributed to the beneficiaries, pursuant to the provisions of the will.

Accession. Accession occurs when the value of personal property increases because it is added to or improved by natural or manufactured means.

Confusion. Confusion occurs if two or more persons commingle fungible goods.
- The owners share ownership in commingled goods to the amount of the goods contributed.

Divorce. Parties obtain property rights in the property of the marital estate.

Mislaid, Lost, and Abandoned Personal Property

People find property belonging to others and ownership rights to the property differs depending on whether the property was mislaid, lost, or abandoned.

Mislaid Property. Property is mislaid when the owner places it somewhere and forgets it.
- The owner will probably return when it is discovered that the property was mislaid.
- The owner of the property where it was found has the right to take possession against all except the rightful owner.
- The owner of the premises becomes an involuntary bailee and must take reasonable care of the property until it is reclaimed.
- The typical situation for this is when a patron leaves their glasses or jacket at a business.

Lost Property. Property is lost when the owner negligently, carelessly, or inadvertently leaves it.
- The finder of the property takes title against the world except the true owner.
- The finder must make efforts to return the property.

Estray Statutes. Most states have an estray statute, which dictates what the finder of lost or misplaced property must do to acquire title to the property.
- This usually includes turning the property over to the police, giving notice that the property was found, and waiting for a time period to pass.
- The finder can then claim ownership.

Abandoned Property. Property is classified as abandoned if the owner discards property with intent to relinquish his rights in it or gives up all attempts to locate lost or misplaced property.

Bailment

A bailment is a transaction where the owner transfers his or her personal property to another to be held, stored, delivered, or for some other purpose.
- Title to the property remains with the owner.
- The owner of the property is the bailor and the party who received the property is the bailee.

Elements Necessary to Create a Bailment. There are three essential elements that must be present to create a bailment:
- Only personal property can be bailed.
- There must be delivery of possession which also involves two elements:
    - The bailee has exclusive control over the personal property.
    - The bailee must knowingly accept the personal property.
- There must be a bailment agreement, which may be either express or implied.

Types of Ordinary Bailments. There are three classifications of ordinary bailments. The importance of these categories is that they determine the degree of care owed by the bailee in protecting the bailed property.
- Bailments for the sole benefit of the bailor. Are gratuitous bailments that benefit only bailor.
    - The typical gratuitous bailment involves the bailee watching the bailor's property as a favor without compensation.
    - The bailee only owed a duty of slight care.
    - If bailee is not grossly negligent, no liability will be incurred for loss or damage
- Bailments for the sole benefit of the bailee. Gratuitous bailments for sole benefit of bailee.
    - This is the typical "borrowing the lawnmower" situation.
    - The bailee owes a duty of great care.
    - The bailee is responsible for even the slightest negligence.
- Mutual benefit bailments. Are made for the benefit of both the bailor and bailee.
    - The bailee has a duty of reasonable care, making the bailee liable for any goods that are lost, damaged, or destroyed because of his or her negligence.
    - This is the typical paid storage or valet parking situation.

Duration and Termination of Bailments. Bailments usually end at a specified time or when a certain purpose has been achieved.

Special Bailments

Special bailees are subject to special liability rules.

Warehouse Companies. These bailees contract for the storage of goods for compensation.
- They are held to a duty of reasonable case.
- They are not liable for the negligence of others that causes loss or damage.
- Warehouse Receipt. This is a written document issued by a warehouseman, containing the terms of the bailment.
    - The warehouse has a lien on the goods until all expenses incurred have been satisfied.

Common Carriers. These bailees offer transportation to the public. They include airlines, railroads, bus companies, trucking companies, and public pipeline carriers.
- The delivery of goods to a common carrier creates a mutual benefit bailment.
- Unlike an ordinary bailment, common carriers are held to a duty of strict liability.
- If goods are lost, damaged, or stolen, the common carrier is liable even if it was not at fault.
- Bill of Lading. Document of title is issued by a carrier when goods are received for shipment.

o Bills of lading are issued by common carriers, contract carriers and others engaged in the business of transporting goods.
o A through bill of lading provides connecting carriers may be used to transport goods.
o Original carrier is liable to bailor for loss or damage caused by the connecting carrier.

Innkeepers Statute. An innkeeper owns a facility that provides lodging for compensation.
- At common law, innkeepers are strictly liability for the loss or damage to property of guests.
- Most all states have innkeepers statutes that limit the liability of innkeepers.
- To limit their liability, the innkeeper must provide a safe and make guests aware of its availability for their use.

Refresh Your Memory

1. Tangible property such as automobiles, furniture, and equipment, and intangible property such as securities, patents, and copyrights are collectively referred to as _____.

2. A building attached to a piece of land would be considered a _____ property.

3. Personal property that is permanently affixed to land or buildings is called a(n) _____.

4. _____ represent rights that cannot be reduced to physical form, such as stock certificates, certificates of deposit, bonds, and copyrights.

5. Real property can become personal property if it is _____.

6. _____ is a method of acquiring ownership, when a manufacturer purchases raw materials and then manufactures a finished good.

7. The voluntary transfer of title to property without payment of consideration by the donee is known as a(n) _____.

8. A gift that is made in contemplation of death is known as a(n) _____.

9. A(n) _____ is an increase in the value of personal property because it is added to or improved by natural or manufactured means.

10. _____ occurs if two or more persons commingle fungible goods.

11. Property that an owner voluntarily places somewhere and then inadvertently forgets is known as _____ property.

12. Property that the owner leaves somewhere due to negligence, carelessness, or inadvertence is referred to as _____ property.

13. A(n) _____ statute permits a finder of mislaid or lost property to clear title to the property if certain prescribed legal formalities are met.

14. A transaction in which an owner transfers his or her personal property to another to be held, stored, or delivered or for some other purpose is known as a _____.

15. A bailment without a fixed term is called a _____.

Critical Thought Exercise

Tom Cruel, chairman of the Central Republican Committee for Rashaw County, was transporting a valuable painting in his trunk to a friend's home where it was to be displayed during a fundraiser. Cruel stopped at the country club for lunch and left his Mercedes in the care of a parking attendant who worked for Jiffy Parking Service, Inc. The attendant left the key box unattended while taking a break. The car and its contents were stolen. The car was recovered by police using a global positioning system, but the trunk was empty upon its return. Cruel was missing the painting worth $30,000, a golf bag and clubs valued at $1,400, and a CD case containing 120 music compact discs worth an estimated $1,500. Cruel has filed suit against Jiffy for the value of all the items taken from the trunk, including the painting. Is Jiffy liable to Cruel? If so, for which stolen items must it pay damages to Cruel?

Please compose your answer to the Critical Thinking Exercise using a separate sheet of paper or your computer word processing program.

Practice Quiz

True/False

16. _____ Personal property includes land and property that is permanently attached to it.

17. _____ Personal property consists of everything that is not real property.

18. _____ Only intangible property qualifies as personal property.

19. _____ A person can acquire ownership of unowned personal property by taking possession of it.

20. _____ For a gift to be considered effective, the donor must be found to have a donative intent.

21. _____ The Uniform Transfers to Minors Act establish procedures for adults to make irrevocable gifts of money and securities to minors.

22. _____ Accession that naturally occurs to a property belongs to the owner.

23. _____ If an accession is mistakenly made by an improver and the improvement cannot be removed from the original article, the owner owns title to the improved property without any payment

24. _____ Title to goods cannot be acquired by confusion.

25. _____ The finder of an abandoned property holds title against the whole world except the owner.

26. _____ In a bailment, the title to the goods passes to the bailee.

27. _____ A consignee is a person to whom a common carrier makes a delivery.

28. _____ Common carriers are held to a duty of strict liability.

29. _____ Common carriers are not liable for the loss, damage, or destruction of goods caused by an act of God.

30. _____ Under the innkeepers' statutes, innkeepers owe a duty of strict liability regarding loss caused to the personal property of transient guests.

Multiple Choice

31. Which of the following is considered real property?

A. a plantation
B. a car
C. furniture
D. a copyrighted song

32. Which of the following methods of acquiring ownership is least in use today?

A. purchase
B. capture
C. gift
D. production

33. What is a gift *inter vivos?*

A. a gift that is made in contemplation of death
B. a gift made during a person's lifetime that is an irrevocable present transfer of ownership
C. a gift that is to be shared by the donor and donee with the payment of consideration by the donee
D. a gift that requires a monetary payment at a set date in the future

34. Which of the following is true of a gift *causa mortis?*

A. It cannot be revoked before the death of the donor.
B. It does not require the actual death of the donor.
C. It represents an irrevocable present transfer of ownership.
D. It takes precedence over a prior conflicting will.

35. Which of the following is true of ownership titles when confusion occurs?

A. Title to the goods can never be shared between the owners involved.
B. Title to goods commingled without permission goes to the innocent party.
C. Title to goods cannot be acquired by confusion.
D. Title to goods can only be acquired if goods were commingled by accident.

36. Which of the following is true of mislaid property with regard to the person who finds it?

A. The finder becomes the owner of the property.
B. The finder has the right to share it with the original owner.
C. The finder is not entitled to possess the property.
D. The finder is absolved of any responsibility of the mislaid property

37. Which of the following is true of ownership rights of an abandoned property?

A. The finder and owner must share ownership of the property.
B. The finder acquires title to the property, even against its original owner.
C. The owner can reclaim his or her property completely from the finder.
D. The owner of the premises where property is mislaid is entitled to possession but does not acquire title.

38. In which of the following processes is the title of goods not transferred?

A. an adverse possession
B. a bailment
C. a sale
D. an acquisition

39. A _____ is a gratuitous bailment that arises when the bailee is requested to care for the bailor's property as a favor.

A. bailment at will
B. mutual benefit bailment
C. bailment for the sole benefit of the bailee
D. bailment for the sole benefit of the bailor

40. What is a warehouse receipt?

A. A receipt received by a warehouse after the bailor has retrieved the bailed goods and payment has been made.
B. A document of title issued by a warehouse company stating that the bailor has title to the bailed goods.
C. An inventory list provided to the warehouse company by the bailor of the bailed goods.
D. A certificate of authenticity issued by a warehouse stating that it is certified to hold bailed goods.

Short Answer

41. What type of property allows a finder to acquire title to it, even against its original owner?

_____

_____

42. When must a bailment be in writing?

_____

_____

43. What three elements must be shown to prove a valid gift?

44. Is a heating system considered a fixture or personal property and why?

45. Most states have an estray statute that permits a finder of lost or misplaced property to clear title to the property (and become the new owner) if what requirements are met?

46. John, who owns fifty Kennedy half dollars, and Marge, who owns thirty Kennedy half dollars, both place their coins in the center of John's dining room table. They both soon realize that they cannot tell whose money is whose. What term is used to describe the situation and how many coins does each now own?

47. What is a bailment for the sole benefit of the bailor?

48. What must a bailee do at the termination of a bailment?

49. If Pricilla borrows Sheila's automatic mixer for a recipe she is making, but leaves it laying in the sink to rust from water constantly being run over it, what type of bailment is this?

50. Using the facts in the previous question, what duty did the bailee owe and what is her liability if any to the bailor?

51. What type of duty does the bailee have in a mutual benefit bailment?

52. When are warehouses liable for loss or damage to the bailed property?

53. Under common law, what standards were innkeepers held to when a transient guest suffered a loss?

54. What must an innkeeper do to take advantage of an innkeeper's statute?

_____

_____

55. Identify who the consignor, consignee, and common carrier are if Busco, a public trucking company, accepts goods from Doug that are to be delivered to Samantha.

_____

_____

Answers to Refresh Your Memory

1. personal property [p. 789]
2. real [p. 789]
3. fixture [p. 789]
4. Intangible properties [p. 789]
5. removed from the land it is situated in[p. 789]
6. Producing [p. 790]
7. gift [p. 790]
8. gift *causa mortis* [p. 790]
9. accession [p. 791]
10. Confusion [p. 791]
11. mislaid [p. 792]
12. lost [p. 792]
13. estray [p. 792]
14. bailment [p. 794]
15. bailment at will [p. 797]

Critical Thought Exercise Model Answer

For liability to be created, a bailment must exist. A bailment is created when personal property is delivered into the possession of a bailee by a bailor for a stated purpose for some period of time. The bailee has the right of exclusive possession, but the bailor retains ownership of the bailed property. Delivery may be accomplished by actual physical delivery of the property or constructive delivery of an item that gives control of the property, such as delivery of a car key to a parking lot attendant. By delivering his car key to the employee of Jiffy Parking, Cruel created a bailment agreement. Mutual benefit bailments are bailments that benefit both parties. The bailee (Jiffy) owes a duty of reasonable care to protect the bailed goods. The bailee is liable for any goods that are lost, stolen, damaged, or destroyed because of his or her negligence. The law presumes that if bailed property is lost, damaged, destroyed, or stolen while in the possession of the bailee, it is because of lack of proper care by the bailee. The typical commercial bailment where someone pays to have his property watched for a fee is this type of bailment. A bailee accepts responsibility for unknown contents of a bailed automobile when the presence of those contents is reasonably foreseeable based on the factual circumstances surrounding the bailment of the automobile. It cannot be said that a country club parking attendant should reasonably foresee the presence of a valuable painting in a member's car trunk. Unless the bailee accepts possession of the property, either expressly or impliedly, there can be no bailment. Therefore, Jiffy Parking had no duty of care to protect the painting in the trunk. The other items lead to a different result. It is quite foreseeable that a club member would have golf clubs in his trunk. Car owners often have cases to carry an assortment of music for them to play in their car. Jiffy Parking will be liable to Cruel for $2,900, the cost of the golf clubs and compact discs.

Answers to Practice Quiz

True/False

16. False. Real property includes land and property that is permanently attached to it. [p. 789]

17. True. Personal property (sometimes referred to as goods or chattels) consists of everything that is not real property. [p. 789]

18. False. Personal property can be either tangible or intangible. [p. 789]

19. True. A person can acquire ownership in unowned personal property by taking possession of it, or capturing it. [p. 789]

20. True. For a gift to be effective, the donor must have intended to make a gift. Donative intent can be inferred from the circumstances or language used by the donor. The courts also consider such factors as the relationship of the parties, the size of the gift, and the mental capacity of the donor. [p. 790]

21. True. The Uniform Transfers to Minors Act establish procedures for adults to make irrevocable gifts of money and securities to minors.[p. 791]

22. True. Accession that occurs naturally belongs to the owner.[p. 791]

23. True. If an improvement is mistakenly made by an improver, and the improvement cannot be removed from the original article, the owner owns title to the improved property and does not have to pay the improver for the improvement. [p. 791]

24. False. Title to goods can be acquired by confusion. [p. 791]

25. False. Anyone who finds abandoned property acquires title to it. The title is good against the whole world, including the original owner. [p. 794]

26. False. A bailment is different from a sale or a gift because title to the goods does not transfer to the bailee. Instead, the bailee must follow the bailor's directions concerning the goods. [p. 794]

27. True. A consignee is a person to whom a common carrier makes a delivery.[p. 798]

28. True. Common carriers are held to a duty of strict liability: If the goods are lost, damaged, destroyed, or stolen, the common carrier is liable even if it was not at fault for the loss.[p. 798]

29. True. Common carriers are not liable for the loss, damage, or destruction of goods caused by an act of God (e.g., a tornado), [p. 798]

30. True. Under the common law, innkeepers owe a duty of strict liability regarding loss caused to the personal property of transient guests. [p. 799]

Multiple Choice

31. A. Answer A is correct. Real property includes land and property that is permanently attached to it. For example, minerals, crops, timber, and buildings that are attached to land are generally considered real property. [p. 789]

32. B. Answer B is correct. A person can acquire ownership in unowned personal property by taking possession of it, or capturing it. The most notable unowned objects are things in their natural state. This type of property acquisition was important when this country was being developed. In today's urbanized society, however, there are few unowned objects, and this method of acquiring ownership in personal property has become less important. [p. 789]

33. B. Answer B is correct. A gift made during a person's lifetime that is an irrevocable present transfer of ownership is a gift *inter vivos*. [p. 790]

34. D. Answer D is correct. A gift *causa mortis* takes precedence over a prior conflicting will. [p. 791]

35. B. Answer B is correct. If goods are wrongfully or intentionally commingled without permission, the innocent party acquires title to them. [p. 792]

36. C. Answer C is correct. The owner of the premises where the property is mislaid is entitled to take possession of the property against all except the rightful owner. This right is superior to the rights of the person who finds it. Such possession does not involve a change of title. [p. 792]

37. B. Answer B is correct, because there is no benefit to the bailee in this situation. Anyone who finds abandoned property acquires title to it. The title is good against the whole world, including the original owner. [p. 794]

38. B. Answer B is correct. Bailment is a transaction in which an owner transfers his or her personal property to another to be held, stored, or delivered, or for some other purpose. Title to the property does not transfer. [p. 794]

39. D. Answer D is correct. A bailment for the sole benefit of the bailor is a gratuitous bailment that arises when the bailee is requested to care for the bailor's property as a favor. [p. 796-797]

40. B. Answer B is correct. A warehouse receipt is a document of title issued by a warehouse company stating that the bailor has title to the bailed goods. [p. 798]

Short Answer

41. Abandoned property. [p. 794]

42. If it is for more than one year. [p. 795]

43. (1) donative intent (2) delivery (3) acceptance. [p. 790]

44. It is considered to be a fixture as it is permanently affixed to a building. Personal property can be removed, as it is more portable. [p. 789]

45. (1) The finder reports the found property to the appropriate government agency and turns over possession. (2) Post notices describing the lost property. (3) A specified time passes without the rightful owner claiming the property. [p. 793]

46. The goods are said to be commingled and each has an ownership interest in proportion to the amount each contributed before the commingling took place. So, John owns fifty and Marge owns 30 of the Kennedy half dollars. [p. 791]

47. A gratuitous bailment is one that only benefits the bailor. [p. 796]

48. The bailee is obligated to do as the bailor directs with the property. Usually, the bailee is obligated to return the identical goods bailed. [p. 798]

49. A benefit for the sole benefit of the bailee (Sheila). [p. 797]

50. Sheila owed a duty of utmost care and is liable to Pricilla for the automatic mixer. [p. 797]

51. A duty of reasonable or ordinary care. [p. 797]

52. Warehousers are liable only for loss or damage to the bailed property caused by their own negligence. They owe a duty of reasonable care. [p. 798]

53. Strict liability. [p. 799]

54. The innkeeper can avoid liability if a safe is provided in which the guests' valuable property may be kept and the guest was aware of the safe's availability. [p. 799]

55. Busco is the common carrier; Doug is the consignor; Samantha is the consignee. [p. 798]

48 | REAL PROPERTY

Chapter Overview

In the Western world, we have come to value real property more than most any other possession. To the ownership of land attaches wealth and influence in Western society. More importantly, the privacy rights associated with property ownership are assigned great personal worth and psychological value. Even in the face of government power, we proclaim, "A man's home is his castle." In this chapter we focus on the legal rights associated with ownership, occupation, use, and transfer of real property.

Chapter Objectives

Upon completion of the exercises contained in this chapter, you should be able to
1. List and describe the different types of real property.
2. Describe the different types of freehold estates and future interests in real property.
3. Identify the different types of concurrent ownership of real property.
4. Explain how ownership interests in real property can be transferred.
5. Describe the zoning laws.

Practical Application

Upon mastering the concepts in this chapter, you should be able to recognize how a piece of real property is held by the owner and what affect that has upon its use, transfer, and value. As an example, real estate that has an easement attached to it is worth less because another party has the right to use the property for their own purposes as specified in the easement. When the property is transferred to another owner, that owner may have to accept the easement, depending on whether legal requirements have been met.

Helpful Hints

There are many rules created by common law, statute, and current case law. A logical order can be created to this large volume of law if you focus on the creation of the right in the land, its transfer, and perfecting the right by giving notice to the rest of the world. When you are faced with a real property problem, you need to know how the person or company obtained its interest in the real property, what rights go with that interest, if any other party claims a joint interest in the same property, and how that interest is protected or sold to another. Unlike personal property that is usually not granted to a beneficiary until a will becomes effective, the transfer of an interest in real property may be dictated by the language and conditions contained in the deed. It is often necessary to look backwards in the line of owners to determine who will own the interest in the future.

Study Tips

The following outline will help you create a mental checklist of the main issues and rights involved in ownership and transfer of rights in real property. This "checklist" is constantly trying to answer the following questions:

- Is this real or personal property?
- In what form is the real property currently owned?
- Does anyone hold a future interest in this land?
- Is anyone a co-owner of this real property?
- Was there a legal transfer of an ownership interest?
- Was the transfer of the ownership interest property recorded by deed?
- Does anyone own a nonpossessory interest in this real property?
- Is any legal action being taken against the real property?

Real Property

Real property is the land itself and any buildings, trees, soil, minerals, timber, plants, and other things that are permanently affixed to the land.

Land and Buildings. Any building or permanent structure that is built upon the land becomes part of the real property.

Subsurface Rights. The owner of the property also owns the subsurface rights to any minerals, oil, gas, or other commodity that may be under the surface.
- These subsurface rights may be sold separate from the rest of the real property.

Plant life and Vegetation. Plants and vegetation growing on the land's surface are real property.
- Both natural and cultivated plants are part of the real property.
- They become personal property if the owner severs them from the land.

Fixtures. Items that are permanently affixed to the land or a building become part of the real property if they cannot be removed without causing substantial damage to the realty.
- A regular refrigerator would remain personal property, to be removed when the realty is sold.
- A built-in commercial refrigerator becomes a fixture and is sold with the realty.

Air Rights. One other type of property is the air space above the surface of realty.
- This space may be sold or leased separate from the realty like a subsurface right.

Estates in Land

The ownership right one possesses in real property is called an estate in land.
- An estate is the bundle of legal rights the owner has to possess, use, and enjoy the property.
- The type of estate an owner possesses is determined by the deed, will, lease, or other document that created or transferred ownership rights.

Freehold Estate. A freehold estate is an estate where the owner has a present possessory interest in the real property. Two types of freehold estates are estates in fee and life estates.

- A Fee Simple Absolute. A type of ownership of real property that grants the owner the fullest bundle of legal rights that a person can hold in real property.
- A Fee Simple Defeasible. Grants the owner all the incidents of a fee simple absolute, except that it may be taken away if a specified condition occurs or does not occur.
- A Life Estate. An interest in land for a person's lifetime.
  - Upon that person's death, the interest will be transferred to another party.
  - A life tenant is treated as the owner of property during the duration of the life estate.

Concurrent Ownership

Two or more persons can own a piece of real property.

Joint Tenancy. On an owner's death, the property passes to the other joint tenants automatically.
- This is called the right of survivorship.

Tenancy in Common. The interest of a surviving tenant in common passes to the deceased tenant's estate and not to the co-tenants.

Tenancy by the Entirety. This form can only be used by married couples.
- This has a right of survivorship, but one tenant cannot sell their interest in the realty.

Community Property. Nine states recognize community property rights.
- Upon the death of one spouse, one-half of the community assets automatically pass to the surviving spouse.
- The other half passes by will or by the state's intestate statute.

Condominium. A form of ownership in a multiple-dwelling building where the purchaser has title to an individual unit and owns the common areas as a tenant in common.

Cooperative. A form of ownership of a multiple-dwelling building where a corporation owns the building and the residents own shares in the corporation.

Future Interests

A person may be given the right to possess property in the future rather than in the present. The two forms of future interests are:

Reversion. A right of possession that returns to the grantor after the expiration of a limited or contingent estate.

Remainder. The right of possession returns to a third party upon the expiration of a limited or contingent estate.

Transfer of Ownership of Real Property

An owner may transfer his/her interest in realty by one of the following methods:

Sale of Real Estate. The passing of title from a seller to a buyer for a price; called a conveyance.

Deeds. Deeds are used to convey property by sale or gift.
- The seller or donor is called the grantor.
- The buyer or recipient is the grantee.
- General Warranty Deed. Has the greatest number of warranties or guarantees.
- Special Warranty Deed. Only protects a buyer from defects in title that were caused by the seller.
- Quitclaim Deed. Provides no protection for the buyer, granting only whatever interest the grantor possesses.

Recording Statute. A recording statute provides that copies of the deed and other documents, such as mortgages and deeds of trust, may be filed with the county recorder's office to give constructive notice of the ownership to the world.
- Recording statutes are intended to prevent fraud and to establish certainty in the ownership and transfer of property.

Quiet Title Action. A quiet title action is a lawsuit for a court to determine the extent of ownership rights in real property.
- Public notice of the hearing must be given so that anyone claiming an interest in the property can appear and be heard.
- The judge declares, or "quiets title" with the decision on who has title to the property.

Marketable Title. A seller has the obligation to transfer marketable title to the grantee.
- Marketable title means that the title is free from encumbrances, defects in title, or other defects that would affect the value of the property.

Tax Sale. The government may obtain a tax lien against property for unpaid property taxes.
- If the lien remains unpaid, a tax sale is held to satisfy the lien.

Gift, Will, or Inheritance. These forms of transfer involve granting title to another without the payment of any consideration.

Adverse Possession. When a person openly possesses the property of another, he/she may acquire title if certain statutory requirements are met.
- The owner must have notice that his or her land is being wrongfully possesses and take no steps to eject the adverse possessor.

Nonpossessory Interests

Nonpossessory interests exist when a person holds an interest in another person's property without actually owning any part of the property.

Easements. An easement is a given or required right to make limited use of someone else's land without owning or leasing it.
- Express Easements. Easements may be expressly created by
  - <u>Grant</u>. Where the owner gives another party an easement across his or her property.
  - <u>Reservation</u> . Where an owner sells his/ her land but keeps an easement on the land.

- Implied Easements. Easements may be implied by
  - Implication. Where an owner subdivides a piece of property with a well, path, road, or other beneficial appurtenant that serves the entire parcel, or by
  - Necessity. Where a landlocked parcel must have egress and ingress.
- Easements Appurtenant. A situation created when the owner of a piece of land is given an easement over an adjacent piece of land.
- Easements in Gross. An easement that authorizes a person who does not own adjacent land the right to use another's land.
  - Examples: Easements granted for power lines, telephone lines, gas lines, cable lines.
  - The easement holder owes a duty to maintain and repair the easement.

Licenses. A license grants a person the right to enter upon another's property for a specified and usually short period of time.
- A ticket to a football game gives a license to use a seat in the stadium for a period of time.

Profit. Grants a person the right to remove something from another's real property.

Zoning

Zoning ordinances regulate land use.
- They generally do the following:
  - establish use districts within the municipality
  - restrict the height, size, and location of buildings on a building site; and
  - establish aesthetic requirements or limitations for the exterior of buildings.
- A zoning commission usually formulates zoning ordinances, conducts public hearings, and makes recommendations to the city council.

Refresh Your Memory

The following exercise will give you the opportunity to test your memory of the principles given in this chapter. Read the question twice and place your answer in the blank provided. Review the chapter material for any question that you are unable to answer or remember.

1. Land, as well as buildings, trees, soil, minerals, timber, plants, and other things permanently affixed to the land are known as _____.

2. _____ is/are an example of real property.

3. The rights to the earth located beneath the surface of the land are defined as _____.

4. Plant life and vegetation growing on the surface of land are considered to be _____.

5. Plant life that is severed from the land is considered _____.

6. The legal rights that the owner has to possess, use, and enjoy the property are known as _____.

7. A(n) _____ is an estate in which the owner has a present possessory interest in the real property.

8. _____ is a type of ownership of real property that grants the owner the fullest bundle of legal rights that a person can hold in real property.

9. A(n) _____ grants the owner all the incidents of a fee simple absolute except that ownership may be taken away if a specified condition occurs or does not occur.

10. _____ is an interest in real property that lasts for a specified person's lifetime.

11. A life estate that is measured by the life of a third party is referred to as _____ .

12. _____ is a form of co-ownership that includes the right of survivorship as well the right of tenants to unilaterally transfer their interest without the consent of co-tenants.

13. _____ is a form of co-ownership of real property that can be used only by married couples.

14. A _____ is a right of possession that returns to the grantor after the expiration of a limited or contingent estate.

15. A _____ is an exception that permits a type of building or use in an area that would not otherwise be allowed by a zoning ordinance.

Critical Thought Exercise

Jim Lewis and Dale Tingle decided to form a partnership for the purpose of entering the restaurant business. Prior to forming the partnership, Lewis and Tingle purchased a large Victorian house in Sacramento with the idea that they would convert the first floor into a restaurant and the upper floors into office space. Lewis contributed $90,000 to the purchase and Tingle contributed $10,000. Lewis and Tingle took title as joint tenants with the right of survivorship. The partnership was formed five months later and the Sacramento property was converted into a restaurant and offices as planned. When Lewis and Tingle purchased another house in Davis, California, they took title as tenants in common. Tingle contributed $100,000 as the down payment for the Davis property. When the partnership was dissolved, the court ordered that both properties be sold. Lewis was given a reimbursement for the Sacramento property in the amount of $80,000. The Davis property was sold for $320,000 and the proceeds of the sale were divided equally between Lewis and Tingle. Did the court divide the proceeds from the sale of the two properties properly?

Please compose your answer to the Critical Thinking Exercise using a separate sheet of paper or your computer word processing program.

Practice Quiz

True/False

16. _____ Buildings constructed on land are considered personal property.

17. _____ A bridge would be an example of real property.

18. _____ Subsurface rights cannot be sold separately from surface rights.

19. _____ Kitchen cabinets in a building are considered fixtures.

20. _____ A fee simple owner has the right to exclusively possess and use his property to the extent that the owner has not transferred any interest in the property.

21. _____ If a person owns real property in fee simple, his or her ownership is limited in duration.

22. _____ If a person owns real property in fee simple, his or her ownership has no limitation on inheritability.

23. _____ A tenant in common can sell his or her interest in the property without the consent of the other co-owners.

24. _____ A general warranty deed contains the greatest number of warranties and provides the highest level of protection to a grantee.

25. _____ In a special warranty deed, the seller is liable for defects in title that existed before the seller obtained the property.

26. _____ If an owner of real property fails to pay property taxes, the government can obtain a lien on the property for the amount of the taxes.

27. _____ The doctrine of adverse possession requires the delivery of deed for transfer of property to be valid.

28. _____ To obtain title under adverse possession, the adverse possessor must physically occupy the property.

29. _____ A new owner of a servient estate cannot inherit the appurtenant easement.

30. _____ An easement in gross does not create a dominant estate.

Multiple Choice

31. What are surface rights in real property?

A. the right to possess the earth beneath the land
B. the right to occupy the land
C. the right to possess personal property
D. the right to convert personal property to negotiable instruments

32. Which of the following is true of subsurface rights in real property?

A. Subsurface rights cannot be used to mine radioactive elements.
B. Subsurface rights can be sold separately from surface rights.
C. Minerals found beneath real property have to be given up to the government.
D. Subsurface rights can only be invoked to dig oil wells.

33. What are fixtures?

A. goods closely associated with a piece of real property
B. intangible properties created inside the premises of a real property
C. parts of a real property that are easily transferrable without substantial damage to the property
D. goods that cannot be classified as personal property or real property

34. Air rights enable the owner of a property to _____.

A. develop natural and cultivated plant life on the land
B. drill into the earth to utilize ground water for personal use
C. rent or sell the space above the property for commercial purposes
D. create fixtures inside the real property that become a part of the sale agreement

35. Which of the following is true of an ownership of real property that is fee simple absolute?

A. It cannot be inherited.
B. It terminates based on the occurrence or nonoccurrence of a specified event.
C. It is infinite in duration.
D. It cannot be transferred at will.

36. Which of the following is true of a life tenant?

A. A life tenant has the right to sell the life estate at will.
B. A person who gives a life estate to another is called a life tenant.
C. A life tenant can possess the life estate to the point of rendering it worthless by permanent damage.
D. A life tenant is treated as the owner of the property for the duration of the life estate.

37. When does a joint tenancy become a tenancy in common?

A. when a joint tenant sells his or her property
B. when a joint tenant dies
C. when two joint tenants swap their share in the tenancy
D. when two joint tenants are bound by a marital relationship

38. Which of the following provisions protects the interest of a joint tenancy upon the death of a joint tenant?

A. the quiet title action
B. the estate in land
C. the right of survivorship
D. the quitclaim deed

39. Which of the following is a form of co-ownership that disallows the right of survivorship and allows unilateral transfer of interest?

A. tenancy in common
B. joint tenancy
C. cooperatives
D. tenancy by the entirety

40. Which of the following is true of a tenancy by the entirety?

A. It can only be formed between corporations.
B. It does not contain the conditional right of survivorship upon the death of a tenant.
C. It cannot be created by the usage of express words alone.
D. It cannot be transferred by any one of the tenants without the consent of the other.

Short Answer

41. List two forms of co-ownership.

_____

_____

42. What happens if Joan, who is a joint tenant of lake front property with Maurice, sells her interest to Cody?

_____

_____

43. What is a form of co-ownership of a multiple-dwelling building in which a corporation owns the building and the residents own shares in the corporation is known as?

_____

_____

44. What determines whether or not community property law applies?

_____

_____

45. How can title to real property be transferred?

_____

_____

46. What does every state have that enables it to provide copies of deeds and other documents concerning interests in real property?

_____

_____

47. Where would things as mortgages, liens, and easements be filed?

_____

_____

48. What is a joint tenancy and how should it be created in a deed?

_____

_____

49. What must a cooperative owner do before selling his or her share or before subleasing his or her unit?

_____

_____

50. What is a reversion?

   _____

   _____

51. Why don't reversions need to be expressly stated?

   _____

   _____

52. What can a person do who is concerned about his or her ownership rights in a parcel of real property?

   _____

   _____

53. What effect does recording a deed to real estate have?

   _____

   _____

54. What is a marketable title?

   _____

   _____

55. When is a gift consideration made?

   _____

   _____

Answers to Refresh Your Memory

1. real property [p. 805]
2. buildings (answer will vary) [p. 805]
3. mineral rights or subsurface rights [p. 805]
4. real property [p. 805]
5. personal property [p. 805]
6. estate in land [p. 806]
7. freehold estate [p. 806]
8. Fee simple absolute [p. 806]
9. fee simple defeasible [p. 807]
10. Life estate [p. 807]
11. *estate pour autre vie* [p. 807]
12. Joint tenancy [p. 808]
13. Tenancy by the entirety [p. 809]
14. reversion [p. 811]
15. variance [p. 818]

Critical Thought Exercise Model Answer

The deed to the Sacramento property created a joint tenancy in the real estate. When a joint tenancy is created, each tenant acquires an equal right to share in the enjoyment of the land during his or her life. A joint tenancy confers equivalent rights on the tenants that are fixed and vested at the time the tenancy is created. These do not change just because an additional agreement is executed to form a partnership. Once a joint tenancy is established between two people and a partition action is undertaken to divide the property, each person owns a one-half interest and they are entitled to one-half of the total proceeds without reimbursement for an unequal down payment. When parties hold property as tenants in common, each tenant's share is fully divisible and fully transferable to a purchaser or an heir upon death. The Davis property was subject to equitable adjustments for the large down payment made by Tingle. When the property is sold, the court must determine the percentage of equity that is attributable to the original down payment. Tingle will be entitled to a substantially greater share of the proceeds from the Davis property. However, the court may consider the Davis property as just one asset in the partnership. The adjustments to the division of the proceeds will consider the partnership contributions and assets as a whole.

Answers to Practice Quiz

True/False

16. False. Buildings constructed on land are real property. [p. 805]

17. True. Such things as radio towers and bridges are usually considered as real property. [p. 805]

18. False. Subsurface rights may be sold separately from surface rights. [p. 805]

19. True. Kitchen cabinets, carpet, and doorknobs are fixtures. [p. 806]

20. True. A fee simple owner has the right to exclusively possess and use his property to the extent that the owner has not transferred any interest in the property [p. 806]

21. False. If a person owns real property in fee simple, his or her ownership is infinite in duration (fee). [p. 807]

22. True. If a person owns real property in fee simple, his or her ownership has no limitation on inheritability (simple). [p. 807]

23. True. A tenant in common can sell, give, devise, or otherwise transfer his or her interest in the property without the consent of the other co- owners. [p. 808]

24. True. A general warranty deed (or grant deed) contains the greatest number of warranties and provides the highest level of protection to a grantee. [p. 812]

25. False. In a special warranty deed, the seller is liable for defects in title that existed before the seller obtained the property. [p. 813]

26. True. If an owner of real property fails to pay property taxes, the government can obtain a lien on the property for the amount of the taxes. [p. 814]

27. False. Under the doctrine of adverse possession, the transfer of the property is involuntary and does not require the delivery of a deed. [p. 815]

28. True. To obtain title under adverse possession, the adverse possessor must physically occupy the property. [p. 815]

29. False. An appurtenant easement runs with the land. If an owner sells the dominant estate, the new owner acquires the benefit of the easement. If an owner sells the servient estate, the buyer purchases the property subject to the easement. [p. 816]

30. True. An easement in gross is a personal right because it does not depend on the easement holder owning adjacent land. Thus, there is no dominant estate. [p. 817]

Multiple Choice

31. D. Answer D is correct. A surface right to the land is, the right to occupy the land. [p. 805]

32. B. Answer B is correct. Subsurface rights may be sold separately from surface rights. [p. 805]

33. A. Answer A is correct. Certain personal property is so closely associated with real property that it becomes part of the realty. Such items are called fixtures. [p. 806]

34. C. Answer C is correct. Air rights enable the owner of a property to rent or sell the space above the property for commercial purposes. [p. 806]

35. C. Answer C is the correct answer. If a person owns real property in fee simple, his or her ownership is infinite in duration (fee). [p. 807]

36. D. Answer D is correct. A life tenant is treated as the owner of the property during the duration of the life estate. [p. 807]

37. A. Answer A is correct. Each joint tenant has a right to sell or transfer his or her interest in the property, but such conveyance terminates the joint tenancy. The parties then become tenants in common. [p. 808]

38. C. Answer C is correct. The most distinguished feature of a joint tenancy is the co-owners' right of survivorship. This means that upon the death of one of the co-owners (or joint tenants), the deceased person's interest in the property automatically passes to the surviving joint tenant or joint tenants. [p. 808]

39. A. Answer A is correct. In a tenancy in common, the interests of a surviving tenant in common pass to the deceased tenant's estate and not to the co-tenants. [p. 808]

40. D. Answer D is correct. Tenancy by the entirety is distinguished from joint tenancy in that neither spouse may sell or transfer his or her interest in the property without the other spouse's consent. Only about half of the states recognize tenancy by the entirety. [p. 809-810]

Short Answer

41. Community property, tenancy in common (answers will vary). [p. 808]

42. The joint tenancy is terminated and Maurice and Cody are now tenants in common. [p. 808]

43. A cooperative [p. 811]

44. Location determines whether or not community property law applies [p. 810]

45. Title to real property can be transferred by sale, tax sale, gift, will, inheritance, adverse possession. [p. 812]

46. Recording statutes. [p. 813]

47. County recorder's office. [p. 813]

48. It is a form of co-ownership that includes the right of survivorship. To create a joint tenancy, words that clearly show a person's intent to create a joint tenancy must be used. Language such as "Marsha Leest and James Leest, as joint tenants" is usually sufficient. [p. 808]

49. Obtain approval of other owners. [p. 811]

50. A reversion is a right of possession that returns to the grantor after the expiration of a limited or contingent estate. [p. 811]

51. Reversions do not have to be expressly stated because they arise automatically by law. [p. 811]

52. Bring a quiet title action. [p. 813]

53. The deed gives constructive notice of the owner's interest in the property. [p. 813]

54. It is title that is free from any encumbrances or other defects that are not disclosed but would affect the value of the property. [p. 814]

55. A gift is made when the deed to the property is delivered by the donor to the donee or to a third party to hold for the donee. [p. 814]

49 | LANDLORD-TENANT LAW AND LAND USE REGULATION

Chapter Overview

The average business does not have the resources to buy land and build its store, offices, manufacturing facilities, or other commercial facilities. Renting or leasing real property is a necessary part of doing business. This chapter covers law in the areas of contracts and real property that relate to the landlord-tenant relationship and discusses the regulation of land use by the government.

Objectives

Upon completion of the exercises in this chapter, you should be able to
1. Explain how a landlord–tenant relationship is created.
2. Identify and describe the various types of tenancy.
3. List and describe the landlord's and tenant's duties under a lease.
4. List and describe the antidiscrimination laws that apply to real estate.
5. Describe the government's power of eminent domain.

Practical Application

Upon learning the objectives in this chapter, you should understand the duties and rights of landlords and tenants in the common leasing of real property. Failure to meet the duties imposed at common law and by statute may cause a tenant to lose his/her tenancy. A landlord who violates his/her duties is subjected to damages and sanctions. A businessperson who is leasing a storefront or commercial building must understand the restrictions on the use of the building and what affirmative tasks must be undertaken to keep him/her out of breach of contract.

Helpful Hints

It is important that you learn the terminology associated with the rights and duties that arise from the landlord-tenant relationship. In each lease of real property, whether you are the landlord or the tenant, you must understand your obligations and know how those obligations are created in a written lease. You must also understand the obligations that are created by statute and remain in effect even if they are not included in the lease. As you examine each right and duty, determine the type of land use that is proper and improper in each situation.

Study Tips

A landlord or tenant can have obligations created by the lease, by statute, or by common law doctrines such as negligence. Examine each of these areas individually to discover the specific rights and duties that are created for the landlord and tenant.

Landlord-Tenant Law and Land Use Regulation

Laws that regulate the ownership, possession, lease, and use of real property have been enacted by federal, state, and local governments, including antidiscrimination laws in leasing and selling real property. Landlord-tenant relationships are created when individuals and businesses rent premises for use as residences or business spaces.
- Lessor. The party who owns or controls the leased space
- Lessee. The party who is renting the space is called the lessee.

Landlord-Tenant Relationship

This relationship is created when the owner of a freehold estate transfers a right to exclusively and temporarily possess the owner's property.
- The tenant receives a leasehold estate.

Lease. The contract between a lessor and lessee is a lease.
- Leases can generally be either oral or written.
- Leases for periods of time longer than one year must be in writing.

Tenancy for Years. A tenancy created when the landlord and the tenant agree on a specific duration for the lease.

Periodic Tenancy. A tenancy created when a lease specifies intervals at which payments are due but does not specify how long the lease is for.

Tenancy at Will. A lease that may be terminated at any time by either party.

Tenancy at Sufferance. A tenancy created when a tenant retains possession of property after the expiration of another tenancy or a life estate without the owner's consent.

Landlord's Duties to a Tenant

Certain duties owed by landlords can be enforced by tenants.

Landlord's Duty to Deliver Possession. A landlord is required to deliver possession of the leased premises to the tenant on the date the lease term begins.
- A landlord may not enter leased premises unless the right is specifically reserved in the lease.

Landlord's Duty Not to Interfere with the Tenant's Right of Quiet Enjoyment. The law implies a covenant of quiet enjoyment in all leases.
- The landlord may not interfere with the tenant's quiet and peaceful possession, use, and enjoyment of the leased premises.

Landlord's Duty to Maintain the Leased Premises. The landlord must comply with the requirements imposed by building and housing codes.

Implied Warranty of Habitability. The leased premise must be fit, safe, and suitable for ordinary residential use.

Tenant's Duties to a Landlord

A tenant owes the landlord the duties agreed to in the lease and any duties imposed by law.

Tenant's Duty to Pay Rent. A tenant owes a duty to pay the agreed-upon amount of rent for the leased premises to the landlord at the agreed-upon time and terms.
- Gross Lease. The tenant pays a gross sum to the landlord, who is responsible for paying the property taxes and assessments on the property.
- Net lease. The tenant is responsible for paying rent and property taxes.
- Double net lease. The tenant is responsible for paying rent, property taxes, and utilities.
- Net, net, net lease (or triple net lease). The tenant is responsible for paying rent, property taxes, utilities, and insurance.
- Upon nonpayment of rent,
    - the landlord is entitled to recover possession of the leased premises from the tenant.
    - the landlord may also sue to recover the unpaid rent from the tenant.
        - The more modern rule requires the landlord to make reasonable efforts to mitigate damages

Tenant's Duty Not to Use Leased Premises for Illegal or Nonstipulated Purposes. A tenant may use leased property for any lawful purposes permitted by the lease.
- If the tenant uses the leased premises for unlawful purposes or nonstipulated purposes, the landlord may terminate the lease, evict the tenant, and sue for damages.

Tenant's Duty Not to Commit Waste. Waste occurs when a tenant causes substantial and permanent damages to the leased premises that decrease the value of the property and the landlord's reversionary interest in it.
- The landlord can recover damages from the tenant for waste.

Tenant's Duty Not to Disturb Other Tenants. A landlord may evict the tenant who interferes with the quiet enjoyment of other tenants.

Premises Liability. Landlords and tenants owe a duty of reasonable care to third parties not to negligently cause injury to them.
- The landlord also owes this duty to the tenant.

Transfer of Rights to Leased Property

Landlords may sell, gift, devise, or otherwise transfer their interests in leased property.
- The new landlord cannot alter the terms of an existing lease.

Assignment of a Lease. The tenant may transfer his or her rights under a lease to another by way of an assignment.
- The new tenant is the assignee and is obligated to perform the duties that the assignor had under the lease.
- The assignor remains responsible for his or her obligations under the lease unless released by the landlord.

Sublease. If a tenant transfers only some of his or her rights under the lease, it is a sublease.

- The sublessor is still responsible under the lease and the sublessee does not obtain any rights under the original lease.

Rent Control. Rent control ordinances stipulate an amount of rent a landlord can charge for residential housing.
- Most of these ordinances fix the rent at a specific amount and provide for minor annual increases.

Civil Rights Acts and Real Estate

Civil rights in the purchase, sale, and lease of real estate, as well as in the use of public property are guaranteed by federal and state laws.

Civil Rights Act. A federal statute that prohibits racial discrimination in the transfer of real property.

Fair Housing Act. A federal statute that makes it unlawful for a party to refuse to rent or sell a dwelling to any person because of his or her race, color, national origin, sex or religion.

Title III of the Americans with Disabilities Act. A federal statute that prohibits discrimination on the basis of disability in places of public accommodation by private entities.

State and Local Antidiscrimination Laws. Many states and local communities have enacted statutes as well as ordinances that prohibit discrimination in the sale or lease of real property.

Eminent Domain and the "Taking" of Real Property

The power of eminent domain allows the government to acquire private property for public purposes.
- The Due Process Clause of the Fifth Amendment to the U.S. Constitution requires the government only take property for "public use."
- The Just Compensation Clause of the Fifth Amendment to the U.S. Constitution requires the government to compensate the property owner.
- In the controversial Kelo case, the U.S. Supreme Court upheld Connecticut's statute that permitted the taking of private property for the purposes of economic development.

Refresh Your Memory

1. An estate where the tenant has a right to possess the real property but does not own title to the property is called _____.

2. A tenant's interest in the real property is called a(n) _____.

3. A transfer of the right to the possession and use of real property for a set term in return for certain consideration is known as a(n) _____.

4. A tenancy created when a landlord and a tenant agree on a specific duration for a lease is known as a _____.

5. A tenancy created when a lease specifies intervals at which payments are due but does not specify how long the lease is for is called a _____.

6. A _____ is a tenancy created when a tenant retains possession of property after the expiration of another tenancy or a life estate without the owner's consent.

7. The _____ is an assurance that provides that leased premises must be fit, safe, and suitable for ordinary residential use.

8. A lease in which the tenant pays a lump sum to the landlord and the landlord is responsible for paying the property taxes and assessments on the property is known as a _____.

9. In a(n) _____ arrangement, the tenant is responsible for paying rent and property taxes.

10. A _____ is a lease where the tenant is responsible for paying the rent, property taxes, utilities, and insurance.

11. The transfer by a tenant of all of his or her rights under a lease to another party is known as a(n) _____.

12. A party to whom a tenant transfers all of his or her rights under a lease is known as a(n) _____.

13. An arrangement in which a tenant transfers some of his or her rights under a lease to another party is known as a _____.

14. The _____ is a clause of the U.S. Constitution that allows the government to take property for "public use."

15. The government's power to take private property for public use, provided that just compensation is paid to the private property holder is known as _____.

Critical Thought Exercise

The city of Peaceful Meadows has numerous historical districts and expensive housing. The architecture is classical with almost no use of neon signs in commercial areas. As the city grows and new commercial areas are developed on streets that intersect with the interstate freeway on the edge of town, the city council is becoming increasingly alarmed with the increase in large electric signs and the typical glass and metal construction used by fast food restaurants and chain stores. Peaceful Meadows passes a zoning ordinance that forbids electrical signs over five feet by eight feet in size and limits the use of neon to the face of opaque signs that must be mounted flush with the ground. The style of the signs must be in conformance with the classical architecture of Peaceful Meadows. Three large chain restaurants desire to place 70-foot tall signs on the property where they are constructing restaurants near the freeway. They also desire to build their restaurants in the style that they always use in other communities because these "cookie-cutter" plans are efficient and economical to build. The Planning Commission of Peaceful Meadows rejects the permits for all signage and building plans proposed by the three restaurants. The restaurants apply for a variance to allow them to avoid the restrictive zoning law. These variance applications are also denied. The restaurants file suit and allege that the zoning ordinance creates an undue hardship and prevents them from making a reasonable use of their land. They also complain that the zoning ordinance is unfairly applied to them due to the numerous other restaurants that already have very tall signs and cheap unsightly construction.

Is aesthetic zoning lawful as used by the city of Peaceful Meadows?

Please compose your answer to the Critical Thinking Exercise using a separate sheet of paper or your computer word processing program.

Practice Quiz

True/False

16. _____ In a landlord–tenant relationship, the tenant receives a nonfreehold estate in the real property.

17. _____ A rental agreement between a landlord and a tenant is called a lease.

18. _____ The Statute of Frauds permits lease contracts that last for less than five years to be orally contracted.

19. _____ Any lease for a stated period irrespective of its duration is called periodic tenancy.

20. _____ A tenancy for years terminates automatically, without notice, upon the expiration of the stated term.

21. _____ A landlord owes a duty to deliver possession of the leased premises to the lessee.

22. _____ If a landlord wrongfully locks the tenant out of the premises of the rented property, it is termed as constructive eviction.

23. _____ In a net lease arrangement, the tenant is responsible for paying rent and property taxes.

24. _____ In a double net lease arrangement, property taxes are shared between the tenant and landlord.

25. _____ In a gross lease, the landlord is responsible for paying the property taxes and assessments on the property.

26. _____ A landlord's right to receive rent is not transferable.

27. _____ An assignee is obligated to perform the duties that the assignor had under the lease.

28. _____ A partial transfer of a tenant's rights under a lease is known as an assignment.

29. _____ In a sublease, no legal relationship is formed between the landlord and the sublessee.

30. _____ The power of the eminent domain allows the government to take private property for public use after paying consideration.

Multiple Choice

31. A landlord–tenant relationship is characterized by _____.

A. the transfer of title to the tenant
B. the receipt of a nonfreehold estate by the tenant
C. the creation of a future interest for the tenant
D. the free simple absolute ownership of the tenant

32. What is a tenancy at will?

A. a tenancy created when a lease specifies intervals at which payments are due but does not specify how long the lease is for
B. a tenancy created by a lease that may be terminated at any time by either party
C. a tenancy created when a tenant retains possession of property after the expiration of another tenancy
D. a tenancy created when a landlord and a tenant agree on a specific duration for a lease

33. What is an unlawful detainer action?

A. a legal process that a tenant must complete before he or she is allowed to sublet
B. a legal lawsuit brought against the landlord for breach of the implied warranty of habitability
C. a lawsuit brought by the tenant against the landlord on wrongful eviction
D. a legal process that a landlord must complete to evict a holdover tenant

34. Which of the following is true of tenancy at sufferance?

A. It can be terminated only after an eviction proceeding.
B. It cannot be terminated as the holdover tenant has the title of transfer.
C. It has a specific time period before expiration.
D. It requires a notice period that equals the length of payment period.

35. Building codes specify the _____.

A. policies of the implied warranty of habitability for residential leases
B. rules on proper delivery of possession to the tenant
C. standards for property owners to maintain and repair leased premises
D. laws regulating the extent to which a landlord can interfere with a tenant's right to quiet enjoyment

36. Which of the following duties has a landlord breached if he leases a rodent-infested warehouse to a farmer?

A. implied warranty of habitability
B. duty not to commit waste
C. duty to deliver possession
D. duty not to interfere with a tenant's right to quiet enjoyment

37. Which of the following clusters of payments are made by a tenant in a double net lease?

A. paying property taxes and assessments on the property
B. paying rent, property taxes, utilities, and insurance
C. paying rent and property taxes
D. paying rent, property taxes, and utilities

38. Who is an assignor of a lease?

A. a tenant who partially transfers his or her rights under a lease
B. a tenant who transfers all of his or her rights under a lease
C. a landlord whose property has been made an assignment
D. a landlord who sells property that has already been leased

39. Which of the following statements is true with regard to a sublease?

A. The sublessee acquires all rights under the original lease agreement.
B. The landlord can sue the sublessee to recover rent payments.
C. The landlord and the sublessee do not have a legal relationship.
D. The sublessee has a duty to pay rent only to the landlord.

40. Which of the following is true of the government's power of eminent domain?

A. It does not allow the owner of the property to make a case for keeping the property.
B. It requires payment of compensation by the government.
C. It does not apply to state and local governments.
D. It allows the government to set up zoning areas.

Short Answer

41. If Karissa subleases her apartment to Mayada, what type of relationship does Mayada now have with Karissa's landlord?

_____

_____

42. What may a landlord recover if his or her tenant has allowed the carpeting in the rented premises to be destroyed by the tenant's four large dogs?

_____

_____

43. When can a periodic tenancy be terminated?

_____

_____

44. What factors are considered in deciding whether a barrier to accessibility for a disabled person must be removed by the owner of an old building that was built before the ADA was enacted?

_____

_____

45. What is the implied warranty of habitability?

_____

_____

46. What may Kerri, a tenant, do if Joe, her landlord, fails to maintain or repair leased premises and it affects the tenant's use and enjoyment of the premises?

_____

_____

47. What is meant by the term net, net, net lease?

_____

_____

48. What are four of the most common types of commercial leases?

_____

_____

49. John, a real estate broker, listed a house in one of the wealthiest cities of Somewhere. He used to live in the particular neighborhood where this listing is and has decided to sell only to Asians. Marla, an African American, qualified for the house and feels that there may be some discrimination going on. What may she base a cause of action on should she decide to sue?

_____

_____

50. What remedy does the landlord have if a sublessee fails to pay rent?

_____

_____

51. Who are the parties to an assignment?

_____

_____

52. Which covenant prevents the landlord from interfering with the tenant's quiet and peaceful possession?

_____

_____

53. Give two examples of things that have been held to breach the implied warranty of habitability.

_____

_____

54. If Kali assigns her rights under a lease that she has with Chad to Edwin, what rights does Edwin now have?

_____

_____

55. What is a rent control ordinance?

_____

_____

Answers to Refresh Your Memory

1. nonfreehold estate [p. 823]
2. leasehold estate [p. 823]
3. lease [p. 823]
4. tenancy for years [p. 823]
5. periodic tenancy [p. 824]
6. tenancy at sufferance [p. 824]
7. implied warranty of habitability [p. 827]
8. gross lease [p. 828]
9. net lease [p. 828]
10. net, net, net lease [p. 829]
11. assignment [p. 830]
12. assignee [p. 830]
13. sublease [p. 830]
14. Due Process Clause of the Fifth Amendment [p. 833]
15. eminent domain [p. 833]

Model Answer to Critical Thought Exercise

Municipalities may enact zoning ordinances pursuant to their police power as reserved to them by the Tenth Amendment. Zoning ordinances may (1) designate the type of land use allowed in an area (residential, commercial, industrial), (2) restrict the height, size, and locations of buildings, and (3) establish aesthetic requirements or restrictions for signs and exteriors of buildings. The owner who wishes to use his land for a use different from that contained in a zoning ordinance may request a variance. The landowner must prove that the ordinance causes an undue hardship by preventing the owner from making a reasonable use or return on investment. Zoning laws are applied prospectively, allowing uses in existence at the time the ordinance is passed to continue. Modifications or renovations often trigger a requirement that the nonconforming use be terminated. A city's planning commission may legally act to protect the character and stability of its neighborhoods. The city may consider what effect any variance may have upon surrounding properties and the overall zoning plan for the city. If a zoning ordinance is enacted pursuant to the city's police power to protect its residents' health, safety, and welfare, then it will be deemed a lawful exercise of constitutional power. The ordinance in Peaceful Meadows was enacted to preserve the quality of the community and to protect the value and use of property in the city. The ordinance only required that the restaurants conform to aesthetic requirements. The ordinance did not prevent the building of the restaurants or the use of signs to announce the location of the restaurants. The restaurants were not deprived of the use of their land and may still obtain a reasonable return on their investment. The zoning ordinance in Peaceful Meadows does not create an undue hardship and is therefore lawful in both design and application.

Answers to Practice Quiz

True/False

16. True. The tenant receives a nonfreehold estate in the real property; that is, the tenant has a right to possession of the property but not title to the property. [p. 823]

17. True. A rental agreement between a landlord and a tenant is called a lease. [p. 823]

18. False. Statutes of Frauds require that leases for periods of time longer than one year be in writing. [p. 823]

19. False. A periodic tenancy is created when a lease specifies intervals at which payments are due but does not specify the duration of the lease. [p. 824]

20. True. A tenancy for years terminates automatically, without notice, upon the expiration of the stated term. [p. 823]

21. True. A landlord owes a duty to deliver possession of the leased premises to the lessee. [p. 825]

22. False. If a landlord causes the leased premises to become unfit for the tenant's intended use (e.g., failing to provide electricity) and the tenant leaves the premises, this is called constructive eviction and constitutes a wrongful eviction. [p. 826]

23. True. In a net lease arrangement, the tenant is responsible for paying rent and property taxes. [p. 828]

24. False. In a double net lease arrangement, the tenant is responsible for paying rent, property taxes, and utilities. [p. 828]

25. True. In a gross lease, the tenant pays a gross sum to the landlord. The landlord is responsible for paying the property taxes and assessments on the property. [p. 828]

26. False. A landlord can sell the right to receive rents. In such case, after proper notice, the tenants are to pay rent to the designated party. The landlord still owes normal duties to the tenants, however. [p. 830]

27. True. The assignee is obligated to perform the duties that the assignor had under the lease. [p. 830]

28. False. If a tenant transfers all of his or her interests under a lease, it is an assignment of a lease. [p. 830]

29. True. In a sublease, no legal relationship is formed between the landlord and the sublessee. Therefore, the sublessee does not acquire rights under the original lease. [p. 830]

30. True. The power of the eminent domain allows the government to take private property for public use after paying consideration.[p. 833]

Multiple Choice

31. B. Answer B is correct. A landlord–tenant relationship is created when the owner of a freehold estate in real estate (i.e., an estate in fee or a life estate) transfers a right to exclusively and temporarily possess the owner's property. The tenant receives a nonfreehold estate in the real property. [p. 823]

32. B. Answer B is correct. A lease that may be terminated at any time by either party creates a tenancy at will. [p. 824]

33. D. Answer D is correct. Eviction proceeding (unlawful detainer action) is a legal process that a landlord must complete to evict a holdover tenant. [p. 825]

34. A. Answer A is correct. A tenant at sufferance is liable for the payment of rent during the period of sufferance. Most states require an owner to go through certain legal proceedings, called an eviction proceeding or unlawful detainer action, to evict a holdover tenant. [p. 825]

35. C. Answer C is correct. States and local municipalities have enacted statutes called building codes, or housing codes. These statutes impose specific standards on property owners to maintain and repair leased premises. [p. 826]

36. A. Answer A is correct. Implied warranty of habitability is a warranty that provides that leased premises must be fit, safe, and suitable for ordinary residential use. [p. 827]

37. D. Answer D is correct. In a double net lease arrangement, the tenant is responsible for paying rent, property taxes, and utilities. [p. 828]

38. B. Answer B is correct. Assignor is a tenant who transfers rights under a lease. [p. 830]

39. C. Answer C is correct. In a sublease, no legal relationship is formed between the landlord and the sublessee. Therefore, the sublessee does not acquire rights under the original lease. [p. 830]

40. B. Answer B is correct. The Just Compensation Clause of the Fifth Amendment to the U.S. Constitution requires the government to compensate the property owner (and possibly others, such as lessees) when it exercises the power of eminent domain. [p. 833]

Short Answer

41. No legal relationship, as Mayada has no rights under the sublease. [p. 830]

42. Damages from the tenant for waste. [p. 829]

43. It can be terminated at the end of any payment interval. [p. 824]

44. With respect to existing buildings, architectural barriers must be removed if such removal is readily achievable. In determining when an action is readily achievable, the factors to be considered include the nature and cost of the action, the financial resources of the facility, and the type of operations of the facility. [p. 833]

45. A warranty that provides that the leased premises must be fit, safe, and suitable for ordinary residential use. [p. 827]

46. The tenant may (1) withhold from his or her rent the amount by which the defect reduced that value of the premises to him or her, (2) repair the defect and deduct the cost of repairs from the rent due for the leased premises, (3) cancel the lease if the failure to repair constitutes constructive eviction, or (4) sue for damages for the amount the landlord's failure to repair the defect reduced the value of the leasehold. [p. 827]

47. The tenant is responsible for paying rent, property taxes, utilities, and insurance. [p. 829]

48. Gross lease, net lease, double net lease, and triple net lease. [p. 828-829]

49. Civil Rights Act 1866. [p. 832]

50. Because there is no legal relationship between the landlord and the sublessee, the landlord must seek the rent from the sublessor. [pp. 830-831]

51. The assignee and assignor. [p. 830]

52. The covenant of quiet enjoyment [p. 825]

53. Unchecked rodent infestation, leaking roofs (answers will vary). [p. 825]

54. All the rights that Kali had under the lease. [p. 830]

55. An ordinance that stipulates what amount of rent a landlord can charge for residential housing [p. 830]

50 | INSURANCE

Chapter Overview

The potential risk of loss that a business or individual faces due to death, fire, or injury may be staggering. Insurance is a crucial part of business planning. This chapter examines the insurance contract, types and uses of insurance, defenses used by insurance companies to avoid liability, and secondary liability for losses. The businessperson should understand the types of insurance coverage that are necessary for the proper protection of personal and business assets.

Objectives

Upon completion of the exercises in this chapter, you should be able to:
1. Describe an insurance contract and define insurable interest.
2. List and describe the various types of life, health, and disability insurance.
3. Identify the risks covered by a standard fire insurance policy and a homeowners' policy.
4. Describe automobile insurance and explain no-fault insurance.
5. List and describe special forms of business insurance.

Practical Application

Even the most successful business has limited resources. This chapter will help you develop a greater understanding of the role that insurance plays in the overall business plan and estate planning of the individual. By understanding the coverage provided by different insurance products, you can make an informed decision as to the type and amount of insurance that is needed to achieve business and personal goals that have been set. Just as important is an understanding of your rights as an insured and the potential defenses that an insurance company will use to avoid paying a claim.

Helpful Hints

You should examine insurance products and incorporate them into any business plan and personal estate plan. When a businessperson is making a decision as to the type and amount of coverage needed, he or she must first determine the asset or risk for which protection is needed. The coverage must then be matched to that risk. The needs of a business will vary depending upon the type of business activity, product produced or sold, importance of key personnel, and exposure to liability based upon the risk created by the business to its employees and members of the general public.

Study Tips

In order to accomplish their business goals, each businessperson should understand the important points contained in the following outline. This laundry list of insurance terms and principles is indispensable.

Insurance

Individuals and businesses can protect themselves against the risk of loss by purchasing various types of insurance.

- Insurance. A contract where one party undertakes to indemnify another against loss, damage, or liability arising from a contingent or unknown event.
- Insurer or Underwriter. The insurance company, which is obligated to pay insurance proceeds to members of the pool who experience losses.
- Policy. An insurance contract.
- Premium. The money paid to the insurance company.
- Insurance Agent. Usually works exclusively for one insurance company.
- Insurance Broker. An independent contractor who represents a number of insurance companies.

Insurable Interest. A person must have an insurable interest in anything he or she insures.

- For life insurance, a person must have a familiar relationship or an economic benefit from the continued life of another.
- For property insurance, anyone who would suffer a monetary loss from the destruction of the property has an insurable interest in that property.

Insurance Policy. The insurance contract, or policy, is a form of third-party beneficiary contract. This policy is purchased by the insured who pays premiums to the insurance company or insurer.

- Mandatory provisions are required by statute and must be included in each policy.
    - If mandatory provisions are omitted from the contract, they will still be implied.
    - Examples. Coverage for certain losses, how limitations on coverage must be worded in the contract.
- Modification of an insurance contract by the parties is usually accomplished by adding an endorsement to the policy or by executing a document called a rider.

Duties of Insured and Insurer. The parties to an insurance contract are obligated to perform the duties imposed by the contract.

- The duties of the insured are:
    - Duty to pay premiums. The insured must pay the agreed-upon premiums.
        - Many policies include a grace period during which an insured may pay an overdue premium.
    - Duty to notify insurer. The insured must notify the insurer after the occurrence of an insured event.
    - Duty to cooperate. The insured must cooperate with the insurer in investigating claims made against the insurer.
- The duties of the insurer are:
    - Duty to defend. The insurer has a duty to defend against any suit brought against the insured that involves a claim within the coverage of the policy.
    - Duty to pay insurance proceeds. The insurer's primary duty is to pay legitimate claims up to the policy limit.

Deductible Clause. A deductible clause provides that insurance proceeds will be paid only after the insured has paid a certain amount toward the damage or loss.

Exclusions from Coverage. Excluding certain events from coverage under a policy is common.

Coinsurance Clause. This clause requires an insured to pay a percentage of the cost of an insured loss.
- Copay clauses require the insured must pay a flat amount rather than a percentage.

Incontestability Clause. Laws that prevent insurers from contesting statements made by insured's in applications for insurance after a certain number of years, usually 2 to 5 years, have been enacted by many states.

Life Insurance

Life insurance is a form of insurance where the insurer must pay a specific sum of money to a named beneficiary upon the death of another.

Parties to a Life Insurance Contract.
- The insurance company issues the policy.
- The owner of the policy is the person who contracts with the insurance company and pays the premiums.
- The insured is the person whose life is insured.
- The beneficiary is the person who is to receive the insurance proceeds when the insured dies.

Suicide Clause. This clause states that if the insured commits suicide within a certain period after taking out a life insurance policy, the insurance company does not have to pay the proceeds to the beneficiary.

Health and Disability Insurance

Health Insurance. Health insurance can be purchased to cover the costs of medical treatment.
- Many companies offer dental insurance.

Disability Insurance. Disability insurance provides a monthly income to an insured who is unable to work due to a nonwork-related disability.

Fire and Homeowners' Insurance

These types of insurance are often required for mortgaged properties.

Standard Fire Insurance Policy. A standard fire insurance policy protects real and personal property against loss resulting from fire and certain related perils.
- Most policies provide for replacement cost insurance that pays the cost to replace the damaged or destroyed property at its current cost.
- It does not provide liability coverage for personal injury.

Homeowner's Policy. A homeowners' policy covers personal liability in addition to the risks covered by the fire insurance policy.

- The homeowners' policy covers losses from a much wider range of causes, including negligence and theft.

Personal Liability Coverage Homeowner's Policy. This policy provides comprehensive personal liability insurance for the insured and members of his or her family.

Personal Articles Floater. An addition to a homeowner's policy that provides insurance for specific valuable items.

Renters' Insurance. A residence contents broad form policy covers losses incurred by renters for damage or destruction to their possessions.

Title Insurance. Title insurance protects against defects in title and liens and encumbrances that are not disclosed on the title insurance policy.

- A lender often requires this insurance before it will fund a loan.

Automobile Insurance

Many states have mandatory automobile insurance statutes. Proof of insurance is required to be kept on file with the state department of motor vehicles.

Collision Insurance. Collision insurance insures the owner's car against the risk of loss or damage.

- The premium varies depending upon the amount of deductible paid towards any loss by the car owner.

Comprehensive Insurance. Comprehensive insurance insures an automobile from loss or damages from causes other than collision, such as fire, theft, hail, falling objects, earthquakes, floods, and vandalism.

Liability Insurance. Liability insurance covers damages that the insured causes to third parties.

- This coverage usually has a limit for injury to each person in an accident, a limit for the total bodily injury for all persons injured, and a limit for property damage.

Medical Payment Coverage. Medical payment coverage covers medical expenses for the driver and his or her passengers who are injured in an accident.

Uninsured Motorist Coverage. Uninsured motorist coverage provides coverage to the driver and passengers who are injured by an uninsured motorist or hit-and-run driver.

No-Fault Automobile Insurance. No-fault automobile insurance has been enacted in some states.

- Under this system, a driver's insurance company pays for any injuries he or she suffered in an accident, no matter who caused the accident.
- Claimants may not sue to recover damages from the party who caused the accident unless the injured party suffered serious injury.

Marine Insurance. Marine insurance protects owners and shippers against loss or damage to their ships and cargo.

Umbrella Insurance. Umbrella insurance coverage pays only if the basic policy limits of a liability policy have been exceeded.
- This insurance is inexpensive and often extends coverage to $5 million.

Business Insurance

The owner of real property and a business should purchase several types of insurance in addition to liability and fire insurance.

Business Interruption Insurance. Business interruption insurance that pays for lost revenues during the period a business is rebuilding after a fire or some other event.

Workers' Compensation Insurance. Workers' compensation insurance pays for injuries and lost wages of employees who are injured on the job.
- This insurance is mandatory in most states.

Key-Person Life Insurance. Key-person life insurance is often purchased by business owners to finance buy-sell agreements upon the death of one of the owners of the business.
- If an insured owner dies, the insurance proceeds are paid to the deceased's beneficiaries.
- The deceased's interest in the business then reverts to the other owners of the business according to the terms of the buy-sell agreement.
- This allows a business to continue upon the death of an owner and prevents the beneficiaries from selling off the assets of the business.

Directors' and Officers' Liability Insurance. Directors' and officers' liability insurance protects directors and officers from liability for their negligent actions that they take on behalf of the corporation.

Professional Malpractice Insurance. Professional malpractice insurance which covers the injuries caused by professionals, such as doctors, lawyers, accountants, and architects, resulting from the negligent performance of their duties.

Product Liability Insurance. Product liability insurance protects against losses incurred by manufacturers and sellers for injuries caused by their defective products.

Refresh Your Memory

The following exercise will give you the opportunity to test your memory of the principles given in this chapter. Read the question twice and place your answer in the blank provided. Review the chapter material for any question that you are unable to answer or remember.

1. _____ is a means for persons and businesses to protect themselves against the risk of loss.

2. An insurance contract is defined as a _____.

3. _____ is a requirement that a person who purchases insurance have a personal stake in the insured item or person.

4. A person who is to receive life insurance proceeds when the insured dies is known as a _____.

5. A(n) _____ is a document that modifies an insurance policy and becomes part of the insurance policy.

6. The _____ is a duty of the insurer to protect the insured against lawsuits or legal proceedings that involve a claim within the coverage of the insurance policy.

7. A(n) _____ is a clause in an insurance policy that provides that insurance proceeds are payable only after the insured has paid a specified amount toward the damage or loss.

8. _____ protects the insurers from intentional or unintentional material or informative misrepresentation from an insurance applicant.

9. The owner of the policy in a life insurance without exception is the _____.

10. An employee of a company that provides _____ insurance to its employees can receive payments, as provided by the policy, for injuries suffered by employees while working on the job.

11. A(n) _____ is a comprehensive insurance policy that includes coverage for the risks covered by a fire insurance policy as well as personal liability insurance.

12. _____ helps an owner of a real property to establish clear ownership over that property.

13. _____ is a form of property insurance that insures an automobile from loss or damage due to causes other than collision.

14. A(n) _____ is an automobile insurance system used by some states in which the driver's insurance company pays for any injuries or death the driver suffers in an accident irrespective of who caused the accident.

15. Insureds who want to increase their liability coverage beyond the original coverage can purchase a(n) _____.

Critical Thought Exercise

The five partners in the law firm of Higgins & Ford, LLP, purchased a $500,000 life insurance policy on the life of each partner from Celestial Insurance. The firm was listed as the beneficiary. On the application forms, the relationship of the beneficiary to the insured was listed as "business/family association." The period of contestability was two years. Three years after the policy on the life of Victor Ford was purchased, Mr. Ford died in an automobile accident. Celestial refused to pay on the policy and filed suit in a federal district court against Higgins &

Ford, seeking to have the policy declared void *ab initio* (from the beginning) on the ground that the law firm lacked an insurable interest.

Does the misleading statement regarding the relationship with the insured by the beneficiary or the lack of a personal relationship with Victor Ford prevent Higgins & ford from having an insurable interest?

Please compose your answer to the Critical Thinking Exercise using a separate sheet of paper or your computer word processing program.

Practice Quiz

True/False

16. _____ Insurance is a form of coverage for loss that is initiated after the loss has occurred.

17. _____ An insurance contract is called a policy.

18. _____ Premiums are based on an estimate of the number of parties within the pool who will suffer the risks insured against.

19. _____ An insurance broker is an agent of the insurer.

20. _____ If the insured does not have an insurable interest in the property being insured, the contract is treated as a wager.

21. _____ An insurable interest is created when the insurer has ownership of the item being insured.

22. _____ For a life insurance, insurable interest is necessary at the time of loss.

23. _____ Insurance coverage is typically suspended during grace periods for payments.

24. _____ Personal injury is not covered under a standard fire insurance policy.

25. _____ Under the replacement cost insurance, the insurer has the right to either pay the insured for the loss or pay to have the property restored.

26. _____ An owner of real property or a mortgagee pays only one premium for title insurance, usually at closing.

27. _____ The uninsured motorist coverage only covers when the accident is the insured's fault.

28. _____ Shippers can purchase comprehensive insurance to cover the risk of loss to their goods during shipment.

29. _____ A directors' and officers' liability insurance helps an organization sue its directors and officers in case of personal negligence.

30. _____ An insurer will issue an umbrella policy only if a stipulated minimum amount of basic coverage on other insurance policies has been purchased by the insured.

Multiple Choice

31. In the context of insurance, what does the term "premium" refer to?

A. the money received from the defaulting party
B. the money paid to the insurance company
C. the money paid to insured after an accidental damage
D. the money paid to insurance brokers as fee

32. Who is an underwriter?

A. a lawyer who represents the insurance company
B. an agent who works for only one insurance company
C. a broker who works on behalf on many insurance companies
D. an insurance company that provides coverage to the insured

33. Which of the following statements is true of insurance?

A. It has to be paid after the risk has been encountered.
B. It can be obtained even if one has no insurable interest in that property.
C. It is a means of transferring and distributing the risk of loss.
D. It cannot be modified once issued.

34. Which of the following statements is true of a life insurance?

A. The insurable interest need not exist at the time of insurance.
B. The insurable interest need not exist at the time of death or loss.
C. The beneficiary and the insured cannot be the same person.
D. The beneficiary and the insured must be bound by a relationship of blood.

35. Which of the following is the insurer's duty to pay?

A. to pay back the insured's money on demand
B. to pay back the premiums paid by the insured upon an endorsement of insurance
C. to pay legitimate claims up to the insurance policy limits
D. to pay interest for the premiums paid by insured on a monthly or yearly basis

36. What is the copay clause in an insurance policy?

A. a clause in a life insurance contract that provides no coverage if the insured commits suicide before a stipulated date
B. a clause in an insurance policy that expressly stipulates the risks that are not covered by the insurance policy
C. a clause that prevents insurers from contesting statements made by insureds in applications after the passage of a stipulated number of years
D. a clause that requires the insured to pay a percentage of an insured loss along with the remainder being paid by the insurer

37. What happens to the life insurance proceeds upon the death of the insured who has not named a beneficiary?

A. The proceeds are given to the state.
B. The proceeds remain with the insurer for the full-term of the insurance.
C. The proceeds are given to charitable organizations.
D. The proceeds go to the insured's estate.

38. Which of the following statements is true of the suicide clause in a life insurance?

A. The insurer is liable to pay in cases of legitimate suicides even if the life insurance policy had elapsed.
B. The suicide clause has a specified date set.
C. The insurer doesn't have to pay the beneficiary even if the suicide takes place after the specified date.
D. The suicide has to occur within the specified date for payment.

39. Which of the following statements is true of a personal articles floater?

A. The insured can insure specific body parts using this policy.
B. The coverage includes insurance of intangible properties.
C. The coverage does not include loss or damage cause during travel.
D. The insurance company will charge an increased premium based on the articles insured.

40. Which of the following statements is true with regard to umbrella insurance?

A. It is cannot be used for liability coverage.
B. It does not require the insured to have already purchased insurance policies.
C. It cannot be used with other insurance policies.
D. It is only paid if the limits on other insurance policies have been exceeded.

Short Answer

41. What is an insurable interest?

_____

_____

42. What is the difference between universal and term life insurance?

_____

_____

43. Explain the two duties owed by an insurer to their insured.

_____

_____

44. What is a double indemnity clause?

_____

_____

45. What is the difference between health insurance and disability insurance?

_____

_____

46. Personal liability coverage under a homeowners' policy will cover what types of losses?

_____

_____

47. What is a personal articles floater?

_____

_____

48. List four standard types of coverage that an automobile owner may purchase.

_____

_____

49. List five types of insurance businesses may purchase for coverage of business –specific events.

_____

_____

50. Why may a manufacturing business located in Denver, Colorado, want to purchase marine insurance?

_____

_____

51. Kyle has automobile liability insurance that pays up to $500,000 per accident and an umbrella policy with an additional $2,000,000 of coverage. If Kyle's negligence causes an accident in which injuries to other persons total $1,500,000, how will the losses be paid?

_____

_____

52. How does no-fault insurance work?

_____

_____

53. What is replacement cost insurance?

_____

_____

54. What is a premium?

_____

_____

55. What is umbrella insurance?

_____

_____

Answers to Refresh Your Memory

1. Insurance [p. 839]
2. policy [p. 839]
3. Insurable interest [p. 839]
4. beneficiary [p. 840]
5. endorsement [p. 840]
6. duty to defend [p. 840]
7. deductible clause [p. 840]
8. Incontestability clause [p. 842]
9. person who pays the premiums [p. 842]
10. disability [p. 844]
11. homeowners' policy [p. 845]
12. Title insurance [p. 846]
13. Comprehensive insurance [p. 847]
14. no-fault insurance [p. 848]
15. umbrella insurance [p. 850]

Critical Thought Exercise Model Answer

A person must have an insurable interest in anything he or she insures. If there is no insurable interest, the contract is treated as a wager and cannot be enforced. In the case of life insurance, a person must have a close family relationship or an economic benefit from the continued life of another to have an insurable interest in that person's life. An insurable interest may be based upon a business relationship. Higgins & Ford not only had a business relationship with Ford, but as a partner in the firm, Higgins & Ford derived an economic benefit from the continued life of Victor Ford. His death created an economic loss for Higgins & Ford, especially if his partnership interest was subject to attachment by creditors. Because the policy was not void *ab initio* and because the period for contesting the policy had passed under the contestability clause, Celestial may not now challenge the terms of the policy or the extent of Higgins & Ford's insurable interest.

Answers to Practice Quiz

True/False

16. False. Insurance is a means for persons and businesses to protect themselves against the risk of loss. [p. 839]

17. True. An insurance contract is called a policy. [p. 839]

18. True. Premiums are based on an estimate of the number of parties within the pool who will suffer the risks insured against. The estimate is based on past experience. [p. 839]

19. False. An insurance broker is an independent contractor who represents a number of insurance companies. The broker is the agent of the insured. [p. 839]

20. True. If the insured does not have an insurable interest in the property being insured, the contract is treated as a wager and cannot be enforced. [p. 839]

21. True. Ownership creates an insurable interest. In addition, mortgagees, lien holders, and tenants have an insurable interest in property. The insurable interest in property must exist at the time of loss. [p. 839]

22. False. The insurable interest must exist when the life insurance policy is issued but need not exist at the time of death. [p. 840]

23. False. Many insurance policies provide a grace period during which an insured may pay an overdue premium. The insurance usually remains in effect during the grace period. [p. 840]

24. True. A standard fire insurance policy protects real and personal property against loss resulting from fire and certain related perils. It does not, however, provide liability insurance for personal injury. [p. 845]

25. True. Replacement cost insurance is an insurance that pays the cost to replace the damaged or destroyed property up to the policy limits. [p. 845]

26. True. An owner of real property or a mortgagee pays only one premium for title insurance, usually at closing. [p. 846]

27. False. Uninsured motorist coverage is an automobile insurance that provides coverage to a driver and passengers who are injured by an uninsured motorist or a hit-and-run driver. [p. 847]

28. False. Shippers can purchase marine insurance to cover the risk of loss to their goods during shipment. [p. 849]

29. False. Directors' and officers' liability insurance (D&O insurance) is an insurance that protects directors and officers of a corporation from liability for actions taken on behalf of the corporation. [p. 850]

30. True. An insurer will issue an umbrella policy only if a stipulated minimum amount of basic coverage on other insurance policies has been purchased by the insured. [p. 850]

Multiple Choice

31. B. Answer B is correct. Premium is the money paid to an insurance company. [p. 839]

32. D. Answer D is correct. Insurer (underwriter) is an insurance company that underwrites insurance coverage. [p. 839]

33. C. Answer C is correct. Insurance is defined as a contract whereby one party undertakes to indemnify another against loss, damage, or liability arising from a contingent or unknown event. It is a means of transferring and distributing risk of loss. [p. 839]

34. B. Answer B is correct. The insurable interest must exist when the life insurance policy is issued but need not exist at the time of death. [p. 840]

35. C. Answer C is correct. The insurer owes the duty to pay legitimate claims up to the policy limits. [p. 840]

36. D. Answer D is correct. Coinsurance clause or copay clause is a clause in an insurance policy that requires the insured to pay a percentage of an insured loss. [p. 842]

37. D. Answer D is correct. Life insurance is really "death insurance" because the insurer is normally obligated to pay a specified sum of money upon the death of the insured. The owner of the policy has the power to name the beneficiary of the insurance proceeds. Most life insurance contracts permit the owner to change beneficiaries. If no beneficiary is named, the proceeds go to the insured's estate. [p. 842]

38. B. Answer B is correct. Life insurance policies usually contain suicide clauses, which state that if the insured commits suicide within a certain period after taking out a life insurance policy on him or her, the insurance company does not have to pay the life insurance proceeds to the named beneficiary. [p. 844]

39. D. Answer D is correct. The insurance company will charge an increased premium based on the articles insured. [p. 846]

40. D. An umbrella policy pays only if the basic policy limits on other insurance policies have been exceeded. [p. 850]

Short Answer

41. An insurable interest is a personal interest in the item or person based upon a family, economic, or ownership interest in the person or property. [p. 839]

42. Term life insurance is effective for a limited period of time and only pays the face value of the policy while universal life combines features of whole life and term life, giving a set face value that is increased by an investment portion of the premium with no set time for expiration of the policy, as in whole life. [p. 843]

43. (1) The insurer must defend the insured in any suit, including paying for a lawyer and the costs associated with the suit. (2) The insurer has a duty to pay legitimate claims up to the policy limit. [p. 840]

44. A clause that stipulates that the insurer will pay double the amount of the policy if death is caused by accident. [p. 843]

45. Health insurance pays for the costs of medical treatment, surgery, and hospital care, while disability insurance pays for lost income and provides a monthly payment when the disabled person cannot work. [p. 844]

46. Personal injury of third persons, property damage caused by the insured or family members, medical expenses resulting from the acts of the insured or family members. [p. 845]

47. It is an addition to a homeowners' policy that covers specific valuable items such as jewelry, paintings, antiques, and collectibles. [p. 845]

48. (1) collision insurance (2) comprehensive insurance (3) liability insurance (4) medical payment coverage. [p. 847]

49. (1) business interruption insurance (2) workers' compensation insurance (3) key-person life insurance (4) directors' and officers' liability insurance (5) product liability insurance. [p. 849-850]

50. If the business engages in shipping of goods by ship or other vessel, the marine insurance will cover the risk of loss to their goods during shipping. Marine inland insurance may be purchased for shipping that uses inland waters such as rivers and lakes. [p. 849]

51. If Kyle has automobile insurance that pays up to $500,000 for each insured event and an umbrella policy with $2 million of coverage, and Kyle causes $1,500,000 in damages to persons in an accident, the liability policy will pay the first $500,000 of the damages and the umbrella policy will cover the remaining $1.0 million in damages. [p. 850]

52. A driver's insurance company pays for any injuries or death he or she suffered in an accident, no matter who caused the accident. [p. 848]

53. Insurance that pays the cost to replace the damage or destroyed property up to the policy limits. [p. 845]

54. Premium is money paid to an insurance company. [p. 839]

55. Umbrella insurance is additional insurance that provides coverage in excess of the basic policy limits of other insurance policies. [p. 850]

51 | ACCOUNTANTS' DUTIES AND LIABILITY

Chapter Overview

Accountants can be held liable to both clients and third parties for breach of contract, negligence, and misrepresentation when they fail to properly perform their duties. These duties may include both auditing of financial statements and rendering opinions based upon those audits. They give tax advice, prepare tax filings, prepare statements for clients, and provide consulting services. In addition to the liability exposure for the common law actions already noted, an accountant may be subject to liability under securities laws and the tax codes. The Sarbanes-Oxley Act has specified additional expectations of accountants with liability for failure to uphold these expectations. The material in this chapter will help you examine the liability of accountants and other professionals.

Objectives

Upon completion of the exercises in this chapter, you should be able to
1. Describe an accountant's liability to his or her client for breach of contract and fraud.
2. Describe an accountant's liability to third parties under the Ultramares doctrine.
3. Describe an accountant's liability to third parties under the Restatement (Second) of Torts and the foreseeability standard.
4. Describe the accountant's civil liability and criminal liability under federal securities laws.
5. Describe the duties of accountants under the Sarbanes-Oxley Act.

Practical Application

This material will help you determine the duty of care owed by an accountant to a business, thereby allowing you to make an initial determination of whether or not an accountant has fulfilled their duties as required by law. By understanding the conduct that triggers liability for accountants, you will be able to question decisions and procedures that could have far reaching implications for the client and the accountant. Businesses that understand accountant liability will have a better understanding of when they can exercise their business judgment based upon representations and decisions made by their accountants. Likewise, accountants need to be aware of the situations that require them to investigate the information supplied to them by the client.

Helpful Hints

Until you understand the duties that are imposed upon an accountant, you will be unable to determine if they have met their duty of care to the client. If you do not understand the duties imposed by statute, you will not know when the accountant has placed the client in jeopardy of civil or criminal liability. In this chapter, focus on the standards that are set and what degree of performance fulfills that standard. Make special note of the trouble areas where mistakes are often made that create liability.

Study Tips

Commence your study of accountant liability by closely examining the following standards, types of auditor's opinions, theories of common law liability, theories establishing liability to third parties, sources of statutory liability, and privileges related to accountants' work.

Accountants' Liability

The primary functions of accountants are auditing financial statements and providing opinions regarding financial statements, but also prepare unaudited financial statements, give tax advice, prepare tax forms, and provide consulting services.

- Lawsuits against accountants are based on common law and statutory violations.
- Accounts can be held liable to clients and third parties.

Public Accounting

A certified public accountant (CPA) is an accountant meeting certain educational requirements, who passes the CPA examination, and has a certain number of years of auditing experience.

- An accountant who is not certified is generally called a public accountant.

Accounting Standards and Principles. Certified public accountants must comply with:

- Generally accepted accounting principles (GAAPs) pertaining to preparation and presentation of financial statements, and
- Generally accepted auditing standards (GAASs) pertaining to audits

Audits. Audits are the verification of a company's books that must be performed by an independent CPA. Auditors render an opinion about how fairly the financial statements:

- present the company's financial position
- result of operations
- change in financial position

Auditor's Opinions. The types of auditor's opinions are:

- *Unqualified opinion.* The most favorable opinion that the auditor can give.
  - o Represents the auditor's finding that the three areas of examination are correct and in conformity with consistently applied generally accepted accounting principles.
- *Qualified opinion.* States that the financial statements are fairly presented except for a departure from generally accepted accounting principles, a change in accounting principles, or a material uncertainty.
  - o The irregularity is noted in the auditor's opinion.
- *Adverse opinion.* Determines that the financial statements do no fairly represent the three areas of examination.
  - o Usually issued when the auditor determines that the company has materially misstated items on its financial statements.
- *Disclaimer of opinion.* Expresses an inability to draw a conclusion as to the accuracy of the company's financial records.
  - o Generally issued when the auditor lacks sufficient information about the financial records to issue an overall opinion.

Limited Liability Partnership (LLP)

Public accounting firms are often organized and operated as limited liability partnerships (LLPs).
- All the partners are limited partners.
- The limited partners are not personally liable for the debts and obligations of the LLP.
- A limited partner is personally liable for his or her own negligent or intentional conduct.

Accountants' Liability to Their Clients

Accountants, who are employed to perform certain accounting services, may be found liable to the clients who hire them under several common law legal theories.

Breach of Contract. An accountant can be held liable for breach of contract and resulting damages when he or she fails to perform as agreed in their engagement, or contract.

Fraud. May be found when there is an actual intent to misrepresent a material fact to a client, if the client relies on the misrepresentation.
- Constructive fraud may be shown if the accountant commits gross negligence in the performance of his or her duties.

Negligence. While performing his or her duties, an accountant must use the care, knowledge, and judgment generally used by accountants in the same or similar circumstances.
- Failure to fulfill this duty is negligence.
- An accountant's violation of GAAPs and GAASs is *prima facie* evidence of negligence.
- An accountant can be held liable for malpractice if he/she reveals confidential information or the contents of working papers without the permission of the client or pursuant to court order.

Accountants' Liability to Third Parties

Many lawsuits against accountants involve liability of accountants to third party plaintiffs, who relied on information supplied by the auditor.

The *Ultramares* Doctrine. Liability will be imposed only if the accountant is in privity of contract, or a privity-like relationship with a third party.
- A relationship would occur where a client employed an accountant to prepare financial statement to be used by a third party, such as by a bank to evaluate a client's loan application.

Section 552 of the *Restatement (Second)* of Torts. Liability will be imposed only if the third party's reliance is foreseen, or known, or if the third party is among a limited class of intended, or known, users.
- This is the rule followed in most states.

The Foreseeability Standard. Liability will be imposed on the accountant if the third party's use of the client's financial statements was reasonably foreseeable.

Fraud. A third party who relies on the accountant's fraud and is injured may bring a tort action against the accountant for damages.

Breach of Contract. Usually, third parties cannot sue accountants for breach of contract, as third parties are incidental beneficiaries, who do not have privity of contract with the accountants.

Securities Law Violations

Accountants can be civilly and criminally liable under various federal and state securities laws.

Section 11(a) of the Securities Act of 1933. An accountant who makes misstatements or omissions of material facts in audited financial statements required for registration of securities or fails to find such misstatements or omissions may be liable to anyone who acquires the securities covered by the registration agreement.
- Accountants can assert a due diligence defense and rely upon a reasonable belief that the work was complete and correct.
- A willful violation of this section is a criminal offense.

Section 10(b) of the Securities Exchange Act of 1934. Accountants are held liable for any manipulative or deceptive practice in connection with the purchase or sale of any security.
- Only intentional conduct and recklessness, but not ordinary negligence, violates this section.

Section 18(a) of the Securities Exchange Act of 1934. An accountant may be liable for any false or misleading statements in any application, report, or document filed with the SEC.
- The accountant can defend against a violation by showing that
  - he or she acted in good faith when making the filing, or
  - the plaintiff had knowledge of the false or misleading statement when the securities were purchased or sold.

Private Securities Litigation Reform Act of 1995. This act changed the liability of accountants
- It makes class action securities lawsuits more difficult to bring.
- It replaces joint and several liability of defendants with proportionate liability.
- Joint and several liability is still imposed if the defendant acted knowingly.

Criminal Liability of Accountants

Section 24 of the Securities Act of 1933. It is a criminal offense to:
- willfully make any untrue statement of material fact in a registration statement
- omit any material fact necessary to ensure that the statements made in the registration statement are not misleading, or
- willfully violate any other provision of the Securities Act of 1933

Section 32(a) of the Securities Exchange Act of 1934. It is a criminal offense for any person willfully and knowingly to make or cause to be made any false or misleading statement in any application, report, or other document required to be filed with the SEC.

Tax Reform Act of 1976. Imposes criminal liability on an accountant for:
- aiding or assisting in the preparation of a false tax return
- aiding and abetting an individual's understatement of tax liability
- negligently or willfully understating a client's tax liability or recklessly or intentionally disregarding IRS rules or regulations

- failing to provide a taxpayer with a copy of a return, failing to sign a return, failing to furnish the appropriate tax identification numbers, or fraudulently negotiating a tax refund check

Racketeer Influenced and Corrupt Organization Act (RICO). Securities fraud is defined as a racketeering activity for which two or more occurrences qualify as a pattern of racketeering.

State Securities Laws. Most states have enacted securities laws which provide for various civil and criminal penalties.

- Many states have enacted the Uniform Securities Act, which makes it a criminal offense for accountants and others to willfully falsify financial statements and other reports.

Sarbanes-Oxley Act

This act imposes new rules that affect public accountants, the goals of which are to improve financial reporting, eliminate conflicts of interest, and provide government oversight of accounting and audit services.

- It established the Public Company Accounting Oversight Board.
- It requires public accounting firms to register with the Public Company Accounting Oversight Board.
- It separates audit and nonaudit services.
- It requires audit report sign-offs.
- It prohibits certain employment.

Accountant Privilege and Work Papers

Accountant-Client Privilege. It is not recognized by the federal courts, but has been enacted in approximately 20 states where it says that an accountant cannot be called as a witness against a client in a court action.

Accountants' Work Papers. Often include a wide array of notes, memos, calculations, and plans concerning audits, work assignments, data collection, client's internal controls, reconciling reports, research, comments, opinions and information regarding the affairs of the client.

- Under federal law these papers are subject to discovery.
- Some states provide work product immunity for accountants, much the same as lawyers, whose work papers on strategy, research, opinions, and trial preparation are not discoverable in a lawsuit involving the client.

Refresh Your Memory

The following exercise will give you the opportunity to test your memory of the principles given in this chapter. Read the question twice and place your answer in the blank provided. Review the chapter material for any question that you are unable to answer or remember.

1. The term _____ applies to persons who perform a variety of services, including bookkeepers, tax preparers, and so on.

2. _____ are standards for the preparation and presentation of financial statements.

3. _____ specify the methods and procedures that are to be used by public accountants when conducting external audits of company financial statements.

4. _____ is a verification of a company's books and records pursuant to federal securities laws, state laws, and stock exchange rules that must be performed by an independent CPA.

5. A(n) _____ is the most favorable opinion an auditor can give.

6. A _____ states that the financial statements are fairly represented except for, or subject to, a departure from GAAPs, a change in accounting principles, or a material uncertainty.

7. A _____ expresses the auditor's inability to draw a conclusion about the accuracy of the company's financial records.

8. _____ occurs when an accountant acts with "reckless disregard" for the truth or the consequences of his or her actions.

9. _____ says that an accountant is liable only for negligence to third parties who are in privity of contract or in a privity-like relationship with the accountant.

10. _____ is the state of two specified parties being in a contract.

11. _____ is a defense an accountant can assert and, if proven, avoids liability under Section 11(a).

12. _____ is a federal act that provides for both criminal and civil penalties for securities fraud.

13. The _____ created the Public Company Accounting Oversight Board.

14. _____ is a state law that provides that an accountant cannot be called as a witness against a client in a court action.

15. Some state statutes provide _____, which means an accountant's work papers cannot be discovered in a court case against the accountant's client.

Critical Thought Exercise

BGT Technologies, Inc., issued stock in a public offering that violated federal securities laws due to material misrepresentations and multiple acts of fraud. When it was discovered that BGT had substantially overstated its assets and failed to report debts owed to foreign banks, the SEC commenced an investigation. Kyle Sawyer was a partner in Jones Bateman, an independent certified public accounting firm. Sawyer was responsible for the BGT account and prepared numerous documents as part of the public offering. The documents filed by Sawyer contained the material misrepresentations. The SEC filed a suit against Sawyer and Jones Bateman, charging them with aiding and abetting the securities fraud perpetrated by BGT. Jones Bateman and Sawyer argue that they relied upon the information supplied to them by BGT to prepare the SEC filings. Jones Bateman did not verify or investigate the debt being carried by BGT. Jones Bateman argues that it should not be liable for aiding and abetting the securities fraud by BGT. What is the likely result when the matter is litigated?

Please compose your answer to the Critical Thinking Exercise using a separate sheet of paper or your computer word processing program.

Practice Quiz

True/False

16. _____ Limited partners are personally liable for the debts and obligations of the LLP.

17. _____ Generally Accepted Accounting Principles (GAAPs) specify the methods and procedures that are to be used by public accountants when conducting external audits of company financial statements.

18. _____ The Generally Accepted Auditing Standards (GAASs) are established by the American Institute of Certified Public Accountants.

19. _____ An unqualified opinion would entail that the company's financial statements have some deviation from GAAPs.

20. _____ A formal entrance into a contract between a client and an accountant is called abatement.

21. _____ An accountant's failure to follow the GAASs when conducting audits constitutes negligence.

22. _____ The Ultramares doctrine provides the broadest standard for holding accountants liable to third parties for negligence.

23. _____ Third parties cannot sue accountants for breach of contract.

24. _____ Only purchasers and sellers of securities can sue under Section 10(b) and Rule 10b-5.

25. _____ The Private Securities Litigation Reform Act of 1995 replaced proportionate liability of the defendant with joint and several liability.

26. _____ A private civil RICO based on securities fraud can only be brought once the defendant has been convicted for the crime.

27. _____ The Sarbanes-Oxley Act of 2002 prohibits the employment of an accountant by a previous audit client for five years after the first appointment.

28. _____ All members of the Public Company Accounting Oversight Board (PCAOB) have to be CPAs.

29. _____ If a state has passed the accountant-client privilege law, it implies that only an accountant can serve as a witness in a case against the client.

30. _____ Federal law allows for discovery of an accountant's work papers in a federal case against the accountant's client.

Multiple Choice

31. Which of the following statements is true with regard to accountants?

A. Accountants who lack CPA certification are called public accountants.
B. Accountants cannot be held liable by provisions of common law.
C. Accountants can be held liable to clients but not to third parties.
D. Accountants cannot be hired to perform nonaudit services.

32. Which of the following statements is true of the GAAP?

A. It sets rules for how corporations must set their accounts on their financial statements.
B. It is the accepted form of accounting principles around the world.
C. It cannot be modified once established by the American Institute of Certified Public Accountants.
D. It is used by auditors as a guide for their nonaudit services only.

33. Holly Lane is an accountant with Mildred & Lane Co. and she has recently been asked to visit Maine Manufacturers to survey their financial records, assess their compliance with federal and state laws, and provide an opinion reflecting the state of the company's financial records. Holly's assessment of the financial records of Maine Manufacturers is called a(n) _____.

A. probate
B. arraignment
C. audit
D. easement

34. Which of the following opinions would an auditor make for a company that, he or she feels, has materially misstated certain items on its financial statements?

A. an unqualified opinion
B. a qualified opinion
C. an adverse opinion
D. a disclaimer of opinion

35. If an auditor makes a disclaimer of opinion, this means that the auditor is _____.

A. favorable to the company's financial statement matching its performance but notes a few departures from GAAPs
B. unfavorable about the financial statement representing the company's position
C. favorable of the company's financial statements representing its performance
D. unable to draw a conclusion about the accuracy of the company's financial records owing to lack of information

36. A(n)_____ is defined as intentional misrepresentation or omission of a material fact that is relied on by the client and causes the client damage.

A. unqualified opinion
B. disclaimer of opinion
C. actual fraud
D. constructive fraud

37. A rule that says that an accountant is liable for negligence to third parties who are projected users of the client's financial statements is known as _____.

A. the Ultramares doctrine
B. the foreseeability standard
C. the due diligence defense
D. the privity of contract

38. Which of the following is true of Section 10A of the Securities Exchange Act of 1934?

A. It prohibits any manipulative or deceptive practice in connection with the process of the probate.
B. It serves as a defense an accountant can assert by claiming due diligence to avoid civil liability.
C. It imposes a criminal liability on accountants for making misstatements or omissions in nonaudit services.
D. It enforces a duty on auditors to detect and report illegal acts committed by their clients.

39. Which of the following can be used by an accountant to counter liability imposed under Section 11(a) of the Securities Act of 1933?

A. the nolo contendere rule
B. the Ultramares doctrine
C. the due diligence defense
D. the foreseeability standard

40. In which of the following ways can an accountant defeat the imposition of liability under Section 18(a)?

A. if he or she can show that the plaintiff had knowledge of the false statement
B. if he or she had acted out of recklessness
C. if he or she was an employee to the plaintiff
D. if he or she can show that the misleading statement was made to protect the company from bankruptcy

41. _____ is a rule that limits a defendant's accountability to his or her equivalent degree of fault.

A. Privity of contract
B. Due diligence defense
C. Ultramares doctrine
D. Proportionate liability

42. Which of the following is a necessity to bring a private civil action against a violator of RICO based on securities fraud?

A. The defendant has to be first criminally convicted in connection with the securities fraud.
B. The accountant must not be a third-party independent contractor.
C. The plaintiff should file the case before the government brings a lawsuit.
D. The defendant has to be tried by the application of the Section 32(a) of the Securities Exchange Act of 1934 first.

43. Which of the following is true of the Public Company Accounting Oversight Board?

A. All members of the Public Company Accounting Oversight Board have to be CPAs.
B. The SEC has oversight and enforcement authority over the board and its functioning.
C. The Public Company Accounting Oversight Board was created by the Tax Reform Act of 1976.
D. The Public Company Accounting Oversight Board lacks the power to initiate any disciplinary actions against defaulting accountants.

44. Under the Sarbanes-Oxley Act, in order to audit a public company, _____.

A. a public accounting firm must register with the PCAOB
B. only public accountants must constitute the audit committee
C. all public accounting firms must assign an accountant who works closely with one client over a long duration of time
D. the law of accountant-client privilege must be accepted by the state legislative mechanism

45. _____ is a state law that provides that an accountant's work papers cannot be used against a client in a court action.

A. Foreseeability standard
B. Accountant–client privilege
C. Work product immunity
D. Noerr Doctrine

Short Answer

46. What are GAAPs?

_____
_____

47. What are the different types of opinions given by an auditor?

_____
_____

48. When does an auditor submit a disclaimer of opinion? What is the significance of an auditor's opinion?

_____
_____

49. Explain accounting malpractice.

_____
_____

50. Explain the Ultramares Corporation v. Touche case.

_____
_____

51. Explain Section 552 of the Restatement (Second) of Torts.

_____
_____

52. Outline Section 10(b) of the Securities Exchange Act of 1934.

_____

_____

53. Give an account of the Private Securities Litigation Reform Act of 1995.

_____

_____

54. What prohibition does the Sarbanes-Oxley Act impose on an accounting firm providing audit and nonaudit services to the same company?

_____

_____

55. What is the accountant-client privilege?

_____

_____

Answers to Refresh Your Memory

1. accountant [p. 857]
2. Generally Accepted Accounting Principles [p. 858]
3. Generally Accepted Auditing Standards [p. 858]
4. Audit [p. 858]
5. unqualified opinion [p. 859]
6. qualified opinion [p. 859]
7. disclaimer of opinion [p. 859]
8. Constructive fraud [p. 860]
9. Ultramares doctrine [p. 861]
10. Privity of contract [p. 864]
11. Due diligence defense [p. 865]
12. Racketeer Influenced and Corrupt Organizations Act [p. 868]
13. Sarbanes-Oxley Act of 2002 [p. 868]
14. Accountant–client privilege [p. 870]
15. work product immunity [p. 870]

Critical Thought Exercise Model Answer

It has been a much-debated issue whether accountants may be held liable in private actions for aiding and abetting violations of securities laws such as Section 10(b) and Rule 10b-5. In *Central Bank v. First Interstate Bank* in 1994, the United States Supreme Court ruled that private parties could not bring actions against accountants for aiding and abetting violations of Section 10(b) of the 1934 Act. The ruling in *Central Bank* was addressed by Congress when it passed the Private Securities Litigation Reform Act of 1995. The act imposed a new statutory duty on accountants. An auditor must use adequate and thorough procedures in any audit performed by them to detect any illegal acts of the customer for whom the audit is being prepared. Any illegality must be disclosed to the company's board of directors, the management audit committee, or even the SEC if the circumstances warrant such action. The act makes aiding and abetting a violation of the Act of 1934 a violation in itself. The Private Securities Litigation Reform Act of 1995 precluded the extension of the ruling in Central bank to SEC actions. Thus, the SEC action against Jones Bateman would be allowed under a theory of aiding and abetting the SEC violations by BGT.

Answers to Practice Quiz

True/False

16. False. In a limited liability partnership all the partners are limited partners who lose only their capital contribution in the LLP if the LLP fails. The limited partners are not personally liable for the debts and obligations of the LLP. [p. 857]

17. False. Generally Accepted Accounting Principles (GAAPs) are standards for the preparation and presentation of financial statements. [p. 858]

18. True. Generally Accepted Auditing Standards (GAASs) are standards for the methods and procedures that must be used to conduct audits. The standards are set by the American Institute of Certified Public Accountants (AICPA). [p. 858]

19. False. An unqualified opinion represents an auditor's finding that the company's financial statements fairly represent the company's financial position, the results of its operations, and the change in cash flows for the period under audit, in conformity with generally accepted accounting principles (GAAPs). [p. 859]

20. False. A formal entrance into a contract between a client and an accountant is called engagement. [p. 859]

21. True. An accountant who does not comply with GAASs when conducting an audit and thereby fails to uncover a fraud or embezzlement by an employee of the company being audited can be sued for damages arising from this negligence. [p. 860]

22. False. The Ultramares doctrine is a rule that says that an accountant is liable only for negligence to third parties who are in privity of contract or in a privity-like relationship with the accountant. [p. 861]

23. True. Third parties usually cannot sue accountants for breach of contract because the third parties are merely incidental beneficiaries who do not acquire any rights under the accountant–client contract. [p. 864]

24. True. Section 10(b) of the Securities Exchange Act of 1934 prohibits any manipulative or deceptive practice in connection with the purchase or sale of any security. Only purchasers and sellers of securities can sue under Section 10(b) and Rule 10b-5. [p. 866]

25. False. The Private Securities Litigation Reform Act of 1995 replaces joint and several liability of defendants (where one party of several at-fault parties could be made to pay all of a judgment) with proportionate liability. [p. 867]

26. True. To bring a private civil RICO action based on securities fraud, the defendant has to have first been criminally convicted in connection with the securities fraud. [p. 868]

27. False. The Sarbanes-Oxley Act of 2002 prohibits employment of an accountant by a previous audit client for certain positions for a period of one year following the audit. [p. 868]

28. False. Two of the members of the Public Company Accounting Oversight Board must be CPAs, and three must not be CPAs. [p. 868]

29. False. The accountant–client privilege is a state law that provides that an accountant cannot be called as a witness against a client in a court action. [p. 870]

30. True. According to most states an accountant's work papers can be discovered. Federal law allows for discovery of an accountant's work papers in a federal case against the accountant's client. [p. 870]

Multiple Choice

31. A. The term accountant applies to persons who perform a variety of services, including bookkeepers, tax preparers, and so on. A person who is not certified is generally referred to as a public accountant. [p. 856]

32. A. Generally Accepted Accounting Principles (GAAPs) are standards for the preparation and presentation of financial statements. These principles set forth rules for how corporations and accounting firms set forth their income, expenses, assets, and liabilities on the corporation's financial statements. [p. 858]

33. C. An audit is a verification of a company's books and records pursuant to federal securities laws, state laws, and stock exchange rules that must be performed by an independent CPA. [p. 858]

34. C. An adverse opinion determines that the financial statements do not fairly represent the company's financial position, results of operations, or change in cash flows in conformity with GAAPs. [p. 859]

35. D. A disclaimer of opinion expresses the auditor's inability to draw a conclusion about the accuracy of the company's financial records. This disclaimer is generally issued when the auditor lacks sufficient information about the financial records to issue an overall opinion. [p. 859]

36. C. Punitive damages may be awarded in cases of actual fraud. Actual fraud is defined as intentional misrepresentation or omission of a material fact that is relied on by the client and causes the client damage. [p. 860]

37. B. Under the foreseeability standard an accountant is liable to any foreseeable user of the client's financial statements. The accountant's liability does not depend on his or her knowledge of the identity of either the user or the intended class of users. [p. 862]

38. D. In 1995, Congress added Section 10A of the Securities Exchange Act of 1934. Section 10A imposes duties on auditors to detect and report illegal acts committed by their clients. [p. 865]

39. C. Due diligence defense is a defense an accountant can assert and, if proven, avoids liability under Section 11(a). [p. 865]

40. A. There are two ways an accountant or another defendant can defeat the imposition of liability under Section 18(a). First, the defendant can show that he or she acted in good faith.

Second, he or she can show that the plaintiff had knowledge of the false or misleading statement when the securities were purchased or sold. [p. 866]

41. D. The proportionate liability is a rule that limits a defendant's liability to his or her proportionate degree of fault. Thus, the accountants are relieved from being the "deep pocket" defendant except up to their degree of fault. [p. 867]

42. A. Persons injured by a RICO violation can bring a private civil action against the violator and recover treble (triple) damages. But to bring a private civil RICO action based on securities fraud, the defendant has to have first been criminally convicted in connection with the securities fraud. [p. 868]

43. B. The SEC has oversight and enforcement authority over the Public Company Accounting Oversight Board. The board has the authority to adopt rules concerning auditing, accounting quality control, independence, and ethics of public companies and public accountants. [p. 868]

44. A. In order to audit a public company, a public accounting firm must register with the Public Company Accounting Oversight Board. [p. 868]

45. C. Some state statutes provide work product immunity, which means an accountant's work papers cannot be discovered in a court case against the accountant's client. [p. 870]

Short Answer

46. Generally Accepted Accounting Principles (GAAPs) are standards for the preparation and presentation of financial statements. These principles set forth rules for how corporations and accounting firms set forth their income, expenses, assets, and liabilities on the corporation's financial statements. There are more than 150 "pronouncements" that comprise these principles. GAAP establishes uniform principles for reporting financial statements and financial transactions. The Financial Accounting Standards Board (FASB), an organization created by the accounting profession, issues new GAAP rules and amends existing rules.
GAAP allies mainly to U.S. companies. Most companies in other counties abide by International Financial Reporting Standards (IFRS). These principles are promulgated by the International Accounting Standards Board (IASB), which is located in London, England. The IFRSs differ in some respects from GAAP. As U.S. companies become more global, and as foreign companies increase their business in the U.S., the International Accounting Standards are replacing GAAP. [p. 858]

47. The various types of opinions are the following:
• Unqualified Opinion – An unqualified opinion represents an auditor's finding that the company's financial statements fairly represent the company's financial position, the results of its operations, and the change in cash flows for the period under audit, in conformity with generally accepted accounting principles (GAAPs). This is the most favorable opinion an auditor can give.
• Qualified Opinion – A qualified opinion states that the financial statements are fairly represented except for, or subject to, a departure from GAAPs, a change in accounting principles, or a material uncertainty. The exception, departure, or uncertainty is noted in the auditor's opinion.
• Adverse Opinion – An adverse opinion determines that the financial statements do not fairly represent the company's financial position, results of operations, or change in cash flows in conformity with GAAPs. This type of opinion is usually issued when an auditor determines that a company has materially misstated certain items on its financial statements. [p. 859]

48. A disclaimer of opinion expresses the auditor's inability to draw a conclusion about the accuracy of the company's financial records. This disclaimer is generally issued when the auditor lacks sufficient information about the financial records to issue an overall opinion. The issuance of other than an unqualified opinion can have substantial adverse effects on the company audited. A company that receives an opinion other than an unqualified opinion may not be able to sell its securities to the public, merge with another company, or obtain loans from banks. The Securities and Exchange Commission (SEC) has warned publicly held companies against "shopping" for accountants to obtain a favorable opinion. [p. 859]

49. Accountants owe a duty to use reasonable care, knowledge, skill, and judgment when providing auditing and other accounting services to a client. In other words, an accountant's actions are measured against those of a "reasonable accountant" in similar circumstances. The development of GAAPs, GAASs, and other uniform accounting standards has generally made this a national standard. An accountant who fails to meet this standard may be sued for negligence (also called accounting malpractice).
Example – An accountant who does not comply with GAASs when conducting an audit and thereby fails to uncover a fraud or embezzlement by an employee of the company being audited can be sued for damages arising from this negligence. [p. 860]

50. The landmark case that initially defined the liability of accountants to third parties was Ultramares Corporation v. Touche.3 In that case, Touche Niven & Co. (Touche), a national firm of certified public accountants, was employed by Fred Stern & Co. (Stern) to conduct an audit of the company's financial statements. Touche was negligent in conducting the audit and did not uncover over $700,000 of accounts receivable that were based on fictitious sales and other suspicious activities. Touche rendered an unqualified opinion and provided 32 copies of the audited financial statements to Stern. Stern gave one copy to Ultramares Corporation (Ultramares). Ultramares made a loan to Stern on the basis of the information contained in the audited statements. When Stern failed to repay the loan, Ultramares brought a negligence action against Touche. [p. 860]

51. Section 552 of the Restatement (Second) of Torts provides a broader standard for holding accountants liable to third parties for negligence than the Ultramares doctrine. Under this standard, an accountant is liable for his or her negligence to any member of a limited class of intended users for whose benefit the accountant has been employed to prepare the client's financial statements or to whom the accountant knows the client will supply copies of the financial statements. In other words, the accountant does not have to know the specific name of the third party. Many states have adopted this standard. [p. 862]

52. Section 10(b) of the Securities Exchange Act of 1934 prohibits any manipulative or deceptive practice in connection with the purchase or sale of any security.9 Pursuant to its authority under Section 10(b), the SEC promulgated Rule 10b-5. This rule makes it unlawful for any person, by the use or means or instrumentality of interstate commerce, to employ any device or artifice to defraud; to make misstatements or omissions of material fact; or to engage in any act, practice, or course of conduct that would operate as a fraud or deceit upon any person in connection with the purchase or sale of any security. The scope of these antifraud provisions is quite broad, and the courts have implied a civil private cause of action. Thus, plaintiffs injured by a violation of these provisions can sue the offending party for monetary damages. Only purchasers and sellers of securities can sue under Section 10(b) and Rule 10b-5. Privity of contract is irrelevant. [p. 866]

53. The Private Securities Litigation Reform Act of 1995, a federal statute, changed the liability of accountants and other securities professionals in the following ways:

1) The act imposes pleading and procedural requirements that make it more difficult for plaintiffs to bring class action securities lawsuits.

2) The act replaces joint and several liability of defendants (where one party of several at-fault parties could be made to pay all of a judgment) with proportionate liability. This new rule limits a defendant's liability to his or her proportionate degree of fault. Thus, the act relieves accountants from being the "deep pocket" defendant except up to their degree of fault. The only exception to this rule—where joint and several liability is still imposed—is if the defendant acted knowingly. [p. 866]

54. The act makes it unlawful for a registered public accounting firm to simultaneously provide audit and certain nonaudit services to a public company. If a public accounting firm audits a public company, the accounting firm may not provide the following nonaudit services to the client: (1) bookkeeping services; (2) financial information systems; (3) appraisal or valuation services; (4) internal audit services; (5) management functions; (6) human resources services; (7) broker, dealer, or investment services; (8) investment banking services; (9) legal services; or (10) any other services the board determines. A certified public accounting firm may provide tax services to audit clients if such tax services are preapproved by the audit committee of the client. [p. 869]

55. Sometimes clients of accountants are sued in court. About 20 states have enacted statues that create an accountant–client privilege. In these states, an accountant cannot be called as a witness against a client in a court action. The majority of the states follow the common law, which provides that an accountant may be called at court to testify against his or her client. The U.S. Supreme Court has held that there is no accountant–client privilege under federal law. Thus, an accountant could be called as a witness in cases involving federal securities laws, federal mail or wire fraud, federal RICO, or other federal criminal statutes. [p. 870]

52 | WILLS, TRUSTS, AND ESTATES

Chapter Overview

Wills and trusts are the two main ways that a person disposes of their assets prior to or upon their death. These assets may include business ownership, intellectual property, stocks and bonds, real estate, and personal property. A person who dies intestate, or without a will, will have his or her estate distributed according to a state statute. A trust may be created before death so that property may be held and managed for the benefit of another.

Objectives

Upon completion of the exercises in this chapter, you should be able to:
1. List and describe the requirements for making a valid will.
2. Describe the different types of testamentary gifts.
3. Identify how property is distributed under intestacy statutes if a person dies without a will.
4. Define trust and living trust and identify the parties to a trust.
5. Describe living wills and health care directives.

Practical Application

When a businessperson acquires assets, it is wise to know how they will be distributed upon their death. The fruits of years of hard work may be wasted if a person does not take adequate steps to preserve their estate and ensure that the estate will be distributed as they wish. As discussed in Chapter 50, insurance, especially key-person insurance, is an integral part of estate planning. A business may have to be dissolved if the owners do not take estate planning into account.

Helpful Hints

The main purpose of entering into business is to acquire wealth and provide the necessities of life for yourself, family, and others that depend upon you. Regardless of the amount of current assets held by a person, everyone should have an estate plan. It may be as simple as a will, or may involve complex estate planning with the use of trusts, tax consultation, and joint tenancy. If an estate plan is in place, it will provide the distribution of assets as desired by the businessperson, even if the assets grow or change. Periodic updates of the estate plan are advisable.

Study Tips

In order to make informed judgments involving estate planning, the individual should understand the following principles of law relating to wills and trusts.

Wills, Trusts, and Elder Law

Wills and trusts are means of transferring property.
- *Wills.* Transfer property upon a person's death.
  - ○ *Intestate.* If a person dies without a will.
    - ▪ The deceased's property is distributed to relatives according to state statute.
    - ▪ The property escheats (goes) to the state if there are no relatives.
- *Trusts.* Are used to transfer property that is to be held and managed for the benefit of another person or persons.
- *Living Will.* States a person's wishes regarding emergency medical treatment and decisions regarding being kept alive on life support systems.
- *Health Care Directive.* Names an individual or individuals who can make health care decisions if the maker of the directive is unable to do so.

Will

A will is a declaration of how a person wants his or her property distributed upon death.
- *Testator/Testatrix.* The person who makes this testamentary disposition of property.
- *Beneficiaries.* The persons designated to receive the property.

Requirements for Making a Will. Every state has a Statute of Wills that sets forth the requirements for a valid will.
- *Testamentary capacity.* The testator must be of legal age and of sound mind.
- *Writing.* The will must be in writing except for nuncupative wills.
- *Testator's signature.* The will must be signed at the end

Attestation by Witnesses. Wills must be attested to by two or three objective and competent persons.
- The person need not live in the same state.
- All the parties must be present when the will is attested to by all witnesses and signed by the testator.

Codicil. Wills may be changed by a codicil, a separate document that must be executed with the same formalities as a will.
- The codicil must incorporate by reference the will it is amending by referring to the testator by name and the date of the previous will.
- The codicil and will become one document that is read as a whole.

Revoking a Will. Any act that shows a desire to revoke a will shall be deemed a revocation.
- Making a new will, burning, tearing, or crossing out the pages are all forms of revocations.
- Wills may also be revoked by operation of law, such as when people get divorced or a spouse is convicted of the murder of the other spouse.

Joint and Mutual Wills.
- *Joint Wills*. Joint wills arise two or more testators execute the same instrument as their will.
    - It may be held invalid as to one testator but not the other(s).
- *Mutual Wills*. Reciprocal wills arise where two or more testators execute separate wills that make testamentary dispositions of their property to each other on the condition that the survivor leave the remaining property on his or her death as agreed by the testators.
    - Because of their contractual nature, mutual wills cannot be unilaterally revoked after one of the parties has died.

Special Types of Wills.
- *Holographic wills*. Are entirely handwritten by the testator, dated, and signed.
    - They need not be witnessed.
- *Nuncupative wills*. Are oral wills made before witnesses during a final illness.
    - They are sometimes call deathbed wills.

Simultaneous Deaths. The question becomes one of inheritance if it is impossible to determine who died first,.
- *The Uniform Simultaneous Death Act*. A model act adopted by many states, provides that each deceased person's property is distributed as though he or she had survived.

Undue Influence. A will may be invalidated if it was made as a result of undue influence upon the testator.
- Undue influence occurs when one person takes advantage of another person's mental, emotional, or physical weakness and unduly persuades that person to make a will.
- The persuasion by the wrongdoer must overcome the free will of the testator.

Videotaped Wills. Videotaped wills do not have any legal force by themselves.
- A written will is still required.
- The videotaped will can be used to supplement the written will to show that the testator had testamentary capacity.

Probate. Probate is the process of a deceased's property being collected, debts and taxes being paid, and the remainder being distributed.
- A personal representative must be appointed to administer the estate.
    - If the person is named in a will, they are called an executor.
    - If the court appoints the representative, they are an administrator.
- A probate proceeding is administered and settled according to the state's probate code.

Testamentary Gifts

- A gift or real property is a *devise*.
- A gift of personal property is a *bequest* or *legacy*.
- *Specific gifts* are specifically named items of personal property, such as a ring.
- *General gifts* do not specify the source, such as a cash gift.
- *Residuary gifts* are established by a residuary clause that leaves the portion of the estate left over after all distributions and costs are satisfied.

Lineal Descendants. When the will leaves the estate to the testator's lineal descendants, it will be distributed either *per stirpes* or *per capita*.

- *Per stirpes.* The lineal descendants inherit by representation of their parents.
- *Per capita.* The lineal descendants equally share the property of the estate without regard to the degree of relationship to the testator. Children share equally with grandchildren.

Ademption. The beneficiary receives nothing when the testator leaves a specific gift and that gift is not in the testator's estate when he or she dies.

Abatement. If the testator's estate is not large enough to pay all of the devises and bequests, the doctrine of abatement applies.

- If the will has general and residuary gifts, the residuary gift is abated first.
- If the will only has general gifts, each gift is reduced proportionately.

Intestate Succession

If a person dies without a will, or a will fails for some legal reason, the property is distributed to his or her relatives pursuant to the state's intestacy statute.

- Relatives who receive property under these statutes are called heirs.
- If there are no heirs, the property escheats (goes) to the state.

Trusts

A trust is a legal arrangement established when one person, the settlor or trustor, transfers title to property to another person to be held and used for the benefit of a third person.

- The property held in trust is called the trust corpus or trust res.
- *Express trust.* A trust created voluntarily by the settler.
- *Implied trust.* A trust that is implied by law or from the conduct of the parties.

Beneficiaries. Trusts often give any trust income to an income beneficiary and the corpus is distributed to a remainder beneficiary upon termination of the trust.

***Inter Vivos* Trust.** A trust that is created while the settlor is alive.

Testamentary Trust. A trust created by will.

Constructive Trust. An equitable trust that is imposed by law to avoid fraud, unjust enrichment, and injustice.

Resulting Trust. A trust created by the conduct of the parties.

Special Types of Trusts.

- *Charitable trust.* Created for the benefit of a segment of society or society in general.
- *Spendthrift trust.* Designed to prevent a beneficiary's personal creditors from reaching his or her trust interest.
- *Totten trust.* Created when a person deposits money in a bank in his/her own name and holds it as trustee for the benefit of another.

Termination of a Trust. A trust is irrevocable unless the settlor reserves the right to revoke it.

- A trust either contains a specific termination date or provides that it will terminate upon the occurrence of an event.
- When terminated, the trust corpus is distributed as provided in the trust agreement.

Living Trust

A living trust, or grantor's trust, is a legal entity used for estate planning.

Benefits of a Living Trust. The primary purpose of using a living trust is to avoid probate.

Funding and Operation of a Living Trust. To fund the trust, the grantor transfers title to his or her property to the trust.

- A trustee, usually the grantor, is responsible for maintaining, investing, buying, or selling trust assets.

Beneficiaries. The beneficiaries are to receive income from the living trust while it is in existence and the property of the trust when the grantor dies.

- The grantor is usually the income beneficiary.

Living Will and Health Care Directive

In 1990, in Cruzan v. Director, Missouri Department of Health, it was recognized by the U.S. Supreme Court that the right to refuse medical treatment is a personal liberty protected by the Due Process Clause of the U.S. Constitution.

- This interest must be expressed through clear and convincing proof that the patient did not want to be sustained by artificial means.

Living Will. People who do not want their lives prolonged indefinitely by artificial means should sign a living will that stipulates their wishes before catastrophe strikes and they become unable to express it themselves.

Health Care Directive. A document that designates an agent to make all health care decisions in accordance with the wishes outlined in the maker's living will.

The Right to Die. In Gonzales, Attorney General v. Oregon, the U.S. Supreme Court upheld, Oregon's Death with Dignity Law in 2006, thereby allowing the law to be administered as written.

Refresh Your Memory

The following exercise will give you the opportunity to test your memory of the principles given in this chapter. Read the question twice and place your answer in the blank provided. Review the chapter material for any question that you are unable to answer or remember.

1. A _____ is a declaration of how a person wants his or her property to be distributed upon death.

2. A person or an organization designated in a will to receive all or a portion of the testator's property at the time of the testator's death is called the _____ .

3. A _____ is a separate document that must be executed to amend a will.

4. If two or more testators execute the same instrument as their will, the document is called a _____.

5. A will that is entirely handwritten and signed by the testator is called a(n) _____.

6. Settlement of the estate is also known as _____.

7. A gift of real estate by will is called a _____.

8. A distribution of an estate in which grandchildren and great-grandchildren of the deceased inherit by representation of their parent is called _____.

9. _____ is a principle that says if a testator leaves a specific devise of property to a beneficiary, but the property is no longer in the estate when the testator dies, the beneficiary receives nothing.

10. _____ is the state of having died without leaving a will.

11. The receiver of property under intestacy statutes is called a(n) _____.

12. A trust that is created while the settlor is alive is called a(n) _____.

13. A _____ is designed to prevent a beneficiary's personal creditors from reaching his or her trust interest.

14. _____ is a situation in which one person takes advantage of another person's mental, emotional, or physical weakness and unduly persuades that person to make a will.

15. _____ is a document that states which life-saving measures the signor does and does not want.

Critical Thought Exercise

Fanny York was unmarried and had no children. Her will made the following bequests: (1) all of the stock she owned in AOL to her friend, Betsy Petersen, (2) all of her stock in Lucent Technologies to her great niece, Molly Burke, (3) her entire doll collection to be sold and the proceeds to be held in trust for the benefit of her two cats, Elmo and Fred, and (4) the residue to Teen Recovery. When the value of her stocks dropped sharply in 2002, York sold the stock and placed the proceeds in separate bank accounts. A piece of paper with Petersen's name is put inside the savings book for the account started from the proceeds from the sale of the AOL stock. Another savings book has a piece of paper with Burke's name on it. The balance of this account came from the sale of the Lucent stock. When York dies in November 2002, Teen Recovery requests that the entire estate, including the proceeds from both savings accounts, be granted to it. Teen Recovery also requests that the proceeds from the sale of the dolls be given to it because the cats are not human and should not be considered a legitimate heir.

Should the probate court give the proceeds from the bank accounts to Burke and Petersen? Should the court uphold the trust for the benefit of Elmo and Fred?

Please compose your answer to the Critical Thinking Exercise using a separate sheet of paper or your computer word processing program.

Practice Quiz

True/False

16. _____ A will can be created to come into effect during one's lifetime.

17. _____ A will has to be composed on legal paper to be considered valid.

18. _____ A beneficiary under the will cannot be the witness of that will.

19. _____ A mutual will cannot be unilaterally revoked after one of the parties has died.

20. _____ A probate can only be conducted by a lineal descendant of the testator.

21. _____ Pursuant to *per capita* distribution, all the lineal descendants equally share the property of the estate.

22. _____ Relatives who receive property under intestacy statutes are called beneficiaries.

23. _____ All trusts are deemed irrevocable on creation.

24. _____ A testamentary trust comes into existence while the settlor is still alive.

25. _____ In a spendthrift trust, all control over the trust is removed from the beneficiary.

26. _____ A Totten trust is considered a tentative trust because the trustee can add or withdraw funds from the account.

27. _____ A living trust does not allow creditors to obtain a lien against the property in the trust.

28. _____ A living trust is subject to property division upon divorce.

29. _____ A living trust is a document that states which life-saving measures the signor does and does not want.

30. _____ Euthanasia pursuant to a living will is considered legal.

Multiple Choice

31. Who is a beneficiary of a will?

A. a person designated in the will to receive the testator's property
B. a person allowed to transfer the testator's legal title property to another person
C. a person assigned in a will to create a trust
D. a person nominated in a living will to make all health care decisions in accordance with the testator's wishes

32. Which of the following statements is true of a testator's signature on a will?

A. The testator's signature must be obtained in the presence of the sole beneficiary as the principal witness.
B. The testator's signature must appear at the end of the will to prevent chances of any fraud.
C. The use of nicknames and honorary titles to sign a will render it unenforceable and invalid.
D. The will need not be signed by the testator if it was already attested by witnesses.

33. What is a codicil?

A. a type of will that cannot be amended once created
B. a duplicate of a will that is used in case the original is destroyed
C. a will that has been attested by the beneficiary of the will
D. a separate document that must be executed to amend a will

34. What is a holographic will?

A. a will that is entirely handwritten and signed by the testator
B. a will that requires the beneficiary to be the witness of the will
C. a will that is revoked on behalf of a testator by a legal attorney
D. a will that is orally declared at a testator's deathbed

35. Bob and Clara were married for 22 years when they died in a car accident, without leaving behind a will. They had no surviving children but they were close to many of their living relatives. According to the Uniform Simultaneous Death Act, how would the couple's properties be distributed following their death?

A. It would be distributed to their respective relatives.
B. It would escheat to the government.
C. It would be made into a charitable fund by a court-appointed trustee.
D. It would be sold by the government and its proceeds would then go to their relatives.

36. A gift of real estate by will is called a(n) _____.

A. bequest
B. abatement
C. devise
D. general gift

37. Which of the following beneficiaries is considered a lineal descendant of the testator?

A. a parent
B. a sibling
C. a spouse
D. a child

38. Reductions under the doctrine of abatement are proportionate for all beneficiaries _____.

A. when there are residuary gifts and special gifts
B. when there are only general gifts
C. when there are residuary and general gifts
D. when there are only residuary gifts

39. When is the deceased's property, in intestacy, necessarily escheated to the government?

A. when the deceased has executed a living will prior to illness or death
B. when the deceased left behind property that has an existing mortgage on it
C. when the deceased has no living relatives
D. when the deceased has no lineal descendants

40. Mr. Rolleck places his estate in a trust while he is alive and he names a local bank as the trustee to administer the trust and invest its assets. The trust designates his wife as the income beneficiary of his estate and stipulates that after his wife's death, their children James and Joyce will receive the trust. James and Joyce are _____ in this scenario.

A. remainder beneficiaries
B. income beneficiaries
C. collateral heirs
D. settlors

41. From which of the following parties can a creditor recover in a spendthrift trust?

A. reminder beneficiary
B. successor trustee
C. trustee
D. income beneficiary

42. Which of the following is a benefit of a living trust?

A. It helps reduce estate taxes more than a will does.
B. It is not subject to property division upon divorce.
C. It helps avoid probate on the property.
D. It does not allow creditors to obtain liens against the property.

43. Which of the following is true of a living trust?

A. It comes in to effect after the death of the grantor.
B. It helps reduce the income tax for the grantor.
C. It is considered a public record subject to probate.
D. It can be revoked during the grantor's lifetime.

44. Horace Holmes died at the age of 85 leaving behind all his property to Joe Baines, his butler. The news of the new will that Horace executed three months before his death naming Joe as the sole beneficiary surprised everyone. By his prior will, he had bequeathed his estate to his two daughters and three grandchildren on a *per capita* basis.

The court took up proceedings to determine the validity of his new will because Horace's rejection of his daughters and grandchildren in his will was uncharacteristic of him. The court most likely suspected this change to be a case of _____.

A. constructive trust
B. undue influence
C. undue hardship
D. spendthrift trust

45. Which of the following does a health care directive outline?

A. which life-saving measures the signor does and does not want
B. who is to make all health care decisions in accordance with the living will on behalf of the signor
C. why the signor has decided to withdraw life-support systems
D. what treatments are to be withdrawn if doctors determine there is no hope of a meaningful recovery

Short Answer

46. What are the requirements of the Statute of Wills?

_____

_____

47. What are the special types of wills?

_____

_____

48. What is probate?

_____

_____

49. What are the different types of testamentary gifts?

_____

_____

50. What is the difference between *per stirpes* distribution and *per capita* distribution?

_____

_____

51. How does the doctrine of abatement work?

_____

_____

52. What is intestate succession?

_____

_____

53. Give an account of the funding and operation of a living trust.

_____

_____

54. What are the different elements a court considers to determine undue influence in making a will?

_____

_____

55. What is a person's right to die? What are the views regarding the legality of euthanasia in the United States?

_____

_____

Answers to Refresh Your Memory

1. will [p. 877]
2. beneficiary of a will [p. 877]
3. codicil [p. 878]
4. joint will [p. 879]
5. holographic will [p. 880]
6. probate [p. 880]
7. devise [p. 881]
8. *per stirpes* distribution [p. 881]
9. Ademption [p. 882]
10. Intestate [p. 884]
11. heir [p. 884]
12. inter vivos trust [p. 885]
13. spendthrift trust [p. 886]
14. Undue influence [p. 888]
15. Living will [p. 890]

Critical Thought Exercise Model Answer

If a testator leaves a specific gift of property to a beneficiary, but the property is no longer in the estate of the testator when he or she dies, the beneficiary receives nothing. This is called the doctrine of ademption. When York sold the stock and opened the two savings accounts, this was an ademption. The stock was a specific gift. Though York may have been trying to preserve the value of the bequest by selling the stock when their values fell significantly, there isn't sufficient proof that York wanted to create a separate gift of money. Petersen and Burke may argue that by putting their names with the savings books, York created Totten trusts for them. However, there is no indication that York held the funds in trust for them. The trust that is to be created for the benefit of the two cats is lawful. In addition to people, trusts may be created for the benefit of animals, groups, social causes, the environment, or any other lawful purpose. As long as a trustee is named and there is a way of fulfilling the testator's wishes, courts have upheld trusts that were created for the care and maintenance of pets. The court should find that the specific gifts to Petersen and Burke were revoked by the sale of the stock and the funds in the accounts are now part of the residue that goes to Teen Recovery.

Answers to Practice Quiz

True/False

16. False. A will is a declaration of how a person wants his or her property to be distributed upon his or her death. [p. 877]

17. False. Wills must be in writing to be valid. The writing may be on legal paper, other paper, scratch paper, envelopes, napkins, or the like. [p. 878]

18. True. Most jurisdictions stipulate that interested parties (e.g., a beneficiary under the will, the testator's attorney) cannot be witnesses. [p. 878]

19. True. Because of their contractual nature, mutual wills cannot be unilaterally revoked after one of the parties has died. [p. 880]

20. False. A personal representative must be appointed to administer an estate during its settlement phase. If a testator's will designates a personal representative, that person is called an executor (male) or executrix (female). [p. 880]

21. True. A distribution of an estate in which each grandchild and great-grandchild of the deceased inherits equally with the children of the deceased is called *per capita* distribution. [p. 882]

22. False. Relatives who receive property under intestacy statutes are called heirs. [p. 884]

23. False. A trust is irrevocable unless the settlor reserves the right to revoke it. This is referred to as an irrevocable trust. [p. 884]

24. False. A testamentary trust is created by will. In other words, the trust comes into existence when the settlor dies. [p. 886]

25. True. A spendthrift trust is designed to prevent a beneficiary's personal creditors from reaching his or her trust interest. All control over the trust is removed from the beneficiary. [p. 886]

26. True. A Totten trust is a tentative trust because (a) the trustee can add or withdraw funds from the account, and (b) the trust can be revoked at any time prior to the trustee's death or prior to completing delivery of the funds to the beneficiary. [p. 887]

27. False. A living trust does not avoid creditors. Thus, creditors can obtain liens against property in the trust. [p. 887]

28. True. A living trust is a method for holding property during a person's lifetime and distributing the property upon that person's death. It is subject to property division upon divorce. [p. 887]

29. False. A living will is a document that states which life-saving measures the signor does and does not want. [p. 890]

30. False. No state permits euthanasia, that is, where a physician or another party administers a lethal injection. [p. 890]

Multiple Choice

31. A. A will is a declaration of how a person wants his or her property to be distributed upon his or her death. The persons designated in the will to receive the testator's property are called beneficiaries. [p. 877]

32. B. Wills must be signed. Most jurisdictions require the testator's signature to appear at the end of the will. This step is to prevent fraud that could occur if someone added provisions to the will below the testator's signature. [p. 878]

33. D. Adding codicils is the legal way to change an existing will. A codicil is a separate document that must be executed with the same formalities as a will. [p. 878]

34. A. Holographic wills are entirely handwritten and signed by the testator. The writing may be in ink, pencil, crayon, or some other medium. [p. 880]

35. A. The Uniform Simultaneous Death Act, a model act adopted by many states, provides that each deceased person's property is distributed as though he or she had survived. [p. 880]
36. C. A gift of real estate by will is called a devise. A gift of personal property by will is called a bequest, or legacy. [p. 881]

37. D. A testator's will often states that property is to be left to his or her lineal descendants (e.g., children, grandchildren, great-grandchildren) either *per stirpes* or *per capita*. [p. 881]

38. B. If a will provides only for general gifts, the reductions are proportionate. [p. 883]

39. C. If the deceased has no surviving relatives, then the deceased's property escheats (goes) to the state. [p. 884]

40. A. The person or entity to receive the trust corpus upon the termination of the trust is called the remainder beneficiary. [p. 884]

41. D. A spendthrift trust is designed to prevent a beneficiary's personal creditors from reaching his or her trust interest. All control over the trust is removed from the beneficiary. [p. 886]

42. C. If a living trust is used, ancillary probate is avoided. [p. 887]

43. D. A living trust is revocable during the grantor's lifetime. Thus, a grantor can later change his or her mind and undo the trust and retake title of the property in his or her own name. [p. 887]

44. B. Undue influence is a situation in which one person takes advantage of another person's mental, emotional, or physical weakness and unduly persuades that person to make a will; the persuasion by the wrongdoer must overcome the free will of the testator. [p. 888]

45. B. Health care directive is a document in which the maker names someone to be his or her health care agent to make all health care decisions in accordance with his or her wishes, as outlined in the living will. [p. 890]

Short Answer

46. Every state has a Statute of Wills that establishes the requirements for making a valid will in that state. These requirements are:
1) Testamentary capacity: The testator must have been of legal age and "sound mind" when the will was made. The courts determine testamentary capacity on a case-by-case basis. The legal age for executing a will is set by state statute.
2) Writing: Wills must be in writing to be valid. The writing may be formal or informal. Although most wills are typewritten, they can be handwritten. The writing may be on legal paper, other paper, scratch paper, envelopes, napkins, or the like. A will may incorporate other documents by reference.
3) Testator's signature: Wills must be signed. Most jurisdictions require the testator's signature to appear at the end of the will. This step is to prevent fraud that could occur if someone added provisions to the will below the testator's signature. [p. 878]

47. The law recognizes several types of wills that do not meet all the requirements discussed previously. The special types of wills admitted by the courts include:
• Holographic wills. Holographic wills are entirely handwritten and signed by the testator. The writing may be in ink, pencil, crayon, or some other medium. Many states recognize the validity of such wills even though they are not witnessed.
• Nuncupative wills. Nuncupative wills are oral wills that are made before witnesses. Such wills are usually valid only if they are made during the testator's last illness and before he or she is about to die. They are sometimes called dying declarations, or deathbed wills. [p. 880]

48. When a person dies, his or her property must be collected, debts and taxes paid, and the remainder of the estate distributed to the beneficiaries of the will or the heirs under the state intestacy statute. This process is called probate, or settlement of the estate. The process and procedures for settling an estate are governed by state statute. A specialized state court, called the probate court, usually supervises the administration and settlement of estates. A personal representative must be appointed to administer an estate during its settlement phase. If a testator's will designates a personal representative, that person is called an executor (male) or executrix (female). If no one is named or if the decedent dies intestate, the court appoints an administrator (male) or administratrix (female). Usually, this party is a relative of the deceased or a bank. An attorney is usually appointed to help administer the estate and to complete the probate. [p. 880]

49. A gift of real estate by will is called a devise. A gift of personal property by will is called a bequest, or legacy. Gifts in wills can be specific, general, or residuary:
• Specific gift – Specific gifts in a will are gifts of specifically named pieces of property. Example – A gift of a ring, a boat, or a piece of real estate in a will is a specific gift.
• General gift – General gifts are gifts that do not identify the specific property from which the gift is to be made. These would be gifts of an amount of money.

Example – A gift of $100,000 to a named beneficiary is an example of a general gift. The cash can come from any source in the decedent's estate.
• Residuary gift – Residuary gifts are gifts that are established by a residuary clause in a will. This means that any portion of the estate left after the debts, taxes, and specific and general gifts have been paid belongs to the person or persons named in the residuary clause. Some wills only contain a residuary gift and do not contain specific or general gifts.
Example – A clause in a will that states "I give my daughter the rest, remainder, and residual of my estate" is an example of a residuary gift. [p. 881]

50. Pursuant to *per stirpes* distribution, the lineal descendants inherit by representation of their parent; that is, they split what their deceased parent would have received. If their parent is not deceased, they receive nothing.
Pursuant to *per capita* distribution, the lineal descendants equally share the property of the estate. That is, children of the testator share equally with grandchildren, great-grandchildren, and so forth. [p. 882]

51. If a testator's estate is not large enough to pay all the devises and bequests, the doctrine of abatement applies. The doctrine works as follows:
• If a will provides for both general and residuary gifts, the residuary gifts are abated first.
Examples – A testator executes a will when he owns $500,000 of property that leaves (1) $100,000 to the Red Cross, (2) $100,000 to a university, and (3) the residual to his niece. If the testator dies with this $500,000 estate, the Red Cross and the university would each receive $100,000, and the niece would receive $300,000. However, if when the testator dies, his estate is worth only $225,000, the Red Cross and the university would each receive $100,000, and the niece would receive $25,000.
• If a will provides only for general gifts, the reductions are proportionate.
Examples – A testator's will leaves $200,000 to each of two beneficiaries. However, when the testator dies, his estate was worth only $100,000. Here, each beneficiary would receive $50,000. [p. 883]

52. If a person dies without a will or trust—that is, intestate—or if his or her will or trust fails for some legal reason, the property is distributed to his or her relatives pursuant to the state's intestacy statute. Relatives who receive property under intestacy statutes are called heirs. Although intestacy statutes differ from state to state, the general rule is that the deceased's real property is distributed according to the intestacy statute of the state where the real property is located, and the deceased's personal property is distributed according to the intestacy statute of the state where the deceased had his or her permanent residence. Intestacy statutes usually leave the deceased's property to his or her heirs in this order: spouse, children, lineal, collateral heirs, and other next of kin. If the deceased has no surviving relatives, then the deceased's property escheats to the state. In-laws do not inherit under most intestacy statutes. [p. 884]

53. To fund a living trust, the grantor transfers title to his or her property to the trust. This property is called the trust corpus. Bank accounts, stock certificates, real estate, personal property, intangible property, and other property owned by the grantor must be retitled to the trust's name. For example, the grantor must execute deeds transferring title to real estate to the trust. Once property is transferred to the trust, the trust is considered funded. A living trust is revocable during the grantor's lifetime. Thus, a grantor can later change his or her mind and undo the trust and retake title of the property in his or her own name. A living trust names a trustee who is responsible for maintaining, investing, buying, or selling trust assets. The trustee is usually the grantor. Thus, the grantor who establishes the trust does not lose control of the property placed in the trust and may manage and invest trust assets during his or her lifetime. The trust should name

a successor trustee to replace the grantor-trustee if the grantor becomes incapacitated or too ill to manage the trust. [p. 887]

54. The court considers elements such as the following to determine the presence of undue influence.
a. The benefactor and beneficiary are involved in a relationship of confidence and trust.
b. The will contains substantial benefit to the beneficiary.
c. The beneficiary caused or assisted in effecting execution of the will.
d. There was an opportunity to exert influence.
e. The will contains an unnatural disposition of the testator's property.
f. The bequests constitute a change from a former will.
g. The testator was highly susceptible to undue influence. [p. 888]

55. One legal issue that has been prominent in the news is whether an individual has the right to choose to die when he or she is terminally ill and has less than a certain time to live. This issue has been debated many times in the past. Today, many persons in the United States support this right to die, while others are against having such a law. The right to die is where a terminally ill person may make a decision to end his or her life. Assisted suicide is where a physician can provide a terminally ill person with the means to end his or her own life. State laws that permit assisted suicide require that physicians make a diagnosis that a person is terminally ill, and that the decision to commit assisted suicide is made by a patient of sound mind. Several states, including Montana, Oregon, and Washington, permit assisted suicide. No state permits euthanasia, that is, where a physician or another party administers a lethal injection. Today, some persons support assisted suicide, while other persons do not. This issue will continue to be debated as states determine whether or not to enact right to die statutes. [p. 890]

53 | FAMILY LAW

Chapter Overview

There are a variety of legal issues that surround the area of family law. This chapter addresses a wide array of topics including premarital issues such as the promise to marry, the engagement, and prenuptial agreements. Though many people have a romantic notion regarding marriage, there are certain state law requirements that must be met before a couple may get married. Once two individuals are married, issues concerning children and parents' rights, duties, and liabilities may also present themselves. These issues, along with topics such as paternity, adoption and foster care, are investigated in your text. A discussion on ways to terminate a marriage, division of assets and debts, spousal and child support, and child custody, are thoroughly examined.

Objectives

Upon completion of the exercises in this chapter, you should be able to:
1. Define marriage and enumerate the legal requirements of marriage.
2. Explain adoption and describe how adoption proceedings work.
3. Define divorce and no-fault divorce and describe divorce proceedings.
4. Describe how assets are distributed upon the termination of marriage and explain the requirements for awarding spousal support.
5. Explain child custody, visitation rights, joint custody of children, and child support.

Practical Application

This chapter will reinforce the concept that marriage is not to be entered into lightly. The responsibilities and life altering consequences a divorce may have are to be taken very seriously. This chapter will better enable you to understand the importance of not only making an educated decision on whom you marry, but also the potential issues that you might have to deal with should the marriage go awry.

Helpful Hints

A majority of people marry for love and companionship. However, many do not recognize the importance of planning before, during, and after the termination of a marriage. In the unfortunate event that a marriage is terminated, it is helpful to be aware of how assets and debts will be divided, as well as the various issues that surround child custody. This chapter methodically takes you through the stages of a relationship from a legal viewpoint.

Study Tips

In order to make informed judgments involving marriage and family law, the individual should understand the following.

Family Law

Marriage, prenuptial agreements, dissolution of marriage, division of property upon dissolution of marriage, spousal and child support, and child custody are topics included in the broad of area of family law and domestic relations.

Premarriage Issues

Promise to Marry. In the 19th century, promises to marry were actionable as a breach of contract, in the event that someone did not fulfill the promise to do so. Modernly, there is no such cause of action.
- The groom, though, may be responsible for costs incurred in the planning of the wedding should he decide to back out of the marriage.

Engagement. The engagement of a couple refers to the period of time prior to the actual marriage of a couple. A proposal accompanied by a ring is the traditional way in which an engagement takes place.
- Fault Rule.
    - If the prospective groom breaks the engagement, the prospective bride may keep the engagement ring.
    - If the prospective bride breaks the engagement, she must return the ring to the prospective groom.
- Objective Rule. The bride must return the ring, regardless of who broke off the engagement.

Prenuptial Agreement. Prenuptial agreements are often considered prior to marriage. A prenuptial agreement is a contract entered into prior to marriage that specifies how property will be distributed upon the termination of the marriage or death of a spouse.
- Requirements:
    - Each party must make full disclosure of his or her assets and liabilities.
    - Each party should be represented by his or her own attorney.
    - Prenuptial agreements should be entered into voluntarily.
    - The agreement must reflect a fair distribution of assets.

Marriage

Simply stated, a marriage is a legal union between a man and woman as per the requirements of the state in which the marriage takes place.

Marriage Requirements. Most states require the following:
- The parties be a man and a woman.
- The parties be of a certain age (usually 18 years of age).
    - Younger parties may marry if emancipated, that is, not supported by his or her parents and provides for himself or herself.
    - All states provide that persons under a certain age like 14 or 15 cannot be married.
    - Marriages between people who are related by blood are prohibited, except in those states allowing cousins to be married.
- Neither party may be married to someone else.

Marriage License. A marriage license must be procured.
- Some states require a marriage ceremony.

Financial Support. Most states require a spouse to financially support the other spouse and their children, which includes food, shelter, clothing, and medical care.

Common Law Marriage. Several states allow common law marriages, that is, a marriage in which the parties have not obtained a valid marriage.
- The requirements for this type of marriage are:
  - the parties are eligible to marry;
  - the parties voluntarily intend to be husband and wife;
  - the parties must live together; and
  - hold themselves out to be husband and wife.
- A court decree of divorce must be obtained to end a common law marriage.

Same-Sex Marriage. Same sex marriages are allowed in several states, whereby gay partners may enter into "civil unions."
- Under the Defense of Marriage Act, states may not be forced to recognize same-sex marriage performed in other states.

Parents and Children

Parents have certain rights and obligations to their children.

Parents' Rights and Duties. They must provide food, shelter, clothing, and medical care until a child reaches the age of 18 or becomes emancipated.
- Parents may be legally responsible beyond the age of 18 if their child has a disability.
- Parental rights include:
  - The right to control the behavior of a child.
  - The right to select the schools for their children and the religion they will practice.
  - Parents may use corporal punishment as long as it does not become child abuse.
- Parental neglect is present when a parent fails to provide a child with the necessities of life or other basic needs.

Parent's Liability for a Child's Wrongful Act. Generally, parents are not liable for the children's negligent acts, unless their negligence caused the child's act.
- Almost half of the states have child liability statutes whereby the parents are financially liable for the intentional torts of their children.
  - Liability, however, is limited to a specific dollar amount.

Adoption. Adoption happens when a person becomes the legal parent of a child who is not his or her biological child.
- The two main ways to become adoptive parents are by agency adoption and independent adoptions.
  - An agency adoption occurs when a person adopts a child from a social service organization of a state.
    - Open-adoption procedures are used whereby the biological and the adoptive parents are introduced prior to adoption.

- The biological parents may screen the prospective adoptive parents to assure suitability for the child.
- Adoptive and biological parents remain in contact with each other with the biological parents having visitation rights to see the child.
  - o An independent adoption occurs when there is a private arrangement between the biological and adoptive parents.
    - A lawyer, doctor, or private adoption agency often introduces the parties.
- Court approval of the adoption must occur in both agency and independent adoptions before the adoption is legal.

Marriage Termination

There are two methods to terminate a marriage:

Annulment. An annulment is an order of the court declaring that the marriage did not exist.
- Annulments are rarely granted.
- Grounds for annulment are: lack of capacity or the marriage was never consummated.
- Children born of a marriage that is annulled are considered to be legitimate.
- Some of the same issues such as child support and custody, spousal support, and property settlement must be agreed upon by the couple or decided by the court.

Divorce. Divorce is a legal proceeding whereby the court issues a decree that legally orders a marriage terminated.
- In the 1960s, states began to recognize no-fault divorce. All one would need to state is that the couple had irreconcilable differences.
- Divorce proceedings. One party files a petition for divorce within the state stating the basic information of parties' names, date and place of marriage, minor children names of and the reason for the divorce.
  - o The petition must be served on the other spouse.
  - o The spouse being served has a certain time frame in which to answer the petition.
  - o The parties can conduct discovery to obtain evidence to support their claims.
  - o A typical waiting period is 6 months before a divorce is final, which gives the parties time to reconcile should they decide to do so.
  - o Restraining orders are issued if there is a showing that one party is likely to injure the other party.
- *Pro se* divorce. Where parties represent themselves. This is usually done for simple divorces.
- Settlement Agreement. About 90 percent of divorce cases are settled before trial.
  - o Some divorce parties use mediation, as it is mandatory in some states.
    - A mediator is a go-between.

Division of Assets

When a marriage is terminated, the parties must reach a settlement regarding assets and debts.
- If the parties cannot reach a settlement, the court will order a division of assets.

Separate Property. Separate property includes property owned by a spouse prior to marriage, and inheritances as well as gifts received during the marriage.
- Each spouse retains his or her own separate property upon dissolution of the marriage.
- However, if separate and marital property is commingled during the marriage or if the owner of separate property places the other spouse's name on the title to property, then the property is considered to be a marital asset.

Marital Property. Marital property is property acquired during the course of the marriage using income from the spouses that was earned during the marriage.
- Marital property is also separate property that has been converted to marital property.
- The two theories of distribution are as follows:
  - Equitable Distribution**.** The court may order the fair distribution of property which does not necessarily mean an equitable distribution. Several factors are considered before the property can be distributed:
    - length of the marriage,
    - occupation of each spouse,
    - standard of living during the marriage,
    - wealth and income-earning ability of each spouse,
    - which party is awarded custody of the children,
    - health of the individuals, and
    - any other relevant factors in the case.
  - Community Property**.** This theory states that all property acquired during the marriage using income earned during the marriage is considered marital property regardless of which spouse earned the income.
    - Those states having community property laws divide property equally between the individuals.

Division of Debts. Each spouse is responsible for his or her own debts acquired prior to marriage.
- Joint debts incurred during marriage are the joint responsibility of each spouse.
  - Additionally, each spouse is jointly liable.
  - If a debt is not paid by the spouse to whom the court has distributed the debt, the third-party creditor may recover payment of the debt from the other spouse.
  - Thereafter the spouse who ultimately paid the debt may seek recourse against the nonpaying spouse.

Spousal Support, Child Support, and Child Custody

Spousal Support. Spousal support is also called alimony.
- Either spouse may collect alimony over a specified period of time.
- Temporary Alimony. The temporary nature enables this to be called rehabilitation alimony or temporary alimony.
  - The amount of the alimony is based on the needs of the individual who will receive the alimony and the income and ability of the other individual to pay.
  - Spousal support terminates if the former spouse dies, remarries, or becomes self-sufficient.
- Permanent Alimony. Permanent alimony is also known as lifetime alimony.
  - This is awarded only if the individual to receive alimony is of an older age and if that person has been a homemaker who has little opportunity to obtain job skills.
  - Permanent alimony lasts until the person dies or remarries.

Child Support. The noncustodial parent is obligated to contribute to the expenses of paying for the financial support of his or her natural and adopted children, including food, shelter, clothing, medical expenses, and other necessities of life.

- If the parents cannot come to an agreement regarding the amount of child support, the court will award an amount to be paid to the custodial parent.
- The court considers the following factors when making its award of child support: number of children, needs of the children, net income of the parents, standard of living of the children prior to the dissolution of the marriage, any special medical needs of the children.
- Child support payments usually continue until the child reaches the age of majority or its equivalent via emancipation or graduation from high school.
- Half of the states have a formula to compute the amount of child support to award.
  - The formula is based upon a percentage of the noncustodial parent's income.
  - Deviation from the formula is allowed where a child has a disability or requires special educational assistance.
- Child support awards can be modified if the noncustodial parent's income or job situation changes or if the child's needs change.

Federal Family Support Act. The federal law states that all original or modified child support orders require automatic wage withholding from a noncustodial parent's income.

- The rationale for this act is to prevent noncustodial parents from failing to pay their required support payments.

Child Custody. Traditionally the mother always got custody of a child. Modernly, fathers are taking a more active role in the raising of their children.

- The court has several factors it looks at to determine the child custody issue:
  - The ability of each parent to provide for the emotional needs of the child.
  - The ability of each parent to provide for the needs of the child, such as education.
  - The ability of each parent to provide for a stable environment for the child.
  - The ability of each parent to provide for the special needs of a child if the child has a disability and requires special care.
  - The desire of each parent to provide for the needs of the child.
  - The wishes of the child. This factor is given more weight the older the child is.
  - The religion of each parent.
  - Other factors the court deems relevant.
- Custody may always be modified and is therefore not permanent.
  - The parent who is awarded custody has legal custody of the child.
  - Day-to-day decisions regarding the child are then made by the custodial parent.
  - Custody will not be awarded to a parent where there has been signs of abuse.
    - Another relative or foster care will be awarded custody.
- **Joint Custody.** Most states allow joint custody whereby both parents are responsible for making major decisions concerning the child, such as education, religion, and other major matters.
  - Joint physical custody is also sometimes awarded whereby the child spends a certain amount of time being raised by each parent.
  - Joint custody is awarded only if the child's best interests are served and if the child remains in the same school while in the physical custody of each parent.

- Visitation Rights. The noncustodial parent usually has visitation rights to see his or her child.
    - o Limited visitation as per the agreement of the court is allowed.
    - o If the safety of the child is an issue, the court will order supervised visitation.
    - o This sort of visitation is implemented if there has been child abuse or if there is a chance that the noncustodial parent will kidnap the child.

Refresh Your Memory

The following exercise will give you the opportunity to test your memory of the principles given in this chapter. Read the question twice and place your answer in the blank provided. Review the chapter material for any question that you are unable to answer or remember.

1. The _____ is a rule which states that if an engagement is broken off, the person who was given the engagement ring must return the ring, regardless of which party broke off the engagement.

2. A minor's act of legally separating from his or her parents and providing for himself or herself is known as _____.

3. _____ is a type of marriage some states recognize, in which a marriage license has not been issued but certain requirements are met.

4. _____ occurs when a parent fails to provide a child with the necessities of life or other basic needs.

5. An order of the court which declares that a marriage did not exist is known as a(n) _____.

6. A divorce recognized by the law of a state whereby neither party is blamed for the divorce is known as a(n) _____.

7. To obtain a no-fault divorce, a couple has to mandatorily prove _____.

8. _____ is a divorce proceeding in which the parties represent themselves in the divorce action.

9. A(n) _____ is a written document signed by divorcing parties that evidences their agreement in the division of property, rights and duties, and other issues of their divorce.

10. Property owned by a spouse prior to marriage, as well as inheritances and gifts received by a spouse during the marriage are referred to as _____.

11. _____ is a law in which the court orders a fair sharing of marital property to the divorcing spouses allowing that the fair share need not be an equal share.

12. _____ is a law used by some states in which the court orders an equal division of marital property to the divorcing spouses.

13. Payments made by one divorced spouse to the other divorced spouse are collectively referred to as _____.

14. Alimony that is ordered by the court to be paid by one divorcing spouse to the other divorcing spouse for a limited period of time is known as _____.

15. The _____ is a federal statute that provides for the automatic wage withholding of child support payments from a noncustodial parent's income.

Critical Thought Exercise

Marissa and Hank, both eighteen years old, decided to get married; however, Hank did not want a traditional marriage ceremony. The couple told all of their friends that they were married and even had a celebration party at their new apartment. Marissa was pregnant at the time of the couple's celebration; however, Hank did not know this fact. After ten months of living together, the couple had acquired a brand new SUV, the down payment of which Marissa put down from a graduation gift of money that her generous parents had given to her. Additionally both Marissa and Hank bought a boat, a new computer, and two Old English Sheepdogs from their earnings at the local Burger King. It should be noted that Marissa had to quit working after two months of marriage, as her ankles became as big as watermelons from standing on her feet all day. The couple also has approximately $28,000 of debt together.

After four months of marriage, Marissa revealed to Hank that she was pregnant and due in three months. Hank became overwhelmed at thought of being a father and left Marissa. Marissa now wants a divorce, plus the SUV and all of the other assets the two have accumulated. Further, she wants full custody of their unborn child and child support and alimony as well. She also wants Hank to pay off their debt since she is no longer working and he has a job now as manager of Burger King making $58,000 a year. Marissa plans on moving back in with her parents and going back to school. Marissa's mother and sister will be able to help with the baby. What advice can you give her regarding her situation with Hank?

Please compose your answer to the Critical Thinking Exercise using a separate sheet of paper or your computer word processing program.

Practice Quiz

True/False

16. _____ A person who backs out of a promise to marry can be liable for punitive damages under the law.

17. _____ According to the fault rule, if the person who gave the engagement ring breaks off the engagement, then the other party can rightfully keep the engagement ring.

18. _____ Under the objective rule, the person who was given the engagement ring must return the ring, regardless of which party broke off the engagement.

19. _____ A prenuptial agreement is a legal document issued by a state which certifies that two people are married

20. _____ Cohabitation is not sufficient in and of itself to establish a common law marriage.

21. _____ Some states that do not permit gay partners to marry provide that they can enter into "civil unions."

22. _____ Parents have the right to use corporal punishment as long as it does not rise to the level of child abuse.

23. _____ A couple that lives separated for a certain time is considered to be divorced.

24. _____ One of the parties being intoxicated at the time of marriage is grounds for a legal annulment.

25. _____ The law considers children born of a marriage that is annulled to be legitimate.

26. _____ A decree of divorce is only granted after division of property and other settlements are finalized.

27. _____ In a pro se divorce, the parties represent themselves in court for the divorce proceedings.

28. _____ A mediator is allowed to make decisions for the divorcing couple.

29. _____ . If a settlement agreement is not reached after mediation, the divorce case goes to trial.

30. _____ The nature and duration of visitation rights is determined by the parent who has legal custody without the involvement of the court.

Multiple Choice

31. Which of the following statements is true with regard to a breach of a promise to marry in the United States?

A. It is considered an unlawful and serious breach of contract.
B. The person who initiates the breach is subjected to legal prosecution.
C. Most courts do not recognize a breach of a promise-to-marry lawsuit.
D. The person who backs out will have to pay permanent alimony.

32. Which of the following statements is true of the fault rule of breaking engagements?

A. If the person who has accepted an engagement ring breaks off the engagement, the ring will be owned by the person who marries first.
B. If the person who has accepted an engagement ring breaks off the engagement, that person can retain the engagement ring.
C. If the person who gave the engagement ring breaks off the engagement, the other side can rightfully keep the engagement ring.
D. If the person who gave the engagement ring breaks off the engagement, the ring is sold at an auction and the proceeds are shared between both parties.

33. Which of the following is a requirement for an ordinary marriage in all states?

A. marriage license
B. marriage ceremony
C. prenuptial agreement
D. parental consent

34. Which of the following is a misconception of a common law marriage?

A. that the parties have to voluntarily intend to be husband and wife in order to establish a common law marriage
B. that only parties who have a marriage license can establish a common law marriage
C. that living together is necessary to establish a common law marriage
D. that cohabitation is sufficient in and of itself to establish a common law marriage

35. Which of the following legislations bars same-sex couples from enjoying federal benefits?

A. Defense of Marriage Act
B. Family Support Act
C. Equal Protection Clause
D. Marriage Protection Act

36. Which of the following can lead to an annulment?

A. if one of the parties has breached the promise to marry
B. if one or both parties were intoxicated at the time of the marriage
C. if one of the parties has children from a prior marriage that was legally terminated
D. if both parties failed to sign a prenuptial agreement in advance of their marriage

37. What is a decree of divorce?

A. a petition filed by the spouse seeking divorce
B. a court order that terminates a marriage
C. a set of rules on how assets are to be divided after divorce
D. a court order placing limitations on a dangerous partner to go near the other partner

38. When is a restraining order issued during a divorce?

A. when both partners have asked for divorce stating irreconcilable differences
B. when one of the partners is financially dependent on the other
C. when one of the partners is disabled and physically dependent on the other
D. when one of the partners is potentially dangerous to the other

39. Which of these legally binding documents are created before a marriage?

A. an annulment
B. a reciprocal will
C. a settlement agreement
D. a prenuptial agreement

40. Upon the termination of a marriage, the separate property owned by spouses is _____.

A. equally divided between the spouses
B. retained by the respective spouses who owned it
C. shared using a fair distribution method for marital assets
D. co-owned by both spouses

Short Answer

41. Under the fault theory, if the prospective groom breaks off the engagement, who gets to keep the engagement ring?

_____
_____

42. What does the modern rule, which is an objective rule, say with regard to broken engagements and the issue of who gets to keep the engagement ring?

_____
_____

43. What is a prenuptial agreement?

_____
_____

44. What is emancipation?

_____
_____

45. List two things that the court will consider when awarding child custody.

_____
_____

46. What is the type of divorce in which the parties represent themselves?

_____
_____

47. What is a decree of divorce?

_____
_____

48. What is a no-fault divorce?

_____
_____

49. When is a restraining order likely to be given?

_____
_____

50. Give an example of separate property.

_____

_____

51. What are the two theories of distribution that are used when dividing marital assets upon termination of a marriage?

_____

_____

52. How do many states determine the amount of child support to be paid to the custodial parent?

_____

_____

53. What does joint custody mean?

_____

_____

54. When will supervised visitation be ordered by the court?

_____

_____

55. What are the two legally recognized ways to terminate a marriage?

_____

_____

Answers to Refresh Your Memory

1. objective rule [p. 896]
2. emancipation [p. 896]
3. Common law marriage [p. 896]
4. Child custody [p. 905]
5. annulment [p. 898]
6. no-fault divorce [p. 898]
7. irreconcilable differences [p. 898]
8. *Pro se* divorce [p. 899]
9. settlement agreement [p. 899]
10. separate property [p. 901]
11. Equitable distribution [p. 901]
12. Community property distribution [p. 901]
13. alimony [p. 903-904]
14. rehabilitation alimony [p. 904]
15. Family Support Act [p. 904]

Critical Thought Exercise Model Answer

Since the facts indicate that Marissa and Hank have not followed the traditional way of getting married by obtaining a marriage license, taking a blood test, and being part of a marriage ceremony, it would appear that the couple has a common law marriage. This is especially evident as both Marissa and Hank are eligible to marry since they are both of legal age (18), and further their intent to be married has been expressed by telling their friends that they were married. The fact that they have an apartment together is indicative that they live together and the fact that the couple is having a party to celebrate their marriage satisfies the requirement that they hold themselves out as husband and wife. Since Marissa now wants a divorce, she will need to file a petition and eventually get a decree of divorce to end her common law marriage to Hank.

When it comes to child support, the court will consider the fact that it is apparently the couple's first child, the baby will be an infant that presumably needs its mother, the standard of living the couple had before their marriage terminated, since the baby is not yet born, as well as other factors like the home the baby will be raised in. Hank's income will be used in computing the amount of child support. As for custody of the unborn child, a variety of factors will be considered including each parent's ability to provide for the emotional and financial needs of the child and whether or not the child will be in a stable environment. Since Marissa's mother and sister will be available to help care for the couple's baby, the baby will presumably be in a stable environment. In all likelihood, Hank will be granted either joint custody or at a minimum visitation rights if the child Marissa is carrying is determined to be his.

As for spousal support, it is obvious from Hank's $58,000 a year salary that he is financially better off than Marissa, who has decided to go back to school. Marissa will probably get temporary alimony from Hank until she is able to obtain the necessary education to enter into the job force. The amount of alimony is based on the needs of the individual who will receive the alimony and the income and ability of the other individual to pay. Arguably Marissa will need alimony to care for the newborn especially since she does not have a job.

In terms of dividing the couple's assets, hence the SUV, boat, computer, and two Old English Sheepdogs, it must be determined whether or not these items are separate or marital property. Arguably the down payment on the SUV is separate property since it appears it was a gift from Marissa's parents, which, according to the law, gifts are separate property. However, even though the facts are silent as to whether Marissa and Hank were making payments together once they declared their relationship to be a marital one; it would seem that they probably were. As such the SUV may be paid for with commingled funds, in which case, Marissa needs to ask for her down payment out of the SUV, provided that the status of the SUV has not been completely changed to where it is the couple's community property. As for the boat, computer, and dogs, these are community property since the couple acquired these items during their marriage. As such, if Marissa and Hank do not reach an agreement as to how these will be divided, then the court will order a division of these assets.

As for the couple's debt of $28,000, the court may equally distribute these debts upon termination of their marriage. Note that if a debt is not paid by the spouse to whom the court has distributed the debt, the third-party creditor may recover payment of the debt from the other spouse

Answers to Practice Quiz

True/False

16. False. Today, most courts do not recognize a breach of a promise-to-marry lawsuit. If the potential groom backs out close to the wedding date, after many of the items for the pending marriage have been purchased or contracted for (e.g., flowers, rental of a reception hall), he may be responsible for paying these costs.[p. 895]

17. True. The fault rule works as follows, if the person who gave the engagement ring breaks off the engagement, the other side gets to keep the engagement ring. [p. 895]

18. True. Objective rule is a rule which states that if an engagement is broken off, the person who was given the engagement ring must return the ring, regardless of which party broke off the engagement. [p. 896]

19. False. A prenuptial agreement (premarital agreement) is a contract entered into prior to marriage that specifies how property will be distributed upon the termination of the marriage by divorce or annulment, or the death of a spouse. [p. 899]

20. True. Cohabitation is not sufficient in and of itself to establish a common law marriage. [p. 897]

21. True. Some states that do not permit gay partners to marry provide that they can enter into "civil unions."[p. 897]

22. True. Parents have the right to use corporal punishment (physical punishment) as long as it does not rise to the level of child abuse. [p. 898]

23. False. Traditionally, a married person who sought a divorce had to prove that the other person was at fault for causing a major problem with continuing the marriage. Grounds for granting an at-fault divorce consisted of adultery, physical or emotional abuse, abandonment, alcohol or other substance abuse, or insanity. [p. 898]

24. True. Certain grounds must be asserted to obtain a legal annulment. One ground is that the parties lacked capacity to consent. Examples are: (1) One of the parties was a minor and had not obtained his or her parents' consent to marry, (2) one of the parties was mentally incapacitated at the time of marriage, (3) one of the parties was intoxicated at the time of the marriage, or (4) the marriage was never consummated. Marriage can also be annulled if the parties are too closely related to one another or there was bigamy (i.e., one of the parties was already married). [p. 898]

25. True. The law considers children born of a marriage that is annulled to be legitimate. [p. 898]

26. False. The decree of divorce may be granted even if the other issues concerning the divorce, such as the division of property or support payments, have not yet been settled or tried. [p. 899]

27. True. In a *pro se* divorce, the parties do not have to hire lawyers to represent them but may represent themselves in the divorce proceeding. [p. 899]

28. False. A mediator is not empowered to make a decision but, instead, acts as a go-between and facilitator to try to help the parties reach an acceptable settlement of the issues.[p. 899]

29. True. If a case is not settled, the case goes to trial. [p. 899]

30. False. If the parents do not have joint custody of a child, the noncustodial parent is usually awarded visitation rights. This means that the noncustodial parent is given the right to visit the child for limited periods of time, as determined by a settlement agreement or by the court. [p. 906]

Multiple Choice

31. C. Answer C is correct. Most courts do not recognize a breach of a promise-to-marry lawsuit. [p. 895]

32. C. Answer C is correct. Some states follow a fault rule, which works as follows: If the person who gave the engagement ring breaks off the engagement, the other side gets to keep the engagement ring; if the person who has accepted an engagement ring breaks off the engagement, that person must return the engagement ring. [p. 895]

33. A. Answer A is correct. State law requires that the parties obtain a marriage license issued by the state. [p. 896]

34. D. Answer D is the correct answer. There are several misconceptions about common law marriages. First, cohabitation is not sufficient in and of itself to establish a common law marriage. Second, the length of time the parties live together is not sufficient alone to establish a common law marriage. [p. 897]

35. A. Answer A is correct. In 1996, the federal Congress enacted the Defense of Marriage Act (DOMA), which bars same-sex couples from enjoying federal benefits (e.g., Social Security benefits due the spouse of a married couple).1 This federal act also provides that states cannot be forced to recognize same-sex marriages performed in other states. [p. 897]

36. B. Answer B is correct. Certain grounds must be asserted to obtain a legal annulment. One ground is that the parties lacked capacity to consent. Examples are: (1) One of the parties was a minor and had not obtained his or her parents' consent to marry, (2) one of the parties was mentally incapacitated at the time of marriage, (3) one of the parties was intoxicated at the time of the marriage, or (4) the marriage was never consummated. [p. 898]

37. B. Answer B is correct. Decree of divorce is a court order that terminates a marriage. [p. 899]

38. D. Answer D is correct. A restraining order places limitations on the ability of the dangerous partner to go near the other partner. Restraining orders may also be issued in nonmarital situations. [p. 899]

39. D. Answer D is correct. A prenuptial agreement is a contract entered into prior to marriage that specifies how property will be distributed upon the termination of the marriage by divorce or annulment, or the death of a spouse. [p. 899]

40. B. Answer B is correct. In most states, upon the termination of a marriage, each spouse is awarded his or her separate property. [p. 901]

Short Answer

41. The prospective bride. [p. 895]

42. The prospective bride must return the engagement ring. [p. 896]

43. A contract that specifies how property will be distributed upon termination of the marriage or death of a spouse. [p. 898]

44. A minor's act of legally separating from his or her parents and providing for himself or herself. [p. 896]

45. The ability of each parent to provide for the emotional needs of the child, The ability of each parent to provide for other needs of the child, such as education, the ability of each parent to provide a stable environment for the child, the ability of each parent to provide for the special needs of a child if the child has a disability or requires special care (answers will vary). [p. 905]

46. A *pro se* divorce. [p. 899]

47. A decree of divorce is a court order that terminates a marriage. [p. 899]

48. A no-fault divorce is a divorce recognized by the law of a state whereby neither party is blamed for the divorce. [p. 898]

49. If there is a showing that one partner is likely to injure the other spouse during a divorce proceeding. [p. 899]

50. Property owned by a spouse prior to marriage (answers will vary). [p. 901]

51. Equitable distribution and community property. [p. 901]

52. The states use a formula usually based on the noncustodial parent's income. [p. 904]

53. Both parents are responsible for making major decisions concerning the child. [p. 905]

54. If there is a history of child abuse or if there is a strong possibility that the noncustodial parent may kidnap the child. [p. 906]

55. Annulment and divorce. [p. 898]

Chapter Overview

This chapter explores the federal government's power under the Foreign Commerce and Treaty Clauses of the U.S. Constitution, as well as the sources of international law. It details the functions and governance of the United Nations. Various economic organizations including the North American Free Trade Agreement are examined. The other international facets that are discussed include international intellectual property rights provided by international treaties, sovereign immunity, and the World Trade Organization's dispute resolution procedure.

Objectives

Upon completion of the exercises in this chapter, you should be able to:
1. Describe the U.S. government's power under the Foreign Commerce Clause and Treaty Clause of the U.S. Constitution.
2. Describe a nation's court jurisdiction over international disputes.
3. Describe the functions and governance of the United Nations.
4. Describe the North American Free Trade Agreement (NAFTA) and other regional economic organizations.
5. Describe the World Trade Organization (WTO) and explain how its dispute-resolution procedure works.

Practical Application

You should be able to appreciate the importance of the Foreign Commerce and Treaty Clauses of the U.S. Constitution, as well as the impact of sovereign immunity. You should be familiar with the names and functions of the various regional organizations. You should be able to state how the World Trade Organization's dispute resolution procedure works.

Helpful Hints

One of the most helpful tools to understanding the importance of this chapter is to focus on the fact that the chapter involves the international spectrum of business. It is helpful to understand functions of various organizations in order to better understand cases discussed in this chapter.

Study Tips

International and World Trade Law

International law is very important with the increase in technology and transportation that is bringing businesses all over the world closer together.
- A legislative source of international law does not exist.

- A separate court for interpreting international law does not exist.
- A world executive branch that could enforce the international laws is also nonexistent.

The United States and Foreign Affairs

The U.S. Constitution divides the power to regulate the internal affairs of this country between the federal and state governments, giving most of the power to the federal government.

Foreign Commerce Clause. The Foreign Commerce Clause allows Congress to regulate commerce with foreign nations.
- States cannot unduly burden foreign commerce.

Treaty Clause. The Treaty Clause gives the president the power to make treaties as long as two-thirds of the senators present agree.
- State and local laws cannot conflict with treaties, as treaties are part of the Constitution.
- Treaties and Conventions. These are like legislations that published by the United Nations and whose subject matter involves human rights, commerce, dispute settlements, foreign aid and navigation.
    - Treaty. An agreement or contract between two or more nations, formally signed and ratified by the supreme power of each nation.
    - Conventions. Treaties that are sponsored by international organizations and are signed by several signatories.

The United Nations

The United Nations (UN) is a very important international organization dedicated toward maintaining peace and security in the world, espousing economic and social cooperation, and protecting human rights.

General Assembly. As a legislative body, the General Assembly governs the UN, adopting resolutions.

Security Council. The council's duty is to maintain peace and security internationally.

Secretariat. The Secretariat administers the day-to-day operations of the UN, headed by the secretary-general.

United Nations Agencies. The United Nations is made up of several agencies including the United Nations Educational, Scientific, and Cultural Organization, the United Nations International Children's Emergency Fund, and the International Monetary Fund, the World Bank International Fund for Agricultural Development.

International Monetary Fund (IMF). The primary function of this UN agency is to promote sound monetary, fiscal, and macroeconomic policies worldwide by providing assistance to needy countries.

World Bank. This UN agency provides money to developing countries to fund projects for humanitarian purposes and to relieve poverty.

International Court of Justice (ICJ). Known as the "World Court", the ICJ hears cases that nations refer to it, as well as cases involving treaties and the UN Charter.
- Only nations, not individuals or businesses, can have cases decided by this court.

Regional International Organizations

The European Union. This international regional organization used to be referred to as the European Community or Common Market.
- It represents more than 300 million people and is made up of several countries of Western Europe.
- The European Commission acts solely in the best interests of the union.
- Customs duties have been_abolished among member nations and customs tariffs have been enacted for European Union trade with the rest of the world.

NAFTA (North American Free Trade Agreement). A three-country free-trade zone which eliminated or reduced most of the duties, tariffs, quotas, and other trade barriers among Mexico, the United States and Canada.
- There is a safety provision in the agreement whereby a country can re-impose tariffs if an import surge from one of the other nations hurts its economy or workers.

Association of South East Asian Nations (ASEAN). Several Asian countries have created the Association of South East Asian Nations (ASEAN).
- China and Japan are not members of this association; however, Japan has given financing for the countries that comprise this organization.
- China may one day become a member of ASEAN.

Organization of Petroleum Exporting Countries (OPEC). This is the best-known Middle Eastern economic organization. The Gulf Cooperation Council was formed to develop an economic trade area.

Other Regional Economic Organizations.
- There are several Latin American and Caribbean countries that have founded many regional organizations to further economic development and cooperation.
- Various economic communities have been formed in Africa.

World Trade Organization (WTO)

The WTO was created as part of the Uruguay Round of trade negotiations concerning the General Agreement on Tariffs and Trade. It is located in Switzerland.
- The WTO is also known as the "Supreme Court of Trade."
  - Its jurisdiction involves the enforcement of comprehensive and important world trade agreements.

WTO Dispute Resolution. The function of the WTO is to hear and decide trade disputes between nations that are members.
- A three-member panel hears the dispute, which then generates a report that is given to the dispute settlement body.
- The WTO has expunged the blocking ability of member nations.
- There is, however, an appellate body to appeal the dispute settlement body.

> o   Only issues of law, not fact, may be appealed.
- If a violation of a trade agreement is found, the offending nation may be ordered to stop participating in the violating practice, as well as to pay damages to the other party.
  > o   If the violating nation does not comply with the order, retaliatory trade sanctions by other nations may be assessed against the offending nation.

National Courts and International Dispute Resolution

National courts of individual nations hear the bulk of disputes involving international law.

Judicial Procedure. The main problems a party seeking judicial resolution of an international dispute faces are which court will hear the case and which law will be applied.
- Most cases are heard in the plaintiff's home country.
- Many international contracts provide for a forum-selection clause as well as a choice of law clause.
- Dispute resolution becomes more difficult and often impossible without these two clauses.

Act of State Doctrine. This act proclaims that judges of one country cannot question the authority of an act committed by another country that occurs within that country's own borders.

Doctrine of Sovereign Immunity. This doctrine states that countries are granted immunity from suits in courts in other countries.
- The Foreign Sovereign Immunities Act codifies restricted, or qualified, immunity applied by the United States.

Exceptions to the Foreign Sovereign Immunities Act. This act provides that countries will not be immune to suits in the U.S. in two situations.
- The first instance in which a foreign country is not immune from lawsuits in the United States courts is if the foreign country has waived its immunity, either explicitly or by implication.
- The second instance is if the action is based upon a commercial activity carried on in the United States by the foreign country or carried on outside the United States but causing a direct effect in the United States.

Jewish Law and the Torah

In addition to abiding by the criminal and civil laws of their host countries, the Jews also obey the legal principles of the Torah.
- The Torah is an exhaustive set of religious and political rules that are formulated from Jewish principles.
- The base of the Torah is to determine the truth.

Islamic Law and the Koran

Saudi Arabia has Islamic law as its only law.
- It is mainly used in matters involving divorce, marriage, and inheritance, with some criminal law.

- One main characteristic of Islamic law is that it prohibits the making of unjustified or unearned profit.

Hindu Law – Dharmasastra

The Hindu law is religious based, using scholarly decisions that have been handed down from century to century.
- It embodies the doctrine of proper behavior.
- Outside of India, Anglo-Hindu law applies in many countries with Hindu populations.

Refresh Your Memory

The following exercise will give you the opportunity to test your memory of the principles given in this chapter. Read the question twice and place your answer in the blank provided. Review the chapter material for any question that you are unable to answer or remember.

1. If a state enacts a law that increases its tax on imported automobiles but not on American-made automobiles, it violates the _____ of the U.S. Constitution.

2. Under the Treaty Clause, the _____ is seen as the agent of the United States in dealing with foreign countries.

3. An agreement between two or more nations that is formally signed by an authorized representative of each nation and ratified by each nation is defined as a(n) _____.

4. Treaties arranged by international organizations like the United Nations are known as _____.

5. The _____ is an international organization created by a multilateral treaty in 1945 to promote social and economic cooperation among nations and to protect human rights.

6. The _____ is a staff of persons that administers the day-to-day operations of the UN.

7. The _____ is a body that prosecutes cases that nations refer to it as well as cases involving treaties and the UN Charter.

8. _____ is a regional international organization that comprises many countries of Western and Eastern Europe and was created to promote peace and security as well as economic, social, and cultural development.

9. The _____ is a trilateral treaty that has removed or reduced tariffs, duties, quotas, and other trade barriers between the United States, Canada, and Mexico.

10. Indonesia, Vietnam, Thailand, and Philippines are members of the _____.

11. Ecuador, Algeria, and the United Arab Emirates are members of the _____.

12. The _____ is an international organization of 153 member nations created in 1995 to promote and enforce trade agreements among member countries and customs territories.

13. _____ is a clause in an international contract that designates which nation's laws will be applied in deciding a dispute arising out of the contract.

14. _____ is a clause in an international contract that designates which nation's court has jurisdiction to hear a case arising out of the contract.

15. _____ is a rule which states that judges of one country cannot question the validity of an act committed by another country within that other country's borders.

Critical Thought Exercise

Scientists at Cornell University engaged in genetic engineering and created a pear called the New York Sweetie, resistant to bruising, browning, and insect infestation. The Sweetie grows about 30 percent larger than known pears and has both a higher water and sugar content, making the Sweetie highly desired by consumers worldwide. The only pear that can compete with the quality of the Sweetie is the Favlaka Beauty, grown exclusively in Favlaka, a large European nation with a population of over 300 million people. Favlaka is a member of the European Union and the World Trade Organization. The residents of Favlaka consume over $1.2 billion worth of pears each year. All pears that are eaten on Favlaka are grown in Favlaka or a neighboring EU country. Favlaka will not allow the importation of fruit that has undergone any genetic engineering. The Favlaka Pear Cartel argues that the introduction of genetically engineered pears into their markets jeopardizes the Favlakan pear industry and the health of all Favlakans. They fear that future crops will become susceptible to insect infestation and attacks by mold and fungus. The U.S. Pear Growers argue that there is no scientific evidence that the NY Sweetie will cause damage to any other variety of pear or humans when it is grown or consumed. They further argue that the actions of the Favlakan government in banning the Sweetie are unfair trade practices under WTO agreements. It is argued that the Favlakan government is only motivated by the goal of preventing international competition for the Favlakan Beauty.

In what forum should this dispute be resolved? What procedure should be used to resolve this international dispute? What law should control the issues in this case? How should the WTO rule in this case?

Please compose your answer to the Critical Thinking Exercise using a separate sheet of paper or your computer word processing program.

Practice Quiz

True/False

16. _____ The U.S. Constitution divides the power to regulate foreign affairs equally between the federal and state governments.

17. _____ Any state or local law that unduly burdens foreign commerce is considered to be in violation of the Foreign Commerce Clause.

18. _____ The Treaty Clause of the U.S. Constitution designates the president of the United States as its agent to deal with foreign affairs.

19. _____ The UN Security Council is composed of all the UN member nations.

20. _____ The UN Secretariat is headed by the secretary-general of the UN.

21. _____ The International Monetary Fund is an example of an autonomous agency that is a part of the UN.

22. _____ The International Court of Justice is composed of 15 judges who serve nine-year terms.

23. _____ A nation can seek redress on behalf of an individual or a business that has a claim against another country in the International Court of Justice.

24. _____ The euro can only be used in countries that are part of the eurozone.

25. _____ The European Union is an example of a multilateral treaty.

26. _____ The North American Free Trade Agreement (NAFTA) is a bilateral treaty between the United States and Mexico.

27. _____ The Organization of the Petroleum Exporting Countries (OPEC) sets quotas on the output of oil production by its individual member nations.

28. _____ The United States follows the doctrine of restricted immunity for suits against foreign nations.

29. _____ The Code of Canon Law of 1983 stipulates the code of conduct to be followed by all Christians around the world.

30. _____ Classical Hindu law heavily rests on civil codes adopted during the reigns of different kings.

Multiple Choice

31. Which of the following statements is true with regard to international law?

A. All legal matters of international importance are prosecuted by a single world court that is responsible for interpreting international law.
B. The enforcement of all international laws is regulated by a unitary world executive branch.
C. There is no single legislative source from which all international laws are created.
D. All countries have to follow the international laws enacted by other countries.

32. Which of the following pairs of constitutional provisions gives the federal government the authority to regulate foreign affairs?

A. the Due Process Clause and Double Jeopardy Clause
B. the Supremacy Clause and Equal Protection Clause
C. the Free Exercise Clause and Establishment Clause
D. the Foreign Commerce Clause and Treaty Clause

33. Which of the following statements is true of the Treaty Clause?

A. It provides that the president can make treaties on his own accord autonomously.
B. It provides that the president can enter into treaties with two-thirds senate approval.
C. It provides that the states have exclusive power to regulate internal and foreign affairs.
D. It provides that the federal government has supremacy over the state in matters of international trade.

34. The General Assembly of the United Nations is _____.

A. a collection of autonomous agencies that deal with the socio-economic problems of the United States
B. the legislative body of the United Nation that is composed of all UN members
C. a group of 15 member nations that is primarily responsible for maintaining international peace and security
D. the staff of persons that administers the day-to-day operations of the UN

35. Which of the following branches of the United Nations is primarily responsible for maintaining international peace and has authority to use armed force for this purpose?

A. the General Assembly
B. the Secretariat
C. the Security Council
D. the International Court of Justice

36. Which of the following is headed by the secretary-general of the UN?

A. the International Court of Justice
B. the Secretariat
C. the Security Council
D. the General Assembly

37. Which of the following statements is true of the International Court of Justice?

A. It is the executive branch of the United Nations that helps interpret international law.
B. It only hears cases of nations, and not of individuals and businesses.
C. It does have the authority to hear cases involving treaties and UN charters.
D. It is headed by the secretary-general of the United Nations.

38. Which of the following replaced the General Agreement on Tariffs and Trade (GATT)?

A. World Bank
B. World Trade Organization
C. International Monetary Fund
D. North American Free Trade Commission

39. Which of the following is an exception to the Foreign Sovereign Immunities Act?

A. sham exception
B. managed trade exception
C. diversity of citizenship exception
D. commercial activity exception

40. Which of the following is true of the Islamic law of *Shari'a*?

A. The *Shari'a* disallows making a reasonable profit from the sale of goods and services.
B. All Islamic countries strictly follow the complete *Shari'a* to govern all aspects of life.
C. The *Shari'a* encourages *riba* through the strict payment and collection of interest on loans within stipulated periods of time.
D. The *Shari'a* is primarily used in the areas of marriage, divorce, and inheritance and, to a limited degree, criminal law.

Short Answer

41. What type of law is Hindu law?

42. What countries make up the European Union?

43. What are the two constitutional provisions that give power to the federal government to regulate international affairs?

44. What is the name of the international organization that was created by a multinational treaty to promote social and economic cooperation among nations and to protect human rights?

45. What is the General Agreement on Tariffs and Trade?

46. What is one of the most well-known oil producing and exploring economic organizations?

47. Which two countries do not belong to any significant economic community?

48. Which large industrialized country in Latin American and the Caribbean have entered into a free trade agreement with all the countries of Central America as well as Chile, Columbia, and Venezuela?

_____

_____

49. What regional international organization that comprises many countries of Western Europe was created to promote peace and security as well as economic, social, and cultural development?

_____

_____

50. For what types of things does the World Bank provide funds?

_____

_____

51. What type of immunity does the United States have to foreign governments?

_____

_____

52. If the Free Trade Area of the Americas were created, what would it eliminate or reduce?

_____

_____

53. Give two United Nations autonomous agencies that deal with a variety of economic and social problems.

_____

_____

54. What is the most notable consequence of _riba_?

_____

_____

55. Which act exclusively governs suits against foreign nations in the United States, whether in federal or state court?

_____

_____

Answers to Refresh Your Memory

1. Foreign Commerce Clause [p. 911]
2. the president [p. 912]
3. treaty [p. 912]
4. conventions [p. 912]
5. United Nations [p. 912]
6. Secretariat [p. 913]
7. International Court of Justice [p. 914]
8. European Union [p. 915]
9. North American Free Trade Agreement [p. 916]

Critical Thought Exercise Model Answer

Both Favlaka and the U.S. are members of the United Nations (UN) and signatories to the General Agreement on Tariffs and Trade that created the World Trade Organization (WTO). The World Court in The Hague is the judicial branch of the UN. One of the functions of the WTO is to hear and decide trade disputes between member nations. Any member nation that believes a trade agreement has been breached can initiate a proceeding that is first heard by a three-member panel of the WTO. The panel issues a report that is referred to a dispute settlement body of the WTO. A seven-member appellate body hears any appeal from the dispute settlement body. The dispute between Favlaka and the U.S. involves a trade barrier imposed by Favlaka. A nation may protect its food sources and livestock from foreign threats that are scientifically proven to exist. A member nation cannot create a barrier that favors its domestic sources of goods over foreign sources for the sole purpose of economic advantage. Favlaka will have to show that the threat of crop destruction from the NY Sweetie is real. According to the facts, there is no scientific proof that the NY Sweetie poses any danger to the Favlaka Beauty. This issue has been decided before. Japan tried to prevent the importation of American apples into Japan by creating apple-testing regulations that acted as a form of tariff or trade barrier. The WTO ruled that the lack of scientific evidence that the American apples posed any threat to the Japanese crops meant that the apple-testing regulations were without merit and improperly impeded entry of foreign-grown apples. The situation with Favlaka is very similar. A judge would likely be compelled to follow the same reasoning and order Favlaka to receive the NY Sweetie for sale in its country.

Answers to Practice Quiz

True/False

16. False. The U.S. Constitution divides the power to regulate the internal affairs of this country between the federal and state governments. On the international level, however, the Constitution gives most of the power to the federal government. [p. 911]

17. True. The Constitution does not vest exclusive power over foreign affairs in the federal government, but any state or local law that unduly burdens foreign commerce is unconstitutional, in violation of the Foreign Commerce Clause. .[p. 911]

18. True. Under the Treaty Clause, only the federal government can enter into treaties with foreign nations. Under the Supremacy Clause of the Constitution, treaties become part of the "law of the land," and conflicting state or local law is void. The president is the agent of the United States in dealing with foreign countries. [p. 912]

19. False. The UN Security Council is composed of fifteen member nations, five of which are permanent members (China, France, Russia, the United Kingdom, and the United States), and ten other countries selected by the members of the General Assembly to serve two-year terms. [p. 913]

20. True. The Secretariat administers the day-to-day operations of the UN. It is headed by the secretary-general, who is elected by the General Assembly. [p. 913]

21. True. The UN is composed of various autonomous agencies that deal with a wide range of economic and social problems. These include the United Nations Educational, Scientific, and Cultural Organization (UNESCO), the United Nations Children's Fund (UNICEF), the International Monetary Fund (IMF), the World Bank, and the International Fund for Agricultural Development (IFAD). [p. 913]

22. True. The International Court of Justice is composed of fifteen judges who serve nine-year terms. [p. 914]

23. True. A nation may seek redress on behalf of an individual or a business that has a claim against another country in the International Court of Justice. [p. 914]

24. True. The euro can be used in all countries of the eurozone. [p. 916]

25. True. The EU treaty creates open borders for trade by providing for the free flow of capital, labor, goods, and services among member nations. Under the EU therefore it is a multilateral treaty.[p. 916]

26. False. On August 12, 1992, the North American Free Trade Agreement (NAFTA) was signed by the leaders of the three countries thereby making it a multilateral treaty. [p. 916]

27. True. OPEC sets quotas on the output of oil production by member nations. [p. 917]

28. True. Originally, the United States granted absolute immunity to foreign governments from suits in U.S. courts. In 1952, the United States switched to the principle of qualified immunity, or restricted immunity, which was eventually codified in the Foreign Sovereign Immunities Act (FSIA) of 1976. [p. 921]

29. False. The *Code of Canon Law of 1983* regulates the conduct of the Church and individual Catholics. [p. 924]

30. False. Classical Hindu law rests neither on civil codes nor on court decisions but on the works of private scholars that were passed along for centuries by oral tradition and eventually were recorded in the *smitris* ("law books"). [p. 924]

Multiple Choice

31. C. Answer C is correct. There is no single legislative source of international law. [p. 911]

32. D. Answer D is correct. On the international level, however, the Constitution gives most of the power to the federal government. Two constitutional provisions establish this authority: the Foreign Commerce Clause and the Treaty Clause. [p. 911]

33. B. Answer B is correct. Article II, Section 2, Clause 2 of the U.S. Constitution—the Treaty Clause—states that the president "shall have power, by and with the advice and consent of the Senate, to make treaties, provided two-thirds of the senators present concur." [p. 912]